Michael A. Stadler is Assistant Professor of Psychology at the University of Missouri in Columbia, where he has been on the faculty since 1992, after 3 years on the faculty at Louisiana State University. He received his B.S. in psychology from Wright State University in 1985 and his Ph.D. in cognitive psychology from Purdue University in 1989. He serves as a consulting editor for the **Journal of Experimental Psychology: Learning, Memory, and Cognition**. His research focuses on human learning and memory.

Peter A. Frensch studied electrical engineering, psychology, and philosophy at the Universities of Darmstadt and Trier, Germany, and at Yale University, where he received his M.S., M.phil., and Ph.D. He worked as an assistant and associate professor in the Department of Psychology at the University of MissouriColumbia, from 1989 until 1994. In 1994, he moved to the MaxPlanckInstitute for Human Development and Education, Berlin, Germany, where he is a senior research scientist. In addition, he is professor of psychology at Humboldt University in Berlin. He is coeditor of the journal **Psychological Research**. His research interests include learning, memory, and problem solving.

HANDBOOK OF IMPLICIT LEARNING

HANDBOOK OF IMPLICIT LEARNING

Edited by
Michael A. Stadler
Peter A. Frensch

SAGE Publications
International Educational and Professional Publisher
Thousand Oaks   London   New Delhi

For information:

SAGE Publications, Inc.
2455 Teller Road
Thousand Oaks, California 91320
E-mail: order@sagepub.com

SAGE Publications Ltd.
6 Bonhill Street
London EC2A 4PU
United Kingdom

SAGE Publications India Pvt. Ltd.
M-32 Market
Greater Kailash I
New Delhi 110 048 India

Printed in the United States of America

Library of Congress Cataloging-in-Publication Data

Main entry under title:

Handbook of implicit learning / edited by Michael A. Stadler and
Peter A. Frensch.
        p.   cm.
Includes bibliographical references and index.
ISBN 0-7619-0197-3 (cloth: acid-free paper)
    1. Implicit learning.   I. Stadler, Michael A. II. Frensch, Peter A.
BF319.5.I45H36 1997
153.1′5—dc21   97-21011

This book is printed on acid-free paper.

98 99 00 01 02 03 04 10 9 8 7 6 5 4 3 2 1

Acquisition Editor:	C. Deborah Laughton
Editorial Assistant:	Eileen Carr
Production Editor:	Astrid Virding
Production Assistant:	Denise Santoyo
Typesetter/Designer:	Christina M. Hill
Indexer:	L. Pilar Wyman
Cover Designer:	Ravi Balasuriya
Print Buyer:	Anna Chin

Contents

Preface

This volume grew out of numerous discussions about implicit learning that we enjoyed at Shakespeare's, a pizza parlor near the campus of the University of Missouri–Columbia, where we were both on the faculty of the Department of Psychology. (Stadler, who remains in Columbia, can still enjoy a slice at Shakespeare's from time to time; alas, Frensch, now at the Max-Planck-Institute for Human Development and Education in Berlin, cannot.) It occurred to us, during one of those discussions, that a comprehensive overview of research in the field would be quite helpful. We hope that this book meets that need.

Arthur Reber named and launched the field of implicit learning in 1967, with the first of his many articles on the topic. For a time after that, Reber *was* the implicit learning literature. According to a PsycINFO search, no one else used the term in a title or abstract until 1980, and the topic did not attract a great deal of interest until later in that decade (when interest in implicit memory was developing rapidly at the same time). Now, interest has grown to the degree that, as the contributions to this volume demonstrate, researchers around the world are applying a variety of approaches and theoretical perspectives to many variants of this very interesting problem. These approaches include basic behavioral studies of the functional characteristics of implicit learning, neuropsychological studies, developmental perspectives, and computational modeling, all of which are represented in this volume. Similarly, many of the different settings in which implicit learning has been studied are represented here, including artificial grammar learning, sequence learning in reaction time tasks, motor learning, the mere exposure effect, and the learning of invariant stimulus features. Finally, research on implicit learning has not gone without controversy, some of which is also represented in chapters in this volume.

In the first section of the book, we try to set the stage with chapters that examine the definition of implicit learning. Frensch's Chapter 2 considers the multiple meanings of the term; Stadler and Roediger's Chapter 3 considers aspects of the definition that hinge on the issue of awareness; and Buchner and Wippich's Chapter 1 considers implicit learning by comparing and contrasting it with implicit memory.

In the second section, we have included chapters that discuss various forms of implicit learning and the paradigms used to study it. Berry and Cock's Chapter 4 looks at recent work on invariance learning; Hoffman and Koch (Chapter 5) consider the important issue of the structure of what subjects learn in implicit learning experiments; Manza, Zizak, and Reber (Chapter 6) review work on artificial grammar learning that uses a preference judgment task as a measure of learning; Mathews and Cochran (Chapter 7) go back to the roots of the most well-used task for studying implicit learning, the artificial grammar learning paradigm, to consider the generativity of implicit knowledge; Reed and Johnson's Chapter 8 looks at implicit learning largely from the perspective of work done with serial reaction time tasks; and finally, Seger (Chapter 9) considers the possibility of multiple forms of implicit learning.

In the third section of the book, various theoretical and empirical issues are considered, including Cleeremans and Jiménez's (Chapter 10) extension of Cleeremans's connectionist model; Curran's (Chapter 11) look at cognitive neuroscientific evidence; Goschke's (Chapter 12) consideration of perceptual and motor mechanisms of implicit learning, a long-standing issue in the field; the developmental perspectives of Hoyer (Chapter 13), Willingham (Chapter 17), and Perruchet and Vinter (Chapter 15); Hsiao and Reber's (Chapter 14) review of evidence on the role of attention in implicit learning; and Shanks and Johnstone's (Chapter 16) consideration of an alternative account of learning in serial reaction time tasks.

Thanks are due to many people, without whose labors this book would not have been possible. We are especially grateful, of course, to the authors of the chapters included here. Our hope was that this book would provide a fairly representative sampling of the research and views of those who do work on this problem; this was only possible because many of them were willing to contribute some of their work for this effort. Moreover, many of the authors also served as reviewers, providing helpful feedback to us and to the authors on early drafts of other chapters. Circulation of these early drafts also allowed for at least a degree of interplay between some of the chapters. Finally, C. Deborah Laughton and her colleagues at Sage contributed to various aspects of the publication process. We are very grateful to them for their help and patience.

—*Michael A. Stadler*
Peter A. Frensch

PART I

DEFINING
IMPLICIT LEARNING

1

Differences and Commonalities Between Implicit Learning and Implicit Memory

Axel Buchner
Werner Wippich

In this chapter, we first suggest a task-related distinction between implicit learning and implicit memory. This distinction is simple and straightforward, and it is not burdened by having to rely on criteria located on different levels such as empirical phenomena, on approaches taken to reconstruct these theoretically, or on the state of consciousness associated with task performance. Subsequently, we provide an overview of the relevant results and approaches in implicit learning and implicit memory research. With these in mind, and based on our task-related distinction between the areas, we first outline the parallels between the areas of implicit learning and implicit memory and then take a look at the differences. However, we go beyond establishing parallels and differences in asking how they may be used for a synergistic transfer of concepts and techniques between the areas of implicit learning and implicit memory.

AUTHORS' NOTE: Preparation of this chapter was supported by grants from the Deutsche Forschungsgemeinschaft to Axel Buchner (Bu 945/1-1) and to Werner Wippich (Wi 943/3-1).

3

TRENDS AND DEFINITIONS

One possible indicator as to whether a particular topic can be considered in vogue is a marked increase in the frequency with which it is referred to in journal titles. A quick look into the PsycLIT database shows that, measured by this criterion, *implicit memory* and *implicit learning* clearly qualify as fashionable topics these days. Before 1986, there is hardly an article that refers to implicit learning in its title, and we found no such articles with implicit memory. This changes considerably during the late 1980s, and a first parallel between implicit memory and implicit learning is a burst of interest in both topics from about 1990 onward (see Figure 1.1).

Of course, such data are of debatable quality. For instance, certain notions may surface in titles, but the authors may have a definition of these notions that differs from our understanding. Indeed, some articles with implicit learning in their titles describe experiments in which participants learned lists of items and later showed performance increases on implicit memory tests for these items (e.g., Beatty, Goodkin, Monson, & Beatty, 1990; Bylsma, Rebok, & Brandt, 1991; Greve & Bauer, 1990). To us, such experiments would seem to be characterized more appropriately as studies of implicit memory as described by Schacter (1987), who defined implicit memory as the facilitation of task performance through prior experiences in the absence of conscious or intentional recollection (cf. Graf & Schacter, 1985).

However, Reber's (1989) remark that Schacter "never came to grips with the distinction between implicit learning and implicit memory" (p. 219) should make us cautious because, without such a distinction, it is difficult to justify our recategorizing the aforementioned studies. In his definition, Reber said that "implicit knowledge results from the induction of an abstract representation of the structure that the stimulus environment displays, and this knowledge is acquired in the absence of conscious, reflective strategies to learn" (p. 219). If the implicit knowledge referred to in this definition is taken as synonymous with Schacter's notion of prior experiences that facilitate task performance in the absence of conscious recollection, then we would conclude that the area of implicit learning would best be understood as a subset of implicit memory research. Shanks and St. John (1994) seem to have adopted a similar position in their analysis of implicit learning research. In this sense, then, the areas of implicit learning and implicit memory would be inseparable.

4

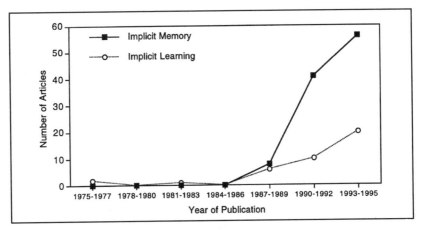

Figure 1.1. Number of articles published with *implicit memory* and *implicit learning* in their titles.

Such an inseparability would be compatible with Berry and Dienes's (1991) conclusion of important commonalities between implicit learning and implicit memory. Specifically, they pointed out five key empirical characteristics with respect to which implicit learning and implicit memory were thought to be parallel. However, the parallels seem less clear now than they appeared then. For instance, Berry and Dienes (1991) pointed out that both implicit learning and implicit memory performance seemed to be very much tied to the *surface characteristics* of the stimuli. This is said not to be the case for explicit learning and explicit memory performance. Indeed, Berry and Broadbent (1988; see also Squire & Frambach, 1990) reported that changing the surface features from an original computer-simulated control task to a structurally identical one resulted in a loss of transfer relative to a condition in which the two tasks were not only structurally identical but also superficially similar. Parallel to this finding runs the assumption that implicit memory of prior experiences would generally involve data-driven processes and thus be susceptible to changes in surface features between study and test, whereas explicit memory performance would mostly draw on conceptually driven processes and thus be relatively immune against changes in surface features (e.g., Jacoby, 1983; Roediger & Blaxton, 1987).

However, it turned out that conceptually driven implicit and data-driven explicit memory performance may be observed just as well (cf. Roediger, 1990b). Furthermore, as Berry and Dienes (1991) already men-

5

tioned, surface characteristics seem to be less relevant for successful performance, at least in implicit grammar-learning tasks. It is perhaps one of
the most fascinating findings in this paradigm that knowledge acquired
from memorizing a particular set of strings can be transferred to a surprisingly large degree to an implementation of the same grammatical structure
with a different alphabet within the same modality (Mathews et al., 1989;
Reber, 1969) and even between implementations in different modalities
(Altmann, Dienes, & Goode, 1995; see also Bright & Burton, 1994;
McGeorge & Burton, 1990).

Considering such difficulties in relating empirical phenomena observed
in implicit memory tasks to those observed in implicit learning tasks (and
vice versa) on the basis of assuming fundamental parallels between both
areas, we think it least controversial to use a task-related distinction for
analyzing the relation between both areas. According to this distinction,
implicit learning refers to the acquisition of knowledge about the structural
properties of the relations between (usually more than two) objects or
events. Knowledge acquisition is incidental, that is, participants are not
informed that there are regularities in the sequences of objects or events to
be processed, let alone are they instructed to search for these regularities.
This is why implicit learning is often described as phenomenally unconscious. The test situation may or may not require intentional retrieval of
previously acquired knowledge. As an example, consider a typical grammar-learning study. Participants first memorize a set of strings generated
by a finite-state grammar. Before the test phase, they are informed of the
regularities in the strings and asked to classify new strings as either grammatical or nongrammatical based on their experiences with the strings
during the acquisition phase.

In contrast to implicit learning, the notion of implicit memory refers
to the effects of past experiences with single events or objects such as words
read or solved as anagrams in the acquisition phase. Most important, the
learning situation does not need to be incidental. Rather, implicit memory
refers to situations in which effects of prior incidental or intentional experiences can be observed despite the fact that participants are not instructed
to relate their current performance to a learning episode (Hintzman, 1990;
Richardson-Klavehn & Bjork, 1988; Roediger, 1990b; Schacter, 1987).
This is why implicit memory is often described as phenomenally unconscious. As an example of an implicit memory test, consider a study by Jacoby
(1983) in which participants were asked to read words out of context, to
read words in the context of antonyms, or to generate words from anto-

nyms. Subsequently, words were briefly presented on a computer screen and had to be reported. This perceptual identification test does not make any reference to the prior study episode, but specific effects of participants' prior experiences with the study words could nevertheless be observed, in that performance was best for words read out of context, and it was worst for words generated from antonyms.

Note that our definitions of implicit learning and memory do not imply anything about the empirical results and their interpretations in terms of the processes that underlie them, and they do not involve assumptions about the state of consciousness associated with the task-relevant processes. We will use these definitions here because we believe that they can lead to some interesting insights, but we also see their limitations. For instance, it is known that reading times decrease as a function of repeatedly reading the same text (for a review, see Levy, 1993). Such repetition effects may be classified as results of implicit learning if the facilitatory effects are due to the acquisition of knowledge about the structural properties of the read text. In contrast, if the reading improvement is tied to the experience with individual words, then we would have to classify it as an effect of implicit memory. Levy (1993) shows that there may be evidence for both types of effects.

OVERVIEW

Implicit Memory

Information acquired during a single episode can facilitate performance on a number of tests that make no explicit reference to the study episode, such as word identification (Jacoby & Dallas, 1981) or category association (Graf, Shimamura, & Squire, 1985). Such facilitation effects have been referred to as priming. Graf and Schacter (1985) introduced the descriptive notions of *explicit* and *implicit* memory to denote the forms of memory involved in recall or recognition, as examples of explicit memory tasks and priming performance, respectively. Unfortunately, these terms have been used to refer to memory tasks, to underlying hypothetical constructs (e.g., different memory systems), and to states of awareness that might accompany memory test performance. For example, Schacter (1987) equated performance facilitation in implicit memory tests with a state of (non) awareness "that does not require conscious or intentional recollection"

(p. 501). In contrast, explicit memory "is revealed when performance on a task requires conscious recollection of previous experiences" (p. 501). In his seminal monograph, Ebbinghaus (1885/1966) foreshadowed this conception by distinguishing

1. Cases in which "we can call back into consciousness by an exertion of the will . . . seemingly lost [mental] states" (p. 1)
2. Cases in which "mental states once present in consciousness return to it with apparent spontaneity and without any act of the will" (p. 2)
3. Cases in which "vanished mental states give indubitable proof of their continuing existence even if they themselves do not return to consciousness at all" (p. 2)

Case 1 is very similar to the definition of explicit memory delivered by Schacter (1987), whereas Cases 2 and 3 may be characterized as implicit test situations because of the missing situational demand to relate the present to the past. Case 2 has been referred to as an instance of involuntary conscious memory within an implicit memory-test situation (Richardson-Klavehn & Gardiner, 1995), whereas Case 3 has been termed unconscious memory (Richardson-Klavehn & Gardiner, 1995). In our view, the type of retrieval orientation and the subjective experience that may accompany performance on memory tests are important issues, but they should be treated separately from the type of test situation. We prefer to use the terms explicit and implicit to refer to different tasks, distinguished operationally by the instructions participants are given during the test. On explicit tests, participants are asked to recall or to recognize previously studied events. On priming tests of implicit memory, participants are not directed to recall past events. Rather, they are asked to perform some task as well and as quickly as possible. Retention is inferred from how the task has been affected by recent experiences relative to a base rate or control condition performance.

Clues regarding a distinction between implicit and explicit memory arose as early as the turn of the century in clinical observations of preserved learning in amnesic patients (Claparède, 1911). It was not until the 1960s, however, that researchers developed experimental paradigms for the analysis of preserved memory functions in amnesia. Densely amnesic patients, who perform very poorly on recall or recognition tests, showed normal priming on tasks that we would call implicit memory tests these days (Warrington & Weiskrantz, 1968, 1970). This dissociation between implicit and explicit memory tasks has been found regularly (see below), and it has also been extended to studies with prosopagnosic and depressed patients or with participants under the influence of alcohol (see, e.g., De Haan, Young, & Newcombe, 1992; Hashtroudi, Parker, DeLisi, Wyatt, & Mutter, 1984; Roediger & McDermott, 1992).

Interestingly, these types of test turned out to be dissociable in normal participants, too. That is, variables that exhibit one pattern of effects on explicit tests show no effects or opposite effects on implicit tests (for reviews, see Richardson-Klavehn & Bjork, 1988; Roediger & McDermott, 1993; Schacter, 1987). Even more important, dissociations have been found between two general classes of implicit tests. Conceptual tests (e.g., category association) are sensitive to manipulations of encoded meaning but are relatively unaffected by manipulations of perceptual attributes (Blaxton, 1989; Hamann, 1990; Rappold & Hashtroudi, 1991). Perceptual tests (e.g., word identification), in contrast, are highly sensitive to manipulations of surface features (e.g., to changes in modality or in symbolic form between study and test or to small changes within a modality between study and test, such as the typography of a word), but priming is largely unaffected by manipulations of encoded meaning (Blaxton, 1989; Jacoby & Dallas, 1981; Roediger & Blaxton, 1987).

There exists a great variety of both perceptual and conceptual implicit memory tests. For instance, Roediger and McDermott (1993) list about a dozen memory tests that have been used relatively widely. The materials used in priming studies are usually visual (words or pictures), but any task, information, or behavior that can be repeated in the same or in similar ways may, of course, be used in implicit memory research. For example, we have demonstrated reliable priming in haptic information processing (Wippich, 1991), in olfaction (Wippich, 1990), in visual image processing (Wippich, Mecklenbräuker, & Halfter, 1989), and in intuitive judgments (Wippich, 1994).

● Implicit Learning

More than half a century after Ebbinghaus's (1885/1966) pioneering work, George Miller (1958) laid the cornerstone of one of the most prominent of the currently active implicit learning paradigms. He investigated the effects of grammatical structures with well-known properties on human learning. Using a finite-state grammar to generate grammatical strings of symbols, he found that it was much easier to memorize syntactically correct strings than random strings. As an interpretation, he offered that learners could exploit the regularities in the syntactically correct sequences to recode them efficiently, lowering the difficulty of the task. For instance, the strings NNSG, NNSXG, NNXSXG, NNXXSG, NNXXSXG, and NNXXXSG could be recoded as 00, 01, 11, 20, 21, and 30 given NNSG and the convention that the digits indicate the numbers of X's preceding and following the S. In this way, several sequences can be derived without having to memorize them individually.

Reber (1967) expressed doubts that participants could discover and use such a recoding system. Also, if participants really used such a system, then there should be at least some verbalizable knowledge about it. In his replication of Miller's (1958) study, Reber (1967) found no evidence of such knowledge. In order to avoid having to rely on introspective reports, Reber (1967) conducted a second study, which can be regarded as the model experiment for a large number of subsequent investigations into implicit grammar learning. Participants were again asked to memorize strings generated by a finite-state grammar. In an unexpected test, participants were informed that the strings memorized were actually formed by a complex set of rules and that their task was to make a decision about the "grammaticality" of a number of test strings. This innovation had two major consequences. First, the memorization phase could be considered incidental with respect to the grammaticality test. Second, Reber could examine whether the grammaticality judgments contained evidence for systematic recoding. No such evidence or hints of other explicit strategies of responding could be found, despite the fact that participants performed better than chance at discriminating grammatical from nongrammatical strings.

This study has stimulated a considerable research program on grammar learning (for reviews, see Berry, 1994; Reber, 1989; Seger, 1994; Shanks & St. John, 1994). Underlying much of the research on the subject are Reber's assumptions that the process of acquiring grammatical knowledge is implicit and occurs without reflective strategies to learn and that the knowledge acquired is (a) a mental representation of the abstract rules contained in the stimuli and (b) tacit, in that it can be expressed in performance but the aspects of the stimuli that determine the performance remain unconscious (Reber, 1989, 1993). However, there have been repeated debates about whether or not there is ground for claiming the contribution of any nonverbalizable knowledge to grammaticality judgments (see below for a few examples).

Similar debates may also be observed in the paradigm of implicit sequence learning. In a typical task in this paradigm (e.g., Nissen & Bullemer,

1987), participants react as fast as possible to event sequences that follow a certain nonobvious pattern. For instance, the events could be asterisks that appear on four different screen locations, each of which is associated with a specific key. Participants' task is to press as fast as possible the key corresponding to the screen location at which an asterisk appears. The screen positions at which the asterisks appear follow a certain pattern that is repeated over and over again. Learning of the repeating pattern is assessed indirectly by contrasting response latencies to events in patterned sequences with response latencies to events in random sequences. If the reaction times are higher when the event sequences are not patterned as opposed to when they are, then sequence learning is said to have occurred. It was surprising that, quite often, this reaction time increase appeared to be independent of the amount of sequence knowledge revealed by direct memory tasks, the most popular version of which is the generate task. In this task, participants no longer respond to the events but rather predict the next event, given the current event, by pressing the key associated with that next event.

Finally, another major implicit learning paradigm originated in problem-solving research. In the 1970s, Broadbent (1977; Broadbent & Aston, 1978) initiated a tradition of research on complex problem solving (cf. Frensch & Funke, 1995) or, more precisely, on how people interact with complex dynamic systems such as computer-simulated factories. One of the most interesting findings was a striking disparity between the often quite satisfactory control performance on the one side and the lack of participants' ability to answer questions about the system they had learned to control on the other. In subsequent studies, Berry and Broadbent (e.g., 1984, 1987, 1988, 1995) were able to pin down a number of factors that appear to influence the development of either control performance or verbalizable knowledge or both. To explain the differences between control performance and verbalizable knowledge, Berry and Broadbent (1988) suggested distinguishing between a selective and a nonselective mode of learning. The selective mode was assumed to be slow and to involve an *abstract working memory* (Hayes & Broadbent, 1988) in which verbalizable associations are formed between individual events. Unselective learning, in contrast, reflects the automatic aggregation of event contingencies.

Obviously, there appears to be a close analogy between the concepts of selective and explicit, and unselective and implicit, learning. However, control tasks clearly differ from other implicit learning tasks in that participants know from the beginning that they have to search for the regularities in the system behavior. Thus, control tasks violate our criterion that

11

the acquisition phase in implicit learning tasks be incidental. In addition, while participants search for the regularities, they also perform an explicit memory test in that they need to recall and use what they already know about how the system works in order to get it into the target state. This raises doubts as to whether control tasks are ideally suited implicit learning tasks. Indeed, Berry (1994; see also Buchner, Funke, & Berry, 1995) reviewed the relevant experimental evidence and concluded that explicit processes may play a larger role in control task performance than was originally thought. With a significant contribution of explicit problem-solving processes to system control performance, the aforementioned results of no transfer between superficially dissimilar systems (Berry & Broadbent, 1988; Squire & Frambach, 1990) resemble more closely the finding of little if any transfer between superficially dissimilar analogical problems in classical problem-solving research (e.g., Holyoak & Koh, 1987) than the transfer findings from typical implicit learning tasks. In the light of these considerations, we do not consider system control tasks, in their present form, to be good instances of implicit learning tasks, and we will ignore the findings obtained with this experimental paradigm in the present chapter.

Beside system control tasks, grammar-learning and sequence-learning tasks are indubitably the major paradigms in which implicit learning has been investigated to date (cf. Berry, 1994), and most of the arguments presented in this chapter refer to these tasks. However, we believe that the basic arguments we put forward in this chapter also apply to the other, less frequently used implicit learning paradigms (e.g., Bright & Burton, 1994; McAndrews & Moscovitch, 1990; McGeorge & Burton, 1990; Reber & Millward, 1968, 1971; Ruhlender, 1989).

PARALLELS BETWEEN IMPLICIT MEMORY AND IMPLICIT LEARNING

Amnesia

Densely amnesic patients perform very poorly on explicit tests of memory, but they perform remarkably well, and frequently normally, on numerous implicit tests. These data provide some of the strongest empirical grounds for distinguishing between implicit and explicit memory. Because there are now many reviews of the relevant literature (e.g., Bowers & Schacter, 1993; Cermak, 1993; Shimamura, 1986, 1993), we only sum-

12

marize the main results. A number of studies have shown normal and long-lasting priming effects on perceptual verbal tests such as word-stem completion or word identification (e.g., Cermak, Talbot, Chandler, & Wolbarst, 1985; Graf, Squire, & Mandler, 1984) and on tests with pictorial materials such as picture naming (Cave & Squire, 1992). It is less clear whether normal priming extends to so-called novel information. Some studies reported a normal acquisition of new verbal associations with implicit test instructions, at least for mild forms of amnesia (Graf & Schacter, 1985), but this was not always replicated (e.g., Mayes & Gooding, 1989). However, there is evidence for normal priming of novel objects or of novel visual information such as dot patterns (Gabrieli, Milberg, Keane, & Corkin, 1990; Schacter, Cooper, Tharan, & Rubens, 1991).

Most of the studies investigating priming on conceptual tests have found a normal pattern of effects with amnesic patients (e.g., Carlesimo, 1994; Graf et al., 1985; Shimamura & Squire, 1984). This is surprising, because amnesia was once thought to damage the conceptual operations needed for successful performance in explicit memory tests, but not the operations supporting perceptual priming. Normal priming in conceptual implicit tests, such as category instance production, does not seem to fit this view (but see Blaxton, 1992).

The pattern of results is less differentiated with respect to implicit learning tasks, but it appears that there are clear parallels to implicit memory research. Under certain circumstances, amnesic patients show performance comparable to that of normals. For instance, in artificial grammar-learning tasks, amnesics show basically the same performance as normal participants if they are asked simply to classify test strings as grammatical and nongrammatical, but not if they are asked to perform the classification task based on the similarity between test strings and strings from the acquisition phase. Presumably, the latter form of the classification task stimulates explicit retrieval of string exemplars from the acquisition phase (Knowlton, Ramus, & Squire, 1992; Knowlton & Squire, 1994). Comparable results have been reported for depressive and schizophrenic patients and for alcoholics with signs of organic brain impairment (Abrams & Reber, 1988). Furthermore, patients suffering from organic amnesia often show normal performance on sequence-learning tasks, as do participants with drug-induced amnesia and patients with Alzheimer's decease (Hartman, Knopman, & Nissen, 1989; Knopman & Nissen, 1987; Nissen & Bullemer, 1987; Nissen, Knopman, & Schacter, 1987; Nissen, Willingham, & Hartman, 1989).

● Divided Attention

It is well-known that the attentional state during the study phase is an important determinant of performance on explicit memory tests, such as recognition (e.g., Fisk & Schneider, 1984) and recall (Baddeley, Lewis, Eldridge, & Thomson, 1984), but this does not seem to be the case for implicit memory tests. For instance, a number of studies have found that implicit tests are more likely than explicit tests to show retention of poorly attended stimuli (Bornstein, Leone, & Galley, 1987; Hawley & Johnston, 1991; Mandler, Nakamura, & Van Zandt, 1987; Merikle & Reingold, 1991). In addition, under most conditions, the amount of priming is equivalent for full and divided-attention conditions (Jacoby, Woloshyn, & Kelley, 1989; Parkin, Reich, & Russo, 1990; Parkin & Russo, 1990; Russo & Parkin, 1993). For example, Parkin et al. (1990) had participants perform a sentence verification task at study. One half of the participants also had to perform a tone monitoring task simultaneously. Retention was assessed a day later, either by an explicit recognition test or an implicit word-fragment completion test on items embedded in the sentences. Dividing attention at study affected recognition, but it had no effect on primed target completion. Parkin and Russo (1990) presented comparable results with pictures as stimuli.

In sum, then, at least perceptual tests of implicit memory may be more immune to dividing attention than comparable explicit tests. We assume that this is so because the processes (or memory systems) relevant for the implicit retrieval of information are left intact by the typically used manipulations of attention. It is, of course, conceivable that methods of "dividing attention" are found that do interfere with the relevant processes or systems, in which case performance decrements may be observed even in implicit memory tests. Nevertheless, implicit memory tests appear more "robust" than explicit memory tests.

Within certain limits, an analog conclusion may be drawn for the area of implicit learning. Most investigations of the role of attention for implicit learning have been conducted in the sequence-learning paradigm. Typically, participants' counting of tones is used as a secondary task to explore the effects of diminished attention for implicit sequence learning. More precisely, participants hear either a low-pitched or a high-pitched tone shortly after each response. They are instructed to count the high-pitched tones and to ignore the other tones, or vice versa. It seems clear that so-called unique or hybrid sequences (i.e., sequences in which each event or at least some of the events, respectively, may be predicted from the preceding event) can be learned under that form of distraction (Cohen, Ivry, & Keele, 1990; Curran & Keele, 1993; Keele & Jennings, 1992). The situation is less clear for ambiguous sequences, that is, sequences in which no event can be predicted perfectly by knowing only one preceding event. On the one hand, detailed analyses show that ambiguous transitions within hybrid sequences may be learned (Curran & Keele, 1993; Frensch, Buchner, & Lin, 1994). On the other hand, Cohen et al. (1990) argue that, in addition to a simple associative learning mechanism, which does not need attention to operate, the learning of ambiguous sequences requires a hierarchic learning mechanism, which does need attention to operate. Indeed, it was shown that when ambiguous sequences are to be learned, the typical reaction-time increase at the transition from systematic to random sequences is not observed with the tone-counting secondary task (Cohen et al., 1990; Nissen & Bullemer, 1987). However, this finding has been difficult to replicate (Mayr, 1996; Reed & Johnson, 1994). One possible alternative view to that of Cohen et al. is that the tone-counting task does not interfere with the learning of ambiguous sequences but rather with the expression of what is learned in the reaction-time measure. In a series of experiments, Frensch, Lin, and Buchner (1996) were able to collect evidence in support of this alternative view. However, the secondary task may still reduce the amount of learning relative to a single task condition. Stadler (1995) showed that this is probably so because the secondary task may interfere with the organization of the sequence elements into higher-order units, and not because the secondary task draws on some general attentional resource that would be necessary for sequence learning to occur (see also Heuer & Schmidtke, in press). He argued that participants' updating of their tone count would be equivalent to inserting a pause, and this forced pause would disrupt the organization of the sequence elements into higher-order units. Consistent with this hypothesis, Stadler found that inserting artificial pauses between half of the trials caused as much interference as the tone-counting secondary task. In addition, there was little interference when participants performed a memory-load task concurrently with the sequence-learning task.

Outside the sequence-learning paradigm, it has been found that random number generation may interfere with grammar learning (Dienes, Broadbent, & Berry, 1991). Dienes et al. speculate that, in their task, the learning of the grammatical strings and the random number-generation task may both have involved an articulatory loop structure, thus leading to interference. Classical sequence-learning tasks differ in that the primary task is visuo-spatial, and the secondary tone-counting task may require an articulatory loop. Thus, one possibility is that interference is observed only to the degree to which primary and secondary tasks require the use of the same working memory structures or processes.

● Temporal Stability

The temporal stability of priming on implicit memory tests may be considerable. For instance, Jacoby and Dallas (1981, Experiment 5) obtained no reliable decrease in priming from an immediate test to testing delayed 24 hours in a word-identification test compared to a significant drop over this interval in recognition memory. Similarly, an often cited study by Tulving, Schacter, and Stark (1982) reported only a slight drop in priming on the word-fragment completion test over an interval of one week, whereas recognition showed a sharp decline. Even more impressively, Mitchell and Brown (1988) showed stable repetition priming over an interval of 6 weeks in picture naming, whereas tests of recognition memory demonstrated reliable forgetting. Research on the re-reading of textual information has found savings over an interval of one year when participants could no longer discriminate between texts that had or had not been read before (Kolers, 1976). Finally, several developmental studies have found infants' and toddlers' memory to be impressively durable as assessed by implicit memory measures, with explicit memory largely lacking (Myers, Clifton, & Clarkson, 1987; Newcombe & Fox, 1994; Perris, Myers, & Clifton, 1990).

However, several studies have also found losses of priming over time. For word-fragment completion tests, Sloman, Hayman, Ohta, Law, and Tulving (1988) showed a rapid loss of priming over short delays (less than 5 minutes) and then more gradual decay thereafter. In one of their experiments, priming lasted over a year, however. On the other hand, complete loss of priming has been found after 2 hours or less with word-stem completion measures (Chen & Squire, 1990; Graf & Mandler, 1984) although there are exceptions to this pattern of results (Roediger, Weldon, Stadler, & Riegler, 1992). For conceptual implicit tests such as category association, Hamann (1990) showed a significant decline in priming over 90 minutes, although priming on this type of test may remain above chance at least over an interval of 24 hours (Rappold & Hashtroudi, 1991). Thus, although the pattern of results is somewhat inconsistent, and priming may not be as completely resistant to forgetting as was once believed, measures of implicit memory have been proven to be extremely long-lasting, at least under certain conditions. It is, indeed, remarkable that even a single presentation of a word can lead to priming that may last months.

Surprisingly long retention has also been reported for knowledge acquired in implicit learning tasks. Allen and Reber (1980) conducted a 2-year follow-up to the grammar-learning study reported by Reber and Allen (1978). Eight out of the original ten participants judged the grammaticality of sequences from the original study. Performance was generally somewhat lower relative to the original study, but participants were still able to distinguish grammatical from nongrammatical letter strings. Similar results, but for smaller retention intervals, have been reported for other variants of the grammar-learning task (Mathews et al., 1989, 1-week intervals over a period of 4 weeks), and for a sequence-learning task (Nissen et al., 1989, 1 week).

● Developmental Patterns

Fagan (1990) used a novelty preference paradigm and found preferential looking to new versus previously exposed patterns in 5-month-olds after delays of 2 weeks. Using an operant conditioning procedure, Rovee Collier and colleagues (e.g., Rovee Collier, 1990) demonstrated retention over 21 days in 6-month-old infants. In a deferred imitation paradigm, Meltzoff (1988) showed that 9-month-old infants were capable of spontaneous imitation after a 24-hour retention interval. Thus, even nonverbal infants may have a rather efficient memory that could be a precursor to adult-like forms of implicit memory, or an "early memory system" (Schacter & Moscovitch, 1984).

Some cross-sectional studies have compared measures of implicit memory across the life span or have compared younger age groups (e.g., preschoolers and school children) or older and younger adults (see e.g., Light & La Voie, 1993; Mitchell, 1993; Naito & Komatsu, 1993; Parkin, 1993). Most of the research with younger children has used picture-identification tasks. Children were to identify pictures from successively presented fragment forms, each successive fragment being more complete than the previous one. At test, this task was repeated with old and with new items. With 5- to 8-year-old children, Wippich, Mecklenbräuker, and Brausch (1989) found developmentally stable priming scores, but explicit memory (e.g., recall and recognition) improved with age.

Unfortunately, there are few studies with children using conceptual implicit tests. Recently, Mecklenbräuker and Wippich (1995) have compared 6- and 10-year-old children on a category-exemplar generation test. Once again, older children produced more category members in explicit cued recall, but priming on the generation test did not vary with age. Given that conceptual tests may be dependent on the development and structure of the knowledge base (e.g., semantic memory), it may be premature to generalize this result to other domains of conceptual priming. Indeed, Perruchet, Frazier, and Lautrey (1995, Experiment 1) have recently shown that older children outperformed the younger ones in priming when the items presented were atypical of their categories.

When younger and older adults are compared on implicit measures of memory, age differences are generally small and significant only in few cases (e.g., Hultsch, Masson, & Small, 1991), but older adults score lower than younger persons on explicit tests of memory (cf. Salthouse, 1988). This pattern suggests that there is a dissociation between explicit and implicit measures of memory in old age too (cf. Light & La Voie, 1993). In general, therefore, we may conclude that compared to explicit tests of memory, age-related differences on implicit tests are generally minimal.

The empirical basis for conclusions about parallel results in implicit learning paradigms is sparse, but what is available suggests that like implicit memory, implicit learning does not vary much as a function of age. In a serial reaction paradigm, Howard and Howard (1989) found that elderly participants learned just as well as younger participants, although the reaction times produced by the elderly participants were generally higher than those of the younger participants. In contrast, the measures used to assess participants' explicit knowledge about the sequences showed clear superiority of the younger over the older participants. Analog results have been obtained by Frensch and Miner (1994) for the standard sequence-learning task. However, when a secondary task was introduced, then differences between the age groups appeared. Another result, which allows for more differentiated conclusions, is Cherry and Stadler's (1995) finding that two groups of older adults who differed in educational attainment, occupational status, and verbal ability also differed in their ability to learn a 10-trial repeating sequence. Whereas the higher-ability group of older adults performed at a level comparable to younger adults, the lower-ability older people showed less sequence learning.

DIFFERENCES BETWEEN IMPLICIT
MEMORY AND IMPLICIT LEARNING

Specificity Versus Abstractness

An intriguing characteristic of perceptual, but not of conceptual, implicit tests of memory is that changes in modality (e.g., from auditory to visual) or changes in symbolic form (e.g., from pictorial to verbal) between study and test can affect performance drastically, even though such changes typically do not affect performance on explicit tests of memory. Moreover, small changes within a particular modality between study and test, such as changes in the physical aspects of a stimulus (e.g., the typography of a word), can attenuate priming on that stimulus in comparison to a stimulus that is simply repeated. Thus, there is clear evidence for specificity in perceptual priming (for a review, see Roediger & Srinivas, 1993). To give just a few examples: No cross-modal (auditory to visual) priming seems to occur in word-identification tests (Jacoby & Dallas, 1981; Rajaram & Roediger, 1993). In word-stem or word-fragment completion tests, the greatest amount of priming results from visual presentations of the words, less from auditory presentations, and least from pictorial presentations (Roediger & Blaxton, 1987). Studying pictures transfers only minimally to words (or not at all in some experiments, see e.g., Weldon, 1991). Finally, in picture-fragment identification tasks, priming was found to be specific to the exact contour presented at study (Srinivas, 1993).

Somewhat surprisingly, priming is unaffected by variations in the size or color of objects between study and test (e.g., Biederman & Cooper, 1992; Cooper, Schacter, Ballesteros, & Moore, 1992; Zimmer, 1995). However, Wippich, Mecklenbräuker, and Baumann (1994) have been able to demonstrate that color information can influence priming on a conceptual test of implicit memory (e.g., a color-choice test for black-and-white versions of studied pictures). Thus, at least some types of perceptual information may be represented, processed, or integrated at a higher, conceptual level.

There appears to be an opposite trend in the results obtained in implicit learning paradigms. As mentioned in the introduction, it has long been shown that knowledge acquired about a finite-state grammar may be transferred between different instantiations of the same grammatical structure (Gomez & Schvaneveldt, 1994; Mathews, Blanchard-Fields, Norris, &

19

Roussel, 1991; Mathews et al., 1989; Reber, 1969). Altmann et al. (1995) have shown that knowledge about a grammar may even be transferred to an implementation of that grammar in a different domain. For instance, hearing grammatical melodies in an acquisition phase helped in the classifying of letter strings generated by the same grammar.

In a similar vein, McGeorge and Burton (1990) showed transfer between different implementations of a nonobvious rule in the composition of number strings. When, in an unexpected test, participants had to select "old" numbers from a set of numbers that were in fact all new, they showed a distinct preference for numbers that conformed to the construction rule of the acquisition-phase numbers. This preference transferred to a format in which the test numbers were presented in their word equivalents. Bright and Burton (1994) induced a preference for clock faces bearing a time between 6 and 12 o'clock, which transferred from analog to digital clock displays. Cock, Berry, and Gaffan (1994) showed that, at least to a large degree, the effect reported by McGeorge and Burton (1990) may be based on participants' choosing test number strings on the basis of their similarity to the acquisition-phase number strings rather than on the implicit abstraction of some rule. This fits with reports by McAndrews and Moscovitch (1985) as well as Vokey and Brooks (1992) that both similarity and grammaticality effects contributed to classifications in a typical grammar-learning task.

Thus, at least based on the current pattern of results, there appears to be evidence for a surprisingly manifest degree of transfer of knowledge between different implementations of implicit learning tasks. This seems to distinguish the area of implicit leaning from that of implicit memory research.

● **State of Awareness**

Implicit memory tests are thought to tap an automatic form of memory, or incidental retrieval. Yet, especially in working with normal participants, it has always been clear that participants may resort to controlled or intentional uses of memory with certain implicit tests (but not with others, see Mecklenbräuker & Wippich, 1995; Mitchell, 1993). For example, while performing a word-fragment completion task, a participant may notice after producing a word that it was studied previously and adopt intentional retrieval attempts on other test items.

In recent years, several criteria have been suggested to establish incidental retrieval in implicit tests of memory. For instance, one may simply ask participants, after the test, about their state of awareness (Bowers & Schacter, 1990). Probably the most common way to show that a test was implicit is to dissociate it from an explicit test within an experiment, but simply showing that two tests are sensitive to different variables does not ensure that the tests require different modes of retrieval (Dunn & Kirsner, 1988). The test dissociation approach may be extended using the retrieval intentionality criterion (Schacter, Bowers, & Booker, 1989), according to which everything is held constant for implicit and explicit groups except for the instructions given at the time of the test. The goal is to establish a dissociation between explicit and implicit versions of a test. Finally, Merikle and Reingold (1991) have proposed a further extension. Their basic idea was to show greater effects of a variable on an implicit than on an explicit test. Such a finding would indicate greater sensitivity to unconscious task-relevant information because, if the information were available for conscious use, it would have been used on explicit tests.

A rather influential approach to the same problem is the process-dissociation procedure proposed by Jacoby (1991). Based on dual-process models of recognition memory (e.g., Mandler, 1980), Jacoby assumed that automatic and controlled memory processes may contribute to task performance. The process-dissociation procedure, in combination with an appropriate measurement model, is a tool to estimate separately the contributions of the two types of processes within one single task, such that one need not rely on dissociations between different tasks. In the measurement model originally suggested by Jacoby (1991), performance was thought to be exclusively determined by the unconscious automatic and the conscious controlled processes. Guessing and, hence, response bias were not taken into account. Recent extensions, however, included guessing parameters and were shown to be more adequate than the original model (e.g., Buchner, Erdfelder, & Vaterrodt-Plünnecke, 1995). Thus, researchers who want to apply the process-dissociation procedure to a memory task should use one of the measurement models that take response biases into account.

It is important to note that the problem of guessing is, of course, also present when different types of tests, such as explicit and implicit memory tests, are compared. If the response biases differ between the two types of tasks, then what looks like a substantive task dissociation could simply be a difference in response biases for the two tasks. Definitely, more attention needs to be devoted to the response bias problem in comparisons of implicit and explicit memory tests.

A final point to be considered is that in implicit memory research, we are always in a position to assess directly whether, at a certain point in time, a certain content of memory is available for recollection. For instance, we may, after an implicit memory test or in a separate control group, simply ask for explicit recognition judgments of the learned material, if we want to find out whether the memories expressed in the implicit test were also available explicitly, and this may yield some very interesting insights about the state of awareness associated with various forms of test performance (Wippich, 1992a).

To summarize, it has always been clear that participants may resort to controlled or intentional uses of memory with certain implicit tests. Attempts to assess empirically the possible contaminations of performance on implicit tests by intentional retrieval are relatively recent. The emphasis has been on estimating how much of the task performance should be attributed to one or the other type of retrieval process. Finally, and most important, we may assess directly whether in fact a certain content of memory is available for explicit recollection.

In contrast, implicit learning research has routinely encompassed attempts to estimate whether the learning that was underlying the task performance may have to be considered explicit, and at least initially, the contribution of explicit learning processes was denied. Furthermore, the debates about the state of awareness associated with the learning process tended to focus on postulating or denying the learning to be unconscious. Finally, and most important, the assessment of the state of awareness associated with the learning process has always been indirect, through the assessment of the knowledge after the learning.

In his early works on implicit learning, Reber (1967; Reber & Allen, 1978; Reber & Lewis, 1977) reported that postexperimental questioning had been done to reveal potentially explicit knowledge. Unfortunately, however, these reports are only fragmentary. In sequence learning, the generate task seemed to be a rather popular method for assessing whether the event regularities that were presumably learned and expressed in the reaction-time measurements could also be reproduced (e.g., Cohen et al., 1990; Frensch et al., 1994; Frensch & Miner, 1994; Nissen & Bullemer, 1987; Nissen et al., 1987; Willingham & Koroshetz, 1993; Willingham, Nissen, & Bullemer, 1989). In system-control tasks, specific post-task questionnaires have been used to assess participants' "verbalizable" knowledge (e.g., Berry & Broadbent, 1984, 1987, 1988).

Why should the state of awareness associated with the knowledge acquired in an implicit learning task be considered important, given the fact that the learning process is the topic of interest? The major reason seems to be a tacit consensus that if a certain learning process should be conceived of as unconscious, then a minimal requirement is to show that the knowledge acquired through this process is also not consciously available. Shanks and St. John (1994) go even further and argue that, if learning is to be called implicit, participants must be unaware of the study episode itself, in addition to the event relations acquired in the study episode. This may appear to be a rather rigid prerequisite, but it should be noted that however rigid the requirement about the state of awareness associated with memories of various aspects of the study episode, the demonstration that participants cannot report such memories at the time of test must not be counted as unequivocal evidence of unconscious learning. Demonstrating no memory of critical study-episode aspects may increase the plausibility of the argument that the learning process itself was also unconscious, but there is always the possibility that participants were quite aware of the critical event relationships during learning, but the relevant knowledge may be inaccessible for any form of explicit retrieval at the time of test because, for instance, some critical cues from the study episode are missing. Additionally, the measures used to assess the potentially explicit knowledge (a) may be insensitive; (b) may not be pure measures of only explicit or only implicit processes; (c) may have inadequate psychometric qualities (e.g., they may be unreliable); or (d) may be directed at knowledge that is irrelevant to successful task performance. It is therefore not surprising to find repeated debates about the state of awareness associated with knowledge acquisition in implicit learning paradigms.

For instance, Dulany, Carlson, and Dewey (1984, 1985) have argued that simple free verbal recall would be an insensitive measure of the knowledge acquired in typical grammar-learning studies (e.g., Reber, 1967; Reber & Allen, 1978; Reber & Lewis, 1977). Dulany et al. (1984) asked their participants to mark the parts of test strings that either defined these as grammatical or violated the grammar's rules. The rules extracted from these marks were only partially valid and limited in scope, but they predicted the grammatical judgments without significant residual. Dulany et al. concluded from this finding that knowledge acquired in typical grammar-learning paradigms consisted of reportable rules that would form so-called correlated grammars. Reber, Allen, and Regan (1985) rejected this interpretation, arguing that Dulany et al.'s measure of grammatical knowledge was not a pure measure of explicit or conscious knowledge. Rather, it may have included intuitions and vague guesses, thereby tapping primarily implicit and unconscious rather than explicit and conscious knowledge. As another example, consider the work by Perruchet and Amorim (1992), who argued that the generate task is an unreliable measure of knowledge. In this task, participants are to demonstrate their explicit knowledge about event systematicities by predicting rather than reacting to an event, given a certain other event. The problem is that few initial trials can be used to estimate how much of what has been learned is explicitly available, because participants may learn through the feedback they receive after each prediction. With only a few reactions on a novel task, one can hardly expect a reliable measure of knowledge, and, of course, an unreliable measure of knowledge cannot be expected to correlate with any other performance measure, such as the indirect reaction-time measure of learning. Finally, Perruchet and Pacteau (1990) suggested that knowledge of permissible letter bigrams can account for classification performance in grammar-learning experiments (but see Gomez & Schvaneveldt, 1994). Thus, asking participants to report the rules underlying their classifications would be misguided because rule knowledge could be irrelevant for successful task performance. All of these examples illustrate why task-appropriate explicit knowledge may exist without being reflected in conventional measures of memory.

● Theoretical Frameworks

A shortcoming of the implicit memory enterprise is the relative scarceness of theoretical specification of the processes and representations assumed to be involved (Ratcliff & McKoon, 1995). The research reports are mainly empirical, with little formal theory. Only rather general "views" or "approaches" have been proposed, which serve as theoretical backgrounds for descriptions of implicit, in contrast to explicit, memory phenomena.

At present, implicit memory research seems to be dominated by two such approaches, which represent complementary rather than competing perspectives: the so-called multiple memory systems view and the transfer-appropriate processing approach. According to the system view, the general faculty of memory must be fractionated into a number of subsystems, such as declarative and procedural (Cohen & Squire, 1980) or episodic and semantic memory (Tulving, 1983). Data from both normal and amnesic participants have caused the number of putative memory systems to grow, so that now most researchers working within this framework would agree that at least half a dozen systems are needed to explain the results of implicit and explicit memory tests. According to Roediger (1990a), the number may extend to about 25. For example, Tulving and Schacter (1990) have argued that three different neural systems account for the findings of implicit memory tests. A word-form perceptual system underlies priming for words, a structural description system is postulated for pictures and objects, and a semantic memory underlies priming on conceptual implicit tests. Considering the available auditory priming results, a presemantic auditory perceptual representation system must be added to this list (Schacter & Church, 1992). The memory systems view is rooted within a neuroscience research tradition, and its proponents often tie their findings and theorizing to what is known from neurological case studies, or to knowledge about brain anatomy and function. In finding converging evidence from neurological measurements (such as from various techniques of neuroimaging), this approach may gain strength (Schacter, 1992).

The systems view has sometimes been criticized for being unparsimonious and for its seemingly arbitrary proliferation of "new" systems. Although we share a first intuition with these critics that an inflation of systems seems less acceptable than a variety of processes to reconstruct task performance theoretically, there is of course no principal reason why one should assume fewer systems than processes. Taken to the extreme, nobody will probably argue that any reasonable theoretical reconstruction of mental performance can be achieved based on only two systems (e.g., a declarative and a procedural system). This is a legitimate starting point for theorizing, but we must be aware that things just cannot be that simple. Thus, we think that there is nothing wrong with the postulating of new memory systems, as long as their characteristics are sufficiently specified for making testable predictions.

One of the most influential processing views in recent research has been a transfer-appropriate processing approach developed by Roediger and his coworkers (e.g., Roediger, 1990b; Roediger, Weldon, & Challis, 1989). The guiding assumptions of this approach have been summarized by Roediger and McDermott (1993) and are as follows:

1. Performance on implicit or explicit memory tests benefits to the extent that the cognitive operations involved in the test recapitulate or overlap those engaged during initial learning.
2. Implicit memory tests usually require different mental processes than do explicit tests and consequently benefit from different types of processing during learning. This is to "explain" dissociations between implicit and explicit measures of memory.
3. The most commonly used implicit tests draw primarily on perceptual processes, whereas the most typical explicit tests draw largely on conceptual processing.
4. The perceptual/conceptual classification of tests is not meant as a dichotomy. Rather, it is more profitable to think of these as two separate dimensions that do not necessarily trade off against one another. Thus, an implicit test may require perceptual as well as conceptual processes.
5. The perceptual/conceptual contrast is not correlated with the implicit/explicit distinction; one can create conceptual implicit tests and perceptual explicit tests. This is to "explain" parallel research findings with implicit and explicit memory tests.

In our view, this approach is useful as a general guiding framework. However, one needs to know more precisely, and a priori, which processes may be required in a given test situation in order to test and to falsify specific hypotheses. For instance, perceptual processes in the verbal domain are certainly different from perceptual processes in the pictorial domain. Furthermore, this approach is mute as to the possible differences between implicit and explicit tests of memory that may overlap in the required processes (i.e., there is no reference to automatic or intentional uses of memory). Interestingly, there are some signs of progress aimed at a specification of processes. For example, Weldon (1991) has analyzed and shown that lexical processes are most important in order to obtain priming on verbal perceptual tests, whereas more superficial features (such as typography) may influence priming to the extent that lexical access has been achieved (but see Wippich, 1995). In sum, it seems to be a good idea to view priming as a phenomenon of transfer. It is indispensable, however, to be as exact as possible in analyzing the tasks used in transferring prior experiences to test performance. Taken together, one can say that implicit memory research has tended to focus on the global cognitive architecture. Detailed task analyses and specific models for these tasks are the exception.

The opposite trend is evident in implicit learning research. Here, we often find elegant but isolated models for specific tasks, and an apparent lack of interest in a more global theoretical framework. For instance,

Servan-Schreiber and Anderson (1990) have suggested a model for grammar learning that explicates how processes relevant in the acquisition phase may support later discriminations between new grammatical and nongrammatical strings. It is proposed in this process model that participants form chunks of letters when asked to memorize the grammatical letter strings. As learning proceeds, longer chunks will be created from more elementary chunks, resulting in a hierarchy of chunks that may then be used to "perceive" new strings generated by the same set of rules. The smaller the number of chunks needed to identify a new string (i.e., the larger the chunks that can be applied to a particular string of a certain fixed length), the easier the string can be perceived, and the more familiar it appears. The probability of a participant classifying a string as grammatical increases as a function of the familiarity associated with that string. Consistent with this model, the systematic grouping of string elements during acquisition leads to better grammaticality judgments, and violations of the syntactical structure of a grammar are detected particularly well if they violate the grouping structure induced during acquisition (Servan-Schreiber & Anderson, 1990). It is also compatible with the model that grammatical strings are better identified than nongrammatical strings in a perceptual identification task (Buchner, 1994).

Certain connectionist models of grammar learning have been evaluated favorably by Dienes (1992). More precisely, he applied models of several classes to the data of Dienes at al. (1991) and of Dulany et al. (1984), and the best class of models considered was that of connectionist models that use the (simultaneous) delta rule as their learning algorithm. In an attempt to give the behavior of the simultaneous delta rule model a more general, substantive interpretation, Dienes (1992) argued that it could best be understood as abstracting a set of representative but incomplete rules for classifying the strings.

Mathews (Druhan & Mathews, 1989; Mathews, 1991) presented a model based on a classifier-system architecture (Holland, Holyoak, Nisbett, & Thagard, 1986) for the grammar-learning task. The model uses a set of weighted rules to classify strings as grammatical or nongrammatical. These rules correspond to fragments of grammatical strings, each of which matches a certain number of strings to be classified. Such fragmentary knowledge is assumed to result from people's less-than-perfect memories of string exemplars. The model fitted the data of two randomly selected participants and their yoked partners in the Mathews et al. (1989) study.

Cleeremans (1993; Cleeremans & McClelland, 1991; Kushner, Cleeremans, & Reber, 1991) suggested a particular connectionist architecture to model implicit sequence learning. He showed that a variant of a simple recurrent network model with hidden units and a back propagation algorithm could account for his experimental data quite well. Like Dienes (1992), Cleeremans conducted extensive analyses of the model's properties. These analyses revealed that the model became more and more sensitive to the context of events (i.e., continuously larger subsequences of events could be distinguished) until finally entire sequences of events were "encoded" by the model.

The models presented in this section represent only a small selection. It should be clear nevertheless that the models of implicit learning phenomena are much more precise and detailed than the theoretical frameworks usually discussed in connection with implicit memory data.

As a final note, we would like to mention that some authors consider their models particularly appropriate for modeling implicit learning phenomena because of the models' particular architecture. For instance, Kushner et al. (1991) argue that "because all the knowledge of the system is stored in its connections, this knowledge may only be expressed through performance" (p. 5), which is seen as a characteristic of implicit learning. Mathews (1991) makes a similar suggestion based on the fact that the mechanisms in his classifier-system model "do not require centralized control" (p. 118). These are certainly appealing statements. Nevertheless, one must be aware that, although these models provide for elegant mechanisms that generate a certain performance pattern that may or may not match the patterns produced in typical experiments, in their current specification, they are mute with respect to the state of awareness associated with the operation of the mechanism.

SYNERGY

In this section, we sketch briefly how the parallels and differences we described between implicit memory and implicit learning research could be exploited by taking methodological or theoretical approaches from one domain into the other. We discuss first the issue of theoretical approaches and subsequently the question of methodological transfer.

● **Theoretical Approaches**

As mentioned above, implicit memory research has tended to focus on the general architecture within which experimental results were interpreted rather than on specific task analyses and models of task performance. More detailed process models are definitely needed. We have mentioned already the progress achieved by Weldon (1991) in her analysis of lexical priming processes. Based on the concept of transfer-appropriate processing, Wippich (1992b) has been able to show which specific component processes in the generation of mental images are responsible for repetition priming effects in imaging tasks. These are the lines along which we see ample room for progress in implicit memory research.

Implicit learning research, in contrast, could gain transparency and coherence from incorporating theoretical frameworks from implicit memory research. For instance, Servan-Schreiber and Anderson's (1990) competitive chunking model may be regarded as an instance of the processing view. More precisely, grammar learning according to this model can be said to be implicit in the sense that the chunking processes relevant during memorization are transfer-appropriate for later string perception and, thus, for later discrimination performance. A similar conclusion has been drawn by Whittlesea and Dorken (1993) based on findings that the type of processing of grammatical strings during an acquisition phase determined what sort of knowledge was acquired and later available for judgments about new strings.

In contrast to grammar learning, there is no clear distinction between acquisition and test phase in sequence-learning tasks. Thus, it may simply not be close at hand to use the concept of transfer to describe performance on such tasks. In addition, a noticeable number of researchers in that area come from a clinical or neuroscience tradition, and it is thus not surprising to find a preference for approaches that may be classified as system views. In the simplest version, procedural and declarative systems are distinguished and thought to be involved in the use of system knowledge for performance speed-up and reportable system knowledge, respectively (e.g., Knopman, 1991; Knopman & Nissen, 1991; Nissen et al., 1987; Squire & Frambach, 1990).

In addition to these more general approaches, it seems that the concept behind dual-process models (e.g., Mandler, 1980) may be applied profitably to implicit learning tasks such as grammar learning (Buchner, 1994; Higham, in press). Consider Higham's (in press) dual-process conception that string classifications in grammar-learning experiments are assumed to be based on both an assessment of the specific similarity of a particular test string with stored instances from the learning phase and on the more abstract grammaticality of the test string. He argues that the classification of new strings on the basis of their similarity to learned instances is based on intentional uses of recollective processes, whereas classification on the basis of grammaticality is familiarity-based.

● Research Techniques

In the typical grammar-learning task, participants first memorize strings generated by a finite-state grammar and then classify strings as grammatically correct or incorrect. Note that the grammaticality judgments are explicit tests of what has been learned. This is so because the instructions need to point out the regularities in the strings, and it is necessary to inform participants about the relationship between study and test. It seems conceivable that participants might try to recall memorized letter strings, either to scan these for "salient" features or to use recallable instances for more global similarity matches. Compatible with this speculation, Higham (in press) found evidence suggesting that similarity-oriented grammaticality judgments are based on intentional uses of recollective processes. Such strategies would undermine the position that an incidental learning process during study was the source of tacit grammatical knowledge relevant at test. In addition, participants might, to a certain degree, successfully identify a few partial rules even during the test phase itself. For example, in a typical grammar-learning study (e.g., Reber, Kassin, Lewis, & Cantor, 1980), grammatical strings usually have a limited number of possible initial and terminal letters, and they often contain runs of identical letters. During test, these features of the strings will be intact more often than not. If this is detected, participants may use such knowledge as a heuristic for their grammaticality judgments without ever having memorized a grammatical string. Interestingly, Dulany et al. (1984) found that even participants who had not memorized any grammatical strings were able to perform above chance on the grammaticality judgments, and Reber (1967) found evidence for continued learning during the test phase.

In other words, grammaticality judgments may, to some unknown degree, be determined by explicit knowledge that does not originate in the acquisition phase. The obvious alternative is to use indirect tests, which do not stimulate the recall of learned instances or the searching for rules. For instance, grammatical and nongrammatical strings may be presented under difficult viewing conditions, and identification times may serve as an indirect measure of the knowledge acquired about grammatical strings. According to Servan-Schreiber and Anderson's (1990) competitive chunking model, larger chunks may be used to support the perceiving of grammatical as opposed to ungrammatical strings. Indeed, the former are identified faster than the latter (Buchner, 1994).

In process-control tasks and grammar-learning tasks, the knowledge test is explicit. That is, participants must use what they have learned about system regularities to get the system into a target state. In addition, as we have mentioned above, the learning situation is intentional. Participants know from the beginning that they have to figure out the regularities in the system behavior. Thus, the problem of performance being based on explicit memories is even more serious. Again, a possible alternative is to use implicit measures of memory (e.g., perceptual identification of a system's output signals), possibly in combination with an incidental learning situation (e.g., the memorizing of sequences of inputs, see Buchner, 1995).

A final example concerns the process-dissociation procedure developed in the context of implicit memory research. In principle, performance on tasks designed to assess post hoc the explicit knowledge acquired in an implicit learning procedure need not be pure measures of knowledge. It seems therefore reasonable to explore whether, and if so how, the process-dissociation procedure may be used in the context of implicit learning tasks. The example we use here is the sequence-learning paradigm. Some researchers have tried to assess participants' explicit knowledge using a recognition task in which participants judge, for a number of sequence fragments, whether these follow the same systematicity as the acquisition-phase sequences (e.g., Perruchet & Amorim, 1992; Reed & Johnson, 1994; Stadler, 1993, 1995; Willingham, Greeley, & Bardone, 1993). One obvious problem with the task of recognizing sequences is that not only explicit recollection but also sequence familiarity (due to greater fluency of processing an "old" sequence) may contribute to recognition judgments. The process-dissociation procedure seems a well-suited tool to separate the two different influences, but a new measurement model had to be developed specifically for that task (Buchner, Steffens, Erdfelder, & Rothkegel, 1996). So far, this measurement model has been evaluated in three experiments, and it seems to reflect accurately the influences of controlled and automatic memory processes on sequence judgments.

The two examples we used to sketch possibilities of a fruitful cross-task between implicit memory and implicit learning concerned the incorporation of implicit memory tests and the process-dissociation procedure into implicit learning research. Another possibility would be to apply Merikle and Reingold's (1991) idea of searching for manipulations that have greater effects on an implicit than on an explicit test of performance to implicit learning paradigms. This route has been taken recently by Jiménez, Méndez, and Cleeremans (in press). Without going into further details, it should be obvious that there is ample room for the synergistic transfer of concepts, research techniques, and methodologies between the areas of implicit learning and implicit memory.

THE PROBLEM OF CONSCIOUSNESS

One of the most exciting—and most troublesome—aspects of research in the domains of implicit learning and implicit memory has been and still is the assertion that these phenomena may reflect unconscious influences of past experiences or knowledge, whereas explicit tests of the learning episode may reflect a conscious influence. Despite this concern with unconscious or conscious states of performance, there have been few attempts to measure conscious experiences directly in relation to performance. This situation may partly reflect what Tulving (1989) has called the doctrine of concordance of behavior, cognition, and experience. In its general form, this doctrine holds that performance, knowledge, and experience are closely correlated. In the past few years, this doctrine has come under debate, and the process-dissociation procedure is one useful methodological consequence of this debate. However, this procedure is an instructional or task manipulation, and it does not assess the state of awareness directly. Given a set of assumptions, consciousness is once again inferred from performance data. An attractive and alternative approach might be to give more weight to the subjective experiences of the participants in our experiments. In fact, Marcel (1988) has proposed a cognitive approach in which phenomenal experiences at the personal level are the most important data. According to Marcel, "psychology without consciousness, without phenomenal experience or the personal level, may be biology or cybernetics, but it is not psychology" (p. 121).

In our view, Marcel's call for a psychology that encompasses phenomenal experiences is challenging, as the conventional way to treat consciousness (if at all) is a functional approach that does identify certain components of information processing (e.g., short-term memory, attention, etc.) with states of consciousness. In doing so, there is a danger of mixing together very different models of the world. Information processing is concerned with a mechanistic system of representations and processes that may be simulated by adequate technologies. This would seem to be very different from the world of subjective personal experiences, in which notions such as (free) will, intention, volition, and so on make sense. Contrary to Marcel, however, we think that first-person accounts of phenomenal experiences can only be meaningful scientific data if they are interpreted within a conception of consciousness. Given that information processing is coordinated with a scientific theory of consciousness (and not with subjective experiences accessible only at a personal level), the problem of contamination of different worlds may be solved.

What is needed, then, is a more differentiated and articulated conception of consciousness in order to be useful for the research about implicit learning and implicit memory phenomena. Until now, most research interests focused on whether something has happened consciously or not. Such demonstrations and their refutations were exciting and attracted much attention. These efforts would gain more theoretical importance if we had a theory of consciousness that would clarify the demarcations between conscious and unconscious systems operating in different modes, on different features, having different formats, capacities, modes of expression, and functions. For example, such a conception would be needed in order to combine different functionalities that have been attributed to consciousness. Within Jacoby's (1991) process-dissociation procedure, the role of consciousness is restricted to control. In our view, there is more to consciousness than control, and we feel that this has been neglected in research of implicit phenomena. Information processing may be based on the parallel operations of specialized and distributed modules with only minimal interactions between subsystems. Consciousness may be the result of processes of integration and construction. That is, the output of modular systems may become synthesized by consciousness and can, thus, be propagated within the entire system. In this way, consciousness may "occur" within the context, and on the basis of, different operations. We may have to say farewell to a conception of consciousness as a stable function at a fixed place. Viewed within such a broader perspective, the study of implicit phenomena may have some potential to be useful for conceptions of consciousness.

REFERENCES

Abrams, M., & Reber, A. S. (1988). Implicit learning: Robustness in the face of psychiatric disorders. *Journal of Psycholinguistic Research, 17,* 425-439.

Allen, R., & Reber, A. S. (1980). Very long-term memory for tacit knowledge. *Cognition, 8,* 175-185.

Altmann, G. T. M., Dienes, Z., & Goode, A. (1995). Modality independence of implicitly learned grammatical knowledge. *Journal of Experimental Psychology: Learning, Memory, and Cognition, 21,* 899-912.

Baddeley, A., Lewis, V., Eldridge, M., & Thomson, N. (1984). Attention and retrieval from long-term memory. *Journal of Experimental Psychology: General, 113,* 518-540.

Beatty, W. W., Goodkin, D. E., Monson, N., & Beatty, P. A. (1990). Implicit learning in patients with chronic progressive multiple sclerosis. *International Journal of Clinical Neuropsychology, 12,* 166-172.

Berry, D. C. (1994). Implicit learning: Twenty-five years on. A tutorial. In C. Umiltà & M. Moscovitch (Eds.), *Attention and performance XV: Conscious and nonconscious information processing* (pp. 755-782). Cambridge: MIT Press.

Berry, D. C., & Broadbent, D. E. (1984). On the relationship between task performance and associated verbalizable knowledge. *The Quarterly Journal of Experimental Psychology, 36A,* 209-231.

Berry, D. C., & Broadbent, D. E. (1987). The combination of explicit and implicit learning processes in task control. *Psychological Research, 49,* 7-15.

Berry, D. C., & Broadbent, D. E. (1988). Interactive tasks and the implicit-explicit distinction. *British Journal of Psychology, 79,* 251-272.

Berry, D. C., & Broadbent, D. E. (1995). Implicit learning in the control of complex systems. In P. A. Frensch & J. Funke (Eds.), *Complex problem solving: European perspective* (pp. 131-150). Hillsdale, NJ: Lawrence Erlbaum.

Berry, D. C., & Dienes, Z. (1991). The relationship between implicit memory and implicit learning [Special Issue: The retirement of Donald Broadbent]. *British Journal of Psychology, 82,* 359-373.

Biederman, I., & Cooper, E. E. (1992). Size invariance in visual object priming. *Journal of Experimental Psychology: Human Perception and Performance, 18,* 121-133.

Blaxton, T. A. (1989). Investigating dissociations among memory measures: Support for a transfer appropriate processing framework. *Journal of Experimental Psychology: Learning, Memory, and Cognition, 15,* 657-668.

Blaxton, T. A. (1992). Dissociations among memory measures in memory-impaired subjects: Evidence for a processing account of memory. *Memory & Cognition, 20,* 549-562.

Bornstein, R. F., Leone, D. R., & Galley, D. J. (1987). The generalizability of subliminal mere exposure effects: Influence of stimuli perceived without awareness on social behavior. [Special Issue: Integrating personality and social psychology]. *Journal of Personality and Social Psychology, 53,* 1070-1079.

Bowers, J. S., & Schacter, D. L. (1990). Implicit memory and test awareness. *Journal of Experimental Psychology: Learning, Memory, and Cognition, 16,* 404-416.

Bowers, J., & Schacter, D. L. (1993). Priming of novel information in amnesic patients: Issues and data. In P. Graf & M. E. J. Masson (Eds.), *Implicit memory: New directions in cognition, development, and neuropsychology* (pp. 303-326). Hillsdale, NJ: Lawrence Erlbaum.

Bright, J. E. H., & Burton, A. M. (1994). Past midnight: Semantic processing in an implicit learning task. *The Quarterly Journal of Experimental Psychology, 47A,* 71-89.

Broadbent, D. E. (1977). Levels, hierarchies, and the locus of control. *The Quarterly Journal of Experimental Psychology, 29,* 181-201.

Broadbent, D. E., & Aston, B. (1978). Human control of a simulated economic system. *Ergonomics, 21,* 1035-1043.

Buchner, A. (1994). Indirect effects of synthetic grammar learning in an identification task. *Journal of Experimental Psychology: Learning, Memory, and Cognition, 20,* 550-565.

Buchner, A. (1995). Basic topics and approaches to the study of complex problem solving. In P. A. Frensch & J. Funke (Eds.), *Complex problem solving: European perspective* (pp. 27-63). Hillsdale, NJ: Lawrence Erlbaum.

Buchner, A., Erdfelder, E., & Vaterrodt-Plünnecke, B. (1995). Toward unbiased measurement of conscious and unconscious memory processes within the process-dissociation framework. *Journal of Experimental Psychology: General, 124,* 137-160.

Buchner, A., Funke, J., & Berry, D. C. (1995). Negative correlations between control performance and verbalizable knowledge: Indicators for implicit learning in process-control tasks? *The Quarterly Journal of Experimental Psychology, 48A,* 166-187.

Buchner, A., Steffens, M., Erdfelder, E., & Rothkegel, R. (1996). *A multinomial model to assess fluency and recollection in a sequence learning task.* Manuscript submitted for publication.

Bylsma, F. W., Rebok, G. W., & Brandt, J. (1991). Long-term retention of implicit learning in Huntington's disease. *Neuropsychologia, 29,* 1213-1221.

Carlesimo, G. A. (1994). Perceptual and conceptual priming in amnesic and alcoholic patients. *Neuropsychologia, 32,* 903-921.

Cave, C. B., & Squire, L. R. (1992). Intact and long-lasting repetition priming in amnesia. *Journal of Experimental Psychology: Learning, Memory, and Cognition, 18,* 509-520.

Cermak, L. S. (1993). Automatic versus controlled processing and the implicit task performance of amnesic patients. In P. Graf & M. E. J. Masson (Eds.), *Implicit memory: New directions in cognition, development, and neuropsychology* (pp. 287-301). Hillsdale, NJ: Lawrence Erlbaum.

Cermak, L. S., Talbot, N., Chandler, K., & Wolbarst, L. R. (1985). The perceptual priming phenomenon in amnesia. *Neuropsychologia, 23,* 615-622.

Chen, K. S., & Squire, L. R. (1990). Strength and duration of word-completion priming as a function of word repetition and spacing. *Bulletin of the Psychonomic Society, 28,* 97-100.

Cherry, K. E., & Stadler, M. E. (1995). Implicit learning of a nonverbal sequence in younger and older adults. *Psychology and Aging, 10,* 379-394.

Claparède, E. (1911). Reconnaissance et moiôté. *Archives de Psychologie, 11,* 79-90.

Cleeremans, A. (1993). *Mechanisms of implicit learning.* Cambridge: MIT Press.

Cleeremans, A., & McClelland, J. L. (1991). Learning the structure of event sequences. *Journal of Experimental Psychology: General, 120,* 235-253.

Cock, J. J., Berry, D. C., & Gaffan, E. A. (1994). New strings for old: The role of similarity processing in an incidental learning task. *The Quarterly Journal of Experimental Psychology, 47A,* 1015-1034.

Cohen, A., Ivry, R. I., & Keele, S. W. (1990). Attention and structure in sequence learning. *Journal of Experimental Psychology: Learning, Memory, and Cognition, 16,* 17-30.

Cohen, N. J., & Squire, L. R. (1980). Preserved learning and retention of pattern-analyzing skill in amnesia: Dissociation of knowing how and knowing that. *Science, 210,* 207-210.

Cooper, L. A., Schacter, D. L., Ballesteros, S., & Moore, C. (1992). Priming and recognition of transformed three-dimensional objects: Effects of size and reflection. *Journal of Experimental Psychology: Learning, Memory, and Cognition, 18,* 43-57.

Curran, T., & Keele, S. W. (1993). Attentional and nonattentional forms of sequence learning. *Journal of Experimental Psychology: Learning, Memory, and Cognition, 19,* 189-202.

De Haan, E. H. F., Young, A. W., & Newcombe, F. (1992). Neuropsychological impairment of face recognition units. *The Quarterly Journal of Experimental Psychology, 44A,* 141-175.

Dienes, Z. (1992). Connectionist and memory array models of artificial grammar learning. *Cognitive Science, 16,* 41-79.

Dienes, Z., Broadbent, D. E., & Berry, D. C. (1991). Implicit and explicit knowledge bases in artificial grammar learning. *Journal of Experimental Psychology: Learning, Memory, and Cognition, 17,* 875-887.

Druhan, B., & Mathews, R. C. (1989). THIYOS: A classifier system model of implicit knowledge of artificial grammars. In *Proceedings of the Eleventh Annual Conference of the Cognitive Science Society* (pp. 66-73). Hillsdale, NJ: Lawrence Erlbaum.

Dulany, D. E., Carlson, R. A., & Dewey, G. I. (1984). A case of syntactical learning and judgment: How conscious and how abstract? *Journal of Experimental Psychology: General, 113,* 541-555.

Dulany, D. E., Carlson, R. A., & Dewey, G. I. (1985). On consciousness in syntactic learning and judgment: A reply to Reber, Allen, and Regan. *Journal of Experimental Psychology: General, 114,* 25-32.

Dunn, J. C., & Kirsner, K. (1988). Discovering functionally independent mental processes: The principle of reversed association. *Psychological Review, 95,* 91-101.

Ebbinghaus, H. (1966). *Über das Gedächtnis.* Amsterdam, Netherlands: E. J. Bonset. (Original work published 1885)

Fagan, J. F. (1990). The paired-comparison paradigm and infant intelligence. *Annals of the New York Academy of Sciences, 608,* 337-364.

Fisk, A. D., & Schneider, W. (1984). Memory as a function of attention, level of processing, and automatization. *Journal of Experimental Psychology: Learning, Memory, and Cognition, 10,* 181-197.

Frensch, P. A., Buchner, A., & Lin, J. (1994). Implicit learning of unique and ambiguous serial patterns in the presence and absence of a distractor task. *Journal of Experimental Psychology: Learning, Memory, and Cognition, 20,* 567-584.

Frensch, P. A., & Funke, J. (1995). Definitions, traditions, and a general framework for understanding complex problem solving. In P. A. Frensch & J. Funke (Eds.), *Complex problem solving: European perspective* (pp. 3-25). Hillsdale, NJ: Lawrence Erlbaum.

Frensch, P. A., Lin, J., & Buchner, A. (1996). *Implicit sequence learning: Evidence against an attentional learning mechanism.* Manuscript submitted for publication.

Frensch, P. A., & Miner, C. S. (1994). Effects of presentation rate and individual differences in short-term memory capacity on an indirect measure of serial learning. *Memory & Cognition, 22,* 95-110.

Gabrieli, J. D., Milberg, W., Keane, M. M., & Corkin, S. (1990). Intact priming of patterns despite impaired memory. *Neuropsychologia, 28,* 417-427.

Gomez, R. L., & Schvaneveldt, R. W. (1994). What is learned from artificial grammars? Transfer tests of simple associations. *Journal of Experimental Psychology: Learning, Memory, and Cognition, 20,* 396-410.

Graf, P., & Mandler, G. (1984). Activation makes words more accessible, but not necessarily more retrievable. *Journal of Verbal Learning and Verbal Behavior, 23,* 553-568.

Graf, P., & Schacter, D. L. (1985). Implicit and explicit memory for new associations in normal and amnesic subjects. *Journal of Experimental Psychology: Learning, Memory, and Cognition, 11,* 501-518.

Graf, P., Shimamura, A. P., & Squire, L. R. (1985). Priming across modalities and priming across category levels: Extending the domain of preserved function in amnesia. *Journal of Experimental Psychology: Learning, Memory, and Cognition, 11,* 386-396.

Graf, P., Squire, L. R., & Mandler, G. (1984). The information that amnesic patients do not forget. *Journal of Experimental Psychology: Learning, Memory, and Cognition, 10,* 164-178.

Greve, K. W., & Bauer, R. M. (1990). Implicit learning of new faces in prosopagnosia: An application of the mere-exposure paradigm. *Neuropsychologia, 28,* 1035-1041.

Hamann, S. B. (1990). Level-of-processing effects in conceptually driven implicit tasks. *Journal of Experimental Psychology: Learning, Memory, and Cognition, 16,* 970-977.

Hartman, M., Knopman, D. S., & Nissen, M. J. (1989). Implicit learning of new verbal associations. *Journal of Experimental Psychology: Learning, Memory, and Cognition, 15,* 1070-1082.

Hashtroudi, S., Parker, E. S., DeLisi, L. E., Wyatt, R. J., & Mutter, S. A. (1984). Intact retention in acute alcohol amnesia. *Journal of Experimental Psychology: Learning, Memory, and Cognition, 10,* 156-163.

Hawley, K. J., & Johnston, W. A. (1991). Long-term perceptual memory for briefly exposed words as a function of awareness and attention. *Journal of Experimental Psychology: Human Perception and Performance, 17,* 807-815.

Hayes, N. A., & Broadbent, D. E. (1988). Two modes of learning for interactive tasks. *Cognition, 28,* 249-276.

Heuer, H., & Schmidtke, V. (in press). Secondary-task effects on sequence learning. *Psychological Research.*

Higham, P. A. (in press). Dissociations of grammaticality and specific similarity effects in artificial grammar learning. *Journal of Experimental Psychology: Learning, Memory, and Cognition.*

Hintzman, D. L. (1990). Human learning and memory: Connections and dissociations. *Annual Review of Psychology, 41,* 109-139.

Holland, J. H., Holyoak, K. J., Nisbett, R. E., & Thagard, P. R. (1986). *Induction: Processes of inference, learning, and discovery.* Cambridge: MIT Press.

Holyoak, K. J., & Koh, K. (1987). Surface and structural similarity in analogical transfer. *Memory & Cognition, 15,* 332-340.

Howard, D. V., & Howard, J. H. (1989). Age differences in learning serial patterns: Direct versus indirect measures. *Psychology and Aging, 4,* 357-364.

Hultsch, D. F., Masson, M. E. J., & Small, B. J. (1991). Adult age differences in direct and indirect tests of memory. *Journal of Gerontology: Psychological Sciences, 46,* P22-30.

Jacoby, L. L. (1983). Remembering the data: Analyzing interactive processes in reading. *Journal of Verbal Learning and Verbal Behavior, 22,* 485-508.

Jacoby, L. L. (1991). A process dissociation framework: Separating automatic from intentional uses of memory. *Journal of Memory and Language, 30,* 513-541.

Jacoby, L. L., & Dallas, M. (1981). On the relationship between autobiographical memory and perceptual learning. *Journal of Experimental Psychology: General, 110,* 306-340.

Jacoby, L. L., Woloshyn, V., & Kelley, C. M. (1989). Becoming famous without being recognized: Unconscious influences of memory produced by dividing attention. *Journal of Experimental Psychology: General, 118,* 115-125.

Jiménez, L., Méndez, C., & Cleeremans, A. (in press). Comparing direct and indirect measures of sequence learning. *Journal of Experimental Psychology: Learning, Memory, and Cognition.*

Keele, S. W., & Jennings, P. J. (1992). Attention in the representation of sequence: Experiment and theory [Special Issue: Sequencing and timing of human movement]. *Human Movement Science, 11,* 125-138.

Knopman, D. S. (1991). Unaware learning versus preserved learning in pharmacologic amnesia: Similarities and differences. *Journal of Experimental Psychology: Learning, Memory, and Cognition, 17,* 1017-1029.

Knopman, D. S., & Nissen, M. J. (1987). Implicit learning in patients with probable Alzheimer's disease. *Neurology, 37,* 784-788.

Knopman, D., & Nissen, M. J. (1991). Procedural learning is impaired in Huntington's disease: Evidence from the serial reaction time task. *Neuropsychologia, 29,* 245-254.

Knowlton, B. J., Ramus, S. J., & Squire, L. R. (1992). Intact artificial grammar learning in amnesia: Dissociation of classification learning and explicit memory for specific instances. *Psychological Science, 3,* 172-179.

Knowlton, B. J., & Squire, L. R. (1994). The information acquired during artificial grammar learning. *Journal of Experimental Psychology: Learning, Memory, and Cognition, 20,* 79-91.

Kolers, P. A. (1976). Reading a year later. *Journal of Experimental Psychology: Human Learning and Memory, 3,* 554-565.

Kushner, M., Cleeremans, A., & Reber, A. S. (1991). *Implicit detection of event interdependencies and a PDP model of the process.* Paper presented at the Thirteenth Annual Meeting of the Cognitive Science Society, Chicago, IL.

Levy, B. A. (1993). Fluent rereading: An implicit indicator of reading skill development. In P. Graf & M. E. J. Masson (Eds.), *Implicit memory: New directions in cognition, development, and neuropsychology* (pp. 49-73). Hillsdale, NJ: Lawrence Erlbaum.

Light, L. L., & La Voie, D. (1993). Direct and indirect measures of memory in old age. In P. Graf & M. E. J. Masson (Eds.), *Implicit memory: New directions in cognition, development, and neuropsychology* (pp. 207-230). Hillsdale, NJ: Lawrence Erlbaum.

Mandler, G. (1980). Recognizing: The judgment of previous occurrence. *Psychological Review, 87,* 252-271.

Mandler, G., Nakamura, Y., & Van Zandt, B. J. (1987). Nonspecific effects of exposure on stimuli that cannot be recognized. *Journal of Experimental Psychology: Learning, Memory, and Cognition, 13,* 646-648.

Marcel, A. J. (1988). Phenomenal experience and functionalism. In A. J. Marcel & E. Bisiach (Eds.), *Consciousness in contemporary science* (pp. 121-158). Oxford, UK: Clarendon Press.

Mathews, R. C. (1991). The forgetting algorithm: How fragmentary knowledge of exemplars can abstract knowledge. *Journal of Experimental Psychology: General, 120,* 117-119.

Mathews, R. C., Blanchard-Fields, F., Norris, L., & Roussel, L. G. (1991, November 23). *Abstractness of implicitly versus explicitly acquired knowledge of artificial grammars.* Paper presented at the Annual Meeting of the Psychonomic Society, San Francisco, CA.

Mathews, R. C., Buss, R. R., Stanley, W. B., Blanchard-Fields, F., Cho, J. R., & Druhan, B. (1989). Role of implicit and explicit processes in learning from examples: A synergistic effect. *Journal of Experimental Psychology: Learning, Memory, and Cognition, 15,* 1083-1100.

Mayes, A. R., & Gooding, P. (1989). Enhancement of word completion priming in amnesics by cueing with previously novel associates. *Neuropsychologia, 27,* 1057-1072.

Mayr, U. (1996). Spatial attention and implicit sequence learning: Evidence for independent learning of spatial and nonspatial sequences. *Journal of Experimental Psychology: Learning, Memory, and Cognition, 22,* 350-364.

McAndrews, M. P., & Moscovitch, M. (1985). Rule-based and exemplar-based classification in artificial grammar learning. *Memory & Cognition, 13,* 469-475.

McAndrews, M. P., & Moscovitch, M. (1990). Transfer effects in implicit tests of memory. *Journal of Experimental Psychology: Learning, Memory, and Cognition, 16,* 772-788.

McGeorge, P., & Burton, A. M. (1990). Semantic processing in an incidental learning task. *The Quarterly Journal of Experimental Psychology, 42A,* 597-609.

Mecklenbräuker, S., & Wippich, W. (1995). Implizites Gedächtnis bei Kindern: Bleiben auch bei konzeptgesteuerten Aufgaben alterskorrelierte Differenzen aus? [Implicit memory in children: Are there age differences with conceptually driven tasks?]. *Zeitschrift für Entwicklungspsychologie und Pädagogische Psychologie, 27*, 29-46.

Meltzoff, A. N. (1988). Infant imitation and memory: Nine-month-olds in immediate and deferred tests. *Child Development, 59*, 217-225.

Merikle, P. M., & Reingold, E. M. (1991). Comparing direct (explicit) and indirect (implicit) measures to study unconscious memory. *Journal of Experimental Psychology: Learning, Memory, and Cognition, 17*, 224-233.

Miller, G. A. (1958). Free recall of redundant strings of letters. *Journal of Experimental Psychology, 56*, 485-491.

Mitchell, D. B. (1993). Implicit and explicit memory for pictures: Multiple views across the lifespan. In P. Graf & M. E. J. Masson (Eds.), *Implicit memory: New directions in cognition, development, and neuropsychology* (pp. 171-190). Hillsdale, NJ: Lawrence Erlbaum.

Mitchell, D. B., & Brown, A. S. (1988). Persistent repetition priming in picture naming and its dissociation from recognition memory. *Journal of Experimental Psychology: Learning, Memory, and Cognition, 14*, 213-222.

Myers, N. A., Clifton, R. K., & Clarkson, M. G. (1987). When they were very young: Almost-threes remember two years ago. *Infant Behavior and Development, 10*, 123-132.

Naito, M., & Komatsu, S.-I. (1993). Processes involved in childhood development of implicit memory. In P. Graf & M. E. J. Masson (Eds.), *Implicit memory: New directions in cognition, development, and neuropsychology* (pp. 231-260). Hillsdale, NJ: Lawrence Erlbaum.

Newcombe, N., & Fox, N. A. (1994). Infantile amnesia: Through a glass darkly. *Child Development, 65*, 31-40.

Nissen, M. J., & Bullemer, P. (1987). Attentional requirements of learning: Evidence from performance measures. *Cognitive Psychology, 19*, 1-32.

Nissen, M. J., Knopman, D. S., & Schacter, D. L. (1987). Neurochemical dissociation of memory systems. *Neurology, 37*, 789-794.

Nissen, M. J., Willingham, D. B., & Hartman, M. (1989). Explicit and implicit remembering: When is learning preserved in amnesia? *Neuropsychologia, 27*, 341-352.

Parkin, A. J. (1993). Implicit memory across the lifespan. In P. Graf & M. E. J. Masson (Eds.), *Implicit memory: New directions in cognition, development, and neuropsychology* (pp. 191-206). Hillsdale, NJ: Lawrence Erlbaum.

Parkin, A. J., Reich, T. K., & Russo, R. (1990). On the differential nature of implicit and explicit memory. *Memory & Cognition, 18*, 507-514.

Parkin, A. J., & Russo, R. (1990). Implicit and explicit memory and the automatic/effortful distinction. *European Journal of Cognitive Psychology, 2*, 71-80.

Perris, E. E., Myers, N. A., & Clifton, R. K. (1990). Long-term memory for a single infancy experience. *Child Development, 61,* 1796-1807.

Perruchet, P., & Amorim, M.-A. (1992). Conscious knowledge and changes in performance in sequence learning: Evidence against dissociation. *Journal of Experimental Psychology: Learning, Memory, and Cognition, 18,* 785-800.

Perruchet, P., Frazier, N., & Lautrey, J. (1995). Conceptual implicit memory: A developmental study. *Psychological Research, 57,* 220-228.

Perruchet, P., & Pacteau, C. (1990). Synthetic grammar learning: Implicit rule abstraction or explicit fragmentary knowledge? *Journal of Experimental Psychology: General, 119,* 264-275.

Rajaram, S., & Roediger, H. L. (1993). Direct comparison of four implicit memory tests. *Journal of Experimental Psychology: Learning, Memory, and Cognition, 19,* 765-776.

Rappold, V. A., & Hashtroudi, S. (1991). Does organization improve priming? *Journal of Experimental Psychology: Learning, Memory, and Cognition, 17,* 103-114.

Ratcliff, R., & McKoon, G. (1995). Bias in the priming of object decisions. *Journal of Experimental Psychology: Learning, Memory, and Cognition, 21,* 754-767.

Reber, A. S. (1967). Implicit learning of an artificial grammar. *Journal of Verbal Learning and Verbal Behavior, 6,* 855-863.

Reber, A. S. (1969). Transfer of syntactic structure in synthetic languages. *Journal of Experimental Psychology, 81,* 115-119.

Reber, A. S. (1989). Implicit learning and tacit knowledge. *Journal of Experimental Psychology: General, 118,* 219-235.

Reber, A. S. (1993). *Implicit learning and tacit knowledge: An essay on the cognitive unconscious.* New York: Oxford University Press.

Reber, A. S., & Allen, R. (1978). Analogic and abstraction strategies in synthetic grammar learning: A functionalist interpretation. *Cognition, 6,* 189-221.

Reber, A. S., Allen, R., & Regan, S. (1985). Syntactical learning and judgment, still unconscious and still abstract: Comment on Dulany, Carlson, and Dewey. *Journal of Experimental Psychology: General, 114,* 17-24.

Reber, A. S., Kassin, S. M., Lewis, S., & Cantor, G. (1980). On the relationship between implicit and explicit modes in the learning of a complex rule structure. *Journal of Experimental Psychology: Human Learning and Memory, 6,* 492-502.

Reber, A. S., & Lewis, S. (1977). Implicit learning: An analysis of the form and structure of a body of tacit knowledge. *Cognition, 5,* 333-361.

Reber, A. S., & Millward, R. B. (1968). Event observation in probability learning. *Journal of Experimental Psychology, 77,* 317-327.

Reber, A. S., & Millward, R. B. (1971). Event tracking in probability learning. *American Journal of Psychology, 84,* 85-99.

Reed, J., & Johnson, P. (1994). Assessing implicit learning with indirect tests: Determining what is learned about sequence structure. *Journal of Experimental Psychology: Learning, Memory, and Cognition, 20,* 585-594.

Richardson-Klavehn, A., & Bjork, R. A. (1988). Measures of memory. *Annual Review of Psychology, 39,* 475-543.

Richardson-Klavehn, A., & Gardiner, J. M. (1995). Retrieval volition and memorial awareness in stem completion: An empirical analysis. *Psychological Research, 57,* 166-178.

Roediger, H. L. (1990a). Implicit memory: A commentary. *Bulletin of the Psychonomic Society, 28,* 373-380.

Roediger, H. L. (1990b). Implicit memory: Retention without awareness. *American Psychologist, 45,* 1043-1056.

Roediger, H. L., & Blaxton, T. A. (1987). Effects of varying modality, surface features, and retention interval on priming in word-fragment completion. *Memory & Cognition, 15,* 379-388.

Roediger, H. L., & McDermott, K. B. (1992). Depression and implicit memory: A commentary. *Journal of Abnormal Psychology, 101,* 587-591.

Roediger, H. L., & McDermott, K. B. (1993). Implicit memory in normal human subjects. In H. Spinnler & F. Boller (Eds.), *Handbook of neuropsychology* (Vol. 8, pp. 63-131). Amsterdam, Netherlands: Elsevier Science.

Roediger, H. L., & Srinivas, K. (1993). Specificity of operations in perceptual priming. In P. Graf & M. E. J. Masson (Eds.), *Implicit memory: New directions in cognition, development, and neuropsychology* (pp. 17-48). Hillsdale, NJ: Lawrence Erlbaum.

Roediger, H. L., Weldon, M. S., & Challis, B. H. (1989). Explaining dissociations between implicit and explicit measures of retention: A processing account. In H. L. Roediger & F. I. M. Craik (Eds.), *Varieties of memory and consciousness: Essays in honor of Endel Tulving* (pp. 3-41). Hillsdale, NJ: Lawrence Erlbaum.

Roediger, H. L., Weldon, M. S., Stadler, M. L., & Riegler, G. L. (1992). Direct comparison of two implicit memory tests: Word fragment and word stem completion. *Journal of Experimental Psychology: Learning, Memory, and Cognition, 18,* 1251-1269.

Rovee Collier, C. (1990). The "memory system" of prelinguistic infants. *Annals of the New York Academy of Sciences, 608,* 517-542.

Ruhlender, P. (1989). Nicht-bewußtes Lernen beim Lösen von Anagrammen [Nonconscious learning in solving anagrams]. *Zeitschrift für experimentelle und angewandte Psychologie, 36,* 494-509.

Russo, R., & Parkin, A. J. (1993). Age differences in implicit memory: More apparent than real. *Memory & Cognition, 21,* 73-80.

Salthouse, T. A. (1988). Resource-reduction interpretations of cognitive aging. *Developmental Review, 8,* 238-272.

Schacter, D. L. (1987). Implicit memory: History and current status. *Journal of Experimental Psychology: Learning, Memory, and Cognition, 13,* 501-518.

Schacter, D. L. (1992). Understanding implicit memory: A cognitive neuroscience approach. *American Psychologist, 47,* 559-569.

Schacter, D. L., Bowers, J., & Booker, J. (1989). Intention, awareness, and implicit memory. In S. Lewandowsky, J. C. Dunn, & K. Kirsner (Eds.), *Implicit memory: Theoretical issues* (pp. 47-65). Hillsdale, NJ: Lawrence Erlbaum.

Schacter, D. L., & Church, B. A. (1992). Auditory priming: Implicit and explicit memory for words and voices. *Journal of Experimental Psychology: Learning, Memory, and Cognition, 18,* 915-930.

Schacter, D. L., Cooper, L. A., Tharan, M., & Rubens, A. B. (1991). Preserved priming of novel objects in patients with memory disorders. *Journal of Cognitive Neuroscience, 3,* 117-130.

Schacter, D. L., & Moscovitch, M. (1984). Infants, anmesics, and dissociable memory systems. In M. Moscovitch (Ed.), *Infant memory* (pp. 173-216). New York: Plenum.

Seger, C. A. (1994). Implicit learning. *Psychological Bulletin, 115,* 163-196.

Servan-Schreiber, E., & Anderson, J. R. (1990). Learning artificial grammars with competitive chunking. *Journal of Experimental Psychology: Learning, Memory, and Cognition, 16,* 592-608.

Shanks, D. R., & St. John, M. F. (1994). Characteristics of dissociable human learning systems. *Behavioral and Brain Sciences, 17,* 367-447.

Shimamura, A. P. (1986). Priming effects in amnesia: Evidence for a dissociable memory function. *The Quarterly Journal of Experimental Psychology, 38A,* 619-644.

Shimamura, A. P. (1993). Neuropsychological analyses of implicit memory: History, methodology, and theoretical interpretations. In P. Graf & M. E. J. Masson (Eds.), *Implicit memory: New directions in cognition, development, and neuropsychology* (pp. 265-285). Hillsdale, NJ: Lawrence Erlbaum.

Shimamura, A. P., & Squire, L. R. (1984). Paired-associate learning and priming effects in amnesia: A neuropsychological study. *Journal of Experimental Psychology: General, 113,* 556-570.

Sloman, S. A., Hayman, C. A. G., Ohta, N., Law, J., & Tulving, E. (1988). Forgetting in primed fragment completion. *Journal of Experimental Psychology: Learning, Memory, and Cognition, 14,* 223-239.

Squire, L. R., & Frambach, M. (1990). Cognitive skill learning in amnesia. *Psychobiology, 18,* 109-117.

Srinivas, K. (1993). Perceptual specificity in nonverbal priming. *Journal of Experimental Psychology: Learning, Memory, and Cognition, 19,* 582-602.

Stadler, M. A. (1993). Implicit serial learning: Questions inspired by Hebb (1961). *Memory & Cognition, 21,* 819-827.

Stadler, M. A. (1995). Role of attention in implicit learning. *Journal of Experimental Psychology: Learning, Memory, and Cognition, 21,* 674-685.

Tulving, E. (1983). *Elements of episodic memory.* Oxford, UK: Clarendon.

Tulving, E. (1989). Memory: Performance, knowledge, and experience. *European Journal of Cognitive Psychology, 1,* 3-26.

Tulving, E., & Schacter, D. L. (1990). Priming and human memory systems. *Science, 247,* 301-306.

Tulving, E., Schacter, D. L., & Stark, H. A. (1982). Priming effects in word fragment completion are independent of recognition memory. *Journal of Experimental Psychology: Human Learning and Memory, 8,* 336-342.

Vokey, J. R., & Brooks, L. R. (1992). Salience of item knowledge in learning artificial grammars. *Journal of Experimental Psychology: Learning, Memory, and Cognition, 18,* 328-344.

Warrington, E. K., & Weiskrantz, L. (1968). New method for testing long-term retention with special reference to amnesic patients. *Nature, 217,* 972-974.

Warrington, E. K., & Weiskrantz, L. (1970). Amnesic syndrome: Consolidation or retrieval? *Nature, 228,* 628-630.

Weldon, M. S. (1991). Mechanisms underlying priming on perceptual tests. *Journal of Experimental Psychology: Learning, Memory, and Cognition, 17,* 526-541.

Whittlesea, B. W. A., & Dorken, M. D. (1993). Incidentally, things in general are particularly determined: An episodic-processing account of implicit learning. *Journal of Experimental Psychology: General, 122,* 227-248.

Willingham, D. B., Greeley, T., & Bardone, A. M. (1993). Dissociation in a serial response time task using a recognition measure: Comment on Perruchet and Amorim (1992). *Journal of Experimental Psychology: Learning, Memory, and Cognition, 19,* 1424-1430.

Willingham, D. B., & Koroshetz, W. J. (1993). Evidence for dissociable motor skills in Huntington's disease patients. *Psychobiology, 21,* 173-182.

Willingham, D. B., Nissen, M. J., & Bullemer, P. (1989). On the development of procedural knowledge. *Journal of Experimental Psychology: Learning, Memory, and Cognition, 15,* 1047-1060.

Wippich, W. (1990). Erinnerungen an Gerüche: Benennungsmaße und autobiographische Erinnerungen zeigen Geruchsnachwirkungen an [Remembering scents: Naming and autobiographical memories reveal effects of prior smelling experiences]. *Zeitschrift für experimentelle und angewandte Psychologie, 37,* 679-695.

Wippich, W. (1991). Haptic information processing in direct and indirect memory tests. *Psychological Research, 53,* 162-168.

Wippich, W. (1992a). Implicit and explicit memory without awareness. *Psychological Research, 54,* 212-224.

Wippich, W. (1992b). Ist ein T immer ein T? [Is a T always a T?]. *Sprache und Kognition, 11,* 38-48.

Wippich, W. (1994). Intuition in the context of implicit memory. *Psychological Research, 56,* 104-109.

Wippich, W. (1995). Priming on verbal perceptual tests: Roles of lexical, surface, and conceptual processes. *Psychological Research, 57,* 250-259.

Wippich, W., Mecklenbräuker, S., & Baumann, R. (1994). Farbwirkungen bei impliziten und expliziten Gedächtnisprüfungen [Color effects in implicit and explicit tests of memory]. *Zeitschrift für experimentelle und angewandte Psychologie, 41,* 315-347.

Wippich, W., Mecklenbräuker, S., & Brausch, A. (1989). Implizites und explizites Gedächtnis bei Kindern: Bleiben bei indirekten Behaltensprüfungen Altersunterschiede aus? [Implicit and explicit memory in children: No age differences in indirect measures of memory?]. *Zeitschrift für Entwicklungspsychologie und Pädagogische Psychologie, 21,* 294-306.

Wippich, W., Mecklenbräuker, S., & Halfter, M. (1989). Implicit memory in spelling from word images. *Psychological Research, 51,* 208-216.

Zimmer, H. D. (1995). Size and orientation of objects in explicit and implicit memory: A reversal of the dissociation between perceptual similarity and type of test. *Psychological Research, 57,* 260-273.

2

One Concept, Multiple Meanings

*On How to Define the
Concept of Implicit Learning*

Peter A. Frensch

It is a truism that scientific concepts do not have absolute, god-given meanings, but only those that science creates for them. Science is not always consistent, however, in its assignment of meanings to concepts. Rather, different meanings are often assigned to the same concept by different scientists. The range of meanings that exists for any concept appears to be a function of the number of scientists showing an interest in the concept, or more accurately, of the number of distinct research backgrounds that are brought to bear on the concept (Frensch & Funke, 1995). As interest in a given concept increases within the research community, thus, the number of meanings that are attached to the concept increases as well.

On the positive side, the existence of multiple meanings for the same concept can stimulate meaningful research, at least as long as the differences

AUTHOR'S NOTE: I thank Hilde Haider-Hasebrink, Michael Stadler, and Dorit Wenke for their insightful comments on previous drafts of this chapter. Correspondence concerning the chapter should be addressed to Peter A. Frensch, Max-Planck-Institute for Human Development and Education, Lentzeallee 94, D-14195 Berlin, Germany. Email may be sent to frensch@mpib-berlin.mpg.de.

among meanings are small relative to their commonalities. However, as the differences among meanings become too large to be ignored, they may seriously undermine scientific progress (e.g., Tulving, 1984). Such is presently the case in the area of implicit learning, I argue, where the lack of a commonly accepted meaning of the concept is one of the primary reasons why researchers cannot even agree on the very existence of the phenomenon.

This chapter is divided into a conceptual part and an empirical part. In the conceptual part, my goal is to clarify which meaning is best to attach to the concept of *implicit learning,* or in other words, how best to define implicit learning. I discuss and evaluate the various meanings of the concept of implicit learning that have been offered in the literature, arguing that most of the existing meanings of implicit learning differ in whether they attach the label *implicit* only to learning processes or to learning and retrieval processes, and in whether they take implicit to be synonymous with *unconscious/unaware* or with *nonintentional/automatic.* There exist thus roughly four distinct classes of meanings for the concept of implicit learning, which differ, I claim, in terms of their scientific usefulness.

I argue that meanings that emphasize only the learning processes are scientifically preferable to those emphasizing both learning and retrieval processes, and that meanings that focus on the nonintentionality/ automaticity of implicit learning are preferable to those emphasizing the unconscious/unaware property of the concept. Taken together, my recommendation is to define the concept of implicit learning as the nonintentional, automatic acquisition of knowledge about structural relations between objects or events.

In the second part of the chapter, I examine the predictive value of the thus formulated meaning of implicit learning by considering whether or not implicit learning adheres to two criteria that have sometimes been used to describe nonintentional automatic processing, effortlessness and ubiquity. On the basis of empirical studies conducted in our lab and elsewhere that directly address these issues, I argue that implicit learning is achieved by nonintentional automatic learning mechanism(s). However, implicit learning does not seem ubiquitous; instead, there appears to exist a preference for learning certain functional relations, reminiscent of the "preparedness" effect observed in animal-learning studies (Seligman, 1970). Preferably learned relations may not reflect the survival value of the relations for the species, however, but instead might reflect functional architectural constraints on how the cognitive system is structured.

CONCEPTUAL PART:
ONE CONCEPT, MULTIPLE MEANINGS

The language scientists initially adopt to describe phenomena of interest frequently becomes an unsuspected source of difficulty in creative thought and an obstacle on the path to progress.

–Tulving, 1984, p. 164

Frensch and Funke (1995) have argued that scientists are ready to accept a given meaning[1] for a given concept if the meaning (a) facilitates communication among researchers, and (b) is perceived as scientifically useful. The degree to which a meaning facilitates communication among researchers is directly related, for example, to how clearly the meaning establishes the boundaries of a concept, that is, makes it clear which aspects are to be included in the concept and which are to be excluded. In this regard, the better a meaning captures the boundaries of a concept, that is, the less fuzzy the boundaries are, the better the meaning facilitates communication.

Although the facilitation of communication among researchers is a necessary prerequisite of any meaning, the primary reason why one particular meaning of a concept is favored over other potential meanings, Frensch and Funke (1995) claim, lies in the perceived usefulness of the meanings. The usefulness of a meaning is not an objective property of the meaning in the sense that a given meaning is judged as more or less useful by everyone in the field. Rather, researchers differ in how useful they believe a meaning to be. Frensch and Funke argue that the perceived usefulness of meanings is affected by researchers' prior knowledge, beliefs, and theoretical goals.

The Frensch and Funke (1995) assessment puts any attempt to objectively and comparatively evaluate distinct meanings of a concept in terms of their scientific usefulness into perspective by pointing out that the perceived usefulness of a meaning may be biased by researchers' personal, subjective backgrounds. Any objective, comparative evaluation of meanings can succeed, thus, only to the extent that researchers share common criteria on how to best achieve progress in a science. This section is divided into three parts. First, I present various definitions of the concept of implicit learning that have been offered in the literature. I argue that most definitions neatly fall into one of four general classes of meanings. Then, I describe a minimal, broadly shared set of criteria for achieving progress in scientific psychology, discuss to what extent the four identified classes of meanings meet these criteria, and present the definition of implicit learning that, in my mind, is the most useful one.

Definitions of Implicit Learning

Consider first some of the better-known definitions of the concept implicit learning that have been offered in the literature. The definitions are listed below in alphabetical order, based on the name of the first author.

- Learning "may be implicit, when people are merely told to memorize the specific material presented, but nevertheless learn about the underlying rules" (Berry & Broadbent, 1988, p. 251).
- Implicit learning is "the acquisition of knowledge about the structural properties of the relations between (usually more than two) objects or events" (Buchner & Wippich, Chapter 1, this volume, p. 6).
- "Implicit learning should designate cases where some knowledge is (1) acquired without intention to learn . . . , and (2) capable of influencing behavior unconsciously" (Cleeremans & Jiménez, 1996).
- "Implicit learning . . . should be identified with evocative mental episodes. It consists of the establishment and use of evocative relations among nonpropositional but fully conscious contents" (Dulany, in press, p. 189).
- Implicit learning is when "subjects are able to acquire specific . . . knowledge . . . not only without being able to articulate what they had learned, but even without being aware that they had learned anything" (Lewicki, Czyzewska, & Hoffman, 1987, p. 523).
- "Implicit learning is thought to be an alternate mode of learning that is automatic, nonconscious, and more powerful than explicit thinking for discovering nonsalient covariance between task variables" (Mathews et al., 1989, p. 1083).
- "The term *implicit learning* designates an adaptive mode in which subjects' behavior is sensitive to the structural features of an experienced situation, without the adaptation being due to an intentional exploitation of subjects' explicit knowledge about these features" (Perruchet & Vinter, Chapter 15, this volume, p. 496).
- Implicit learning is "characterized as a situation-neutral induction process whereby complex information about any stimulus environment may be acquired largely independently of the subjects' awareness of either the process of acquisition or the knowledge base ultimately acquired" (Reber, 1993, p. 12).

50

- "Implicit learning (a) happens in an incidental manner, without the use of conscious hypothesis-testing strategies, (b) happens without subjects acquiring sufficient conscious knowledge to account for their performance on tests of their learning, (c) is of novel material, rather than involving activation of previously acquired representations, and (d) learning is preserved in patients with amnesia" (Seger, Chapter 9, this volume, p. 296).

- "We will reserve the term unconscious learning for learning without awareness, regardless of what sort of knowledge is being acquired" (Shanks & St. John, 1994, p. 367).

- "Essentially, we argue that learning is implicit when the learning process is unaffected by intention" (Stadler & Frensch, 1994, p. 423).

The definitions listed are examples selected from literally dozens of definitions that have been offered and continue to be offered in the literature. Although I cannot claim the list of definitions to be exhaustive, I argue that one of the many possibilities to classify most definitions is in terms of three aspects that I refer to as the What Is It About?, Type of Knowledge Representation, and Type of Phenomenon issues.

THE WHAT IS IT ABOUT? ISSUE

In any learning episode, implicit or other, three types of processes can be conceptually distinguished: perceptual processes that encode the constituents of learning, cognitive processes that underlie the acquisition of knowledge, and cognitive processes that underlie the retrieval of what was learned. The constituents of learning are the basic elements (i.e., stimuli, responses) among which some systematic relation holds that needs to be learned. The acquisition of knowledge refers to the actual learning of this relation by the organism, and the retrieval of the learned refers to the access to some temporally stable representation of the acquired knowledge. Definitions of implicit learning differ on which of these three types of processes the label implicit is applied to.

As Table 2.1 shows, there exist, in principle, seven distinct possibilities to assign the label implicit to any one of the types of processes in isolation, to combinations of two, or to all three types of processes. In practice, definitions of implicit learning use only two of the seven possible combinations (highlighted by italics in Table 2.1), namely a subset of those three combinations that do not refer to the perception of the constituents of learning as implicit. The avoidance of the remaining four of the seven

TABLE 2.1 The Implicit Character of Three Distinct Processes Involved in Any Learning Situation

Perception	Learning	Retrieval
I	N	N
N	I	N
N	N	I
N	I	I
I	N	I
I	I	N
I	I	I

NOTE: I refers to an implicit process; N refers to a nonimplicit process. Italics indicate the two combinations of processes that are used in implicit learning.

possibilities reflects a perceived difference in the research community between learning that occurs below and above the perceptual threshold of the constituents among which relations are learned, and it delineates the distinction between the concepts of implicit learning and *subliminal learning*. Implicit learning, thus, and here all existing definitions are in agreement, refers to a learning situation where the constituents of learning are presented above perceptual threshold.

The definitions differ, however, in whether they assign the label implicit to the acquisition processes only or to both acquisition and retrieval processes. In the listing above, for instance, Cleeremans and Jiménez (1996), Lewicki et al. (1987), Reber (1993), Seger (Chapter 9, this volume), and Shanks and St. John (1994) suggest definitions of implicit learning in which both the acquisition of knowledge and the subsequent access to the acquired knowledge are referred to as implicit. The remaining definitions focus on the implicit character of the knowledge acquisition process only and can be divided into two more or less distinct subcategories. In Dulany's (in press) and Perruchet and Vinter's (Chapter 15, this volume) definitions, access to the acquired knowledge is considered decidedly nonimplicit, whereas in Buchner and Wippich's (Chapter 1, this volume) and Stadler and Frensch's (1994) definitions, the status of the access to the learned is left open and has no bearing on the definition. In essence, therefore, existing definitions of the concept of implicit learning differ in whether they demand the learning, or both the learning and the retrieval, of the acquired knowledge to be implicit.

THE TYPE OF KNOWLEDGE REPRESENTATION ISSUE

Some definitions make explicit reference to the nature of the knowledge representation that is associated with implicit learning. In the list of definitions above, for instance, Dulany (in press) demands that the knowledge representation be nonpropositional. Reber (1989), at times, refers to the abstract nature of the knowledge representation when he writes that the acquired "knowledge patterns are manifestations of abstract generative rules for symbol ordering" (p. 229; see also Mathews et al., 1989), and Perruchet (see also Vokey & Brooks, 1992) argues that the knowledge representation consists of fragmentary, episodic knowledge that the learner is aware of. Although Dulany and sometimes Reber make the type of knowledge representation part of their definition of implicit learning, most researchers in the area consider the type of knowledge representation an issue that needs to be settled empirically. This stance is perhaps most obvious in Shanks and St. John's (1994) definition, where implicit learning is explicitly defined independent of the type of knowledge that is acquired in an implicit learning episode. I find myself very much in agreement with the prevailing general view that empirical issues should have no bearing on definitions of concepts.[2]

THE TYPE OF PHENOMENON ISSUE

The type of phenomenon issue is arguably the most interesting theoretical dividing line among existing definitions of implicit learning. Basically, this issue concerns the meaning of the term implicit, whether it applies to the process of acquiring knowledge only or to accessing the stored knowledge as well. Essentially four meanings of implicit appear in the literature. For many researchers in the area, the meaning of implicit is equivalent either to *unconscious* (Berry & Broadbent, 1988; Shanks & St. John, 1994; Seger, Chapter 9, this volume, in part) or *unaware* (Lewicki et al., 1987; Reber, 1993). For others, implicit means *nonintentional, automatic* (Cleeremans & Jiménez, 1996; Perruchet & Vinter, Chapter 15, this volume; Stadler & Frensch, 1994), or *incidental* (Seger, Chapter 9, this volume, in part). If one considers unawareness a potential indicator of the more general term *unconsciousness,* and *incidental* an operational, rather than content-related attribute of learning or retrieval, then the basic distinction is one between unconscious/unaware on the one side and nonintentional/automatic on the other side.

When viewed as equivalent to unconscious/unaware, implicit refers, in the context of knowledge acquisition, to a learning process that occurs outside of consciousness, which is often presumed to be indicated by the fact that the learner is not aware that learning occurs. In the context of accessing stored knowledge, unconscious/unaware is meant to imply that the acquired knowledge is accessible through an unconscious retrieval process, that is, a process that the learner is not aware of as it occurs. When viewed as equivalent to nonintentional/automatic, in contrast, implicit refers to automatic learning and/or retrieval processes that are not intentionally controlled and that meet certain criteria for automaticity as outlined, for example, by Hasher and Zacks (1979, 1984).

Below, my argument will be that the distinction between the unconscious/unaware and the nonintentional/automatic meanings of implicit is important because definitions focusing on the two meanings differ in their scientific usefulness. My argument rests on the assumption, of course, that the meanings of unconscious/unaware and nonintentional/automatic are distinct. To many this may seem odd. Awareness is often thought of as the sine qua non of intentional control, and the oldest theory of control holds that a nonmaterial conscious mind is directing the activities of the material body. However, phenomenological experience, as well as relevant empirical data, attest to the separability of the two meanings.[3] First, phenomenologically, dreaming serves as a good example for the separability of unconscious/unaware and nonintentional/automatic. Control of a dream's content is, apparently at least, completely automatic, although the result of this automatic control may well be experienced as conscious. Indeed, Humphrey (1992) has recently claimed that phenomenal awareness is intrinsically associated with certain kinds of sensations but not intentions.

Second, empirical support for the separability of unconscious/unaware and nonintentional/automatic comes from a variety of sources (Monsell, 1996). To mention just a few: Fehrer and Raab (1962) demonstrated, for example, that initiation of a voluntary act does not require awareness of the stimulus that triggers it. Neumann and Klotz (1994), in a series of elegant experiments, have extended these findings by showing that metacontrast suppressed stimuli, which subjects cannot discriminate even by the most sensitive measure, can influence choice as well as simple reactions, even when the stimulus-response mapping varies from trial to trial. At least one possible interpretation of these results is to assume that intentional control can occur unconsciously. Findings reported in the neurological literature support such an assumption. For example, one can find cases in which coordinated actions by one hand, that to an observer appear intentional in the sense that they are appropriate to both their target and their context (e.g., grasping a door knob and pulling), are surprising and upsetting to patients who feel that they have not intended them, and therefore disown them—the so-called "alien hand" phenomenon (e.g., Goldberg, Mayer, & Toglia, 1981). Furthermore, blindsight patients frequently make movements toward targets that they report not to see. These movements appear to be intentionally controlled; yet, the patients are not aware of any intentions (e.g., Farah, 1994).

In a different realm, the allocation of attention can be triggered by the sudden appearance or change of externally presented cues. Here, behavior appears to be controlled automatically and nonintentionally although one is aware of both the triggering stimulus and the result of control (e.g., Cowan, 1988). Examples such as these (see also Frith, 1992, who has argued that some of the delusions of the schizophrenic are due to a loss of awareness of intention) show that the unconscious/unaware and nonintentional/automatic meanings of implicit are at least partially separable. Because the interpretation of the term implicit as either nonintentional/automatic or unconscious/unaware thus changes the meaning of the concept of implicit learning, the distinction may, in principle, have some bearing on the scientific usefulness of meanings of implicit learning.

Conclusion 1: Existing definitions of the concept of implicit learning differ in their assigned meaning to the term implicit, just as they differ in whether they demand the learning process or both learning and knowledge retrieval processes to be implicit. Most of the existing definitions of the concept of implicit learning fall into one of the four possible categories that result from crossing the unconscious/unaware versus nonintentional/automatic distinction with the learning-only versus learning-plus-retrieval distinction.

● **The Acceptability of Scientific Concepts**

Scientific concepts are often mentalistic concepts and as such are "checks drawn on an empty epistemic bank account" (Kimble, 1996, p. 23). For concepts to become scientifically acceptable, they need to meet a set of criteria; many scientists agree that, at minimum, they need to be (a) operationalizable and (b) unique and to (c) have predictive value (Kimble, 1996). The three criteria of scientific acceptability, operationalizability, uniqueness, and predictive value, I argue below, can be used to evaluate not only the scientific acceptability of concepts, but, by extension, the scientific usefulness of meanings of concepts as well.

OPERATIONALIZATION

Concepts are operationalizable when they can be mapped onto the operational level, that is, when they can be measured by some means. Both the link between concept and operationalization and the reverse, the link between operationalization and concept, are usually dependent upon theoretical assumptions that are often not made explicit. To illustrate, consider the concept of *intelligence,* which for our purposes may be defined as the ability to think abstractly and deal effectively with the environment. The concept is typically operationalized in form of some IQ test. In order for the mapping between the concept of intelligence and the measurement of intelligence to be valid, a number of assumptions must be met that are partly specific to the IQ test used. Typical assumptions involve the validity of the assessment of abstract thinking in (a) questionnaire format, (b) the presence of other testpersons, and (c) multiple-choice format, for example. In general, concepts are the more acceptable, scientifically, the fewer unproven theoretical assumptions are required to unambiguously operationalize the concepts.

UNIQUENESS

Sometimes the same concept may, in different contexts, go by different names, or the same name may refer to different concepts. To avoid confusion, scientific concepts need to be unique. Concepts are unique if they are distinguishable from other related concepts at both the conceptual and the operational level. Uniqueness does not imply complete conceptual and operational independence from other concepts, of course. It merely requires that the overlap with other concepts not be complete.

PREDICTIVE VALUE

Scientific concepts disappear in oblivion, and rightly so, if they turn out not to have predictive value, that is, if they do not have a predictive relation to other concepts. Kimble (1996) describes an example that Gustav Bergmann used in courses at the University of Iowa to make this point. Kimble (1996) writes,

> In approximately Bergmann's words: I can define a concept, Beta (for Bergmann), as follows: Beta is equal to the square root of the number of hairs on my head (a small number), multiplied by the ratio of my systolic to my diastolic blood pressure. The operational definition of Beta . . . is impeccable, but the concept never caught on in psychology because it lacks significance. (pp. 23-24)

In summary, thus, concepts may be considered more or less scientifically acceptable according to the extent to which they are unique, operationalizable, and of predictive value. By extension, I argue that meanings of concepts can be evaluated on a dimension of scientific usefulness. Meanings may be considered useful when (a) they distinguish a concept from related concepts, both at the conceptual and operational level, (b) they require few assumptions for the mapping from the conceptual to operational level and reverse, and (c) they demonstrate predictive value.

Before I compare the four distinct classes of meanings of implicit learning identified above in terms of their uniqueness, mapping assumptions, and predictive value, two preliminary remarks are in order. First, the predictive value of concepts is, at least primarily, an empirical issue. To what extent a measure of, say the concept of intelligence, is predictive of measures of other concepts cannot be known a priori, that is, before extensive empirical research is conducted. Because much of the empirical research on implicit learning has been concerned primarily with trying to establish the phenomenon rather than with the predictive value of the concept, I will, in my evaluation of the different meanings of implicit learning, not consider the predictive value criterion, concentrating instead on the two remaining criteria. However, I will return to the issue of predictive value in the empirical part of this chapter, where I examine whether or not the particular meaning of implicit learning that I consider scientifically the most useful is consistent with existing empirical research on the topic.

Second, instead of comparing the four classes of meanings of the concept of implicit learning, my approach will be to evaluate to what extent the learning-only versus learning-plus-retrieval and the unconscious/unaware versus nonintentional/automatic distinctions affect the uniqueness and operationalization of the concept implicit learning. In other words, I will discuss whether or not these two distinctions have any bearing on the uniqueness and operationalization of implicit learning.

● Uniqueness/Distinguishability of the
Implicit Learning Concept

Before different meanings of implicit learning can be evaluated in terms of their uniqueness, one needs to know which other concepts implicit learning needs to be distinguished from. Primarily, these appear to be the concepts of explicit learning, incidental learning, learning without awareness, and implicit memory. Although there is considerable disagreement on the meanings of these other concepts, as well, explicit learning typically refers to the intentional, frequently hypothesis-guided acquisition of knowledge. Incidental learning is often operationally defined as learning that occurs in the absence of learning instructions (but see Jenkins, 1933, who defines incidental learning as "learning which occurs in the absence of a specific intent to remember" [p. 471]). Learning without awareness refers to learning that occurs "without awareness of what is being learned or intent to learn it" (Thorndike & Rock, 1934, p. 1), and implicit memory, finally, refers to memory effects "that occur primarily in the absence of a conscious intention to recollect prior episodes" (Graf, 1994, p. 682).

The primary message conveyed in the following subsection will be that the four distinct meanings of implicit learning, identified above, differ in their distinguishability from these related concepts. For instance, the learning-only meaning of implicit learning appears to be conceptually similar to, but operationally different from, incidental learning in Jenkins's (1933) sense and learning without awareness. The learning-plus-retrieval meaning is operationally difficult to distinguish from both explicit learning and implicit memory, and the unconscious/unaware meaning has a number of well-known problems when it comes to operationally distinguishing it from explicit learning. The nonintentional/automatic meaning appears to be most easily distinguished from related concepts.

LEARNING-ONLY VERSUS LEARNING-PLUS-RETRIEVAL DISTINCTION

In his 1993 book, Reber, who first used the term implicit learning in the published literature (Reber, 1967), briefly discusses the distinguishability of the concept implicit learning from other, related concepts:

Other related terms like incidental learning and learning without awareness had already been co-opted and, anyway, were really different kinds
of phenomena. The neutral term implicit learning was chosen simply to
differentiate the processes from the explicit learning research on concept
formation and categorization that others, such as Bruner, Goodnow, and
Austin (1956), were doing. (p. 10)

From this quotation, it is apparent that, for Reber, the uniqueness of the
concept of implicit learning was an important issue. Focusing predominantly on the implicit-explicit learning distinction and following Gibson
and Gibson (1955), Reber viewed implicit learning as similar to perceptual
learning and as distinguishable from explicit learning, which he took as
reflecting subjects' use of "conscious, reflective strategies to learn" (Reber,
1989, p. 219).

The quotation also indicates that at least in his earlier writings, Reber
viewed the difference between implicit learning, on the one hand, and
incidental learning and learning without awareness, on the other hand, as
tied to the nature of the stimulus material used. In other words, his argument
was that the terms differed at the operational level. Noting that most studies
on incidental learning and on learning without awareness involved the use
of repeated trial designs, in which subjects were presented with complex,
usually linguistic, meaningful stimuli and were differentially reinforced for
certain stimulus-response associations, Reber emphasized the use of complex stimuli that were composed of unpronounceable sequences of letters
whose order was determined by arbitrary rules in his own studies. Reber
writes,

> When ordered stimuli are presented to a S who has appropriate coding
> schemes available, then he will use such schemes to organize the stimuli.
> . . . In our case, the stimuli were patterned but in a fashion which biased
> against the possibility of there being appropriate coding schemes available.
> (1967, p. 863)

or

> Optimally, implicit learning should be examined in a setting in which the
> acquisition process is unlikely to have been contaminated by previous
> learning or preexisting knowledge. (1993, p. 12)

Early on then, Reber seems to have viewed implicit learning as a learning-only process that, conceptually, differed primarily from explicit learning, and operationally, differed from the related concepts of incidental learning and learning without awareness.

As is often the case in psychology, however, the operationalization of the concept subsequently altered the definition of the very concept. That is, Reber's and others' empirical finding that subjects seem to be capable of learning without being able to verbalize what they have learned subsequently achieved the status of a conceptual definition of implicit learning. The definition thus changed from emphasizing a learning-only interpretation to emphasizing a learning-plus-retrieval interpretation. Subjects' inability to verbalize what they have learned, which was originally merely taken to support the assumption that learning was implicit, now became a component of the definition.

This change in definition has had three serious consequences. First, the new definition has made implicit learning conceptually more easily distinguishable from incidental learning and learning without awareness. Indeed, Cleeremans and Jiménez (1996) have argued that the assumption of implicitness for both learning and retrieval is needed if implicit learning is to be distinguished from other forms of learning. Based on Stadler and Frensch's (1994) proposition that the implicit or explicit nature of learning and the implicit or explicit nature of memory retrieval are functionally independent, Cleeremans and Jiménez argue that by crossing implicit and explicit acquisition and retrieval processes, four different human learning behaviors can be distinguished. In their classification scheme, explicit acquisition and retrieval of knowledge defines *rule-following behavior* and explicit acquisition coupled with implicit retrieval characterizes *automatization. Human conditioning* refers to implicit acquisition, but explicit retrieval of information, and *implicit learning* stands for implicit acquisition coupled with implicit retrieval.

Second, by enhancing uniqueness at the conceptual level, Reber and Cleeremans and Jiménez, among many others, may, however, have run the risk of reducing uniqueness at the operational level. In fact, Shanks and St. John (1994), who seem to be in basic agreement with Reber and Cleeremans and Jiménez in their own conceptual definition of implicit learning (although they do not recognize the abstract nature of the tacit knowledge representation), have recently argued that implicit learning and implicit memory cannot be distinguished at the operational level and that implicit learning is therefore best regarded as a proper subset of implicit memory.

Third, changing its definition has considerably narrowed the scope of the concept of implicit learning because an empirically testable component has been added to the definition. In fact, much subsequent work by researchers adhering to the new definition (this excludes Reber himself and researchers such as Perruchet and Dulany) became concerned with testing whether or not the knowledge acquired in an implicit learning episode is truly implicit.

When judged on this background, I argue that the advantage of the learning-plus-retrieval over the learning-only view of implicit learning in terms of an increased conceptual uniqueness is more then outweighed by the concomitant decline in operational distinguishability, both from the concept of explicit learning (Eriksen, 1958, 1960; Holender, 1986) and from the concept of implicit memory (Shanks & St. John, 1994). Implicit learning research, I believe, demands a return to Reber's original conception. In Reber's original sense, implicit learning is a learning phenomenon, not a memory retrieval phenomenon. As such, implicit learning is conceptually indistinguishable from the earlier concepts of unconscious learning and learning without awareness but differs from the earlier concepts in that operationally, learning and the application of preexisting knowledge are unconfounded.

UNCONSCIOUS/UNAWARE VERSUS
NONINTENTIONAL/AUTOMATIC DISTINCTION

Whereas the learning-only versus learning-plus-retrieval distinction primarily affects the distinguishability of implicit learning from a variety of other concepts, the unconscious/unaware versus nonintentional/automatic distinction has more immediate bearing on the distinction that has been at the heart of implicit learning since Reber's (1967) early studies, namely the distinction between implicit and explicit learning. In order to decide which of the two views, unconscious/unaware or nonintentional/automatic, is scientifically more useful, it needs to be clear, at minimum, how unconscious/unaware (i.e., implicit) is to be distinguished from conscious/aware (i.e., explicit), and respectively, how nonintentional/automatic (i.e., implicit) is to be distinguished from intentional/nonautomatic (i.e., explicit). First, I turn to the distinction between unconscious/unaware and conscious/aware, a distinction that is grounded in the concept of consciousness.

Unconscious/Unaware Versus Conscious/Aware. Both the use of the term consciousness and the status of the concept remain, as many theorists have noticed (e.g., Marcel & Bisiach, 1988), notoriously unclear and inconsistent. Mandler (1992), for example, distinguishes between four general positions that have been taken toward conscious phenomena. Natsoulas (1978) distinguishes seven conceptual uses of the term consciousness, and it is not difficult to find additional usages. Generally, consciousness appears to be defined in either a functionalist way, such that it is equivalent to concepts such as attention, short-term memory, representation, or control, or in a phenomenological way, such that it is equivalent with subjective experience, qualia, the contents of awareness, the experience of intentionality, or personal unity.

In the literature on unconscious cognition, the phenomenological stance toward consciousness is perhaps the one with the longer tradition. Greenwald (1992) has argued that the most often used meaning of unconscious is *unaware of* and that there are two distinct senses of unaware of that appear widely in cognitive psychological research, namely outside of attention and lack or failure of introspection. I view Greenwald's outside of attention view as one of many functional stances toward understanding consciousness that I discuss below. If unconsciousness is interpreted as lack or failure of introspection, that is, the ability to report experience validly, then one is unconscious or unaware of the occurrence, causes, or other attributes of actions, objects, or events, when one cannot report those properties validly. The entire thrust of the distinction between learning (or learning-plus-retrieval) processes that are unconscious/unaware and those that are conscious/aware, thus, hinges on the verbal reportability of the occurrence, type, and/or result of learning.

As Adams (1957), Eriksen (1960), Holender (1986), and most recently Shanks and St. John (1994), among many others, have argued, the validity of verbal report data is often questionable. In fact, if history has taught us any lesson, then it is that verbal reports, be they free recall or cued recall, are often unreliable and invalid measures of consciousness. Shanks and St. John (1994) have therefore proposed two criteria for establishing the phenomenal state of unawareness, the Information Criterion and the Sensitivity Criterion. The Information Criterion states that in order to conclude that subjects are unaware of the information they have learned, it needs to be established that the information asked for by awareness tests is the same information that has led to the demonstrated learning. The Information Criterion is essentially a reformulation of the notion of *correlated hypotheses,* stated earlier by Adams (1957) and Dulany (1961). Shanks and St. John's second criterion, the Sensitivity Criterion (for earlier formulations see Brewer, 1974; Eriksen, 1960; Reingold & Merikle, 1988) demands that tests of awareness have an adequate level of sensitivity, that is, a level of sensitivity comparable to that of tests demonstrating learning in the first place. Thus, Shanks and St. John argue in essence, that the distinction between unconscious/unaware and conscious/aware learning is empirically meaningful only if verbal reports of awareness meet these two criteria. The authors then go on to argue on the basis of an extensive literature review, as Adams (1957), Eriksen (1960), and Holender (1986) have done before that empirically valid demonstrations of unconscious/unaware learning do not exist.

Even if one does not entirely agree with Shanks and St. John's (1994) assessment, one does well to acknowledge that taking the phenomenological stance toward consciousness has historically not served the distinction between unconscious (i.e., implicit) and conscious (i.e., explicit) cognition well. I cannot see any reason why this route would be any more useful now, scientifically speaking, than it has been in the recent and more remote past, notwithstanding recent attempts to find new and better measures of awareness (e.g., Chan, 1992, cited in Berry, 1994).

The alternative stance toward distinguishing between conscious and unconscious cognition is a functionalist one. However, whereas the phenomenological stance demonstrates at least some compactness and commonality to the outside observer, the functional stance does not. Atkinson and Shiffrin (1971; see also Waugh & Norman, 1965), for instance, identify consciousness with the contents of an all-purpose short-term store. Neisser (1963) argues that there are two modes of processing, one generally serial and conscious, and the other one generally parallel and unconscious. Posner and Klein (1973) view consciousness as corresponding to the operation of a general purpose, limited-capacity system. Greenwald (1992), as mentioned above, views unconscious as meaning outside of attention, implying that consciousness and attention are more or less synonymous terms. Shallice (1978) takes consciousness to be the component that selects which of many parallel-operating action systems dominates its competitors through mutually inhibitory competition.

In contrast to these limited views on the function of consciousness, Mandler (1975) presents a much broader and wider range of functions that a consciousness system must have. These functions are derived from a phenomenological analysis of a range of mental processes, and include (a) choice and selection of action systems, (b) modification and interrogation of long-term plans, (c) the initiation of retrieval from long-term memory, (d) commentary on the organism's current activity, (e) the construction of storable representations of the current activity, (f) the accessing of cognitive processes to language, and (g) trouble-shooting about the inappropriate operation of structures not normally represented in consciousness.

Finally, at the neurological level, Farah (1994) discusses three different stances toward consciousness, (a) a privileged role account, in which only certain privileged brain regions play a role on mediating consciousness; (b) integration accounts, in which consciousness integrates activity across different brain systems, and (c) quality of presentation accounts, in which consciousness requires a relatively higher quality of perceptual representation than nonconscious types of performance. After reviewing much of the empirical literature on several syndromes in which visual perception and awareness of perception appear to be dissociated (e.g., blindsight, covert recognition of faces in prosopagnosia, unconscious perception of extinguished or neglected stimuli, implicit reading in pure alexia), Farah concludes that they are "probably a heterogeneous set of phenomena, and unlikely to be explainable by a single common type of account" (p. 37).

This brief overview of some of the many functions that have been associated with consciousness indicates that it would probably be unwise to try to integrate the various potential functions of consciousness into one super-function. Thus, there is unlikely to be one single set of criteria, based on the functions of consciousness, that would let us distinguish implicit from explicit, unconscious/unaware from conscious/aware, processes. In other words, a general assessment of the scientific usefulness of the unconscious/unaware meaning of implicit that is based on a functional stance toward consciousness appears impossible, at least unless a specific function of consciousness is selected (for a similar recent argument, see, for instance, Cleeremans & Jiménez, 1996).

Nonintentional/Automatic Versus Intentional/Nonautomatic. The notion of intentional, nonautomatic mental processes was introduced into modern information-processing models of cognition by Atkinson and Shiffrin (1968), who distinguished between memory structures on the one hand and control processes on the other hand. The basic distinction between control processes and memory processes, writes Shallice (1994), "was introduced by the analogy of the relation between what a human programmer writes at a remote console and the computer hardware and built-in program that the written program controls" (p. 395). Control processes were defined as processes that "are not permanent features of memory, but are transient phenomena under the control of the subject" (Atkinson & Shiffrin, 1968, p. 106).

The idea of different types of processes was refined in two ways during the 1970s and 1980s. First, the idea that a separable system may be responsible for the operation of control was introduced into memory models (Baddeley & Hitch, 1974; LaBerge, 1975). Second, the contrast between intentionally controlled and nonintentional/automatic processes in terms of both empirical criteria and theoretical distinctions was developed (Fisk & Schneider, 1983; Posner & Snyder, 1975; Schneider & Fisk, 1982, 1984; Schneider & Shiffrin, 1977; Shiffrin & Schneider, 1977).

The significance of the distinction between nonintentional/automatic and intentionally controlled processing for the purpose of this chapter is twofold. First, there now exist a number of theoretical accounts of the control of processing that may provide a much-needed background for the distinction between implicit and explicit learning (e.g., Detweiler & Schneider, 1991; Newell, 1990; Norman & Shallice, 1986). Second, based partly on these models, a number of important functional characteristics have been identified that are correlated with the difference between nonintentional/automatic and intentionally controlled processes, and may therefore be used to operationally distinguish between implicit and explicit cognition. The exact list of these characteristics is not invariant among authors, but there is considerable overlap. For example, Hasher and Zacks (1979) draw the distinction between automatic and controlled processes as follows:

> Operations that drain minimal energy from our limited-capacity attentional mechanism are called automatic; their occurrence does not interfere with other ongoing cognitive activity. Automatic operations function at a constant level under all circumstances. They occur without intention and do not benefit from practice. . . . Contrasted with these processes are effortful operations, such as rehearsal and elaborative mnemonic activities. They require considerable capacity and so interfere with other cognitive activities also requiring capacity. They are initiated intentionally and show benefits from practice. (p. 356)

Regardless of whether one accepts Hasher and Zacks's (1979, 1984) criteria for distinguishing between nonintentional/automatic and intentional/controlled processing or not, the above discussion indicates that the nonintentional/automatic meaning of the term implicit holds considerable promise. It is, or at least can be, grounded in meaningful and established theories of control, can lead to widely accepted operational criteria for distinguishing implicit from explicit processing, and is correlated, although not perfectly, with phenomenological awareness. The latter is important if the nonintentional/automatic meaning of implicit is not to lose all contact with the empirical phenomena that have been established in the implicit learning literature during the last four decades.

Conclusion 2: Meanings of implicit learning differ in terms of the uniqueness/distinguishability they provide for the concept. Meanings that treat implicit learning as a learning-only rather than learning-plus-retrieval phenomenon and meanings that regard implicit as equivalent with nonintentional/automatic rather than unconscious/unaware show greater promise in distinguishing the concept of implicit learning from existing concepts, such as explicit learning, incidental learning, learning without awareness, or implicit memory.

● **Operationalization of the Implicit Learning Concept**

As argued above, meanings of concepts are the more useful the less ambiguous their translation into operationalization, that is, the fewer assumptions are needed to measure the meanings. Ideally, of course, both the translation of a concept into its operationalization and the reverse are free of assumptions. In practice, this is never achieved, however. The question of interest in this subsection is, therefore, to what extent the learning-only versus learning-plus-retrieval and unconscious/unaware versus nonintentional/automatic meanings of implicit learning influence the assumptions that are needed to measure the concept.

One possibility to seemingly circumvent this entire complex of problems is to operationally define a concept. Buchner and Wippich (Chapter 1, this volume) suggest just such a route for implicit learning when they define implicit learning as "the acquisition of knowledge about the structural properties of the relations between (usually more than two) objects or events" (p. 6). Note that although this approach does indeed eliminate the need for assumptions that govern the mapping from conceptual to operational level, it does not eliminate the reverse. That is, in order to attach a conceptual meaning to the operational definition, which is necessary if empirical results generated under the definition are ever to be theoretically interpretable, assumptions governing the mapping from operational to conceptual level are inescapable. In essence, thus, operational definitions do not remove the need for mapping assumptions; they only move them.

LEARNING-ONLY VERSUS
LEARNING-PLUS-RETRIEVAL DISTINCTION

The learning-only versus learning-plus-retrieval distinction influences primarily what needs to be demonstrated in a learning episode in order to call it an implicit learning episode. The learning-only meaning of implicit learning implies that any learning episode can only be called implicit if it is demonstrated that (a) learning occurs, and (b) the learning process is implicit. The learning-plus-retrieval meaning implies, in contrast, that it can be demonstrated that (a) learning occurs, (b) the learning process is implicit, and (c) retrieval of the acquired knowledge is implicit as well. The difference between the two meanings of implicit learning is obvious: It hinges on the demonstration that access to the learned is implicit, which needs to be demonstrated only under the latter, but not the former view.

Although this difference might appear straightforward, in practice it has generated considerable confusion and debate. Both the confusion and debate have arisen because of the apparent difficulty of cleanly separating the assessment of implicit learning and implicit retrieval. This difficulty is perhaps best understood by reference to the typical experimental arrangement by which implicit learning has been assessed (see Shanks & St. John, 1994, for details). In the typical implicit learning situation, subjects have the opportunity to learn a predictive relation between Event A and Event B. Learning takes place, presumably, during or after presentation of Event B. The assessment of whether learning is implicit is difficult because it cannot, or typically is not, done at just the moment when learning presumably occurs, but rather at some time after learning has taken place. Assessment cannot be done at the time of learning because the assessment would be intrusive, in the sense that it would influence the nature of the learning it assesses. Asking subjects, for example, whether they are aware of the relation between Events A and B is likely to direct their attention to the relation and thus alter the type of learning that occurs.

In the absence of nonintrusive measures of type of learning, type of learning is typically assessed at some later point in time. Measures therefore necessarily reflect memory of learned knowledge, rather than learning itself. Here, the difficulty to operationally distinguish implicit learning and implicit retrieval becomes apparent. According to the learning-only view of implicit learning, the implicitness of learning is measured by the implicitness of subjects' memory retrieval. According to the learning-plus-retrieval view, however, the memory-based measure assesses the implicitness of retrieval and thus cannot serve as an independent measure of the implicitness of learning. For example, within the unconscious/unaware view of implicitness, proponents of the learning-only view would argue that subjects' being unaware of the relation between Events A and B at a later time indicates their being unaware of the relation at the earlier time of learning. Proponents of the learning-plus-retrieval view could argue, in contrast, that subjects' being unaware of the relation between Events A and B at the later time indicates the implicitness of retrieval of their acquired knowledge but has no bearing on whether the learning process was implicit or not.

The problems in operationalizing the concept of implicit learning differ thus for the learning-only and learning-plus-retrieval views. At minimum, the former needs to make the assumption that the memory measure of implicitness is a valid measure of the implicitness of learning. The latter view, at least in principle, has a valid measure of the implicitness of memory retrieval but does not have any independent measure of the implicitness of learning, and therefore it needs to either adopt the assumption of the former view, which, however, would make learning and retrieval indistinguishable, or needs to argue that a measure of the implicitness of learning is unnecessary or is in principle unattainable.

The latter is indeed the view endorsed by Reber (1993), who has essentially argued that the implicitness of learning needs to be "guaranteed" by arranging the experimental learning situation in the proper way, whereas the implicitness of memory retrieval can be measured directly and validly. Reber states,

> Ideally, in order to obtain insight into a process such as implicit learning, it is essential to present the learner with a stimulus domain that has the following properties: 1. The stimuli need to be novel, . . . 2. The rule system that characterizes the stimulus domain needs to be complex. . . . 3. The stimuli should be meaningless and emotionally neutral, . . . 4. The stimuli should be synthetic and arbitrary. (p. 26)

In summary, the learning-only versus learning-plus-retrieval distinction of the meaning of implicit learning influences what needs to be demonstrated in an implicit learning episode in order to label the learning implicit. Although conceptually the difference between the two meanings is straightforward, operationally, separately assessing the implicitness of learning and retrieval by valid and independent measures has proven to be very difficult. Consequently, the learning-only and learning-plus-retrieval views differ dramatically in how they are operationalized. In the former, the implicitness of learning is measured on the basis of the implicitness of memory retrieval, thereby indirectly recategorizing the concept of implicit learning as a subset of the concept of implicit memory or implicit retrieval (Shanks & St. John, 1994). In the latter, implicit retrieval is assessed more or less directly, but the implicitness of learning is typically not assessed at all, leaving it up to experimental arrangement to guarantee the occurrence of implicit learning.

It is evident that both views would profit immensely from a nonintrusive measure of the implicit character of learning itself, and from, perhaps, the development of clever experimental arrangements and paradigms within which implicit learning can be assessed. Although it is much too early at the present time to even speculate, recent results of a number of neuro-imaging studies using Positron Emission Tomography (e.g., Grafton, Hazeltine, & Ivry, 1995; Hazeltine, Grafton, & Ivry, 1996; cited after Curran, Chapter 11, this volume), indicating that different brain areas may be involved in explicit and implicit learning, are extremely encouraging along those lines. If nonintrusive measures of type of learning can indeed be developed, the differences between the learning-only and learning-plus-retrieval views at the operational level might disappear. Up until then, however, measuring type of learning indirectly (learning-only view) appears to be preferable to measuring the type of learning not at all (learning-plus-retrieval), unless it can be demonstrated empirically that Reber's incidental learning arrangement does indeed have a higher likelihood of being accompanied by implicit rather than explicit learning (see comments below).

UNCONSCIOUS/UNAWARE VERSUS
NONINTENTIONAL/AUTOMATIC DISTINCTION

Whether implicit learning is considered an unconscious/unaware or a nonintentional/automatic process has obvious and strong implications for how implicit learning is measured. The issues that belong under the current heading map on to the issues that were discussed earlier when the unconscious/unaware versus nonintentional/automatic distinction was evaluated with regard to its impact on the distinguishability of implicit from explicit learning. What I concentrate on in this subsection are two questions: (a) which measures of implicitness are suggested by the unconscious/unaware view of implicit learning, and (b) which measures are suggested by the nonintentional/automatic view?

The Unconscious/Unaware Meaning. Cleeremans and Jiménez (1996) argue that "the development of theories about how to best assess implicit learning is not separable from the development of theories about consciousness." I see little reason to disagree with this assessment. Although consciousness can be and has been defined in both a functionalist and phenomenological manner, implicit learning research has, since the early work by Reber (1967), concentrated almost exclusively on the latter. The general idea has been to use measures of the degree to which subjects are conscious, typically assessed as awareness of the content of learning, as indicators of explicit learning. Following a dissociation logic (Reingold & Merikle, 1988), implicit learning is said to be demonstrated when learning of some contingency occurs either in subjects who show zero scores (no difference to chance) on the measure of explicit learning ($\alpha > \beta$ where $\beta = 0$ logic, see Erdelyi, 1986) or when the information available to the conscious system (α), as expressed in the explicit learning score, is not sufficient to explain subjects' degree of learning of the contingency ($\alpha > \beta$ where β is unconstrained).

It should be evident that a number of important assumptions characterize this approach. First, whether the first or the second type of logic is adopted is dictated, although this is frequently not acknowledged, by the theoretical assumptions about the relation between the unconscious and conscious systems one is willing to make (see Cleeremans & Jiménez, 1996, for a recent excellent discussion on this topic). Second, it must be assumed that the measure of explicit learning one uses is process-pure, that is, influenced by subjects' conscious knowledge of the content of learning alone (e.g., Reingold & Merikle, 1990). If process purity cannot be assumed, then the first type of logic may be completely misleading, and the second type of logic, although still attainable, might seriously underestimate the degree of implicit learning. Which measure of explicitness is used is thus of critical importance. In the words of Reber (1993), "Just how such measures are made and what kinds of psychometric defenses of them are provided will prove to be extremely difficult yet critical areas of investigation" (p. 9).

The main problem with the unconscious/unaware interpretation of the term implicit is that there does not exist a commonly agreed upon measure, or set of measures, of consciousness, or even awareness. Put differently, the theoretical meaning of consciousness is not specific enough to determine how consciousness should be measured. This is not necessarily a problem, of course, because it might be the case that all measures that supposedly assess consciousness agree empirically, that is, lead to the same pattern of findings. Unfortunately, however, this is not the case at all, as the following brief discussion of the different measures of consciousness that have been used reveals, thus leaving considerable doubts that a nonambiguous mapping of the concept of consciousness from the conceptual to the operational level can ever be achieved unless the concept of consciousness is defined more specifically.

In general, three types of measures of consciousness or awareness have been used, verbal reports, objective tests, and subjective tests (St. John & Shanks, in press). First, and most straightforward, one can take verbal reports as a measure of awareness, by asking subjects, via a series of probing questions, to indicate what they have learned. Use of verbal reports generally provides robust evidence of unconscious learning (via both types of logic described above), but as many critics have noticed (e.g., Eriksen, 1960; Holender, 1986), verbal reports suffer from a variety of empirical and methodological problems. St. John and Shanks (in press) list five such problems, most important among which are that verbal reports may be insensitive, that is, they may not exhaustively assess all of subjects' conscious knowledge due, for instance, to individual response bias (e.g., Eriksen, 1960; but see Erdelyi, Finks, & Feigin-Pfau 1989; Roediger, Srinivas, & Waddill, 1989), and that they may not meet Shanks and St. John's (1994) Information Criterion discussed earlier.

In light of these concerns, a number of researchers (e.g., Eriksen, 1960; Reed & Johnson, 1994; Stadler, 1989; Willingham, Nissen, & Bullemer, 1989) have advocated the use of so-called objective measures of awareness. Objective measures are identical to the measures used to assess learning in an implicit learning episode except that instructions given to subjects encourage the access of all relevant conscious knowledge. Objective measures have the obvious methodological problem, alluded to above, that they may not be process-pure measures of conscious knowledge. They also have the empirical problem that evidence in favor of implicit learning begins to evaporate when objective measures are used to assess consciousness. As Eriksen (1960; see also Holender, 1986; Shanks & St. John, 1994), in his influential review of the literature on unconscious perception and learning, has persuasively argued already, empirical evidence for implicit learning, when implicit is interpreted in terms of unconscious/unaware, is at best scarce and at worst nonexistent when objective measures of awareness are used. In light of the empirical problems to find evidence for implicit learning and the methodological problem that objective measures are unlikely to be process-pure, the "status of objective tests as acceptable indices of awareness seems very fragile" (St. John & Shanks, in press).

The third measure of consciousness that has been proposed in the literature are so-called subjective tests. In subjective tests, information is assumed to be unconscious when subjects claim to be unaware of it (Cheesman & Merikle, 1984). Although quite appealing, one often-pointed to problem with the use of subjective measures as tests of consciousness is that the criteria used to distinguish guessing from nonguessing are not specified and might thus vary across subjects. If different subjects do indeed have different guessing thresholds, then their data cannot be compared and aggregated. Reingold and Merikle (1990), among many others (e.g., Adams, 1957; Eriksen, 1960; Holender, 1986) have addressed this issue in depth.

The clear impression that this brief discussion of the various measures of consciousness/awareness conveys is that unambiguous operationalization of the concept of implicit learning, when implicit is taken to mean unconscious/unaware, is currently not attainable and most likely will not be attainable unless an unambiguously operationalizable concept of consciousness has been developed (Cleeremans & Jiménez, 1996).

The Nonintentional/Automatic Meaning. Nonintentional/automatic processing is often defined by listing dichotomous properties that distinguish it from some other kind of processing (e.g., attentional, Logan, 1980; controlled, Shiffrin & Schneider, 1977; effortful, Hasher & Zacks, 1979; strategic, Posner & Snyder, 1975; and even conscious, Posner & Klein, 1973). As one might expect, different researchers use somewhat different lists of criteria and also disagree on the necessity and sufficiency of the criteria they list. To mention the extremes, Posner and Snyder (1975) list only 3 criteria, whereas Hasher and Zacks (1984) list 6, and Schneider, Dumais, and Shiffrin (1984) list 12. Hasher and Zacks (1979, 1984) have argued that all criteria must be present in a truly nonintentional/automatic process, but other researchers have been less restrictive.

Although the exact list of nonintentionality/automaticity criteria is thus clearly not invariant among authors, there is, in general, considerable overlap in terms of the properties that tend to be viewed as indicating nonintentionality/automaticity. Among the conceptual properties perhaps mentioned most frequently are autonomy, lack of control, unconditionality, obligatoryness, effortlessness, unconsciousness, and poor memory (Logan, 1988), with the key properties perhaps being effortlessness and oblig-atoryness. Effortlessness refers to the assumption that nonintentional/ automatic processes do not drain mental energy; obligatoryness means that, given the proper external and/or internal conditions, nonintentional/auto-matic processes are initiated. The properties are not independent from each other, and some researchers have questioned the agreement between prop-erties, showing, for example, that an obligatory process need not be effortless (e.g., Kahneman & Chajzyck, 1983; Paap & Ogden, 1981; Regan, 1981).

At least some of the confusion concerning the proper criteria for non-intentional/automatic processing is cleared up when one considers the possibility that there exist different types of nonintentionality/automaticity. Hasher and Zacks (1979), for example, argue for two different origins of automatic processes, heredity and practice. Hasher and Zacks (1979) state,

> With regard to the former source, it may be that the nervous system is wired in such a way to maximize the processing of certain types of infor-mation. By this we mean that minimal experience is required for the acquisition of some automatic processes. Speculations concerning the relative ease of passage into the automatic state find some basis in the concept of "preparedness" in animal learning (Seligman, 1970). Prepar-edness to learn a particular association reflects the survival value of the association for the species. For example, rats are prepared to associate gastric distress with novel tastes and odors but not with sights or sounds (Garcia, Ervin, & Koelling, 1966).
>
> The second source for the origin of automatic processes is practice. Recent discussions of skilled readings (Kolers, 1975; LaBerge & Samuels, 1974), of communication (Shatz, 1977), of detection skills (Shiffrin & Schneider, 1977), and of individual differences in intelligence (Hunt, 1978) have supposed that large amounts of practice will under some circumstances result in the development of automatic processes. (pp. 359-360)

Hasher and Zacks's (1979, 1984) distinction between *learned* and *innate* automaticity leads to the possibility that these are two types of nonintentional/automatic processes that are not necessarily indicated by the same set of criteria. Hasher and Zacks (1979) argue,

> These considerations give rise to the suggestion that . . . processes occur along a continuum from effortful to automatic, with the "learned" automatic processes sharing some but not all of the attributes of processes at the automatic terminus of the attentional demand continuum. (p. 360)

It should be evident that innate automaticity, rather than learned automaticity, is the focus of the present discussion. Hasher and Zacks (1984) list six criteria which they argue all have to be met in order to conclude that a process, in their case the encoding of frequency information, is automatic in the innate automaticity sense:

> (a) People are sensitive to this information without necessarily intending to be; (b) the information encoded in this way is no different than it is when intention is activated; (c) training at processing such information does not improve encoding and neither does explicit feedback; (d) people differ very little in their ability to encode this information . . . ; (e) encoding of this information will be invariant across a wide range of ages; and (f) disruptions due to arousal, stress, and/or additional simultaneous processing demands will have no impact on the processing of such information. (p. 1373)

With the exception of (b) and (c), Hasher and Zacks's (1984) criteria for evaluating innate automaticity appear to be directly applicable to implicit learning research. Criteria (b) and (c) need to be excluded because, in contrast to a frequency encoding situation, voluntary, effortful learning strategies lead to enhanced learning in most tasks that have been studied in the laboratory. At the operational level, the remaining four criteria imply, for example, that learning in a particular research paradigm can be obtained under incidental instructions, shows little variability across individuals and age, and is unaffected by secondary tasks.

It follows that the nonintentional/automatic interpretation of implicit learning can lead to the formulation of relatively strict criteria for implicit learning at both the conceptual and the operational level. However, this advantage relative to the unconscious/unaware view is masked by the problem to integrate the criteria with the dissociation logic typically employed in implicit learning research. In the unconscious/unaware tradition, implicit learning is said to be demonstrated when learning occurs either in subjects who show zero awareness of what was learned or in subjects for which the acquired knowledge is not sufficient to explain all of the learning that they show. A similar dissociation logic seems plausible for some but not all of the automaticity criteria listed above. For example, it is conceivable, in principle, that learning could be demonstrated in subjects who show zero susceptibility to the presence of secondary tasks. Such a demonstration demands, however, a different experimental arrangement than the one used in the unconscious/unaware tradition. At minimum, subjects' learning would need to be assessed both with and without distraction, and subjects showing less learning in the presence of distraction would need to be discarded because for them, learning had not occurred automatically. The situation worsens when one considers that there exist additional criteria for automaticity that have an equal "right" to be the basis for distinguishing automatic from nonautomatic forms of learning.

A pragmatically more interesting alternative, therefore, would be a two-step approach where one would first demonstrate that learning proceeds nonintentionally/automatically for a given experimental paradigm and would then, in a second step, use the paradigm to explore potentially interesting properties of automatic learning. It is of utmost importance, when such an approach is selected, of course, that the experimental situation be arranged such that the likelihood for demonstrating automaticity is maximized and the likelihood for demonstrating nonautomaticity is minimized. Reber's (1993) aforementioned necessary properties of an implicit learning situation (i.e., complexity of rules, novelty, neutrality, and arbitrariness of stimuli) offer valuable hints at how such a learning situation might need to be arranged.

Summary. The preceding section has demonstrated that both the learning-only versus learning-plus-retrieval and the unconscious/unaware versus nonintentional/automatic distinctions influence how implicit learning is operationalized. The learning-only versus learning-plus-retrieval distinction affects primarily what needs to be demonstrated in order to label a learning episode an implicit learning episode. In contrast, the unconscious/unaware versus nonintentional/automatic distinction affects primarily how—that is, by which measures—whatever needs to be demonstrated *is* demonstrated. Regarding the what question, it appears that measuring the implicit character of learning indirectly (learning-only view) seems preferable to not assessing the implicitness of learning at all (learning-plus-retrieval). Regarding the how question, it appears that the unconscious/ unaware meaning of implicit learning is currently not unambiguously operationalizable. The nonintentional/automatic view of implicit learning might have the potential of providing strong operational criteria for the evaluation of implicitness.

Conclusion 3: Meanings of implicit learning differ in terms of how they are operationalized. Meanings that treat implicit learning as a learning phenomenon and meanings that interpret implicit as equivalent with nonintentional/automatic are more easily and less ambiguously operationalized than meanings treating implicit learning as a learning-plus-retrieval phenomenon and meanings interpreting implicit as unconscious/unaware.

● Putting It All Together

The general result of my evaluation of different meanings of the concept of implicit learning is relatively straightforward: Meanings that emphasize only the learning processes appear to be scientifically more useful than those emphasizing both learning and retrieval processes, and meanings that focus on the nonintentionality/automaticity of implicit learning appear to be more useful than those emphasizing the unconscious/unaware property of the concept. Taken together, my recommendation is thus *to define the concept of implicit learning in terms of the nonintentional, automatic acquisition of knowledge about structural relations between objects or events* (for a similar recent view see Perruchet & Gallego, in press). It is important to point out that this recommendation does by no means imply that the learning-only and nonintentional/automatic views are the correct views of implicit learning and that the learning-plus-retrieval and unconscious/ unaware views are incorrect views; my general point is rather that the former views are scientifically more useful than the latter ones because they more effectively distinguish implicit learning from related concepts and because they are more easily and less ambiguously operationalizable.

A conceptual analysis of the meanings of a concept is one thing; empirical support for the conceptually preferred meaning is a completely different thing, however. As I pointed out earlier, a meaningful scientific concept needs not to only be unique and operationalizable, it also needs to have predictive value. The question of interest thus becomes: does the concept of implicit learning, defined as the nonintentional automatic acquisition of knowledge about structural relations between objects or events, have empirical support, that is, does there exist empirical evidence that is consistent with the view that implicit learning is best characterized in terms of a nonintentional/automatic learning process? In the second part of this chapter, I consider empirical studies, primarily of my own group, that address some of the most pressing questions originating from the above definition of implicit learning. A much more exhaustive recent review of the applicability of the automaticity concept to implicit learning and memory can be found, for example, in Underwood and Bright (1996).

EMPIRICAL PART: THE NONINTENTIONALITY/ AUTOMATICITY OF IMPLICIT LEARNING

Any definition of implicit learning in terms of nonintentionality/ automaticity demands validation in terms of the criteria that indicate nonintentionality/automaticity. Two criteria that are frequently encountered in the literature are effortlessness and ubiquity. Effortlessness refers to the assumption that nonintentional/automatic processes do not require mental energy. Ubiquity is a criterion that is specific to innate automaticity (Hasher & Zacks, 1984), capturing the idea that nonintentional/automatic processes are not tied to specific content. With regard to implicit learning, ubiquity means that the relation between any two (or more) objects or events is acquired nonintentionally/automatically, regardless of the nature of the objects or events. Whether or not a process proceeds without effort is typically assessed in a dual-task (DT) situation in which subjects are to perform the process of interest together with a secondary task. Examining whether or not a process is ubiquitous requires an experimental setup in which subjects have a choice of learning different functional relations. There have been a considerable number of recent DT studies in the implicit learning domain but virtually none on the ubiquity of implicit learning. I discuss the former studies, along with some of my own, in the first subsection of the empirical part of this chapter and concentrate on the latter topic in the second subsection, where I explore the possibility that functional relations between pure phonological sequences and between pure visual sequences are more likely to become implicitly acquired than relations between mixed phonological and visual sequences.

● **Effortlessness of Implicit Learning**

In an often cited article, Nissen and Bullemer (1987) demonstrated that all sequence learning, explicit and implicit, is completely eliminated in normal, healthy individuals when a secondary tone-counting task is performed concurrently with the serial reaction time (SRT) task (Experiments 2 and 3). Referring to a capacity notion of attention, the authors argued that the secondary tone-counting task reduces the amount of attention that is available for performing the SRT task, and that because no learning is obtained under DT conditions, the implicit learning mechanism must require at least some attention in order to operate (for a recent overview on this and similar positions, see Hsiao & Reber, Chapter 14, this volume). If this interpretation is correct, then implicit learning can, of course, not be interpreted in terms of a nonintentional/automatic process, and consequently, my conceptual analysis above has little empirical support. In other words, the nonintentional/automatic meaning of implicit learning would have no predictive value. It is therefore important to ask (a) whether the original Nissen and Bullemer (1987) finding is replicable, and (b) if so, whether the findings can be explained in an alternative manner that do not require modifying my view of implicit learning as nonintentional/automatic.

The basic Nissen and Bullemer (1987) finding of a difference between ST and DT conditions on the SRT task has been replicated in a number of subsequent studies. Frensch and Miner (1994), for example, reported that the increase in response times (RTs) following the replacement of the structured repeating sequence by random sequences was significantly larger under ST than DT conditions. Similar findings have been reported by Cohen, Ivry, and Keele (1990), Frensch, Buchner, and Lin (1994), Keele and Jennings (1992), and Stadler (1995). In addition, Curran and Keele (1993, Experiment 1) showed that when ST practice was followed by DT practice in a within-subjects design, the amount of learning demonstrated under ST conditions was about twice that demonstrated under DT conditions for participants who reported very little awareness of the repeating sequence.

However, replications of the original finding have added two important qualifications to the difference between the ST and DT situations that had been reported by Nissen and Bullemer. First, it has been shown that, in general, implicit learning is not completely absent under DT conditions, but rather that it is only smaller than under ST conditions (roughly by the factor 2 to 3; see, e.g., Cohen et al., 1990; Frensch et al., 1994; Frensch & Miner, 1994; Keele & Jennings, 1992). Second, it has been demonstrated that the ST versus DT difference holds for different types of sequences (e.g., Cohen et al., 1990; Frensch et al., 1994), and not only for the sequence type used by Nissen and Bullemer (1987).

Notwithstanding the empirical reliability of the Nissen and Bullemer (1987) finding, the authors' interpretation of the difference between the ST and DT learning situations, namely that the mechanism(s) underlying implicit learning in the SRT task require(s) attention in order to operate, can in principle be challenged from at least two angles. First, it can be argued that the learning deficit in the DT situation relative to the ST situation might have been caused by specific interference effects rather than by a general lack of capacity. In order for this counterposition to be taken seriously, of course, the mechanisms of interference need to be specified. Indeed, Cohen et al. (1990), Cleeremans and McClelland (1991), Frensch et al. (1994), Frensch and Miner (1995), Heuer and Schmidtke (1996), Keele and Jennings (1992), and Stadler (1992, 1995) have described various ideas on how specific interference effects may operate in the SRT task. For example, Cleeremans and McClelland (1991) and Keele and Jennings (1992) were able to mimic the DT deficit in the SRT task by introducing nonspecific noise into their computational models. Stadler (1995) suggested that the tone-counting task interferes with sequence learning because it disrupts organization. Frensch et al. (1994) argued that the tone-counting task limits the amount of time that consecutive stimuli in the SRT task are simultaneously held in short-term memory. Heuer and Schmidtke (1996; Schmidtke & Heuer, in press) suggested that the need to integrate primary and secondary task may account for DT deficits in learning.

The second argument that can be leveled against the Nissen and Bullemer (1987) interpretation of their results is a methodological one, namely that their experimental manipulation did not allow for a separation of learning and expression-of-learning (i.e., performance) effects. More specifically, it can be argued that the secondary tone-counting task may impair sequence learning in the SRT task, the behavioral expression of what was learned, or both. This argument implies the methodological requirement that test conditions following ST and DT learning be identical when learning is to be compared under the two situations. This methodological requirement is widely recognized in the area of motor learning (e.g., Schmidt, 1988), for instance, but it has so far received very little attention in studies of implicit learning (but see Heuer & Schmidtke, 1996).

Our goal was therefore to assess to what extent a secondary tone-counting task affects implicit learning, the behavioral expression of what was learned, or both in the SRT task. Separating the influences of tone counting on learning and the behavioral expression of the learned calls for a logical separation of practice and testing phases in the SRT task, and it requires that the manipulation of ST versus DT be crossed with the two phases. Consequently, we had participants in two experiments practice the SRT task under both ST and DT conditions. The total amount of practice was the same for all participants (seven trial blocks with a repeating sequence), but different groups of participants received different schedules of ST and DT practice. In the first experiment, the assessment of how much had been learned (two random blocks) occurred under ST testing conditions; in the second experiment, it was done under DT testing conditions (Frensch, Lin, & Buchner, in press).

If tone counting affects learning, but not the expression of what was learned, then different practice schedules should lead to differences in the learning scores, assessed in the testing phase. In addition, the qualitative and quantitative patterns of the learning scores should be the same for ST and DT testing, that is, they should be identical for the two experiments. Conversely, if tone counting affects performance but not learning, then the different practice schedules should not affect learning differently. That is, the degree of learning should be the same for all practice schedules of Experiment 1, and it should be the same for all practice schedules of Experiment 2. However, the effects should generally be larger in Experiment 1 than in Experiment 2. Finally, if tone counting affects both learning and performance, then one would expect the manipulation of practice schedule to affect the amount of learning demonstrated under ST and DT testing conditions. Furthermore, the pattern of results should qualitatively be the same for the ST and DT testing conditions but should quantitatively be stronger for the ST than the DT testing situation.

Figure 2.1 captures the results of Experiment 1; Figure 2.2 those of Experiment 2. As can be seen, the overall RTs differed dramatically during the learning phase of the experiments (Blocks 1 to 7), depending on whether participants performed the SRT task alone or simultaneously with the tone-counting task. More important, the increase in RT when systematic sequences were replaced by random sequences (difference between Blocks 7 and 8) was not different for the three groups tested under single-task (ST) conditions (Figure 2.1) and was also not different for the three groups tested under DT conditions (Figure 2.2). These findings are relatively

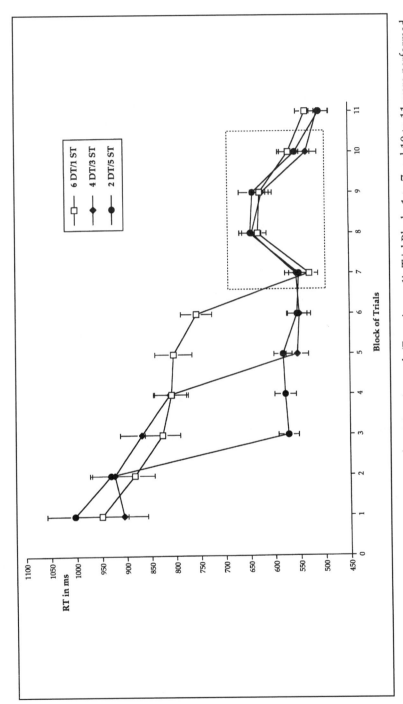

Figure 2.1. Mean reaction times (RTs) on serial reaction time task (Experiment 1). Trial Blocks 1 to 7 and 10 to 11 were performed with a repeating sequence; Trial Blocks 8 and 9 were performed with random sequences.

NOTE: ST = single-task condition; DT = dual-task condition.

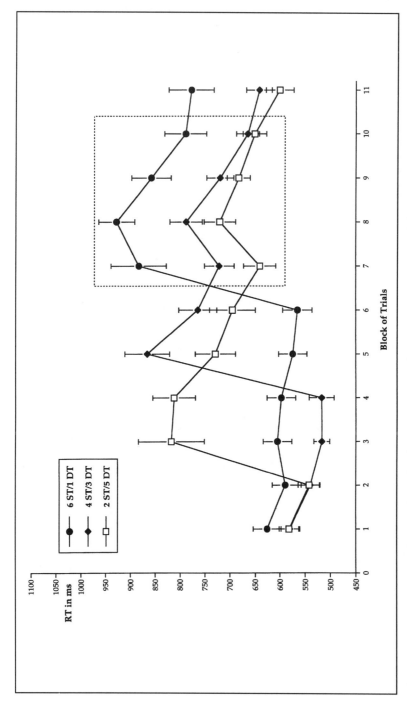

Figure 2.2. Mean reaction times (RTs) on serial reaction time task (Experiment 2). Trial Blocks 1 to 7 and 10 to 11 were performed with a repeating sequence; Trial Blocks 8 and 9 were performed with random sequences.
NOTE: ST = single-task condition; DT = dual-task condition.

straightforward, and clearly indicate that tone counting affects the expression of the learned and not learning per se.

This interpretation is inconsistent with findings presented by Curran and Keele (1993). In their Experiment 3, Curran and Keele showed that the amount of learning did not differ when participants were first tested under DT conditions and were then retested under ST conditions. A performance interpretation would need to predict, in contrast, that when freed from the restraining secondary tone-counting task, the amount of learning demonstrated in a subsequent ST testing situation should exceed that demonstrated in a DT testing situation. Although Heuer and Schmidtke (1996) have recently provided evidence that is consistent with our expectation and contradicts the Curran and Keele findings, it was important for us to replicate the Curran and Keele experiment.

Two more experiments were therefore designed to test the performance hypothesis in the Curran and Keele experimental situation. The experiments differed from the first two experiments in three aspects. First, the two testing situations, ST and DT, were now administered in a within-subjects design, rather than a between-subjects design. Thus, participants were either first tested under ST conditions and then retested under DT conditions, or vice versa.

Second, instead of using hybrid repeating sequences (Cohen et al., 1990), we now varied the type of sequence. In Experiment 3, we used ambiguous sequences; in Experiment 4, we used unique sequences (see Cohen et al., 1990). Other than that, Experiments 3 and 4 were identical. Cohen et al. (1990) have argued that implicit learning of unique and ambiguous sequences is accomplished by learning mechanisms that differ in part. The manipulation of sequence type, therefore, lets us explore the generalizability of our findings.

Third, we systematically varied the amount of practice participants received before they underwent their first learning test. Participants practiced either one or five trial blocks with a repeating sequence in either the presence or absence of the tone-counting task before learning was assessed. The assumption that tone counting affects the expression of what was learned predicts that the learning scores obtained under ST testing conditions will exceed those obtained under DT testing conditions. Thus, when participants are first tested under DT conditions and are then retested under ST conditions, their learning scores should be larger under ST conditions. The difference between the two sets of learning scores should be more apparent after much practice (i.e., five trial blocks) than after little practice (i.e., one trial block), assuming that not much is learned in the first place in the low-practice condition. The exact same pattern of results is expected for participants who are first tested under ST conditions and are then retested under DT conditions. Furthermore, these predictions hold regardless of whether the repeating sequence is of an ambiguous (Experiment 3) or a unique (Experiment 4) sequence type.

Figure 2.3 captures the results of Experiment 3; Figure 2.4 those of Experiment 4. In all conditions, Trial Blocks 1 through 5, 7, and 10 were performed with a systematic sequence; Trial Blocks 6, 8, and 9 were performed with random sequences. The findings were again straightforward; in six out of eight cases, ST testing led to higher learning scores than DT testing, the exception being the 1-ST condition in both Experiments 3 and 4. Second, the difference between ST testing and DT testing varied generally with task practice and was the larger the more trials participants had practiced at the time of testing. Third, all effects were larger with unique than with ambiguous sequences, although the general pattern of results was virtually identical for the two sequence types. Thus, on the whole, these findings clearly do not replicate the Curran and Keele (1993, Experiment 3) findings. Instead, they are consistent with recent results by Heuer and Schmidtke (1996), who also reported increased learning scores under ST relative to DT testing conditions for both unique and ambiguous sequence transitions.

Overall, our findings thus agree with the assumption that tone counting affects the behavioral expression of what has been learned and not implicit learning per se. Implicit learning is thus likely achieved by nonattentional, automatic learning mechanism(s) (see also Cleeremans, in press). Ultimately, of course, the best empirical arguments to refute the involvement of attention in implicit learning are to demonstrate (a) that multiple secondary tasks that do not differ in terms of their complexity differ nevertheless, in a predictable manner, in their effects on performance in the SRT task or (b) that varying the demands of a single secondary task does not affect SRT task performance. The former, I believe, has recently been reported by Heuer and Schmidtke (1996), who have shown that learning in the SRT task and the behavioral expression of the learned were not affected by secondary verbal memory and visuospatial tasks, but were affected by an auditory go/no-go distractor task (see also Goschke, 1992). The latter result has been reported by Cohen et al. (1990), who found that implicit learning was unaffected by variation of tone-counting difficulty. The Heuer and Schmidtke finding is consistent with the view of a response-

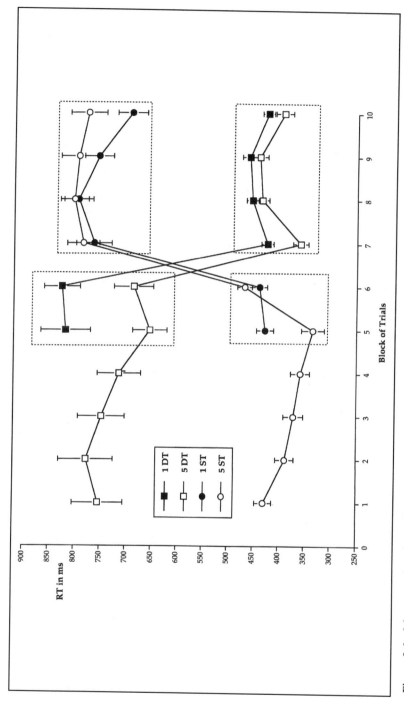

Figure 2.3. Mean reaction times (RTs) on serial reaction time task (Experiment 3). Trial Blocks 1 to 5, 7, and 10 were performed with a repeating sequence; Trial Blocks 6, 8, and 9 were performed with random sequences.

NOTE: ST = single-task condition; DT = dual-task condition.

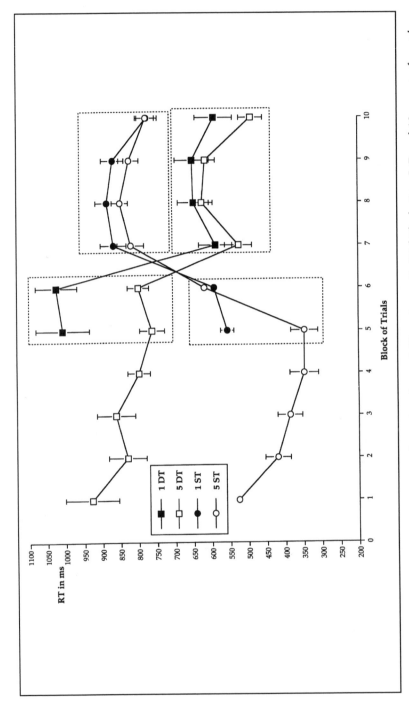

Figure 2.4. Mean reaction times (RTs) on serial reaction time task (Experiment 4). Trial Blocks 1 to 5, 7, and 10 were performed with a repeating sequence; Trial Blocks 6, 8, and 9 were performed with random sequences.

NOTE: ST = single-task condition; DT = dual-task condition.

selection bottleneck in human cognition (e.g., Pashler, 1994) and begins to tease apart the important question of how exactly secondary tasks might interact with SRT task performance.

● **Ubiquity of Implicit Learning**

Animals seem to be "prepared" (Seligman, 1970) to learn particular functional relations more quickly and durably than others. For example, rats are much more likely to associate gastric distress with novel tastes and odors than with sights or sounds (Garcia, Ervin, & Koelling, 1966). In the animal learning literature, preferred functional relations are argued to reflect the survival value of the relations for the species. In the studies I present next, Caroline Miner and I explore the possibility that preparedness can be found in implicit learning as well. In some sense, such a finding would qualify the nonintentionality/automaticity of the implicit learning mechanism(s) argued for above, because it would indicate that the nonintentional/automatic process is not ubiquitous, an assumption typically endorsed, although often implicitly, for innate automatic processes. Hasher and Zacks (1984), for instance, argue that frequency information is automatically encoded for any event that is attended to, regardless of the nature of the event. The preferred functional relations examined in Frensch and Miner's (1995) studies do not reflect evolutionary ideas, as in the animal learning research; rather, they may reflect functional architectural considerations of how our cognitive system is structured.

In an earlier attempt to theoretically capture the concept of implicit learning, Miner and I (Frensch & Miner, 1994) have argued that learning in the Nissen and Bullemer (1987) paradigm, both explicit and implicit, involves the operation of (a) two functionally separable memory stores, short-term memory and long-term memory; and (b) a central executive that directs attention and controls intentional processing. We assumed that short-term memory represents an activated subset of long-term memory (e.g., Cowan, 1993; Hebb, 1949) and that only a subset of the activated long-term memory may be in the focus of attention at any point in time. Learning, whether explicit or implicit, was assumed to occur only in that subset of long-term memory that is active (i.e., short-term store). Explicit learning was viewed as occurring only in the subset of short-term memory that is also in the focus of attention, and as achieved through active processes (e.g., hypothesis testing) that are controlled by the central executive. Implicit learning, in contrast, was theorized as involving activated information inside and/or outside the focus of attention and as achieved through a passive, strictly associative process (e.g., Cleeremans & McClelland, 1991), capable of detecting and storing covariational environmental information. Implicit learning was thus seen as not guided by the central executive.

The central point in our earlier theorizing, as viewed from the present theoretical interest, was that we adhered to the ubiquity assumption. That is, by viewing implicit learning mechanisms as operating on the contents of activated memory representations, we indirectly endorsed the assumption that the relation between any two or more knowledge representations can, in principle, be learned, and that there is no reason to assume that it should be more difficult to acquire the same functional relation between memory representations A and B than between A and C.

This ubiquity assumption has not been unique to our own previous theorizing. For example, Berry and Broadbent (1988; see also Hayes & Broadbent, 1988) distinguish two modes of learning, which the authors label *s-mode* (selective mode) and *u-mode* (unselective mode). The selective mode of learning corresponds to what Miner and I refer to as explicit learning mode; the unselective mode refers to our implicit learning mode. Berry and Broadbent argue that only the selective mode of learning operates within a decay-prone and capacity-limited type of working memory, whereas the unselective learning mode "does not reflect the operation of a cognitive subsystem such as AWM" (Hayes & Broadbent, 1988, p. 251), where AWM refers to an *abstract working memory* (Broadbent, 1984). The difference between Berry and Broadbent's view and our earlier view lies thus in the memory structure implicit learning is assigned to; the commonality between the two views is that they both adhere to the ubiquity assumption, or at least do not formulate criteria that would constrain the ubiquity of the implicit learning mechanism(s).

Similarly, Mathews et al. (1989) argue that implicit learning reflects a process that automatically extracts family resemblances among exemplars stored in long-term memory (see the memory-array models described by Estes, 1986, and Dienes, 1992, for instance, for how such a process might operate). Mathews et al. agree with Berry and Broadbent (1988) and with recent connectionist models of serial learning (e.g., Cleeremans & McClelland, 1991; Keele & Jennings, 1992) that implicit learning should not be affected by properties of short-term memory. However, Mathews et al.'s model, like all others, accepts the ubiquity assumption.

What functional architectural reasons are there to assume that ubiquity might not characterize implicit learning? The one I will concentrate on is the working memory model proposed by Baddeley and Hitch (1974, 1994; see also Baddeley, 1986, 1992). Baddeley and Hitch proposed to abandon the earlier idea (e.g., Atkinson & Shiffrin, 1968) of a single, unitary working-memory system, proposing instead a tripartite model. Their model assumed an attentional controller, termed the central executive, aided by two active slave systems, the articulatory or phonological loop (which maintains speech-based information) and the visuospatial scratchpad or sketchpad (which is capable of holding and manipulating visuospatial information). According to Baddeley and Hitch, the phonological loop has two components: a brief speech-based store that holds a memory trace, which fades within approximately 2 seconds (Baddeley, 1992), coupled with an articulatory control process. This process, which resembles subvocal rehearsal, is capable of maintaining the material in the phonological store by a recycling process and, in addition, is able to feed information into the store by a process of subvocalization. One additional assumption regarding the phonological loop is that auditory spoken information gains obligatory access to the store.

Similar to the phonological loop, the visuospatial sketchpad is also assumed to involve a brief store, together with control processes responsible for registering visuospatial information and for refreshing it by rehearsal. Visuospatial information is assumed to gain obligatory access to the store. Recently, Farah (1988) has presented evidence for two separate subcomponents of the sketchpad from studies of both normal subjects and neuropsychological patients and argues for the anatomical and functional separation of a pattern-based ("what") and a spatial ("where") component of visual working memory. The visuospatial sketchpad and phonological loop are assumed to operate independently from each other.

The Baddeley and Hitch (1974, 1984) model generates a number of interesting questions regarding the mechanism(s) underlying implicit learning if one is willing to treat seriously the possibility that these mechanisms may operate in working memory. One of these questions concerns the ubiquity assumption. For functional and/or architectural reasons, it is possible to argue from within the model that sequences of phonological information may be implicitly learned independently from sequences of visuospatial information, and furthermore, if Farah's (1988) analysis is correct, that spatial sequences may be learned independently from visual nonspatial sequences. Furthermore, learning of sequences that combine phonological with visuospatial information might be more difficult to achieve than learning of "pure" sequences.

Evidence supporting the independence of implicit learning of spatial and nonspatial visual regularities comes from a recent study by Mayr (1996), who demonstrated that "the joint learning of spatial and object sequences was as efficient as learning of single sequences and that it even occurred when learning required memory for past sequence elements and attention was blocked through a secondary tone-counting task" (p. 350). The three experiments I briefly present next were designed to examine whether functional relations between pure phonological sequences and between pure visual sequences are more likely to become implicitly acquired than relations between mixed phonological and visual sequences. A straightforward approach to investigating this question is to have three different subject groups implicitly learn pure phonological, pure visuospatial, and mixed phonological-visuospatial regularities. This is indeed what we did, using a modified version of the Nissen and Bullemer (1987) task. Participants performed a sequential matching task in which the sequence of target symbols, which were either letters or nonpronounceable visual patterns of equal size, followed a systematic pattern. An additional benefit of using the matching-task modification of Nissen and Bullemer's task was that motor learning influences were excluded because the mapping of matching symbols to response keys was randomly rearranged for each trial.

Figure 2.5 captures the results of the first experiment in this series. As can be seen, sequences of phonological targets and sequences of alternating phonological-visual targets were learned; sequences of visual targets were not learned. This result is surprising, at first sight, because it fits neither the prediction of the ubiquity assumption, nor the prediction of the Baddeley and Hitch model. There are at least two different possible interpretations of the findings. First, one might argue that only sequences of phonological targets can be learned implicitly, but not sequences of nonpronounceable visual targets. Learning in the mixed group would in this case be exclusively based on the learning of the letter target sequence. Second, one might argue that both sequences of phonological and sequences of visual targets can be learned and that the empirical difference between the two is merely a function of a difference in familiarity with the target symbols. According to the latter explanation, by experimentally equating familiarity with letters and nonpronounceable visual targets, one should be able to eliminate the obtained learning difference. In two subsequent experiments, we tested both interpretations.

In Experiment 2 of this series, we used only sequences of nonpronounceable visual targets, but we manipulated both amount of familiarity

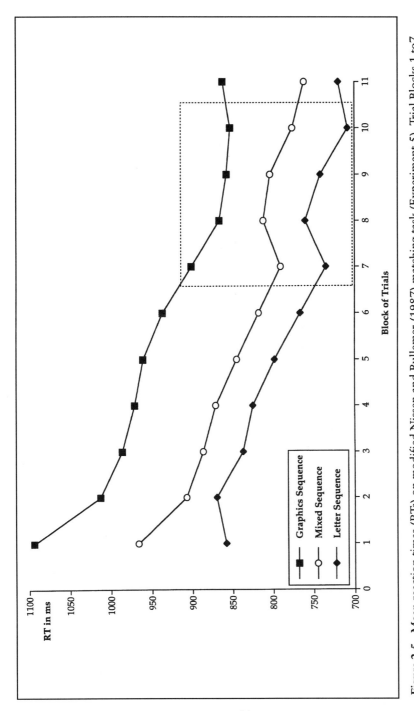

Figure 2.5. Mean reaction times (RTs) on modified Nissen and Bullemer (1987) matching task (Experiment 5). Trial Blocks 1 to7 and 10 to 11 were performed with a repeating sequence; Trial Blocks 8 and 9 were performed with random sequences.

91

with the targets and availability of a phonological label. Participants in the Label groups learned a nonsense phonological label for each target before the experiment began; participants in the No Label groups did not learn labels. Participants in the Low Familiarity groups were asked to accurately copy each of the used target symbols 20 times preexperimentally; participants in the High Familiarity groups copied each symbol 40 times. By crossing the two manipulations we ended up with four different subject groups.

If indeed a lack of familiarity accounted for the lack of learning in the visual group of the first experiment, then we should find a significant main effect of Familiarity in this experiment. If, on the other hand, the lack of learning in the visual group was due to the nonavailability of phonological labels, then we should find a significant main effect of Label. Moreover, if learning of both sequences of letters and of nonpronounceable targets is possible and occurs independently from each other, then the two main effects should not be qualified by a statistical interaction between Familiarity and Label.

Figure 2.6 displays the main results from this experiment in terms of the increase in RT that resulted in the four experimental conditions when the systematic sequence was replaced by random sequences. As can be seen, both the main effect of Familiarity and the main effect of Label were significant. The interaction between Familiarity and Label was not, however. These findings are consistent with the view that implicit sequence learning occurs independently in the two working-memory slave systems, phonological loop and visuospatial sketchpad. If this is indeed the case, then one might expect that implicit learning in the mixed condition of Experiment 1 might have been due primarily to learning of the phonological target sequence and that implicit learning of functional relations that cross the two slave systems might not be possible, or at least might be impaired.

In the final experiment, we used only mixed phonological and non-pronounceable target sequences. Of interest here was primarily whether, within the mixed sequences, phonological-visual relations would be learned as well as phonological-phonological and visual-visual relations. To this end, two different transfer conditions were realized after all participants had gone through the same learning phase. In the Letter Change group, participants received transfer sequences in Blocks 8 and 9 that differed from the original sequences in that the sequence of target letters was now random; the sequence of visual targets was identical in learning phase and

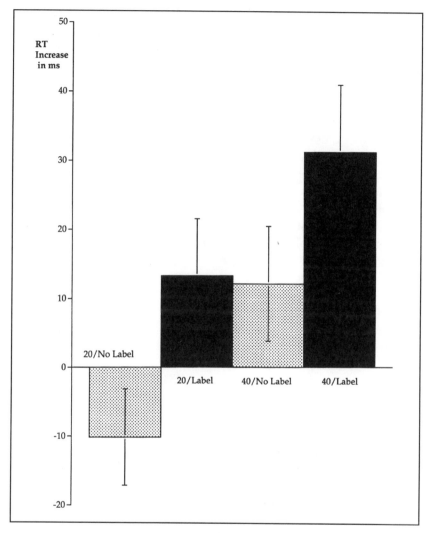

Figure 2.6. Mean reaction time (RT) increase (RT random – RT repeating) on modified Nissen and Bullemer (1987) matching task (Experiment 6).

transfer phase. In the Graphics Change group, participants received transfer sequences in Blocks 8 and 9 that differed from the original sequences in that the sequence of visual targets was now random; the sequence of letter targets was identical in learning phase and transfer phase.

In addition, participants' responses to letter targets and nonpronounce-able visual targets were analyzed separately. If implicit learning occurs independently for letter and visual sequence information and a crossover is not possible, then participants' RTs to letter targets should be affected by the modification of the letter sequence but not by the modification of the graphic sequence. Conversely, participants' RTs to graphic targets should be affected by the modification of the graphic sequence but not by the modification of the letter sequence. If letter-graphic and graphic-letter combinations can be learned implicitly, however, then both modifications should show effects, regardless of whether responses to letter targets or graphic targets are involved. Figure 2.7 displays the main findings from this experiment. The results show that implicit sequence learning occurs independently for letter target and graphic target sequences and that learning of letter-graphic and graphic-letter relations does not occur at all—in other words, the ubiquity assumption appears to be incorrect.

These findings are reminiscent of the preparedness effect obtained in animal learning studies (Seligman, 1970), although the preferred functional relations that are learned do not necessarily reflect evolutionary appropriate adaptive behavior; instead, they reflect functional architectural constraints of how our cognitive system might be structured.

● Summary

The series of experiments reported in the empirical part of this chapter was motivated by the definition of implicit learning, argued for in the first part of the chapter, in terms of the nonintentional/automatic acquisition of knowledge about structural relations between objects or events. Our findings indicate that such a definition has predictive value. Experiments 1 through 4 demonstrated that a secondary task affects the behavioral expression of what has been learned, and not implicit learning per se. Implicit learning is thus likely achieved by nonattentional/automatic learning mechanism(s). Experiments 5, 6, and 7 demonstrated that implicit learning is not ubiquitous, however. Rather, there exists a preference for learning certain functional relations, similar to the preparedness effect observed in animal learning studies (Seligman, 1970). Preferably learned relations may not reflect the survival value of the relations for the species, however, but instead may reflect functional architectural constraints on how the cognitive system is structured.

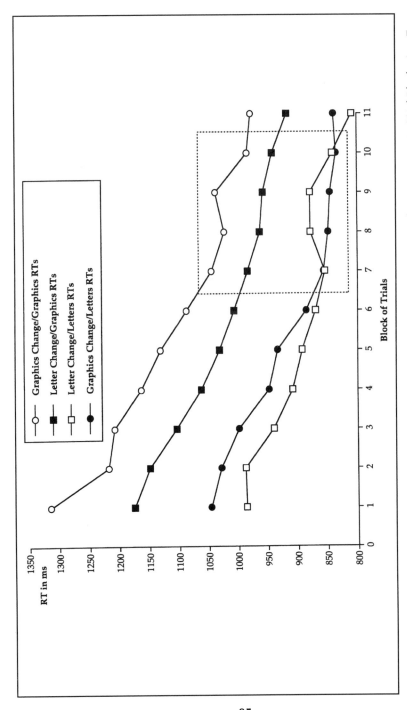

Figure 2.7. Mean reaction times (Rts) on modified Nissen and Bullemer (1987) matching task (Experiment 7). Trial Blocks 1 to 7 and 10 to 11 were performed with a repeating sequence; Trial Blocks 8 and 9 were performed with random sequences.

SUMMARY AND CONCLUSIONS

The present chapter was divided into a conceptual part and an empirical part. In the conceptual part, my goal has been to clarify which meaning best to attach to the concept of implicit learning, or, in other words, how best to define implicit learning. I have discussed and evaluated the various meanings of the concept of implicit learning that have been offered in the literature and have argued that most of the existing meanings of implicit learning differ in whether they attach the label implicit only to learning processes or to learning and retrieval processes, and in whether they take implicit to be synonymous with unconscious/unaware or with nonintentional/automatic. There exist thus roughly four distinct classes of meanings of the concept of implicit learning, which differ, I have claimed, in terms of their scientific usefulness.

I have argued that meanings that emphasize only the learning processes are scientifically preferable to those emphasizing both learning and retrieval processes, and that meanings that focus on the nonintentional/automatic property of implicit learning are preferable to those emphasizing the unconscious/unaware property of the concept. Taken together, my recommendation was to define the concept of implicit learning as the nonintentional and automatic acquisition of knowledge about structural relations between objects or events.

In the second part of the chapter, I examined the predictive value of the thus formulated meaning of implicit learning by considering whether or not implicit learning adheres to two criteria that have sometimes been used to describe innate automatic processing, effortlessness and ubiquity. On the basis of empirical studies conducted in our lab and elsewhere that directly address these issues, I have argued that implicit learning is indeed achieved by automatic learning mechanism(s). However, implicit learning does not seem ubiquitous; instead, there exists a preference for learning certain functional relations, reminiscent of the preparedness effect observed in animal learning studies (Seligman, 1970). Preferably learned relations may not reflect the survival value of the relations for the species, however, but instead may reflect functional architectural constraints on how the cognitive system is structured.

NOTES

1. According to *Webster's New Twentieth Century Dictionary* (1983), a definition is "an explanation or statement of what a word or word phrase means or has meant." Definitions, thus, formally capture the meaning of a concept, and henceforth the terms *definition* and *meaning* will be used interchangeably.

2. Consequently, I do not consider Seger's part (d) of her definition of implicit learning as relevant to any definition of the concept either.

3. The question of whether intentional control and consciousness/awareness are functionally separable is quite complex, and in the past, it has been taken to refer to the relation between intentional control and either awareness of the act of controlling, awareness of the result of controlling, or awareness of the intention guiding control. In the present context, I am interested in whether or not intentional control and consciousness can be separated in principle. Therefore, the questions of interest to me are whether or not intentional control is always accompanied by awareness of any kind, be it the act or result of control or the intention guiding control, and whether automatic, nonintentional control is always accompanied by a lack of any kind of awareness. In order to demonstrate the functional separability of intentional control and consciousness in principle, one thus needs to find situations where (a) intentional control is accompanied by the lack of awareness of the act of control, as well as of the result of control and of the intention guiding control, and where (b) nonintentional control is accompanied by awareness of either the act of control, of the result of control, or of the intention guiding control.

REFERENCES

Adams, J. K. (1957). Laboratory studies of behavior without awareness. *Psychological Bulletin, 54,* 383-405.

Atkinson, R. C., & Shiffrin, R. M. (1968). Human memory: A proposed system and its control processes. In K. W. Spence & J. T. Spence (Eds.), *The psychology of learning and motivation: Advances in research and theory* (Vol. 2). New York: Academic Press.

Atkinson, R. C., & Shiffrin, R. M. (1971). The control of short-term memory. *Scientific American, 224,* 82-90.

Baddeley, A. D. (1986). *Working memory.* Oxford, UK: Clarendon.

Baddeley, A. D. (1992). Working memory. *Science, 255,* 556-559.

Baddeley, A. D., & Hitch, G. J. (1974). Working memory. In G. Bower (Eds.), *The psychology of learning and motivation* (Vol. 8, pp. 47-90). San Diego, CA: Academic Press.

Baddeley, A. D., & Hitch, G. J. (1994). Developments in the concept of working memory. *Neuropsychology, 8,* 485-493.

Berry, D. C. (1994). Implicit learning: Twenty-five years on. A tutorial. In C. Umiltà & M. Moscovitch (Eds.), *Attention and performance XV: Conscious and non-conscious information processing* (pp. 755-782). Cambridge: MIT Press.

Berry, D. C., & Broadbent, D. E. (1988). Interactive tasks and the implicit-explicit distinction. *British Journal of Psychology, 79,* 251-272.

Brewer, W. F. (1974). There is no convincing evidence for operant or classical conditioning in adult humans. In W. B. Weimer & D. S. Palermo (Eds.), *Cognition and the symbolic processes* (pp. 1-42). Hillsdale, NJ: Lawrence Erlbaum.

Broadbent, D. E. (1984). The Maltese cross: A new simplistic model for memory. *Behavioral and Brain Sciences, 7,* 55-94.

Bruner, J. S., Goodnow, J., & Austin, G. (1956). *A study of thinking.* New York: John Wiley.

Chan, C. (1992). *Implicit cognitive processes: Theoretical issues and applications in computer system design.* D.Phil. thesis, University of Oxford.

Cheesman, J., & Merikle, P. M. (1984). Priming with and without awareness. *Perception and Psychophysics, 36,* 387-395.

Cleeremans, A. (in press). Sequence learning in a dual-stimulus setting. *Psychological Research.*

Cleeremans, A., & Jiménez, L. (1996). *Implicit cognition with the symbolic metaphor of mind: Theoretical and methodological issues.* Unpublished manuscript.

Cleeremans, A., & McClelland, J. L. (1991). Learning the structure of event sequences. *Journal of Experimental Psychology: General, 120,* 235-253.

Cohen, A., Ivry, R. I., & Keele, S. W. (1990). Attention and structure in sequence learning. *Journal of Experimental Psychology: Learning, Memory, and Cognition, 16,* 17-30.

Cowan, N. (1988). Evolving conceptions of memory storage, selective attention, and their mutual constraints within the human information-processing system. *Psychological Bulletin, 104,* 163-191.

Cowan, N. (1993). Activation, attention, and short-term memory. *Memory & Cognition, 21,* 162-167.

Curran, T., & Keele, S. W. (1993). Attentional and nonattentional forms of sequence learning. *Journal of Experimental Psychology: Learning, Memory, and Cognition, 19,* 189-202.

Detweiler, M., & Schneider, W. (1991). Modeling the acquisition of dual task skills in a connectionist/control architecture. In D. Damos (Ed.), *Multiple-task performance: Selected topics* (pp. 69-99). London, UK: Taylor & Francis.

Dienes, Z. (1992). Connectionist and memory-array models of artificial grammar learning. *Cognitive Science, 16,* 41-79.

Dulany, D. E. (1961). Hypotheses and habits in verbal "operant conditioning." *Journal of Abnormal and Social Psychology, 63,* 251-263.

Dulany, D. E. (in press). Consciousness in the explicit (deliberative) and implicit (evocative). In J. Cohen & J. Schooler (Eds.), *Scientific approaches to the study of consciousness.* Hillsdale, NJ: Lawrence Erlbaum.

Erdelyi, M. H. (1986). Experimental indeterminacies in the dissociation paradigm of subliminal perception. *Behavioral and Brain Sciences, 9,* 30-31.

Erdelyi, M. H., Finks, J., & Feigin-Pfau, M. B. (1989). The effect of response bias on recall performance, with some observations on processing bias. *Journal of Experimental Psychology: General, 118,* 245-254.

Eriksen, C. W. (1958). Unconscious processes. In M. R. Jones (Ed.), *Nebraska symposium on motivation* (Vol. 6, pp. 169-228). Lincoln: University of Nebraska Press.

Eriksen, C. W. (1960). Discrimination and learning without awareness: A methodological survey and evaluation. *Psychological Review, 67,* 279-300.

Estes, W. K. (1986). Memory storage and retrieval processes in category learning. *Journal of Experimental Psychology: General, 115,* 155-174.

Farah, M. J. (1988). Is visual memory really visual? Overlooked evidence from neuropsychology. *Psychological Review, 95,* 307-317.

Farah, M. J. (1994). Visual perception and visual awareness after brain damage: A tutorial overview. In C. Umiltà & M. Moscovich (Eds.), *Attention and performance XV* (pp. 37-76). Cambridge: MIT Press.

Fehrer, E., & Raab, E. (1962). Reaction time to stimuli masked by metacontrast. *Journal of Experimental Psychology, 63,* 143-147.

Fisk, A. D., & Schneider, W. (1983). Category and word search: Generalizing search principles to complex processes. *Journal of Experimental Psychology: Learning, Memory, and Cognition, 2,* 177-195.

Frensch, P. A., Buchner, A., & Lin, J. (1994). Implicit learning of unique and ambiguous serial transitions in the presence and absence of a distractor task. *Journal of Experimental Psychology: Learning, Memory, and Cognition, 20,* 567-584.

Frensch, P. A., & Funke, J. (1995). Definitions, traditions, and a framework for understanding complex problem solving. In P. Frensch & J. Funke (Eds.), *Complex problem solving: The European perspective* (pp. 3-25). Hillsdale, NJ: Lawrence Erlbaum.

Frensch, P. A., Lin, J., & Buchner, A. (in press). Learning versus behavioral expression of the learned: The effects of a secondary tone-counting task on implicit learning in the serial reaction task. *Psychological Research.*

Frensch, P. A., & Miner, C. S. (1994). Effects of presentation rate and individual differences in short-term memory capacity on an indirect measure of serial learning. *Memory & Cognition, 22,* 95-110.

Frensch, P. A., & Miner, C. S. (1995). Zur Rolle des Arbeitsgedächtnisses beim impliziten Sequenzlernen [The role of working memory in implicit sequence learning]. *Zeitschrift für Experimentelle Psychologie, 17,* 545-575.

Frith, C. D. (1992). *The cognitive neuropsychology of schizophrenia.* Hove, UK: Lawrence Erlbaum.

Garcia, J., Ervin, F. R., & Koelling, R. A. (1966). Learning with prolonged delay of reinforcement. *Psychonomic Science, 5,* 121-122.

Gibson, E., & Gibson, J. J. (1955). Perceptual learning: Differentiation or enrichment? *Psychological Review, 62,* 32-41.

Goldberg, G., Mayer, N. H., & Toglia, J. U. (1981). Medial frontal cortex and the alien hand sign. *Archives of Neurology, 38,* 683-686.

Goschke, T. (1992, April). *The role of attention in implicit learning of structured event sequences.* Paper presented at the Annual Conference for Experimental Psychologists. Osnabrück, Germany.

Graf, P. (1994). Explicit and implicit memory: A decade of research. In C. Umiltà & M. Moscovich (Eds.), *Attention and performance XV* (pp. 681-696). Cambridge: MIT Press.

Grafton, S. T., Hazeltine, E., & Ivry, R. (1995). Functional mapping of sequence learning in normal humans. *Journal of Cognitive Neuroscience, 7,* 497-510.

Greenwald, A. G. (1992). New look 3: Unconscious cognition reclaimed. *American Psychologist, 47,* 766-779.

Hasher, L., & Zacks, R. T. (1979). Automatic and effortful processes in memory. *Journal of Experimental Psychology: General, 108,* 356-388.

Hasher, L., & Zacks, R. T. (1984). Automatic processing of fundamental information: The case of frequency of occurrence. *American Psychologist, 39,* 1372-1388.

Hayes, N. A., & Broadbent, D. E. (1988). Two modes of learning for interactive tasks. *Cognition, 28,* 249-276.

Hazeltine, E., Grafton, S. T., & Ivry, R. (1996). *Neural loci of motor learning depend on stimulus characteristics.* Unpublished manuscript.

Hebb, D. O. (1949). *The organization of behavior: A neuropsychological theory.* New York: John Wiley.

Heuer, H., & Schmidtke, V. (1996). Secondary-task effects on sequence learning. *Psychological Research, 59,* 119-133.

Holender, D. (1986). Semantic activation without conscious identification in dichotic listening, parafoveal vision, and visual masking: A survey and appraisal. *Behavioral and Brain Sciences, 9,* 1-66.

Humphrey, N. (1992). *A history of the mind.* London: Chatto & Windus.

Hunt, E. (1978). Mechanics of verbal ability. *Psychological Review, 85,* 109-130.

Jenkins, J. G. (1933). Instruction as a factor in "incidental" learning. *The American Journal of Psychology, 45,* 471-477.

Kahneman, D., & Chajzyck, D. (1983). Tests of the automaticity of reading: Dilution of Stroop effects by color-irrelevant stimuli. *Journal of Experimental Psychology: Human Perception and Performance, 9,* 497-509.

Keele, S. W., & Jennings, P. J. (1992). Attention in the representation of sequence: Experiment and theory. *Human Movement Science, 11,* 125-138.

Kimble, G. A. (1996). *Psychology: The hope of a science.* Cambridge: MIT Press.

Kolers, P. A. (1975). Memorial consequences of automatized learning. *Journal of Experimental Psychology: Human Learning and Memory, 1,* 689-701.

LaBerge, D. (1975). Acquisition of automatic processing in perceptual and associative learning. In P. M. A. Rabbitt & S. Dornic (Eds.), *Attention and performance* (Vol. 5). New York: Academic Press.

LaBerge, D., & Samuels, S. J. (1974). Toward a theory of automatic information processing in reading. *Cognitive Psychology, 6,* 293-323.

Lewicki, P., Czyzewska, M., & Hoffman, H. (1987). Unconscious acquisition of complex procedural knowledge. *Journal of Experimental Psychology: Learning, Memory, and Cognition, 13,* 523-530.

Logan, G. D. (1980). Attention and automaticity in Stroop and priming tasks: Theory and data. *Cognitive Psychology, 12,* 523-553.

Logan, G. D. (1988). Toward an instance theory of automatization. *Psychological Review, 95,* 492-527.

Mandler, G. (1975). Consciousness: Respectable, useful, and probably necessary. In R. Solso (Ed.), *Information processing and cognition: The Loyola symposium* (p. 229-254). Hillsdale, NJ: Lawrence Erlbaum.

Mandler, G. (1992). Toward a theory of consciousness. In H.-G. Geissler, S. W. Link, & J. T. Townsend (Eds.), *Cognition, information processing, and psychophysics: Basic issues* (pp. 43-66). Hillsdale, NJ: Lawrence Erlbaum.

Marcel, A. J., & Bisiach, E. (1988). *Consciousness in contemporary science.* Oxford, UK: Oxford University Press.

Mathews, R. C., Buss, R. R., Stanley, W. B., Blanchard-Fields, F., Cho, J. R., & Druhan, B. (1989). Role of implicit and explicit processes in learning from examples: A synergistic effect. *Journal of Experimental Psychology: Learning, Memory, and Cognition, 15,* 1083-1100.

Mayr, U. (1996). Spatial attention and implicit sequence learning: Evidence for independent learning of spatial and nonspatial sequences. *Journal of Experimental Psychology: Learning, Memory, and Cognition, 22,* 350-364.

Monsell, S. (1996). Control of mental processes. In V. Bruce (Ed.), *Unsolved mysteries of the mind: Tutorial essays in cognition* (pp. 93-148). Hove, UK: Lawrence Erlbaum.

Natsoulas, T. (1978). Consciousness. *American Psychologist, 33*, 906-914.

Neisser, U. (1963). The multiplicity of thought. *British Journal of Psychology, 54*, 1-14.

Neumann, O., & Klotz, W. (1994). Motor responses to nonreportable, masked stimuli: Where is the limit of direct parameter specification? In C. Umiltà & M. Moscovich (Eds.), *Attention and performance XV* (pp. 123-150). Cambridge: MIT Press.

Newell, A. (1990). *Unified theories of cognition.* Cambridge, MA: Harvard University Press.

Nissen, M. J., & Bullemer, P. (1987). Attentional requirements of learning: Evidence from performance measures. *Cognitive Psychology, 19*, 1-32.

Norman, D. A., & Shallice, T. (1986). Attention to action: Willed and automatic control of behavior. In R. J. Davidson, G. E. Schwartz, & D. Shapiro (Eds.), *Consciousness and self-regulation* (Vol. 4). New York: Plenum.

Paap, K. R., & Ogden, W. C. (1981). Letter encoding is an obligatory but capacity-demanding operation. *Journal of Experimental Psychology: Human Perception and Performance, 7*, 518-527.

Pashler, H. (1994). Dual-task interference in simple tasks: Data and theory. *Psychological Bulletin, 116*, 220-244.

Perruchet, P., & Gallego, J. (in press). A subjective unit formation account of implicit learning. In D. Berry (Ed.), *How implicit is implicit learning?* Oxford, UK: Oxford University Press.

Posner, M. I., & Klein, R. M. (1973). On the functions of consciousness. In S. Kornblum (Ed.), *Attention and performance* (Vol. 4, pp. 21-35). New York: Academic Press.

Posner, M. I., & Snyder, C. R. R. (1975). Facilitation and inhibition in the processing of signals. In P. M. A. Rabbitt & S. Dornic (Eds.), *Attention and performance* (Vol. 5). New York: Academic Press.

Reber, A. S. (1967). Implicit learning of artificial grammars. *Journal of Verbal Learning and Verbal Behavior, 6*, 855-863.

Reber, A. S. (1989). Implicit learning and tacit knowledge. *Journal of Experimental Psychology: General, 118*, 219-235.

Reber, A. S. (1993). *Implicit learning and tacit knowledge: An essay on the cognitive unconscious.* New York: Oxford University Press.

Reed, J., & Johnson, P. (1994). Assessing implicit learning with indirect tests: Determining what is learned about sequence structure. *Journal of Experimental Psychology: Learning, Memory, and Cognition, 20*, 585-594.

Regan, J. E. (1981). Automaticity and learning: Effects of familiarity on naming letters. *Journal of Experimental Psychology: Human Perception and Performance, 7*, 180-195.

Reingold, E. M., & Merikle, P. M. (1988). Using direct and indirect measures to study perception without awareness. *Perception and Psychophysics, 44,* 563-575.

Reingold, E. M., & Merikle, P. M. (1990). On the interrelatedness of theory and measurement in the study of unconscious processes. *Mind and Language, 5,* 9-28.

Roediger, H. L., III, Srinivas, K., & Waddill, P. (1989). How much does guessing influence recall? Comment on Erdelyi, Finks, and Feigin-Pfau. *Journal of Experimental Psychology: General, 118,* 255-257.

Schmidt, R. A. (1988). *Motor control and learning: A behavioral emphasis.* Champaign, IL: Human Kinetics Publishers.

Schmidtke, V., & Heuer, H. (in press). Task integration as a factor in secondary-task effects on sequence learning. *Psychological Research.*

Schneider, W., Dumais, S. T., & Shiffrin, R. M. (1984). Automatic and control processing and attention. In R. Parasuraman & R. Davies (Eds.), *Varieties of attention* (pp. 1-27). New York: Academic Press.

Schneider, W., & Fisk, A. D. (1982). Concurrent automatic and controlled visual search: Can processing occur without resource cost? *Journal of Experimental Psychology: Learning, Memory, and Cognition, 8,* 261-278.

Schneider, W., & Fisk, A. D. (1984). Automatic category search and its transfer. *Journal of Experimental Psychology: Learning, Memory, and Cognition, 10,* 1-15.

Schneider, W., & Shiffrin, R. M. (1977). Controlled and automatic human information processing: I. Detection, search, and attention. *Psychological Review, 84,* 1-66.

Seligman, M. E. P. (1970). On the generality of the laws of learning. *Psychological Review, 77,* 406-418.

Shallice, T. (1978). The dominant action-system: An information-processing approach to consciousness. In K. S. Pope & J. L. Singer (Eds.), *The stream of consciousness: Scientific investigations into the flow of human experience* (pp. 117-157). New York: Plenum.

Shallice, T. (1994). Multiple levels of control processes. In C. Umiltà & M. Moscovich (Eds.), *Attention and performance XV* (pp. 395-420). Cambridge: MIT Press.

Shanks, D. R., & St. John, M. F. (1994). Characteristics of dissociable human learning systems. *Behavioral and Brain Sciences, 17,* 367-447.

Shatz, M. (1977). The relationship between cognitive processes and the development of communication skills. In B. Keasey (Ed.), *Nebraska symposium on motivation* (Vol. 25). Lincoln: University of Nebraska Press.

Shiffrin, R. M., & Schneider, W. (1977). Controlled and automatic human information processing: II. Perceptual learning, automatic attending, and a general theory. *Psychological Review, 84,* 127-190.

Stadler, M. A. (1989). On learning complex procedural knowledge. *Journal of Experimental Psychology: Learning, Memory, and Cognition, 15,* 1061-1069.

Stadler, M. A. (1992). Statistical structure and implicit serial learning. *Journal of Experimental Psychology: Learning, Memory, and Cognition, 18,* 318-327.

Stadler, M. A. (1995). Role of attention in implicit learning. *Journal of Experimental Psychology: Learning, Memory, and Cognition, 21,* 674-685.

Stadler, M. A., & Frensch, P. A. (1994). Whither learning, whither memory? *Behavioral and Brain Sciences, 17,* 423-424.

St. John, M. F., & Shanks, D. R. (in press). Implicit learning from an information processing standpoint. In D. Berry (Ed.), *How implicit is implicit learning?* Oxford, UK: Oxford University Press.

Thorndike, E. L., & Rock, R. T., Jr. (1934). Learning without awareness of what is being learned or intent to learn. *Journal of Experimental Psychology, 17,* 1-19.

Tulving, E. (1984). Multiple learning and memory systems. In K. M. J. Lagerspetz & P. Niemi (Eds.), *Psychology in the 1990s: In honour of Professor Johan von Wright on his 60th birthday, March 31, 1984* (pp. 163-184). Amsterdam: Elsevier Science.

Underwood, G., & Bright, J. E. (1996). Cognition with and without awareness. In G. Underwood (Ed.), *Implicit cognition* (pp. 1-40). Oxford, UK: Oxford University Press.

Vokey, J. R., & Brooks, L. R. (1992). Salience of item knowledge in learning artificial grammars. *Journal of Experimental Psychology: Learning, Memory, and Cognition, 18,* 328-344.

Waugh, N. C., & Norman, D. A. (1965). Primary memory. *Psychological Review, 72,* 89-104.

Willingham, D. B., Nissen, M. J., & Bullemer, P. (1989). On the development of procedural knowledge. *Journal of Experimental Psychology: Learning, Memory, and Cognition, 15,* 1047-1060.

3

The Question of Awareness in Research on Implicit Learning

●————————————————————————————————

Michael A. Stadler
Henry L. Roediger III

Memory is not to be identified with the act of remembering, or with conscious awareness that one is remembering something from the past, although it includes this. Any measure of change in behavior that reflects the effect of prior experience is a valid index of a memory or a memory trace or an engram. We tend to emphasize too much the use of recall or recognition, which is a highly personal kind of thing, as measures of learning and memory. It seems to me that a measure of change in performance such as is involved in the "relearning" method, where progressive changes in performance occur as a result of experience in the situation but where the subject need not be aware of the use of prior experience, is also acceptable as an index of the presence of a memory trace.

Arthur Melton made this statement as part of his opening remarks at the Second International Interdisciplinary Conference on Learning, Remembering and Forgetting, which was held in 1964 (Kimble, 1967, p. 25). To illustrate his point that measures of change in performance would be good measures of memory, Melton presented experiments patterned on the Hebb (1961) repetition effect, in which subjects' memory of a list of digits that is repeated intermittently among nonrepeated lists improves relative to that of the nonrepeated lists. After presenting his results, Melton heard a now familiar question. Another participant at the conference, Donald Broadbent (who was later to become one of the early leaders in the field of implicit learning; see, e.g., Berry & Broadbent, 1988; Broadbent, Fitzgerald, & Broadbent, 1986; Hayes & Broadbent, 1988) raised the issue of awareness: "I have heard it asserted by people who have repeated this experiment, that in their experience, the only people who showed the Hebb effects were the ones who caught onto what was happening" (Kimble, 1967, p. 41). Melton's response to the awareness question (also on p. 41) was that

> the subject in an experiment of this sort is reacting to each stimulus as though all he has to do is to remember it long enough to write it down. We are in the midst of some further studies of this kind, and, in one study, we have waited until the eighth eight-consonant stimulus before introducing for the very first time, the one that is going to be repeated. When this eighth stimulus is repeated, it occurs again after five intervening eight-consonant units. By the time the subject sees the stimulus a second time, he has had thirteen of these strings of eight consonants, all from the same limited set of nine consonants, and ought to be thoroughly confused. Nevertheless, the second trial on that repeated eight-consonant stimulus shows an improved recall, as compared with the first trial or a control.

Melton's response was based on the plausible argument that the structure of the task made it unlikely that subjects were deliberately using memory for the first presentation of the repeated list in their attempts to remember it the second time. Of course, it is one thing to assume subjects are not doing this, another to prove it to the avowed skeptic. The awareness question, that is, the question of how to rule out the possibility that conscious processing contaminates what is presumed to be nonconscious processing, is a serious issue confronting researchers interested in implicit learning. It has been suggested that concerns about awareness in tests of implicit memory may have reached levels greater than is warranted (see Roediger & McDermott, 1993), but given that there have been several well-known and well-cited criticisms of how research on implicit learning has addressed the awareness question (Dulany, Carlson, & Dewey, 1984; Perruchet & Amorim, 1992; Perruchet, Gallego, & Savy, 1990; Perruchet & Pacteau, 1990; Shanks & St. John, 1994), it is an issue that must be dealt with carefully and convincingly. The difficulties Melton had concerning the issue of awareness are difficulties the field still grapples with (e.g., Dienes & Berry, 1997; Neal & Hesketh, 1997; Shanks & St. John, 1994; Stadler, 1997).

Melton was arguably presenting evidence for implicit learning (in her 1994 review, Seger included as an example of implicit learning the Hebb task that Melton used), although the term would not be introduced until a few years later (Reber, 1967). At the time, however, the paradigm Hebb used would more likely have been described as one involving *incidental learning* (in contrast to *intentional learning*). Interestingly, issues similar to those being considered here were also important in that literature. In a review, Postman (1964) wrote that "a basic obstacle to the definition of the term 'incidental' has been that its connotations are negative, i.e., it refers to the *absence* of a set or intent to learn" (p. 185) and that "in then assuming that learning under these conditions occurs without any intent to learn, one is essentially in the position of accepting the null hypothesis" (p. 185). He concluded by noting that "it is hazardous ever to assert that learning is incidental in an absolute sense. We can accept this point without abandoning a substantive problem which is implied in the distinction between intentional and incidental learning" (p. 185). Our view is that researchers interested in implicit learning should similarly focus on the differential effects of implicit and explicit orientations on learning, rather than on attempts to demonstrate that learning is implicit in some absolute sense.

To date, inquiries into subliminal perception and implicit memory have perhaps dealt more effectively with the question of awareness than those into implicit learning (see Reingold & Merikle, 1988, and Roediger & McDermott, 1993, for examination of this issue in the subliminal perception and implicit memory literatures, respectively). Researchers in these areas have used approaches seldom used in studies of implicit learning, so these related literatures may offer some lessons for future research on implicit learning. The reasons for the different levels of progress on this question are not clear. They may owe to the different interests of researchers in the various areas. Or they may simply owe to a difference in levels of activity in the areas. In the 10 years after Graf and Schacter (1985) coined the term implicit memory, the terms *implicit learning* and *implicit memory* have been used in the titles or abstracts of 443 papers indexed in PsycINFO. The overwhelming majority of those publications were concerned with implicit memory (362, or 82% of the 443). In any case, it is worth considering what these other literatures have to offer as help in answering the awareness question.

DEFINITIONS AND ASSUMPTIONS

The first definitions of the terms implicit learning and implicit memory seem quite similar to Melton's idea that memory is not confined to "the act of remembering." Reber (1967) wrote that implicit learning is a process in which "information is abstracted out of the environment . . . without recourse to explicit strategies for responding or systems for recoding the stimuli" (p. 863). Thus, encoding occurs without the subject's intention to learn, and learning is measured by the influence of that knowledge on another task.

Graf and Schacter (1985) wrote that "implicit memory is revealed when performance on a task is facilitated in the absence of conscious recollection; explicit memory is revealed when performance on a task requires conscious recollection of previous experiences" (p. 501). Here, retrieval, rather than encoding, occurs without the subject's intention and, as in implicit learning, memory is inferred from a change in performance on a transfer task rather than being tested with recall or recognition.

Some differences do exist from one author to the next in the precise use of the term implicit. It has been used with reference to task instructions, so that implicit learning would refer to essentially the same thing as incidental learning (see Postman, 1964), or with reference to mental processes, to indicate a characteristic of those processes or a form of learning (see Frensch, Chapter 2, this volume, for a detailed discussion of this issue). This state of affairs could, of course, lead to some confusion. Richardson-Klavehn and Bjork (1988) outlined several potential difficulties that similar confusion over the term implicit memory might cause and so recommended the use of the term *indirect* to refer to the task distinction and the term *implicit* to refer to the form of learning distinction. Those objections could apply just as readily to the term implicit learning. However, such problems are not new and may not be that problematic. Roediger and McDermott (1993) pointed out that the term *episodic memory,* for example, is used to describe both a hypothetical memory system and a class of memory tasks without much confusion. The manner in which the term implicit is used is usually clear from the context.

Without putting too much emphasis on purely definitional concerns, it is worth distinguishing implicit learning from implicit memory (see also Buchner & Wippich, Chapter 1, this volume). Despite the apparent similarity in the terms, implicit learning and implicit memory were defined at different times by different people for different purposes. The implicit learning literature has traditionally focused on learning of relatively complex novel information over many (even thousands) experimental trials. To the extent that it has been compared to explicit learning (see below), it has focused on encoding processes, following Reber's idea that implicit encoding occurs without the use of conscious strategies. The implicit memory literature, in contrast, has focused largely on effects of single presentations of already familiar stimuli (e.g., words) and has emphasized the nature of retrieval. Encoding of material often occurs under intentional learning conditions, although the intentional or incidental nature of encoding often does not affect performance (measured by priming) on implicit memory tests (e.g., Roediger, Weldon, Stadler, & Riegler, 1992).

The distinction between encoding and retrieval is especially important in distinguishing implicit learning and implicit memory. For example, the typical test of learning in the artificial grammar-learning situation used by Reber (see Reber, 1989, for a review) was one in which subjects were informed that the stimuli they had seen in the first part of the experiment were composed according to complex rules and that they should then attempt to classify new stimuli according to whether they followed those rules or not. In the 1967 study, each subject "was instructed to make his decisions on the basis of what he had learned about the grammar from the 20 sentences he had previously memorized" (p. 860). This test meets Graf and Schacter's (1985) definition of an explicit, not implicit, retrieval test. At least as originally defined, subjects might or might not be aware of implicitly acquired knowledge; Reber only said that the information could be applied on a transfer test, not necessarily that it could be applied without awareness. (In other parts of that article, however, Reber did also make the claim that subjects were not aware of and could not verbalize what they had learned.)

The operational definitions of implicit learning and implicit memory cited above may be combined in various ways (implicit encoding with implicit retrieval; implicit encoding with explicit retrieval; explicit encoding with implicit retrieval; explicit encoding with explicit retrieval; see Stadler & Frensch, 1994). Thus, implicit learning as studied in the standard artificial grammar-learning paradigm is a case of implicit encoding and explicit (intentional) retrieval, although Reber (e.g., Reber, Allen, & Regan, 1985) has typically argued that even with instructions for explicit retrieval, subjects are unable to do this, so their judgments are influenced by nonconscious knowledge. In other procedures, such as implicit sequence learning in reaction time (RT) tasks (e.g., Nissen & Bullemer, 1987; Stadler, 1995), both encoding and retrieval occur under implicit instructions. Most recently, Shanks and St. John's (1994) definition of implicit learning focused on conditions at test; they held that implicit learning occurred when, at the time of the test, subjects were unaware of both the to-be-learned information and the episode in which it was learned. Their definition was mute on the nature of encoding, so it could presumably be either implicit or explicit. Thus, we have covered with these various definitions of implicit learning three of the four cells in the matrix: implicit encoding with explicit retrieval (in the typical artificial grammar-learning experiment), implicit encoding with implicit retrieval (in the usual serial reaction time [SRT] experiment), and explicit encoding with implicit retrieval (a possibility allowed for in Shanks & St. John's definition but not yet realized in the implicit learning literature). There is agreement, at least, that explicit encoding with explicit retrieval does *not* qualify as a case of implicit learning.

Part of the confusion here may stem from the different purposes for which claims concerning awareness have been used. Recall Postman's (1964) definition of incidental learning. One reason to measure subjects' awareness is to be able to make strong claims about *learning without awareness,* defining implicit learning in the absolute sense that Postman cautioned against. Another, we believe better, reason for making such a claim is to allow for the investigation of *unintentional learning,* in the sense of investigating the functional differences between deliberate, strategy-driven encoding and incidental, automatic (i.e., obligatory) encoding. In the latter case, claims about awareness are made as assurance that encoding was unintentional; subjects cannot intentionally encode something of which they are not aware. Thus, the interest is not in learning without awareness per se, just in being as sure as possible that subjects did not use intentional learning strategies.

LEARNING WITHOUT AWARENESS

To make claims about learning without awareness, researchers obviously need adequate measures of awareness (which, because they require intentional processing, are explicit measures). Reingold and Merikle (1988) examined two important assumptions that can be made about explicit measures. One is the exhaustiveness assumption, which is that the explicit measure completely measures subjects' conscious knowledge. This has been important in the implicit learning literature, because without some demonstration that subjects have no explicit knowledge, critics will be able to claim that what is said to be implicit learning is actually explicit learning that went undetected by the researcher. And of course, many criticisms of claims for nonconscious processing are based on a claim that this assumption has not been met (e.g., Holender, 1986; Shanks & St. John, 1994). Unfortunately, it is probably impossible to guarantee that this assumption is met by any particular measure.

The other assumption is the exclusiveness assumption, which is that the explicit measure only measures explicit knowledge and is not influenced by implicit knowledge. Proponents of nonconscious processing in implicit learning tend to focus more on this assumption. The problem with some explicit measures, particularly recognition and other forced-choice discriminations, is that they may not be process-pure (Jacoby, 1991). That is, they may also be influenced by nonconscious processing. For example, recognition judgments might be influenced by a nonconscious fluency of processing, thus contaminating a purportedly explicit measure with implicit processing.

There are several good reasons to be concerned about the exclusiveness assumption. Fluency at least potentially influences recognition judgments (Fendrich, Healy, & Bourne, 1991; Johnston, Dark, & Jacoby, 1985; Johnston, Hawley, & Elliott, 1991). Also, there are nonconscious influences on performance that cannot be controlled by explicit instruction (e.g., Jacoby, 1991; Jacoby, Woloshyn, & Kelly, 1989). Finally, subjects are reliably able to distinguish recognition judgments based on "remembering" of an item from those based only on "knowing" that an item was previously presented (Gardiner, 1988; Gardiner & Java, 1993; Tulving, 1985). These two classes of responses have been systematically dissociated from one another in ways that suggest that remember responses reflect explicit processing, whereas know responses depend on implicit processing (Rajaram, 1993). All of these factors show that it would be treacherous indeed to assume that the exclusiveness assumption is met by a given explicit test.

Fortunately, Reingold and Merikle (1988) also offered a solution to these problems, one that would be based on a much simpler and more reasonable assumption. Their logic requires first that the implicit and explicit measures be comparable, differing only in that subjects are instructed to rely on conscious knowledge for the explicit measure but not the implicit measure. Comparability means that subjects must receive the same stimuli under the same conditions, that the tests must be the same except for the presence or absence of the instruction to use conscious recollection, that the tests must use the same number of alternatives and the same scale of measurement, and so on. Such comparability may be difficult to achieve in some cases, but the ability to do without the exclusiveness and exhaustiveness assumptions makes this approach worth pursuing. Using this logic, one need only assume that the explicit measure is at least as sensitive to conscious knowledge as the implicit measure. If so, then any result in which the implicit measure is more sensitive to knowledge than the explicit measure implies the existence of nonconscious processing.

Merikle and Reingold (1991, Experiment 2) reported an implicit memory study in which, after studying a list of words, subjects were tested on words displayed against a background mask of varying contrast. Subjects in the explicit test group were instructed to indicate whether each word was old or new. Subjects in the implicit test group were instructed to indicate whether each word had high or low contrast. Following Jacoby, Allan, Collins, and Larwill (1988), the expectation was that words seen previously in the experiment would tend to be judged as having high contrast, words not seen as having low contrast. Both groups of subjects were tested over three blocks of trials. As shown in Figure 3.1, for the first two blocks, the implicit test was more sensitive to prior presentation than the recognition test; this pattern reversed in the third block. Given that the testing conditions were identical except for instructions, and given the very reasonable assumption that the recognition test was at least as sensitive to conscious memory as the contrast test, this study clearly demonstrates a case of nonconscious memory.

As a further illustration of this approach, consider a study by Mandler, Nakamura, and Van Zandt (1987) of the subliminal mere exposure effect. It also meets the conditions set forth by Reingold and Merikle (1988). In the first phase of this experiment, subjects were presented with five 1 ms exposures to each of 10 irregular octagons. In the second phase, four groups of subjects were shown pairs of these shapes, one of which was presented during the first phase of the experiment, one of which was not. One group was asked to make a recognition judgment, indicating which of the shapes had been presented during the first phase of the experiment. Another group was asked to indicate which of the two figures they liked the best. A third group was instructed to indicate which figure appeared to be brighter, and a fourth to indicate which appeared to be darker. The performance of subjects in the recognition condition was not different from chance, whereas subjects in the other groups reliably selected the shape that had been

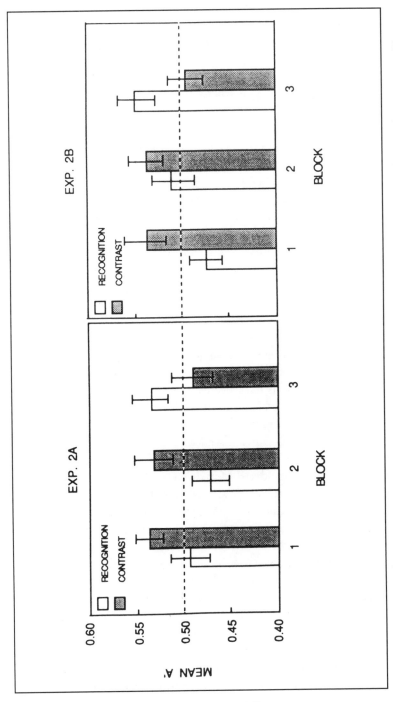

Figure 3.1. Mean sensitivity (A′) of the recognition and contrast tasks at each trial block in Experiment 2A and Experiment 2B. (Bars indicate standard errors.)

SOURCE: From "Comparing Direct (Explicit) and Indirect (Implicit) Measures to Study Unconscious Memory," by P. M. Merikle and E. M. Reingold, 1991, *Journal of Experimental Psychology: Learning, Memory and Cognition, 17,* p. 230. Copyright 1991 by the American Psychological Association. Used with permission.

previously presented. Here again, an implicit measure was more sensitive than an explicit measure taken under comparable conditions, thus demonstrating nonconscious memory.

There are not, to our knowledge, many published studies of implicit learning that meet all of Reingold and Merikle's (1988) criteria. One that meets many of them is an experiment by Stadler (1989), which was the only study that Shanks and St. John (1994) acknowledged to have demonstrated implicit learning with procedures not open to one or another of their methodological criticisms. That study used a prediction measure to test explicit learning in an SRT task modeled after Lewicki, Czyzewska, and Hoffman's (1987) study. In that task, subjects looked for a target presented in one of four locations and pressed a key that corresponded to the location in which the target appeared. Subjects were trained on 24 different seven-trial repeating sequences over several days. An implicit measure showed that subjects learned the patterns; when the patterns were changed, RT increased dramatically. In a final phase of the experiment, however, subjects responded to the first six trials of each sequence exactly as they had in training, but on the seventh trial were shown a blank display and asked to indicate where the target would have appeared. Although the implicit (RT) measure indicated that subjects had learned these repeating sequences, they performed at chance on this prediction task. Thus, the implicit measure appears to have been more sensitive than the explicit measure. The one way in which this study does not meet Reingold and Merikle's criteria is the difference in response metrics between the implicit (RT) and explicit (four-alternative forced-choice recognition) measures.

Jiménez, Méndez, and Cleeremans (1996) recently reported a study based specifically on Reingold and Merikle's (1988) logic. In a six-choice RT task in which the sequence of stimuli was determined by complex probabilistic rules, they found that although there was a positive correlation between comparable implicit and explicit measures of knowledge of sequential structure, when the explicit scores were partialed out, there was still a significant relation between the implicit scores and the to-be-learned sequential structure. They concluded that the knowledge reflected in that partial correlation was nonconscious. Thus, although this approach has not been used extensively in the study of implicit learning, it appears to hold promise that can only be realized with additional research.

Reber's (1976) study of artificial grammar learning used similar but not identical logic. Two groups of subjects were tested under identical conditions, one given implicit (incidental) study instructions during the study phase of an artificial grammar-learning experiment, the other given explicit (intentional) study instructions. In the test phase, both groups of subjects were shown new grammatical and nongrammatical items and asked to indicate whether each item was grammatical or nongrammatical. The implicit study group was accurate on about 77% of the items, the explicit group on only about 65% of them. Part of a later study (Reber, Kassin, Lewis, & Cantor, 1980) that replicated the conditions of Reber's (1976) study produced the same pattern of results, although not at a statistically significant level. It is tempting, given Reingold and Merikle's (1988) reasoning, to conclude that because the implicit study condition produced better performance on the test, subjects in that condition learned more. Note, however, as Reber (1976) did, that subjects in the explicit study condition may have formed incorrect hypotheses about the structure of the stimuli, attempted to use those hypotheses at the time of test, and thus performed more poorly. A critic might argue that both the implicit and the explicit study groups have conscious knowledge about, say, individual items (e.g., Brooks, 1978) or parts of grammatical items (e.g., Perruchet & Pacteau, 1990), but that knowledge is not expressed in the explicit condition because subjects choose to base their judgments on whatever hypotheses they developed in the study phase.

● Definitions of Awareness

As we have noted, there have been few attempts to use Reingold and Merikle's (1988) logic to demonstrate implicit learning. More studies have attempted to apply Cheesman and Merikle's (1984) distinction between the *subjective* and *objective* thresholds of awareness. Often, positive demonstrations of subliminal perception could be criticized on the grounds that measures of subjects' awareness of the subliminal stimuli were not reliable or sensitive enough. Cheesman and Merikle conducted an experiment with more stringent threshold-setting measures and demonstrated that with those measures, no evidence for subliminal perception was obtained. Then, to account for differences between their negative finding and previous positive findings, they distinguished between an objective definition of awareness, at which subjects' performance on a forced-choice discriminative test is at chance, and a subjective definition, at which subjects' belief is that their performance on the forced-choice discrimination is at chance. They suggested that previous studies reporting positive evidence for subliminal perception had employed equivalents of subjective definitions of

115

awareness. They then performed a second experiment that revealed no evidence of subliminal perception with an objective definition, but positive evidence with a subjective definition. Merikle and Cheesman (1986) subsequently argued that the subjective criterion might be preferable because it most closely reflects subjects' phenomenological experiences.

Several studies have adopted this approach to investigate implicit learning. The study by Stadler (1989) included a subjective measure. Based on Cheesman and Merikle's (1984) findings, the expectation was that subjects might be judged unaware by the subjective measure but aware by the objective measure. Instead, subjects appeared to be unaware of the repeating patterns by either measure. More recently, several studies that used subjective measures of awareness have been done on artificial grammar learning. After reviewing this evidence, and some suggestive evidence from other tasks used to study implicit learning, Dienes and Berry (1997) tentatively concluded, in line with Cheesman and Merikle (1984), that whereas subjects would often be judged aware by an objective definition of awareness, they would not be by a subjective definition. This pattern of results, aware by an objective measure but not by a subjective measure, reinforces concerns about the exclusiveness assumption. Subjects appear to have little or no metaknowledge about what has been learned in an implicit learning task, yet by the objective tests, they might be judged aware. This suggests again that implicit knowledge is contaminating performance on the objective tests, in violation of the exclusiveness assumption discussed above. Although critics of the notion of implicit learning are concerned that implicit measures are contaminated by explicit knowledge, the evidence would seem to suggest that the opposite is at least as much of a problem. Roediger and McDermott (1993) have made this same argument in implicit memory research.

Which is the best criterion, subjective or objective? Stadler (1997) argued that although the subjective definition may have more face validity (this will always be open to debate, of course), use of the objective definition of awareness is most likely to convince the skeptics, simply because it is more conservative. Recall, too, that even if the objective test is somewhat contaminated by implicit knowledge, implicit learning can still be demonstrated if a comparable implicit measure is more sensitive to learning than the explicit measure (Reingold & Merikle, 1988).

The real difficulty here may be that in this debate, implicit learning is defined in terms of awareness (i.e., it occurs when subjects are not aware that knowledge has been encoded and retrieved) instead of in terms of intention (i.e., knowledge was acquired unintentionally, as an automatic consequence of performing some task; see Reber's [1967] definition). The most effective answer to the awareness question may actually sidestep it and deal instead with the more empirically tractable question of intention, which we consider next (see also Frensch, Chapter 2, this volume; Stadler & Frensch, 1994).

UNINTENTIONAL LEARNING

To this point, we have reviewed ways of defining implicit learning and assumptions that may be used to construct measures of implicit learning and checks on explicit learning. One reason for doing this, recall, is to provide assurance that conditions presumed to involve unintentional encoding of information do not actually involve intentional encoding. However, definitions and assumptions such as those reviewed so far may seem reasonable to some but unreasonable to others and so must be put to empirical test for validation. Ultimately, we need a series of converging operations to support a theoretical construct (when Garner, Hake, and Eriksen introduced the idea of converging operations in 1956, they used subliminal perception and issues related to those being reviewed in this chapter to illustrate some of their points). Converging operations can be provided by dissociating the construct of interest (implicit learning) from related or competing ideas (explicit learning). Such converging operations provide support for the assumptions and definitions but at the same time provide valuable information about the nature of the processes being studied and how they are similar to and different from other processes.

Cheesman and Merikle (1986) noted that their distinction between the objective and subjective thresholds, which were identifiably and reliably different (Cheesman & Merikle, 1984), still raised the question of whether those definitions of awareness meaningfully distinguished between different perceptual states, conscious and nonconscious. That is, was perception under conditions when subjects were not aware by a subjective definition meaningfully different from conditions when they were aware? If this question is answered affirmatively, then we have converging operations for the distinction, and we have learned something about the theoretical constructs in question.

For example, Cheesman and Merikle (1986), building on their earlier experiments (Cheesman & Merikle, 1984), measured subjects' latency to name the color of color patches in a Stroop (1935) experiment. In one condition, masked color-word primes were presented briefly, at the subjective threshold, right before presentation of the color patch; in another, the primes were presented supraliminally before the color patch. As shown in Figure 3.2, Stroop interference was found in both conditions; naming latencies were longer when the prime was incongruent with the color patch (the prime *green* before a blue patch) than when the prime was congruent with the patch (the prime *green* before a green patch).

Cheesman and Merikle's (1986) main finding, however, was that the size of the Stroop effect could be manipulated by manipulating the proportion of trials when the prime was congruent with the patch, but only in the supraliminal conditions. Under conditions where subjects are aware of the stimuli, they might be expected to use various strategies, to form expectations or hypotheses, or to make inferences and judgments that subjects would not make if they did not believe they were perceiving any stimuli in the first place. Consistent with this, in the supraliminal condition, the difference between the naming latencies on congruent and incongruent trials was smaller when incongruent trials were frequent, larger when they were infrequent. This suggests that subjects' expectancies influenced their strategies in performing the task, but only when the prime was presented supraliminally. Presumably, subjects do not adopt such strategies when they think there was no prime stimulus. Thus, subjects' behavior is quite different in the subliminal and supraliminal conditions. If no such differences could be found, then there would be little reason to be interested in a distinction between subliminal and supraliminal perception. But because these two forms of perception are in fact different, the distinction has been one of great interest (e.g., Greenwald, 1992; Kihlstrom, 1987).

Jacoby and Whitehouse (1989, Experiment 2) provided another interesting and convincing example of qualitative differences between conscious and nonconscious information processing. In the first phase of the experiment, subjects read a list of words. In the second phase, subjects made recognition judgments about test words. In an unaware condition, test trials were arranged so that test words were preceded by context items that were masked so that subjects could (presumably) not consciously read them. In an aware condition, the context items were presented for longer durations, and subjects were instructed to try to remember them for a later test. The context items could match the test word, be another nonmatching word, or, as a control, consist of the letter string xoxoxox. As shown in Table 3.1, the context items influenced subjects' performance, particularly on new test words (words not presented in Phase 1) and did so differentially

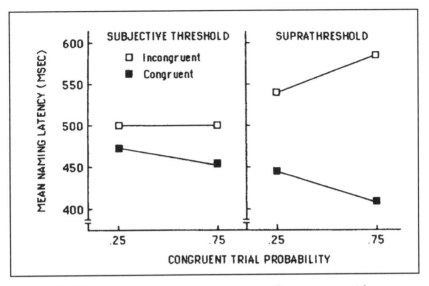

Figure 3.2. Mean naming latencies for congruent and incongruent trials as a function of congruent-trial probability under subjective and suprathreshold conditions.

SOURCE: From "Distinguishing Conscious From Unconscious Perceptual Processes," by J. Cheesman and P. M. Merikle, 1986, *Canadian Journal of Psychology, 40,* p. 343. Copyright 1986 by the Canadian Psychological Association. Used with permission.

depending on whether subjects were aware of them. In the unaware condition, presentation of a matching context item increased the probability that subjects would call a new test word "old" (i.e., that they would make a false alarm) whereas in the aware condition, presentation of a matching context item decreased the probability of a false alarm. This pattern of findings strongly suggests that subjects in the unaware condition were actually not aware of the context items. Had they been, their performance presumably would have been more comparable to that of the aware condition. Again, qualitative differences such as these are important because they demonstrate that it is theoretically meaningful to distinguish conscious and nonconscious perception. The ways in which various factors influence subjects' behavior change depending on whether subjects are aware of the stimuli or not.

The implicit memory literature has thrived on the discovery of such dissociations between implicit and explicit tests (for reviews, see Richardson-Klavehn & Bjork, 1988; Roediger & McDermott, 1993; Schacter, 1987).

TABLE 3.1 Probability of Calling a New Test Word "Old"

Condition	Match	Nonmatch	Control
Aware	.21	.36	.33
Unaware	.26	.17	.17

SOURCE: From "An Illusion of Memory: False Recognition Influenced by Unconscious Perception," by L. L. Jacoby and K. Whitehouse, 1989, *Journal of Experimental Psychology: General, 118*, p. 129. Copyright 1989 by the American Psychological Association. Adapted with permission.

For example, performance on perceptual implicit memory tests tends to be influenced by manipulations of surface structure and modality, whereas performance on explicit memory tests tends not to be; performance on implicit memory tests tends *not* to be influenced by manipulations of elaborative processing during study, whereas performance on explicit memory tests does tend to be influenced by such manipulations (Schacter, 1987). These and many other dissociations provide convincing converging evidence for the distinction between implicit and explicit memory and have been influential in the vigorous debate about competing theories.

In contrast, there has been very little work in the implicit learning literature directly contrasting implicit and explicit learning.[1] Thus, we know relatively little about what kinds of dissociations might exist between them and what kinds of differences in processing those dissociations might imply. This may also account for why the field is caught up in a debate over whether implicit learning exists in the first place (see Shanks & St. John, 1994, and the subsequent commentary); compared to work on implicit memory, there have been relatively few converging operations, specifically studies of qualitative differences, to support the distinction.

One difficulty with the dissociation approach in implicit memory research has been that implicit and explicit testing conditions have often differed in more ways than the nature of the retrieval conditions (Neely, 1989). Consider a typical experiment in which two groups of subjects study a list of words and are then given a test, either a free-recall test of explicit memory or a word-fragment completion test of implicit memory (e.g., Roediger & Blaxton, 1987). The retrieval instructions differ, as implied by Graf and Schacter's (1985) definition of implicit memory, but so do many other things: the types of cues present on the test (or the lack thereof), the order and pace of subjects' responses, and so on. Thus, such studies suffer from the same problem as any experiment with a confound: There are potential alternative explanations for any observed differences between implicit and explicit memory. As when using Reingold and Merikle's (1988) approach, the logic of dissociation works best when the only difference between conditions is, in implicit memory, the retrieval instructions. In studies of implicit learning, of course, the difference would be in the encoding instructions. Many studies comparing explicit and implicit memory tests have overcome this difficulty (e.g., Roediger et al., 1992). Unfortunately, there are relatively few such studies in the implicit learning literature.

Another difficulty has sometimes been the relative lack of control of possible contamination by intentional retrieval strategies (Schacter, Bowers, & Booker, 1989). Schacter and his colleagues delineated several scenarios that could occur during implicit testing, should conscious knowledge of the relation between study and test occur and depending on whether and how the subject acted on that knowledge. These ranged from cases in which awareness was essentially epiphenomenal, such that the subjects notice that they have studied some of the items before but do not act on that fact, to cases in which such conscious knowledge poses serious problems because subjects act on their awareness by deliberately attempting to use memory for the study episode in performing the implicit task. To circumvent this problem, Schacter et al., like Reingold and Merikle (1988) and Neely (1989), advised that implicit and explicit test conditions should differ only in the instructions given to subjects; everything else should be comparable across conditions. Then, a variable must be found that dissociates performance on the two tests. For example, if variable X influences the explicit test but not the implicit, or if it has a different effect on the implicit test, then it can be inferred that subjects did not use intentional retrieval in the implicit condition. If they had, their performance would have been influenced by variable X in the same way as that of the subjects in the explicit test condition. Further investigations can then use such a finding as a benchmark to guard against possible contamination of the implicit measure by explicit retrieval strategies.

Roediger et al. (1992, Experiment 1) applied this logic in studies comparing the word-fragment and word-stem completion tasks. For both the implicit and explicit tests, subjects were tested under identical conditions. Everything, including the cues given at test, was the same except for the instructions. Subjects in the implicit testing conditions were instructed to complete the word fragments or word stems with the first item that came to mind, whereas subjects in the explicit testing conditions were instructed to use the fragments or stems as cues to help them remember the study items. The key finding for present purposes was that for both tests, when the study stimuli were printed words, a level of processing manipulation had a strong effect on the explicit test, but no effect on the implicit test (even with $n = 60$ in each condition). If subjects engaged in intentional retrieval of study items, they should have shown the same levels of processing effect found in the explicit test condition.

Similarly, Java (1994, Experiment 2) manipulated study conditions by having subjects read words or generate them from cues and then tested both groups with word-stem cues, giving one group implicit retrieval instructions and another explicit retrieval instructions. For the implicit test, reading the word produced better performance than generating, but for the explicit test, generating produced better performance than reading (see Table 3.2). This is a key result because the study manipulation produced opposite effects on the implicit and explicit tests. It would thus be difficult to argue that subjects in the implicit test condition were using explicit retrieval strategies; if that were so, their performance should have been similarly affected by the study manipulation. These results also provide important converging evidence for the distinction between retrieval modes. Following Cheesman and Merikle's (1986) argument, there would be little reason for interest in the distinction between implicit and explicit retrieval if they differ only in whether or not subjects are aware of the prior study episode. There is much more reason for making the distinction if, as in Java's study, the two modes of retrieval produce qualitatively different patterns of results.

Studies of implicit learning have generally not compared implicit learning to explicit learning (for some exceptions see Curran & Keele, 1993; Frensch & Miner, 1994; Jiménez et al., 1996; Reber, 1976; Reber et al., 1980), so Stadler (1997) suggested the adoption of an *encoding intentionality criterion* to complement Schacter et al.'s (1989) retrieval intentionality criterion. The logic would be to test two groups, manipulating encoding instructions while holding everything else constant. One group would be instructed to intentionally encode the to-be-learned material; the other would simply be instructed in how to do the task and thus exposed to the to-be-learned material incidentally. If, under these conditions, a variable were found to influence the intentional encoding condition differently than the incidental encoding condition, then the argument could be made that processing in the incidental condition was implicit; if subjects in that condition had intentionally learned the material, then results in that condition

TABLE 3.2 Proportion Correct on Explicit and Implicit Tests (Implicit Scores Are Priming Scores)			
Test	*Nonstudied*	*Read*	*Generate*
Explicit	0.04	0.22	0.41
Implicit	0.14/0.15	0.33	0.19

SOURCE: From "States of Awareness Following Word-Stem Completion," by R. I. Java, 1994, *European Journal of Cognitive Psychology, 6*, p. 86. Copyright 1994 by Lawrence Erlbaum Associates Limited. Adapted with permission.

would be expected to parallel those in the intentional learning condition. Note the shift in emphasis from awareness to intention. Awareness is something that must be measured, but for which no widely agreed upon measure has been found, as discussed above. Intention is something that can be manipulated with instructions and should not invite the kind of debate that surrounds measures of awareness.

Reber et al.'s (1980) study essentially took this approach. This study replicated the manipulation of study intentionality used in Reber's (1976) experiment but also manipulated the format in which items were presented, so that for some subjects, presentation order was random, but for others, presentation order systematically reflected the structure of the grammar. Reber et al. found that structured presentation produced much better performance than random presentation for the explicitly instructed subjects but that there was no difference between these conditions for implicitly instructed subjects. This suggests that the implicitly instructed subjects did not engage in any intentional learning strategies. Unfortunately, Dulany et al. (1984) failed to replicate this result, and, to our knowledge, this manipulation has not been tested again. Similarly, a study by Hayes and Broadbent (1988), which also satisfied the logic of the encoding intentionality criterion, could not subsequently be replicated (Green & Shanks, 1993). Other recent studies (e.g., Curran & Keele, 1993; Frensch & Miner, 1994; Jiménez et al., 1996) have manipulated intention and found some differences between implicit and explicit learning orientations, although not qualitative differences. Still, given the positive results from the use of the retrieval intentionality criterion in the implicit memory arena, the encoding intentionality criterion holds promise, but it is at present unrealized.

The dissociation logic can be extended even further. Jacoby has employed what he calls the method of opposition (e.g., Jacoby, 1991; Jacoby et al., 1989). The idea is to give subjects instructions that oppose or discourage the use of the implicit knowledge. Jacoby et al.'s (1989) experiments involved two phases, a study phase in which subjects read aloud a list of nonfamous names, and test phase in which they decided whether each name in another list was famous or nonfamous. The test list included some old nonfamous names that had been presented in the study phase, and some new nonfamous names that had not been. Subjects knew that if an item was in the study list, it is nonfamous, so they could use their memory of study list items to help make the fame judgments. In Experiment 2, the study phase was conducted in conjunction with a secondary task for half the subjects; the other half of the subjects did the study task alone. As shown in Table 3.3, subjects in the secondary task condition incorrectly called more old nonfamous names "famous" than did subjects in the single-task condition. Because subjects knew that any name they recognized from the first phase of the experiment was nonfamous, this greater propensity to call an old nonfamous name famous indicates an influence of prior experience that could not be consciously controlled and was thus automatic or nonconscious. This study also compares implicit and explicit memory directly, but by manipulating subjects' ability to rely on explicit memory with the presence or absence of a secondary task requirement. The key feature of this study and the others reviewed in this section is the direct comparison of implicit and explicit retrieval modes.

In another extension of this logic, Jacoby (1991) examined how conscious and nonconscious processes might contribute to performance under two specific conditions. Consider an experiment with two phases, a study phase during which subjects are exposed somehow to a set of items and a test phase during which subjects are asked to respond to some kind of cue or test item. The dependent variable is the probability that subjects will respond to the test item with a previously studied item. In one condition, which Jacoby termed inclusion, subjects are instructed to respond to the test items with the first thing that comes to mind, including items they may have encountered during the study phase of the experiment. In the second condition, termed exclusion, subjects are instructed to respond to the test items with the first thing that comes to mind that was *not* encountered during the study phase. Thus, any response in the exclusion condition that consists of an item from the study phase is assumed to be due to nonconscious processing. Furthermore, assuming that the conscious and nonconscious processes are independent, it is possible to estimate the contributions of each of these to performance. Performance in the inclusion condition,

TABLE 3.3 Probability of Calling a Name "Famous"			
		Nonfamous Name	
Condition	Famous Name (New)	New	Old
Full attention	.62	.31	.19
Divided attention	.49	.17	.27

SOURCE: From "Becoming Famous Without Being Recognized: Unconscious Influences of Memory Produced by Dividing Attention," by L. L. Jacoby, V. Woloshyn, and C. Kelley, 1989, *Journal of Experimental Psychology: General, 118,* p. 119. Copyright 1989 by the American Psychological Association. Adapted with permission.

I, may depend on both conscious (C) and nonconscious (N) influences of the study item, so that $I = C + N - NC$. In the exclusion condition (E), in contrast, the study item will only be produced if it influenced the nonconscious process and not the conscious process, so that $E = N (1 - C)$, or $E = N - NC$. The parameter C can then be estimated by $I - E$; an estimate of N can then be calculated using simple algebra.

Jacoby and his colleagues have done numerous studies exploring various possible uses of the process dissociation procedure (e.g., Debner & Jacoby, 1994; Jacoby, Toth, & Yonelinas, 1993; Toth, Reingold, & Jacoby, 1994; Yonelinas & Jacoby, 1995; Yonelinas, Regehr, & Jacoby, 1995). However, the status of the procedure is somewhat uncertain at present. There have been several critiques and extensions of it (e.g., Buchner, Erdfelder, & Vaterrodt-Plünnecke, 1995; Cowan & Stadler, 1996; Dodson & Johnson, 1996; Ratcliff, Van Zandt, & McKoon, 1995). Further research will be required to tell whether this and related procedures will help distinguish conscious and nonconscious processing. One step in this direction has been taken by Buchner, Steffens, Erdfelder, and Rothkegel (1996), who recently extended Jacoby's (1991) approach by developing a multinomial model of implicit learning in the SRT task.

CONCLUSIONS

How then should we answer the awareness question? Generally, a promising strategy will be to follow the lead of researchers interested in implicit memory and subliminal perception, who have to date dealt with this question quite effectively. More specifically, we see two possible approaches worth pursuing. One is to try to answer the awareness question directly, using the logic outlined by Reingold and Merikle (1988). If an implicit measure is more sensitive to learning than a comparable explicit measure, and we assume that the explicit measure is at least as sensitive to conscious knowledge as the implicit measure, then we have demonstrated implicit learning. This approach does not say that a particular explicit measure or particular type of explicit measure is absolutely correct; indeed, this approach allows for the possibility that the explicit measure is contaminated by implicit knowledge. It also has the important advantage that it meets the demands of critics, at least some of whom have acknowledged that Reingold and Merikle's logic is convincing (e.g., Shanks & St. John, 1994). This approach alone, however, still leaves unanswered the question of whether there are any functional differences between these two modes of learning.

The other approach to answering the awareness question is to shift the focus from awareness to intention. An important element of this approach is the direct comparison of implicit and explicit learning orientations through the use of the encoding intentionality criterion (Stadler, 1997). Indeed, Reber (1967) originally defined implicit learning in terms of intention, some of his later investigations focused on this variable (Reber, 1976; Reber et al., 1980), and the manipulation of subjects' intentions is consistent with and complements current approaches to studying implicit memory. What we do not yet know is precisely whether and how implicit and explicit learning are different, although several chapters in this book begin to offer some answers. As Stadler (1997) argued, this requires two things, an experimental methodology for finding out the differences and development of theories that account for processing under the different learning orientations. The encoding intentionality criterion may help on the methodology side. On the theoretical side, there are several information-processing models of implicit learning (e.g., Cleeremans, 1993; Cleeremans & Jiménez, Chapter 10, this volume; Keele & Jennings, 1992; Servan-Schreiber & Anderson, 1990). These models do not account for explicit learning or the differences between it and implicit learning but could perhaps be expanded to do so.

The approach we recommend for studying implicit learning is essentially the same as the one used by Melton, although it has been greatly refined since then. What we must do is establish conditions that make unlikely, and even rule out, the possibility that subjects use intentional learning strategies so that we can see how implicit learning is different from explicit learning.

NOTE

1. In his 1964 review of research on incidental and intentional learning, Postman concluded that any differences between the two were differences of degree, not differences in kind. However, the prominent theoretical questions and experimental paradigms of that time may not have lent themselves to the discovery of such differences in kind. Given the differences researchers have observed between incidental and intentional retrieval reviewed in this chapter, it seems likely that similar kinds of differences may be found for incidental and intentional encoding.

REFERENCES

Berry, D. C., & Broadbent, D. E. (1988). Interactive tasks and the implicit-explicit distinction. *British Journal of Psychology, 79,* 251-272.

Broadbent, D. E., Fitzgerald, P., & Broadbent, M. H. (1986). Implicit and explicit knowledge in the control of complex systems. *British Journal of Psychology, 77,* 33-50.

Brooks, L. R. (1978). Nonanalytic concept formation and memory for instances. In E. Rosch & B. B. Lloyd (Eds.), *Cognition and categorization* (pp. 169-211). Hillsdale, NJ: Lawrence Erlbaum.

Buchner, A., Erdfelder, E., & Vaterrodt-Plünnecke, B. (1995). Toward unbiased measurement of conscious and unconscious memory processes within the process dissociation framework. *Journal of Experimental Psychology: General, 124,* 137-160.

Buchner, A., Steffens, M., Erdfelder, E., & Rothkegel, R. (1996). *A multinomial model to assess fluency and recollection in a sequence learning task.* Manuscript submitted for publication.

Cheesman, J., & Merikle, P. M. (1984). Priming with and without awareness. *Perception & Psychophysics, 36,* 387-395.

Cheesman, J., & Merikle, P. M. (1986). Distinguishing conscious from unconscious perceptual processes. *Canadian Journal of Psychology, 40,* 343-367.

Cleeremans, A. (1993). *Mechanisms of implicit learning: Connectionist models of sequence processing.* Cambridge: MIT Press.

Cowan, N., & Stadler, M. A. (1996). Estimating unconscious processes: Implications of a general class of models. *Journal of Experimental Psychology: General, 125,* 195-200.

Curran, T., & Keele, S. W. (1993). Attentional and nonattentional forms of sequence learning. *Journal of Experimental Psychology: Learning, Memory, and Cognition, 19,* 189-202.

Debner, J. A., & Jacoby, L. L. (1994). Unconscious perception: Attention, awareness, and control. *Journal of Experimental Psychology: Learning, Memory, and Cognition, 20,* 304-317.

Dienes, Z., & Berry, D. (1997). Implicit learning: Below the subjective threshold. *Psychonomic Bulletin and Review, 4,* 3-23.

Dodson, C. S., & Johnson, M. K. (1996). Some problems with the process-dissociation approach to memory. *Journal of Experimental Psychology: General, 125,* 181-194.

Dulany, D. E., Carlson, R. A., & Dewey, G. I. (1984). A case of syntactical learning and judgment: How conscious and how abstract? *Journal of Experimental Psychology: General, 113,* 541-555.

Fendrich, D. W., Healy, A. F., & Bourne, L. E. (1991). Long-term repetition effects for motoric and perceptual procedures. *Journal of Experimental Psychology: Learning, Memory, and Cognition, 17,* 137-151.

Frensch, P. A., & Miner, C. S. (1994). Effects of presentation rate and individual differences in short-term memory capacity on an indirect measure of serial learning. *Memory & Cognition, 22,* 95-110.

Gardiner, J. M. (1988). Functional aspects of recollective experience. *Memory & Cognition, 16,* 309-313.

Gardiner, J. M., & Java, R. I. (1993). Recognizing and remembering. In A. F. Collins, S. E. Gathercole, M. A. Conway, & P. E. Morris (Eds.), *Theories of memory* (pp. 163-188). Hillsdale, NJ: Lawrence Erlbaum.

Garner, W. R., Hake, H. W., & Eriksen, C. W. (1956). Operationism and the concept of perception. *Psychological Review, 63,* 149-159.

Graf, P., & Schacter, D. L. (1985). Implicit and explicit memory for new associations in normal and amnesic subjects. *Journal of Experimental Psychology: Learning, Memory, and Cognition, 11,* 501-518.

Green, R. E., & Shanks, D. R. (1993). On the existence of independent explicit and implicit learning systems: An examination of some evidence. *Memory & Cognition, 21,* 304-317.

Greenwald, A. G. (1992). New Look 3: Unconscious cognition reclaimed. *American Psychologist, 47,* 766-779.

Hayes, N. A., & Broadbent, D. (1988). Two modes of learning for interactive tasks. *Cognition, 28,* 249-276.

Hebb, D. O. (1961). Distinctive features of learning in the higher animal. In J. F. Delafresnaye (Ed.), *Brain mechanisms and learning* (pp. 37-46). Oxford, UK: Blackwell.

Holender, D. (1986). Semantic activation without conscious identification in dichotic listening, parafoveal vision, and visual masking: A survey and appraisal. *Behavioral and Brain Sciences, 9,* 1-66.

Jacoby, L. L. (1991). A process dissociation framework: Separating automatic from intentional uses of memory. *Journal of Memory and Language, 30,* 513-541.

Jacoby, L. L., Allan, L. G., Collins, J. C., & Larwill, L. K. (1988). Memory influences subjective experience: Noise judgments. *Journal of Experimental Psychology: Learning, Memory, and Cognition, 14,* 240-247.

Jacoby, L. L., Toth, J. P., & Yonelinas, A. P. (1993). Separating conscious and unconscious influences of memory: Measuring recollection. *Journal of Experimental Psychology: General, 122,* 139-154.

Jacoby, L. L., & Whitehouse, K. (1989). An illusion of memory: False recognition influenced by unconscious perception. *Journal of Experimental Psychology: General, 118,* 126-135.

Jacoby, L. L., Woloshyn, V., & Kelley, C. (1989). Becoming famous without being recognized: Unconscious influences of memory produced by dividing attention. *Journal of Experimental Psychology: General, 118,* 115-125.

Java, R. (1994). States of awareness following word stem completion. *European Journal of Cognitive Psychology, 6,* 77-92.

Jiménez, L., Méndez, C., & Cleeremans, A. (1996). Comparing direct and indirect measures of sequence learning. *Journal of Experimental Psychology: Learning, Memory, and Cognition, 22,* 948-969.

Johnston, W. A., Dark, V. J., & Jacoby, L. L. (1985). Perceptual fluency and recognition judgments. *Journal of Experimental Psychology: Learning, Memory, and Cognition, 11,* 3-11.

Johnston, W. A., Hawley, K. J., & Elliott, J. M. (1991). Contribution of perceptual fluency to recognition judgments. *Journal of Experimental Psychology: Learning, Memory, and Cognition, 17,* 210-223.

Keele, S. W., & Jennings, P. J. (1992). Attention in the representation of sequence: Experiment and theory. *Human Movement Science, 11,* 125-138.

Kihlstrom, J. F. (1987). The cognitive unconscious. *Science, 237,* 1445-1452.

Kimble, D. P. (Ed.). (1967). *The organization of recall: Proceedings of the Second International Interdisciplinary Conference on Learning, Remembering, and Forgetting.* New York: New York Academy of Sciences.

Lewicki, P., Czyzewska, M., & Hoffman, H. (1987). Unconscious acquisition of complex procedural knowledge. *Journal of Experimental Psychology: Learning, Memory, and Cognition, 13,* 523-530.

Mandler, G., Nakamura, Y., & Van Zandt, B. J. (1987). Nonspecific effects of exposure on stimuli that cannot be recognized. *Journal of Experimental Psychology: Learning, Memory, and Cognition, 13,* 646-648.

Merikle, P. M., & Cheesman, J. (1986). Consciousness is a "subjective" state. *Behavioral and Brain Sciences, 9,* 42-43.

Merikle, P. M., & Reingold, E. M. (1991). Comparing direct (explicit) and indirect (implicit) measures to study unconscious memory. *Journal of Experimental Psychology: Learning, Memory, and Cognition, 17,* 224-233.

Neal, A., & Hesketh, B. (1997). Episodic knowledge and implicit learning. *Psychonomic Bulletin and Review, 4,* 24-37.

Neely, J. H. (1989). Experimental dissociations and the episodic/semantic memory distinction. In H. L. Roediger III & F. I. M. Craik (Eds.), *Varieties of memory and consciousness: Essays in Honour of Endel Tulving* (pp. 229-270). Hillsdale, NJ: Lawrence Erlbaum.

Nissen, M. J., & Bullemer, P. (1987). Attentional requirements of learning: Evidence from performance measures. *Cognitive Psychology, 19,* 1-32.

Perruchet, P., & Amorim, M.-A. (1992). Conscious knowledge and changes in performance in sequence learning: Evidence against dissociation. *Journal of Experimental Psychology: Learning, Memory, and Cognition, 18,* 785-800.

Perruchet, P., Gallego, J., & Savy, I. (1990). A critical reappraisal of the evidence for unconscious abstraction of deterministic rules in complex experimental situations. *Cognitive Psychology, 22,* 493-516.

Perruchet, P., & Pacteau, C. (1990). Synthetic grammar learning: Implicit rule abstraction or explicit fragmentary knowledge? *Journal of Experimental Psychology: General, 119,* 264-275.

Postman, N. (1964). Short-term memory and incidental learning. In A. W. Melton (Ed.), *Categories of human learning* (pp. 146-201). New York: Academic Press.

Rajaram, S. (1993). Remembering and knowing: Two means of access to the personal past. *Memory & Cognition, 21,* 89-102.

Ratcliff, R., Van Zandt, T., & McKoon, G. (1995). Process dissociation, single-process theories, and recognition memory. *Journal of Experimental Psychology: General, 124,* 352-374.

Reber, A. S. (1967). Implicit learning of artificial grammars. *Journal of Verbal Learning and Verbal Behavior, 6*(6), 855-863.

Reber, A. S. (1976). Implicit learning of synthetic languages: The role of instructional set. *Journal of Experimental Psychology: Human Learning and Memory, 2,* 88-94.

Reber, A. S. (1989). Implicit learning and tacit knowledge. *Journal of Experimental Psychology: General, 118,* 219-235.

Reber, A. S., Allen, R., & Regan, S. (1985). Syntactical learning and judgment, still unconscious and still abstract: Comment on Dulany, Carlson, and Dewey. *Journal of Experimental Psychology: General, 114,* 17-24.

Reber, A. S., Kassin, S. M., Lewis, S., & Cantor, G. (1980). On the relationship between implicit and explicit modes in the learning of a complex rule structure.

Journal of Experimental Psychology: Human Learning and Memory, 6, 492-502.

Reingold, E. M., & Merikle, P. M. (1988). Using direct and indirect measures to study perception without awareness. *Perception and Psychophysics, 44,* 563-575.

Richardson-Klavehn, A., & Bjork, R. A. (1988). Measures of memory. *Annual Review of Psychology, 39,* 475-543.

Roediger, H. L., & Blaxton, T. A. (1987). Effects of varying modality, surface features, and retention interval on priming in word-fragment completion. *Memory & Cognition, 15,* 379-388.

Roediger, H. L., & McDermott, K. (1993). Implicit memory in normal human subjects. In F. Boller & J. Grafman (Eds.), *Handbook of neuropsychology* (Vol. 8, pp. 63-130). Amsterdam: Elsevier Science.

Roediger, H. L., Weldon, M. S., Stadler, M. L., & Riegler, G. L. (1992). Direct comparison of two implicit memory tests: Word fragment and word stem completion. *Journal of Experimental Psychology: Learning, Memory, and Cognition, 18,* 1251-1269.

Schacter, D. L. (1987). Implicit memory: History and current status. *Journal of Experimental Psychology: Learning, Memory, and Cognition, 13,* 501-518.

Schacter, D. L., Bowers, J., & Booker, J. (1989). Intention, awareness, and implicit memory: The retrieval intentionality criterion. In S. Lewandowsky, J. C. Dunn, & K. Kirsner (Eds.), *Implicit memory: Theoretical issues* (pp. 47-65). Hillsdale, NJ: Lawrence Erlbaum.

Seger, C. A. (1994). Implicit learning. *Psychological Bulletin, 115,* 163-196.

Servan-Schreiber, E., & Anderson, J. R. (1990). Learning artificial grammars with competitive chunking. *Journal of Experimental Psychology: Learning, Memory, and Cognition, 16,* 592-608.

Shanks, D. R., & St. John, M. F. (1994). Characteristics of dissociable human learning systems. *Behavioral and Brain Sciences, 17,* 367-447.

Stadler, M. A. (1989). On learning complex procedural knowledge. *Journal of Experimental Psychology: Learning, Memory, and Cognition, 15,* 1061-1069.

Stadler, M. A. (1995). Role of attention in implicit learning. *Journal of Experimental Psychology: Learning, Memory, and Cognition, 21,* 674-685.

Stadler, M. A. (1997). Distinguishing implicit and explicit learning. *Psychonomic Bulletin and Review, 4,* 56-62.

Stadler, M. A., & Frensch, P. A. (1994). Whether learning, whither memory? *Behavioral and Brain Sciences, 17,* 423-424.

Stroop, J. R. (1935). Studies of interference in serial verbal reactions. *Journal of Experimental Psychology, 18,* 643-662.

Toth, J. P., Reingold, E. M., & Jacoby, L. L. (1994). Toward a redefinition of implicit memory: Process dissociations following elaborative processing and self-generation. *Journal of Experimental Psychology: Learning, Memory, and Cognition, 20,* 290-303.

Tulving, E. (1985). Memory and consciousness. *Canadian Psychology, 26,* 1-12.

Yonelinas, A. P., & Jacoby, L. L. (1995). Dissociating automatic and controlled processes in a memory-search task: Beyond implicit memory. *Psychological Research, 57,* 156-165.

Yonelinas, A. P., Regehr, G., & Jacoby, L. L. (1995). Incorporating response bias in a dual-process theory of memory. *Journal of Memory and Language, 34,* 821-835.

PART II

METHODOLOGIES

4

Implicit Learning of Invariant Features?

●————————————————————————————

Dianne Berry
Josephine Cock

Implicit learning is said to have occurred when a person learns about the structure of a fairly complex stimulus environment without necessarily intending to do so, and in such a way that the resulting knowledge is difficult to express (Berry & Dienes, 1993). Over the past 20 years, implicit learning has been demonstrated using a number of now well-established paradigms, including artificial grammar learning (e.g., Mathews et al., 1989; Reber, 1967, 1976, 1989), control of complex systems (e.g., Berry & Broadbent, 1984, 1988; Stanley, Mathews, Buss, & Kotler-Cope, 1989), and sequence learning (e.g., Nissen & Bullemer, 1987; Reed & Johnson, 1994; Willingham, Nissen, & Bullemer, 1989). A newer paradigm, which has been receiving increasing attention over the last few years, is that of implicit learning of invariant characteristics. The original study was conducted by McGeorge and Burton (1990), who argued that performance on their task could best be accounted for in terms of unconscious abstraction of an abstract rule.

Since then, a number of more recent experiments have investigated the kind of knowledge acquired in the McGeorge and Burton task, as well

AUTHORS' NOTE: We are very grateful to Irene Michas for her helpful comments on an earlier version of this chapter. The experiments conducted by Josephine Cock were supported by the Biotechnology and Biological Sciences Research Council.

as the mechanisms underlying performance (e.g., Bright & Burton, 1994; Cock, Berry, & Gaffan, 1994; Wright & Burton, 1995). This chapter reviews these studies and also reports some recent unpublished findings. It assesses whether the pattern of results can best be explained in terms of implicit rule abstraction or in terms of some form of instance- or similarity-based processing. It also addresses the question of the accessibility of the acquired knowledge.

THE McGEORGE AND BURTON STUDY

In the initial experiment, subjects were first exposed to 30 sequentially presented four-digit strings, for example, 2134, 3786 (McGeorge & Burton, 1990). Unbeknownst to subjects, who concentrated on a cover task involving mental arithmetic on each number string, this was the learning phase of the experiment. In the subsequent test phase, subjects carried out a forced-choice recognition test on 10 pairs of new strings. For example, subjects were asked, "Which do you think you saw previously, 6417 or 1532?" and so on, in such a way that they were led to believe that one string of each pair had actually appeared in the learning phase. This was not the case; however, one string of each pair did contain a particular invariant digit that had appeared in each learning string. This fact was not drawn to subjects' attention at any stage. (In the example just given, the invariant digit was 3). McGeorge and Burton reported that subjects selected significantly more strings that contained the invariant digit than would be expected by chance alone, even though they expressed considerable surprise when the hidden rule was subsequently explained.

In a second experiment, McGeorge and Burton (1990) investigated whether the effect was mediated at a semantic rather than a perceptual level. All subjects were again presented with 30 four-digit strings in the learning phase, but three different types of test string were used. In one condition, subjects saw the new pairs of four-digit number strings as in the initial experiment; in a second condition, they saw the test strings printed in a different numerical script; and in the third condition, they saw word equivalents of the number strings. The results showed that subjects performed equally well in all conditions, suggesting that the effect was mediated at a semantic rather than a perceptual level. Finally, the third experiment showed that the same effect was obtained at a lower, yet still significant level when subjects were given a more perceptual orienting task in the learning phase, which did not encourage verbalization of the stimulus elements. The task required subjects to count the number of horizontal lines in each number string. McGeorge and Burton used this last finding as support for the claim that the learning was not mediated by phonological recoding of the stimuli and that semantic encoding of the stimulus items was automatic.

SOPHISTICATED RULE ABSTRACTION OR SIMPLE FREQUENCY COUNTING?

Although McGeorge and Burton (1990) interpreted their findings in terms of implicit rule abstraction, it is possible that the results could be accounted for by a simpler (nonconscious) feature-frequency counting mechanism (e.g., Kellogg & Dowdy, 1986). Given that their choice of invariant feature involved the presence of a constant digit in the same form in each learning string, subjects may have become primed to respond to this digit. As Bright and Burton (1994) argued, a more sensitive test of implicit learning of invariance would be to use a less rigidly defined rule that employs a constant feature but that does not give rise to unduly high occurrences of any particular surface pattern. This should discourage the use of feature-frequency counting strategies and reveal any deeper processing of the invariant aspects of the learning set.

To do this, Bright and Burton (1994) devised a new task in which the stimulus material was a series of clock faces. The invariant feature of the clock faces shown in the learning phase was that the displayed time was always between 6 and 12 o'clock. The particular times shown (set at 5-minute intervals) varied randomly within these limits, thus avoiding the high occurrence of any one particular time. Subjects were presented with 30 clock faces and were simply asked to write down the time shown on each clock face. In the test phase, they were shown 10 pairs of new clock faces and were asked to select the one from each pair that they had seen in the preceding phase of the experiment.

As with the original McGeorge and Burton (1990) study, none of the test-phase stimuli had been seen before, but one of each pair conformed to the hidden rule (i.e., displayed a time between 6 and 12 o'clock). Bright and Burton (1994) found that subjects were more likely to select as "old" clock faces that conformed to the hidden rule than those that did not. Again, on the basis of subjects' responses to detailed post-task questions, there was no indication that they were at all aware of the invariant feature at any stage.

Bright and Burton (1994, Experiment 2) went on to show that the effect was just as strong when the test-phase stimuli were presented in digital rather than analog form, even though the learning stimuli were always presented in analog form. They also found that the effect persisted (although at a reduced level) when the distractor task was changed so that subjects had to rate how much they liked each clock face (Experiment 3). On the basis of these findings, they argued that learning was not mediated by a primarily perceptual process but was due to automatic encoding of semantic features of the clocks. Unfortunately, Bright and Burton did not run a control group of subjects who performed the forced-choice test without prior exposure to the hidden rule during the learning phase. This might have ascertained more conclusively whether or not subjects were actually basing their test responses on the criterion intended by the experimenters. On the other hand, there was no obvious indication, either from subjects' comments or from their responses to questioning, that (relevant) alternative strategies had been used. A particularly important finding in their final experiment was that subjects showed no preference for previously seen times over times that were novel but nevertheless conformed to the underlying rule. Bright and Burton used this latter finding as support for implicit rule abstraction rather than for memory-based similarity processing. We will return to this interpretation later.

CAN PEOPLE LEARN OTHER
TYPES OF INVARIANCE RULES?

If people can learn that all learning phase stimuli contain a particular digit, or display a time within a certain range, can they learn other types of invariance rules? Josephine Cock has recently carried out two experiments (as part of her Ph.D. thesis) to investigate this question. In the first of these, subjects were again presented with 30 four-digit number strings in a learning phase. Unbeknownst to them, half of the stimuli contained the digit 4 and were printed in red ink, whereas the other half contained the digit 3 and were printed in green ink. The red stimuli never contained a 3 and the green stimuli never contained a 4: all other digits occurred at random. In the subsequent test phase, subjects saw 10 pairs of new stimuli, printed in black, with one of each pair containing a 3 (but never a 4) and one containing a 4 (but never a 3). They were asked to say which of the two stimuli had appeared in red in the learning phase and which in green. Unfortunately, subjects were not able to do this; performance was not significantly different from chance, suggesting that they were not able to learn two underlying rules at once in an incidental way, or at least were not able to distinguish between them when required to do so. It remains possible, of course, that given more practice, the color rules might have been learned. Roberts and MacLeod (1995) claimed to find evidence of nonconscious categorization when subjects were trained at length (about 200 trials) to distinguish between nonexemplars and exemplars that were green and featured a parallelogram, and additionally (i.e., in the same experiment) between nonexemplars and exemplars that were red and featured a triangle. A major difference (apart from amount of exposure to the learning stimuli), however, was that one rule was learned incidentally and the other intentionally. Roberts and MacLeod found that whereas subjects could subsequently break down the intentionally acquired rule into its component parts, they were only able to process exemplars of the incidentally acquired rule in a more holistic way. Another difference between the two studies was that Roberts and MacLeod gave subjects feedback on performance as part of their training procedure, which did not happen in the study by Cock.

In the second experiment carried out by Cock, subjects were allocated to one of two conditions. In both cases, they were presented with 30 five-digit number strings in the learning phase. In one condition, each learning string contained five different digits, whereas in the other condition each string contained one or more repeated digits. Subjects were then presented with 10 pairs of new five-digit number strings, with one of each pair containing five different digits and one containing one or more repeated digits. Subjects were told to select, from each pair, the string that had appeared in the preceding phase. The results showed that the two learning conditions produced different levels of performance. Subjects whose learning strings featured five different digits performed significantly above chance at test, whereas those whose learning strings contained one or more repeated digits performed at chance level in the test phase.

Taking the two experiments together, it seems that people are limited in the types of invariance rule they can learn, at least with the amount of exposure given in these experiments (30 learning strings). Apparently, subjects were not able to learn the more complex rule that every red string must contain a 4 and every green string must contain a 3; nor were they able to learn that every string contains a repeated digit. In contrast, they performed significantly above chance at test when the underlying rule was that each learning string contained five different digits. The fact that subjects were able to learn this, but not that each learning string contained one or more repeated digits, is interesting. Why should they be able to learn one rule but not the other? One possible explanation for this anomaly could be that subjects' decisions at test were influenced by preexisting expectations. For example, if subjects believed that all strings had been generated at random, then the occurrence at test of some strings in which all the digits differed would not appear "wrong" in any way. However, for subjects who had seen only strings featuring different digits, the occurrence of some strings at test featuring repeated digits might have been more noticeable. Hence, above-chance performance in this condition might actually depend on processes of rejection rather than selection. We will return to this issue later.

THE ROLE OF ATTENTION
IN INVARIANCE LEARNING

Another possible reason why invariance learning sometimes fails to "work" could be that subjects' attention to the necessary features and associations (i.e., those that make up the "rule") is not sufficiently engaged. For example, in the original McGeorge and Burton (1990) study, subjects carried out mental arithmetic on the learning stimuli and although this cover task successfully distracted subjects from noticing the invariant digit, all the digits in all the strings were at least processed to some degree. When the cover task was changed to something more perceptual (i.e. counting the number of straight lines occurring in each string), performance deteriorated on the recognition task. In retrospect, another explanation why Josephine Cock failed to find learning on the red-green number string task could be that the prerequisite color-digit associations were not reinforced in any way; that is, the mental arithmetic task did not necessitate attention to color. In line with this suggestion, Musen and Squire (1993) found evidence for implicit learning of color-word associations, using the Stroop paradigm, when subjects were required to attend to the colors by naming them aloud. In contrast, a prior study by Treisman (1992) had found no learning of color-object associations, but subjects in that study were not required to name the colors overtly (see also Logan, Taylor, & Etherton, 1996).

The role of attention in implicit learning is far from clear. Although Reber and colleagues (e.g., Reber, Kassin, Lewis, & Cantor, 1980) reported evidence of artificial grammar learning when subjects passively observed the letter strings in the learning phase, Berry (1991) found that observation alone was not sufficient for people to learn how to control the sugar production and person interaction tasks. Subjects had to interact with the tasks themselves in order for learning to occur. Several authors have claimed that attention is not necessary for learning of structured sequences to occur (e.g., Cohen, Ivry, & Keele, 1990; Curran & Keele, 1993). In these studies, degree of attention has usually been manipulated by requiring subjects to carry out a secondary tone-counting task that varied in difficulty. However, it could be argued that even when the secondary task was very demanding, subjects still "attended" to the positions of the asterisks, in that they carried out a serial reaction time task that involved responding to the location of each asterisk. Furthermore, Hartman, Knopman, and Nissen (1989) reported data on the implicit learning of new verbal associations suggesting that attention played a vital role; in fact, learning of the sequence without awareness only occurred when the stimulus-response mapping required an attention-demanding activity. Similarly, Chapnik Smith, Besner, and Miyoshi (1994) found that semantic priming of words was not automatic but depended largely on subjects paying attention to the context in which the words were read.

An experiment recently carried out by two undergraduate students (Stephen Hatter and Colin Tennant) in our laboratory suggests that attention could play an important role in invariance learning. In the experiment, the learning stimuli were two different dart boards shown side by side and each displaying the positions of three darts. The three darts were always on three different numbers and each configuration differed from all the others. One board was always labeled "John" and the other "David," although their respective left-right position varied from trial to trial. John's board always conformed to the underlying rule that all three darts should fall on the right-hand side of the board (a rule similar to that used by Bright and Burton), whereas David's always conformed to the rule that all three darts should fall on even numbers. (The rules were mutually exclusive because the small number of combinations that fitted both rules were not used.) At test, subjects chose between new exemplars that fitted John's rule and random exemplars, and between new exemplars that fitted David's rule and other random exemplars. Attention was manipulated during the learning phase; in one condition, subjects were encouraged to focus on John's board (by getting them to add up John's two highest-scoring darts on each trial); in the second condition, they were encouraged to focus on

David's board (by adding up David's two highest-scoring darts on each trial); and in the third condition, they were encouraged to focus on both boards at the same time (by getting them to say which player scored higher on each trial). In all three conditions, subjects saw the same learning and test stimuli.

The results showed that when the cover task required subjects to attend to just one player, the rule for the attended player was learned, in that subjects scored significantly above chance in the test phase when they had to distinguish between new boards that corresponded to the attended player's rule and new random boards. Nothing was learned about the unattended player's rule; performance here was at chance level only. Interestingly, in the condition where subjects attended to both players' boards in the learning phase, both rules appeared to be learned; subjects performed significantly above chance in both parts of the test phase (i.e., when tested on John's rule and on David's rule). Following the unexpected test phase, subjects were asked a series of graduated questions aimed at tapping any explicit knowledge relating to the two rules, or any other rules that subjects might have been using when making their forced-choice test decisions. For example, they were asked, "Did you notice anything about the positioning of the darts in the first part of the experiment? Over the 30 trials, did you notice anything different about the general patterns of David's and John's dart positions? David's dart positions followed a simple rule. Have you any idea about what this might have been?" It was found that about one third of subjects attending to just David's board in the learning phase (i.e., when all three darts were on even numbers), and half of the subjects attending to just John's board (i.e., when the darts were on the right-hand side of the board) appeared to have explicit knowledge of the relevant rule. In the former case, the performance of the remaining "implicit" subjects was still significantly above chance, but this was not the case for those who attended to just John's board in the learning phase. A particularly interesting finding was that subjects who attended to both rules in the learning phase appeared to have no explicit knowledge of either rule and claimed to be very surprised when the nature of the task was revealed to them.

At first sight, these results seem to support Reber's (1989, 1993) contention that implicit (rather than explicit) learning is induced when more complex stimuli are used—after all, attending to both players at once would have made the separate rules far less salient. However, before drawing firm conclusions, we will consider the task in relation to the two criteria for implicit learning put forward by Shanks and St. John (1994).

APPLYING SHANKS AND ST. JOHN'S
CRITERIA TO INVARIANCE LEARNING

Shanks and St. John (1994) put forward two criteria that they argue need to be applied when considering implicit learning studies. The first criterion (the Information Criterion) concerns the match between the information that is responsible for performance changes and the information that is revealed by the test of awareness. Shanks and St. John suggest that if learning involves acquisition of information I, but the experimenter is focusing on information I*, then subjects may appear to be unaware of the relevant knowledge when in fact they are. This is similar to Dulany's (1961) notion of correlated hypotheses. The second criterion (the Sensitivity Criterion) states that to show that the test of conscious knowledge and task performance relate to dissociable underlying systems, we must be able to demonstrate that our test of awareness is sensitive to all of the relevant conscious knowledge. Clearly, many of the studies that have commonly been cited as evidence in favor of implicit learning would fail these two criteria. However, as Berry (1994) and others have argued, it may be that Shanks and St. John have gone too far in their rejection of the evidence. Despite some problems with individual experiments, it is still the case that many of the tasks labeled as being implicit are associated with a fairly distinct set of features that do not apply to tasks currently labeled as being explicit (Berry & Dienes, 1993; see also, Dienes & Berry, 1997). Nevertheless, we still believe that it is useful to look at implicit learning of invariance in relation to the two criteria. We will discuss the Sensitivity Criterion later in this chapter when we look more closely at evidence for the accessibility of subjects' knowledge. As far as the Information Criterion is concerned, above-chance selection of positive test stimuli (i.e., those containing the invariant digit in the McGeorge and Burton, 1990, experiment) in the absence of any explicit knowledge of the rule, only indicates implicit learning to the extent that it can be demonstrated that test performance is governed by knowledge about the presence of the invariant digit, rather than by other correlated information. In other words, we need to be sure that subjects are making their test decisions primarily on the basis of the presence (or absence) of the invariant feature.

Returning to the dart boards experiment, in the conditions where subjects attended to the single dart boards, we know that many had learned the rule the experimenters intended them to learn because they were able to state the rule explicitly. What about the subjects who seemed to learn David's rule (that darts should always fall on even numbers) implicitly? Was their above-chance performance in the test phase also a result of having learned the experimenters' rule, but in their case implicitly? It is difficult to think of alternative rules that these subjects could have been using that would not have been picked up in the explicit knowledge testing phase, but at the same time, the possibility cannot be totally excluded. What about subjects who attended to both dart boards during the learning phase? Were they making their test decisions on the basis of having learned that John's darts always fall on the right-hand side of the board and that David's always fall on even numbers, or did they learn something else that could account for their above-chance performance? One possibility is that these subjects may simply have learned that certain numbers did not appear in the learning phase. Given the nature of the two rules, darts were never positioned on odd numbers on the left-hand side of the board in the learning phase. Subjects could therefore have made their decisions at test by applying a single rule such as "do not select dart boards if any of the darts landed on 5, 7, 9, 11 or 19." There was no obvious evidence (e.g., from the explicit knowledge testing) that subjects did actually learn and apply this simpler rule, but again we cannot exclude the possibility. Thus, it is difficult to draw a firm conclusion as to whether or not this study did satisfy Shanks and St. John's (1994) Information Criterion. Furthermore, there is a growing body of evidence that studies demonstrating the original McGeorge and Burton (1990) effect might not satisfy the criterion.

IS ABOVE-CHANCE PERFORMANCE ON THE MCGEORGE AND BURTON TASK REALLY DUE TO SEMANTIC RULE ABSTRACTION?

McGeorge and Burton (1990) and Bright and Burton (1994) interpreted their findings in terms of implicit rule abstraction, that is, semantic knowledge acquired across the set of learning exemplars. Their findings do not, however, exclude the possibility that subjects could have gained some advantage at test by performing post hoc comparisons between each new string presented and those partially remembered from the learning phase. After all, subjects were led to believe that they were taking part in a memory test. Performance might well be related to the salience of the test strings vis-à-vis those already learned. A sense of familiarity (or lack of it) might guide decisions, rather than implicit abstraction of the hidden rule. Such an explanation would be in line with recent instance-based accounts of concept learning (e.g., Medin & Florian, 1992; Perruchet, 1994; Shin & Nosofsky, 1992; Vokey & Brooks, 1992).

Vokey and Brooks (1992) discussed the salience of item knowledge in the learning of artificial grammars, arguing that grammaticality of test strings and specific similarity to previously learned exemplars were confounded in the Reber studies (e.g., Reber, 1967, 1976). They demonstrated that it was possible to differentiate between the two effects, and both were found to be major determinants of performance. Similarly, McAndrews and Moscovitch (1985), also working on the implicit induction of syntactic rules, showed that, for some subjects, classification judgments were based solely on analogy to stored exemplars, whereas others could unwittingly discriminate between grammatical and nongrammatical items that were all highly similar to actual remembered exemplars. Therefore, it seems possible that either, or both, of these effects could contribute to the findings of McGeorge and Burton (1990) and Bright and Burton (1994).

One feature of Bright and Burton's (1994) results that at first sight supports rule abstraction rather than memory-based similarity processing is the finding that subjects showed no preference for previously seen times over times that were novel but nevertheless conformed to the underlying rule. It could be argued, however, that the lack of preference for previously seen instances in their final experiment might be due to the fact that subjects encoded the times in the learning phase in a rather approximate way. This is particularly likely, given that half of the clock faces did not feature any numbers at all. Subjects might have interpreted some of the times slightly differently from what was intended by the experimenters, especially if the placing of the clock hands was ambiguous. This approximate encoding, coupled with unreliable memory, could result in subjects showing little in the way of preference for previously seen exemplars. These partial and approximate memories, however, would still be sufficient to allow for some perceptually based similarity processing to occur (Perruchet & Pacteau, 1991; Whittlesea & Dorken, 1993).

THE ROLE OF SIMILARITY PROCESSING

Cock et al. (1994) carried out three experiments to investigate the role of exemplar similarity in the original McGeorge and Burton paradigm. Our first experiment was a replication of McGeorge and Burton's (1990) procedure, in that subjects were presented with 30 four-digit number strings in the learning phase (each containing an invariant digit) and were required to carry out the mental arithmetic cover task. In the subsequent test phase, they were presented with 10 pairs of new strings (one containing the invariant digit and one not) and were required to select the one from each pair that they believed had appeared in the earlier phase. In line with McGeorge and Burton, the results showed that subjects selected significantly more strings at test that conformed to the hidden rule than those that did not. Again, none of the subjects reported explicit awareness of the invariant digit at any stage of the experiment, and in general, they expressed surprise when it was revealed.

In order to investigate the role of similarity in the experiment, Cock et al. (1994) went on to compute four simple indices of similarity between the test strings and the set of learning strings seen by each subject. Each test string was examined, digit by digit, and compared with each of the 30 learning strings in turn. The indices were total digits in common regardless of position, digits in the same position within the two strings, adjacent pairs of digits in common regardless of position, and adjacent pairs of digits in the same position. The four indices were summed separately for each test string, across the 30 learning strings, for each subject. The scores were then averaged separately for the four categories of test string: positive test strings (i.e., those containing the invariant digit) that were selected, positive strings that were rejected, negative strings (i.e., those that did not contain the invariant digit) that were selected, and negative strings that were rejected. Unsurprisingly, the analysis showed that both types of positive strings had higher similarity scores than negative strings (because of the presence of the invariant digit). More interesting, negative strings that were selected had higher scores, on all four indices, than did negative strings that were rejected, showing that similarity to the set of learning strings could influence subjects' choices even when the invariant digit was absent.

Although the results of this post hoc analysis were interesting, it is possible to criticize the way in which similarity was scored. Cock et al. (1994) therefore conducted a second experiment in which the strings were deliberately structured to manipulate the degree of similarity between stimuli. Given the difficulty of contriving strings in accordance with some notion of general similarity (Whittlesea & Dorken, 1993), the test strings were constructed on the basis of specific similarity to individual learning strings. The test strings therefore varied on two dimensions: whether posi-

146

tive or negative, and on how closely they matched a learning phase string. "Similar" strings had three digits in common with a learning string, and the digits occurred in the same locations, whereas "dissimilar" strings had only two digits in common and the digits occurred in new locations. It was hoped that contriving the strings in this way would allow the two possible factors influencing performance at test (namely, decisions based on similarity to stored exemplars and those mediated by rule abstraction) to be separated.

It was expected that if the presence of the invariant digit alone were influencing performance, then subjects should simply select positive over negative strings, irrespective of their degree of similarity to the learning strings.

However, the results showed that this was not the case. In the two conditions in which degree of similarity to previously processed strings was held constant (i.e., where both the positive and negative strings had comparable levels of similarity to the learning strings), positive versus negative selection was at chance level only. Furthermore, although performance was significantly above chance (in terms of the selection of positive strings) in the condition where subjects had to choose between positive similar strings and negative dissimilar strings, it was significantly below chance in the condition where they had to choose between positive dissimilar strings and negative similar strings. In other words, subjects did seem to be influenced by the relative similarity of the test strings. In all test conditions where similar strings were paired with dissimilar strings, subjects were significantly more likely to select the similar strings, irrespective of the presence or absence of the invariant digit.

In the final experiment in this study, Cock et al. (1994) examined whether the same results held when subjects were not led to believe that the final phase of the experiment was a memory test. Thus, in the test phase, subjects were given an instruction similar to that used in typical artificial grammar-learning studies. They were told that the strings seen during the learning phase all conformed to a simple rule (but they were not told what the rule was), and they were told that on each of the subsequent trials, they should indicate which item out of the two was more likely to conform to the same rule as before. The results showed a very similar pattern of performance to that found in the previous experiment. Again, there was no appreciable sign that the invariant digit was influencing performance over and above the similarity effect. Hence, even though the subjects were instructed to judge which of two test strings might fit a certain unknown rule, they were still choosing on the basis of similarity or dissimilarity to strings seen earlier. On the basis of the results of the three experiments, Cock et al. concluded that performance on the McGeorge and Burton (1990) task can be largely accounted for in terms of some form of similarity-based processing rather than in terms of implicit rule abstraction.

If performance on the McGeorge and Burton (1990) task is largely based on similarity matching, it is necessary to account for their finding of transfer across different scripts (Experiment 2). McGeorge and Burton found that performance was still significantly above chance, even when the test strings were presented in word rather than digit form. As described earlier, they used this as evidence that the acquired knowledge was held at a semantic rather than a perceptual level. Bright and Burton (1994) put forward a similar argument to account for their finding of transfer between analog and digital representations of time.

As discussed in the Cock et al. (1994) article, we believe that there are two ways in which such transfer effects could depend on similarity. One possibility is that subjects carried out some form of mental translation on the test stimuli so that they could "picture" them in their original form. Alternatively, it might be necessary to draw on some notion of abstract or relational similarity and assume that exemplars are stored in an abstract way (i.e., not tied to the surface characteristics of the original stimuli). In this latter case, any instance-based model would need to incorporate the semantic content of the individual exemplars on which decisions are based.

REJECTION OF DISTINCTIVE ITEMS

According to Cock et al. (1994), subjects make their decisions at test on the basis of how similar or dissimilar test items are to strings seen during the preceding learning phase. That is, they select a particular string because it resembles one or more previously processed learning strings, or because the string that it is paired with does not resemble the learning set. An alternative (but related) account has recently been put forward by Wright and Burton (1995). Wright and Burton argue that, rather than selecting or rejecting strings on the basis of similarity/dissimilarity, subjects make their decisions at test purely on the basis of rejection. Specifically, they propose that subjects reject very distinctive strings containing repeated digits (e.g., 6366, 7557). Wright and Burton's argument (as does Cock et al.'s) rests on the fact that constraining one of the test strings to contain an invariant digit changes other properties of the strings. In particular, they note that it produces an imbalance in the number of repeated digits contained in positive and negative strings, with the probability of a repetition being noticeably higher in negative strings. Subjects can then score at an above-chance level simply by rejecting strings that contain repeated digits (i.e., on the grounds that this kind of string had not been very common during the learning phase).

Wright and Burton (1995) conducted two experiments in order to test their hypothesis. In their first experiment, they compared performance on a standard version of the McGeorge and Burton (1990) task (using random strings) with a version where the learning and test strings did not contain any repeated digits. They argued that if above-chance performance on the task relies solely on subjects learning (implicitly) about the presence of the invariant digit (i.e., a semantic rule), there should be no differences in performance between the original and repetition-free conditions. On the other hand, if subjects were using repeated digits as a basis for rejecting test items, then performance should be better in the original condition. The results were in line with this latter position: performance was significantly above chance in the original condition but at chance level in the repetition-free condition.

Further evidence for the use of the "reject repeated digits" strategy came from a post-hoc analysis of subjects' responses in the original (random string) condition. The analysis involved ranking all test strings according to how many repeated digits they featured. When the negative test items contained more repeated digits than the positive test items, the positive strings were selected on 76% of occasions, but when the positive strings contained more repeated digits than the negative strings, positive strings were selected on only 33% of occasions (i.e., they were rejected 67% of the time). Although these numbers are interesting, it was not possible for Wright and Burton to carry out any statistical analysis of this data as there was no control over the rate of inclusion of repeated digits in the positive and negative strings. Furthermore, their results cannot be completely accounted for in terms of rejection of repeated digits. On occasions when the positive and negative strings in the test phase featured comparable numbers of digit repetitions, significantly more positive than negative strings were chosen (61%).

In their second experiment, Wright and Burton (1995) controlled the rate of occurrence of repeated digits at test so that inferential statistical tests could be used. They also probed subjects as to what strategies they had used at test in the hope of distinguishing between analogical (i.e., instance-based) and rule-based behavior. In the learning phase of their experiment, all subjects were exposed to randomly generated strings selected from the original set for Experiment 1.

However, the test strings were contrived so that each subject was exposed to 12 test pairs made up of four pairs of three types of combination: the positive string contained a repeated digit but the negative did not, the negative string contained a repeated digit but the positive did not, neither contained a repeated digit. The results showed that subjects' performance was significantly influenced by the type of test-string combination. They performed best (in terms of selection of positive over negative test items) for pairs where the negative string (but not the positive) contained a repeated digit, and worst for pairs where the positive string (but not the negative) contained a repeated digit. The results were not that clear-cut, however, with the effects generally being smaller than would be predicted on the basis of a pure rejection model. Post-task questioning suggested that some subjects were using a rule-based rather than analogical strategy but, as Wright and Burton (1995) admitted, it was extremely difficult to differentiate between the two types of process in practice.

SIMILARITY VERSUS
REJECTION OF REPETITIONS

Cock et al.'s (1994) similarity account requires that subjects evaluate the similarity of both items in a test pair to items in the learning set and then make their selection on the basis of this. This approach therefore combines both selection and rejection and takes into consideration various different features of the number strings. In contrast, Wright and Burton's account is solely based on rejection of one particular feature. Josephine Cock recently carried out an experiment (as part of her Ph.D. thesis) in an attempt to distinguish between these two different views. In the learning phase of the experiment, all subjects saw 32 randomly generated four-digit number strings. At test, half of the subjects were given randomly generated strings, and half were given contrived strings: in both cases, a positive string was always paired with a negative string. In addition, half of each of these two groups of subjects were instructed to use memory at test and half were given rule-guessing instructions. The contrived test strings were made by altering each of the 32 learning strings (in much the same way as in Experiments 2 and 3 of Cock et al., 1994). Half of the contrived test strings were made to be very similar to at least one of the learning strings, and the other half were contrived to be dissimilar. In addition, half of all contrived strings were constructed so that they contained a repeated digit, and half were constructed so that they always featured four different digits. This gave rise to four different kinds of contrived positive string (either similar or dissimilar, with or without a repeated digit) and four different kinds of negative string. Subjects in the contrived test-string conditions received all possible combinations of the different types of test string; those in the random test-string conditions did not necessarily receive all the different kinds of string, nor all the different kinds of test-pair combinations.

Both the similarity and the reject-repeats accounts predict that subjects should select significantly more positive than negative strings in the random test-string conditions, whereas they should select equal numbers of positive and negative strings in the two contrived test-string conditions. In addition, the similarity account predicts that subjects will tend to select similar over dissimilar strings, whereas the reject-repeats account predicts that subjects will select only strings without repeated digits over those with repeated digits. Although much of the time, the two accounts make similar predictions, they do make opposing predictions for certain types of test-pair combinations. For example, when a positive similar string with a repeated digit is pitted against a negative dissimilar string without a repeated digit, the similarity account predicts that subjects will be more likely to select the positive string, whereas according to Wright and Burton's (1995) account, subjects should be more likely to select the negative string. Similarly, when a positive dissimilar string without a repeated digit is pitted against a negative similar string with a repeated digit, the similarity account predicts that subjects will be more likely to select the negative string, whereas Wright and Burton's account predicts that subjects should be more likely to select the positive string.

The results showed that, as predicted, in the two random-string conditions more positive than negative strings were selected, whereas in the two contrived conditions, overall performance was at chance level. In all four conditions, subjects were found to favor similar over dissimilar strings, and in three of the four conditions they also favored strings featuring four different digits over those featuring repeated digits. Regarding the opposing predictions made by the two models, it was found that when positive similar strings with repeated digits were paired with negative dissimilar strings without repeated digits, more positive than negative strings were chosen, as would be predicted on the basis of the Cock et al. (1994) account. However, when positive dissimilar strings without repeated digits were pitted against negative similar strings with repeated digits, performance was at chance level only, which would not be predicted by either of the two accounts.

Taken together, the results provide some support for both the string similarity/dissimilarity and the reject-repeated-digits accounts, with the former account doing slightly better. Neither model, however, was conclusively superior and it is likely that performance is based on a combination of the two processes.

ARE SUBJECTS USING EXPLICIT OR IMPLICIT STRATEGIES?

The preceding sections have shown that performance on the McGeorge and Burton (1990) task can be better accounted for in terms of some form of memory-based processing rather than in terms of semantic rule abstraction. However, nothing has yet been said about whether this memory-based processing is carried out implicitly or explicitly. Some investigators (e.g., Perruchet, 1994; Shanks & St. John, 1994) seem to assume that instance-based learning is essentially an explicit process, whereas others (e.g., Reber & Allen, 1978) suggest that it remains implicit because "subjects are not consciously aware of the aspects of the stimuli which lead them to their decisions" (Reber & Allen, 1978, p. 218).

As discussed earlier, one issue to bear in mind when discussing the accessibility of subjects' knowledge is whether or not the experimental methods satisfy Shanks and St. John's (1994) Sensitivity Criterion. This criterion states that the test of awareness must be sensitive to all of the relevant conscious knowledge; it must be just as sensitive to tapping explicit knowledge as the performance measure is to assessing performance. Many of the early studies in the area of implicit learning (e.g., Reber, 1967) would have failed this criterion, in that they simply asked subjects what the underlying rules were. The same criticism might also be applied to the original McGeorge and Burton (1990) study. More recent studies, however, have used a series of graduated questions to attempt to tap any task-relevant explicit knowledge that subjects might have. Although Shanks and St. John would probably argue that these more recent studies still do not meet their Sensitivity Criterion, other investigators (including ourselves) would argue that useful information can be gained from the use of such graduated questions.

Cock et al. (1994) gave subjects a structured post-task questionnaire that asked about their level of explicit awareness of the nature of the strings, both during the learning and test phases, and about how decisions had been made. The questions were graduated so that three kinds of knowledge could be evaluated: the level of general awareness of the string properties, any explicit awareness of the rule itself, and any *aide-memoire* heuristics used at test. In particular, before the possibility of the presence of a rule was mentioned, subjects were asked to consider how they had made their decisions each time. An examination of questionnaire responses from the three experiments showed that none of the subjects could describe the hidden rule when asked, nor any other rule that could consistently account for their actual performance. When asked more generally what strategies they had used, not surprisingly, over half of the subjects in Experiment 2 (50 out of 96) mentioned relying on "memory" or "familiarity." Many of the remaining subjects said that they had simply guessed. The number mentioning memory or familiarity decreased to 14 out of 72 in Experiment 3, which used the rule-guessing rather than the memory instruction at test. Thus, there was no evidence that the majority of subjects were explicitly aware of using a memory-based strategy. In both experiments, a few subjects mentioned other strategies, such as checking the sums of the pairs, but in each case, use of such strategies could not have conferred any significant advantage at test. When subjects were told the nature of the hidden rule and asked what the invariant digit might be, very few produced the correct response by itself. Some subjects mentioned the correct number, but they usually mentioned two or three other numbers at the same time. In all experiments, there was no evidence that subjects who guessed the invariant digit performed better at test than those who did not. However, given that we do not believe that subjects' performance is being driven by semantic rule abstraction, it is not really surprising that there was no evidence for explicit awareness of the invariant digit.

Wright and Burton (1995) also looked at the question of whether the processes underlying performance in their experiments were explicit or implicit. They argued that a similarity-based account does not necessarily imply one thing or the other, whereas their rejection account seems naturally to favor explicit processing. They asked subjects a series of post-task questions, including whether they were aware of using any strategies when guessing. On the basis of these post-task interviews, Wright and Burton classified 2 subjects (out of 13) in Experiment 1 and 6 (out of 30) in Experiment 2 as having explicit knowledge that was relevant to the rejection of test items containing repeated digits (usually adjacent). Furthermore, they argued that these were not just post-hoc rationalizations: the behavior of the subjects matched their verbalizations.

Finally, in her most recent experiment (described above), Josephine Cock tried to assess subjects' level of explicit awareness in relation to the three different strategies for carrying out the McGeorge and Burton (1990) task (rule abstraction, similarity processing, and rejection of repeated digits). She asked subjects a series of graduated questions after completing the test phase of the task. As usual, there was no evidence that subjects were aware of the nature of the hidden rule, nor of the invariant digit itself. When asked how they made their decisions, no subject mentioned the presence of an invariant digit. When told the nature of the hidden rule and asked what the invariant digit might be, 13 out of 72 subjects responded with the correct digit, but many also mentioned other digits as well.

In terms of evidence for similarity processing, 30 out of 72 subjects mentioned relying on memory or familiarity when making their decisions, the numbers being greater for the two groups given memory instructions at test than for the two groups given rule-guessing instructions. It was not always clear, however, whether subjects were referring to memory of what they had or had not seen. In terms of rejection, 13 of the 72 subjects spontaneously mentioned relying on rejection as a strategy used to make their decisions. Subjects were then explicitly asked whether they thought they had relied more on processes of selection or rejection during the test phase. As might be expected, many subjects found this a difficult question to answer. However, when pressed to respond, 42 subjects claimed to use mostly selection, whereas 30 subjects claimed to use mostly rejection. The final question in the series tried to ascertain in a more indirect way whether subjects had used predominantly processes relying on string similarity or those relying on the rejection of repeated digits. Subjects were given a series of statements describing different strategies (e.g., I usually chose one rather than the other because the two strings differed in the degree to which they resembled the learning set), and they were asked to select the one that most closely corresponded to how they carried out the task. Their responses suggested that a combination of string similarity/dissimilarity was used more than rejection of repeated digits alone.

Although there are considerable difficulties with interpreting data such as these, it seems clear that the majority of subjects were not using an explicit strategy to carry out this task in the way suggested by Wright and Burton (1995). Given the potential difficulties of interpreting verbal statements, Josephine Cock also used another index in an attempt to determine whether subjects' performance should be classified as being implicit or explicit. This involved measuring the correlation between subjects' accuracy on the task and their level of confidence in their responses. This method was first introduced by Chan (1992) in relation to artificial grammar learning, and has subsequently been used by Dienes, Altmann, Kwan, and Goode (1995). Chan suggested that the relationship between objective accuracy and subjective confidence can be used as a criterion for deciding whether performance is explicit or implicit. Explicit processes usually produce a positive correlation, whereas implicit processes produce no correlation. One reason why this measure is potentially interesting is that it can be used to distinguish between different types of performance that might be viewed as being the same on the basis of other measures. For example, Chan showed that different forms of training on the artificial grammar-learning task (e.g., bigrams versus whole strings) can give rise to equal levels of classification knowledge but to different relationships between confidence and accuracy.

Cock asked subjects to rate their level of confidence (on a 5-point scale) in each test decision during her experiment. She then computed three separate correlations; one for positive versus negative test decisions, one for similar versus dissimilar test decisions, and one for repeated digits versus no repeated digits test decisions. She found that none of the correlations was significant at the 0.05 level, suggesting that subjects were not using any of these processes in a predominantly explicit way. Too much emphasis should not be placed on this interpretation, however, as no explicit control groups were included in the experiment. We could be more confident in interpreting the lack of correlations if other subjects had been given explicit information about the true nature of the task and provided with a possible strategy for success and had produced positive correlations.

CONCLUSIONS

So what can we conclude about implicit learning of invariant features? There now seems to be abundant evidence that the McGeorge and Burton (1990) effect cannot be accounted for solely (or even largely) in terms of implicit abstraction of a semantic rule. Rather, the effect seems to depend on stimulus structure: constraining one of the test strings to contain an invariant digit changes other properties of the strings. Subjects can then make above-chance selections on the basis of features of the strings other than the presence or absence of the invariant digit. Two interpretations have been discussed in this chapter, namely Cock et al.'s (1994) similarity account and Wright and Burton's (1995) rejection account. At present, it is not possible to decide conclusively between these two explanations; in fact, it seems more likely that performance is based on a combination of the two processes. What is even less clear at the moment is whether the processes are carried out in a primarily implicit or explicit way.

So what about future research in this area? Maybe we need to look for other ways of assessing implicit learning of invariant features, rather than relying on the forced-choice pseudo-memory task. One possibility would be to use a categorization procedure similar to the one used by Roberts and MacLeod (1995), in which subjects would be informally required (i.e., without hypothesis testing) to indicate which stimuli (taken from a pool of rule-fitting and rule-breaking exemplars) would be more likely to belong to the experimental category. An approach of this kind might facilitate abstraction of the invariance rule. Whatever experimental procedure is used, it seems clear that future experiments should look more closely at what happens during the encoding of the stimuli, by varying the nature of the orienting task, the amount of exposure to the stimuli, and the level of feedback given. One particular issue that requires further investigation is the role of attention in experiments of this kind, and, indeed, in implicit learning in general.

REFERENCES

Berry, D. C. (1991). The role of action in implicit learning. *Quarterly Journal of Experimental Psychology, 43,* 881-906.

Berry, D. C. (1994). A step too far. *Behavioral and Brain Sciences, 17,* 397-398.

Berry, D. C., & Broadbent, D. E. (1984). On the relationship between task performance and associated verbalisable knowledge. *Quarterly Journal of Experimental Psychology, 36,* 209-231.

Berry, D. C., & Broadbent, D. E. (1988). Interactive tasks and the implicit-explicit distinction. *British Journal of Psychology, 79,* 251-272.

Berry, D. C., & Dienes, Z. (1993). *Implicit learning: Theoretical and empirical issues.* Hove, UK: Lawrence Erlbaum.

Bright, J. E. H., & Burton, A. M. (1994). Past midnight: Semantic processing in an incidental learning task. *Quarterly Journal of Experimental Psychology, 47,* 71-89.

Chan, C. (1992). *Implicit cognitive processes: Theoretical issues and applications in computer systems design.* Unpublished D.Phil. Thesis, University of Oxford.

Chapnik Smith, M., Besner, D., & Miyoshi, H. (1994). New limits to automaticity: Context modulates semantic priming. *Journal of Experimental Psychology: Learning, Memory and Cognition, 20,* 104-115.

Cock, J. J., Berry, D. C., & Gaffan, E. A. (1994). New strings for old: The role of similarity processing in an incidental learning task. *Quarterly Journal of Experimental Psychology, 47,* 1015-1034.

Cohen, A., Ivry, R. I., & Keele, S. W. (1990). Attention and structure in sequence learning. *Journal of Experimental Psychology: Learning, Memory and Cognition, 16,* 17-30.

Curran, T., & Keele, S. W. (1993). Attentional and nonattentional forms of sequence learning. *Journal of Experimental Psychology: Learning, Memory and Cognition, 19,* 189-202.

Dienes, Z., Altmann, G., Kwan, L., & Goode, A. (1995). Unconscious knowledge of artificial grammars is applied strategically. *Journal of Experimental Psychology: Learning, Memory and Cognition, 21,* 1322-1338.

Dienes, Z., & Berry, D. C. (1997). Implicit learning: Below the subjective threshold? *Psychonomic Bulletin and Review, 4,* 3-23.

Dulany, D. E. (1961). Hypotheses and habits in verbal operant conditioning. *Journal of Abnormal and Social Psychology, 63,* 251-263.

Hartman, M., Knopman, D. S., & Nissen, M. J. (1989). Implicit learning of new verbal associations. *Journal of Experimental Psychology: Learning, Memory and Cognition, 15,* 1070-1082.

Kellogg, R. T., & Dowdy, J. C. (1986). Automatic learning of the frequencies of occurrence of stimulus frequencies. *American Journal of Psychology, 99,* 111-126.

Logan, G. D., Taylor, S. E., & Etherton, J. L. (1996). Attention in the acquisition and expression of automaticity. *Journal of Experimental Psychology: Learning, Memory and Cognition, 22,* 620-638.

Mathews, R. C., Buss, R. R., Stanley, W. B., Blanchard-Fields, F., Cho, J. R., & Druhan, B. (1989). Role of implicit and explicit processes in learning from examples: A synergistic effect. *Journal of Experimental Psychology: Learning, Memory and Cognition, 15,* 1083-1100.

McAndrews, M. P., & Moscovitch, M. (1985). Rule-based and exemplar-based classification in artificial grammar learning. *Memory & Cognition, 13,* 469-475.

McGeorge, P., & Burton, A. M. (1990). Semantic processing in an incidental learning task. *Quarterly Journal of Experimental Psychology, 42,* 597-610.

157

Medin, D. L., & Florian, J. E. (1992). Abstraction and selective coding in exemplar-based models of categorization. In A. F. Healy, S. M. Kosslyn, & R. M. Schiffrin (Eds.), *From learning processes to cognitive processes: Essays in honor of William K. Estes* (Vol. 2, pp. 207-234). Hillsdale, NJ: Lawrence Erlbaum.

Musen, F., & Squire, L. R. (1993). Implicit learning of color-word associations using a Stroop paradigm. *Journal of Experimental Psychology: Learning, Memory and Cognition, 19,* 789-798.

Nissen, M. J., & Bullemer, P. (1987). Attentional requirements of learning: Evidence from performance measures. *Cognitive Psychology, 19,* 1-32.

Perruchet, P. (1994). Learning from complex rule-governed environments: On the proper functions of nonconscious and conscious processes. In C. Umiltà & M. Moscovitch (Eds.), *Attention and performance XV: Conscious and unconscious information processing* (pp. 811-835). Cambridge: MIT Press.

Perruchet, P., & Pacteau, C. (1991). Implicit acquisition of abstract knowledge about artificial grammar: Some methodological and conceptual issues. *Journal of Experimental Psychology: General, 120,* 112-116.

Reber, A. S. (1967). Implicit learning of artificial grammars. *Journal of Verbal Learning and Verbal Behavior, 6,* 855-863.

Reber, A. S. (1976). Implicit learning of synthetic languages: The role of instructional set. *Journal of Experimental Psychology: Human Learning and Memory, 2,* 88-94.

Reber, A. S. (1989). Implicit learning and tacit knowledge. *Journal of Experimental Psychology: General, 118,* 219-235.

Reber, A. S. (1993). *Implicit learning and tacit knowledge.* New York: Oxford University Press.

Reber, A. S., & Allen, R. (1978). Analogic and abstraction strategies in synthetic grammar learning: A functionalist interpretation. *Cognition, 6,* 189-221.

Reber, A. S., Kassin, S. M., Lewis, S., & Cantor, G. (1980). On the relationship between implicit and explicit modes of learning a complex rule structure. *Journal of Experimental Psychology: Human Learning and Memory, 6,* 492-502.

Reed, J., & Johnson, P. (1994). Assessing implicit learning with indirect tests: Determining what is learned about sequence structure. *Journal of Experimental Psychology: Learning, Memory and Cognition, 20,* 585-594.

Roberts, P. L., & MacLeod, C. (1995). Representational consequences of two modes of learning. *Quarterly Journal of Experimental Psychology, 48,* 296-319.

Shanks, D. R., & St. John, M. F. (1994). Characteristics of dissociable human learning systems. *Behavioral and Brain Sciences, 17,* 367-447.

Shin, H., & Nosofsky, R. M. (1992). Similarity scaling studies of "dot pattern" classification and recognition. *Journal of Experimental Psychology: General, 121,* 278-304.

Stanley, W. B., Mathews, R. C., Buss, R. R., & Kotler-Cope, S. (1989). Insight without awareness: On the interaction of verbalization, instruction, and practice in a simulated process control task. *Quarterly Journal of Experimental Psychology, 41,* 553-577.

Treisman, A. (1992). Perceiving and reperceiving objects. *American Psychologist, 47,* 862-875.

Vokey, J. R., & Brooks, L. R. (1992). Salience of item knowledge in learning artificial grammars. *Journal of Experimental Psychology: Learning, Memory and Cognition, 18,* 328-344.

Whittlesea, B. W. A., & Dorken, M. D. (1993). Incidentally, things in general are particularly determined: An episodic-processing account of implicit learning. *Journal of Experimental Psychology: General, 122,* 227-248.

Willingham, D. B., Nissen, M. J., & Bullemer, P. (1989). On the development of procedural knowledge. *Journal of Experimental Psychology: Learning, Memory and Cognition, 15,* 1047-1060.

Wright, R. L., & Burton, A. M. (1995). Implicit learning of an invariant: Just say no. *Quarterly Journal of Experimental Psychology, 48,* 783-796.

5

Implicit Learning of Loosely Defined Structures

●————————————————————————

Joachim Hoffmann
Iring Koch

Learning in general can be defined as a behavioral change resulting from individual information processing (e.g., Klix, 1971). For example, classical conditioning changes the probability of the conditioned response as a result of processing information about the contingency between the unconditional and the conditional stimulus (cf. Holyoak, Koh, & Nisbett, 1989; Rescorla, 1988). In comparison to such a precise description, the content of implicit learning is far less accurately defined. Some current citations might illustrate this point. In his influential review article, Reber (1989) provides the following definition: "Implicit learning represents a . . . fundamental operation whereby critical covariations in the stimulus environment are picked up" (p. 233). Berry and Dienes (1993) describe implicit learning as a process where "a person typically learns about the structure of a fairly complex stimulus environment" (p. 2). In the view of Cleeremans (1993), "implicit learning is thought of as an essentially unintentional process by which a system acquires information about the structure of the stimulus environment" (p. 14), and Seger (1994) states, in a comprehensive review of recent research, that "implicit learning involves learning complex information in an incidental manner" (p. 163). Thus, it appears that the content of implicit learning is rather fuzzily paraphrased as "critical covariations in the stimulus environment," "the structure of a fairly complex environment," "the structure of the stimulus environment," or simply as "complex information."

There are at least two reasons for the vagueness of definitions of implicit learning. First, reports of implicit learning have been taken rather skeptically in cognitive psychology (e.g., Hoffmann, 1993a; Perruchet, Gallego, & Savy, 1990; Shanks & St. John, 1994); as a result, research has primarily striven for demonstrations of the mere existence of the phenomenon, while the question of what exactly it is that has been learned received comparably less attention. Second, various experimental paradigms have been used in demonstrating implicit learning, so that it is difficult to provide a general description of the content of learning that holds for all settings. The most frequently used paradigms are (a) covariation learning, (b) artificial grammar learning, (c) learning in the control of dynamic systems, and (d) serial learning, each of which we will briefly exemplify next.

A typical example of covariation learning is provided by a study by Lewicki, Hill, and Sasaki (1989). In a learning phase, simulated brain scans (that is, patterns of randomly distributed computer graphics characters resembling the shape of a brain) were presented to the subjects. For each brain scan, subjects were informed whether it was from an intelligent or a nonintelligent person. The scans of the two groups differed only in a tiny detail: A certain graphics character occurred in the scans of one group with a frequency of 13% and in the scans of the other group with a frequency of 17%; that is, in the learning phase, a hardly detectable visual feature of the scans was completely correlated with the intelligence of the respective individuals. After the learning phase, subjects had to rate the intelligence of new brain scans (that is, of the respective individuals). The data indicated that the intelligence ratings were systematically biased by the relative frequency of the critical character in the given scan, in accordance with the previously experienced covariation. However, the subjects were not aware of this influence. Some subjects reported that they had experienced intuitive feelings about the intelligence of the brain scans, but they were completely unable to articulate the origins of those feelings (cf. also Lewicki, 1986).

The early studies of Reber and his colleagues serve well to illustrate implicit learning of an artificial grammar (Reber, 1967, 1969, 1976; Reber & Allen, 1978). In these studies, letter strings were presented. Unknown to the subjects, the strings followed certain grammatical rules. In the learning phase, subjects had to memorize sets of strings until a fixed learning criterion was attained. After memorization, the existence of grammatical rules was revealed to the subjects. Then, new grammatically well-formed strings, as well as strings where the order of letters violated the grammatical rules were presented, and subjects were asked to judge whether a given string was a grammatical or an agrammatical one. Subjects usually achieved performance levels of 60% to 70%, that is, clearly above chance, without being able to penetrate the motivations of their judgments. Obviously, subjects had acquired some intuitive knowledge about the grammaticality of the strings they had memorized before.

An experiment by Berry and Broadbent (1984) may serve to illustrate implicit learning in system control. Subjects had to control the production of a simulated sugar factory. The structure of the task was rather simple: There was only one control variable, the number of workers employed (W), and only one variable to be controlled, the amount of sugar produced (P). The "sugar factory" operates according to the following equation: $P_t = 2 \times W_t - P_{t-1} + r_t$. In Trial t, the output of the factory (P_t) is a function of the number of actually employed workers (W_t), its output at the preceding trial (P_{t-1}), and a random component (r_t). Subjects were required to choose, trial for trial, the number of workers to be employed in such a way that the production reached and maintained a prespecified target value. The data reveal that some subjects attained reasonably satisfactory performance during practice, despite their inability to answer questions about concrete relations between their input and the output of the system. Again, these subjects seem to have acquired some intuitive knowledge of how to act properly, without knowing exactly why.

Finally, in serial learning tasks, stimuli are successively presented to subjects who are asked to respond as quickly as possible. Regular sequences of stimuli are compared with random sequences. For example, in an experiment by Nissen and Bullemer (1987), the stimuli were asterisks, presented on a computer screen at four horizontally aligned locations. The stimuli were mapped onto four keys in a spatially congruent fashion, such that subjects had to press the key that was approximately below the respective asterisk. In a regular sequence, 10 subsequent locations were cyclically repeated, whereas in a control condition, the locations followed each other randomly. The data showed that in the course of training, reaction time (RT) decreased remarkably more with the repeating than with the random sequence, indicating that learning is at least partly due to the sequential regularities in the repeating sequence. Most subjects noticed the repetitive character of the sequence, but the learning effect, although smaller, was still present in subjects who did not report noticing repetitions (Willingham, Nissen, & Bullemer, 1989). These subjects seem to have learned how to use the sequential regularities for speeding up their responses without noticing them.

The examples manifest the diversity of information that is to be learned in the various experimental settings. In covariation learning, it is a covariation between a hidden stimulus feature and the required response that is to be learned. In grammar learning, restrictions in the succession of stimuli should be learned. In the control of dynamic systems, learning refers primarily to relations between control and output variables, that is, between acts and their outcomes. Finally, in serial RT tasks, subjects learn, similar to grammar learning, about regularities either in the experienced stimulus sequences or in the executed response sequences. If one wants to refer jointly to what is being learned in all these different tasks, the term *structure* seems to be indeed appropriate: In all cases subjects adapt to structures in the environment. However, cognitive psychology in general deals with adaptation to environmental structures so that the use of the term structure is hardly helpful to designate a specific performance. To elucidate the specific mechanisms underlying the phenomena of implicit learning, a differentiation of various types of structure seems to us to be indispensable. The present chapter is designed to contribute to this aim. In the next section, various concepts of structure, which all have been proven to be of psychological significance, will be discussed. Then, we will show that all the distinguishable structural components are involved in one of the most frequently used implicit learning tasks, namely in serial choice reactions. Finally, we will propose a research strategy that we believe is more appropriate to the complexity of the phenomena in question than the current concentration on certain narrow issues.

THE CONCEPT OF STRUCTURE IN PSYCHOLOGY

The concept of structure is used in many ways in psychology. For example, it refers to perceptual structures, to the structure of a problem space, to the structure of concepts, to the structure of social groups, to the structure of intelligence, and so on. In a comprehensive analysis, Klix and Krause (1969) compared the various applications of the concept and depicted what they all have in common. According to the authors, the definition of structure presupposes determinations of a finite set of elements and of a finite set of relations as possible *morphisms* between the elements. Then, structure is defined by the total number of relations between the given set of elements. Thus, what composes a structure depends on the elements and the relations that are regarded. For the present purpose, it is sufficient to distinguish three types of structures according to the specificity of the relations under consideration: (a) structures based on dependencies between the sheer occurrence of elements, (b) structures based on significant relations between the appearances of elements, and (c) structures based on the spatial and temporal distributions of elements. We will now discuss in some detail the psychological significance of each of the three types of structure.

● Structure in Terms of Information Theory

In a small book titled *The Mathematical Theory of Communication*, Claude E. Shannon and Warren Weaver (1949) developed a metric for the measurement of information. They proposed to determine the information that is transmitted by the occurrence of an event as a function of its probability in such a way that information should be zero when the event occurs with certainty and that information should increase as the probability of the event decreases. These properties are met if the information of an event (I) is calculated as the logarithm (in fact the logarithm dualis was used) of its reciprocal probability:

$$(1) \quad I(x_i) = \text{ld } 1/p(x_i)$$

If a situation with several alternative events is considered, $X = \{x_1, x_2, ..., x_i, ... x_n\}$, the information of the situation, its entropy (H), is computed as the weighted mean across the information of all single events.

$$(2) \quad H(X) = \Sigma \, p(x_i) \, \text{ld } 1/p(x_i)$$

The maximum possible information occurs when each event is equally likely, and the entropy becomes zero if only one event occurs with certainty:

$$(3) \quad H_{max}(X) = \text{ld}(n) \text{ and } H_{min}(X) = 0$$

Another important term of information theory is *redundancy* (R), which expresses how much of the maximal possible entropy of a situation is actually realized:

$$(4) \quad R(X) = 1 - (H(X)/H_{max}(X))$$

Redundancy ranges from 0 to 1. It will be 0 when $H(X)$ is equal to $H_{max}(X)$, that is, when each event is equally likely, so that there is a maximum of uncertainty. Redundancy will be 1 when $H(X)$ is 0, that is, when one event appears with certainty. Thus, redundancy provides a direct measure of the amount of certainty or regularity that is given in a situation.

The computation of information can be extended to event sequences, as well, which can be easily illustrated by the example of a traffic light (in Germany, the regular sequence of traffic lights is as follows: green-yellow-red-yellow-green . . .): There are three events to be distinguished, the signals red, yellow, and green. According to Equation 3, the maximal entropy is ld 3 = 1.58496. However, the signals do not occur with equal probabilities. Rather, the signal yellow occurs twice as frequently as red and green. Therefore, the actual entropy has to be computed according to Equation 2 as $H_1(X) = (0.5_{yellow} \times$ ld $1/0.5) + (0.25_{red} \times$ ld $1/0.25) + (0.25_{green} \times$ ld $1/0.25) = 1.5$. The measure is termed the entropy of first order, and the index 1 indicates that not only the number of alternatives is considered but also their likelihood. To consider additional dependencies in the occurrence of two consecutive signals, the entropy for pairs of signals (bigrams) is calculated, and the entropy of first order is then subtracted.

$$(5) \quad H_2(X) = H(bigram) - H_1(X)$$

In sequences of traffic lights, the bigrams red-yellow, yellow-green, green-yellow, and yellow-red occur with equal likelihood, such that H(bigram) = ld 4 = 2 and $H_2(X) = 2.0 - 1.5 = 0.5$. The second-order entropy expresses the average information that is transmitted by the occurrence of an event when the previous event is known. In the given example, the entropy decreases from 1.5 to 0.5 because only after the signal yellow does there remain uncertainty about what comes next. Analogously, dependencies between three consecutive signals can be considered by calculating the third-order entropy as $H_3(X) = H$(trigram) $- H$(bigram). What results in the present case is an entropy of zero because at a traffic light, every signal can be absolutely reliably predicted if the previous two signals are known.

The example illustrates how regularities in the occurrence of events are precisely captured by the indices of the information theory. Generally speaking, the entropy of order n holds the amount of uncertainty as to the occurrence of events that remains when the information of $n - 1$ previous events is completely considered. Regularities in the occurrence of single stimuli are captured by the first-order entropy. The additional entropies of higher orders capture dependencies in the succession of events. If such dependencies exist, the entropy decreases with increasing n until the consideration of additional previous events provides no further information. Thus, the indices of entropy, and complementarity of redundancy, express the strength of dependencies between events, regardless of what kind of events they are and where the dependencies originate. Entropy and redundancy can therefore be regarded as being abstract indices of structure in the sense of the general definition given above.

It was primarily this measurability of structure and organization that made the information theory so attractive for psychology (cf. Attneave, 1959; Miller, 1953, 1956, 1958; Miller & Frick, 1949; Welford, 1976). As soon as the theory became public, an intensive search for relations between entropy and performances was initiated. Against this background, it is easy to imagine how enthusiastically the seminal result of Hick (1952) was regarded: He varied the number of alternative stimuli in a choice RT task and found a linear relationship between the mean RT and the entropy of the stimulus source. Further investigations manipulated the frequency distributions of the stimuli as well as sequential dependencies between them (e.g., Crossman, 1953; Hyman, 1953; Klemmer & Muller, 1953): In each case, a monotonic increase of RTs in dependence on the entropy of the stimulus source was always found. Thus, information, as measured in terms of entropy and redundancy, was proven to be of psychological relevance. The general conclusion was that the processing of stimuli is to be understood as information processing (cf. also Mandler, 1985).

Beside choice RT tasks, various other experimental settings have been used to explore the influence of entropy on performance (for reviews, see, e.g., Attneave, 1959; Berlyne, 1957; Garner, 1962; Hartman, 1954; Pollack, 1952; Quastler, 1953). For the present purpose, serial recall experiments are of special importance. For example, in a famous experiment, Miller and Selfridge (1950) presented lists of words that increasingly approximated the redundancies in word sequences of ordinary English. The results indicated that the number of correctly recalled words increased as more higher-order dependencies were taken into account. Likewise, recall of letter and digit sequences, as well as of sequences of meaningless syllables, was found to be improved by redundancies of first and higher order (Aborn & Rubenstein, 1952; Rubenstein & Aborn, 1954). In brief, there are numerous experiments that convincingly indicate that those structural components which are expressed in the measures of entropy and redundancy have remarkable effects on the processing of stimulus sequences.

● Structural Information Theory

The metric proposed by Shannon and Weaver is based on the consideration that *information* can be measured by the amount of uncertainty that is resolved by the occurrence of an event. Consequently, information is defined as a function of probability. However, simple considerations easily make plain that human beings also use other kinds of structure to reduce uncertainty.

For example, consider a sequence of digits such as 24816 . . . , which is cyclically repeated. The redundancies of the sequence can be determined as a function of the likelihood and of the conditional probabilities by which the digits 1, 2, 4, 6, and 8 occur. However, any attentive subject will quickly notice that the sequence forms a part of a geometric row, where each next element is generated by doubling the previous one: 2-4-8-16. By this knowledge about the relation between consecutive digits any uncertainty is abruptly reduced as the whole sequence can be easily generated from its first element. This way of reducing uncertainty by considering relational patterns between events cannot be handled by information theory. It needs a description that is not based on probabilities but rather on the way events can be generated.

The determination of the structure of a stimulus sequence by the effort that is necessary for its generation requires a standard that can be equally applied to any sequence. Such a standard was proposed by Hans Buffart, Emanuel Leeuwenberg, and Frank Restle under the term *structural information theory* (SIT). The authors applied SIT mainly to visual configurations. The general procedure can be depicted as follows (cf. Buffart & Leeuwenberg, 1983; Buffart, Leeuwenberg, & Restle, 1981; Leeuwenberg, 1969, 1971; Leeuwenberg & Buffart, 1983): Any visual configuration is described as a sequence of elementary units that are strung together, starting from one point of the configuration and proceeding in one direction. Consequently, the code of the configuration arises as a string of its basic coding elements. This string is called the primitive code. Further processing is directed toward detecting regularities (that is, structure) in the primitive code in order to reduce its length. For example, let us take a string like abababab, whereby the letters a and b refer to any elementary coding units.

The string consists of four repetitions of the pair ab, hence it can be described by applying a repetition operator: R_4(ab). Other operators refer to further regularities in the primitive code. For example, a sequence like abccba can be reduced by applying a symmetry operator SYM(abc), which specifies that the substring abc has to be repeated in the reverse order to complete the sequence. A sequence like cabdabeabfabg contains the ab subsequence several times at regular positions. This can be described by a distribution operator DIST(ab)[(c)(d)(e)(f)(g)], which specifies that the substring ab has to be inserted between the elements given in the rectangular brackets. In general, applying such "redundancy operators" reduces the length of the primitive code. The code that allows the description of the sequence by the smallest number of symbols is called the minimal code. Its length provides a measure for the informational content of the original sequence.

The proponents of SIT successfully applied the theory to account for phenomena of visual perception (Buffart et al., 1981; Leeuwenberg, 1971; Leeuwenberg & Buffart, 1983). These applications are not of primary concern in the present context. Rather, we are interested in effects of *structural* information on serial learning. The influence of relational patterns on serial learning has been demonstrated in numerous studies: No matter whether it was sequences of tones (Jones, Boltz, & Kidd, 1982; Jones, Summerell, & Marshburn, 1987), letter strings (Simon & Kotovski, 1963), lists of words (Hoffmann, 1979; Kintsch, 1971, 1972; Underwood, Shaughnessy, & Zimmermann, 1974), or sequences of keystrokes (Collard & Povel, 1982; Povel & Collard, 1982; Rosenbaum, Kenny, & Derr, 1983, Ziessler, Hänel, & Hoffmann, 1988; Ziessler, Hänel, & Sachse, 1990), it was always shown that the presence of systematic relational patterns between consecutive events improves learning and retention (Hoffmann, 1996). As an illustration, we will discuss a pertinent study by Restle and Brown (1970a, 1970b) in some detail.

Subjects sat in front of a series of six horizontally aligned lamps (1-2- . . . -6). The lamps were flashed in a certain order, and the subjects were required to predict which lamp would flash next. There were significant relations between consecutive flashes that were easily recognized, for example the repetition, when the same lamp flashes again (R(1)→11), the transposition, when the light moves to the next position right or left, (T(1)→12), or the mirroring, when the rightmost lamp flashes after the leftmost lamp (M(1)→16). By a recursive application of these relations, hierarchically organized sequences of flashes can be generated as illustrated in Figure 5.1. The start element 1 is first transposed: T(1)→12. The pair

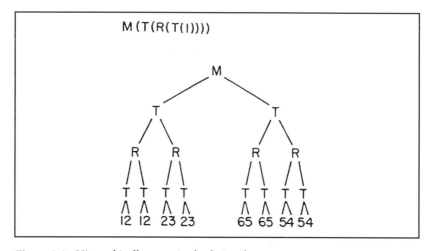

Figure 5.1. Hierarchically organized relational pattern.
SOURCE: From "Theory of Serial Pattern Learning: Structural Trees" by F. Restle, 1970, *Psychological Review, 77,* p. 487. Copyright 1970 by the American Psychological Association. Reprinted with permission.

is then repeated, R(12)→1212, and the resulting quadruple again transposed, T(1212)→12122323. The subsequence of eight elements is finally mirrored so that the whole sequence can be completely described by the following minimal code: M(T(R(T(1))))→1212232365655454.

Such hierarchically structured sequences were cyclically presented and subjects tried to continuously predict the next flash. In the data analysis, the authors aggregated the relative frequencies of correct predictions across those serial positions that are determined by transformations on the same hierarchic level: The second elements of all pairs are jointly determined by transpositions on the lowest Level 4. The first elements of every second pair are jointly determined by repetitions on Level 3, and the first elements of the quadruples are jointly determined by transpositions on Level 2. Finally, the first element of the second subsequence of eight elements is determined by mirroring on Level 1. In Figure 5.2, the averaged prediction performance for various hierarchies with five levels each are presented. The picture of a clear dependency arises: The number of correct predictions systematically increases with the depth of the hierarchic level by which the events to be predicted are determined.

The results indicate that the generative structure of the presented sequences is indeed used by the subjects to make predictions more reliable. Evidently, subjects learn that the sequences are composed of parts that share

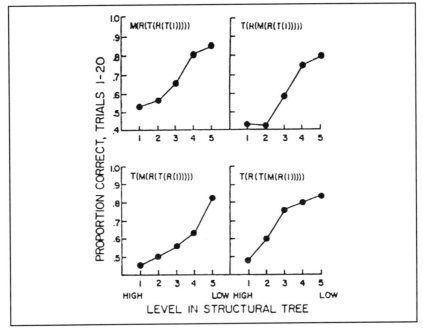

Figure 5.2. Averaged prediction performance, arranged by the hierarchic level for various sequences with five levels.

SOURCE: From "Theory of Serial Pattern Learning: Structural Trees" by F. Restle, 1970, *Psychological Review, 77,* p. 489. Copyright 1970 by the American Psychological Association. Reprinted with permission.

the same relational patterns among their elements. Furthermore, that the prediction of events is better the deeper the level is by which the occurrence of the events has been determined indicates that the relational patterns are learned from the bottom to the top of the hierarchy. The systematicity of relations between adjacent elements seems to be learned before relations between these elementary patterns are taken into account. Thus, the results confirm and substantiate what George Miller had already claimed in 1956, namely that parsing of a sequence in mutually related subsequences or chunks is a basic component of serial learning.

So far, our discussion has led to a differentiation of two factors of chunking: Redundancy as it is expressed in the indices of information theory, on the one hand, and relational patterns as they are described by the minimal codes of SIT, on the other hand. The basic difference between the two approaches can once again be illustrated by an example from the repeating sequence 1212232365655454, which was used by Restle and

Brown: According to information theory, the stimuli 3 and 4 should be least predictable because they belong to the group of stimuli that seldom occur and because they are not predictable on the basis of their respective antecedents (the antecedent of 3 is 2, which is also followed by 1 and 2, and the antecedent of 4 is 5, which is also followed by 6 and 5). That nevertheless 3 and 4 are reliably predicted cannot, therefore, be due to probabilities. Rather, it is due to the fact that every second stimulus in consecutive pairs is generated by a transposition of the first stimulus in the pair, which renders all second stimuli and thus also 3 and 4 highly predictable. The essential difference between the information theory and the SIT is that the former describes the reduction of uncertainty exclusively as a function of dependencies between the sheer occurrence of stimuli, whereas the latter emphasizes the *quality* of relations between stimuli instead.

● **Patterns in Space and Time**

Structures according to the spatial configuration of stimuli are omnipresent in visual perception: Stimuli that are close together are more likely integrated into a perceptual chunk than stimuli that are further apart. Gestalt psychologists have explicitly postulated a law of proximity to account for this basic perceptual phenomenon, and there are numerous demonstrations of this law in vision and visual search (Boring, 1942; Koffka, 1935; Köhler, 1929; Metzger, 1975; Palmer, 1977; Treisman, 1982; Wertheimer, 1923). In the same way as proximity in space supports chunking of spatially distributed stimuli, proximity in time supports chunking of successive stimuli. This is especially obvious in music: Pauses between otherwise homogeneously presented tones let us perceive the pauses as incisions that separate chunks of unitary subsequences from each other. Human beings are ordinarily highly sensitive to rhythms and to deviations from them (cf. Johnson, 1965; Jones, 1976; Neisser, 1967; Wilkes & Kennedy, 1970). Thus, there is no doubt at all as to the structuring effects of spatial and temporal configurations. Therefore, it should be sufficient to illustrate the corresponding research by just one example by which research in implicit learning has been motivated (cf. Stadler, 1993).

Bower and Winzenz (1969, Experiment 3) investigated the influence of temporal patterns on serial recall. Eight sequences of 12 digits each were successively presented to the subjects. Each sequence had to be recalled immediately after presentation. Every second sequence was identical, so that there were five different sequences overall, from which one was repeated four times in alternation with a different sequence each time. The presentation of the digits was rhythmically designed by interspersing pauses in different positions. The critical variation involved the rhythm of the repeatedly presented sequence. It was repeated always either in the same or in different rhythms. For example, the sequence 176839452386 was either always repeated in the rhythm 17-683-945-2386 or instead, at the second repetition, in the rhythm 176-8-3945-2386 and at the third and fourth repetition, with the rhythms 1768-39-45-2386 and 176-839-4-52-386, respectively. In general, recall should improve with every repetition. However, this happened only when the sequence was repeated in a constant rhythm. There was no improvement of recall when the rhythms were changed between the repetitions. The result clearly indicates that the subject's perception of the digit sequences was essentially affected by their rhythmical presentation. Clearly, it was not sequences of single digits that were perceived, but sequences of substrings seperated by pauses. This immediate parsing of the sequence seemed to be so dominant that identical sequences were not perceived as being identical when they differed in rhythm, so that any repetition effect failed to appear.

● Summary

In this section, various possibilities of grasping the concept of structure have been discussed. Information theory defines structure in terms of unconditional and conditional probabilities. For the SIT, structures depend on transformative rules for the generation of events from events. Finally, structures refer also to spatial and temporal patterns. In a formal way, all these considerations aim at a metrical description of structure, which is actually accomplished by information theory only. The SIT provides at best an ordinal metric, and there are, to our knowledge, only tentative accounts of a formal description of spatial and temporal patterns (e.g., Palmer, 1977). From a psychological perspective, the main interest is in an elucidation of the mechanisms that mediate the influence of the distinguishable components on the formation of structures. It is reasonable to assume that the formation of structures generally serves the purpose of predicting forthcoming events (e.g., Cleeremans, 1993). In this sense, the reported effects of informational redundancies demonstrate mechanisms of predicting events on the basis of their likelihood. The reported effects of relational patterns refer to mechanisms of predicting forthcoming events by transformations of current events, and the effects of patterns in time and space indicate mechanisms that not only predict what will happen next but also where and when it will happen.

If, as mentioned above, implicit learning is thought of as being an incidental acquisition of environmental structures, and if it is also acknowledged that the acquisition of structure serves the purpose of reducing uncertainty, the question arises as to what extent the various mechanisms of reducing uncertainty, which all are proven to be of psychological relevance, are involved in implicit learning. In the following, we will pursue this question in detail with regard to one of the most commonly used paradigms in implicit learning research, the serial reaction time (SRT) task. First, we will show that the distinguishable structural components are all involved in these tasks. Second, we will review some selected studies that demonstrate the actual influence of the distinguished components on learning. Finally, we will argue that a careful control of structural components is an indispensable condition for a further progress in implicit learning research.

CONFUSIONS OF VARIOUS STRUCTURAL COMPONENTS IN SERIAL CHOICE REACTION TIME TASKS

Nissen and Bullemer (1987) reported an experiment that became a standard for many subsequent studies (e.g., Cohen, Ivry, & Keele, 1990; Curran & Keele, 1993; Frensch, Buchner, & Lin, 1994; Frensch & Miner, 1994; Hoffman & Koch, 1997; Howard, Mutter, & Howard, 1992; Perruchet & Amorim, 1992; Stadler, 1992, 1993, 1995; Willingham et al., 1989) and therefore can be regarded as being prototypical for a great part of implicit learning research. The experimental setting was already mentioned above. To reiterate: asterisks that could appear on four horizontally aligned positions on a screen (1 to 4 from left to right) served as stimuli. Four response keys were spatially congruently assigned to the four stimulus positions. Subjects were requested to press as quickly as possible that key that was mapped to the position of the respectively presented asterisk. The keys were to be pressed from left to right by the middle and the index fingers of the left hand, and by the index and the middle fingers of the right hand. The critical variation was the succession of stimuli. A control group received the asterisks presented at randomly selected positions, with the only restriction being that no position appeared twice in a row. For an experimental

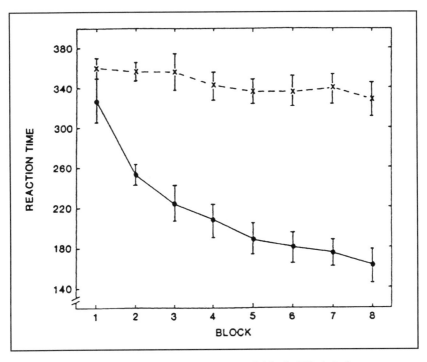

Figure 5.3. Mean of median reaction time in each block. Filled circles: repeating sequence; x's: random sequence. Bars represent standard errors.

SOURCE: From "Attentional Requirements of Learning: Evidence From Performance Measures," by M. J. Nissen & P. Bullemer, 1987, *Cognitive Psychology, 19,* p. 8. Copyright 1987 by Academic Press. Reprinted with permission.

group, the deterministic 10-trial sequence of the positions 4231324321 was cyclically repeated. The experiment was run in eight blocks of 100 individual trials each. Figure 5.3 shows the mean RTs plotted against blocks for both groups of subjects. The data clearly indicate that subjects in the experimental group responded increasingly quicker than subjects in the control group. This growing advantage of the repeating over the random sequence was taken as indicating structural learning. There is nothing wrong with this conclusion, as the quicker responses must indeed be due to differences in the structures of the repeating and the random sequences. But what are these differences in detail?

A first difference regards the relative frequencies of the four stimuli. In the random sequence, all stimuli are equally likely so that the entropy of first order is maximal: $H_1(R) = ld4 = 2$. In contrast, in the repeating sequence, the positions 3 and 2 appear three times in each run of the sequence, whereas the positions 1 and 4 appear only twice in each run. According to Equation 2, the entropy of first order of the repeating sequence results in $H_1(S) = 1.970954$, that is, it contains redundancy.

A second difference regards redundancies of higher order. In the random sequence, each of the four stimuli has three equally likely successors (repetitions of the same position were excluded). Thus, there are 12 equally likely bigrams with an entropy of $H(bigram) = ld\ 12 = 3.58496$. According to Equation 4, the second-order entropy is calculated as $H\ (bigram) - H_1(R) = 3.58496 - 2 = 1.58496$, which simply expresses the fact that the number of alternatives is reduced from four to three if the current stimulus is used in predicting the next one ($ld\ 3 = 1.58496$). Nothing is changed if further preceding stimuli are taken into account: Each of the 12 bigrams can again be succeeded in three different equally likely ways, such that all higher-order entropies will result in the value of ld 3. In contrast, the repeating sequence includes nine bigrams, from which the pair 32 appears twice and all other pairs only once within each run of the cycle. Accordingly, the entropy of the bigrams results in $H(bigram) = 3.12193$ and the second-order entropy of the sequence in $H_2(S) = 1.150976$. If trigrams are taken into account the entropy is further reduced to $H_3(S) = 0.2$, which reflects that there only remains uncertainty after the pair 32, that is, whether the position 1 or the position 4 comes next. Finally, if three preceding stimuli are taken into account, the entropy becomes zero because now all stimuli are completely predictable. Thus, the repeating sequence differs from the random one not only in its first-order redundancy but also in its redundancies of higher order.

Furthermore, the repeating sequence contains consistent relational patterns that are not present in the random sequence. For example, the first three stimuli are mirrored against the fourth stimulus, that is, they are repeated in reversed order: 423 (1) 324. Another salient pattern is formed by the last four stimuli of the sequence. It is a continuous transposition of the asterisk from the rightmost to the leftmost position (4321). If one considers relations between successive keystrokes, regular patterns appear again. Thus, the responses on the first seven stimuli are executed by both hands in alternation: $right_4$-$left_2$- $right_3$-$left_1$-$right_3$-$left_2$-$right_4$. Moreover the repeating sequence may also allow spatial patterns to become effective as the successive stimuli can be viewed as a movement of an asterisk over the screen. It appears as a vivid picture of regular movement that is illus-

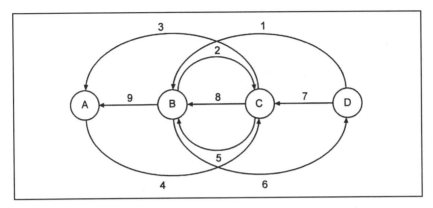

Figure 5.4. Illustration of the regular movement pattern arising from the repeating 10-trial sequence used by Nissen and Bullemer (1987).

trated in Figure 5.4: the asterisk first jumps back and forth before closing a cycle by moving continuously to the left.

In summary, the structure of the repeating sequence differs in several aspects from the random sequence. All these structural components, beginning with the redundancy of first order up to spatial patterns, affect serial learning, as has been convincingly demonstrated by numerous experiments reviewed above. Thus, each of the components may have contributed to the observed learning effect, and it remains a completely unsolved issue as to which of the components learning is actually based on, and to what degree, as long as the effects of the participating components are not disentangled (cf. also Reed & Johnson, 1994; Shanks & St. John, 1994). In the following, we will discuss some selected studies that contribute to this important enterprise of assessing the effects of the various structural components on implicit learning in isolation.

INFLUENCES OF VARIOUS STRUCTURAL COMPONENTS ON LEARNING IN SERIAL REACTION TIME TASKS

First-Order Redundancy in Serial Reaction Time Tasks

The first-order redundancy of a series of stimuli is determined by the frequencies with which the single stimuli occur. It has been variously demonstrated that people are extremely sensitive to frequency of occurrence information. Hasher and Zacks (1984) reviewed the corresponding literature, which reveals among other things that information about frequency is recorded in memory without a person's intention to do so, that the ability to encode frequency information is neither improved by training nor deteriorated by dual task demands, and that most people have no awareness of having this information (cf. Zacks, Hasher, & Sanft, 1982). Summarizing the given evidence, Hasher and Zacks (1984) concluded that the acquisition of information about frequency of occurrence is presumably an implicit, or automatic, process, which functions independently of access to consciousness (p. 1385). Furthermore, psychologists have known since Hick's law about the monotonic function between the entropy of a stimulus source and RT. Thus, from all that we know, the acquisition of frequency information is a good candidate to account for the observed reduction of RT in responding to redundant sequences of stimuli. Correspondingly, in recent studies of implicit learning, the frequency of the stimuli has been considered (e.g., Frensch et al., 1994; Reed & Johnson, 1994; Stadler, 1993, Experiment 2, 1995). However, we know of only one study in which the influence of frequency variations on implicit learning was explicitly investigated.

In this study, conducted by Shanks, Green, and Kolodny (1994, cited after Shanks & St. John, 1994, p. 384), the standard Nissen and Bullemer task was administered. In one condition, subjects responded to the repeating sequence that was used by Nissen and Bullemer, in which, as described above, the stimuli 2 and 3 appeared three times and the stimuli 1 and 4 appeared twice in one cycle of 10 presentations. In order to control for the first-order redundancy, a second group received a "pseudorandom" sequence in which the frequencies of single stimuli were matched to the repeating sequence, that is, in each 10 consecutive stimuli, the stimuli 2 and 3 also appeared three times and the stimuli 1 and 4 also twice, but in a random rather than in a deterministic order (except that stimuli never appeared twice in a row, as in the repeating sequence). Finally, as in the original study of Nissen and Bullemer (1987), a "truly" random sequence was presented to a third group, where all stimuli appeared equally often in random order with the only restriction being again that no stimulus occurred twice on consecutive trials. After training, the subjects of the repeating sequence group were classified on the basis of a structured interview as having no explicit knowledge of the sequence, some knowledge or full knowledge. The critical comparison with regard to implicit learning is between the repeating sequence/no-knowledge group, on the one hand,

and the pseudorandom and truly random groups, on the other hand: It appears that there was no significant RT difference between the repeating sequence/no-knowledge group and the pseudorandom group, whereas RTs of both groups improved more than those of the truly random group.

The results allow at least two conclusions: first, the advantage of the pseudorandom over the truly random group indicates that first-order redundancy is indeed sufficient to speed up responses. Thus, first-order redundancy is proven to be a basic factor in mediating phenomena of implicit learning in SRT tasks. Second, the fact that the repeating sequence/no-knowledge group improved no more than the pseudorandom group makes plain that the improvement does not necessarily indicate *sequence* learning; it may instead be based solely on event frequency information. Consequently, Shanks and St. John (1994, p. 384) suspected that most if not all of the supposedly implicit learning in the standard SRT tasks may be simply due to the development of response biases reflecting knowledge of the frequencies of the different stimuli.

● **Second- and Higher-Order Redundancies in
Serial Reaction Time Tasks**

One of the most common assumptions made to account for implicit learning phenomena in SRT tasks is that subjects learn to anticipate forthcoming stimuli on the basis of sequential constraints (Cleeremans, 1993; Cleeremans & McClelland, 1991). This assumption renders the predictability of stimuli in dependence of preceding stimuli, that is, second- and higher-order redundancies, a crucial experimental variable. Especially in the last few years, several studies were reported where the influence of this variable on learning was carefully analyzed. We start the discussion of this research with a study of Cohen et al. (1990), which focused on effects of second-order redundancies on implicit learning. Then, we turn to studies indicating that higher-order redundancies also contribute to implicit learning.

Cohen et al. (1990) again used the standard Nissen and Bullemer (1987) task, where a sequence of stimulus locations was cyclically repeated. The nature of the sequences was varied. There were *unique, ambiguous,* and *hybrid* sequences. In unique sequences (e.g., 15243), each stimulus had only one successor, so that from any given stimulus in the sequence the next one could be predicted with certainty. In ambiguous sequences (e.g., 132312), each stimulus had at least two successors. Now, two predecessors in the sequence had to be taken into account respectively in order to predict the next stimulus with certainty. Finally, hybrid sequences (e.g., 142312) contained both unique and ambiguous transitions between consecutive stimuli. In terms of information theory, it was mainly the second-order redundancy of the sequences that is varied in this way, from totally redundant unique sequences to informative ambiguous sequences (but, as Reed & Johnson, 1994, correctly criticized, sequence length as well as the number of alternative stimuli were confounded with second-order entropy).

The experiment was performed under dual task conditions. In addition to the response signals, high- and low-pitched tones were presented in the interval between any response and the presentation of the next stimulus (response stimulus interval, RSI), and subjects were asked to keep count mentally of the number of high-pitched tones during each block of trials. This tone-counting task was originally introduced by Nissen and Bullemer (1987) and became a standard task to distract attention from the stimulus sequence (e.g., Cohen et al., 1990; Reed & Johnson, 1994). After several blocks of practice with the repeating sequences, subjects received two blocks with a random sequence of the same stimuli. Sequence-specific learning is indicated by an increase of RTs when subjects were transferred from the repeating to the random sequence. The results show learning with the unique and the hybrid sequences only. With ambiguous sequences, switching from the repeating to the random sequence caused no increase of RTs. In other words, under attentional distraction, sequence-specific learning seemed to take place only if there were unique transitions between succeeding stimuli in the sequence.

On the basis of this differential effect of attentional distraction on learning unique and ambiguous transitions, the authors deduced that two learning mechanisms could be separated: one basic associative mechanism that is sensitive to unique transitions and does not need attention to operate, and a second learning mechanism that also takes into account dependencies between substrings of stimuli and requires that attention is focused on the sequence (cf. also Curran & Keele, 1993). However, subsequent studies did not confirm the dissociation between learning of unique and ambiguous transitions (Keele & Jennings, 1992; Reed & Johnson, 1994).

Frensch et al. (1994) replicated parts of the Cohen et al. (1990) study under slightly changed conditions. The subjects were first trained with a hybrid sequence, that is, a sequence that contains unique as well as ambiguous transitions. After training had been completed, a transfer sequence was introduced. In the transfer sequence, either the unique or the ambiguous transitions of the preceding training sequence were altered. This procedure allowed a separate assessment of the degree of learning for the two types of transitions. The results clearly indicate that both unique and ambiguous transitions were learned, even if the subject's attention was distracted from the stimulus sequence by a secondary tone-counting task. Moreover, unattentional learning of both transitions appeared to be equally influenced by manipulations of the time of onset of the distracting tones as well as by manipulations of the length of the RSI, which favors a common instead of separate learning mechanisms.

An experiment of Reed and Johnson (1994) provides still stronger evidence for unattentional learning of ambiguous transitions, as completely ambiguous instead of hybrid sequences were used and as the sequences were additionally controlled for their first- and second-order entropy (that is, for stimulus frequencies and serial transitions). Subjects were first trained with what the authors called a repeating second-order conditional (SOC) sequence. In an SOC sequence, every stimulus can be predicted exclusively on the basis of its two predecessors. For example, in the SOC sequence 121342314324, every stimulus appears three times, and it is followed by every other stimulus except itself. Thus, stimuli are neither predictable by their frequencies nor by their transitions. But every pair of stimuli has only one definite successor; that is, all stimuli of the sequence are completely predictable on the basis of two predecessors. After an extensive training of 17 blocks, subjects were transferred to another SOC sequence. The transfer sequence was completely new in terms of SOC information but identical to the training sequence in relation to stimulus frequency and serial transitions. Thus, for the above-mentioned training sequence, the following transfer sequence was used: 123413214243. Again, every stimulus appears three times and is followed by every other stimulus except itself. Again, every pair of stimuli has one definite successor. But, the successors were replaced. For example, the pair 12 is now followed by 3 instead of 1, the pair 13 by 2 instead of 4, and so on. The introduction of the transfer sequence led to a significant increase in RT, which is due to the SOCs, because only these have been changed. Obviously, in the training session, subjects have learned somehow to use the SOCs in order to speed up their responses. This learning took place despite a distracting tone-counting task that was used and despite other tests indicated that no subject was aware of any sequential regularity.

In the preceding studies, repeating deterministic sequences were always used. In deterministic sequences, the predictability of stimuli increases as more preceding stimuli are taken into account (a repeating sequence of n elements is completely predictable if $n-1$ preceding elements are regarded). Consequently, the effects of redundancies of lower order are always confounded with possible effects of redundancies of higher order. For example in the above-mentioned study of Reed and Johnson (1994), subjects could have learned not only that the stimulus pair 12 is always followed by the stimulus 1, that 21 is always followed by 3, and that 13 is always followed by 4, but also that the string 12134 is repeated. To avoid such confounding of redundancies of different order, probabilistic sequences are to be used, as was done in the following two studies.

Stadler (1992, Experiment 2) used a method that was already introduced by Miller and Selfridge in 1950. He started with a repeating 10-trial sequence. To disentangle the effects of statistical constraints of different orders, he constructed several quasirandom nonrepeating sequences, which increasingly approximated the statistical structure of the repeating sequence. The orders of approximation were constructed by using the conditional probabilities that each stimulus would follow the preceding run of n stimuli in the repeating sequence. For example, in the first-order approximation, the stimuli in the quasirandom sequence appeared with the same relative frequencies as in the repeating sequence. In the second-order approximation, the relative frequencies of stimuli were additionally matched in dependence on their predecessors in the repeating sequence. In the third-order approximation, another predecessor was also taken into account in order to match the relative frequencies of stimuli in the repeating and in the quasirandom sequence, and so on, until in the fifth order of approximation, all stimuli could be predicted with certainty such that the quasirandom sequence actually became a repeating one. The data showed that as the redundancy of the quasirandom sequences increases, the rate of learning also increases.

The second experiment of interest in this context was reported by Cleeremans and McClelland (1991). Again, probabilistic sequences of stimuli were used, which were generated on the basis of a finite state grammar. There is not enough space here to describe the grammar in detail. For the present purpose, it is sufficient to know that the grammar restricts the set of succeeding stimuli at every position in the generated sequences, whereby the restrictions depend not only on the current but also on the preceding stimuli. Thus, the grammar generates varying sequences of stimuli that jointly represent the sequential restrictions that are imposed by the grammar. Needless to say, the data again revealed that subjects are sensitive to the grammatical restrictions, as they respond increasingly faster to grammatically than to agrammatically placed stimuli. Furthermore, the authors showed that in the course of training, subjects' RTs were increasingly influenced by the conditional probabilities of stimulus occurrence, first in dependence of the preceding stimulus and later in dependence of two preceding stimuli. A fine-grained analysis of selected substrings revealed evidence for the influence of even three preceding stimuli at the end of training. This pattern of results is consistent with the idea that subjects are encoding increasingly large amounts of temporal context in order to predict the next stimulus. In terms of information theory, subjects learn to use statistical redundancies in increasing order.

In summary, the available evidence demonstrates convincingly that statistical redundancies in the order of stimuli contribute to learning in SRT tasks. The experiments by Stadler (1992, Experiment 2) and Cleeremans and McClelland (1991) also show that the effects of statistical redundancy are not restricted to repeating deterministic sequences only. Rather, they can also be observed if probabilistic sequences of stimuli are used. Furthermore, learning is not only sensitive to unique transitions between consecutive stimuli, but it also takes conditional probabilities into account, up to the second order at least. Thus, statistical redundancy, as it is defined by information theory as redundancies of second and higher order, has been shown to be an important factor of implicit learning in SRT tasks.

● Relational Patterns in Serial Reaction Time Tasks

We turn now to the question of whether, aside from statistical redundancies, relational patterns are also used to reduce uncertainty in SRT tasks. Earlier, we referred to numerous studies that convincingly demonstrated the influence of relational patterns on learning stimulus as well as response sequences. Despite this overwhelming evidence, the potential effects of relational patterns have played no role in implicit learning research so far. Presumably, it is assumed that relational patterns must be explicitly detected to become effective and thus can be neglected in the context of implicit learning. However, there are several hints that even in studies on implicit learning, relational patterns were effective.

For example, Cleeremans and McClelland (1991, p. 240) asked their subjects, after completion of the SRT task, whether they had noticed any regularity in the way the stimulus moved on the screen. All subjects reported noticing that short sequences of alternating stimuli did occur frequently, and five of six subjects were able to specify that they had noticed two pairs of positions between which the alternating pattern was taking place. In a replication of the Nissen and Bullemer (1987) task with the repeating sequence (4231324321), there were 16 of 20 subjects who recalled spontaneously the regular subsequence 4321 (that is, the asterisk is moving from the rightmost to the leftmost position) when they were asked for substrings they eventually became aware of (Hoffmann & Koch, 1997). Perruchet et al. (1990) reported evidence that relational patterns might mediate learning, even if subjects do not explicitly refer to them. In their experiment, subjects had to respond to the locations of a target within four quadrants. In subsequences of five consecutive locations, the last three locations were perfectly predictable on the basis of the first two locations, corresponding to a set of rules. This task was originally introduced by Lewicki, Hill, and Bizot (1988) for demonstrating implicit rule learning. Learning of the rules was indeed indicated by a rule-specific acceleration of responses to the predictable locations in the course of training. However, Perruchet et al. analyzed the patterns of target movements that resulted from the rules (e.g., horizontal displacements or back and forth movements) and could show that the decrease of RTs corresponded to the frequencies with which these patterns occurred. They argued that subjects may not have learned any kind of rules but rather the frequencies of movement patterns.

Finally, it has been frequently reported that if subjects repeatedly execute a sequence of keystrokes that is systematically patterned, the interresponse times adapt to the respective pattern. For example, if a first pair of strokes is to be repeated before another pair has to be repeated and so on (abab cdcd . . .) the pairs are increasingly more quickly executed, whereas interresponse times between the pairs remain relatively long, especially long between the quadruples. Obviously, the systematicity of relations between the keystrokes is used in order to structure the control of their execution (Collard & Povel, 1982; Povel & Collard, 1982; Rosenbaum et al., 1983; Ziessler et al., 1990). Altogether, these observations point to at least the possibility that relational patterns in the stimulus and/or in the response sequences may affect learning in SRT tasks, even if learning is incidental and possibly even without awareness (cf. also Hartman, Knopman, & Nissen, 1989; Reed & Johnson, 1994).

Despite these various hints regarding potential effects of relational patterns on learning in SRT tasks, there is, to our knowledge, only one recent study that tried systematically to analyze these influences. In this study, Hoffmann and Sebald (1996) used the letters K, L, M, N, O, and P as stimuli and keystrokes with the index-, middle-, and ringfingers of both hands as responses in a standard SRT task. To impose relational patterns on the sequence of stimuli, the letters were presented in subsequences of three letters each corresponding to their alphabetic order: KLM MLK NOP PON KLM LMN MNO NOP. More precisely, the first alphabetic triple, KLM, was subsequently presented in reversed order, MLK. Then, the next alphabetic triple was presented and again was repeated in reversed order, NOP PON. Finally, four alphabetic triples followed whereby each triple moved one step further in the alphabet, KLM LMN MNO NOP. Correspondingly, a well-structured sequence of responses was introduced where the relational patterns were based on spatial instead of alphabetic adjacency. If one designates the response fingers from left to right with the digits 1, 2, 3, 4, 5, and 6, the well-structured response sequence was: 123 321 456 654 123 234 345 456. Again, a first and a second systematic triple were to be repeated in reversed order, followed by four systematic triples that "moved" from left to right by one position. Both the well-structured stimulus sequences and the well-structured response sequence were contrasted with irregular sequences that were constructed to match the statistical redundancies of the well-structured sequences. Furthermore, a quasi-random sequence of stimuli and responses was introduced where frequencies as well as conditional probabilities of occurrence were equalized.

The relational structures of the stimulus and the response sequences were orthogonally varied. To do so, in four groups of subjects, the stimulus response mappings were chosen in such a way that in the one case, the structured stimulus sequence (that is, KLM . . .) triggers either a structured (123 . . .) or an irregular response sequence (642 . . .) and in the other case, the irregular stimulus sequence (PNL . . .) triggers either a structured (123 . . .) or an irregular response sequence (642 . . .) as well. After an introductory training of two blocks with a quasirandom sequence, three experimental blocks followed where the variations of the relational structures of the stimulus and the response sequences were administered. Finally, the session ended with a last block, where a quasirandom sequence was presented again.

The main result of the experiment is presented in Figure 5.5. The data clearly indicate a strong effect of the relational patterns in the sequence of responses on learning: The decrease of RTs is steeper with patterned than with irregular response sequences. Moreover, a closer inspection of the interresponse times reveals that in the patterned sequences, responses are fast within the triples, and they increase by about 140 ms between the

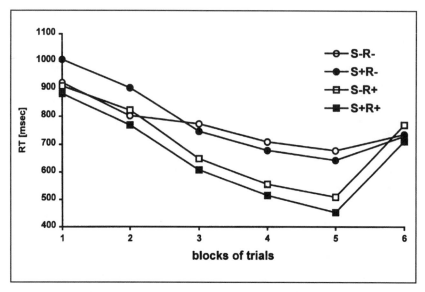

Figure 5.5. Mean choice reaction times as a function of the relational structure of the stimulus sequence (S+, S−) and the relational structure of the response sequence (R+, R−), plotted over block of trials. In Blocks 1, 2, and 6, quasirandom sequences were presented.
SOURCE: Adapted from Hoffmann & Sebald (1996).

triples. There is no such regularity of the RTs with respect to the same sequential positions in executing irregular response sequences. The authors conclude that the relational pattern in the response sequence supports the formation of motor programs that integrate the execution of three consecutive adjacent keystrokes each into one unit, making execution within the units fast and switches between the units relatively slow (cf. Keele, 1968, 1986; Rosenbaum et al., 1983; Shaffer, 1982).

In comparison, the effects of relational patterns in the stimulus sequence are much weaker and statistically not reliable. It would be premature to conclude that relational patterns in stimulus sequences do not affect sequential learning at all. For example, it might be that the alphabetic patterns used were not salient enough to become effective. Here is not the place, however, to discuss this issue in detail. Rather, it was the aim of this section to point out the influences relational patterns in the sequences of stimuli and responses can have on learning in SRT tasks. As already mentioned, it might be argued that these effects are of no relevance for the mechanisms of implicit learning because relational patterns may need explicit detection to become effective. In the Hoffmann and Sebald (1996) study all (except one) of the subjects who performed the structured response sequence were indeed aware of the repetitive nature of the sequences. But simply from the observation that relational patterns are mostly explicitly detected, one cannot deduce that they do not exert influence if they are not detected. Especially the consideration that relational patterns in response sequences may contribute to the formation of motor programs should give us enough reason for a careful experimental control of this variable.

● Temporal and Spatial Patterns in Serial Reaction Time Tasks

Patterns in space and time are subordinated factors in current research on implicit learning, simply because the spatial and temporal parameters of stimulus presentation were seldom varied. However, in all cases where they were varied, strong effects on learning have been found. In the following, we will present one example each for experimental demonstrations of the influence of temporal and spatial patterns on learning in SRT tasks.

Stadler (1993) investigated effects of variations of the time interval between a response and the presentation of the following stimulus (RSI) in a standard SRT task. In each block of trials, presentations of a repeating sequence alternated with presentations of a randomly generated sequence of the same length. Additionally, three different RSI schedules were used. In the first condition, the RSIs were kept constant throughout the experiment, so that there were no demarcations of the beginning and the end of the repeating and the random sequences, that is, they ran together. In the second condition, the RSIs at the end of each repeating sequence and of each random sequence were remarkably longer than elsewhere (2000 ms vs. 400 ms), so that the beginning and end of the sequences were marked by an inserted pause. In the last condition, pauses were randomly inserted so that different subsequences were marked across consecutive cycles. A similar manipulation was used in the serial recall experiment by Bower and Winzenz (1969) already mentioned above. The reader may remember that the improvement of recall due to repetitions of a sequence completely vanished in this study if the sequence was differently parsed across repetitions. In comparison, the present experiment was designed in order to explore the issues of whether implicit learning appears at all if the repetitions of a sequence are intervened by random sequences and whether it is influenced by the way the sequences are parsed by interspersed pauses.

The results of both this and another experiment clearly indicate implicit learning of the repeating sequence, although it is alternated with random sequences. Furthermore, the variation of the way in which pauses were interspersed into the sequence had a clear impact on the amount of learning. The repetition of the repeating sequence led to a much stronger decrease of RTs if the sequence was consistently marked by pauses. If the sequence was instead randomly parsed into different subsequences each time it occurred, learning was reduced but not eliminated. If there were no pauses at all, the repetition effect was in between. Thus, if one considers the homogeneous presentation of stimuli without any pauses as the baseline condition, one can claim that a consistent parsing of the sequences by pauses facilitates learning and an inconsistent parsing reduces learning.

The second experiment to be mentioned here demonstrates effects of spatial instead of temporal parsing. The experiment was reported by Ziessler (1995). The subjects performed an SRT task with four different letters as stimuli and keystrokes by the index and middle fingers of both hands as responses. Again, a sequence of six letters was cyclically presented. If one designates the letters that were assigned to the response fingers from left to right with A, B, C, and D (in actuality, other letters were used; this does not matter here, however), the two repeating sequences used were ACACBD and DBDBCA. The critical variation regards the spatial presentation of the letters. In Condition 1, the letters were presented at a fixed location in the center of the screen. In Condition 2, there were six horizontally aligned locations on the screen. The first letter of the repeating sequence was presented at the leftmost location. The second letter at the next right location, the third letter at the next right location, and so on until the last letter of the sequence was presented at the rightmost location. Then, with the beginning of a new cycle, the presentation jumped back to the leftmost position with the presentation of the first letter and so on. Thus, like pauses, the jump to the leftmost position marked the end as well as the beginning of the repeating sequence. Condition 3 was identical to the second one except that the presentation of the sequence started at the rightmost position, so that the jump back to the leftmost location always appeared with the second letter of the repeating sequence throughout the experiment. It should be noted that in both conditions the jump parsed the continuously running repeating sequence into consistent strings. The strings differ from each other, however. In Condition 2, the jump suggests the repeating string ACACBD, for example, whereas in Condition 3, the substring CACBDA is cyclically presented from left to right. It should also be noted that in all conditions, the subjects perform exactly the same response sequences.

Learning of the repeating sequence was assessed by the decrease of RTs in the course of training. The data reveal that learning was indeed influenced by the way the response signals were presented. In Condition 2, learning was fastest. In Condition 1, where the letters did not "move" on the screen, learning was somewhat decelerated, but the same RT level was approached at the end of training as in Condition 2. In Condition 3, learning was further decelerated, and the RTs approached an asymptotic level, which was on average about 130 ms above those of the other two conditions. To account for these effects, Ziessler (1995) analyzed in detail the interresponse times across the six serial positions of the repeating sequences. In Conditions 1 and 2, the RT profiles clearly indicate a parsing of the sequences in three strings of two events each, which are easy to rehearse as well as easy to perform: A first pair of stimuli/keystrokes is repeated, followed by second pair ((AC AC) BD)). In contrast, in Condition 3 the profile hardly specifies any special parsing of the sequence. If at all, a parsing into two strings of three events each is indicated (CAC BDA). The results suggest that the locational pattern of stimulus presentation primarily influences the way in which the repeating sequence is parsed into consistent substrings. If a parsing into substrings is advanced that is easy to perform and easy to repeat, learning is accelerated. If, however, the locational pattern distracts subjects from an appropriate parsing, learning is slowed down.

Both experiments demonstrate the strong influence that locational as well as temporal patterns of stimulus presentation have on the parsing of the event sequences in SRT tasks. This is by no means surprising, not only because effects of locational and temporal patterns on learning artificial miniature languages, that is, on learning grammatical restrictions, is a well-established fact (Morgan, 1986; Morgan & Newport, 1981; Morgan, Meier, & Newport, 1987; Riegle, 1969; Weinert, 1990), but also because temporal and spatial proximity simply *are* the most obvious factors for the spontaneous structuring of our phenomenal world in general. What is of importance, however, is that parsing does interact that strongly with learning. This gives support for a renaissance of the classic consideration that sequential learning includes a process of parsing or chunking sequences of events, if possible, into related substrings (e.g., Hoffmann, 1996; Lashley, 1951; Miller, 1956; Servan-Schreiber & Anderson, 1990; Stadler, 1993, 1995).

CONCLUSIONS

It was the aim of the present chapter to call attention to the diversity of components of structure that may contribute to implicit learning. We did so in reference to one of the most frequently used paradigms in implicit learning research, the SRT task, which we believe can be regarded as being representative of other experimental settings in implicit learning research as well. Covariation learning can be considered as being to a certain extent a serial learning task that is reduced to short sequences of a stimulus (the event), a response (its classification), and a next stimulus (the accuracy feedback). In process-control tasks, subjects generate successive process states by successive control acts, and learning refers to regularities in the joined S-R-S sequences in the same way as in SRT tasks (cf. Buchner & Funke, 1993, for a formal description of equivalency of process-control and SRT tasks). Finally, that learning in SRT tasks is comparable to grammar learning is evident, because in both cases, learning refers to redundancies in event sequences. Thus, we believe that the structural components that are involved in SRT tasks represent the totality of components that contribute to learning in the other settings, too.

The various experimental settings that are used in implicit learning research are not only comparable with regard to their structural components but also with regard to the demands they entail: In all settings the required performance can be improved by predicting forthcoming events and/or behavioral demands. Recall the examples mentioned in the introduction. The classification of a brain scan is improved if the intelligence can be predicted on the basis of the graphic appearance; the control of the sugar factory is improved if the effect of a currently chosen number of employed workers on the output of the factory can be predicted; the recollection of a grammatically generated letter string is improved if, from a part of the string, the remaining letters can be predicted; and finally, the responses to sequentially presented stimuli are accelerated if forthcoming events can be predicted.

In general, the need for predictability can be regarded as being a basic learning motive. For example, Tolman (1949) argued that latent learning involves the formation of so-called field expectancies, so that "upon the comprehension of a first group of stimuli [the animal] becomes prepared for the further to come groups of stimuli" (p. 145). Berlyne (1950, 1958) introduced a need for exploration, White (1959) discussed an instinct to master, and Hoffmann (1993b) argued that a need for anticipation is an indispensable presupposition of any behavioral adaptation. An elaboration of this motivational background is beyond the scope of this chapter (cf. Hoffmann, 1993b). We simply want to state here that the learning mechanisms that are analyzed under the topic of implicit learning are presumably just those mechanisms by which organisms reduce uncertainty by a steady adaptation of expectations about what might happen to what really happens.

Reliable predictions require reliable relations between events, that is, they require structure. There is no predictability without structure. We have argued that different types of structural components can be distinguished. There are structures that refer to relations between the mere occurrence of events, structures that refer to significant relations between individual events, and, finally, structures that refer to the spatial and temporal distribution of events. In the present chapter, we have referred to ample evidence that all these structural components are indeed used to improve performance. As we would like to claim now, they are used to make the predictions on which the performance rests more reliably. Consequently, if one is interested in assessing the impact of only one of these components on learning, all other components should be carefully controlled, which has so far seldom been considered (cf. also Reed & Johnson, 1994; Shanks & St. John, 1994).

However, the matter is still more intricate, because not only are there various structural components to be distinguished but also various "events" to which these structural components refer. We have already pointed to the fact that in SRT tasks, the sequential structure is given in the sequence of stimuli as well as in the sequence of responses, and it is still an unsolved issue whether learning is based primarily on the redundancies in the stimulus or in the response sequences (e.g., Cohen et al, 1990; Howard et al., 1992; Mayr, 1996; Nattkemper & Prinz, 1993, in press; Willingham et al., 1989). For example, Figure 5.3 presents the structure of the repeating stimulus sequence used by Nissen and Bullemer (1987) in terms of a movement trajectory over the screen. The corresponding sequence of keystrokes is structured as well. In the first seven strokes of the 10-trial sequence, the hands alternate as explained above. Learning may refer to one or the other structure or to both. Also, not only do relations between successive stimuli and successive responses establish structures, but relations between stimuli and responses do as well. For example, in order to account for contradictory evidence in favor of and opposed to learning of response sequences in an SRT task, Willingham et al. (1989) concluded that "what is learned may be thought of as a series of condition-action statements mapping stimuli onto responses" (p. 1058). Whereas Willingham et al. emphasized by this conclusion the importance of successive S-R mappings, Ziessler (1994, 1995) referred to the importance of consistent R-S mappings. He reported data that convincingly suggest that implicit learning can be based solely on associations between responses and their outcomes. In summary, the relations between successive stimuli (S-S), between successive responses (R-R), between successive stimulus response mappings (S-R), and between responses and their outcomes (R-S) may all cause redundancy, and all of them seem to be used by human subjects to improve predictions.

Against this variety of relations among a variety of events that may each contribute to learning, the simple dichotomies that currently dominate the discussions about implicit learning, as, for example, between attentional and nonattentional learning (Curran & Keele, 1993), between associative and hierarchical learning (Cohen et al., 1990), between one-process and two-process accounts (Frensch et al., 1994), between sensory or motor learning (e.g., Howard et al., 1992; Willingham et al., 1989), or between predicting and clustering (Cleeremans & McClelland, 1991; Servan-Schreiber & Anderson, 1990) appear at best to be oversimplifications of the true state of affairs. Rather than setting one simplification against another, a more sophisticated research strategy seems to be required to meet the complexity of the matter in question. First, we need a careful analysis of the learning effects of the various structural relations between stimuli and/or responses in isolation, that is, under conditions where other possible influences on learning are strictly controlled. Second, we should analyze to what extent the effects of the different components are modulated by intentional and attentional circumstances of the task. In other words, we need to investigate which of the different components automatically contribute to learning and which components require control to become effective. We can hope that such systematic research will then let us understand the mechanisms on which the reduction of uncertainty are finally based.

REFERENCES

Aborn, M., & Rubenstein, H. (1952). Information theory and immediate recall. *Journal of Experimental Psychology, 44,* 260-266.

Attneave, F. (1959). *Applications of information theory to psychology.* New York: Holt, Rinehart, & Winston.

Berlyne, D. E. (1950). Novelty and curiosity as determinants of exploratory behavior. *British Journal of Psychology, 41,* 68-80.

Berlyne, D. E. (1957). Uncertainty and conflict: A point of contact between information-theory and behavior-theory concepts. *Psychological Review, 64,* 329-339.

Berlyne, D. E. (1958). The present status of research on exploratory and related behavior. *Journal of Individual Psychology, 14,* 121-126.

Berry, D. C., & Broadbent, D. E. (1984). On the relationship between task performance and associated verbalizable knowledge. *Quarterly Journal of Experimental Psychology, 36A,* 209-231.

Berry, D. C., & Dienes, Z. (1993). *Implicit learning: Theoretical and empirical issues.* Hove, UK: Lawrence Erlbaum.

Boring, E. G. (1942). *Sensation and perception in the history of experimental psychology.* New York: Appleton.

Bower, G. H., & Winzenz, D. (1969). Group structure, coding, and memory for digit series. *Journal of Experimental Psychology, Monograph Supplement, 80,* 1-17.

Buchner, A., & Funke, J. (1993). Finite-state automata: Dynamic task environments in problem-solving research. *Quarterly Journal of Experimental Psychology, 46,* 83-118.

Buffart, H., & Leeuwenberg, E. (1983). Structural information theory. In H. G. Geissler, H. Buffart, E. Leeuwenberg, & V. Sarris (Eds.), *Modern issues in perception* (pp. 48-74). Amsterdam: North-Holland.

Buffart, H., Leeuwenberg, E., & Restle, F. (1981). Coding theory of visual pattern completion. *Journal of Experimental Psychology: Human Perception and Performance, 7,* 241-274.

Cleeremans, A. (1993). *Mechanisms of implicit learning.* Cambridge: MIT Press.

Cleeremans, A., & McClelland, J. L. (1991). Learning the structure of event sequences. *Journal of Experimental Psychology: General, 120,* 235-253.

Cohen, A., Ivry, R., & Keele, S. W. (1990). Attention and structure in sequence learning. *Journal of Experimental Psychology: Learning, Memory, and Cognition, 16,* 17-30.

Collard, R., & Povel, D. (1982). Theory of serial pattern production: Tree traversal. *Psychological Review, 89,* 693-707.

Crossman, E.R.F.W. (1953). Entropy and choice time: The effect of frequency unbalance on choice-response. *Quarterly Journal of Experimental Psychology, 5*, 41-51.

Curran, T., & Keele, S. W. (1993). Attentional and nonattentional forms of sequence learning. *Journal of Experimental Psychology: Learning, Memory, and Cognition, 19*, 189-202.

Frensch, P. A., Buchner, A., & Lin, J. (1994). Implicit learning of unique and ambiguous serial transitions in the presence and absence of a distractor task. *Journal of Experimental Psychology. Learning, Memory, and Cognition, 20*, 567-584.

Frensch, P. A., & Miner, C. S. (1994). Effects of presentation rate and individual differences in short-term memory capacity on an indirect measure of serial learning. *Memory & Cognition, 22*, 95-110.

Garner, W. R. (1962). *Uncertainty and structure as psychological concepts.* New York: John Wiley.

Hartman, E. B. (1954). The influence of practice and pitch-distance between tones on the absolute identification of pitch. *American Journal of Psychology, 67*, 1-14.

Hartman, M., Knopman, D. S., & Nissen, M. J. (1989). Implicit learning of new verbal associations. *Journal of Experimental Psychology: Learning, Memory, and Cognition, 15*, 1070-1082.

Hasher, L., & Zacks, R. T. (1984). Automatic processing of fundamental information: The case of frequency of occurrence. *American Psychologist, 39*, 1372-1388.

Hick, W. E. (1952). On the rate of gain of information. *Quarterly Journal of Experimental Psychology, 4*, 11-26.

Hoffmann, J. (1979). Klassifizierung und Übertragbarkeit semantischer Relationen im menschlichen Gedächtnis. In M. Bierwisch (Ed.), *Psychologische Effekte sprachlicher Strukturkomponenten* (pp. 145-190). Berlin: Akademie Verlag.

Hoffmann, J. (1993a). Unbewußtes Lernen—eine besondere Lernform? *Psychologische Rundschau, 44*, 75-89.

Hoffmann, J. (1993b). *Vorhersage und Erkenntnis: Die Funktion von Antizipationen in der menschlichen Verhaltenssteuerung und Wahrnehmung.* Göttingen: Hogrefe.

Hoffmann, J. (1996). Sequentielles Lernen. In J. Hoffmann & W. Kintsch (Eds.), *Enzyklopädie der Psychologie:* Vol. 2.8: *Lernen* (pp. 237-274). Göttingen: Hogrefe.

Hoffmann, J., & Koch, I. (1997). S-R compatibility and sequential learning in the serial reaction time task. *Psychological Research, 60*, 87-97.

Hoffmann, J., & Sebald, A. (1996). Reiz- und Reaktionsmuster in seriellen Wahlreaktionen. *Zeitschrift für experimentelle Psychologie, 63*(1), 40-68.

Holyoak, K. J., Koh, K., & Nisbett, R. E. (1989). A theory of conditioning: Inductive learning within rule-based default hierarchies. *Psychological Review, 96,* 315-340.

Howard, J. H., Mutter, S. A., & Howard, D. V. (1992). Serial pattern learning by event observation. *Journal of Experimental Psychology: Learning, Memory, and Cognition, 18,* 1029-1039.

Hyman, R. (1953). Stimulus information as a determinant of reaction time. *Journal of Experimental Psychology, 45,* 188-196.

Johnson, N. (1965). The psychological reality of phrase-structure rules. *Journal of Verbal Learning and Verbal Behavior, 4,* 469-475.

Jones, M. R. (1976). Time, our lost dimension: Toward a new theory of perception, attention, and memory. *Psychological Review, 83,* 323-355.

Jones, M. R., Boltz, M., & Kidd, G. (1982). Controlled attending as a function of melodic and temporal context. *Perception & Psychophysics, 32,* 211-218.

Jones, M. R., Summerell, L., & Marshburn, E. (1987). Recognizing melodies: A dynamic interpretation. *The Quarterly Journal of Experimental Psychology, 39A,* 89-121.

Keele, S. W. (1968). Movement control in skilled motor performance. *Psychological Bulletin, 70,* 387-403.

Keele, S. W. (1986). Motor control. In K. R. Boff, L. Kaufmann, & J. P. Thomas (Eds.), *Handbook of perception and performance: Vol. 2. Cognitive processes and performance.* New York: John Wiley.

Keele, S. W., & Jennings, P. J. (1992). Attention in the representation of sequence: Experiment and theory. *Human Movement Studies, 11,* 125-138.

Kintsch, W. (1971). Models for free recall and recognition. In D. A. Norman (Ed.), *Models of human memory.* New York: Academic Press.

Kintsch, W. (1972). Notes on the structure of semantic memory. In E. Tulving & W. Donaldson (Eds.), *Organization of memory.* New York: Academic Press.

Klemmer, E. T., & Muller, P. F. (1953). The rate of handling information. Key-pressing responses to light patterns. *HFORL Memo report,* No. 34.

Klix, F. (1971). *Information und Verhalten.* Berlin: Verlag der Wissenschaften.

Klix, F., & Krause, B. (1969). Zur Definition des Begriffs "Struktur," seiner Eigenschaften und Darstellungsmöglichkeiten in der Experimentalpsychologie. *Zeitschrift für Psychologie, 176,* 22-54.

Koffka, K. (1935). *Principles of gestalt psychology.* New York: Harcourt.

Köhler, W. (1929). *Gestalt psychology.* New York: Liveright.

Lashley, K. S. (1951). The problem of serial order in behavior. In L. A. Jeffress (Ed.), *Cerebral mechanisms in behavior.* New York: John Wiley.

Leeuwenberg, E. (1969). Quantitative specification of information in sequential patterns. *Psychological Review, 76,* 216-220.

Leeuwenberg, E. (1971). A perceptual coding language for visual and auditory patterns. *American Journal of Psychology, 84,* 307-349.

Leeuwenberg, E., & Buffart, H. (1983). An outline of coding theory, summary of some related experiments. In H. G. Geissler, H. Buffart, E. Leeuwenberg, & V. Sarris (Eds.), *Modern issues in perception* (pp. 25-47). Amsterdam: North-Holland.

Lewicki, P. (1986). Processing information about covariation that cannot be articulated. *Journal of Experimental Psychology: Learning, Memory, and Cognition, 12,* 135-146.

Lewicki, P., Hill, T., & Bizot, E. (1988). Acquisition of procedural knowledge about a pattern of stimuli that cannot be articulated. *Cognitive Psychology, 20,* 24-37.

Lewicki, P., Hill, T., & Sasaki, I. (1989). Self-perpetuating development of encoding biases. *Journal of Experimental Psychology: General, 118,* 323-337.

Mandler, G. (1985). *Cognitive psychology. An essay in cognitive science.* Hillsdale, NJ: Lawrence Erlbaum.

Mayr, U. (1996). Spatial attention and implicit sequence learning: Evidence for independent learning of spatial and nonspatial sequences. *Journal of Experimental Psychology: Learning, Memory, and Cognition, 22,* 350-364.

Metzger, W. (1975). *Die Gesetze des Sehens.* Frankfurt am Main: Kramer.

Miller, G. A. (1953). What is information measurement? *American Psychologist, 8,* 3-11.

Miller, G. A. (1956). The magical number seven, plus or minus two: Some limits on our capacity for processing information. *Psychological Review, 63,* 81-97.

Miller, G. A. (1958). Free recall of redundant strings of letters. *Journal of Experimental Psychology, 56,* 485-491.

Miller, G. A., & Frick, F. C. (1949). Statistical behavioristics and sequences of responses. *Psychological Review, 56,* 311-324.

Miller, G. A., & Selfridge, J. A. (1950). Verbal context and the recall of meaningful material. *American Journal of Psychology, 63,* 176-185.

Morgan, J. L. (1986). *From simple input to complex grammar.* Cambridge: MIT Press.

Morgan, J. L., Meier, R. P., & Newport, E. L. (1987). Structural packaging in the input to language learning: Contributions of prosodic and morphological marking of phrases to the acquisition of language. *Cognitive Psychology, 19,* 498-550.

Morgan, J. L., & Newport, E. L. (1981). The role of constituent structure in the induction of an artificial language. *Journal of Verbal Learning and Verbal Behavior, 20,* 67-85.

Nattkemper, D., & Prinz, W. (1993). Processing structured event sequences. In C. Bundesen & A. Larsen (Eds.), *Proceedings of the sixth conference of the European Society for Cognitive Psychology* (pp. 21-22). Copenhagen: European Society for Cognitive Psychology.

Nattkemper, D., & Prinz, W. (in press). Stimulus and response anticipation in a serial reaction task. *Psychological Research*.

Neisser, U. (1967). *Cognitive psychology*. New York: Appleton.

Nissen, M. J., & Bullemer, P. (1987). Attentional requirements of learning: Evidence from performance measures. *Cognitive Psychology, 19*, 1-32.

Palmer, S. (1977). Hierarchical structure in perceptual representation. *Cognitive Psychology, 9*, 441-474.

Perruchet, P., & Amorim, M.-A. (1992). Conscious knowledge and changes in performance in sequence learning: Evidence against dissociation. *Journal of Experimental Psychology: Learning, Memory, and Cognition, 18*, 785-800.

Perruchet, P., Gallego, J., & Savy, I. (1990). A critical reappraisal of the evidence for unconscious abstraction of deterministic rules in complex experimental situations. *Cognitive Psychology, 22*, 493-516.

Pollack, I. (1952). The information of elementary auditory displays. *Journal of the Acoustical Society of America, 24*, 745-749.

Povel, D. J., & Collard, R. (1982). Structural factors in patterned finger tapping. *Acta Psychologica, 52*, 107-124.

Quastler, H. (1953). *Essays on the use of information theory in biology*. Urbana: University of Illinois Press.

Reber, A. S. (1967). Implicit learning of artificial grammars. *Journal of Verbal Learning and Verbal Behavior, 6*, 855-863.

Reber, A. S. (1969). Transfer of syntactic structure in synthetic languages. *Journal of Experimental Psychology, 81*, 115-119.

Reber, A. S. (1976). Implicit learning of synthetic languages: The role of instructional set. *Journal of Experimental Psychology: Human Learning and Memory, 2*, 88-94.

Reber, A. S. (1989). Implicit learning and tacit knowledge. *Journal of Experimental Psychology: General, 118*, 219-235.

Reber, A. S., & Allen, R. (1978). Analogic and abstraction strategies in synthetic grammar learning: A functionalist interpretation. *Cognition, 6*, 189-221.

Reed, J., & Johnson, P. (1994). Assessing implicit learning with indirect tests: Determining what is learned about sequence structure. *Journal of Experimental Psychology: Learning, Memory, and Cognition, 20*, 585-594.

Rescorla, R. A. (1988). Pavlovian conditioning, it's not what you think it is. *American Psychologist, 43*, 151-160.

Restle, F. (1970). Theory of serial pattern learning: Structural trees. *Psychological Review, 77*, 481-495.

Restle, F., & Brown, E. R. (1970a). Organization of serial pattern learning. In G. H. Bower (Ed.), *Psychology of learning and motivation* (Vol. 4, pp. 249-332). New York: Academic Press.

Restle, F., & Brown, E. R. (1970b). Serial pattern learning. *Journal of Experimental Psychology, 83*, 120-125.

Riegle, E. M. (1969). *Some perceptual characteristics of phrase structure rule learning.* Unpublished doctoral dissertation, University of Minnesota.

Rosenbaum, D. A., Kenny, S. B., & Derr, M. A. (1983). Hierarchical control of rapid movement sequences. *Journal of Experimental Psychology: Human Perception and Performance, 9,* 86-102.

Rubenstein, H., & Aborn, M. (1954). Immediate recall as a function of degree of organization and length of study period. *Journal of Experimental Psychology, 48,* 146-152.

Seger, C. A. (1994). Implicit learning. *Psychological Bulletin, 115,* 163-196.

Servan-Schreiber, E., & Anderson, J. R. (1990). Learning artificial grammars with competitive chunking. *Journal of Experimental Psychology: Learning, Memory, and Cognition, 16,* 592-608.

Shaffer, L. H. (1982). Rhythm and timing in skill. *Psychological Review, 89,* 109-122.

Shanks, D. R., Green, R. E., & Kolodny, J. (1994). A critical examination of the evidence for nonconscious (implicit) learning. In C. Umiltà & M. Moscovitch (Eds.), *Attention and performance XV: Conscious and nonconscious information processing.* Cambridge: MIT Press.

Shanks, D. R., & St. John, M. F. (1994). Characteristics of dissociable learning systems. *Behavioral and Brain Sciences, 17,* 367-395.

Shannon, C. E., & Weaver, W. (1949). *The mathematical theory of communication.* Urbana: University of Illinois Press.

Simon, H. A., & Kotovski, K. (1963). Human acquisition of concepts for sequential patterns. *Psychological Review, 70,* 534-546.

Stadler, M. A. (1992). Statistical structure and implicit serial learning. *Journal of Experimental Psychology: Learning, Memory, and Cognition, 18,* 318-327.

Stadler, M. A. (1993). Implicit serial learning: Questions inspired by Hebb (1961). *Memory & Cognition, 21*(6), 819-827.

Stadler, M. A. (1995). Role of attention in implicit learning. *Journal of Experimental Psychology: Learning, Memory, and Cognition, 21,* 674-685.

Tolman, E. C. (1949). There is more than one kind of learning. *Psychological Review, 56,* 144-155.

Treisman, A. (1982). Perceptual grouping and attention in visual search for objects. *Journal of Experimental Psychology: Human Perception and Performance, 8,* 194-214.

Underwood, B. J., Shaughnessy, J. J., & Zimmermann, J. (1974). The locus of the retention differences associated with degree of hierarchical conceptual structure. *Journal of Experimental Psychology, 102,* 850-862.

Weinert, S. (1990). *Zum Erwerb sprachanaloger Regeln: Lernmechanismen und Einflußfaktoren.* Dissertation, Fakultät für Psychologie und Sportwissenschaft, Bielefeld.

Welford, A. T. (1976). *Skilled performance: Perceptual and motor skills.* Glenview, IL: Scott Foresman.

Wertheimer, M. (1923). Untersuchungen zur Lehre von der Gestalt II. *Psychologische Forschung, 4,* 301-350.

White, R. W. (1959). Motivation reconsidered: The concept of competence. *Psychological Review, 66,* 297-333.

Wilkes, A. L., & Kennedy, R. A. (1970). The relative accessibility of list items within different pause-defined groups. *Journal of Verbal Learning and Verbal Behavior, 9,* 197-201.

Willingham, D. B., Nissen, M. J., & Bullemer, P. (1989). On the development of procedural knowledge. *Journal of Experimental Psychology: Learning, Memory, and Cognition, 15,* 1047-1060.

Zacks, R. T., Hasher, L., & Sanft, H. (1982). Automatic encoding of event frequency: Further findings. *Journal of Experimental Psychology: Learning, Memory, and Cognition, 8,* 106-116.

Ziessler, M. (1994). The impact of motor responses on serial learning. *Psychological Research, 57,* 30-41.

Ziessler, M. (1995). *Die Einheit von Wahrnehmung und Motorik.* Frankfurt am Main: Peter Lang.

Ziessler, M., Hänel, K., & Hoffmann, J. (1988). Die Programmierung struktureller Eigenschaften von Bewegungsfolgen. *Zeitschrift für Psychologie, 196,* 371-388.

Ziessler, M., Hänel, K., & Sachse, D. (1990). The programming of structural properties of movement sequences. *Psychological Research, 52,* 347-358.

6

Artificial Grammar Learning and the Mere Exposure Effect

Emotional Preference Tasks and the
Implicit Learning Process

●————————————————————

Louis Manza
Diane Zizak
Arthur S. Reber

The past decade has seen a virtual explosion of research concerning the similarities and differences between implicit thought processes, which are relatively passive and automatic, occurring primarily outside the realm of conscious awareness, and explicit processes, which are decidedly more conscious and attention-demanding (Dienes, Broadbent, & Berry, 1991; Jacoby, 1988; Jacoby, Toth, & Yonelinas, 1993; Joordens & Merikle, 1993; Mandler, 1989; Reber, 1989; Seger, 1994). One issue of critical importance that has continually surfaced in discussions surrounding these topics concerns the nature of the tasks that have been used to measure implicit and explicit learning (Reber, 1989; Seger, 1994; Shanks & St. John, 1994). Insofar as explicit thought is concerned, establishing a conscious cognitive ability has been relatively easy to demonstrate;

AUTHORS' NOTE: We would like to thank Robert Bornstein, Michael Stadler, and Bob Mathews for helpful commentary on a previous draft of this chapter. Please address all correspondence to Louis Manza, Department of Psychology, Lebanon Valley College, Annville, PA 17003.

have an individual attend to some stimuli, then test their knowledge of the original stimuli with a task that requires them to explicitly refer back to the initial study episode (Jacoby, 1991; Schacter, 1989; Schacter & Graf, 1986; Tulving, 1983). The controversy here has primarily focused on whether or not abilities deemed to be implicit are indeed occurring outside of conscious awareness. Within the framework of implicit learning processes, the task that has raised the most controversy has been the artificial grammar-learning task.

THE "CONTROVERSY" OF
ARTIFICIAL GRAMMAR LEARNING

Artificial grammar learning essentially involves presenting subjects with a set of rule-governed stimuli for initial observation, although the nature and/or existence of the rule system underlying the stimuli is typically not mentioned to subjects during this initial presentation. Following this task, subjects are informed as to the existence of the rule system (although no actual rules are provided) and are then typically presented additional, but novel, grammar-generated stimuli and asked to decide whether or not these additional items conform to the structure of the grammar. Because subjects (a) are not asked to provide explicit rationales for their decisions, (b) frequently fail to consciously report any valid rules of the grammar, and (c) must rely on generalizations from study task items to complete this classification task at above-chance levels, successful above-chance performance on this task is taken as an indicator of implicit learning ability (Reber, 1989). However, others have suggested that the learning that is occurring during the rule-decision task is moderated by conscious forces, as the initial exposure to the grammar involves conscious attention, and subjects are aware of the existence of the grammar at the time of their rule-based classification decisions (Dulany, Carlson, & Dewey, 1984; Perruchet & Pacteau, 1990). In addition, one of the primary criteria that has recently been offered to distinguish implicit from explicit processes suggests that the test of one's knowledge should not make reference to the previous study episode if the learning that is said to be demonstrated during the task is to be considered implicit (Schacter & Graf, 1986). Fortunately, a possible modification of the artificial grammar-learning task does exist and lies within a procedure that yields what is referred to as a mere exposure effect (Bornstein, 1989).

THE MERE EXPOSURE EFFECT:
BASICS AND EXTENSIONS

The mere exposure effect is defined as an increased affect toward a stimulus that is a result of nonreinforced, repeated exposure to the stimulus (Bornstein, 1989; Bornstein & D'Agostino, 1992; Seamon, Williams, Crowley, Kim, Langer, Orne, & Wishengrad, 1995). The experiment that brought the mere exposure effect into the realm of modern psychology was conducted by Zajonc (1968, Experiment 1). In this experiment, participants were exposed to nonsense words at frequencies of 0 to 25 presentations each; following each exposure, subjects had to rate each stimulus on a 7-point scale on the degree to which the stimulus suggested "good" or "bad" affect. The results indicated that a positive relationship existed between the mean goodness rating and the frequency of stimulus exposure.

Since this seminal investigation, the mere exposure effect has been explored in over 200 investigations (Bornstein, 1989) using additional stimuli, such as line drawings (Stang & O'Connell, 1974), Chinese ideographs (Saegert & Jellison, 1970), and polygons (Hamid, 1973) to support the mere exposure effect. In addition, other studies in this vein have involved the subliminal (e.g., 1-5 ms) presentation of stimuli, followed by affective judgments of old and new items. In support of the mere exposure effect, these investigations have also found that increased exposure results in a greater level of affect for exposed stimuli compared to novel items, despite the fact that subjects are not consciously aware of their initial exposure (Bornstein & D'Agostino, 1992; Bornstein, Leone, & Galley, 1987; Kunst-Wilson & Zajonc, 1980; Mandler, Nakamura, & Van Zandt, 1987). These investigations connect to the current dilemma in artificial grammar learning, because the rating task used in mere exposure experiments seemingly satisfies Schacter and Graf's (1986) criteria that a measure of implicit cognition should not refer to a previous study episode; one does not necessarily need to think back to previous stimuli to decide how much they like a particular stimulus. Consequently, if the theoretical foundation of the mere exposure effect (i.e., repeated exposure to stimuli creating increased affect for said stimuli in relation to novel stimuli) could be applied to artificial grammar learning, the data obtained in such investigations could provide some clarity in the debate concerning the nature of implicit learning.

Such an approach was initially attempted by Gordon and Holyoak (1983), who merged existing research on the mere exposure effect with implicit learning. One goal here was to determine if the emotional preferences for certain types of stimuli that individuals acquire in a variety of laboratory and real-world settings would generalize to the artificial grammar learning task. Following initial exposure to artificial grammar-generated stimuli, Gordon and Holyoak had subjects rate the degree to which they liked grammar-generated items on a scale ranging from 1 to 6 (with higher numbers indicating positive degrees of affect and lower numbers indicating negative degrees of affect). The logic behind using the liking rating task as a measure of implicit learning was twofold. If (a) subjects are detecting differences between items that do and do not conform to the structure of the grammar, and, therefore, developing a preference for one stimulus type over another, and (b) the primary principle of the mere exposure effect holds true, then such discrimination ability may be evidenced by subjects reporting higher ratings for items they are more familiar with (items that conform to the rule structure) compared to ones they are not familiar with (items that violate the structure of the grammar). Remember, however, that such a result would be extending the mere exposure effect and showing how preferences emerge from more than strict familiarity, as these test items are not identical to study items; they are similar in the sense that they are generated from the same rule system as study items and therefore share structural but not identical surface-based information with training items. Assuming that the two item types do not possess any inherent likability that would lead to the aforementioned rating differential, using such a task as a measure of implicit learning ability could also be seen as a valid assessment of nonconscious cognition, as subjects are never made aware of the existence of the rule structure underlying stimuli, and explicit recollection of the initial study episode would not be necessary to provide emotion-based ratings of test stimuli.

Supporting these postulations, Gordon and Holyoak (1983) found that subjects provided significantly higher liking ratings to novel items that conformed to the structure of the grammar (M rating = 4.41), compared to those items that violated the structure of the grammar (M rating = 3.96). Being that these results supported the aforementioned logic behind using the liking task to assess implicit learning, this study set the stage for future investigations into the validity of the liking task as a measure of implicit learning and as a means to investigate the emergence of affect-based preferences. However, for unknown reasons, Gordon and Holyoak's finding did not have an impact on the implicit learning field until recently.

Using Gordon and Holyoak's (1983) work as a benchmark, recent work has attempted to study implicit learning within the context of the mere exposure effect. What follows is a review of some of the work, in our respective labs, that has dealt with this issue. However, being that much of the work to be described shares various methodological elements, a brief review of the liking task-oriented artificial grammar-learning procedure is in order.

OVERVIEW OF THE AFFECT-BASED
ARTIFICIAL GRAMMAR-LEARNING TASK

The entire artificial grammar-learning procedure, as we have conceptualized it, consists of several different tasks. Initially, subjects are informed that the experiment they will participate in is nothing more than a simple memory investigation. Subjects are then presented with a set of stimuli (e.g., typically 15 to 20 individual letter sequences consisting of three to eight elements each) that they are asked to attend to and commit to memory. At this time, subjects are typically not aware that the stimuli they are studying are generated by a complex rule system (the artificial grammar), such as the one depicted in Figure 6.1. For this study task, the complete stimulus set typically contains exemplars covering all state-to-state transitions of the grammar, providing the subject with exposure to all of the rules of the grammar, albeit in an indirect fashion. The processes said to be occurring here are concurrent; while subjects are explicitly learning the symbols of the stimulus set, they are also acquiring the underlying rules of the grammar in an automatic, implicit fashion.

Once the study task has been completed, subjects are presented with a novel set of 50 to 75 stimuli generated from the same grammar as study task items. As with the study task, no mention is made as to the existence of the grammar. Half of these stimuli are referred to as *grammatical* items (as they conform to the structure of the grammar), whereas the remaining items contain a violation of the structure of the grammar (a violation is typically defined as a symbol, e.g., a letter, appearing in a position not possible according to the rules of the grammar) and are referred to as *nongrammatical* items. Each item is presented individually, with the subjects' task being to provide an emotion-based liking rating for each stimulus.

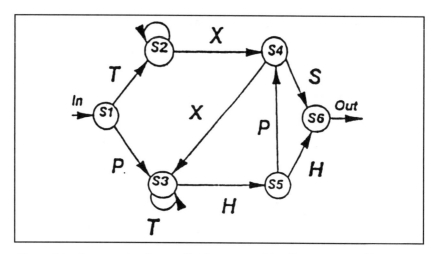

Figure 6.1. An example of an artificial grammar. Stimuli are generated by entering the grammar at State 1 (S1) and then following the arrows to the terminal position, State 6 (S6). Letters are "picked up" in between states, with the resulting sequences being termed grammatical. Nongrammatical items are generated by simply replacing a permissible letter with one that is not permissible in a particular position.

This decision requires subjects to rate each item according to the following scale: 6 = *I really like this item,* 5 = *I like this item,* 4 = *I sort of like this item,* 3 = *I sort of do not like this item,* 2 = *I do not like this item,* 1 = *I really do not like this item.* After the full set of liking-task items have been rated, subjects are asked to report any criteria they used to assist them in making their liking decisions. This manipulation check allows for the determination of any explicit retrieval/rule awareness processes that subjects may have used during the preceding task, as such processes could possibly contaminate the data and make the liking task slightly less implicit than its intended nature.

In addition, before valid conclusions could be drawn from the data, the grammatical and nongrammatical stimuli are typically pretested for any inherent likability; that is, are subjects' affective ratings based on their implicit detection of the underlying rule system, or do the grammatical and/or nongrammatical items possess some inherent, non-rule based qualities that allow for subjects to provide different ratings for these items? By having subjects rate the degree to which they liked grammatical and nongrammatical items independent of participating in the study portion of each experiment (when the acquisition of the rule system, and preferences, is said to occur), the inherent likability of grammar-generated items could be determined. The implementation of such a control condition has been undertaken in several of the studies reported in the current review (Manza & Bornstein, 1995; Zizak & Reber, 1995) and several pilot experiments undertaken to test the liking task's reliability (Manza, Carson, Druckenmiller, & Sparaco, 1996; Manza & McCullough, 1995; Manza & Skypala, 1996), and in each case, analyses of the ratings given to grammatical and nongrammatical items by these control subjects have not yielded significant differences between the two item types, suggesting that any observed differences in the ratings given to grammatical and nongrammatical stimuli is most likely due to the presence of implicit discriminations between items that conform to the rule structure and those that do not.

MERGING THE MERE EXPOSURE EFFECT
WITH ARTIFICIAL GRAMMAR LEARNING

Using the above procedure, recent work in our labs has attempted to merge the theoretical concepts developed within the confines of the mere exposure effect with implicit learning via the artificial grammar-learning task. One such area of investigation has looked at the effect that stimulus type has on implicit learning. In his review of mere exposure-effect research, Bornstein (1989) outlined research on the type of stimuli used in mere exposure experiments. Looking at a cross-section of over 200 experiments, Bornstein was able to show how significant mere exposure effects have been obtained using stimuli such as ideographs, nonsense syllables, polygons, real objects, photographs, meaningful words, and paintings. In addition, Bornstein's review revealed that subliminal initial exposure to experimental stimuli typically leads to larger mere exposure effects compared to supraliminal presentation. However, drawing from this collective database, it seems that the critical aspect in obtaining the mere exposure effect is the previous exposure to stimuli, and not the specific stimuli themselves or the nature of the initial exposure.

In an attempt to generalize these findings to artificial grammar learning, Zizak and Reber (1995) conducted a pair of experiments designed to investigate whether or not the alphabetic nature of the stimuli typically used in artificial grammar-learning experiments (see Reber, 1989, for a review) would somehow predispose subjects to use some type of semantic prejudice in processing stimuli. To avoid any such bias, Zizak and Reber replaced the usual English letters in their grammar with five Japanese Kana characters. They then presented these truly novel sequences to participants and instructed them to attend to and reproduce each sequence; this served as their study task. Following this initial exposure to grammar-generated exemplars, half of the participants were shown additional grammar-generated items and asked to provide liking ratings for them on a 6-point scale with higher ratings indicating more positive affect. However, this stimuli list consisted of one third novel grammatical items, one third novel nongrammatical items, and one third old grammatical items (these final stimuli were items that appeared as study-task items). As a final task, these participants were presented with the test stimuli once again, but on this second presentation, they were asked to simply decide whether or not each item conformed to the structure of the grammar. The remaining individuals participated in the liking and rule judgment tasks as outlined above, but in the reverse order (rule judgment first, followed by liking ratings).

This study yielded several interesting results. First, there was no task-order effect; that is, those individuals participating in the liking task before the rule-judgment task did no better or worse on either task compared to those participants who underwent those two tasks in the opposite order. In addition, although participants did perform above chance in making rule-judgment decisions (M proportion correct for grammatical items $= .69$, M for nongrammatical items $= .56$), Zizak and Reber (1995) failed to find a significant mere exposure effect, as the use of Japanese Kana characters produced a null effect on individuals' liking ratings for the three item types. One possible explanation why this result does not merge well with Bornstein's (1989) review might lie in the notion that typical mere exposure-effect experiments do not, in their use of indirect affective ratings, measure learning ability; these tasks are more memory based. However, the rating task used in artificial grammar learning is a measure of learning; one must be able to generalize knowledge about the initially presented items to the novel test items.

In an attempt to explore this issue, a second experiment used the more common English letters in place of the Japanese Kana characters; all other elements were identical to the first experiment. As with the first experiment, there was no task-order effect present; explicit knowledge of the grammar did not influence subjects' liking ratings. More important, however, the change to a more familiar stimulus type had its desired effect; participants in the second experiment reported greater affect for grammatical items

(M rating = 4.01, SD = 1.64), compared to nongrammatical items (M = 3.56, SD = 1.73). When taken together, the results of these two experiments suggest that within the context of implicit artificial grammar learning, the mere exposure effect cannot occur implicitly when subjects are completely unfamiliar with the stimulus environment (i.e., being exposed to the Japanese Kana characters). Rather, some degree of familiarity must be present (i.e., letters) in order for participants to attend to the structure of stimuli and develop an emotional preference for more structured, as opposed to less structured, stimuli. This suggestion marks a distinction between artificial grammar-learning and standard mere exposure-effect tasks, but, as mentioned earlier, because the tasks are somewhat different in their orientation as to what they are measuring, such a conclusion may not be totally unwarranted.

PRIMING, MERE EXPOSURE, AND IMPLICIT LEARNING

Another area of investigation studied within the construct of the mere exposure effect involves the cognitive process of priming. Priming studies typically involve exposing subjects to some set of stimuli during an initial exposure phase (e.g., word pairs such as cow-automobile) and then testing their memory for the initial material by presenting, in either a sub- or supraliminal manner, some type of information intended to assist subjects in recalling target material (e.g., presenting *cow* alone for 4 ms, followed by the supraliminal presentation of *automobile;* this latter event may involve having subjects rate how much they like the word, decide if they have seen it before, etc.). The point behind the procedure is that the priming stimulus activates the connection in memory between the prime and the target, and targets that are primed are typically responded to in a different manner than stimuli that are not primed. Within the context of the mere exposure effect, this phenomenon has recently been explored by studying whether or not the affective nature of a priming stimulus influences subjects' affective preference for more familiar items over less familiar items. Specifically, Murphy, Monahan, and Zajonc (1995) initially exposed subjects to Chinese ideographs, following this exposure phase with a test of subjects' affect for the ideographs. However, prior to the presentation of each test item, subjects were presented with either no prime, a face conveying a positive emotion, or a face conveying a negative emotion. Subjects' affective ratings for the text stimuli revealed two interesting results. First, as in previous experiments (Bornstein, 1989), subjects demonstrated the mere exposure effect in all three priming conditions by providing higher liking ratings for stimuli that they were initially exposed to at a higher frequency compared to less frequent stimuli. However, the nature of the prime influenced subjects' ratings in the sense that items with positive primes were rated higher than items with no primes, which in turn were rated higher than items with negative primes. Clearly, this experiment demonstrates that whatever process underlies the mere exposure effect, be it an affective process or a cognitive process (Marcel, 1983a, 1983b; Meyer & Schwaneveldt, 1971; Murphy & Zajonc, 1993; Neeley, 1977; Seamon et al., 1995), subjects' ability to discriminate between items of different familiarity can be influenced by prior activation of relevant information.

Applying this priming process in theory to implicit learning and the mere exposure effect, two recent studies have shown that nonconscious learning processes can both be primed and serve as a prime within the context of artificial grammar learning. First, in an extension of the work of Gordon and Holyoak (1983), Manza and Bornstein (1995) had their subjects initially observe a set of grammar-generated stimuli, following this task with either a liking task or a rule-decision task. The liking task was similar to that of Gordon and Holyoak (1983), whereas the rule-decision task was modified from the form outlined earlier to allow for a degree of similarity between the liking and rule tasks. Specifically, rule judgments here were made on a 6-point scale, where 6 was high certainty that the item was grammatical and 1 was high certainty that the item was nongrammatical. The prediction was that because the rule task makes reference to the existence of the grammar, possible explicit processing components may integrate with the implicit nature of the task, and participants may emerge from this task with more explicit knowledge about the nature of the grammar compared to liking participants, who remained theoretically unaware of the existence of the grammar during their classification task. In other words, the rule-decision task was predicted to act as a prime for subjects' explicit knowledge of the grammar. To test this hypothesis, following their respective classification tasks, both liking-task and rule decision-task participants completed a fragment-completion task designed to assess their explicit knowledge of the grammar. Here, after being instructed as to the existence of the grammar, all participants were given a set of grammar-generated items with one letter missing in a certain location (e.g., MXT_), and their task was to fill in the blank space with the letter they thought

TABLE 6.1 Summary of Experimental Results of Liking Tasks

Experiment	Condition	Item Type Grammatical M	SD	Nongrammatical M	SD
Manza & Bornstein (1995)	Liking	3.58	0.54	3.39	0.46
	Rule	3.56	0.39	3.04	0.55
Manza et al. (1995)	Liking first	3.99	0.55	3.89	0.58
	Rule first	4.01	0.87	3.48	0.99
Manza, Power et al. (1996)	Full attention	3.76	0.44	3.36	0.65
	Divided attention	3.58	0.52	3.31	0.63
Manza, Moretti et al. (1996)	Attention deficit disorder	3.78	0.44	3.49	0.73
	Control	3.92	0.40	3.56	0.57

NOTE: Data in the table represent the results of the liking tasks from the experiments described herein, with the exception of Manza and Bornstein (1995), which report data from both the liking and rule-judgment tasks, and Manza, Power, et al. (1996). The data from this latter experiment are the mean grammatical and nongrammatical ratings collapsed across the liking and rule-judgment tasks, as analyses indicated nonsignificant differences between the two tasks.

would appear there, according to the rules of the grammar. As this task made explicit reference to the grammar and to the previously presented study items, it was a decidedly explicit task. Results, shown in the top row of Table 6.1, found that both liking task and rule decision-task subjects could detect structural differences between grammatical and nongrammatical items, as the former were rated significantly higher than the latter by subjects in both conditions. In addition, despite a nonsignificant interaction of the ratings between grammatical and nongrammatical items and the nature of the classification task (rule or liking), subjects in the rule-decision condition (M percent correct $= 40$, $SD = 5$) performed significantly better than liking subjects ($M = 33$, $SD = 9$) on the explicit fragment-completion task. This finding supported the initial hypothesis that the rule-decision task somehow primes explicit knowledge of the rules of the grammar, as the rule-decision subjects, but not their liking-task counterparts, entered the fragment-completion task with prior knowledge of the grammar.

This priming effect has also been explored in regard to whether or not knowledge of the grammar can prime subjects' affective ratings of grammatical and nongrammatical items in a manner that would influence the nature of the mere exposure effect during artificial grammar learning. Manza, Parton, Moretti, and LaPierre (1995) investigated the priming issue explored in Manza and Bornstein (1995) by initially requiring participants to attend to, and then attempt to reproduce, grammar-generated stimuli. This study task was followed by both the liking-rating task and the rule-judgment task, with half of the participants undergoing the liking task first and the remaining individuals proceeding through the rule-judgment task first. The hypothesis behind this design was that because the rule-judgment task involves explicit awareness of the existence of the grammar and possible processing mechanisms that may activate explicit knowledge of the grammar, this task may activate rule-based knowledge of the grammar that the liking task requires if subjects are to favor grammatical over nongrammatical items during the liking task. For this experiment, the data from the rule-judgment task showed no order effect and also revealed that participants could discriminate between the two item types, as grammatical stimuli were rated significantly higher ($M = 3.71, SD = 0.62$) than nongrammatical items ($M = 3.14, SD = 0.80$). More interesting, however, were the analyses of the liking-task data, shown in the second row of Table 6.1. This analysis revealed that although participants in both conditions rated grammatical items significantly higher than nongrammatical items, this effect was significantly more pronounced in those individuals participating in the rule-judgment task prior to the liking task. Apparently, engaging in the type of processing necessary for completion of the rule-judgment task, and having the nature of the rule-judgment task correspond closely with the nature of the liking task, primes the mechanisms responsible for the emotion-based preferences for grammatical items over nongrammatical stimuli on the liking task that correspond to an implicit learning mere exposure effect.

EVOLUTIONARY EXPLORATIONS OF MERE EXPOSURE AND IMPLICIT LEARNING

Thus far, this review has presented data supporting the existence of the mere exposure effect and the connection of implicit artificial grammar learning to this process. A question that remains, however, is why the mere exposure effect occurs as it does, and, relatedly, what purpose implicit learning ability serves. A possible answer lies in evolutionary theory. Both Bornstein (1989) and Reber (1992) have offered evolution-based explanations for the mere exposure effect and implicit learning, respectively, and these two theories demonstrate the connection between the mere exposure effect and artificial grammar learning that has been developed in the present exposition.

Bornstein (1989) contends that the preference that subjects demonstrate for familiar items over unfamiliar items in mere exposure experiments is suggestive of an adaptive ability that allows one to minimize the risk of potential danger in unfamiliar situations. His position is highlighted by the following example:

> Who was likely to survive longer, reproduce, and pass on genetic material (and inherited traits) to subsequent generations, the cave dweller who had a healthy fear of the strange and unfamiliar beasts lurking outside, or the more risk-taking (albeit short-lived) fellow who, on spying an unfamiliar animal in the distance, decided that he wanted a closer look? (p. 282)

A similar type of reasoning has been employed by Reber (1992), who has suggested that implicit learning's role in evolution is one that allows an organism to extract information from a stimulus environment and then apply the knowledge obtained in the initial knowledge extraction to guide its actions in novel circumstances. In addition, having such an ability would, in an analogous fashion to Bornstein's (1989) assertion, give an organism an advantage over another organism who lacked such knowledge and might not know how to behave under the same circumstances. At the core of Reber's theory is the notion that this evolutionary utility of implicit learning suggests that such processes existed prior to the appearance of conscious abilities and, therefore, are more vital to survival than conscious abilities. This latter suggestion has led to a robustness view of implicit learning (Abrams & Reber, 1988; Reber, 1992; Reber, Walkenfeld, & Hernstadt, 1991), which suggests that implicit abilities should demonstrate different responses to experimental manipulations when compared to explicit processes; specifically, those manipulations that impair explicit abilities should have little or no effect on implicit abilities.

Several recent experiments have attempted to test these evolutionary theories by comparing implicit learning mere exposure effects and explicit abilities, in the face of experimental manipulations. One such study has investigated the effects of attentional manipulations on implicit and explicit processes (Manza, Power, et al., 1996). Findings of impaired explicit ability in response to a divided attention manipulation is a fairly robust phenomenon (Ashcraft, 1994), but the effects of such a manipulation are unknown on mere exposure-based tasks. If data were to reveal that implicit learning mere exposure abilities remain relatively stable in comparison to decreased explicit capacities, when both are exposed to a divided attention manipulation, such a finding could be taken as support for Bornstein's (1989) and Reber's (1992) evolutionary theories of human cognition. To test this possibility, Manza, Power, et al. (1996) had participants initially exposed to grammar-generated stimuli under either full or divided attention conditions. Participants in the full attention condition were initially required to attend to and then reproduce grammar-generated letter sets; their divided attention counterparts were presented with the same requirement, with the added task of computing the sum of three random two-digit numbers with each grammar-generated item. Following this study task, participants rated either (a) the degree to which they liked novel grammatical and nongrammatical items, or (b) the degree to which they felt items conformed to the rule structure (such as in Manza et al., 1995, mentioned earlier). If the evolutionary position was to be supported, the divided attention manipulation should have had differential effects on participants' explicit recall of study-task items and implicit classifications during the liking and rule-judgment tasks.

Results here supported such a dissociation perspective, as full attention participants were significantly more accurate in terms of their percentage of correct reproductions on the initial study task ($M = 86$, $SD = 10$) compared to their divided attention cohorts ($M = 44$, $SD = 16$), but participants' implicit liking ratings and rule judgments were not significantly influenced by the attention manipulation at the time of initial study, as both full and divided attention subjects were able to discriminate between grammatical and nongrammatical stimuli with relatively equal ability (see Table 6.1, panel 3).

An additional experiment testing the possible evolutionary underpinnings of implicit mere exposure effects has focused on the role of attention deficit disorder (ADD) in implicit and explicit learning. The purpose of this line of research within the evolutionary framework is that it has been suggested (Reber, 1992) that data showing preserved implicit abilities but impaired explicit abilities in the face of neurological dysfunction can be taken as support of the evolutionary necessity of implicit cognition. To date, artificial grammar-based mere exposure studies have not looked at clinical populations to test Reber's theory, so investigating the nature of implicit mere exposure effects within a neurologically impaired population could support Reber's robustness principle.

ADD is a neurological impairment that causes individuals to become highly distractible and unable to exert total control over impulses (Hallowell & Ratey, 1994). Because individuals with this condition, when untreated, tend to have difficulties in terms of their explicit processing of information (as a result of their distractibility), there is an analogy here with other individuals with different neurological conditions, such as amnesia, Alzheimer's disease, schizophrenia, and anxiety (Abrams & Reber, 1988; Knowlton, Ramus, & Squire, 1992; Rathus, Reber, Manza, & Kushner, 1994), who also show explicit impairment. Where the connection to implicit learning stems from in the case of ADD is that these other neurological dysfunctions, while impairing explicit learning, tend not to have a negative impact on participants' implicit learning ability. Therefore, to determine if the implicit/explicit performance differential observed in other neurological conditions also pertains to ADD, recent research has explored this connection using the artificial grammar-learning liking task as a measure of implicit cognition.

Manza, Moretti, et al. (1996) conducted an implicit artificial grammar-learning experiment, comparing a group of college students with self-reported ADD (the ADD group) to a group of college students without ADD (the control group). Prior to the experiment, all subjects completed an ADD symptom questionnaire (maximum score = 20; Hallowell & Ratey, 1994), with the results indicating that the ADD group ($M = 14.0$, $SD = 2.6$) reported a significantly greater number of attention-related dysfunctions when compared to the control group ($M = 2.7$, $SD = 1.6$). It was predicted that these attentional disturbances would disrupt the explicit processing of those with ADD but spare their implicit abilities, supporting a dissociation pattern among clinical populations observed elsewhere (Abrams & Reber, 1988; Knowlton et al., 1992; Rathus et al., 1994).

After completing the above-mentioned questionnaire, all participants were presented with a set of grammar-generated stimuli to observe and reproduce. Following this study phase, all individuals rated the degree to which they liked novel grammatical and nongrammatical stimuli. The results from these tasks supported part of the initial dissociation prediction. Participants were able to discriminate grammatical from nongrammatical items on the liking task, with no interactions between the groups (see Table 6.1, row 4), supporting the assumptions about preserved implicit abilities in the face of neurological dysfunction. However, despite the symptomatic differences between the ADD and control groups, the accuracy of their explicit reproductions of study items did not differ significantly, as the overall mean proportion correct was .80 ($SD = 0.14$). One possible explanation for this latter result stems from the presence of medication in the ADD group. Specifically, 83% of the ADD participants were taking some form of stimulant medication to regulate their condition, and although subjects consented to abstaining from their medication for 24 hours prior to the experiment, that time period was most likely not sufficient to observe their ADD symptoms in a nonmedicated form. Future work in this area should attempt to rectify this problem by studying the cognitive effects of ADD in nonmedicated patients.

When taken together, therefore, the previous two experiments using the artificial grammar-based mere exposure procedure seem to offer some support for Bornstein's (1989) and Reber's (1992) evolutionary perspectives of human cognition. We hope that future work in this regard will add to the database concerning the utility of implicit processes, and the studies reported herein seem to serve as a functional base.

CONCLUSIONS, SPECULATIONS, AND FUTURE DIRECTIONS

At the outset of the present discussion, the possibility that implicit thought processes might not exist entirely beyond conscious awareness was raised. Although some possibly valid points have been made in support of this perspective (Dulany et al., 1984; Perruchet & Pacteau, 1990), a large body of evidence, including the studies reported herein, goes beyond attempting to demonstrate the existence of implicit cognition, suggesting instead the possible mechanisms behind nonconscious thought (Greenwald, 1992; Jacoby, Lindsay, & Toth, 1992; Joordens & Merikle, 1993; Kihlstrom, 1987; Klinger & Greenwald, 1995; Mandler, 1989; Roediger, 1990). In this vein, the artificial grammar-learning procedure has been used to understand the nature of implicit learning.

Can the artificial grammar-learning procedure be used to demonstrate implicit learning? Although some might respond in the negative to this question (Dulany et al., 1984; Perruchet & Pacteau, 1990), such a response would most likely be based on the use of the standard rule-judgment task, which has been the primary task used in artificial grammar-learning experiments over the past 30 years, as the measure of implicit learning. As mentioned earlier, although this task does involve awareness of the rule system underlying experimental stimuli, this awareness does not necessarily imply the use of conscious decision-making strategies when making rule-based classification decisions during the testing portion of the artificial grammar-learning task. However, the possibility of explicit contamination does arise within the task due to subjects' awareness of the grammar. How does one lessen such contamination? The preceding review has offered a possible answer to this question, by drawing a theoretical and procedural bridge between tasks used to generate the mere exposure effect and artificial grammar learning.

This connection has resulted in the development of an affect-based discrimination task in the context of the artificial grammar-learning procedure that permits experimental participants to make generalizations about novel grammatical and nongrammatical stimuli without deliberate, concurrent awareness of the existence of the rule system underlying such stimuli. The findings from the experiments reported herein, with subjects demonstrating greater affect for grammatical items than nongrammatical items, similar to the mere exposure effect's demonstration of greater affect for more familiar items over less familiar items, seems to address critics' questions concerning whether performance on the artificial grammar-learning task can be taken as evidence of implicit learning for two reasons. First, because experimental subjects have been shown to prefer novel grammatical items to novel nongrammatical items, and at rates greater than chance, they are demonstrating some type of learning. With this in mind, because subjects are not aware of the grammar and the liking task does not require participants to explicitly recall the initial study phase of the procedure (from which the affect-based generalizations are based), the task satisfies criteria (Schacter & Graf, 1986) for a task being implicit in nature.

In a broader sense, as outlined earlier in the discussion of evolutionary theory and cognitive ability, the use of the liking task in the context of the artificial grammar-learning task may offer some explanatory power of preference development. Why, for instance, would an individual prefer the musical compilations of Mozart over the Grateful Dead? Why do some sports enthusiasts prefer the high-speed action of ice hockey over the comparatively sedentary rate of golf? The data presented here clearly illustrate that subjects can indeed acquire and demonstrate a preference for novel well-structured stimuli over ill-structured stimuli, with two possible processes moderating such preferences. Familiarity (Bornstein, 1989) may be playing a role here, as research on the mere exposure effect has illustrated that simple exposure to information increases one's emotional affinity for that stimuli over less familiar information. In addition, the research on implicit learning suggests that humans may develop positive affect for

217

structured displays once they have become inculcated with the underlying structure of those displays. For example, we like the poetry of Emily Dickinson and favor it over, say, the work of Robert Frost, once we learn to understand the depths of form and expression that are embodied in it. We like Mozart after hearing his work enough that we have implicitly formed a tacit representation of the basic structures and forms of his music. This alternative suggests that structural systems that are deep and sophisticated—which we can interpret in our hard-nosed scientific manner as systems that are based on complex, stochastic, and multileveled patterns of covariation (e.g., the artificial grammars used in the experiments described herein)—are going to become part of a culture's *oeuvre,* once the people within the culture acquire the structure. Conversely, those systems that have a trivial and shallow structure will merely have their Warholian 15 minutes and quietly retire.

Such an explanation for the development of implicit emotional preferences is, of course, speculative in nature at this time, although it does suggest a path toward future research exploring affect-based implicit learning ability. In addition, this theory does, however, seem to correlate with the laboratory-based hybrid mere exposure/artificial grammar-learning task that initially exposes subjects to highly structured and complex information and then allows subjects to demonstrate their affect-based affinities for stimuli that adhere to the structure over those that do not, in the absence of explicit awareness of the existence/nature of the rule structure generating the stimuli. One aim of the research, however, is to offer some generalized prediction/explanation about behavior outside the lab, and the liking-oriented artificial grammar-learning task does seem to provide some basis for understanding real-world emotional preferences. Future work, therefore, can now aim toward trying to find additional support for this explanation concerning real-world preference acquisition, with the ultimate goal leaning in the direction of our acquiring a deeper understanding of the human mind.

REFERENCES

Abrams, M., & Reber, A. S. (1988). Implicit learning: Robustness in the face of psychiatric disorders. *Journal of Psycholinguistic Research, 17,* 425-439.

Ashcraft, M. H. (1994). *Human memory and cognition* (2nd ed.). New York: HarperCollins.

Bornstein, R. F. (1989). Exposure and affect: Overview and meta-analysis of research, 1968-1987. *Psychological Bulletin, 106,* 265-289.

Bornstein, R. F., & D'Agostino, P. R. (1992). Stimulus recognition and the mere exposure effect. *Journal of Personality and Social Psychology, 63,* 545-552.

Bornstein, R. F., Leone, D. R., & Galley, D. J. (1987). The generalizability of subliminal mere exposure effects: Influence of stimuli perceived without awareness on social behavior. *Journal of Personality and Social Psychology, 53,* 1070-1079.

Dienes, Z., Broadbent, D., & Berry, D. (1991). Implicit and explicit knowledge bases in artificial grammar learning. *Journal of Experimental Psychology: Learning, Memory, and Cognition, 17,* 875-887.

Dulany, D. E., Carlson, R. A., & Dewey, G. I. (1984). A case of syntactical learning and judgment: How conscious and how abstract? *Journal of Experimental Psychology: General, 113,* 541-555.

Gordon, P. C., & Holyoak, K. J. (1983). Implicit learning and generalization of the "mere exposure" effect. *Journal of Personality and Social Psychology, 45,* 492-500.

Greenwald, A. G. (1992). New look 3: Unconscious cognition reclaimed. *American Psychologist, 47,* 766-779.

Hallowell, E. M., & Ratey, J. J. (1994). *Driven to distraction: Recognizing and coping with attention deficit disorder from childhood through adulthood.* New York: Simon & Schuster.

Hamid, P. N. (1973). Exposure frequency and stimulus preference. *British Journal of Psychology, 64,* 569-577.

Jacoby, L. L. (1988). Memory observed and memory unobserved. In U. Neisser & E. Winograd (Eds.), *Remembering reconsidered: Ecological and traditional approaches to the study of memory* (pp. 145-147). Cambridge, UK: Cambridge University Press.

Jacoby. L. L. (1991). A process dissociation framework: Separating unconscious from intentional uses of memory. *Journal of Memory and Language, 30,* 513-541.

Jacoby, L. L., Lindsay, D. S., & Toth, J. P. (1992). Unconscious influences revealed: Attention, awareness, and control. *American Psychologist, 47,* 802-809.

Jacoby, L. L., Toth, J. P., & Yonelinas, A. P. (1993). Separating conscious and unconscious influences of memory: Measuring recollection. *Journal of Experimental Psychology: General, 122,* 139-154.

Joordens, S., & Merikle, P. M. (1993). Independence or redundancy? Two models of conscious and unconscious influences. *Journal of Experimental Psychology: General, 122,* 462-467.

Kihlstrom, J. F. (1987). The cognitive unconscious. *Science, 237,* 1445-1452.

Klinger, M. K., & Greenwald, A. G. (1995). Unconscious priming of association judgments. *Journal of Experimental Psychology: Learning, Memory, and Cognition, 21,* 569-581.

Knowlton, B. J., Ramus, S. J., & Squire, L. R. (1992). Intact artificial grammar learning in amnesia: Dissociation of classification learning and explicit memory for specific instances. *Psychological Science, 3,* 172-179.

Kunst-Wilson, W. R., & Zajonc, R. B. (1980). Affective discrimination of stimuli that cannot be recognized. *Science, 207,* 557-558.

Mandler, G. (1989). Memory: Conscious and unconscious. In P. R. Solomon, G. R. Goethals, C. M. Kelly, & B. R. Stephens (Eds.), *Memory: Interdisciplinary approaches* (pp. 84-106). New York: Springer-Verlag.

Mandler, G., Nakamura, Y., & Van Zandt, B. (1987). Nonspecific effects of exposure to stimuli that cannot be recognized. *Journal of Experimental Psychology: Learning, Memory, and Cognition, 13,* 646-648.

Manza, L., & Bornstein, R. F. (1995). Affective discrimination and the implicit learning process. *Consciousness and Cognition, 4,* 399-409.

Manza, L., Carson, J., Druckenmiller, K., & Sparaco, S. (1996). *Implicit and explicit cognition: Reduced and preserved abilities through adulthood.* Manuscript submitted for publication.

Manza, L., & McCullough, P. (1995). *Implicit learning and retroactive interference: Evidence for distinct implicit and explicit learning modes.* Poster session presented at the annual meeting of the Eastern Psychological Association, Boston.

Manza, L., Moretti, M., Holladay, P., D'Uva, Y., Gilpin, T., Daniels, T., & Parsons, A. (1996). *Attention Deficit Disorder and implicit learning: Preserved cognitive abilities in the face of attentional dysfunction.* Poster session presented at the annual meeting of the Eastern Psychological Association, Philadelphia.

Manza, L., Parton, K., Moretti, M., & LaPierre, K. (1995). *Implicit and explicit tests of artificial grammar-based knowledge.* Poster session presented at the annual meeting of the American Psychological Society, New York.

Manza, L., Power, M., Ryan, S., Balstra, D., Witmer, A., & Twining, B. (1996). *Divided attention and artificial grammar learning: Dissociation of implicit and explicit thought processes.* Paper presented at the annual meeting of the Eastern Psychological Association, Philadelphia.

Manza, L., & Skypala, D. (1996). *Attention and artificial grammar learning: Interdependence of implicit and explicit knowledge systems.* Manuscript submitted for publication.

Marcel, A. J. (1983a). Conscious and unconscious perception: An approach to the relation between phenomenal experience and perceptual process. *Cognitive Psychology, 15,* 238-300.

Marcel, A. J. (1983b). Conscious and unconscious perception: An approach to the relation between visual masking and word recognition. *Cognitive Psychology, 15,* 197-237.

Meyer, D., & Schwaneveldt, R. (1971). Facilitation in recognizing pairs of words: Evidence of dependence between retrieval operations. *Journal of Experimental Psychology, 90,* 227-234.

Murphy, S. T., Monahan, J. L., & Zajonc, R. B. (1995). Additivity of nonconscious affect: Combined effects of priming and exposure. *Journal of Personality and Social Psychology, 69,* 589-602.

Murphy, S. T., & Zajonc, R. B. (1993). Affect, cognition, and awareness: Affective priming with suboptimal and optimal stimulus. *Journal of Personality and Social Psychology, 64,* 723-739.

Neeley, J. H. (1977). Semantic priming and retrieval from lexical memory: Roles of inhibitionless spreading activation and limited-capacity attention. *Journal of Experimental Psychology: General, 106,* 226-254.

Perruchet, P., & Pacteau, C. (1990). Synthetic grammar learning: Implicit rule abstraction or explicit fragmentary knowledge. *Journal of Experimental Psychology: General, 119,* 264-275.

Rathus, J. R., Reber, A. S., Manza, L., & Kushner, H. M. (1994). Implicit and explicit learning: Differential effects of affective states. *Perceptual and Motor Skills, 79,* 163-184.

Reber, A. S. (1989). Implicit learning and tacit knowledge. *Journal of Experimental Psychology: General, 118,* 219-235.

Reber, A. S. (1992). An evolutionary context for the cognitive unconscious. *Philosophical Psychology, 5,* 33-51.

Reber, A. S., Walkenfeld, F. F., & Hernstadt, R. (1991). Implicit learning: Individual differences and IQ. *Journal of Experimental Psychology: Learning, Memory, and Cognition, 17,* 888-896.

Roediger, H. L. (1990). Implicit memory: Retention without remembering. *American Psychologist, 96,* 341-357.

Saegert, S. C., & Jellison, J. M. (1970). Effects of initial level of response competition and frequency of exposure on liking and exploratory behavior. *Journal of Personality and Social Psychology, 16,* 553-558.

Schacter, D. L. (1989). On the relation between memory and consciousness: Dissociable interactions and conscious experience. In H. L. Roediger & F. I. M. Craik (Eds.), *Varieties of memory and consciousness: Essays in honor of Endel Tulving* (pp. 355-389). Hillsdale, NJ: Lawrence Erlbaum.

Schacter, D. L., & Graf, P. (1986). Effects of elaborative processing on implicit and explicit memory for new associations. *Journal of Experimental Psychology: Learning, Memory, and Cognition, 12,* 432-444.

Seamon, J. G., Williams, P. C., Crowley, M. J., Kim, I. J., Langer, S. A., Orne, P. J., & Wishengrad, D. L. (1995). The mere exposure effect is based on implicit memory: Effects of stimulus type, encoding conditions, and number of exposures on recognition and affect judgments. *Journal of Experimental Psychology: Learning, Memory, and Cognition, 21,* 711-721.

Seger, C. A. (1994). Implicit learning. *Psychological Bulletin, 115,* 163-196.

Shanks, D. R., & St. John, M. F. (1994). Characteristics of dissociable human learning systems. *Behavioral and Brain Sciences, 17,* 367-447.

Stang, D. J., & O'Connell, E. J. (1974). The computer as experimenter in social psychology research. *Behavior Research Methods and Instrumentation, 6,* 223-231.

Tulving, E. (1983). *Elements of episodic memory.* New York: Oxford University Press.

Zajonc, R. B. (1968). Attitudinal effects of mere exposure. *Journal of Personality and Social Psychology Monographs, 9*(2, Pt. 2), 1-27.

Zizak, D., & Reber, A. S. (1995). *Implicit learning task manipulations: The formation of emotional preferences.* Manuscript in preparation.

7

Project Grammarama Revisited

Generativity of Implicitly Acquired Knowledge

●────────────────────────────────

Robert C. Mathews
Barbara P. Cochran

One of the curious things about artificial grammar research is that the major researchers who have developed it as a laboratory task, spending many hours doing experiments with it, usually have a strange ambivalence about artificial grammar learning as a research paradigm. For example, one time when the first author mentioned to Arthur Reber that some students had acquired the habit of referring to finite state grammars as "Reber grammars," he was appalled. Even given his special status as a lexicographer of psychology, his reaction was strong. This love-hate relation is also apparent in George Miller's (1968) writings about this extensive involvement with artificial grammars, known as Project Grammarama. Perhaps, some of this ambivalence comes from the fact that artificial grammar learning *seems* to capture something deep. Many of us who have explored the paradigm are drawn to it by an instinctive feeling that it may lead to an important discovery. Perhaps, a key piece of the puzzle that enabled human thinking and language to evolve lies buried in the attempts of subjects to learn these artificial grammars. However, the paradigm seems too artificial, too removed from anything people care about. Memorizing or judging strings of letters is a boring, tiresome task. It's not exciting, like eyewitness testimony research or subliminal perception studies. It's not even clear why an audience would care to hear about it.

In this chapter, we will briefly recount George Miller's flirtation with artificial grammars in the 1950s and 1960s in Project Grammarama. In doing so, we will conjecture why he missed finding the key secrets of the natural language mystery (or NLM), and subsequently abandoned the whole paradigm as having little relevance to learning language. We will also explain why even the recent resurgence of work on artificial grammars, although it comes close to revealing the secrets of the NLM, is now also off the main trail. Then, we will point the way to what we believe is the true path to the Holy Grail of the NLM, and we will describe our first expeditions into the new domain of experiments in artificial grammar learning focused on generativity.

PROJECT GRAMMARAMA AND THE SEARCH FOR THE NATURAL LANGUAGE MYSTERY

The Initial Project

Following about 7 years of on and off research on the project, George Miller (1968) began his chapter on Project Grammarama by expressing his ambivalence toward the paradigm. He begins with an anecdote about a friend being asked after an hour's lecture, Why would anyone do this research? Then he asks himself, why would anyone undertake Project Grammarama? His answer:

> I would characterize Project Grammarama as a pleasant field trip through some rather exotic psycholinguistic meadows; I have collected a few specimens that look interesting, but so far not much has been accomplished by way of taxonomy. In more literal terms, it is a program of laboratory experiments to investigate how people learn the grammatical rules underlying artificial languages. (p. 126)

In the end of the chapter, he admits that whereas earlier he may have had some notions that these experiments might tell us something about learning human languages, he has been persuaded that there is insufficient common ground between artificial grammar experiments and natural languages to generalize from one to the other. Among the many differences he lists, he is especially convinced by the lack of meaning and phonetics in artificial grammars.

In retrospect, the absence of phonetics in artificial grammars may not be as damning as Miller thought, given that we now know sign language has most of the components of spoken language, without being spoken. The absence of meaning may be more important. However, it is tantalizing that chimps taught sign language easily mastered the meaning component but faltered on syntax. Because artificial grammar strings have no meaning, syntax is the focus of artificial grammar experiments. Perhaps there are more important secrets in humans' ability to detect and employ meaningless constraints in artificial grammars than Miller suspected.

Project Grammarama began in 1957 when Miller and Chomsky began a study of algebraic systems that led to the formalization of what we now know as finite-state grammars. His first artificial grammar-learning experiment was designed to replicate an earlier finding of Aborn and Rubenstein (1952), showing that strings generated by more restrictive grammars were easier to memorize. Miller succeeded in replicating this phenomenon and published an article on it (Miller, 1958). Then he put Project Grammarama aside for a while because it didn't seem to be taking him anywhere and his subjects weren't having fun memorizing meaningless strings. The curse of the boring task bothered him early on. Thinking about an alternative to rote memorization of strings, Miller was inspired by the classic study of concept formation by Bruner, Goodnow, and Austin (1956). Bruner et al. distinguished between reception and selection situations versus a production situation. Reception and selection situations are those, like 99% of all studies on artificial grammar learning reported in the literature, where subjects select instances provided by the experimenter for classification, or they attempt to discriminate instances from noninstances of a concept. In a production situation, subjects generate instances and are provided feedback about their status by the experimenter. Miller's instinct was to follow the production paradigm in designing artificial grammar experiments, having subjects generate strings that may belong to the grammar.

However, in bringing this idea to practice, Miller once again hit several brick walls. First, it quickly became obvious that only the very simplest grammars could be mastered in the short time period that one could get subjects to work on the task. Also, whereas memorizing strings was no fun, it is even worse to generate many strings and be constantly told "wrong, wrong, wrong. . . . " Yet subjects were only given dichotomous feedback—right or wrong—patterned after the procedure used in the concept formation literature. Thus, the experiments consisted of mostly failed attempts to generate valid strings. Quoting Miller (1968), "Moreover, a person who is told twenty or thirty times in a row that he is wrong has an understandable urge to strangle the experimenter" (p. 144).

Various ways of circumventing these problems were tried in subsequent years by Miller and his colleagues. For example, Eva Shipstone avoided giving negative feedback entirely by having subjects devise their own classification schemes for sets of valid strings printed on cards. She also had them talk aloud, generating rich protocols on their developing classification schemes. However, rich as these protocols were in detail, they seemed to offer little in generalizations across subjects. Mostly, it seemed that idiosyncratic strategies were being employed.

One of the most creative efforts toward developing a production task that involved a meaning component was the work by Suppes (1966). He had children attempt to produce a pattern of lights, working with four buttons that rearranged an initial light pattern according to four transformation rules associated with each of the four buttons. The most interesting feature of Suppes's data was that first-grade children's error patterns showed sudden learning curves that are typically associated with insight learning. Some researchers have assumed that sudden learning curves might be associated with higher learning processes as compared to the more gradual changes associated with progressive conditioning (see Mathews, Buss, Chinn, & Stanley, 1988). However, it is not clear what the significance of sudden learning curves is. Harlow (1949) demonstrated that monkeys also show sudden learning curves after experiencing a series of different problems of the same general type. The shape of the learning curves for Harlow's monkeys showed a continuous shift from slow to sudden or insight-like as they gained experience with different problems of the same general type. However, the Suppes light task seems quite novel for his first-grade subjects, and yet their learning appeared to reflect sudden insight without prior experience with the task. Is this an important feature of the difference between minds of humans versus monkeys? We still don't know.

Early on, Miller realized that some type of automation was essential for effective grammar-production experiments. He enlisted the help of Newman to design what must have been one of the first precursors of the laboratory computer that runs most experiments today. Newman's black box enabled subjects to type in strings and get feedback (right or wrong) after each response. However, being on the edge of technology, it didn't work reliably enough to make the experiments practical. Later, when the first reliable laboratory computers did become available, Miller again tried to create an effective paradigm for studying grammar production. He once again patterned the design of his experiments after the concept-learning tradition. His subjects generated strings, and they received dichotomous feedback. To avoid long training periods, the grammars were kept simple. In retrospect both of these approaches (dichotomous feedback and over-simplified grammars) probably contributed to the lack of interesting results.

Once again, Miller became frustrated with the task. He wrote:

> Surely we have here discovered the most inefficient way to teach a set of rules—the way of pure induction—almost beautiful in its unadorned ugliness. Those poor subjects, working so long, thinking so hard, failing so often. . . . But even beyond pragmatic questions of efficiency it is difficult to suppress a feeling that the whole interaction is grotesquely stupid. (Miller, 1968, p. 163)

Still he persisted in collecting data. His subjects' general behavior in this task reflected a long search for a correct string and then a more focused search for more instances of a similar nature. Miller catalogued various strategies of searching for instances, which he rightly concluded probably have little to do with language learning. At this point in Project Gramma-rama, he moved in the direction of examining conscious discovery of rules corresponding to symbolic logic. From this point on, Project Grammarama appears to have traveled down a blind alley leading further away from anything reflecting natural language learning.

IMPLICIT LEARNING OF ARTIFICIAL GRAMMARS

The artificial grammar-research story might well have ended here were it not for Arthur Reber. In contrast to Miller's search for active, conscious mechanisms of discovering grammatical rules, Reber (1969, 1976) was fascinated by the apparent ease with which subjects exposed to exemplars could later distinguish new valid from invalid strings. He decided to focus his attention on this passive learning process, now known as implicit learning. In many of his experiments, he contrasted memorization or observation of instances with active rule discovery. Generally, he found that active attempts at rule discovery rarely led to more knowledge of the grammar than could be gained by memorizing instances. Also, he argued that subjects were generally unaware of the rules they were using to discriminate valid from invalid strings (see Reber, 1993, for a summary of this work). Throughout most of the 1970s and early 1980s, Reber and his colleagues kept this research topic alive, amid skeptics who periodically blasted the whole idea of two distinct learning systems as a hoax.

Then, at the close of the 1980s, there began a boom in artificial grammar studies, along with several other paradigms of implicit learning research (see Berry & Dienes, 1993, or Reber, 1993, for a summary of implicit learning research). The popularity of implicit learning experiments occurred for a variety of reasons. Partly, it followed the success of the implicit memory paradigms and interesting findings of dissociations between implicit and explicit memory (see Roediger, 1990). It also received stimulus from modular theories of mind (e.g., Fodor, 1986) and from connectionism's demonstrations of the power of simple decentralized learning mechanisms (e.g., Cleeremans, 1993; McClelland & Rumelhart, 1986). We think this last decade of implicit learning research has been very productive. We have learned that subjects can often provide consciously expressed evidence of their implicitly acquired knowledge (Dulany, Carlson, & Dewey, 1984; Mathews et al., 1989). However, the amount of knowledge they have usually exceeds their ability to express it (Reber, 1993), and confidence about implicit knowledge appears lacking (Chan, 1992; Dienes, Altmann, Kwan, & Goode, 1995). Also, implicitly acquired knowledge seems to depend heavily on seeing instances during training (Brooks & Vokey, 1991; Vokey & Brooks, 1992).

However, just as Miller's turn toward studying rules reflecting symbolic logic marked a turn away from the direction of discovering secrets of the NLM, we think the implicit learning literature is now moving away from relevance to the NLM. We believe the current focus of this research on the conscious versus nonconscious character of implicitly acquired knowledge marks another detour that is not likely to yield increasing returns. Also, because the ability to recognize strings develops faster than the ability to produce them, implicit learning studies have focused on string discrimination rather than production paradigms. Even a pigeon can learn to make complex discriminations among stimuli (e.g., Herrnstein, Loveland, & Cable, 1976). However, if even our closest animal relative, a chimpanzee, cannot learn to use symbols generatively, then perhaps therein lies the key to the NLM.

COGNITIVE EVOLUTION PERSPECTIVE

It might be useful to summarize our view of the history of attempts to find the beginnings of human capacity to think consciously and communicate with language. The NLM has intrigued mankind for centuries, probably because language is the most obvious discontinuity between humans and other species. We see ourselves as unique, and our language abilities seem to support this view. Some researchers have tried to close the gap by demonstrating language abilities outside our species, but efforts have largely failed to do so. No other species has a communication system that rivals the level of displacement and generativity found in natural human language (Griffin, 1976; Hailman & Ficken, 1986; Nottenbohm, 1972). Neither has any other species demonstrated language learning comparable to human children, even though much time and effort has gone into trying to train some animals to use language (Gardner & Gardner, 1969; Hayes, 1952; Premack, 1971; Savage-Rumbaugh, 1984). There is, however, another source of debate associated with natural language, which may have more to say about the nature of language ability itself.

Noam Chomsky (1966), as well as several other noted theorists (Bickerton, 1984; Lenneberg, 1967; Pinker & Bloom, 1990), has suggested that in addition to being unique to humans, natural language is also unique among human activities. That is, storage and processing of language, according to Chomsky, is qualitatively different from all other cognitive activities in which humans engage. According to this view, language as we know it arose very late in human evolution, perhaps due to some random genetic mutation (Piatelli-Palmarini, 1989). The adaptation of generative language, however, was such an advancement over other forms of animal communication that it provided H. sapiens sapiens an advantage over other species competing for the same resources, resulting in extinction of all other hominid species. In addition, this new ability turned out to be a powerful new tool for organizing thought. The so-called evolutionary explosion of some 35,000 years ago, which produced a proliferation of stone tools and the famous cave paintings in France, is supposedly due to this newfound generative thought process based on linguistic abilities (Davidson & Noble, 1989; Stringer & Andrews, 1988).

Although it is enticing to believe that the skill that seemingly sets us apart from other species is itself unique among our abilities, not everyone agrees with this Chomskian notion. An alternative view dates the beginning of language development over 2.5 million years ago. According to this account, human language had its beginnings in a communication system that may have been similar to that of modern day chimpanzees (Hewes, 1973). Chimpanzees in the wild use pointing, gesturing, and facial expressions, as well as a variety of vocalizations to convey meaning to other members of the troop (Goodall, 1986; Snowden, Brown, & Peterson, 1982). Although quite complex in nature, chimp communication is different from human language in that it is very much tied to the here and now, classifying it as a system of signals rather than symbols (Corballis, 1991). Furthermore, the components are strung together into stereotypical combinations that have specific meanings, rather than being combined in novel ways to produce an unlimited number of meanings, which is considered to be a hallmark of human communication. Thus, the question arises as to exactly how a communication system such as that used by chimps could develop into the symbolic, generative system we know as language.

The latter view of language evolution holds that language is based on a general cognitive ability that preceded the appearance of true language. Bipedalism, along with restructuring of the social order brought about by climate changes between 4 and 5 million years ago, produced radical changes in the lifestyle of apelike species living in eastern Africa (Johanson & Edey, 1982; Lovejoy, 1988). This change in the complexity of daily life is thought to have altered thought processes, producing a new way of encoding information, which gradually led to more complex forms of communication. The most important property of this radical new way of thinking is said to be *generativity* (Corballis, 1991; Donald, 1991).

There are two views of the rise of generative thought that we find particularly interesting. Donald (1991) describes the evolution of mental processes as influenced by social evolution, whereas Corballis (1991) attributes the change in cognitive abilities to the advancements in tool use brought about by bipedalism. These theories do not contradict, but rather complement each other, focusing on different aspects of evolution. Below, we provide a summary that includes important features of both theories.

According to Donald (1991), the human mind underwent several key changes as human evolution proceeded. First, there was only procedural knowledge, a direct stimulus-response type of knowledge that does not require intervention of conscious control nor the ability to communicate or even to think about one's own knowledge. Next came the episodic mind, which adds the ability to remember past incidents and use this information to guide behavior in new circumstances. The ability to remember and use information from past events seems to presuppose some level of conscious awareness of the remembered events, in order to choose which one to respond to and to decide how it can be applied to different situations.

However, the episodic mind is thought to be stimulus bound. Memory of previous events is evoked by environmental stimuli or retrieval cues present in new situations. We assume that the purely episodic mind, epitomized by the chimpanzee, has no capabilities for searching (self-cueing) its episodic memories in the absence of environmentally provided retrieval cues. Thus, the structure and organization of the episodic mind directly reflects the environment in which a creature lives. There is, at this point, very little in the way of structure consciously imposed by the mind. That is, there is no thinking in the sense of creatively rearranging or producing new ideas.

Creative or generative control of thinking begins, according to Donald (1991), with the mimetic stage. This is where early humans began to mime or act out important events. Such acting out behavior provided a physical way of re-presenting events to others. The adaptive value of mime lies in its ability to rehearse and perhaps improve upon behaviors. It also opens the door for increased communication. Although mimetic knowledge originated from actual events (e.g., reenactments of hunting incidents), these reenactments were reproduced and eventually changed and stereotyped across time by processes similar to Bartlett's (1932) notions of leveling and sharpening. Thus, mimetic reenactments became a form of knowledge adapted more to the needs of communication and culture (e.g., in ritual song and dance) than to veridical preservation of environmental information.

Corballis (1991) agrees that generative thought processes began as a restructuring of mental representation, which occurred during the same historical period in which Donald places the beginning of the mimetic stage; however, Corballis claims that this reorganization of thought has its roots in praxis and tool making. Praxis is defined as voluntary actions that consist of internally generated sequences of movements unconstrained by the spatial features of the environment. A prime example of praxis in humans is speech. Praxis in itself, however, does not distinguish us from other species. Bird song can be described as praxic, and even though manual praxis is most highly developed in humans, many of our closest relatives, such as chimpanzees and gorillas, are very good at skilled movements of the hands. Corballis (1991) contends, however, that freeing of the hands from their role in locomotion as a result of bipedalism increased the scope of praxis, thus increasing the opportunity for the development of generative thought.

In this scenario, as early humans moved about on two legs, they discovered the advantage of carrying a tool over stopping to make a new tool each time the need arose, as apes who use their forepaws for locomotion must do. Using a tool more than once emphasized the fact that some methods of making tools are more efficient or result in better tools, leading humans to practice these techniques, trying to repeat the movements that resulted in better tools. This would have advanced their praxic skills, yielding even better tools, but more important, it would have changed their mental representation of the tool-making activity. No longer was tool making a matter of choosing a stick or stone from the immediate surroundings that seemed appropriate for the job at hand. Rather, tool making became a process of imposing on the stone a shape that already existed in the mind of the tool maker and that was brought about by specific features of the process itself. According to Corballis, storing mental representations of actions in terms of basic features is a necessary precursor to the generative thought processes used in language (see also Holloway, 1985).

Recoding activities in terms of basic features was not the only change that accompanied the rise of tool making. In addition, humans soon realized that combining features of the activity in various ways yielded different types of tools suited to different purposes. Archeological evidence indicates that early tool makers applied the features of their tool-making techniques in a generative fashion (Leakey, 1981). According to Corballis (1991), generative knowledge systems require fragmentary representations that are capable of being recombined in new ways. In his view, stone tools bear a record of such a knowledge system. Just as the concept of replaceable parts caused an irrevocable qualitative change in the nature of human artifacts following the industrial revolution, the invention of generative forms of knowledge representation dramatically opened up new possibilities for thinking and communication, which put our ancestors on the path to development of language. Mimetic knowledge, although using entirely physical forms of representation (e.g., different facial gestures and body movements), has the quality of fragmentary representations that are infinitely recombinable (see Mathews & Roussel, in press).

Both Donald (1991) and Corballis (1991) date the actual invention of language (and its accompanying high level of conscious control of communication and thought) much later than the rise of generative thought. Donald sees language as resulting from increasing pressure on the need for symbolic representation during the mythic stage, in which reenactments were elaborated into stories. Corballis contends that language arose from the need for more complex forms of communication to pass tool-making techniques from generation to generation. Therefore, both Donald and Corballis place the first seeds of generative thought deep in the prelinguistic mechanisms of mind. According to Donald, these prelinguistic generative mechanisms of mind are still operative in the modern human mind (see also Reber, 1993).

● Where Are the Secrets of the Natural Language Mystery?

If the theories described above are correct in their conclusion that generativity of knowledge is the key to understanding evolution of language ability, and that generative knowledge systems evolved long before language and conscious symbolic representation, then Project Grammarama, with its focus on generative production of strings, was on target for discovering the secrets of the NLM.

Imagine that the mind consists of geographical strata, laid out according to Donald's (1991) stages. The lowest or deepest layer is procedural knowledge. Next comes the episodic layer, followed by mimetic, then mythic, then symbolic, and theoretic levels. The seeds of human thinking abilities, the NLM, lies buried in the mimetic layer. Miller's Project Grammarama began digging in just the right spot, digging down from the top (theoretic) layer by examining conscious discovery of grammar rules. However, after hitting the bedrock associated with the problems in developing a viable paradigm for studying generativity, he became discouraged and changed direction, missing his chance to reach the NLM. Implicit learning research was a little off center where it began (focusing on a discrimination paradigm rather than generativity). However, the angle of digging was such that this line of work came very close to revealing the hidden NLM. Now, however, with the current focus on nonconscious knowledge, most implicit learning research has gone too deep, into the procedural level, missing the NLM.

● Focusing on Generativity

Generativity is defined by Corballis (1991) as the ability to produce an unlimited number of representations from a small number of components and a set of rules for combination of components. A major advantage of such a system is its flexibility. But language is only one of several domains in which a generative representation may be advantageous. A generative representational system for perception, for example, would have been much better for dealing with the rapidly changing technological environment in which early humans found themselves (Corballis, 1991).

● Generativity in Perception

   If generativity is a prelinguistic ability, there should be evidence of it in nonlinguistic domains. Much of the work in the ecological approach to perception attempts to demonstrate that perception involves the detection of sets of invariant relationships and associated transformations over which the invariant relationships are maintained. If we look at perception in this way, it seems very similar to a grammar. Grammars are often described as having deep structures that are invariant across acceptable transformations. Grammatical rules are thought to be sets of acceptable transformations. From the ecological perspective, perception is like a dialogue between an organism and its environment (see Neisser, 1976).

   Among the most compelling and insightful experiments related to this way of looking at perception are the experiments on perception of moving dots of light. Johansson (1973) filmed a person with several light sources attached to different body joints. When the film was shown with the contrast turned all the way up, it appears to be a set of random dots. However, when the person being filmed begins walking, it is immediately perceived as a person walking. Even the gender of the person walking can be detected from the pattern of moving dots. The amazing thing about this experiment is that we have never seen a person under these conditions before. Yet, we instantly see the moving dots of light as a person walking. Thus, we must respond perceptually to complex interrelations among the positions of joints while observing people walking. Our perceptual system self-tunes to detect appropriate abstract invariances without help from the central executive. Perception of such abstract invariant relations appears to be central to normal perception.

   While the invariant relations among the moving dots tell us that it is a person walking, this pattern can be modulated by other factors or transformations. The person could walk faster, or run, or limp. In each of these cases, the pattern of moving dots would be altered by an acceptable transformation that alters the perception but does not prevent us from perceiving that it is still a person walking. Just as the cues used in perception can be quite complex, the sets of acceptable transformations necessary to perceive real world concepts, such as growing things, smiling faces, and bending fingers, can also be very complex (see Michaels & Carello, 1981).

Recall that generativity, according to Corballis (1991), requires fragmentary representations in which parts can be recombined in new ways. There is extensive evidence that perception involves analysis of a stimulus into reusable parts. The classic Gestalt laws of perception (similarity, closure, proximity, figure ground segregation) may all be considered ways of parsing a stimulus into features. Evidence that we use feature perception in processing language is quite compelling. The standard classroom demonstration in which one searches for the letter *t* in different backgrounds (see Figure 7.1) demonstrates that we automatically process the minimum necessary features to distinguish a *t* from its background. Thus, it is much more difficult to find *t*s in a background of many different letters versus in a background of sets of a single letter. Adjustments of the features used to find the *t*s is automatic and effortless. Thus, the use of specific features to identify letters seems to be under adaptive control of some nonconscious mechanism (implicit) used to guide perception of letters, but perception of nonlinguistic stimuli seems to have these generative qualities as well (see bottom of Figure 7.1). Two important theories of perception are based on just such ideas.

According to Marr's (1982) theory of visual perception, because of the infinite variability of patterns created by light reflecting off objects in the visual array, recognition of objects would be impossible without first parsing objects into primitive units as they pass through various levels of bottom-up visual processing. To complete the process of recognizing the object, however, the image must be matched to a stored representation, which is a top-down process. For this to occur, the representation of the object in memory must be flexible enough to match, no matter what orientation the object is viewed from or what the lighting conditions are, and so forth. According to Marr (1982), top-down generation of objects from stored representations of some generalized set of components can solve the problem. This theory has much in common with many theories of language processing (e.g., see Liberman, 1984); however, Biederman (1986) proposes a similar theory of visual perception, which draws a direct parallel to language.

Biederman (1986) proposes that visual objects and scenes are parsed into components, which are then matched to a set of geometric ions or *geons* stored in memory. Just as human languages contain from 16 to 44 phonemes, Biederman proposes that most objects and scenes can be repre-

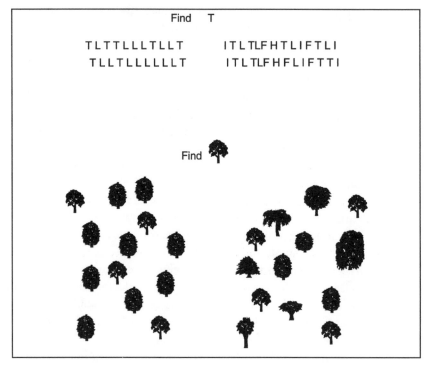

Figure 7.1. Adaptive feature processing with linguistic and nonlinguistic stimuli.

sented using 38 geons. Furthermore, the process of combining geons is said to be hierarchical, in that geons are embedded within each other to form objects that are embedded to form entire visual scenes, just as language uses embedded structures for representing complex meanings. The rules for combining geons, according to Biederman, are dictated by the way we understand physical reality, and the number of meaningful combinations is limitless. The fact that recognition of distorted pictures is better if geons are preserved rather than mutilated is seen as evidence supporting this theory. In addition, Biederman has shown that people recognize simple line drawings composed of geons as quickly as they recognize full color, detailed photographs of the objects.

Apparently, this generative ability is *not* limited to processing language. As demonstrated in Figure 7.1, the same adaptive feature-processing effect can be obtained with nonlinguistic stimuli. Perception, like language, appears to involve fragmentary representations (features) that can be recombined to perceive different shapes or similar shapes in different contexts. According to Corballis (1991), the power of such a component-based system lies in its unlimited ability to produce, as well as recognize new combinations. This type of representation is well-adapted to a technological environment that is constantly changing. Because of flexibility, the high level of generativity in human perception would have been an excellent adaptation for early humans as they began to make tools and shape their own environment.

● Generativity in Memory

What about human memory? We are used to thinking of memory as a mechanism for preserving records of past events. Thus, we might think about memory more in terms of consistency or preserving accurate details than in terms of generating new combinations. Yet, there seems to be a generative side of memory as well as perception. Both theories of perception described above include the idea of long-term storage of some set of basic components. According to Corballis (1991), storing some basic "vocabulary" of idealized components while discarding unnecessary information could have aided early humans in solving the problems of memory limitations as their social order became increasingly complex.

One study examining repeated tellings of the same ballad by experienced ballad singers in North Carolina (Wallace & Rubin, 1988) demonstrated that the stability in ballads across time and different singers is not maintained by rote memory of the material. Instead, it is maintained by constraints imposed by music, poetics, narrative structure, and imagery. Within these constraints, repeated singing of a ballad may vary both by the same and by different singers. Also, when the experiment was repeated with untrained college students as the memorizers of the ballads, the same types of constraints governed their retellings of the story. For example, when rhythmical information was emphasized in the stimulus, recalls were more accurate. Wallace and Rubin concluded that "the memory for the ballads is not the exact song, nor is it a collection of words; rather, it is a collection of rules and constraints" (p. 303). Such findings suggest that memory for events may involve generative processes that permit variation within constraints.

Another experiment by Shaw, Wilson, and Wellman (1986) illustrates the generative side of memory. The point of their experiment was to demonstrate that the mind is tuned to sets of possibilities, acquiring generative concepts, rather than remembering specific events. In their intriguing experiment, they showed subjects a sequence of eight cards, each containing a simple geometric shape in one of the corners. In the set, designed to stimulate the set of all possible figures rotating around the four corners, each card contained a figure in the next corner rotating around the cards (see Figure 7.2). In the oscillating groups, the shape alternated between the upper left and lower right corners across the sequence of cards. Thus, whereas any of the four shapes in any of the four corners might be acceptable if the concept acquired was shapes rotating around corners, no shapes ever occurred in the upper right or lower left corners in the oscillating group. In the Shaw et al. study, the shapes used were a simple square, circle, heart, and cross. The shapes in Figure 7.2 are from a replication of the Shaw et al. study in our lab that will be discussed below. The locations of the shapes exactly replicate those used by Shaw et al. in the rotating and oscillating groups.

Shaw et al. (1986) showed the sequences of eight cards corresponding to the rotating and oscillating conditions to groups of subjects, who were instructed to memorize the stimuli so that they could draw them later. However, instead of having them draw the cards after viewing the set of cards, they were actually given a discrimination task in which they attempted to tell which exact cards they had experienced during training from a set of 25 cards. There were three types of test items. Eight cards were the actual old items from their study list. Another eight cards were new cards that were possible for the set of all shapes rotating around all four corners, but they did not occur in the study list. These possible-new items all occurred in the upper right or lower left corners, so that they would be impossible in the oscillating condition, if subjects had noticed that the cards in their set only used the other two corners. Finally nine cards were "noncases" that involved different shapes, different size shapes, or shapes in the center of a card, which were quite different from the training stimuli.

Everyone did well on the actual old items and the noncases. The interesting results concern the possible-new items. These items were easily detected in the oscillating condition but were often falsely identified as old in the rotating condition. In a second experiment, Shaw et al. (1986) manipulated the number of study trials before the discrimination test. It is especially interesting that false recognition of these items in the rotating condition increased with additional study trials. With a single study trial, they falsely recognized the possible-new items as old 50% of the time. With

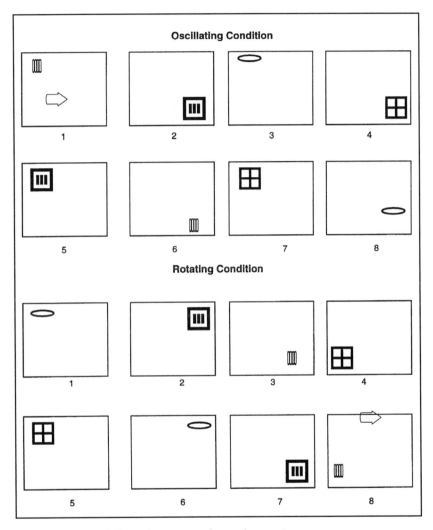

Figure 7.2. Stimuli from the memory for cards experiment.

two study trials, the false recognition rate rose to 75%, and with three trials it was 80%. We know of no other memory experiment showing that memory actually declines with additional practice. Thus, here we have a situation where subjects are trying to remember exact individual items, but the nature of the study set causes them to generate the whole set of possible items, increasing false recognition of the possible-new items.

239

We found this result very interesting and wondered if we could replicate it, given that this result seems unlike most memory experiments. In our replication of this study, we included one additional condition beside the rotating and oscillating conditions. The new condition, which we will call the no pattern condition, used all four corners but did not rotate around the four corners in succession. Shaw et al. (1986) suggested that it was the sequential rotating of corners that made the presentation series a "generator set" that induced the rotation concept in their subjects' minds and, thereby, caused false recognition of the possible-new items. However, if the same result was found in the no pattern condition, we would conclude that it was simply recognition of all four corners being used, rather than induction of the rotating concept that produced the effect. We also manipulated number of study trials (one trial, three trials, or six study trials) before the discrimination test as another between-subjects variable.

We added an additional test, given after the discrimination test, to see if subjects would actually generate sets of items following the constraints they were exposed to during training (oscillating or rotating). In this test, we gave subjects a paper containing four new shapes and eight blank rectangles representing a new sequence of cards. The rectangles were numbered one through eight to indicate their order in a study list. Subjects were asked to draw a set of cards as similar as possible to their training set, except that only the four new shapes could be used. By requiring subjects to transfer to a new set of shapes, we tried to avoid their use of rote memory to create the new set of cards. We were interested in seeing if subjects would draw sets of cards having the rotating or oscillating pattern that they were exposed to during the study phase of the experiment.

The draw test was scored for presence of both the oscillating and rotating patterns in the stimuli drawn, irrespective of which condition a subject was in. Thus, all drawings received an oscillating score and a rotating score. Each drawn card was scored as following ($+1$) or not following ($+0$) the pattern based on the previous card. For example, if the first card contained a shape in the upper left corner, the rotating score was increased by 1 if the next card was in the upper right corner. The oscillating score was incremented by 1 if the next card was in the lower right corner. Each score ranged from 0 to a maximum of 7.

The results of the discrimination test replicated several of the Shaw et al. (1986) findings. All conditions did well on the old items and the non-case items. The possible-new items, the items of main interest, were easily detected in the oscillating groups, who classified these items 81% correct with one study trial, 95% correct with three study trials, and 97% correct with six study trials. As in Shaw et al. (1986), possible-new items were correctly classified as new items at a lower level in the rotating condition as compared to the oscillating condition, 69% with one study trial, 71% when subjects had three study trials, and 96% with six study trials. However, the random condition was very similar to the rotating condition, achieving 66% correct with one study trial, 79% correct with three study trials, and 94% with six study trials. Because the rotating and random pattern conditions were so similar, we are forced to conclude that results were not caused by a special quality activated by the rotating pattern. Instead, it seems that the same results can be produced when random corners are used. Also, it was disappointing that we did not find a drop in performance on the new-possible items in the rotating condition as a function of more practice. Our subjects did slightly better on these items with three versus one trial and much better with six learning trials. Thus, with more practice subjects got better at remembering exactly what they saw (as one would expect in any memory experiment) in all three conditions. We plan to continue these experiments in a richer domain (more study items, variety of shapes and locations). Perhaps it was just too easy to learn the exact items with only eight unique study cards.

The drawing test indicated that subjects in both the oscillating and rotating conditions used the pattern they were exposed to during training in generating a set of new training cards. Subjects in the rotating condition tended to draw rotating patterns (mean rotating score of 4.4 in the single-study trial condition, 5.8 in the three-study trial condition, and 6.7 in the six-trial rotating condition). Subjects in the oscillating condition tended to use the oscillating pattern in their drawings (mean oscillating scores of 3.8, 6.3, and 6.5 in the one-, three-, and six-trial conditions, respectively). The no pattern condition had low scores on both measures, irrespective of number of study trials (mean of 1.4 on the rotating pattern and 1.9 on the oscillating pattern). Interestingly, however, the correlations between the appropriate response on the drawing test and recognition of the new-possible items were quite low (.27 in the rotating condition and .31 in the oscillating conditions). This suggests that conscious awareness of the patterns may not have played a major role in recognizing the new-possible items.

PROJECT GRAMMARAMA REVISITED

Having argued that important secrets still lie in the direction initially investigated by George Miller in Project Grammarama, it remains to break through the brick walls of problems he faced in order to explore generativity with experiments on artificial grammars. Below we report on a recent series of experiments we have been conducting, with Lewis Roussel and Anne Cook, that is directed toward developing a viable artificial grammar paradigm for studying generativity (Cochran, Mathews, Roussel, & Cook, 1997).

One major obstacle to studying generativity with artificial grammars, which was emphasized by Miller (1968), was the absence of a meaning element. The lack of meaning of generated strings is related to a second recurrent problem—the boring nature of the artificial grammar-learning task. We attempted to solve both of these problems by incorporating generation of strings into a game that gave meaning to the strings and made the task more exciting. Our cover story places the task in a starship. Subjects were given instructions containing the following story:

> We are on a military transport vessel attempting to bring remnants of a space colony back home. Unfortunately, we are short on food for the long trip. Making matters worse, much of the food that we took on board from the colony has been contaminated by a radioactive poison. Your job is to learn to distinguish poison from nonpoisoned food by recognizing poison food labels.

Explicit groups were told that the poisoning of the food was done by spies and that spies have a secret code for discriminating poison from nonpoison food labels. We know this because spies never eat poison food. Thus, explicit groups were encouraged to crack the spies' code to discriminate poison from nonpoison food labels. In Experiment 3 described below, we went further in assigning meaning to each letter in a string in terms of movements of the food through control points on the spaceship. In the implicit groups, subjects were led to believe that the poisoning was accidental; there was no mention of spies. They were also led to expect that memorizing poison can labels would be helpful because poison can labels "look alike."

The second key problem that blocked progress with Miller's Project Grammarama was the fact that it takes too long to learn complex artificial grammars, making it practically impossible to do experiments in the short time we can keep volunteer subjects in the lab. A related problem was that continued failure in attempts to generate valid strings, which is bound to occur when subjects attempt to generate strings from a complex grammar without any previous experience, is frustrating and discouraging. In our attempt to solve these problems, we took an idea from mothers' interactions with their toddlers learning to speak. Mothers often help children by guessing what they are trying to say and repeating the inferred message back to the child.

Our computerized version of "motherese" also did not require a completely accurate generated string for positive feedback. Instead, whenever a subject generated a string that was close to a valid string, we had the computer find the nearest valid string and return the corrected string to the subject. We thought this form of computerized motherese would facilitate the learning process and avoid uninteresting search behaviors (e.g., trying slight changes in a generated string to find an exact match to a valid string), which dominated the behavior of subjects in the earlier Project Grammarama experiments. Of course, our motherese idea had to be implemented in the starship game. To accomplish this the following information was included in the instructions:

> The poisoned food is highly radioactive. Although all of the food supply was initially contaminated, each time it is passed through a working decontamination device, the amount of radioactivity is reduced. Thus, when tested with a special geiger counter on the ship, radioactivity levels in individual cans of food may range from 0 to 10. Each can label generated during training will be located by computer and tested for radioactivity. Only cans that test at level 10 are poison. Any can with a radioactivity reading lower than 10 is safe to eat. Also, since cans that have readings above 7 are similar to a poison can label (a 10), the computer is capable of tracking down the related poison can and giving the exact label.

The radioactivity reading returned by the computer for each label was 10 times the proportion of letters in a generated string that matched a valid string not previously found by the subject. Because valid strings get readings of 10 and the score declines with fewer matching letters, it is also a simple

243

measure of string goodness or degree of grammaticality of the generated string.

One more twist was added to the game to avoid subjects repeatedly generating the exact same string and to encourage exploring the whole space of potential strings (poison cans) generated by the grammar. Once a subject found a poison can of food, the computer eliminated that can from its list of valid strings. Thus, if a subject typed the same can label again, the computer would not find the same poison can again. Instead, the reading would be based on the closest remaining valid string not yet generated by the subject.

● Experiment 1

In the first experiment of this series, we explored subjects' ability to generate valid strings (find poison cans of food) without any prior training or exposure to instances of the grammar. In Experiment 1, we used the grammar previously used by Reber (1967), which generates a total of 43 valid strings. Subjects in the explicit group were told the spy story described above. The implicit groups were given the same radioactive food scenario but were led to believe that the poisoning was accidental. Thus, there was no secret code to break. Their instructions told them to memorize poison food can labels that they found because labels of poison cans tend to look alike. We implemented our motherese approach in this experiment, setting a cutoff of greater than seven on the radioactivity score for the computer to find the valid string. That is, more than 70% of the letters in the generated string must match a poison can (grammatical string) in order for the computer to find the poison can. Subjects played the game in three successive 25-minute sessions. Each session they began the game again, attempting to find all 43 valid strings.

What we discovered from the results of Experiment 1 was that the brick walls preventing development of a useful paradigm for studying generativity of artificial grammars were much harder to break through than we imagined. Even with the "exciting" starship game format and our motherese assistance in finding valid strings, subjects found the task very hard and frustrating. In the third session, subjects generated a mean of 246 strings. However, they found only an average of 13.4 of the 43 valid strings. Thus, their hit rate was only 5.5%. Whether they were given the explicit spy story or the implicit memorization instructions had little effect. Very little was learned about the grammar.

● Experiment 2

In the second experiment, we applied a lesson from the implicit learning literature to push learning to a higher level. People often seem to learn more quickly about a grammar from viewing sets of valid strings (learning implicitly) than by carefully thinking about grammar rules (e.g., see Reber, 1993). As stated earlier, acquiring grammatical knowledge seems to rely more on instances than inferences (Brooks & Vokey, 1991; Vokey & Brooks, 1992). Thus, in the second experiment, we exposed subjects to series of valid strings, presented as a military training exercise for learning to identify poison food, before letting them play the starship game (the generate task). This procedure also provided us with an opportunity to explore the effects of different types of string study tasks on resulting generativity of the acquired knowledge. At this point, we also switched to the grammar used by Mathews et al. (1989) because it generates more valid strings (177). Thus, it gave subjects more targets (poison cans) to look for.

The study task for all subjects involved viewing 30 valid strings, one study string at a time, on a computer screen for 3 seconds each. After each string was presented, the screen was erased and several blanks corresponding to the length of the string appeared. The subjects then typed letters to fill in the blanks for all or part of the string they had just viewed, depending on their assigned training condition. The *whole recall group* was instructed to remember and type in the entire string they had just seen on the screen. They were permitted only one key press to type each letter of the string in order, from left to right, in the spaces provided. Each letter they got correct appeared in its correct blank on the screen. Each letter they typed wrong did not appear. Instead a # sign appeared to occupy positions of incorrectly typed letters. The *familiar fragment finding group* was instructed to look for familiar letter patterns in the strings displayed across training trials. Their task on each trial was to type in a familiar chunk of up to six letters in the string that they remembered seeing in strings on earlier trials. On the first few trials, they were instructed to type in any fragment of the string they wished if they didn't recognize any chunks. This group's instructions externalized the process of chunk finding thought to be a key learning process in implicit learning of artificial grammars (e.g., Perruchet & Pacteau, 1990; Servan-Schreiber & Anderson, 1990). The *familiar fragment yoked group* involved yoking each subject in this group to one subject in the familiar fragment-finding group. Each of the subjects in this yoked group saw the entire string with the chunk previously identified (typed in) by their yoked partner highlighted. Their job was to type in the highlighted part of the string. The *random fragment yoked group* was also yoked to a subject in the original familiar fragment-finding group. However, instead of having the chunks they found highlighted, a randomly selected chunk of the same length was highlighted in the string for them to type. Thus, this group was exposed to an unsystematic parsing of the training strings (Stadler, 1995). Finally, one additional group, the *informed fragment-finding group*, performed the same task as the fragment-finding group except that they were told the spy-secret code story (the others got the same story without mentioning how the food became poisoned), and they were encouraged to discover the secret code. We conceptualized this group's training as a synergistic combination of implicit learning (memory processing) and explicit processing (consciously looking for rules). The nature of the training task itself, typing fragments of each string back into the computer and looking for familiar chunks, engages implicit processes. Yet the spy story sensitized them to look for rules (the secret code). We have argued previously that combinations of both types of learning may be optimal for learning some tasks (Mathews et al., 1989).

After training, subjects took either a string-classification test or a string-generation test. They were told it was time to feed the troops. In the classification test, they were shown 120 can labels and asked to label as poisoned whichever cans they thought were poison so that they could be discarded. In the generate test, they were told to generate labels of 100 cans of food to be eliminated before the troops were fed.

The first finding of importance is that subjects in this experiment did much better on the generation task than did subjects in Experiment 1. In several conditions in this experiment, subjects generated strings with a 30% to 40% hit rate (in terms of finding valid strings). In Experiment 1, they had only a 5.5% hit rate after three study sessions. This finding highlights the point that grammatical knowledge is acquired better from exposure to instances than by trying to figure out the rules of the grammar. Instances rather than inferences are the wellspring of grammatical knowledge.

The second finding of importance is that generally speaking, what is good for discrimination is good for generation. In both generation and discrimination tests, the groups that studied whole strings for recall, found familiar fragments, or were provided familiar fragments found by their yoked partners, all performed well. However, in both discrimination and generation, the random fragment yoked group did much worse. Finally, all of the trained groups did better than the untrained control groups.

Additionally, in both discrimination and generation, there was evidence that the informed fragment-finding group did better than the uninformed fragment-finding group; however, the difference between these two groups was greater in discrimination than in generation.

The finding of similar patterns of results in discrimination and in generation across the various conditions is good news. It means that the large literature on implicit grammar learning, based almost entirely on string discrimination or classification tests, may be generalizable to generation of grammatical strings. Of course, more work is needed to verify that similar effects are found for both discrimination and generation—and we may find some differences as well. Still, it appears that findings in the implicit learning literature may have relevance to the important issue of generativity.

The finding of similar patterns of results for string discrimination and string generation is also consistent with our view that generativity occurs in perceptual processes. In a string-discrimination task, subjects look at the strings and decide which ones look like "poison" (more like a valid string) versus ones that look safe (invalid strings). Theories of implicit learning have linked this ability to perceptual processes, such as chunking, used to recognize the strings (e.g., Servan-Schreiber & Anderson, 1990). The above results suggest that the same variables that enhance discrimination of strings also enhance string generation. We suspect this is true because generativity is rooted in perception. We discover patterns by learning to perceive the relative invariants and "slippable" qualities of the patterns (Hofstadter, 1995). This same knowledge of invariants and acceptable transformations forms the basis for generating strings.

The finding that learning random chunks retarded both discrimination and string generation is consistent with the view that consistent parsing of the strings is crucial to implicit learning (Servan-Schreiber & Anderson, 1990; Stadler, 1995). It is also consistent with the view that implicit learning depends on learning to recognize familiar or frequent chunks in the sequence (Perruchet & Pacteau, 1990; Servan-Schreiber & Anderson, 1990) and acquiring information about how the pieces are put together into valid strings (Cleeremans, 1993; Dienes, 1992; Mathews & Roussel, in press).

● Experiment 3

The generally poor showing of explicit learning instructions in most artificial grammar experiments might reflect the rather limiting experimental conditions under which most of these experiments have been conducted. Usually explicit instructions involve telling subjects to look for rules to distinguish valid from invalid strings. Subjects are not provided with any notions about the type of rules they should look for, nor are they given the opportunity to use paper and pencil to help figure out the rules. Norman (1993) has noted that testing mental capacities in the absence of the normal cognitive artifacts on which our thinking depends may give false impressions about human abilities. In Experiment 3, we gave our explicit groups instructions on what types of rules to look for and how to find them. We also allowed them the use of paper and pencil to decipher the rules of the grammar.

The extent to which the strings generated by the grammar were meaningful was also limited in the first two experiments. The strings did have a nominal meaning, in that they were defined as labels on cans of food. However, the actual letters that made up the strings, the components of the strings, did not have meaning. In Experiment 3, we attached meaning to the individual letters in terms of movements of the food through control points about the starship. Thus, we added something like a meaningful graphemic level to the strings. This was done by elaborating the starship story as described below:

The food taken on board our vessel came originally from another vessel on which all of the passengers died from the poisoned food. Before they all perished, in a last-ditch effort to save themselves, members of that ship had installed decontamination devices throughout the ship. These decontamination devices were placed at several control points on the ship where food was moved from one location to the next. However, the spies on board who had originally poisoned the food made many of the decontamination devices inoperative. Every can of food that passed through at least one working decontamination device in its travels about the ship was and still is safe to eat. Cans that passed through only nonworking decontamination devices are still poisonous and must not be eaten.

The strings of letters represent labels on cans of food that were stamped as the food was moved from one control point to another. The stamps indicate the squad that the food inspector at each control point belonged in. Thus, the same letter could be used by more than one inspector at different control points. Nonetheless, the letter sequences in the labels remain as a cryptic but accurate record of movements of the cans of food around the large ship. Your task is to learn to recognize poison food cans so that we can avoid feeding them to the people on board our vessel.

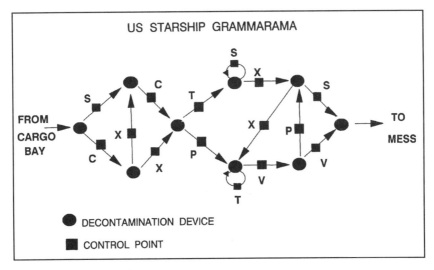

Figure 7.3. Unsafe path map.

Figure 7.3 provides an unsafe path map, listing all the failed decontamination units. Thus, any can of food that moved about the ship only along these paths is still poison. Any can of food that is moved through any path (from one control point to another) that is not included on this map must have gone through at least one safe decontamination unit, and it is safe to eat. To readers familiar with the implicit learning literature, this unsafe path map will look familiar. It is the finite-state grammar used by Mathews et al. (1989), which generates 177 valid strings, or in this case, poison cans of food. Any label that has at least one transition not included on the unsafe path map (i.e., contains at least one violation of the grammar) is safe to eat. In the experiment, subjects did not get to see the unsafe path map. They had to learn to discriminate (classify cans of food provided for them) or generate poison food labels in order to find and eliminate all the unsafe cans of food.

We gave subjects a large set of strings (80 valid strings) to study and ample time (three 2-hour sessions) to learn something about the grammar. Our contrasting memory processing or implicit groups were similarly endowed with time and cognitive artifacts to try to memorize the 80 study strings. Practice on the task was interspersed with practice tests (either string discrimination or generation tests), in which they attempted to find or produce all 80 test strings. Upon reaching a criterion of 80% correct on their study list or after completing three study-test sequences, subjects attempted to find or produce all of the strings generated by the grammar (177 strings).

Under these optimal conditions for model building, we expected our explicit subjects to quickly discover the rules of the grammar and outperform the memorizers (implicit groups). Observations of the subjects participating in the experiment seemed to confirm our expectations. The model builders were more confident and seemed to enjoy the task much more than the memorizers. They drew maps that became increasingly complex over sessions. When it came to the final test, they confidently seemed to be using their maps to perform the test. The memorizers, on the other hand, seemed to get increasingly frustrated with the task. Eighty strings seemed like too many to memorize, and they all looked very similar. They spent a lot of time organizing the items for recall but did not seem to enjoy the task. We were quite surprised when we looked at the results of the final test.

In the final test, the results for the discrimination test were: model builders with discrimination practice during training classified 83% of the strings correctly; model builders with generate training classified 85% correct. Memorizers with discrimination practice classified 74% correct; and memorizers with generate practice classified 90% correct.

On the generate test, the model builders with discriminate practice produced 45% of the valid strings (with the help of the computer's motherese), and model builders with generate practice produced 45% of the strings. Memorizers with discriminate training produced 38% of the strings, and memorizers with generate practice produced 64% of the strings, significantly more than all the other conditions.

The above data reflect how good subjects were at producing or "finding" the entire set of valid strings that can be generated by the grammar. It does not take into account the number of tries or number of strings generated by a subject. Recall that subjects were allowed to generate as many strings as they wished on the generate test, trying to find all the valid strings. The mean number of strings generated by the memorizers with discrimination training (117) was considerably lower than those of subjects in the other four conditions, who generated mean numbers of strings ranging from 159 to 171 strings. Therefore, we also looked at the data in terms of hit rate. This way of looking at the data produces a slightly different pattern: The model builders with discriminate practice had a hit rate of 43%. The model builders with generate training had a hit rate of 50.3%.

The memorizers with discriminate training had a hit rate of 57%, and the memorizers with generate training had a hit rate of 71%.

Thus, no matter how you look at the data, the memorizers with generative practice are the best. The memorizers with discriminative practice come in second when looking at hits per try (a measure of quality of each generated string), but they come in last when looking at total number of poison cans found, because they produced fewer strings. Thus, in terms of ability to generate good strings (disregarding the number of strings produced), it appears that, contrary to our expectations, we replicated the standard implicit learning finding: The implicit mode (memorizing strings) led to greater knowledge of the set of grammatical strings; moreover, the knowledge that subjects in this mode gained was better able to support generating good strings than the explicit mode. This occurred in spite of our efforts to attach meaning to the strings, train subjects on how to build models of the grammar, allow them to use paper and pencil during training to develop a model of the grammar, and allow them to use their model on the final test. However, it should be noted that, although building models of the grammar did not improve generativity, it did not greatly interfere with learning the grammar. The model-building groups were only slightly inferior to the memorizing groups in our measure of string goodness and did better than the memorizers with discriminative training in terms of total number of valid strings produced in the final test.

Curiously, model building seemed to greatly enhance the confidence of the subjects in their ability to perform the task. They seemed to enjoy the task more and found it less frustrating. They also appeared to spend less time studying the strings. Thus, we might speculate, in this paradigm, mental models served as a motivational function more than as a tool for classifying strings. We suspect that the same type of memory-based knowledge used in the memorizing group was also at work in helping the model builders classify and generate strings. That is, when actually performing the task, subjects may have relied more on their implicitly acquired knowledge than their mental model or cognitive artifact (their map of the grammar devised during training). We have seen this pattern of behavior before in other paradigms, such as process control tasks, in which modification of subjects' mental model of a task often has little effect on their performance (Mathews & Roussel, in press).

It is also interesting to ask what differentiates the memorizing generate practice group from the other groups, allowing it to outproduce all the other groups substantially on the final generate test. Initial analysis of the strings generated by subjects in all the groups shows that the differences lie primarily in the beginnings or first five letters in the strings generated. The memorizers with generate practice were getting these prefixes of strings correct 95% of the time, whereas the other groups were considerably lower (ranging from 70% to 80%). Thus, it appears that generative practice during training got memorizers to concentrate their attention on the beginning of strings. They got to know the initial branches in the grammatical tree structure better than did the other groups. It makes sense that knowledge of this initial structure of the grammar would be most beneficial in a generation test if strings were generated from the beginning (left to right).

One more pattern in the generated strings of subjects in all the groups is quite interesting. If subjects were memorizing good strings, we would expect that their sets of generated strings would begin with good ones—the ones they remembered well—and the quality would deteriorate rapidly when they exhausted their list of remembered strings. Actually, the pattern of quality of strings generated remained fairly constant across successive sets of generated strings. This pattern is consistent with the notion that subjects are not using rote memory of instances to generate strings. Instead, they have learned about the grammar in terms of constraints and allowable transformations. Thus, the nth string they generated follows pretty much the same constraints as the first several strings.

The results of this experiment support the conclusion that there is a similar level of generativity associated with implicit versus explicit instructions in this task. This result contrasts with findings in process control tasks that have found little evidence of generality in implicitly acquired knowledge. For example, Dienes and Fahey (1995) found that performance in situations involving different exact levels of workers used during training were at a chance level on the sugar production task. Perhaps the difference in generalizability between the sugar task and the present experiment lies in the fact that in the grammar task, subjects were exposed to a representative set of instances during training. The set of strings subjects were exposed to during training in these experiments may correspond to what Shaw et al. (1986) have called a generator set. Thus, knowledge acquired about the nature of valid strings generalizes well to the complete set of strings generated by the grammar.

In the sugar production task, the set of situations experienced by a learner is under the learner's control. Each output level is dependent on the prior response of the learner. Thus, learners may adopt strategies that avoid sampling certain areas of the problem space (Buckner, Funke, &

Berry, 1995). However, one would still expect some transfer to new situations. Thus, this difference in generalizability of acquired knowledge may represent deeper differences between the knowledge used in the two tasks. Perhaps the knowledge acquired in process-control tasks is limited to the episodic level (see Mathews & Roussel, in press). However, the knowledge acquired in artificial grammar tasks seems to have very different qualities that enable relatively good generalization to new situations.

LESSONS

1. Generativity involves perception of relative invariance against a background of predictable changes. It requires representations that consist of reusable parts that are highly constrained in their ways of being recombined (Corballis, 1989). There is evidence of this type of generativity in perception, memory, and implicitly acquired knowledge of grammars.

2. Conscious efforts to discover the rules of the grammar have little effect on the nature or quality of generated strings, even when subjects are trained in model building and are allowed to use cognitive artifacts (paper and pencil) during study. We think this is true because natural language generativity at the syntactic level is largely a nonconscious process rooted in perception. Conscious control of language is primarily at the meaning level. The type of generativity explored in our experiments involves trying to generate all the strings allowed by the grammatical syntax, not trying to generate a string with a specific meaning (e.g., a specific path through the grammar). Consequently, the natural nonconscious mechanisms by which we learn to recognize and produce grammatical strings dominated in this task.

3. Mental models seemingly served primarily a motivational or emotional function. They seemed to act like a security blanket to prevent frustration with the immensity of the task. They gave subjects confidence but had little impact on the quality or quantity of generated strings.

4. The pattern of strings generated by subjects appears to reflect true generativity in the sense of constrained regularities rather than rote memory for instances. The sets of strings generated by subjects tended to display a fairly flat progression in string quality. If rote memory were being used, we would have expected high quality of generated strings initially, followed by a drop in quality when subjects used up their list of well-remembered instances. Instead, as in the case of memory for ballads (Wallace & Rubin,

1988) or sequences of cards (Shaw et. al., 1986), the sequences of generated strings were constant in quality, suggesting that they reflect knowledge of constraints (invariants) and allowable recombinations of reusable parts rather than memory of good cases followed by strategic guessing.

We think this type of knowledge fits Donald's (1991) description of mimetic level knowledge, which marks the first point of departure in the evolutionary history of humans versus apes. We conceptualize the mimetic controller as a presemantic perceptual representation system (e.g., Schacter, 1990, 1992a, 1992b; Tulving & Schacter, 1990). It is similar to Mandler's (1992) concept of image schemas. Its primary function is to build simplified conceptual representations that preserve temporal or spatial relationships. It produces nonlinguistic mental representations that provide us with information about object structure, location, and affordances (e.g., Gibson, 1977; Schacter & Cooper, 1995). It has capabilities for limited mental inferences (e.g., object trajectory) and mental operations (e.g., delayed imitation of a rhythm). Thus, the mimetic controller has some degree of internal structure or syntax that can be imposed on representations of stimuli such that different representations can be compared or combined. There is also evidence that the presemantic structural representation system (mimetic controller) is separate from symbolic or linguistic knowledge. For example, Warrington (1975) found that patients with dementia or severe visual object agnosia, who performed poorly on naming the functions of everyday objects, performed normally on tests of knowledge of object structure.

Thus, mimetic representations seem to be the beginning of rule-based representations that afford mental computation. Such internally constrained and recombinable representations appear to be what separates human from chimpanzee (Donald, 1991). Implicitly acquired knowledge of artificial grammars appears to be tapping into this basic-level knowledge system that is the direct precursor of language.

SUMMARY

Generativity can be defined as the ability to learn an activity or skill in terms of a set of separable features together with a rule system for combining those features. The advantage of such a system is the possibility of generating an infinite number of productions from a finite set of representations. Processing natural human language is said to be the most advanced form of generative thinking. There is no question that language is a generative system used by humans for communication, as well as for other purposes, such as social bonding. The debate surrounding generativity does not involve whether humans possess this ability, nor does it question whether learning and using language is generative. The point of debate has been whether generative thinking arose as a result of developing linguistic skills, or whether generative thinking is a prelinguistic ability that gave rise to the unique communication system of humans.

If generative thinking predates language as we know it, evidence of generativity should be found in cognitive processes thought to have preceded language. Previous research has provided evidence that both perception and memory involve generative thinking. We believe that research involving the generative nature of knowledge acquired in artificial grammar learning tasks can support the idea that generative thinking is a skill that predates the advent of language. Now that we have broken through some of the problems in developing a paradigm for studying generativity of implicit knowledge, we hope many studies will follow. We think this work will help eventually solve the NLM.

REFERENCES

Aborn, M., & Rubenstein, H. (1952). Information theory and immediate recall. *Journal of Experimental Psychology, 54,* 260-266.

Bartlett, F. (1932). *Remembering.* Cambridge, UK: Cambridge University Press.

Berry, D. C., & Dienes, Z. (1993). *Implicit learning: Theoretical and empirical issues.* Hillsdale, NJ: Lawrence Erlbaum.

Bickerton, D. (1984). The language bioprogram hypothesis. *Behavior and Brain Sciences, 7,* 173-221.

Biederman, I. (1986). Recognition-by-components: A theory of human image understanding. *Psychological Review, 94,* 115-147.

Brooks, L. R., & Vokey, J. R. (1991). Abstract analogies and abstracted grammars: Comments on Reber (1989) and Mathews et al. (1989). *Journal of Experimental Psychology: General, 120,* 316-323.

Bruner, J. S., Goodnow, J. J., & Austin, G. A. (1956). *A study of thinking.* New York: John Wiley.

Buckner, A., Funke, J., & Berry, D. C. (1995). Negative correlations between control performance and verbalizable knowledge: Indicators for implicit learning in process control tasks? *Quarterly Journal of Experimental Psychology: Human Experimental Psychology, 48A,* 166-187.

Chan, C. (1992). *Implicit cognitive processes: Theoretical issues and applications in computer systems design.* Unpublished D.Phil. thesis, University of Oxford.

Chomsky, N. (1966). *Language and mind.* New York: Harcort Brace Jovanovich.

Cleeremans, A. (1993). *Mechanisms of implicit learning: Connectionist models of sequence processing.* Cambridge: MIT Press.

Cochran, B. P., Mathews, R. C., Roussel, L. G., & Cook, A. E. (1997). *Learning artificial grammars or learning grammars artificially: Focus on generativity.* Manuscript in preparation.

Corballis, M. C. (1989). Laterality and human evolution. *Psychological Review, 96,* 492-505.

Corballis, M. C. (1991). *The lopsided ape.* New York: Oxford University Press.

Davidson, I., & Noble, W. (1989). The archeology of perception: Traces of depiction and language. *Current Anthropology, 30,* 125-155.

Dienes, Z. (1992). Connectionist and memory array models of artificial grammar learning. *Cognitive Science, 16,* 41-79.

Dienes, Z., Altmann, G. T. M., Kwan, L., & Goode, A. (1995). Unconscious knowledge of artificial grammars is applied strategically. *Journal of Experimental Psychology: Learning, Memory, and Cognition, 21,* 1322-1328.

Dienes, Z., & Fahey, R. (1995). Role of specific instances in controlling a dynamic system. *Journal of Experimental Psychology: Learning, Memory, and Cognition, 21,* 848-862.

Donald, M. (1991). *Origins of the modern mind: Three stages in the evolution of culture and cognition.* Cambridge, MA: Harvard University Press.

Dulany, D. E., Carlson, R. A., & Dewey, G. I. (1984). A case of syntactical learning and judgment: How conscious and how abstract? *Journal of Experimental Psychology: General, 113,* 541-555.

Fodor, J. A. (1986). *The modularity of mind.* Cambridge: MIT Press.

Gardner, R. A., & Gardner, B. T. (1969). Teaching sign language to a chimpanzee. *Science, 165,* 664-672.

Gibson, J. J. (1977). The theory of affordances. In R. E. Shaw & J. Bransford (Eds.), *Perceiving, acting, and knowing.* Hillsdale, NJ: Lawrence Erlbaum.

Goodall, J. (1986). *The chimpanzees of Gombe.* Cambridge, MA: Harvard University Press.

Griffin, D. R. (1976). *The question of animal awareness: Evolutionary continuity of mental experience.* New York: Rockefeller University Press.

Hailman, J. P., & Ficken, M. S. (1986). Combinatorial animal communication with computable syntax: Chik-a-dee calling qualifies as "language" by structural linguistics. *Animal Behavior, 34,* 1899-1901.

Harlow, H. F. (1949). The formation of learning sets. *Psychological Review, 56,* 51-65.

Hayes, C. (1952). *The ape in our house.* London: Gollanez.

Herrnstein, R. J., Loveland, D. H., & Cable, C. (1976). Natural concepts in pigeons. *Journal of Experimental Psychology: Animal Behavior Processes, 2,* 285-302.

Hewes, G. W. (1973). Primate communication and the gestural origins of language. *Current Anthropology, 14,* 5-24.

Hofstadter, D. (1995). *Fluid concepts and creative analogies.* New York: Basic Books.

Holloway, R. L. (1985). The past, present, and future significance of the lunate sulcus in early hominid evolution. In P. V. Tobias (Ed.), *Hominid evolution: Past, present, and future* (pp. 47-62). New York: Alan R. Liss.

Johanson, D., & Edey, M. (1982). *Lucy: The beginnings of human kind.* New York: Warner Books.

Johansson, G. (1973). Visual perception of biological motion and a model for its analysis. *Perception and Psychophysics, 14,* 201-211.

Leakey, R. E. (1981). *The making of mankind.* New York: E. P. Dutton.

Lenneberg, E. (1967). *Biological foundations of language.* New York: John Wiley.

Liberman, P. (1984). *The biology and evolution of language.* Cambridge, UK: Cambridge University Press.

Lovejoy, O. (1988). Evolution of human walking. *Scientific American, 259*(5), 82-89.

Mandler, J. M. (1992). How to build a baby: II. Conceptual primitives. *Psychological Review, 99,* 587-604.

Marr, D. (1982). *Vision.* San Franscisco: Freeman.

Mathews, R. C., Buss, R. R., Chinn, R., & Stanley, W. B. (1988). The role of explicit and implicit learning processes in concept discovery. *The Quarterly Journal of Experimental Psychology, 40,* 135-165.

Mathews, R. C., Buss, R. R., Stanley, W. B., Blanchard-Fields, F., Cho, J. R., & Druhan, B. (1989). The role of implicit and explicit processes in learning from examples: A synergistic effect. *Journal of Experimental Psychology: Learning, Memory, and Cognition, 15,* 1083-1100.

Mathews, R. C., & Roussel, L. G. (in press). Abstractness of implicit knowledge: A cognitive evolutionary perspective. In D. Berry (Ed.), *How implicit is implicit learning.* New York: Oxford University Press.

McClelland, J., & Rumelhart, D. (1986). *Parallel distributed processing: Explorations in the microstructure of cognition* (Vol. 2). Cambridge: MIT Press.

Michaels, C. F., & Carello, C. (1981). *Direct perception.* Englewood Cliffs, NJ: Prentice Hall.

Miller, G. A. (1958). Free recall of redundant strings of letters. *Journal of Experimental Psychology, 56,* 485-491.

Miller, G. A. (1968). *The psychology of communication: Seven essays.* Harmondsworth, UK: Penguin Books.

Neisser, U. (1976). *Cognition and reality.* San Francisco: W. H. Freeman.

Norman, D. A. (1993). *Things that make us smart: Defending human attributes in the age of the machine.* Reading, MA: Addison-Wesley.

Nottenbohm, F. (1972). Neural lateralization of vocal control in a passerine bird: II. Subsong, calls, and a theory of vocal learning. *Journal of Experimental Zoology, 179,* 25-50.

Perruchet, P., & Pacteau, C. (1990). Synthetic grammar learning: Implicit rule abstraction or explicit fragmentary knowledge? *Journal of Experimental Psychology: General, 119,* 264-275.

Piatelli-Palmarini, M. (1989). Evolution, selection, and cognition: From "learning" to parameter setting in biology and the study of language. *Cognition, 31,* 1-44.

Pinker, S., & Bloom, P. (1990). *Natural language and natural selection.* Cambridge: Center for Cognitive Science, Massachusetts Institute of Technology.

Premack, D. (1971). Language in chimpanzee? *Science, 172,* 808-822.

Reber, A. S. (1967). Implicit learning of artificial grammars. *Journal of Verbal Learning and Verbal Behavior, 6,* 855-863.

Reber, A. S. (1969). Transfer of syntactic structure in synthetic languages. *Journal of Experimental Psychology, 81,* 115-119.

Reber, A. S. (1976). Implicit learning of synthetic languages: The role of instructional set. *Journal of Experimental Psychology: Human Learning and Memory, 2,* 88-94.

Reber, A. S. (1993). *Implicit learning and tacit knowledge: An essay on the cognitive unconscious.* New York: Oxford University Press.

Roediger, H. L., III. (1990). Implicit memory: Retention without remembering. *American Psychologist, 45,* 1043-1056.

Savage-Rumbaugh, E. S. (1984). Acquisition of functional symbol usage in apes and children. In H. L. Roitblat, T. G. Bever, & H. S. Terrace (Eds.), *Animal cognition* (pp. 291-310). Hillsdale, NJ: Lawrence Erlbaum.

Schacter, D. L. (1990). Perceptual representation systems and implicit memory: Toward a resolution of the multiple memory systems debate. *Annals of the New York Academy of Sciences, 608,* 543-571.

Schacter, D. L. (1992a). Priming and multiple memory systems: Perceptual mechanisms of implicit memory. *Journal of Cognitive Neuroscience, 4,* 244-256.

Schacter, D. L. (1992b). Understanding implicit memory: A cognitive neuroscience approach. *American Psychologist, 47,* 559-560.

Schacter, D. L. & Cooper, L. A. (1995). Bias in the priming of object decisions: Logic, assumptions, and data. *Journal of Experimental Psychology: Learning, Memory, and Cognition, 21,* 768-776.

Servan-Schreiber, E., & Anderson, J. R. (1990). Learning artificial grammars with competitive chunking. *Journal of Experimental Psychology: Learning, Memory, and Cognition, 16,* 592-608.

Shaw, R. E., Wilson, B. E., & Wellman, H. (1986). Abstract conceptual knowledge: How we know what we know. In V. McCabe & G. J. Balzano (Eds.), *Event cognition: An ecological perspective.* Hillsdale, NJ: Lawrence Erlbaum.

Snowden, C. T., Brown, C. H., & Peterson, M. R. (Eds.). (1982). *Primate communication.* Cambridge, UK: Cambridge University Press.

Stadler, M. A. (1995). The role of attention in implicit learning. *Journal of Experimental Psychology: Learning, Memory, and Cognition, 3,* 674-685.

Stringer, C. B., & Andrews, P. (1988). Genetic and fossil evidence for the origin of modern humans. *Science, 239,* 1263-1268.

Suppes, P. (1966). Mathematical concept formation in children. *American Psychologist, 21,* 139-150.

Tulving, E., & Schacter, D. L. (1990). Priming and human memory systems. *Science, 247,* 301-306.

Vokey, J. R., & Brooks, L. R. (1992). Salience of item knowledge in learning artificial grammars. *Journal of Experimental Psychology: Learning, Memory, and Cognition, 18,* 328-344.

Wallace, W. T., & Rubin, D. C. (1988). "The wreck of the old 97": A real event remembered in song. In U. Neisser & E. Winograd (Eds.), *Remembering reconsidered: Ecological and traditional approaches to the study of memory* (pp. 283-310). Cambridge, UK: Cambridge University Press.

Warrington, E. (1975). The selective impairment of semantic memory. *Quarterly Journal of Experimental Psychology, 27,* 635-657.

8

Implicit Learning

Methodological Issues and
Evidence of Unique Characteristics

Jonathan M. Reed
Peder J. Johnson

This chapter begins with a discussion of what we think is a central issue in implicit learning research. Our intent here is to clarify what is implied by the statement, "learning requires consciousness." In the next section, we define two a priori hypotheses a researcher may adopt in investigating the role of consciousness in learning. We discuss how there has been a bias favoring the hypothesis that learning does require consciousness (referred to as the *explicit hypothesis*) and go on to critique the basis for this assumption. This is followed by a discussion of how the explicit hypothesis has influenced the interpretation of findings in the implicit learning literature. This sets the stage for the final section of the chapter, which describes a series of recently completed experiments conducted so as to characterize implicit learning, in an attempt to more clearly distinguish it from explicit learning.

WHAT IS AT ISSUE?

What is at issue in the implicit learning literature is whether learning requires consciousness. As perhaps most readers are aware, this issue has been the subject of a great deal of controversy in the recent literature. It is our contention that most, if not all, of this controversy stems from two problems. One is related to whether participants in this controversy adopt a first- or third-person perspective regarding the role of consciousness, and the other concerns the ambiguity of all three concepts in the statement learning requires consciousness.

● First- Versus Third-Person Perspectives

We can view consciousness either from a first-person perspective (how the world appears from the subject's point of view) or from a third-person perspective (how events relating to the subject appear to an external observer, such as the experimenter). In writing this chapter from the perspective of researchers investigating implicit learning, we assumed that we should take a third-person perspective. In doing so, we quite likely stacked the deck toward concluding that consciousness does not play an important role in learning. This becomes quite apparent in the content of the peer commentary to Velmans (1991). Velmans explicitly adopts a third-person perspective in concluding that consciousness appears to have no causal influences on any cognitive process, from perceptual encoding to problem solving and decision making.

Several of the commentaries that disagree most strongly with Velmans's (1991) conclusion often take a first-person perspective. A good example of this is MacKay's (1991) claim that consciousness is king in the sense that it "issues the commands," "sets the goals," and then steps aside to allow the nervous system to implement the details that result in the intended action. Or so it appears from the first-person perspective. It should not surprise us that from the first-person perspective, where we use conscious introspection to reveal the role of consciousness, our consciousness tells us it is omniscient. Given its limited access to cognitive processing, it is difficult to imagine what else we could have expected.

However, from the third-person perspective, it is not at all clear that consciousness is king. Rather, we must ask MacKay (1991) how consciousness sets goals and issues commands and why such functions could not be performed by the brain. From this third-person perspective, the role of consciousness seems to be greatly diminished as a causal agent in cognitive processing. In fact Baars (1991), in his peer commentary to Velmans's (1991) article, states that Velmans's conclusion regarding the role of consciousness may be more a matter of his pretheoretical assumptions than the empirical findings. In effect, Baars is telling us that the issue regarding the role of consciousness in any cognitive process may become a moot point, once one takes a third-person perspective.

The Meaning of Learning Requires Consciousness

Much of the debate surrounding implicit learning has centered around a few methodological issues. Much of this controversy stems from the ambiguity of what is meant by *learning, requires,* and *consciousness* in the statement, learning requires consciousness. Unless each of these concepts is clearly defined, it is unlikely that the evidence for or against implicit learning can be considered in a coherent manner. Here we define what we mean by learning, requires, and consciousness in the context of the implicit learning literature.

WHAT IS MEANT BY LEARNING?

Statements in the literature regarding the evidence for implicit learning have ranged from claims that there is no evidence of any implicit learning, thereby implying that all learning is explicit (Dulany, 1991), to claims that a wide range of tasks, including abstract rules, can be learned implicitly (Reber, 1989). Between these extremes, some researchers have claimed that only certain very limited types of simple events may be learned implicitly (Perruchet & Amorim, 1992; Shanks & Johnstone, Chapter 16, this volume), whereas others have allowed that procedural types of knowledge may be acquired implicitly (Mandler, Nakamura, & Van Zandt, 1987; Squire, 1987). Interestingly, we have not found anyone claiming that all learning is implicit and that there is no explicit learning.

For purposes of this chapter, we define learning as acquiring an association that is at least of the complexity of the second-order conditional (SOC) learning we demonstrated in an earlier work (Reed & Johnson, 1994a). Here, using a serial location reaction-time task, we found that subjects were able to learn target locations that were determined by the previous two locations. Later, we discuss the methods and findings of this study in greater detail, but for the moment, we can think of this as a type of configural procedural learning.

There are two obvious interpretations of what is implied by the verb required in the statement, learning requires consciousness. One, which we may consider the strong interpretation, is that consciousness enters into the process of learning and plays a causal role. The other, the weak interpretation, is that consciousness often or always accompanies learning, and in this sense, it could be said to be "empirically necessary." In this role, consciousness functions more as a placeholder, distinguishing those processes that are accompanied by consciousness from those that are not.

It is important to be clear that in the case of the weak interpretation, consciousness does not enter into the process of learning, nor does it play a causal role. Consciousness, from this perspective is epiphenomenal as it relates to learning.

Therefore, there would be no necessity to include consciousness in our models of learning. Perhaps this explains Stanovich's (1991) observation that there does not exist one single model in cognitive psychology where consciousness plays a necessary role. Only the strong interpretation has empirical implications that could potentially lead to a better understanding of learning. Thus, we shall interpret the phrase learning requires consciousness to imply that what is at issue is whether consciousness enters into the process of learning as a causal agent.

WHAT IS MEANT BY CONSCIOUSNESS?

When viewed from various perspectives, ranging from folk psychology to philosophy of mind to cognitive psychology and neuroscience, consciousness appears as a mongrel concept taking on a hopeless variety of meanings. However, as studied in the context of implicit learning, consciousness is typically viewed as a state of awareness. It is within this restricted sense of consciousness that we discuss two properties of its meaning that have contributed to the controversy regarding its influence on learning.

Process or Product. First, do we view consciousness as a product or process, and second, if viewed as a process, can consciousness be dissociated from other cognitive processes, such as focal-attentive processing, that it may covary with? To the extend that consciousness is viewed as awareness, it suggests that it may be difficult to separate consciousness from the product that is the content of awareness. It is difficult to think of awareness in the absence of content. Research findings, such as those reported by Libet (1985), suggest that consciousness is the consequence or product of the extensive unconscious neural processing that preceded it. This is consistent with the widely held notion of large-scale preattentive processing preceding the occurrence of consciousness perception (Neisser, 1967).

Viewed as a product, we are probably less inclined to think of consciousness as exerting a causal influence. However, it remains possible that once an event becomes a conscious product, it is processed differently than if it had not become conscious. For example, Rozin (1976) has speculated that conscious events are broadcast more extensively throughout the information-processing system. In this manner, the product may influence the process and could be said to be part of the causal chain.

We shall take the view that consciousness in the statement learning requires consciousness is only theoretically interesting when it is assumed that consciousness "enters into processing." If viewed exclusively as a product, it is only implied that we may become aware of the consequences of learning. There are probably few who would disagree with such a claim.

● Dissociation of Consciousness

Proceeding on the assumption that consciousness is a process (or that it at least can enter into a process), we now consider whether this process can be dissociated from the other processes it may covary with. If the concept of consciousness carries with it the meaning of all the concepts that covary with it, it would seem rather pointless to debate the role of consciousness in any cognitive function. This is true whether we are thinking of information-processing concepts such as focal-attentive processing (Velmans, 1991) or neural systems such as levels of activation in the hippocampus (Moscovitch, 1994). Questioning the role of consciousness in learning does not require one to also question the role of focal-attentive processing or the hippocampus.

For this reason, it is necessary that we restrict the definition of consciousness to awareness and show that awareness can be dissociated from other correlated processes that may play a causal role in learning. To illustrate this point, there is abundant evidence that focal-attentive processing can be dissociated from awareness. This perhaps is most clearly demonstrated with so-called preattentive processes such as perceptual encoding, which is generally agreed to be unconscious but has been demonstrated to require attentional resources (e.g., Johnson, Forester, Calderwood, & Weisgerber, 1983; Paap & Ogden, 1981). Later in this chapter, we present some findings that extend this dissociation to implicit learning.

The important implication of these and similar findings is that once focal-attentive processing has been dissociated from awareness, it becomes the responsibility of those who believe them to be one and the same to provide evidence to support that view. We conclude this section, proposing that for purposes of evaluating the claim that learning requires consciousness, we restrict the definition of consciousness to awareness.

● Summary

We can now restate with a greater degree of clarity what we propose is at issue in the implicit learning literature. The claim that learning requires consciousness is interpreted to imply that to learn something as complex as SOC sequences, it is necessary for awareness to enter into the learning process.

CHOOSING AN A PRIORI HYPOTHESIS

Having defined what is at issue regarding the role of consciousness in learning, researchers may proceed by framing the issue in terms of one of two working hypotheses. They may either adopt the *implicit* default hypothesis that learning does not require consciousness, and this view will be held until there is compelling evidence to the contrary. Alternatively, they may adopt the *explicit* default hypothesis that learning does require consciousness and maintain this view until there is contradictory evidence. In this section, we argue that there has been a strong tendency for researchers to adopt the explicit default hypothesis and that this choice has largely been based on a pretheoretic first-person perspective that assumes the primacy of conscious over unconscious processing. We shall refer to this view as the consciousness as king (CasK) assumption. We go on, in the next section, to show that opting for the explicit default hypothesis has had a profound influence on how research findings on implicit learning have been interpreted.

● The "Consciousness as King" Assumption

In examining the cognitive literature over the past several decades, there appears a consistent skepticism regarding virtually all evidence of unconscious processing (e.g., Eriksen, 1960; Shanks & St. John, 1994). This skepticism regarding unconscious processing seems to go hand-in-hand with an aversion to the view that consciousness maybe epiphenomenal (see peer commentary to Velmans, 1991). We introduce the CasK assumption to reflect this perspective. We can only speculate as to the roots of CasK in cognitive psychology. The skepticism regarding unconscious processing may reflect a reaction to psychoanalytic theory, and the rejection of epiphenomenalism may reflect a reaction to behaviorism. More likely, both views reflect the trickle of first-person perspective into what is essentially a third-person approach.

CasK manifests itself in its most subtle form in folk psychology. In its full-blown "person-on-the-street" manifestation, it entails the first-person perspective that we have conscious access and control over all important cognitive processes. We are, indeed, the captains of our ships. This view, as noted earlier, is supported by an insidious trick that consciousness plays when we introspect about what determines our thinking and behavior. Not surprisingly, we find that we are consciously aware of all influential factors.

We assume that most cognitive psychologists are well-aware of the pitfalls of attempting to introspect upon motives and cognitive processes (Nisbitt & Wilson, 1977). Moreover, most would be quick to agree that there is more to cognitive processes than meets the conscious eye. However, from an examination of the content of the peer commentary to Velmans's (1991) article, there is clearly an attitude that a third-person perspective necessarily denies the validity of a first-person perspective. We do not have the space to discuss this issue here but refer you to Velmans's response to the peer commentary. The upshot of his reply is that taking a third-person perspective toward understanding the role of consciousness in information processing does not require one to reject the importance of the first-person perspective in achieving a more complete understanding of cognition. One can deny the causal role of consciousness from a third-person perspective without endorsing an epiphenomenal view of consciousness.

● The Case for the Explicit Default Hypothesis

The importance of CasK to implicit learning research is that it promotes a preference for the default hypothesis that learning requires consciousness. This is seen most clearly in the arguments against unconscious processing, which on occasion have been stated so strongly as to suggest that proponents of the view that some processing may occur without consciousness are of dubious scientific credibility (Dulany, 1991). More specifically, as this view pertains to learning, it is claimed that learning requires consciousness and that claims to the contrary are unsubstantiated by empirical evidence (e.g., Dulany, Carlson, & Dewey, 1984; Perruchet, Gallego, & Savy, 1990; Shanks & St. John, 1994). Proponents of this view are particularly critical of the methods employed in demonstrations of implicit learning. The criticisms primarily focus on whether the tests of awareness were sufficiently sensitive. Clearly, we all support the most rigorous application of available scientific methods. But this is a two-edged sword and must be applied equally to both default hypotheses (Reingold & Merikle, 1990). We discuss this problem in some detail later in the chapter. At this juncture, we only wish to make the point that there has been a far greater concern about conscious processing contaminating implicit learning than about unconscious information contaminating conscious performance.

● The Case for the Implicit Default Hypothesis

Here we make the case that the implicit default is the more reasonable of the two a priori hypotheses. To begin with, the preference for the explicit default is largely based on the CasK assumption, which assumes a first-person perspective that is inappropriate in the context of the present controversy, which concerns the empirical (third-person perspective) evidence for implicit learning.

Second, we believe that the plausibility of the explicit hypothesis was largely based on a misunderstanding regarding what is at issue regarding implicit learning. If all that was being claimed is that awareness accompanies learning, it is understandable how first-person knowledge may be marshaled to support this claim. However, if what is at issue is whether awareness is a necessary antecedent for learning to occur, it seems far less self-evident that this is, indeed, the case.

Third, parsimony alone would dictate that it would be more reasonable to begin with the assumption that animate systems, from flatworms to humans, are all capable of learning without awareness. After all, as noted earlier, there is good evidence that numerous other cognitive processes appear to function without the benefit of consciousness (e.g., preattentive processes, Neisser, 1967; implicit memory, Schacter, 1987). Why, other than the subjective experience that learning is usually accompanied by conscious awareness, would it be the case that consciousness is required for learning? It may be reasonable to conclude that certain kinds of learning require consciousness, but only when there are compelling theoretical and empirical reasons for noting exceptions to this generalization.

It might be countered that it would be more parsimonious to begin with the assumption that all human learning requires consciousness because we already know that some human learning requires consciousness. Once again, although there is evidence, as in the classical conditioning literature (e.g., Brewer, 1974), that learning only occurs when there is awareness of the conditioned stimulus-unconditioned stimulus contingency, this only involves a correlation; it does not tell us that awareness enters into the processing to play a causal role.

Fourth, the explicit hypothesis introduces dualist-interactionism issues. If it is being claimed that consciousness does play a causal role in learning, how does consciousness, a mental process, interact with the brain to produce behavioral effects? More likely, it is not being proposed that consciousness plays a direct causal role but rather functions as a placeholder (e.g., consciousness is indicative of hippocampal processing). If this is what is being proposed, then the claim that consciousness is critical only begs the question of what are the mechanisms (ideally in terms of a model) by which consciousness influences the learning process. However, once these mechanisms have been identified, we would no longer refer to the role of consciousness in the same manner.

Fifth, if consciousness is necessary for learning, we should expect to see it playing an explicit role in our theories of learning. This, however, does not appear to be the case, as evidenced by Stanovich's (1991) observation that "there does not exist one single model in cognitive psychology where 'consciousness' plays a necessary theoretical role" (p. 696). Although consciousness is often alluded to, as in Atkinson and Shiffrin's (1968) notion of controlled processing, consciousness-related mechanisms or processes play the critical roles and not consciousness itself.

269

Finally, and possibly at the crux of the issue, what legitimate inferences regarding the role of consciousness in learning can be made, given the available methods and results from implicit learning studies? Our conclusions regarding the role of consciousness are based on the results of some direct test that informs us regarding conscious access to information learned as a consequence of previous training. If direct test performance is above some baseline control, we conclude that subjects have some awareness of what they learned. Once again, we only have a correlation between learning and awareness. When detected, such a correlation may have resulted due to the fact that awareness was a product or consequence of the learning. The results certainly cannot be taken to necessarily imply that awareness was necessary for the learning to have occurred.

On the other hand, if the results from the direct test fail to show any evidence of awareness, we may be in a stronger position to conclude that awareness is not always necessary for learning to occur. This point will be discussed in greater detail later in the chapter; however, on the basis of what has been presented thus far, it appears that the implicit default hypothesis is more amenable to empirical testing than the explicit default hypothesis.

In conclusion, we find no compelling reason to approach implicit learning research with the assumption that learning requires consciousness. Rather, we find a number of factors suggesting that it would be far more reasonable to approach the area with the assumption that awareness may not be necessary for learning to occur.

INFLUENCE OF THE EXPLICIT HYPOTHESIS ON IMPLICIT LEARNING RESEARCH

The preceding discussion of the CasK assumption and its influence on the selection of an appropriate default hypothesis is relevant to the manner in which research on implicit learning has been evaluated. This section focuses upon discussion of three methodological issues that have been viewed as often (if not always) undermining research that has been interpreted by some as evidence of implicit learning. We discuss these issues as they relate to the CasK assumption and conclude by presenting the general methodological approach we adopted in conducting the research described in the final section of this chapter.

● The Task-Dissociation Method

Cognitive psychologists have usually employed the task-dissociation methodology to investigate implicit learning. This paradigm requires that subjects engage in a task during which they are exposed to potentially learnable information that could be used to enhance performance. Next, learning of the task-embedded information (about which subjects have remained uninformed) is assessed using both indirect and direct tests. Direct tests encourage performance based on consciously available information, and indirect tests avoid encouraging the use of conscious knowledge. Implicit learning is demonstrated when indirect tests indicate that learning has occurred, whereas direct tests do not.

The procedure used by Cohen, Ivry, and Keele (1990) illustrates the task-dissociation method. Subjects pressed keys corresponding to the locations of serially presented visual targets as they appeared in one of several positions on a computer screen. Response latencies of subjects trained on a repeating sequence became faster with practice and then slowed significantly when a series of random target locations were introduced. This negative transfer effect, a type of indirect test, was interpreted as evidence that subjects had learned about the sequence, and subsequent direct tests of conscious awareness indicated that the learning was implicit.

Task dissociations have been presented as evidence of implicit learning of diverse types of information (e.g., sequence structures, Reber & Squire, 1994; the complex rules used to construct "legal" or "grammatical" letter strings, Reber, 1989; and the critical relationships among inputs and outputs in artificial control systems, Berry & Broadbent, 1988). Usually, however, task dissociations have not been considered strong demonstrations of implicit learning. This is because dissociative performance on indirect and direct tests can result for a number of reasons and therefore cannot always be considered compelling evidence for implicit learning. We consider three situations in which one would expect to observe task dissociations that might be interpreted inaccurately as evidence for implicit learning.

CONSTRAINING MEASURES OF LEARNING

Researchers are often interested in examining the implicit acquisition of particular types of information. However, in providing subjects with the opportunity to learn, it is usually not possible to present the information of interest in isolation. If subjects have been exposed to multiple sources of information, then measures of learning might reflect the acquisition of some or all of the available information. That is, it may not be possible to specify which type of information has been learned.

Consider a study in which subjects trained on a serial reaction time (SRT) task that involved the use of sequences of predictable and unpredictable trials (Lewicki, Hill, & Bizot, 1988). Because response latencies for the predictable subsequences decreased with training and those associated with unpredictable subsequences did not, Lewicki et al. concluded that subjects had learned the rules of predictable subsequence construction. Because subjects could not articulate these rules, it was concluded that they had been acquired implicitly. In a replication study, however, Perruchet et al. (1990) demonstrated that all of the improvement in response latencies occurred for those movements that had a relatively high probability in the predictable subsequences. Because the indirect measure of learning was not sufficiently constrained in the original study, it was not possible to determine which type of information had been learned.

Task dissociations that reflect the sensitivity of indirect and direct tests to different types of information do not provide evidence for implicit learning (Shanks & St. John, 1994). In contrast, if indirect and direct tests are constrained such that they are sensitive to the learning of the same type of information, task dissociations may reflect implicit learning. For example, Reed and Johnson (1994a) gave subjects extensive training on an SRT task that exposed them to a variety of information. Afterward, subjects continued to perform the SRT task for a series of transfer trials in which the probabilistic structure of the original sequence was maintained. It was, therefore, possible to specifically attribute the RT disruption associated with the sequence change to the learning of the manipulated information. In addition, the direct tests were designed to assess explicit awareness of the same information. Thus, because the dissociation between performance on the two types of learning measures was not ascribable to differences in the types of information to which they were sensitive, the results were interpretable as a demonstration of implicit learning.[1]

It is possible that task dissociations reflect the sensitivity of indirect and direct tests to different types of information whenever ambiguity exists regarding the type of information accessed by the two types of learning measures. It is interesting to note that although researchers have often expressed concern regarding such ambiguity involving the interpretation of indirect measures of learning (Perruchet, Gallego, & Pacteau, 1992; Shanks & St. John, 1994), this concern has not always been adequately focused on the use of direct measures of learning. For example, Perruchet and Amorim (1992) used a direct test of sequence learning (i.e., the free-generation task) in which subjects made a series of 100 key presses after having been instructed to repeatedly reproduce the sequence of target locations encountered during SRT training trials. It was found that sequence-trained subjects produced certain chunks of the training sequence more reliably than subjects who had received random training trials. It was concluded, therefore, that indirect measures of learning actually reflected explicit rather than implicit learning of these sequence chunks. The manner in which the free-generation task was employed, however, does not necessitate such an interpretation.

Subjects in the random training condition were likely to have been exposed to different probabilistic information than those who trained with the repeating sequence (Reed & Johnson, 1994a). Because of the unconstrained nature of the free-generation task, performance on this direct test may have reflected the acquisition of such nondeterministic structure rather than explicit learning of sequence chunks.

To test this hypothesis, we engaged two groups of subjects in the SRT task. One group received training with a repeating sequence, and the other trained on a series of nonrepeating trials that shared the same probabilistic structure as the sequence encountered by the first group (i.e., nonrandom training). For both groups, SRT training was followed by the completion of the free-generation task. We found that although sequence-trained subjects did produce certain sequence chunks more often than those who trained with the nonrepeating trials, other chunks were reproduced more reliably by subjects who trained with nonrepeating trials. This pattern of results indicates that when free-generation task performance is not compared between groups of subjects that have been exposed to the same probabilistic information, differences in performance do not necessarily inform one regarding the acquisition of consciously available deterministic sequence structure.

In general, like indirect tests, direct tests can be insufficiently constrained in that they may be free to reflect the learning of more than one type of information. Therefore, in order to appropriately interpret comparisons of performance on indirect and direct tests, both types of learning measures need to be constrained so as to measure the learning of the same type of information. This principle applies equally to situations in which task dissociations are observed and those in which they are not.

SIMILARITY OF TESTING CONTEXTS

Task dissociations can also be anticipated when direct and indirect tests differ in relation to the extent to which they allow individuals to express what they have learned. Typically, critics of implicit learning research have focused upon the suggestion that studies of implicit learning often involve direct tests that are insufficiently sensitive to explicit knowledge (Holender, 1986; Reingold & Merikle, 1990; Shanks & St. John, 1994). For example, when subjects' verbal reports of explicit knowledge acquired during the performance of a nonverbal task are used as measures of explicit knowledge (Nissen & Bullemer, 1987), observed task dissociations may reflect the relative insensitivity of the direct test to the acquired knowledge and not necessarily implicit learning.

In general, direct tests that do not maintain the experimental context encountered during training are likely to be undersensitive to explicit awareness (Schacter & Graf, 1986; Shanks & St. John, 1994). Therefore, researchers have begun using direct measures that provide performance contexts that closely match those of indirect tests (e.g., Cohen et al., 1990; Stadler, 1989). For example, Reed and Johnson (1994a) used a recognition test of sequence structure that involved a retrieval context that closely matched that of the indirect test. On each recognition-test trial, subjects performed the SRT for a small number of trials and then rated the series of target locations as either part of the original sequence (old) or not (new). Thus, the context in which the direct test was performed was similar to that of the indirect test.

If direct and indirect tests provide similar retrieval contexts, task dissociations are less likely to reflect the undersensitivity of direct tests to explicit knowledge. On the other hand, when the retrieval context associated with a direct test is highly similar to that of the indirect test, the direct test may be oversensitive to implicit knowledge (Richardson-Klavehn & Bjork, 1988). Using a direct test that is oversensitive to implicit knowledge could result in the failure to observe a task dissociation and lead to the inappropriate conclusion that all learning was explicit.

The selection of an appropriate direct test depends upon ensuring that the associated retrieval context is similar enough to that of the indirect tests to allow for full expression of explicit knowledge, while not allowing the measure to reflect the expression of implicit knowledge. In the strictest sense, direct tests need to be exclusively and exhaustively sensitive to consciously available information (Reingold & Merikle, 1990). Unfortunately, it is never possible to be confident that one has employed measures of learning that satisfy these criteria. Therefore, in evaluating the evidence for implicit learning resulting from studies that employ the task-dissociation method, one must decide whether a direct test has met these criteria to a reasonable degree.

We expect that, at least in part, how well one believes the use of a particular direct test comes to achieving these ends will depend upon the particular theoretical perspective adopted by the reader. If one is invested in a perspective that assumes that all learning is accompanied by awareness, then task dissociations are likely to be viewed as resulting from the use of a direct test that is insensitive to the relevant consciously available knowledge (i.e., the test failed to met the exhaustiveness criteria). In contrast, if one adopts the view that learning does not require conscious awareness, the lack of a task dissociation might be interpreted as resulting from the use of a direct test that was oversensitive to the influence of implicit knowledge (i.e., the test failed to met the exclusivity criterion).

In the studies described later, we attempted to adopt a middle-ground perspective with respect to this issue. Direct tests were designed to maintain performance contexts that were highly similar to those of indirect tests, but subjects were instructed to perform the tasks based upon consciously available knowledge. We rely on the reader to judge the adequacy of this approach, but we hope that caution will be exercised in doing so, such that verdicts are not based solely upon preconceptions regarding the cognitive unconscious.

TEMPORAL APPROPRIATENESS OF DIRECT TESTS

A final methodological issue that we consider involves decisions regarding the appropriate point in time at which direct tests should be administered. Assuming that one is confident that direct and indirect tests have measured learning of the same information, and that the direct test employed was appropriately sensitive, the interpretation of an observed task dissociation remains somewhat ambiguous. This is because one could claim that learning was explicit but that subjects lost conscious awareness of the acquired information prior to the administration of the direct test.

How might one address such a criticism? One approach would be to administer the direct test after less exposure to the learned information and look for evidence of explicit knowledge at earlier points in time. Assume that this approach was taken and that the direct test was administered at a number of earlier time points. If in every case no evidence of explicit knowledge was obtained, would this demonstration provide unequivocal evidence of implicit learning? It would not, because, if so inclined, one could simply suggest that the particular times at which the direct tests were administered remained inappropriate.

Without supporting empirical evidence, reliance upon arguments of this sort belies the biases inherent in the adoption of the CasK assumption. In addition, the pervasiveness of the CasK assumption appears to have obscured the dual implications of this argument. If one were to assume that awareness is inessential to learning, the same argument could be used to undermine demonstrations of explicit learning. That is, if appropriate direct and indirect tests each provided evidence of learning (i.e., no task dissociation was observed), one could argue that learning occurred implicitly but that subjects acquired awareness of the information at some time prior to the administration of the direct test.

How temporally appropriate one deems the administration of a direct test to be is likely to depend upon which default hypothesis is adopted. If one adopts the CasK assumption, then direct tests are likely to be considered temporally appropriate only when a task dissociation is not observed. Alternatively, if one assumes that awareness is inessential to learning, then direct tests will be seen as temporally appropriate only when task dissociations are observed. In the absence of a clear solution to this problem, we have proceeded with our research by adopting the following perspective.

We assume neither that all learning is implicit nor that all learning is explicit. In addition, we suggest that those who adopt the CasK assumption are faced with the challenge of providing a demonstration of explicit learning that can meet all of the criteria usually reserved for judging the soundness of demonstrations of implicit learning.

● Comments on Methodology

As the above discussion suggests, methodological inadequacies can be viewed as prohibiting one from confidently concluding that task dissociations provide evidence for implicit learning. Nevertheless, when these methodological shortcomings are avoided, task dissociations can be interpreted as reflecting implicit learning with greater certainty. With this assumption in mind, we have conducted numerous studies in an attempt to characterize implicit learning processes. This research, described in the next section, was conducted by adhering to the following guidelines.

First, we attempted to use experimental procedures that would satisfy the information criterion (Shanks & St. John, 1994). That is, in every case, the indirect and direct tests were constrained such that we were confident that each test measured the particular information in which we were interested. Second, direct tests were designed so as to recreate the retrieval context associated with the indirect tests and thereby provide sensitive tests of explicit knowledge (Schacter & Graf, 1986). Third, we assumed that the amount of exposure to information that subjects received was insufficient to result in the proceduralization of explicit knowledge and therefore that subjects were not likely to have lost conscious access to explicitly acquired information prior to performing the direct tests. Fourth, the experimental circumstances created in these studies were intended to maximize the opportunity to observe implicit learning. This was done by making a secondary tone-counting task (Cohen et al., 1990) an integral part of the procedures used in all the experimental conditions, with one exception. By including the secondary task, we hoped to prevent the content of learning from becoming consciously available (Reed & Johnson, 1994a) and thereby to maximize the opportunities for observing implicit learning. Finally, and more generally, we attempted to work from a theoretical perspective that was broad enough to allow for the possibility of implicit learning, while recognizing the importance of the methodological issues discussed above.

CHARACTERIZING IMPLICIT LEARNING

Reber (1989, 1992) has described implicit learning as a relatively automatic process whereby perceptual regularities (often highly complex) are abstracted from the environment without conscious awareness. Although the results of numerous studies have been interpreted as being consistent with various aspects of this theoretical characterization (e.g., Reber, 1969), in general, these studies have been criticized in relation to the methodological issues discussed earlier (Shanks & St. John, 1994). We have undertaken the investigation of implicit learning with two primary goals in mind. First, we intended to conduct experiments using procedures that would result in unambiguously interpretable observations. Second, we sought to explore the nature of implicit learning processes. In particular, we were interested in determining the attentional requirements and complexity-related limits of implicit learning. The remainder of this chapter is devoted to describing these experiments and discussing the implications of their results.

● Attention and Implicit Learning

Secondary tasks have sometimes been employed as a means of manipulating the availability of attentional resources. Some studies indicate that such tasks can interfere with or eliminate implicit learning of complex sequence structures (Cohen et al., 1990; Nissen & Bullemer, 1987), whereas others have indicated that learning persists during dual-task performance (Keele & Jennings, 1991; Reed & Johnson, 1994a). Alternatively, it has been suggested that dual-task performance specifically interferes with attentionally driven organizational processes required for the learning of certain sequence structures (Stadler, 1995).

In a recent experiment, we manipulated the inclusion of a tone-counting task across conditions to determine whether or not implicit sequence learning is influenced by the availability of processing resources (Reed, Johnson, & Ottaway, 1995). Performance on indirect and direct tests of sequence learning was compared across three types of conditions. In some conditions (dual-task), the SRT task was always performed in conjunction with the tone-counting task. In other conditions (single-task), subjects only performed the SRT task. In a third set of conditions (dual-single-task), the tone-counting task was used during most of the SRT trials but not during the last block of training or during transfer trials (i.e., a dual-task learning phase was followed by a single-task testing phase). Each of these types of conditions was associated with either an indirect test (i.e., RT disruptions associated with transfer trials) or a direct test (recognition, Reed & Johnson, 1994a).

The results are summarized in Table 8.1. Disruptions in RTs were significantly greater for the single-task condition compared to the dual-task condition, $t(19) = 2.65$, $p < .05$, whereas RT disruptions did not differ reliably between the dual-task and dual-single-task condition, $t(19) = 1.32$, $p > .05$. This outcome indicated that, as assessed by the indirect test, subjects in the dual-task conditions learned less about the sequence structure than those in the single-task condition. In contrast, performance on the direct test indicated that subjects did not acquire explicit awareness of the sequence structure in any of the conditions (i.e., ratings for old and new

TABLE 8.1 Summary of Results From Reed, Johnson, and Ottaway (1995)			
		Mean (SE) Ratings for Recognition Items	
Condition	Mean (SE) RT Disruption	Old Triad[a]	New Triad[a]
Single-task, indirect test	130.7 ms (14.06)	NA	NA
Dual-task, indirect test	76.2 ms (14.22)	NA	NA
Dual-single-task, indirect test	55.2 ms (5.94)	NA	NA
Single-task, direct test	NA	2.08 (.06)	2.01 (.06)
Dual-task, direct test	NA	2.03 (.10)	2.01 (.08)
Dual-single-task, direct test	NA	2.10 (.10)	2.07 (.10)

NOTE: a. Recognition-task ratings represent subjects' judgments of 12 target triads consistent with the training sequence (old) and 12 triads not encountered during SRT training (new) on a 4-point scale (1 = *definitely part of original sequence* to 4 = *definitely not part of original sequence*).

recognition-task trials did not differ for any of the conditions, all $ps > .05$). Thus, although implicit learning occurred in all instances, the inclusion of the secondary task did result in attenuated learning as indirectly measured.

We have also examined the attentional demands of implicit learning using a different type of dual-task paradigm. In particular, we provided subjects with two types of information and determined whether or not the acquisition of one type of information disrupted learning of the other. In the first of these studies, we examined the acquisition of probabilistic structure that accompanied deterministic sequence structure (Reed & Johnson, 1994b). In Reed and Johnson (1994a, Experiment 1) it was demonstrated that probabilistic structure[2] was learned when no deterministic structure was provided. It was, therefore, argued that to accurately assess deterministic structure learning, the probabilistic structure of training and transfer sequences must be equated. This, however, assumed that acquisition of the more useful deterministic structure did not eliminate probabilistic learning.

To test this assumption, we trained subjects with a repeating deterministic sequence structure and then transferred them to a series of nonrepeating trials that provided only probabilistic structure (Reed & Johnson, 1994b). In one condition, the probabilistic structure of the transfer trials was different from that of the training sequence. In the other condition, the probabilistic structure of the transfer sequence was virtually the same as that of the training trials. If learning of the more useful repeating sequence structure during training trials eliminates learning of the less useful probabilistic structure, then one would expect equivalent RT disruptions for both conditions. However, if both types of information are learned concurrently, then greater RT disruptions would be expected for the condition in which the probabilistic structure changed. The results were consistent with this latter prediction in that greater mean RT disruptions were observed when the probabilistic structure of the transfer trials was different from those of training trials (97 ms) compared to the condition in which the probabilistic structure was the same during training and transfer (65 ms). Because the training procedures were identical for this experiment and a previous study that demonstrated deterministic learning (Reed & Johnson, 1994a, Experiment 2), we assume that both types of structure were learned concurrently.

An additional study was designed to determine whether or not two different types of deterministic information would be implicitly acquired concurrently (Reed, 1995, Experiment 8). During an SRT task, subjects indicated the location of a target (square) that appeared in one location of a display that was divided into equal-size quadrants. Each quadrant consisted of a centered black figure (i.e., target or distractor—circle, triangle, or diamond) presented on a colored background (red, yellow, green, or blue). Subjects were assigned to one of three different conditions. In the sequence learning condition, the target appeared according to a repeating sequence during training trials but according to a new sequence during transfer trials (as in Reed & Johnson, 1994a). In the perceptual learning condition, the target always appeared diagonal to the quadrant with the blue background during training but vertical to blue during transfer trials.[3] In a third condition (concurrent learning), subjects were exposed to both the repeating sequence and the perceptual relationship during all training trials. Three different types of transfer trials were used in an order that was completely counterbalanced across subjects. The transfer trials measured sequence learning (i.e., the sequence but not the perceptual rule was different from that used during training), perceptual learning (i.e., the perceptual rule but not the sequence was different from that used during

TABLE 8.2 Summary of Results From Reed (1995)		
Condition	Mean (SEM) Reaction Time Disruption	Mean (SEM) Correct Responses on Cued-Recall Task
Rule 1, indirect test	53.0 ms (5.10)	NA
Rule 2, indirect test	48.6 ms (7.37)	NA
Rule 3, indirect test	49.6 ms (7.77)	NA
Rule 1, direct test	NA	5.8 (.42)
Rule 2, direct test	NA	5.9 (.34)
Rule 3, direct test	NA	5.9 (.23)

Note: Cued-recall test results represent the number of rule-consistent responses made on 24 trials and were compared to chance performance of six correct responses.

training), or both (i.e., the sequence and perceptual rule were different from those used during training).

RT disruptions associated with the three conditions are presented in Table 8.2. Reliable disruptions were observed for all types of transfer (all $ps < .05$). However, RT disruptions associated with the introduction of the new sequence were greater when training trials were not consistent with any perceptual rule, $t(58) = 3.26$, $p < .01$. Similarly, RT disruptions associated with the change in the perceptual rule were greater when training trials were not consistent with any repeated sequence, $t(58) = 2.27$, $p < .05$. These results indicate that both types of deterministic information were learned concurrently but that learning of each type of information was attenuated by the presence of the other.

Based on the outcomes of these studies, we draw three primary conclusions. First, multiple types of information can be implicitly acquired simultaneously, even when one type of information is less useful (i.e., probabilistic) or completely redundant with the other. Second, implicit learning processes are influenced by the availability of cognitive resources and therefore cannot be considered automatic in a strict sense (Posner, 1978). Third, because the secondary task influenced implicit learning but not performance on the direct test (see Table 8.1), conscious awareness and attention appear to be at least partially independent.

● **Complexity and Implicit Learning**

Reed and Johnson (1994a) demonstrated implicit learning of a particular type of sequence structure, referred to as SOC structure. Each target location in these sequences was predicted by the two previous locations but not by the previous location alone. This type of sequence structure can be considered complex compared to first-order conditional structures, in which each location is exactly specified by the previous location. Thus, the complexity of sequence structures has been defined in terms of the number of discrete events that need to be considered to correctly anticipate the location of an upcoming target location (cf., Cohen et al., 1990).

Because methodological constraints made further examination of the relationship between implicit learning and sequence-structure complexity unwieldy, we decided to continue our investigation of the complexity-related limitations of implicit learning by employing the perceptual learning task (Reed, 1995, Experiment 1). In particular, we compared implicit and explicit learning of two different perceptual relationships (Reed, 1995, Experiment 2). In the first (Rule 2), the target appeared diagonally to the blue when an upper quadrant was blue, but otherwise appeared vertically to the blue quadrant. In the second (Rule 3), the location of the target was determined by which particular quadrant was blue: The target appeared in the upper-left quadrant if the upper-left quadrant was blue, the target appeared in the lower-right quadrant if the lower-left quadrant was blue, the target appeared in the lower-left quadrant if the lower-right quadrant was blue, and the target appeared in the upper-right quadrant if the lower-left quadrant was blue.

The previously examined relationship (Rule 1) was considered simpler than either of these relationships because only one general rule was needed in order to exactly specify the location of the target based on the color information. Rule 2 was considered more complex because it required the use of two less general subrules, and Rule 3 the most complex because it required four rather specific relationships.

In the implicit learning experiment, subjects were assigned to one of four conditions defined by the particular rule associated with training trials and the type of learning measure used (indirect or direct). For indirect test conditions, the perceptual rules never applied during SRT task-transfer trials and RT disruptions were measured.[4] For direct test conditions,

TABLE 8.3 Summary of Results From Reed (1995)		
Condition	Proportion of Subjects Learning Rule	Mean (SEM) Trials to Criterion
Rule 1	19/20	207.8 (43.74)
Rule 2	7/20	506.8 (54.88)
Rule 3	1/20	744.4 (31.51)

the cue-recall task described above was employed instead of transfer trials. The results of the experiment are summarized in Table 8.2. For both of the indirect test conditions, reliable RT disruptions were observed (all $ps <$ .05), but subjects never expressed awareness of the perceptual relationships on the direct tests (all $ps > $ .05). Because each consecutive perceptual relationship can be considered increasingly complex, and even the most complex rule was learned, the data suggested that implicit learning processes are powerful in relation to the complexity of the information that is acquired.

In the explicit learning experiment, we encouraged three groups of subjects to intentionally learn one of the three different perceptual rules (Reed, 1995, Experiment 4). On each experimental trial, subjects were presented with four different colored quadrants, and they indicated where they thought the target belonged. After each trial, feedback was provided (error tone for incorrect responses, but none for correct), and the target appeared in the correct location. Explicit learning of the rules was considered complete when subjects had made 24 consecutive correct responses. The number of trials completed after 45 minutes of training was used if subjects failed to meet the learning criterion within this time.

The results are presented in Table 8.3. Rule 3 required more training trials than Rule 2, $t(19) = 3.65, p < .01$, and more trials were required for Rule 2 than Rule 1, $t(19) = 4.15, p < .001$. Also, more subjects learned Rule 1 than Rule 2, and more subjects learned Rule 2 than Rule 3. Thus, the manipulation of rule complexity had a dramatic effect on explicit learning. Comparison of these results and those of the previous experiments suggests that the same manipulation of complexity had a powerful influence upon explicit learning, but none upon the degree of implicit learning.

Although this conclusion is consistent with the outcome of the two experiments, we doubted this interpretation because each rule appeared to have been implicitly learned equally well (i.e., the RT disruptions did not differ across the three conditions). Whereas we had been prepared to accept the possibility that the most complex rule could be learned implicitly, we did not anticipate a complete lack of an effect of rule complexity upon the indirect measure of learning. That is, because we considered Rule 3 to be sufficiently more complex than Rule 1, we anticipated that if subjects became sensitive to the perceptual consistencies described by Rule 3, learning would not be as great as observed for the other rules.

An alternative explanation of these results requires one to suppose that subjects in the implicit learning conditions had overtrained on the SRT task. If subjects had overlearned the more complex rules, then possible differences in learning across conditions could have been obscured. Therefore, the conditions from the original experiments (Reed, 1995, Experiments 1 and 2) were used in a replication study, but subjects received only half as many training trials (Reed, 1995, Experiment 3). The resulting RT disruptions were reduced (by about 32 ms), but no reliable differences among disruptions were observed, $F(2, 57) = .97, p > .05$. We, therefore, concluded that the similarity among the magnitudes of the RT disruptions observed in the original experiments was not the result of overlearning but that indeed each perceptual relationship had been learned equally well in the implicit learning conditions.

Such an observation is consistent with Reber's (1989, 1992) contention that implicit learning processes are capable of abstracting highly complex information from the environment. This interpretation, however, appears to require one to assume that unlimited attentional resources are available to implicit learning processes. That is, the four abstract contingencies of Rule 3 were implicitly acquired as easily as the single contingency of Rule 1 because the acquisition of the multiple relationships did not compete for attentional resources. Although this account may be accurate, it is inconsistent with the findings from the previously described experiments, which indicated that manipulations of attentional resources influence the degree to which implicit learning occurs. As an alternative, we offer an interpretation that does not rely upon such an assumption.

We begin by concluding that the pattern of data does support the notion that implicit and explicit learning processes involve different cognitive processes. In addition, however, we suggest that these distinct processes

TABLE 8.4	Three Possible Representational Forms of the Three Perceptual Rules From Reed (1995)		
		Type of Representation	
Rule	*Abstract*	*Less Abstract*	*Exemplar*
1	T diagonal to blue Q	Q 1 blue, T diagonal Q 2 blue, T diagonal Q 3 blue, T diagonal Q 4 blue, T diagonal	24 exemplars
2	Upper Q blue, T diagonal Lower Q blue, T vertical	Q 1 blue, T diagonal Q 2 blue, T diagonal Q 3 blue, T vertical Q 4 blue, T vertical	24 exemplars
3	Q 1 blue, T in blue Q 2 blue, T vertical Q 3 blue, T horizontal Q 4 blue, T diagonal	Q 1 blue, T in blue Q 2 blue, T vertical Q 3 blue, T horizontal Q 4 blue, T diagonal	24 exemplars

NOTE: For the Abstract and Less Abstract formulations, the perceptual relationships are described as relating the blue quadrant (Q) to the location of the target (T).

result in the acquisition of different types of cognitive representations of the learned information. In particular, the data are consistent with the notion that implicit learning processes yield less abstract knowledge representations than do explicit processes. This is suggested by the lack of a complexity effect for the implicit learning conditions. If the implicitly acquired perceptual relationships were represented in a relatively less abstract manner, then the three perceptual relationships can be viewed as equally complex.

For example, all three perceptual relationships may be represented as four less abstract rules, each of which relates the specific location of the target to the particular location of the blue quadrant (see Table 8.4). Alternatively, each relationship may be represented as the entire set of 24 exemplars used to illustrate the more general rules during SRT training. In either case, the three relationships, which differ in complexity at the more abstract level of analysis, can be considered equally complex at a less abstract level. Therefore, if implicit learning is assumed to result in less abstract representations than explicit learning, the differential effects of the complexity manipulation are easily interpreted. By this account, complexity is in the eye of the beholder, and the complexity discerned by the conscious explicit eye does not necessarily generalize to that ascertained by the unconscious implicit eye.

Unfortunately, the designs of our experiments do not allow us to specify more precisely the manner in which the implicitly acquired perceptual rules were represented. In addition, observations made by other researchers also do not allow one to draw firm conclusions in this regard. Reber (1969) has found that learning in the artificial grammar paradigm allows subjects to accurately judge the grammaticality of letter strings that are formed by the same underlying set of rules used to form training strings, but that differ completely in relation to the specific letter constituents of test items. These results imply that implicitly acquired representations may not be so specific as to be isomorphic to the particular set of stimuli encountered during training. In contrast, reports that all learning observed in artificial grammar studies can be accounted for in terms of explicit learning of letter-string fragments are consistent with the notion of exemplar representations (Gomez & Schvaneveldt, 1994; Perruchet, 1994). Regardless of the exact nature of the implicitly acquired representations, we suggest that the data presented above can only be accounted for by assuming that implicit learning results in less abstract representations of information than explicit learning and that definitions of complexity are inextricably tied to the manner in which information is represented by the cognitive system.

Finding that implicitly acquired information is less abstract than explicitly learned information may have some potentially important implications regarding our theoretical conceptualization of implicit learning. As we discussed earlier, meeting the information criterion requires knowing precisely what subjects have learned. If one assumes that abstract information is learned, then it is critical to demonstrations of implicit learning that subjects be unaware of this abstract structure. In contrast, this assumption does not require that subjects be unaware of the stimuli presented during the learning situation. However, if it is the case that only concrete exemplars are learned, then direct tests need to assess memory for specific stimulus instances rather than knowledge of abstract structure. In the extreme case, subjects' awareness of stimuli encountered during learning situations would be sufficient to undermine a demonstration of implicit learning. Moreover, this would have the effect of blurring the distinction between implicit learning and implicit memory. Implicit memory is generally defined as a situation in which a previously consciously experienced event subsequently influences behavior at a point in time when one fails to recall the event.

Therefore, it becomes critical to demonstrate that what is learned implicitly is more abstract than the specific exemplars that were experienced.

This would seem to be the case with sequence learning because of subjects' apparent inability to distinguish SOC structural elements encountered during SRT training from the new structural elements used in the recognition task. We also have evidence that subjects learned more than specific exemplars in the perceptual learning paradigm. In a single-condition experiment, subjects were exposed to half of the original set of training exemplars used in the original study of Rule 1 learning (Reed, 1995, Experiment 5). Learning was indirectly assessed by discontinuing the presentation of these exemplars and introducing the Rule 1 exemplars that had not been previously encountered. Observed RTs for these trials did not differ from those associated with the final block of training trials involving the previously trained set of exemplars, $t(19) = .74$, $p = .46$, suggesting that learning was somewhat more abstract than the acquisition of the specific set of training exemplars.

Summary of Findings

Historically, the cognitive investigation of learning has concentrated upon the examination of explicit forms of such processes (e.g., hypothesis testing and category learning). The large body of research regarding explicit learning has resulted in a particular characterization of these processes. Probably the most obvious is that they are typically accompanied by conscious awareness of the information that is acquired. Additionally, they can be characterized as directive and highly influenced by the availability of attentional resources. Furthermore, they appear to be sensitive to the complexity of available information in that less complex information is acquired with relative ease compared to highly complex material. Finally, they are generally considered to result in the acquisition of abstract representations of learned information.

The experiments we have described were designed to examine the characteristics of implicit learning. In contrast with explicit learning, the defining feature of implicit learning processes is the apparent lack of concomitant conscious awareness of acquired information. The results of our studies are consistent with this characterization but also provide information regarding other ways in which implicit learning can be contrasted to explicit learning processes.

As regards the relationship between implicit learning and attention, we reported three primary observations. First, implicit learning was influenced by a manipulation of available attentional resources and therefore, like explicit learning processes, appeared to be nonautomatic. Second, implicit learning resulted in the assimilation of multiple sources of simultaneously presented information and accordingly was characterized as a nonselective process. This characteristic can be viewed as contrasting with the directive and selective nature of explicit learning processes. Finally, conscious awareness was at least partially dissociated from attention in that the inclusion of a secondary task influenced the degree of implicit learning observed without affecting measures of explicit awareness. In this manner, implicit learning processes are divergent from explicit learning in that conscious awareness and the allocation of attentional resources appear to covary in the latter form of learning.

Regarding the complexity-related limitations of implicit learning, we observed that sequence structure and strictly perceptual relationships that can be considered complex were acquired implicitly. It was suggested, however, that the appropriate characterization of information in terms of its complexity is dependent upon the manner in which the cognitive system represents the knowledge that it acquires. In particular, it was proposed that when information is encoded in a relatively nonabstract manner, the acquired knowledge might best be considered less complex. In this regard, issues of information complexity and representational abstractness appear to be highly related. In accord with this view, we have suggested that implicit learning results, at least in certain circumstances, in the acquisition of relatively specific and simple information. This stands in contrast with explicit learning processes, which are capable of representing highly complex information in abstract forms.

In general, the results of our research suggest that implicit learning processes can be characterized as unique in a number of ways as compared with explicit forms of learning. This conclusion is based upon research that we consider to be rigorous in relation to the methodological concerns that have frequently appeared to undermine the interpretation of task-dissociation studies. It is acknowledged that by necessity, the methods employed cannot be deemed as allowing for entirely unambiguous interpretation of the results presented. However, we suggest that they can be viewed as informative if the biases inherent in the adoption of the CasK assumption are avoided.

SUMMARY

The way we frame a question, and the underlying (often implicit) assumptions that guide our thinking, will always shape the manner in which we conduct research. This inescapable fact makes it particularly important for researchers to make explicit the nature of the issues they hope to investigate and to recognize and address the validity of the assumptions that guide their pursuits. In the first sections of our chapter, we described our perspective on implicit learning research. These considerations struck us as necessary given the controversial status of demonstrations of implicit learning.

At the start, we considered questions regarding the relationship between consciousness and learning to be of particular interest when they examine the role of consciousness as a force that exerts an influence upon learning processes. Given this, we considered two alternative default research hypotheses from which one can approach the investigation of implicit learning. The intent was not to champion a particular choice of default hypothesis, but rather to illustrate that arguments can be made favoring either one. The implications of adopting either of these choices were presented, and it was suggested that those who choose to adopt the default hypothesis that learning requires consciousness until proven otherwise are faced with serious theoretical challenges. By our assessment, the CasK assumption is adopted by the many critics of implicit learning research, and we suggest that they have not provided adequate justification for this position.

If universally agreed-upon methods were available for potentially demonstrating implicit learning in an unambiguous manner, we probably would not have felt the need to include the preceding discussion. Because this is not the case, however, we felt the need to review the methodological issues of particular relevance. In doing so, we highlighted the kinds of decisions concerning experimental design that one needs to make and how one's choice of default hypothesis can influence these. In addition, we attempted to make an explicit justification for the methods we adopted and the criteria we used in establishing evidence for implicit learning in the research described in the final section of the chapter.

The studies we described focused on two particular issues: (a) the attentional requirements of implicit learning, and (b) the complexity-related limits of implicit learning. The data we reported regarding implicit learning have been interpreted as suggesting that (a) consciousness can be dissociated, at least in part, from attention, (b) manipulations of attention can influence implicit learning processes, and (c) complex information regarding sequence structure and perceptual relationships can be acquired implicitly. The difficulty in establishing a metric of complexity independent of considerations of mental representations was also discussed.

NOTES

1. These results stand in contrast to those reported by Shanks and Johnstone (Chapter 16, this volume). In particular, the results of their direct test suggested that many SOC elements were learned explicitly. To explore this discrepancy, we reanalyzed our data by examining all 10 responses observed on each of the 24 cued-generation task trials, thus approximating the use of the free-generation task used by Shanks and Johnstone. This analysis revealed two particularly interesting findings. First, subjects generated reversals (e.g., 121, 212, etc.) on only 13% of their responses. In fact, even the reversal encountered during training (i.e., 121) was rarely generated. We interpret this finding as indicating that subjects acquired sensitivity to the global statistical constraints of the training sequence. This interpretation is consistent with previous evidence of learning of such statistical constraints within this paradigm (Reed & Johnson, 1994a; Stadler, 1989). Given that subjects are sensitive to such constraints, an adjustment must be made in what is considered "chance" correct responding (i.e., when a subject has encountered two previous locations, the probability of guessing the next location is closer to .50 than the .33 used by Shanks and Johnstone).

Second, our analysis of all 10 responses generated in the cued-generation task revealed some evidence in support of Shanks and Johnstone's (Chapter 16, this volume) contention that subjects may explicitly learn some SOC elements. Specifically, there was evidence for explicit knowledge of 2 of the 12 SOC elements. However, the observation that subjects had acquired conscious knowledge of a subset of the SOC elements does not imply that all learning was explicit. Instead, the fact that significant RT disruptions were associated with changes in all 12 SOC elements indicates that learning was primarily implicit.

2. Previously referred to as simple frequency information.

3. Previous research indicated that this perceptual relationship (referred to as Rule 1) was implicitly learned (Reed, 1995, Experiment 1). For an indirect test condition, a 53 ms RT disruption was associated with the change of the perceptual relationship, $t(19) = 10.39, p < .01$. In a direct test condition, subjects performed a cued-recall task in which they responded to displays of colored quadrants (without

figures) by indicating where they thought the target belonged. On average, subjects produced 5.8 training-consistent responses for the 24 trials. This level of performance did not differ reliably from that expected by chance responding (6 correct), $t(38) = .47$, $p > .05$, indicating that subjects did not have consciously available knowledge of the perceptual relationship.

4. In the indirect test conditions, all irrelevant perceptual consistencies provided during training and transfer were held constant. This was accomplished by constraining the location of the target figure such that it (a) appeared in each possible location with equal frequency; (b) appeared in, vertical to, and horizontal to all colors, except blue, with equal frequency; and (c) appeared vertical to, horizontal to, and diagonal to each of the distractor figures with equal frequency.

REFERENCES

Atkinson, R. C., & Shiffrin, R. M. (1968). Human memory: A proposed system and its control processes. In K. W. Spence & J. T. Spence (Eds.), *Advances in the psychology of learning and motivation: Research and theory* (Vol. 2). New York: Academic Press.

Baars, B. J. (1991). A curious coincidence? Consciousness as an object of scientific scutiny fits our personal experience remarkably well. *Behavioral and Brain Sciences, 14,* 669-670.

Berry, D. C., & Broadbent, D. E. (1988). Interactive tasks and the implicit-explicit distinction. *British Journal of Psychology, 79,* 251-272.

Brewer, W. F. (1974). There is no convincing evidence for operant and classical conditioning in human beings. In W. B. Weimer & D. J. Palermo (Eds.), *Cognition and the symbolic processes* (pp. 1-42). Hillsdale, NJ: Lawrence Erlbaum.

Cohen, A., Ivry, R. I., & Keele, S. W. (1990). Attention and structure in sequence learning. *Journal of Experimental Psychology: Learning, Memory, and Cognition, 16,* 17-30.

Dulany, D. E. (1991). Conscious representations and thought systems. In R. S. Wyer, Jr., & T. K. Srull (Eds.), *Advances in social cognition.* Hillsdale, NJ: Lawrence Erlbaum.

Dulany, D. E., Carlson, R. A., & Dewey, G. I. (1984). A case of syntactical learning and judgment: How conscious and how abstract. *Journal of Experimental Psychology: General, 113,* 541-555.

Eriksen, C. W. (1960). Discrimination and learning without awareness: A methodological survey and evaluation. *Psychological Review, 67,* 279-300.

Gomez, R. L., & Schvaneveldt, R. W. (1994). What is learned from artificial grammars? Transfer tests of simple association. *Journal of Experimental Psychology: Learning, Memory, and Cognition, 20,* 396-410.

Holender, D. (1986). Semantic activation without conscious identification of dichotic listening, parafoveal vision, and visual masking: A survey and appraisal. *Behavioral and Brain Sciences, 9,* 1-23.

Johnson, P. J., Forester, J. A., Calderwood, R., & Weisgerber, S. A. (1983). Resource allocation and the attentional demands of letter encoding. *Journal of Experimental Psychology: General, 112,* 616-638.

Keele, S. W., & Jennings, P. J. (1991). Attention in the representation of sequence: Experiment and theory. *Human Movement Sciences, 11,* 14-27.

Lewicki, P., Hill, T., & Bizot, E. (1988). Acquisition of procedural knowledge about a pattern of stimuli that cannot be articulated. *Cognitive Psychology, 20,* 24-37.

Libet, B. (1985). Unconscious cerebral initiative and the role of conscious will in voluntary action. *Behavioral and Brain Sciences, 8,* 529-566.

MacKay, W. A. (1991). Consciousness is king of the neuronal processors. *Behavioral and Brain Sciences, 14,* 687-688.

Mandler, G., Nakamura, Y., & van Zandt, B. J. S. (1987). Nonspecific effects of exposure on stimuli that cannot be recognized. *Journal of Experimental Psychology: Learning, Memory, and Cognition, 13,* 646-649.

Moscovitch, M. (1994). Memory and working with memory: Evaluation of a component process model and comparisons with other models. In D. L. Schacter, & E. Tulving (Eds.), *Memory models* (pp. 269-310). Cambridge: MIT Press.

Neisser, U. (1967). *Cognitive psychology.* New York: Appleton-Century-Crofts.

Nisbitt, R. E., & Wilson, T. D. (1977). Telling more than we can know: Verbal reports on mental processes. *Psychological Review, 84,* 231-259.

Nissen, M. J., & Bullemer, P. (1987). Attentional requirements of learning: Evidence from performance measures. *Cognitive Psychology, 19,* 1-32.

Paap, K. R., & Ogden, W. G. (1981). Letter encoding is an obligatory but capacity-demanding operation. *Journal of Experimental Psychology: Human Perception and Performance, 7,* 518-528.

Perruchet, P. (1994). Learning from complex rule-governed environments: On the proper functions of nonconscious and conscious processes (pp. 811-835). In C. Umiltà & M. Moscovitch (Eds.), *Attention and performance XV: Conscious and nonconscious information processing* (pp. 811-835). Cambridge: MIT Press.

Perruchet, P., & Amorim, M. (1992). Conscious knowledge and changes in performance in sequence learning: Evidence against dissociations. *Journal of Experimental Psychology: Learning, Memory, and Cognition, 18,* 785-800.

Perruchet, P., Gallego, J., & Pacteau, C. (1992). A reinterpretation of some earlier evidence for abstractiveness of implicitly acquired knowledge. *Quarterly Journal of Experimental Psychology, 44A,* 193-210.

Perruchet, P., Gallego, J., & Savy, I. (1990). A critical reappraisal of the evidence for unconscious abstraction of deterministic rules in complex experimental situations. *Cognitive Psychology, 22,* 493-516.

Posner, M. I. (1978). *Chronometric exploration of mind.* Hillsdale, NJ: Lawrence Erlbaum.

Reber, A. S. (1969). Transfer of syntactic structure in synthetic languages. *Journal of Experimental Psychology, 81,* 115-119.

Reber, A. S. (1989). Implicit learning and tacit knowledge. *Journal of Experimental Psychology: General, 118,* 219-235.

Reber, A. S. (1992). An evolutionary context for the cognitive unconscious. *Philosophical Psychology, 5,* 33-51.

Reber, P. J., & Squire, L. R. (1994). Parallel brain systems for learning with and without awareness. *Learning & Memory, 1,* 217-229.

Reed, J. (1995). *An empirical examination of four theoretical characteristics of implicit learning.* Unpublished doctoral dissertation, University of New Mexico, Albuquerque.

Reed, J., & Johnson, P. (1994a). Assessing implicit learning with indirect tests: Determining what is learned about sequence structure. *Journal of Experimental Psychology: Learning, Memory, and Cognition, 20,* 585-594.

Reed, J., & Johnson, P. (1994b, April). *Concurrent learning of deterministic and probabilistic sequence structure.* Paper presented at the sixty-fourth annual meeting of the Rocky Mountain Psychological Association, Las Vegas, NV.

Reed, J., Johnson, P., & Ottaway, S. (1995, November). *Attentional demands of implicit learning.* Poster session presented at the thirty-sixth annual meeting of the Psychonomic Society, Los Angeles.

Reingold, E. M., & Merikle, P. M. (1990). On the interrelatedness of theory and measurement in the study of unconscious processes. *Mind & Language, 5,* 9-28.

Richardson-Klavehn, A., & Bjork, R. A. (1988). Measures of memory. *Annual Review of Psychology, 39,* 475-542.

Rozin, P. (1976). The evolution of intelligence and access to the cognitive unconscious. In J. M. Sprague & A. N. Epstein (Eds.), *Progress in psychobiology and physiological psychology.* New York: Academic Press.

Schacter, D. L. (1987). Implicit memory: History and current status. *Journal of Experimental Psychology: Learning, Memory, and Cognition, 13,* 501-518.

Schacter, D. L., & Graf, P. (1986). Effects of elaborative processes on implicit and explicit memory for new associations. *Journal of Experimental Psychology: Learning, Memory, and Cognition, 12,* 432-444.

Shanks, D. R., & St. John, M. F. (1994). Characteristics of dissociable human learning systems. *Behavioral and Brain Sciences, 17,* 367-447.

Squire, L. R. (1987). *Memory and brain.* New York: Oxford University Press.

Stadler, M. A. (1989). On learning complex procedural knowledge. *Journal of Experimental Psychology: Learning, Memory, and Cognition, 15,* 1061-1069.

Stadler, M. A. (1995). Role of attention in implicit learning. *Journal of Experimental Psychology: Learning, Memory, and Cognition, 21,* 674-685.

Stanovich, K. E. (1991). Damn! There goes that ghost again! *Behavioral and Brain Sciences, 14,* 696-698.

Velmans, M. (1991). Is human information processing conscious? *Behavioral and Brain Sciences, 14,* 651-726.

9

Multiple Forms of Implicit Learning

●————————————————————————————

Carol A. Seger

"Now, don't you see the difference? It wasn't anything but a wind reef. The wind does that."

"So I see. But it is exactly like a bluff reef. How am I ever going to tell them apart?"

"I can't tell you. It is an instinct. By and by you will just naturally know one from the other, but you will never be able to explain why or how you know them apart."

—Mark Twain (1896/1944), Life on the Mississippi

This chapter investigates the degree to which implicit learning is a unified phenomenon. I argue that there are at least three different forms of implicit learning: abstract, perceptual, and motor learning. In the first portion of the chapter, a working definition of implicit learning is given, and each of the three forms of learning is described. The middle portion of this chapter presents research investigating whether abstract, motor, and perceptual implicit learning are separate processes. The final portion of this chapter discusses differences between these forms of implicit learning in terms of the flexibility of the knowledge acquired, the complexity of the relations learned, the spatial and temporal relations that must exist between stimulus features for learning to occur, the automaticity of learning, and the neural dependencies of each form of learning.

WORKING DEFINITIONS

Researchers disagree as to which tasks should be considered examples of implicit learning. For the purposes of this chapter, I follow the definition I put forward earlier (Seger, 1994b). Implicit learning (a) happens in an incidental manner, without the use of conscious hypothesis-testing strategies; (b) happens without subjects acquiring sufficient conscious knowledge to account for their performance on tests of their learning; (c) is of novel material, rather than involving activation of previously acquired representations; and (d) is preserved in patients with amnesia. Criteria (a) and (b) are a relatively lenient version of the strict criteria adopted by some researchers, such as Shanks and St. John (1994), whose main goal is to prove or disprove the existence of unconscious learning. I have argued (Seger, 1994a) that some forms of implicit learning are potentially on the fringe of consciousness; therefore, I do not emphasize conscious accessibility in this chapter. These criteria also limit implicit learning to situations in which the information learned is not verbalizable throughout the learning process, as opposed to learning of skills in which consciously held knowledge becomes unconscious through automatization (Anderson, 1987). Criterion (c) is intended to distinguish implicit learning tasks from implicit memory tasks in which novel material is not learned (e.g., most repetition-priming experiments) and in which performance may be due to activation of previously acquired knowledge rather than induction of new knowledge. Criterion (d), that implicit learning be preserved in cases of global amnesia, limits implicit learning to being a form of nondeclarative memory (Knowlton & Squire, 1994, 1996; Reber & Squire, 1994).

It is important to keep in mind the distinction between theoretically proposed mental processes and tasks that are hypothesized to tap these mental processes. Tasks are seldom process-pure: any given task may involve many cognitive processes. Below, I will talk about forms of learning (abstract, perceptual, and motor) and measures of these forms of learning (e.g., a grammaticality test of artificial grammar learning that is hypothesized to be a measure of abstract implicit learning).

The terms *abstract, motor,* and *perceptual* were chosen to refer to types of learning. These terms differ from those used in Seger (1994b). In that earlier work, I discussed three kinds of implicit learning which I called conceptual fluency, efficiency, and prediction and control, which were collectively termed *response modalities*. Abstract implicit learning corresponds to *conceptual fluency,* motor implicit learning corresponds to *efficiency,* and perceptual implicit learning is a new category. Prediction and control is not discussed in this chapter.

FORMS OF IMPLICIT LEARNING

Abstract Implicit Learning

Tests classified as measures of abstract learning are those that require the subject to make a judgment about a stimulus rather than measuring motor reaction time or measuring the ability to perceive the stimulus. Artificial grammar learning is the paradigm case of abstract learning within the implicit learning literature. In a standard artificial grammar-learning experiment, subjects study a set of letter strings formed according to a finite-state automaton. Then subjects observe novel strings and decide for each one whether it is grammatical or not. Subjects usually perform at above-chance levels on this grammatical judgment test; they perform better on the test than can be accounted for by their verbalizable knowledge of the grammar (Seger, 1994b). Amnesic patients show normal learning on artificial grammar tasks (Knowlton & Squire, 1994, 1996).

A connotation of the term abstract is that learning should not be bound to surface features of stimuli. Several experiments have shown that subjects can transfer their knowledge of the grammar to strings in which the underlying grammar is the same but the letters used in the strings have been changed (Gomez & Schvaneveldt, 1994; Knowlton & Squire, 1996; Mathews et al., 1989). Furthermore, some studies show transfer to novel letter-like symbols (Altmann, Dienes, & Goode, 1995; Chan, cited in Berry & Dienes, 1993) and across sensory modalities (Altmann et al., 1995; Manza & Reber, 1992). Letter-set transfer occurs normally even in amnesic subjects (Knowlton & Squire, 1996).

Judgments about strings other than judgments of grammatical well-formedness are also affected by implicit grammatical knowledge. Gordon and Holyoak (1983) found that making an affective judgment about a string, such as whether one likes it or not, tapped the same knowledge as making a grammaticality judgment about the string. However, Manza and Bornstein

(1995) showed in an artificial grammar paradigm after letter-set transfer that grammaticality judgments were a more sensitive test of grammatical knowledge than liking judgments.

A theory of how different judgments can be made about stimuli on the basis of unconscious knowledge has been developed in experiments investigating the subliminal mere exposure effect. In the subliminal mere exposure paradigm, subjects are first presented subliminally with geometric figures. Later, subjects are shown pairs of figures, one of which is repeated from the learning phase and one of which is novel. For each pair, subjects indicate which one they like the most. Subjects prefer previously seen figures more often than novel figures, despite conscious recognition of the repeated figures being at chance levels (Kunst-Wilson & Zajonc, 1980). Implicit knowledge also influences other judgments, including judgments of familiarity (Bonanno & Stillings, 1986) and judgments of lightness or darkness of the stimulus (Mandler, Nakamura, & Van Zandt, 1987). Bornstein (1992) proposed a two-stage theory of how judgments are made in a subliminal mere exposure paradigm: in the first stage, unconscious knowledge of the stimulus is activated; in the second stage, this knowledge is attributed to liking the stimulus, familiarity of the stimulus, or other features of the stimulus. Seger (1994b) extended this theory to implicit learning, proposing that abstract judgments may be made in a two-part process. First, unconscious knowledge is activated and is available to the subject in terms of an intuitive sense or "feeling of knowing." Second, subjects, noting the absence of explicit knowledge of the stimulus, attribute this feeling or sense to the grammatical legality, pleasantness, or other properties of the stimulus.

It is unknown what cognitive information the intuitive sense or feeling of knowing is based on. Potentially, it could be the output of early level perceptual systems that is accessible to higher-order thinking or an independent computation of higher-level cognitive systems. There is some evidence against the former possibility. Recent research has shown that perceptual fluency contributions toward recognition, which may be related to the feeling of knowing in artificial grammar learning, are independent of some aspects of lower-level processing of stimuli. Wagner, Gabrieli, and Verfaellie (1997) have found that perceptual identification priming is independent of the perceptual fluency component of recognition. In one of their experiments, M.S., a patient with a right occipital lobe lesion who showed no perceptual identification priming, showed normal contribution of perceptual fluency to recognition. In addition, Poldrack and Logan (1997) have found that speed of processing of words is independent of the fluency component of recognition. Seamon et al. (1995) found qualitatively different results when implicit knowledge of possible and impossible figures was measured via a possible/impossible decision task than when it was measured via preference judgments. In the possible/impossible decision task, priming was found only for possible objects, whereas preference increased for both impossible and possible objects. Finally, after extensive training, subjects show good performance on familiarity measures on studied novel words in a novel script, to the degree that their performance on the novel language words is close to their performance on English words. However, despite this good learning on the familiarity measure, subjects do not show changes in processing of these novel words in the visual word-form area (Posner, Abdullaev, McCandliss, & Sereno, in press).

Zajonc (1980; Murphy & Zajonc, 1993) proposed that tasks involving judgments of liking are part of an emotional processing system that is qualitatively different from cognitive systems. There are many cases in which learned information can be shown to affect subjects' judgments of liking without subjects being aware of the basis of their judgments. For example, Van der Bergh, Vrana, and Eelen (1990) found that typists preferred letter combinations that were typed with different fingers, whereas nontypists had no such preference; the typists did not have conscious knowledge of the basis of their preference. Zajonc takes such cases as evidence for the primacy of emotional processing.

● **Perceptual Implicit Learning**

Recently, several perceptual implicit memory tests have been developed that meet the criteria for implicit learning used in this chapter. A perceptual implicit learning measure is one in which learning is measured by changes in the perceptual processing of stimuli up to the level of basic identification of stimulus identity. Rather than requiring subjects to make judgments about stimuli, these experiments attempt to measure the ability to perceive a stimulus. Very little research has been performed in traditional implicit learning tasks using perceptually linked measures of learning. However, Buchner (1994) found that subjects were faster to identify a grammatical string than a nongrammatical string in a perceptual clarification procedure. Within the field of implicit memory, however, there are several tasks that meet the definition of implicit learning. Below, I discuss repetition-priming effects for nonwords, repetition priming for novel objects, and association-specific repetition priming for word pairs.

PERCEPTUAL IDENTIFICATION PRIMING

Recent research has found repetition priming for nonword letter strings, including orthographically and phonologically legal strings (Bowers, 1994; Dorfman, 1994) and orthographically illegal strings (Keane, Gabrieli, Noland, & McNealy, 1995). These studies usually use the perceptual identification procedure, in which subjects are exposed to the letter strings, then at test are presented with rapidly presented or degraded strings and have to indicate the string's identity. Subjects are more accurate for strings that they have previously seen. Nonword priming meets the criteria for implicit learning in that learning happens incidentally and without conscious awareness being necessary, learning involves the acquisition of new information (a particular pattern of letters), and learning is preserved in amnesia (Keane et al. 1995; Smith & Oscar-Berman, 1990). Perceptual identification priming is strongly linked to perceptual features of stimuli and disappears if characteristics such as type font are changed (Tenpenny, 1995). Gabrieli, Fleischman, Keane, Reminger, and Morrell (1995) found a right occipital lobe locus for perceptual identification priming: Patient M.S., an otherwise cognitively normal patient who had his right occipital lobe resected in treatment for intractable epilepsy, showed no perceptual identification priming.

NOVEL OBJECT PRIMING

Schacter, Cooper, and colleagues (Schacter, Cooper, & Delaney, 1990) have identified a perceptual system that can show learning of novel visual forms. In their experiments, subjects study line drawings of possible and impossible objects. An impossible object drawing violates rules of edge or surface representation and cannot exist in a three-dimensional form. Subjects are tested by showing them novel and repeated objects and having them decide for each if it is possible or impossible. Priming is defined as making more accurate decisions about repeated objects than novel objects; priming only occurs for possible objects. The researchers postulate that the priming they find is due to activation in a visual structural representation system that computes object form from visual input, which can only occur if the drawing is of a possible object. Object decision priming is not affected by changes in size or reflection of drawings between study and test, but it is greatly reduced by rotation of the drawing in the picture plane (Cooper

& Schacter, 1992). Object decision priming meets the criteria for implicit learning in that learning happens incidentally, learning involves the acquisition of new information (a particular shape formed by a novel conjunction of line segments), and learning is preserved in amnesia (Schacter, Cooper, Tharan, & Rubens, 1991). In a positron emission tomographic (PET) brain-imaging study, Schacter and colleagues (Schacter et al., 1995) found an inferior temporal region that was differentially active when possible and impossible objects were observed. They postulated that this could be the neural basis for a visual structural representation system.

ASSOCIATIVE PRIMING

Goshen-Gottstein and Moscovitch (1995b, 1995c) found relational priming for unrelated words paired in learning and at test. Lexical decision times were faster when subjects were presented with an intact pair (one that was presented at study) than when subjects were presented with a recombined pair (one in which each word was presented at study, but in different pairs). They argued that this form of priming is perceptually linked because it was not affected by levels of processing manipulation (which indicates the involvement of conceptual or semantic processes in priming; Roediger & McDermott, 1993) and because it was interfered with when the stimuli were altered in spatial and temporal presentation (i.e., were presented simultaneously during study but sequentially during testing). Gabrieli, Keane, Zarella, and Poldrack (1997) found similar association-specific priming for word pairs in a perceptual identification task. Word-pair relational priming meets the criteria for implicit learning in that learning happens incidentally and without conscious awareness being necessary, learning involves the acquisition of new information (a particular pairing of stimuli), and learning is preserved in amnesia on both lexical decision and perceptual identification measures (Goshen-Gottstein & Moscovitch, 1995a; Gabrieli et al., 1996).

● Motor Implicit Learning

Motor implicit learning is learning that is accessible to and can facilitate motor responses. The best-studied motor implicit learning task is the serial reaction time (SRT) task; it qualifies as motor implicit learning in that learning is measured via motor response facilitation. In this task, subjects are presented with visual stimuli, usually dots or asterisks, that can appear in one of several discrete locations. The subject's task is to press a button corresponding to each stimulus location as quickly as possible after a stimulus is presented. The stimuli can be presented in a pattern, and learning of the pattern can be determined by decreased reaction times across blocks or by comparison of reaction times on pattern and random blocks.

A line of research has been aimed at investigating whether subjects must produce motor responses during the learning phase for motor learning to occur. It might be more parsimonious for the brain to learn only what is of immediate use (Seger, 1994b). However, the experiments indicate that subjects learn patterns that are later accessible to motor responses equally well through observation of the stimuli as through making responses to the stimuli (Howard, Mutter, & Howard, 1992), even when explicit knowledge is controlled for (Seger, 1996a).

The existence of motor implicit learning is supported by research in patients with brain damage in regions primarily associated with motor processing. Two kinds of patient groups are often studied: those with Huntington's disease and those with Parkinson's disease. In Huntington's disease, patients have damage to the basal ganglia; in Parkinson's disease, there is damage to the substantia nigra. Both diseases interrupt processing loops between the frontal lobes, basal ganglia, substantia nigra, and thalamus. These patients are typically intact on measures of perceptual and conceptual priming but show motor learning deficits. In addition to impairments on SRT tasks (Huntington's: Knopman & Nissen, 1991; Willingham & Koroshetz, 1993; Parkinson's: Jackson, Jackson, Harrison, Henderson, & Kennard, 1995), patients with these disorders are impaired on other motor learning tasks, such as weight biasing (Heindel, Salmon, Shults, Walicke, & Butters, 1989) and pursuit rotor (Gabrieli, 1995). However, subjects with Huntington's disease perform normally on the mirror-tracing task (Gabrieli, 1995).

Motor learning itself may also consist of several submechanisms. Willingham (1992) identifies three potential components to motor learning: learning mappings between stimuli and associated motor responses, learning higher-order motor plans such as serial order, and learning involved in making movements spatially and temporally invariant. Implicit learning research has usually been concerned with investigating acquisition of higher-order motor plans; however, Willingham, Koroshetz, and Peterson (1996) found that subjects with Huntington's disease showed normal learning of novel mappings but impaired learning of higher-order motor plans.

EVIDENCE FOR SEPARATE
LEARNING MECHANISMS

Abstract Versus Perceptual

Within standard implicit learning paradigms, no research has been performed intended to investigate whether abstract and perceptual learning involve separate processes. However, Buchner (1994) performed research that can be interpreted as providing such evidence. Subjects studied strings formed according to an artificial grammar, then performed two tests with novel strings, a perceptual clarification test and a grammatical judgment test. In the perceptual clarification test, subjects were shown a solid black rectangular mask from which pixels were gradually removed, revealing a letter string. Subjects indicated at which point in this clarification process they were able to identify the string; they required less clarification of the string to identify grammatical strings than nongrammatical strings. Buchner further found that clarification speed was not related to judgment of grammatical correctness, in that for grammatical strings, clarification times were the same for hits (strings classified as grammatical) and for misses (strings classified as nongrammatical), and for nongrammatical strings, clarification times were equally fast for correct rejections (strings classified as nongrammatical) and for false alarms (strings classified as grammatical).

Research in other aspects of implicit learning show a similar pattern of findings such that judgments about stimuli are independent of perceptual processing of stimuli. As discussed above in the section on abstract learning, the perceptual fluency component of recognition is independent of perceptual identification priming (Wagner et al., 1997) and speed of processing of words (Poldrack & Logan, 1997). In addition, the affective judgment measure of knowledge about possible and impossible objects behaves qualitatively differently from the measure of performance on the object decision task (Seamon et al., 1995).

Perceptual Versus Motor

Very little research has directly compared perceptual learning with motor learning. In SRT, there is a body of research investigating transfer of learning across changes in perceptual features and motor features of the task. This research usually finds separate contributions of perceptual and motor aspects of the task to task performance (Mayr, 1996). Another body of research in SRT has shown that subjects can learn information about a sequence through observation of stimuli alone (Howard et al., 1992, Seger, 1996a). One problem with interpreting these studies within the framework set up by this chapter is that the same motor response measure is used as the dependent measure in the perceptual and motor conditions; a measure of perceptual facilitation is not included. The experiments can only show differences in motor responding attributable to changes in visuospatial features or in purely motor features; any perceptual effect that may exist is filtered through the motor response system.

● **Abstract Versus Motor**

Seger (1996b, 1997) performed research in both the artificial grammar and SRT paradigms investigating whether abstract and motor-linked learning were independent. These tasks were chosen for several reasons, the most important of which was that the measure usually used in artificial grammar learning is a grammaticality test, which may tap abstract knowledge, whereas the measure usually used in SRT tasks is reaction time, which is more likely to tap motor knowledge. In each paradigm, subjects were tested with a motor-linked and an abstract measure of learning in order to investigate independence within task.

Two different sources of evidence for independence are usually used in implicit memory research (Tulving, 1985). One type of independence is functional independence: Performance on one of the tasks is affected by a variable that has less or no effect on the other task (a single dissociation) or, even stronger, has the opposite effect on the other task (a double dissociation). Another type is stochastic independence: Performance on the different tests is uncorrelated. Stochastic independence can be evaluated by taking individual subjects or individual test items as the basis for calculating scores on the different tests, and these scores can then be subjected to correlation analysis by subjects or items, respectively. Stochastic independence provides a stronger argument for independence (Tulving, 1985).

To control for the effects of explicit learning on the tasks, subjects in each experiment completed tests of explicit knowledge that examined how aware they were of the pattern presented. This made it possible to divide subjects into low and high explicit knowledge groups and to confirm that learning occurred in the low-awareness groups. This method is similar to the retrieval intention criterion in implicit memory research (Bowers &

Schacter, 1990) and has often been used in SRT research (Curran & Keele, 1993) and recently in artificial grammar research (Gomez, in press).

METHODS

In the SRT experiment, the stimuli were four circles in a horizontal row on the computer screen: The circles darkened one at a time in a set sequence. Three different learning tasks were examined: observe, in which subjects merely watched the stimuli; respond, in which subjects pressed a key corresponding to each stimulus; and dual task, in which subjects made key presses and performed a dual task. The dual task was a tone-counting task: after each trial, a high or low tone was played, and subjects were required to count the number of high tones. Length of study was also manipulated, with subjects training across 3, 6, or 12 blocks of five repetitions of the sequence each. Finally, the instantiation of the sequence in terms of assignment of sequence elements to screen locations was manipulated. The underlying structure of the sequence was the same for all subjects, ABCDBCBDBC, but it was presented as one of five sequences: 1324323432, 1342343234, 2143141314, 3412414241, or 3142141214, where 1 and 4 correspond respectively to the farthest left and farthest right screen locations.

In the test phase, subjects first completed a motor response test in which they responded to stimulus elements in the same way that the respond group did on the learning task. They then completed a dual-task test in which they made responses and performed the tone-counting task. For both tests, subjects were given both random and sequence stimuli; learning was defined as the difference between reaction times for random and sequence stimulus blocks. The third test was the explicit knowledge questionnaire, which was followed by a free-generation test (this test was included for exploratory purposes and will not be discussed further here) and finally the pattern-recognition test. The pattern-recognition test was intended to be as similar as possible to an artificial grammar grammaticality test. Subjects were shown correct and incorrect sequence fragments and were asked to indicate for each whether it was legal or illegal.

In the artificial grammar experiments, the method was similar to the SRT experiment. The stimuli were letter strings formed by an artificial grammar, shown in Figure 9.1. The strings were presented letter by letter until the whole string was visible. Subjects performed one of two learning tasks: observe, in which they watched the strings appear on the screen letter

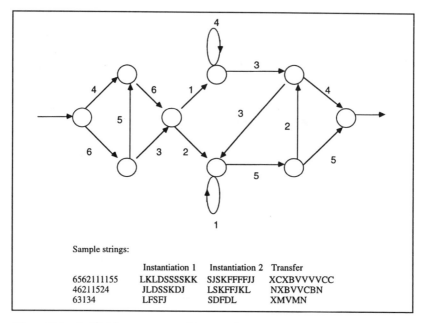

Figure 9.1. Artificial grammar used in experiments.

by letter; or type, in which they typed each letter on the keyboard as it appeared. The letters used to instantiate the strings were assigned to the grammar locations in one of two ways, shown in Figure 9.1. In the testing phase, subjects performed both a motor test (speeded typing of grammatical and nongrammatical strings) and an abstract test (the usual grammatical judgment test). At the end, they filled out a questionnaire examining their awareness of the existence of a pattern in the stimuli and their ability to describe it. A control group of subjects was run on just the testing phase tasks to ensure that the learning shown by the experimental groups was due to information acquired during the learning phase.

In the artificial grammar experiment, the complexity of knowledge acquired by subjects was examined to investigate whether first-order sequential information (information about legal and illegal pairwise transitions) would be learned differently from higher-order sequential information. Early research (Cohen, Ivry, & Keele, 1990) implied that subjects performing SRT tasks under conditions of divided attention could learn pairwise relationships but not higher-order relations, whereas subjects performing SRT tasks with full attention learned both kinds of relationships;

however, more recent research indicates that both pairwise and higher-order relationships can be learned in conditions of divided attention (Reed & Johnson, 1994). In artificial grammar learning, Gomez and Schvaneveldt (1994) showed that subjects were sensitive to both pairwise and higher-order information on a grammaticality test, even when the letter set used to instantiate the grammar was changed between study and test.

In the grammatical judgment test of the present experiment, for some of the nongrammatical strings, all pairwise transitions were grammatical and the string was nongrammatical as a result of violating higher-order sequential dependencies among the letters; performance on these strings was the measure of higher-order knowledge. The rest of the nongrammatical strings had at least one illegal pairwise transition; performance on these strings was the measure of pairwise knowledge. For the typing test, the pairwise measure was calculated by taking the difference between the mean typing speed for illegal transitions (i.e., a letter that cannot legally follow the preceding letter) within nongrammatical strings and the mean typing speed for legal transitions within grammatical strings. The higher-order measure was calculated by taking the difference between mean typing speed for legal transitions within nongrammatical strings and mean typing speed for legal transitions within grammatical strings.

STOCHASTIC MEASURES OF INDEPENDENCE

For both the SRT and the artificial grammar experiment, correlations were computed for the measures of motor and abstract knowledge. Subjects with relatively high explicit knowledge were not included in the analyses because subjects may use explicit knowledge to increase their performance on both kinds of tests. For the SRT experiment, the correlation between the single task respond test and the pattern judgment test was .05; the correlation between dual-task respond and pattern judgment was −.04. In the artificial grammar experiment, the correlations between higher-order and pairwise typing test measures and higher-order grammatical judgment measures were .04 and −.01, respectively; the correlations between higher-order and pairwise typing measures and pairwise grammatical judgment measures were −.25 and .13, respectively. Thus, in both the SRT task and the artificial grammar experiment, performance on measures postulated to tap motor-linked knowledge did not correlate significantly with measures postulated to tap abstract knowledge, which is consistent with the hypothesis that the tests access separate learning mechanisms.

A second stochastic measure was performed on the SRT experiment. Because one of the variables manipulated was length of learning phase, it was possible to examine whether acquisition of one kind of knowledge was dependent on the previous acquisition of another kind of knowledge. A criterion for learning was set for both the pattern-recognition and single-task respond tests as one standard deviation above chance performance; subjects scoring above the critical value were classified as high-level learners. Then the distribution of subjects who met criteria on each task was examined across the length of learning phase, to see whether attaining a criterion on one test was dependent on attaining a criterion on the other test. There was no evidence that performance on either task was dependent on the other: An equal proportion of subjects was classified as having abstract knowledge but not motor knowledge as subjects classified as having motor knowledge but not abstract knowledge across learning phase length.

Further evidence for stochastic independence comes from an artificial grammar experiment in which subjects performed a single test in which they first typed a string and then a grammatical judgment about it. This test design made it possible to perform an item-level analysis examining whether rapid typing is associated with grammatical judgments. For grammatical items, hits (items judged as being grammatical) were typed equally rapidly as misses (items judged as being nongrammatical), indicating that typing and grammatical judgment were independent. For nongrammatical items, however, there was a trend for correct rejections to be typed more slowly than false alarms, indicating a possible relationship between typing speed and grammatical judgment for processing of nongrammatical items.

FUNCTIONAL MEASURES OF INDEPENDENCE

Functional dissociations between measures were also found. In the SRT experiment, three variables were manipulated: length of study, type of study task, and the assignment of sequence elements to screen locations. The length of study and type of study variables led to single dissociations. Each of these variables had a significant effect on the abstract measure but no effect on the motor measure. The screen-location assignment variable led to especially rich results. A double dissociation was found such that two screen-location assignment types (1324323432 and 1342343234) led to high performance on the motor test but poor performance on the abstract test, whereas the other three assignment types (2143141314, 3412414241, and 3142141214) led to high performance on the abstract test but low performance on the motor test. A post hoc analysis of the sequences that led to good performance on the typing test but poor performance on the grammaticality test indicated that these two sequences each had a back and forth pattern (323432 or 2343234) that may have been easily learned by a motor test because it involves "natural" movements of the fingers in sequence. In the three sequences that led to good performance on the grammaticality test but poor performance on the typing test, the sequence is such that the stimulus often alternates between end positions, and the end positions appear more frequently than the middle positions. These end positions might be more salient than the middle positions, enabling participants to learn more about the sequences that later is accessible by the pattern-judgment test.

In the artificial grammar experiments, the variables of study type (observe and typing), letter assignment type, and complexity (pairwise versus higher-order information) were examined. On the grammatical judgment test, observe learning led to a bigger difference between pairwise and higher-order knowledge than respond learning; knowledge of pairwise relations after observe learning was significantly higher than knowledge of higher-order relations after observe learning or knowledge of either sort of relationship after typing learning. Conversely, on the typing test, observe learning again led to a bigger difference between pairwise and higher-order knowledge, but in this case, higher-order knowledge after observe learning was significantly lower than the other three conditions. Overall, there was a single dissociation between typing and grammatical judgment such that observe learning was better than respond learning for the acquisition of knowledge accessible to grammatical judgments, whereas there was no significant difference for observe and respond learning on the typing test (although there was a slight trend for respond learning to be superior to observe).

An additional experiment examined whether subjects could transfer their knowledge of the grammar to a set of strings in which the underlying grammar remained the same, but in which a different set of letters was used to instantiate the grammar. Previous research showed that subjects could transfer significant amounts of knowledge across letter sets when performance was tested on a grammatical judgment test (Gomez & Schvaneveldt, 1994; Knowlton & Squire, 1996; Mathews et al. 1989; Reber, 1969; Whittlesea & Dorkin, 1993). It was hypothesized that the typing test of motor knowledge would be more sensitive to changes in letter set and that subjects would not show learning on that measure.

Two experimental and two control groups of subjects were run. The experimental groups performed an observational learning task; one group then performed the grammatical judgment test and typing test on strings instantiated in a different letter set than in the learning phase, and the other group performed the tests on strings instantiated in the same letter set as in the learning phase. Separate control groups performed the testing phase for each letter set. Subjects performed significantly better than controls on the grammaticality test, both when the same letters and different letters were used in the testing phase. On the typing test, however, only subjects in the same letter-set group showed above control-level performance. This result indicates that grammatical knowledge could not be used to facilitate motor responses across letter sets. Gomez (in press) also investigated typing speed for grammatical and nongrammatical strings after letter-set transfer and also found no evidence for learning.

In conclusion, there is little evidence that motor-linked (key pressing or typing) and abstract (pattern judgment or grammatical judgment) measures access the same forms of implicit learning. The majority of the evidence is consistent with the motor-linked and abstract measures being independent measures of separate sources of learning. It should be noted that, in attempting to prove that two processes are independent, one must prove the null hypothesis. Nevertheless, the results consistently show a lack of dependence of the measures.

FACTORS THAT DISSOCIATE
FORMS OF IMPLICIT LEARNING

The preceding section discussed the degree to which abstract, motor, and perceptual implicit learning can be dissociated from each other. The following section discusses several of the features that were used to dissociate these forms of implicit learning: the flexibility and complexity of the knowledge acquired, the degree to which learning is sensitive to spatial and temporal contiguity of stimulus features, the degree to which learning is automatic, and the neural substrates underlying forms of learning.

Flexibility

The issue of whether implicit knowledge is flexible or not has been a controversial issue in the areas of implicit memory and implicit learning.

Some theorists have argued as part of the definition of nondeclarative memory (a term used to refer to implicit memory, implicit learning, and other cognitive tasks that are preserved in cases of amnesia) that it consists of inflexible knowledge that contrasts with the flexible knowledge acquired with the use of hippocampal processing (Cohen, Poldrack, & Eichenbaum, 1997; Holyoak & Spellman, 1993; Squire, 1992; for a criticism of this view, see Willingham & Preuss, 1995). However, some implicit knowledge is either inherently flexible or, at a minimum, can be applied flexibly. Most notable are the studies discussed above that find transfer across letter sets, novel symbols, and sensory modalities in artificial grammar experiments using a grammaticality test (Altmann et al., 1995; Chan, cited in Berry & Dienes, 1993; Gomez & Schvaneveldt, 1994; Knowlton & Squire, 1996; Manza & Reber, 1992; Mathews et al., 1989).

Although transfer is well-established for grammatical judgments, motor and perceptual measures of learning may be more stimulus-bound. Hence, flexibility of implicit knowledge may be one of the bases on which different forms of implicit learning differ. As described above, Seger (1996b) studied motor (typing) and abstract (grammaticality) measures of learning in an artificial grammar paradigm. Subjects could transfer knowledge across letter sets on a grammatical judgment test, but not on the typing test (subjects' performance on strings after the letters were changed did not differ from controls). Gomez (in press) also found no letter-set transfer when a typing test was used.

● **Structural Complexity**

Another property that may differentiate between forms of implicit learning is the complexity or specific structural properties of the stimuli. One common way of examining complexity is through information-theory analysis of the sequential structure of stimuli. Much research has investigated the degree to which subjects learn pairwise relations between adjacent items, versus learning higher-order relations (e.g., learning that position 1 follows position 2, versus learning the sequence 4 2 1; Cohen et al., 1990; Gomez & Schvaneveldt, 1994). The artificial grammar experiments presented above indicated that typing test performance was especially poor for higher-order information after an observational learning task, whereas grammatical judgment test performance was especially good for pairwise information after an observational learning task.

Other aspects of stimulus structure undoubtedly affect learning, but they have not yet been identified and studied. One tantalizing finding discussed above was the finding that different assignments of sequence items to screen locations led to different patterns of performance on a typing test (motor learning) and a grammaticality test (abstract learning).

● Spatial and Temporal Contiguity

There is some evidence that tests may be differentially sensitive to the spatial and temporal relations between stimulus features. Gomez (in press) found that subjects did not learn information that was accessible to a grammaticality test after performing a string typing task, whereas Seger (1996b) found that subjects did learn information accessible to grammaticality judgments after performing a similar task. In both experiments, subjects demonstrated learning when tested on a typing speed measure. The main difference between the learning procedures was that in the Gomez experiment, subjects saw letters individually, and each letter was presented only for the amount of time needed to type it, then disappeared from view, whereas in the Seger experiment, each letter string stayed on the screen until the last letter in the string was presented, and the entire string remained on the screen for an additional 2.5 seconds. These results taken together indicate that simultaneous presentation of letters is necessary for acquisition of knowledge accessible to grammatical judgment tests, but not necessary for knowledge accessible to motor responses. Furthermore, Goshen-Gottstein and Moscovitch (1995c) found priming of associations between unrelated words only when the pair of words was presented simultaneously, not if they were presented sequentially. This implies that spatial and temporal contiguity plays a role in perceptually based implicit learning as well as abstract implicit learning.

Another sense in which contiguity of stimuli can affect implicit learning is in the purity of the stimulus input to the learning system. Is learning best when only positive exemplars are studied, or can learning be accomplished equivalently well when positive and negative items are mixed? In artificial grammar learning, Dienes, Broadbent, and Berry (1991) found that subjects who studied a mixed list of grammatical and ungrammatical strings performed worse on a grammatical judgment test than subjects who studied only grammatical strings, indicating that knowledge accessible to an abstract measure is affected by purity of input to the system. In SRT tasks, learning of a sequence occurs when the sequence alternates with random stimuli

(Stadler, 1993), indicating that motor learning can occur even with mixed input to the learning system; however, no study has compared learning of sequences alone to mixed sequences and random stimuli. Gomez (in press) found a dissociation between motor and abstract learning of an artificial grammar that could be due to the effects of mixed input to a learning system. She found that subjects showed some learning of an artificial grammar during a typing speed test in which they typed both legal and illegal stimuli, but no learning during a grammatical judgment test in which they judged both legal and illegal strings.

● **Automaticity**

Another way that forms of implicit learning may differ is in terms of how automatic learning is in each. One meaning of automatic is that stimulus regularities are learned, regardless of the subject's mental state, for example, regardless of whether attention is deployed to the stimuli. Abstract measures may be less automatic than motor or perceptual measures. Artificial grammar learning accessible to a grammatical judgment test is reduced under conditions of attentional division (Dienes et al., 1991). However, in SRT, attentional division does not affect learning measured by motor response speed for at least some kinds of sequences (Cohen et al., 1990; Reed & Johnson, 1994). For implicit memory tasks, attentional division does not affect perceptual identification priming but does affect more conceptual priming tasks (Gabrieli et al., 1996).

A second sense of automaticity concerns whether implicit learning is automatically applied in relevant future situations, what Dienes, Altmann, Kwan, and Goode (1995) term having intentional control over the use of the knowledge. In an artificial grammar paradigm using a standard grammaticality test, they found that subjects could control whether implicit knowledge was applied. In one experiment, subjects studied two grammars sequentially, then received a test in which they were presented with legal and illegal strings from both grammars. Subjects were told to indicate which strings were grammatical according to the first or the second grammar they had studied. Subjects were able to ignore the other grammar and judge strings on the basis of the indicated grammar. In an additional experiment, subjects completed the learning phase of a grammar study and were told that the experiment was over. As they left, they were invited by a different experimenter to be in a different experiment in a different building. In fact, the second experiment was the testing phase, in which subjects were asked to classify strings as to whether they were grammatical. Subjects who were unaware of the relation between the two experiments performed at control levels on the grammaticality test, indicating that the knowledge learned in the first portion was not automatically applied to the strings in the second portion. It would be interesting to investigate whether subjects in motor or perceptual implicit learning tasks have intentional control over the application of their knowledge; a priori, it seems doubtful that they would.

● **Neural Substrates**

Implicit learning forms may differ in their reliance on particular neural systems. First, it should be noted that part of the working definition of implicit learning used in this chapter is that implicit learning is preserved in patients with amnesia; hence, all of the forms of learning discussed in this chapter do not depend on the hippocampal-diencephalic systems implicated in amnesia. Research on the cognitive features of Huntington's and Parkinson's diseases has shown one way that motor and abstract implicit learning dissociate. Patients with these diseases are impaired in motor implicit learning and implicit memory tasks, including SRT and pursuit-rotor motor learning tasks (Knopman & Nissen, 1991; Willingham & Koroshetz, 1993). However, Huntington's disease patients are unimpaired in artificial grammar learning measured by grammatical judgment (Knowlton, Squire, & Butters, 1994).

Other brain areas that may be of interest for differentiating forms of implicit learning include primary sensory cortices and association cortices. The patient M.S., who has a right occipital lobe lesion, showed a specific deficit in perceptual identification priming (Gabrieli et al., 1995). In Alzheimer's disease, there is relative sparing of primary sensory and motor cortex with more extensive damage to frontal and temporo-parietal association areas. Perceptual learning, such as perceptual identification priming for pseudowords (Keane, Gabrieli, Growdon, & Corkin, 1994), is preserved in Alzheimer's disease, as is motor learning on the SRT task (Knopman & Nissen, 1987). However, higher-level cognitive processes are impaired, including conceptual priming, priming that relies on the activation of semantic information associated with a stimulus rather than perceptual aspects of a stimulus (Keane, Gabrieli, Fennema, Growdon, & Corkin, 1991).

CONCLUSION

In this chapter, I presented an argument that implicit learning is not a single unified learning process. Rather, implicit learning consists of separate forms of learning, which may include abstract learning and forms linked to perceptual or motor processing. Performance on tasks measuring different forms of learning can be dissociated from each other and show stochastic independence. Different forms of implicit learning may differ qualitatively in terms of the neural substrates underlying learning, the flexibility and automaticity of learning, and the particular features of a stimulus that are learned.

REFERENCES

Altmann, G. T. M., Dienes, Z., & Goode, A. (1995). Modality independence of implicitly learned grammatical knowledge. *Journal of Experimental Psychology: Learning, Memory, and Cognition, 21*, 899-912.

Anderson, J. R. (1987). Skill acquisition: Compilation of weak-method problem solutions. *Psychological Review, 94*, 192-210.

Berry, D. C., & Dienes, Z. (1993). *Implicit learning: Theoretical and practical issues.* Hillsdale, NJ: Lawrence Erlbaum.

Bonanno, G. A., & Stillings, N. A. (1986). Preference, familiarity, and recognition after repeated brief exposures to random geometric shapes. *American Journal of Psychology, 99*, 403-415.

Bornstein, R. F. (1992). Subliminal mere exposure effects. In R. F. Bornstein & T. S. Pittman (Eds.), *Perception without awareness: Cognitive, clinical, and social perspectives* (pp. 191-210). New York: Guilford.

Bowers, J. S. (1994). Does implicit memory extend to legal and illegal nonwords? *Journal of Experimental Psychology: Learning, Memory, and Cognition, 20*, 534-549.

Bowers, J. S., & Schacter, D. L. (1990). Implicit memory and test awareness. *Journal of Experimental Psychology: Learning, Memory, and Cognition, 16*, 404-416.

Buchner, A. (1994). Indirect effects of synthetic grammar learning in an identification task. *Journal of Experimental Psychology: Learning, Memory, and Cognition, 20*, 550-566.

Cohen, A., Ivry, R. I., & Keele, S. W. (1990). Attention and structure in sequence learning. *Journal of Experimental Psychology: Learning, Memory, and Cognition, 16*, 17-30.

Cohen, N. J., Poldrack, R. A., & Eichenbaum, H. (1997). Memory for items and memory for relations in the procedural/declarative memory framework. *Memory, 5,* 131-178.

Cooper, L. A., & Schacter, D. L. (1992). Dissociations between structural and episodic representations of visual objects. *Current Directions in Psychological Science, 1,* 141-146.

Curran, T., & Keele, S. W. (1993). Attentional and nonattentional forms of sequence learning. *Journal of Experimental Psychology: Learning, Memory, and Cognition, 19,* 189-202.

Dienes, Z., Altmann, G. T. M., Kwan, L., & Goode, A. (1995). Unconscious knowledge of artificial grammars is applied strategically. *Journal of Experimental Psychology: Learning, Memory, and Cognition, 21,* 1322-1338.

Dienes, Z., Broadbent, D., & Berry, D. (1991). Implicit and explicit knowledge bases in artificial grammar learning. *Journal of Experimental Psychology: Learning, Memory, and Cognition, 17,* 875-887.

Dorfman, J. (1994). Sublexical components in implicit memory for novel words. *Journal of Experimental Psychology: Learning, Memory, and Cognition, 20,* 1108-1125.

Gabrieli, J. D. E. (1995). Contribution of the basal ganglia to skill learning and working memory in humans. In J. C. Houk, J. L. David, & D. G. Beiser (Eds.), *Models of information processing in the basal ganglia* (pp. 277-294). Cambridge: MIT Press.

Gabrieli, J. D. E., Fleischman, D. A., Keane, M. M., Reminger, S. L., & Morrell, F. (1995). Double dissociation between memory systems underlying explicit and implicit memory in the human brain. *Psychological Science, 6,* 76-82.

Gabrieli, J. D. E., Keane, M. M., Zarella, M. M., & Poldrack, P. A. (1997). Preservation of implicit memory for new associations in global amnesia. *Psychological Science, 8,* 326-329.

Gabrieli, J. D. E, Stone, M. V., Shackleton, K., Galan, J. B., Thompson-Schill, S. L., Seeley, W. W., & Chari, A. (1996). *Attention and implicit memory for words.* Manuscript submitted for publication.

Gomez, R. L. (in press). Transfer and complexity in artificial grammar learning. *Cognitive Psychology.*

Gomez, R. L., & Schvaneveldt, R. W. (1994). What is learned from artificial grammars? Transfer tests of simple association. *Journal of Experimental Psychology: Learning, Memory, and Cognition, 20,* 396-410.

Gordon, P. C., & Holyoak, K. J. (1983). Implicit learning and generalization of the "mere exposure" effect. *Journal of Personality and Social Psychology, 45,* 492-500.

Goshen-Gottstein, Y., & Moscovitch, M. (1995a). Intact implicit memory for newly-formed verbal associations. *Society for Neuroscience Abstracts, 21,* 566.

Goshen-Gottstein, Y., & Moscovitch, M. (1995b). Repetition priming effects for newly formed associations are perceptually based: Evidence from shallow encoding and format specificity. *Journal of Experimental Psychology: Learning, Memory, and Cognition, 21,* 1249-1262.

Goshen-Gottstein, Y., & Moscovitch, M. (1995c). Repetition priming for newly formed and preexisting associations: Perceptual and conceptual influences. *Journal of Experimental Psychology: Learning, Memory, and Cognition, 21,* 1229-1248.

Heindel, W. C., Salmon, D. P., Shults, C. W., Walicke, P. A., & Butters, N. (1989). Neuropsychological evidence for multiple implicit memory systems: A comparison of Alzheimer's, Huntington's and Parkinson's disease patients. *The Journal of Neuroscience, 9,* 582-587.

Holyoak, K. J., & Spellman, B. A. (1993). Thinking. *Annual Review of Psychology, 44,* 265-315.

Howard, J. H., Mutter, S. A., & Howard, D. V. (1992). Serial pattern learning by event observation. *Journal of Experimental Psychology: Learning, Memory, and Cognition, 18,* 1029-1039.

Jackson, G. M., Jackson, S. R., Harrison, J., Henderson, L., & Kennard, C. (1995). Serial reaction time learning and Parkinson's disease: Evidence for a procedural learning deficit. *Neuropsychologia, 33,* 577-593.

Keane, M. M., Gabrieli, J. D. E., Fennema, A. C., Growdon, J. H., & Corkin, S. (1991). Evidence for a dissociation between perceptual and conceptual priming in Alzheimer's disease. *Behavioral Neuroscience, 105,* 326-342.

Keane, M. M., Gabrieli, J. D. E., Growdon, J. H., & Corkin, S. (1994). Priming in perceptual identification of pseudowords is normal in Alzheimer's disease. *Neuropsychologia, 32,* 343-356.

Keane, M. M., Gabrieli, J. D. E., Noland, J. S., & McNealy, S. I. (1995). Normal perceptual priming of orthographically illegal nonwords in amnesia. *Journal of the International Neuropsychological Society, 1,* 425-433.

Knopman, D. S., & Nissen, M. J. (1987). Implicit learning in patients with probable Alzheimer's disease. *Neurology, 37,* 784-788.

Knopman, D., & Nissen, M. J. (1991). Procedural learning is impaired in Huntington's disease: Evidence from the serial reaction time task. *Neuropsychologia, 29,* 245-254.

Knowlton, B. K., & Squire, L. R. (1994). The information acquired during artificial grammar learning. *Journal of Experimental Psychology: Learning, Memory, and Cognition, 20,* 79-91.

Knowlton, B. K., & Squire, L. R. (1996). Artificial grammar learning depends on implicit acquisition of both abstract and exemplar-specific information. *Journal of Experimental Psychology: Learning, Memory, and Cognition, 22,* 169-181.

Knowlton, B. K., Squire, L. R., & Butters, N. (1994). Intact artificial grammar learning in patients with Huntington's disease. *Society for Neuroscience Abstracts, 20,* 1075.

Kunst-Wilson, W. R., & Zajonc, R. B. (1980). Affective discrimination of stimuli that cannot be recognized. *Science, 207,* 557-558.

Mandler, G., Nakamura, Y., & Van Zandt, B. J. S. (1987). Nonspecific effects of exposure on stimuli that cannot be recognized. *Journal of Experimental Psychology: Learning, Memory, and Cognition, 13,* 646-648.

Manza, L., & Bornstein, R. F. (1995). Affective discrimination and the implicit learning process. *Consciousness and Cognition, 4,* 399-409.

Manza, L., & Reber, A. S. (1992, November). *Implicit learning: Transfer across form and sensory modality.* Paper presented at the meeting of the Psychonomic Society, St. Louis, MO.

Mathews, R. C., Buss, R. R., Stanley, W. B., Blanchard-Fields, F., Cho, J. R., & Druhan, B. (1989). Role of implicit and explicit processes in learning from examples: A synergistic effect. *Journal of Experimental Psychology: Learning, Memory, and Cognition, 15,* 1083-1100.

Mayr, U. (1996). Spatial attention and implicit sequence learning: Evidence for independent learning of spatial and nonspatial sequences. *Journal of Experimental Psychology: Learning, Memory, and Cognition, 22,* 350-364.

Murphy, S. T., & Zajonc, R. B. (1993). Affect, cognition, and awareness: Affective priming with optimal and suboptimal stimulus exposures. *Journal of Personality and Social Psychology, 64,* 723-739.

Poldrack, R. A., & Logan, G. D. (1997). Fluency and response speed in recognition judgments. *Memory & Cognition, 25,* 1-10.

Posner, M. I., Abdullaev, Y. G., McCandliss, B. D., & Sereno, S. C. (in press). Anatomy, circuitry, and plasticity of word reading. In J. Everatt (Ed.), *Visual and attentional processes in reading and dyslexia.*

Reber, A. S. (1969). Transfer of syntactic structure in synthetic languages. *Journal of Experimental Psychology, 81,* 115-119.

Reber, P. J., & Squire, L. R. (1994). Parallel brain systems for learning with and without awareness. *Learning and Memory, 1,* 217-229.

Reed, J., & Johnson, P. (1994). Assessing implicit learning with indirect tests: Determining what is learned about sequence structure. *Journal of Experimental Psychology: Learning, Memory, and Cognition, 20,* 585-594.

Roediger, H. L., & McDermott, K. B. (1993). Implicit memory in normal human subjects. In H. Spinnler & F. Boller (Eds.), *Handbook of neuropsychology* (Vol. 8). Amsterdam: Elsevier.

Schacter, D. L., Cooper, L. A., & Delaney, S. M. (1990). Implicit memory for unfamiliar objects depends on access to structural descriptions. *Journal of Experimental Psychology: General, 119,* 5-24.

Schacter, D. L., Cooper, L. A., Tharan, M., & Rubens, A. B. (1991). Preserved priming of novel objects in patients with memory disorders. *Journal of Cognitive Neuroscience, 3,* 118-131.

Schacter, D. L., Reiman, E., Uecker, A., Polster, M. R., Yun, L. S., & Cooper, L. A. (1995). Brain regions associated with retrieval of structurally coherent visual information. *Nature, 376,* 587-590.

Seamon, J. G., Williams, P. C., Crowley, M. J., Kim, I. J., Langer, S. A., Orne, P. J., & Wishengrad, D. L. (1995). The mere exposure effect is based on implicit memory: Effects of stimulus type, encoding conditions and number of exposures on recognition and affect judgments. *Journal of Experimental Psychology: Learning, Memory, and Cognition, 21,* 711-721.

Seger, C. A. (1994a). Criteria for implicit learning: De-emphasize conscious access, emphasize amnesia. *Behavioral and Brain Sciences, 17,* 421-422.

Seger, C. A. (1994b). Implicit learning. *Psychological Bulletin, 115,* 163-196.

Seger, C. A. (1996a). *Implicit learning through observation on the serial reaction time task.* Manuscript submitted for publication.

Seger, C. A. (1996b). *Independent judgment-linked and motor-linked mechanisms in artificial grammar learning.* Manuscript submitted for publication.

Seger, C. A. (1997). Two forms of sequential implicit learning. *Consciousness and Cognition, 6,* 108-131.

Shanks, D. R., & St. John, M. F. (1994). Characteristics of dissociable human learning systems. *Behavioral and Brain Sciences, 17,* 367-447.

Smith, M. E., & Oscar-Berman, M. (1990). Repetition priming of words and pseudowords in divided attention and in amnesia. *Journal of Experimental Psychology: Learning, Memory, and Cognition, 16,* 1033-1042.

Squire, L. R. (1992). Memory and the hippocampus: A synthesis from findings with rats, monkeys, and humans. *Psychological Review, 99,* 195-231.

Stadler, M. A. (1993). Implicit serial learning: Questions inspired by Hebb (1961). *Memory & Cognition, 21,* 819-827.

Tenpenny, P. L. (1995). Abstractionist versus episodic theories of repetition priming and word identification. *Psychonomic Bulletin & Review, 2,* 339-363.

Tulving, E. (1985). How many memory systems are there? *American Psychologist, 40,* 385-398.

Twain, M. (1944). *Life on the Mississippi.* New York: Heritage Press. (Originally published in 1896)

Van der Bergh, O., Vrana, S., & Eelen, P. (1990). Letters from the heart: Affective categorization of letter combinations in typists and nontypists. *Journal of Experimental Psychology: Learning, Memory, and Cognition, 16,* 1153-1161.

Wagner, A. D., Gabrieli, J. D. E., & Verfaellie, M. (1997). Dissociations between familiarity processes in explicit-recognition and implicit-perceptual memory.

Journal of Experimental Psychology: Learning, Memory, and Cognition, 23, 305-323.

Whittlesea, B. W. A., & Dorkin, M. D. (1993). Incidentally, things in general are particularly determined: An episodic-processing account of implicit learning. *Journal of Experimental Psychology: General, 122,* 227-248.

Willingham, D. B. (1992). Systems of motor skill. In N. Butters & L. R. Squire (Eds.), *Neuropsychology of memory* (2nd ed.). New York: Guilford.

Willingham, D. B., & Koroshetz, W. J. (1993). Evidence for dissociable motor skills in Huntington's disease patients. *Psychobiology, 21,* 173-182.

Willingham, D. B., Koroshetz, W. J., & Peterson, E. W. (1996). Motor skills have diverse neural bases: Spared and impaired skill acquisition in Huntington's disease. *Neuropsychology, 10,* 315-321.

Willingham, D. B., & Preuss, L. (1995, October). The death of implicit memory. *Psyche* [On line Serial], *1*(14). Available at http://psyche.cs.monash.edu.au/ volume2-1/ psyche-95-2-15-implicit-1-willingham.

Zajonc, R. B. (1980). Feeling and thinking: Preferences need no inferences. *American Psychologist, 35,* 151-175.

PART III
THEORETICAL AND EMPIRICAL ISSUES

10

Implicit Sequence Learning

The Truth Is in the Details

●————————————————————————————

Axel Cleeremans
Luis Jiménez

A lthough sequence learning has not yet received as much
attention as other tasks (such as artificial grammar learning,
for instance) as a paradigm through which to study implicit learning, it is
nevertheless increasingly in focus today (e.g., Frensch, Buchner, & Lin,
1994; Frensch & Miner, 1994; Jackson & Jackson, 1995; Jiménez, Men-
dez, & Cleeremans, 1996; Mayr, 1996; Reed & Johnson, 1994; Stadler,
1995) and is producing an increasing number of empirical results that are
relevant to many of the central issues with which the field is concerned.
Indeed, the sequence learning paradigm has been used to attempt to answer
questions such as whether implicit learning produces unconscious knowledge (e.g., Jiménez et al., 1996; Perruchet & Amorim, 1992; Reed &
Johnson, 1994; Shanks & Johnstone, Chapter 16, this volume), whether
this knowledge should be characterized as rule based or instance based
(e.g., Ferrer-Gil, 1994; Lewicki, Hill, & Bizot, 1988; Perruchet, Gallego,
& Savy, 1990), and whether its acquisition depends on participants' orientation to learn (e.g., Curran & Keele, 1993; Frensch et al., 1994; Jiménez
et al., 1996) or on the amount of attentional resources allocated to the
processing of relevant stimuli (e.g., Frensch et al., 1994; Stadler, 1995).
Some authors have recently pointed out that sequence learning appears to
be particularly well-suited to explore implicit learning, because it provides

us with truly incidental learning conditions (Cleeremans, 1993b) and because it makes it possible to compare learning effects obtained through similar direct and indirect measures (e.g., Jiménez et al., 1996; see also Shanks & Johnstone, Chapter 16, this volume).

An issue that remains largely unresolved today, however, is to determine exactly what participants exposed to a sequence learning situation learn about the material. At least two contrasting positions about this issue have been expressed over the years: Some authors have argued that participants induce rules that define the legal transitions between successive stimuli (e.g., Lewicki et al., 1988), whereas others have claimed that sequence knowledge consists essentially of memorized chunks or runs of sequence elements (e.g., Perruchet et al., 1990). It also remains unclear whether sequence learning involves essentially motor or perceptual representations.

In this chapter, we address this issue of sequence representation and defend a third position. We start by briefly summarizing the main results obtained with the different variants of the sequence learning paradigm. Next, we focus on the processes involved in sequence representation and acquisition. We suggest that sensitivity to the sequential structure of the stimulus material (i.e., sequence learning) is a result of the acquisition of a representation of its *statistical* constraints and that this sensitivity emerges through the operation of mechanisms that are well-instantiated by connectionist models such as the Simple Recurrent Network (SRN; see Cleeremans, 1993b), which has already been widely used to model implicit learning in general (Altman, Dienes, & Goode, 1995; Cleeremans & McClelland, 1991; Cleeremans, 1993a, 1993b; Jiménez et al., 1996). In this chapter, we present new simulation work meant to explore to what extent the SRN model can account for specific empirical data better than alternative theories based, for instance, on sensitivity to frequency information, on memory for instances, or on rule induction.

In addition, we also present experimental results meant to explore in a systematic way the impact of various factors on sequence learning performance, such as attention, the availability of explicit knowledge, and the sequential structure of the stimulus material. Like the simulation work, these experiments suggest that implicit sequence learning develops based on an automatic process of acquisition of statistical knowledge about the relative likelihood of appearance of different successors in the context defined by an eventually optimal number of previous trials. This perspective does not rule out the possibility that sequence learning simultaneously involves additional sources of explicit knowledge, such as serial knowledge or some kind of ruled-based knowledge (cf. Perruchet et al., 1990), but instead only states that what is implicit in implicit sequence learning is best characterized as statistical learning—a position shared by other authors, such as Stadler (1992).

AN OVERVIEW OF SEQUENCE LEARNING

The sequence-learning paradigm can broadly be defined as consisting of several types of situations that share the common features of presenting participants with a speeded task during which (a) they have to respond to the location of a target stimulus that may appear at one of several possible locations on a computer screen on each trial, and (b) in which the series of locations follows a regularity that is not revealed to participants. Although in most studies, the series of locations is structured to follow a fixed and repeating sequence (e.g., Nissen & Bullemer, 1987), some authors have used sequential material generated on the basis of a complex set of rules from which one can produce several different alternative deterministic sequences (e.g., Lewicki et al., 1988; Stadler, 1989), or based on the output of probabilistic and noisy finite-state grammars (Cleeremans & McClelland, 1991; Jiménez et al., 1996).

Hence, one may distinguish three main subparadigms: the Simple Repeating Sequence paradigm, the Deterministic Rule-Based paradigm, and the Probabilistic Rule-Based paradigm.

In general, the results obtained in each of these three paradigms have uniformly shown that participants' performance with the serial reaction time (SRT) task expresses sensitivity to the sequential constraints regardless of the nature of the generation rules and that this sensitivity is not necessarily accompanied by conscious awareness of the relevant sequential constraints when assessed by a comparable direct measure. This last issue, however, remains one of the most contentious ones in the relevant literature (see Jiménez et al., 1996; Perruchet & Amorim, 1992; Shanks & Johnstone, Chapter 16, this volume). It should come as no surprise, therefore, that most research conducted in this area has been concerned with the problem of collecting evidence to either confirm or refute the claim that some part of the learning obtained under these circumstances can be cast as unconscious learning, that is, whether awareness is necessary for learning, and whether knowledge acquired in sequence learning is available to awareness.

Considerable research has also been dedicated, however, to exploring additional factors thought to be significant with respect to the nature of implicit learning processes in general. Among these factors, the most important ones are probably as follows:

1. The role of orientation (i.e., incidental vs. intentional learning conditions)
2. The role of attention (i.e., typically, whether sequence learning is to be performed concurrently with a demanding secondary task or not)
3. The nature of sequence representation (e.g., whether it is abstract, based on instances, or statistical; whether it is based on motor or perceptual sequences)
4. The nature of the underlying learning mechanisms (e.g., chunking, memory for instances, connectionist-based learning mechanisms)

In the rest of this section, we briefly review research relevant to the first three issues (awareness, orientation to learn, and attention). In a later section, we focus on issues of representation and process.

● Sequence Learning and Awareness

Implicit learning has typically been defined as acquisition of knowledge that takes place independently of conscious attempts to learn and largely in the absence of explicit knowledge of what has been acquired (e.g., Reber, 1993). The two components of this definition (i.e., the role of orientation and the nature of the resulting knowledge) have both been addressed extensively within the sequence-learning paradigm. In the following paragraphs, we address each in turn.

The question of whether sequence learning can be considered as an instance of implicit learning has often taken the form of a more specific question: Is knowledge expressed in SRT tasks unconscious? As hinted above, the field at present appears to be openly divided about what the best answer may be to this question. The main debate is essentially methodological and focuses on the important issue of determining which measure best reflects conscious learning. Most authors seem to share the assumption that a comparison between corresponding direct and indirect measures of sequence learning might constitute the best way to address this question (see Jiménez et al., 1996; Reed & Johnson, 1994). Likewise, there is widespread agreement that improvement in reaction times (RTs) resulting specifically from responses to sequentially structured trials constitutes the best indirect measure of sequence learning. Authors differ substantially, however, on the issue of choosing the best direct measure through which to assess explicit knowledge about the material.

The most widespread direct measure is probably one of the several different versions of the generation task first proposed by Nissen and Bullemer (1987). In the standard generation task, participants are exposed to the same stimulus material as during the SRT task but are asked to try to predict the location at which the next stimulus will appear instead of merely reacting to the current one (e.g., Cleeremans & McClelland, 1991; Cohen, Ivry, & Keele, 1990; Jiménez et al., 1996; Perruchet & Amorim, 1992; Willingham, Nissen, & Bullemer, 1989). Other authors have favored measures involving recognition of fragments of the sequence, based on the argument that such tests could be more sensitive to the relevant knowledge than any of the generation-task variants, because the latter can globally be cast as cued-recall measures and because cued-recall measures have typically been found to be less sensitive to memory information than recognition tasks are (e.g., Perruchet & Amorim, 1992; Stadler, 1995; Willingham, Greeley, & Bardone, 1993).

This methodological controversy is made particularly problematic because there is no obvious reason to assume that RT speedup, recognition, or generation measures are process-pure measures in the sense that they exclusively involve either conscious or nonconscious knowledge. For instance, both recognition and generation may be sensitive to some nonconscious information, and response times collected during the SRT task may just as well be similarly influenced by conscious knowledge (e.g., Curran & Keele, 1993). If no measure can be safely taken as reflecting exclusively either implicit or explicit knowledge, then selecting the appropriate direct measure based on its presumed global sensitivity may result in failing to distinguish conscious from unconscious sensitivity.

Elsewhere (Jiménez et al., 1996, see also Reingold & Merikle, 1988), we have argued that the only way to circumvent this problem involves the following steps. First, one should identify a dimension that can be considered a priori as theoretically relevant to separating conscious from unconscious sensitivity. Second, one should compare two similar measures that differ only in that specific dimension. Any difference in performance as assessed by two such measures can then be unequivocally attributed to their different sensitivity to variation in the underlying dimension. There are reasons to believe that the direct versus indirect dimension may be such a theoretically relevant dimension, and the studies that have begun to use this logic have produced compelling dissociations between otherwise similar direct and indirect measures of sequence learning. Such results, there-fore, appear to entail the conclusion that some knowledge about the stimu-lus material is acquired and used unconsciously (e.g., Jiménez et al., 1996).

A related strategy to assess the role of awareness during sequence learning tasks has consisted of manipulating participants' orientation to learn. Several studies using simple repeating sequences as the stimulus material have shown large advantages for participants who were informed that the material contained regularities. Frensch and Miner (1994), for instance, showed that participants who knew that the material was sequen-tially structured, and who were asked to look for rules in a four-location SRT task in which the sequence of locations followed a fixed sequence of 12 elements, performed substantially better than uninformed participants. However, the advantages provided by intentional orientation disappear entirely when the material involves more complex, probabilistic sequences. For instance, no differences were observed between intentional and inci-dental learners, even after as many as 62,000 trials of training with a six-location SRT task (Jiménez et al., 1996). This contrast between tasks involving deterministic or probabilistic sequences suggests that the benefits of an intentional orientation to learn may interact with the complexity and structure of the stimulus material and may only be actually beneficial when the material is simple enough to be memorized.

From this perspective, sequence learning could therefore involve two different kinds of learning: One process involves memorizing a series of successive events, and another involves a developing sensitivity to the statistical structure of the material. The plausibility of this hypothesis is strengthened by results such as those obtained by Curran and Keele (1993). Curran and Keele used simple sequences of six elements in a four-location SRT task and contrasted the performance of intentional and incidental participants. Intentional participants were asked to memorize the actual sequence they would be exposed to before the onset of the SRT task, whereas incidental participants were kept uninformed about the existence of sequential structure in the task material. Not surprisingly, intentional participants performed much better than incidental participants—a result that clearly indicates that conscious knowledge of the stimulus sequence can have a strong effect on RT performance. The performance advantage observed with intentional participants disappeared entirely, however, when both groups were subsequently asked to perform the same RT task, but in the presence of a demanding secondary tone-counting task that had to be performed concurrently. Conscious knowledge, therefore, only appears to be beneficial when attentional resources are available. These results were interpreted by the authors as evidence that two separate forms of learning could indeed be influencing RT responses. The first process would depend on the availability of attentional resources, as well as conscious awareness of the stimulus sequence and intention to learn, whereas the second, non-attentional process would not be influenced by such factors. The role of attention in such experiments, however, is often hard to assess and has sometimes been confounded with the availability of explicit information. We examine this issue more closely in the next section.

Sequence Learning and Attention

A third question about sequence learning concerns its sensitivity to the availability of attentional resources. If sequence learning is a good example of implicit learning as typically defined, then one would expect it to be relatively insensitive to the availability of attentional resources, because implicit learning presumably involves automatic processes.

Most studies designed to address the issue of the role of attentional resources in sequence learning have relied on some variant of the dual-task procedure briefly described in the previous section, during which a secondary task has to be performed concurrently with the main sequence learning task in order to divert attention from the latter. Typically, the secondary task consists of asking participants to monitor auditory stimuli presented during the interval between two visual RT trials. For instance, one can ask participants to keep a running count of the number of high-pitched tones presented so far and to report the total number at the end of a block.

The first study to use this methodology in the context of sequence learning was reported by Nissen and Bullemer (1987). They observed that the presence of a secondary tone-counting task interfered with sequence learning and concluded that attention was therefore necessary for sequence learning to occur (in contrast to awareness). Subsequent research has led to a significant reappraisal of this conclusion, however.

For instance, Cohen et al. (1990) observed that sequence learning could remain unaffected by distraction when the sequence was simple enough, that is, when it contained at least one simple association between two consecutive items. By the same token, Reed and Johnson (1994; see also Shank & Johnstone, Chapter 16, this volume) confirmed that sequence learning could be produced under dual-task conditions even when more complex sequences containing exclusively ambiguous dependencies (i.e., dependencies such that two previous sequence elements are always necessary to predict the location of the next one) were presented. Finally, other authors (e.g., Frensch et al., 1994) showed that although learning can indeed be expressed under both single-task and dual-task conditions and for both simple and ambiguous sequences, the learning effect was nevertheless significantly reduced under distraction. At first sight, this ensemble of results could be taken to indicate that implicit sequence learning is modulated by how participants allocate attentional resources, but several other results and theoretical developments have led different authors to reject this idea.

First, if one agrees with the notion that any measure of performance can potentially reflect a blend of implicit and explicit knowledge (e.g., Jiménez et al., 1996; Reingold & Merikle, 1988), then a plausible account for the interference effect observed under dual-task conditions can simply be that distraction selectively influences explicit learning, thereby reducing its influence on the overall measure of performance.

Second, it may also be the case that distraction influences implicit sequence learning. Even if this is the case, however, it may still be that the interference stems from mechanisms that do not involve a reduction in the hypothetical pool of attentional resources necessary for implicit sequence learning. For instance, Stadler (1995) has provided a convincing demonstration that the effects of the tone-counting secondary task were more similar to the effects of disrupting the temporal organization of the sequence by allowing variability in response stimulus interval (RSI) than to the effects of increasing the memory load by asking participants to memorize unrelated material for the duration of the task. Stadler also observed that limiting attentional resources by means of a different attentional manipulation that does not require participants to monitor continuously incoming stimuli produced fewer interference effects, and that this interference was more specific to the direct measures. Based on these results, he concluded that implicit sequence learning can be cast as an obligatory and automatic process that associates the representation of all the events simultaneously activated in short-term memory and that may contribute to improving performance together with any other ongoing source of explicit learning.

Finally, some other authors have simply rejected the notion that sequence learning is sensitive to the availability of attentional resources and have instead argued that the effects of a secondary task simply consists of interfering with the expression of the acquired knowledge (e.g., Frensch, Lin, & Buchner, in press).

To summarize, then, the results we have reviewed so far can be taken to indicate that some (implicit) sequence-learning processes may be resilient to distraction, whereas some other processes of (explicit) sequence learning may be truly dependent on the amount of resources allocated to the relevant task. We have also argued that there may be some (implicit) sequence-learning processes that may operate independently of participants' intention to learn and produce some unconscious knowledge, whereas some other (explicit) learning processes would depend on participants' intention to learn and would produce essentially conscious knowledge. Implicit and explicit sequence-learning processes are assumed to operate simultaneously, both contributing to improved performance.

Although these claims may be plausible in the face of current empirical data, they leave open two important additional issues. First, what kind of mechanism may result in implicit sequence learning? Second, how is the resulting implicit sequence knowledge represented? Addressing these issues will be our main focus for the rest of this chapter, in which we provide a discussion of different approaches to these issues and report on both simulation and empirical work aimed to clarify them.

REPRESENTATIONAL ISSUES IN IMPLICIT SEQUENCE LEARNING

What is learned in implicit sequence learning? Does the fact that people exhibit sensitivity to sequential constraints somehow mean that they have developed a representation of the sequence, either in the form of serial knowledge about the sequence itself or about fragments of this sequence, or in the form of the general rules based on which the material was generated? Before we attempt to answer these questions, it should be pointed out that sequence learning, as we indicated in the previous section, is not a unitary paradigm. Several cases probably need to be distinguished according to the structure of the stimulus material.

For instance, whenever straightforward rules can be spelled out to describe the structure of the sequence, as they can for the sequences designed by Lewicki et al. (1988; see also Ferrer-Gil, 1994; Perruchet et al., 1990), then it is also plausible that participants induce these rules and use them as a way to improve their efficiency in coping with the task. Rule-based knowledge could also possibly be acquired whenever the sequences are deterministic, because rules can provide summary, abstract descriptions of several types of transitions between successive stimulus locations (i.e., stimulus movements). For instance, general descriptions such as "the same location is never repeated," "big jumps often occur" or "the target moves from left to right" could presumably be induced by any system equipped with high-level, symbolic regularity-detection mechanisms whenever such a system is exposed to the typical short repeating deterministic sequences used in the standard paradigm. If this is indeed the case, one would expect human participants to be able to report on such rules, and they often are (e.g., Cleeremans, 1993b).

Similarly, when the material is simple enough and the task is performed without distraction, it is also likely that participants will be capable of memorizing the entire repeating sequence, or shorter fragments (e.g., particularly salient subsequences) thereof. Such explicit exemplar-like knowledge is less likely to be acquired by participants when they are presented with probabilistic sequences, such as those used by Cleeremans and McClelland (1991) or by Jiménez et al. (1996), because in this case every possible transition can occur with some finite probability. Rule-based knowledge is similarly difficult to induce when the material is probabilistic in that potential local rules tend to be systematically invalidated by new instances where they fail to apply, thereby hindering participants' attempts to induce them. Learning of such noisy sequences is therefore most likely accounted for by the acquisition of statistical knowledge about the probabilities with which different successors appear in the context defined by a given number of previous trials.

Although it is thus plausible that sequence learning involves different kinds of representations and learning processes depending on the nature of the stimulus material, we would nevertheless like to defend the notion that the acquisition of statistical knowledge represents the core process with which to characterize sequence-learning mechanisms in general. To do so, we first describe the kind of empirical situation used by Cleeremans and McClelland (1991), in which it is unlikely that participants acquired any other knowledge than statistical knowledge because the stimulus material was generated probabilistically. Next, we briefly describe how the SRN model, which instantiates a process of statistical learning, is capable of learning in such a situation. Finally, we focus on the question of determining whether such learning processes are also at play when participants are exposed to much simpler rule-based, deterministic stimulus material, as typically used in sequence learning research.

● **Learning Statistical Knowledge With Probabilistic Sequences**

In hopes of reducing participants' ability to develop conscious knowledge about the stimulus material they are exposed to in sequence-learning situations, Cleeremans and McClelland (1991) proposed to use inherently noisy, probabilistic material instead of simple repeating sequences. This kind of material can be generated based on a finite-state grammar, such as the one shown in Figure 10.1. Finite-state grammars consist of nodes connected by labeled arcs, and sequences of stimuli can be generated simply by following a random path through the graph. Stimulus generation with such a system involves (a) randomly selecting an arc emanating from the current node, (b) recording the corresponding label as a screen location for the stimulus to appear at, and (c) setting the current node to be the node that the arc selected in Step (a) points to. With the further assumption that the grammar is re-entrant, that is, that the first and last nodes are identical, a probabilistic sequence that is not limited in length and that never repeats exactly over great lengths can easily be generated. To assess learning with this kind of material, one can substitute random screen locations to the screen locations that had been selected based on the generation procedure described above in a given proportion of the trials (typically, 15% to 20%). Learning is then measured by comparing performance on the grammatical trials with performance on the nongrammatical trials interspersed throughout training—a procedure that makes control data available continuously throughout training.

The main advantage of this procedure, however, is that it also makes it impossible for participants to memorize more than a few frequent salient patterns or to induce reliable rules. Hence, they cannot develop full knowledge of which specific elements can follow other elements. Despite the complexity of the material, participants still tend to become sensitive to the statistical regularities contained in the sequence. For instance, grammatical elements (such as D in the context of C; see Figure 10.1) tend to be responded to faster than the nongrammatical elements resulting from the substitution procedure (e.g., D in the context of A). Jiménez et al. (1996) showed that, after extensive training, participants further learned to discriminate between grammatical and nongrammatical successors of contexts of Length 2, thus responding faster to a (grammatical) D in the context of AC than to a (nongrammatical) D in the context of EC, even though all the transitions in this latter subsequence (i.e., E-C, C-D) were grammatical,

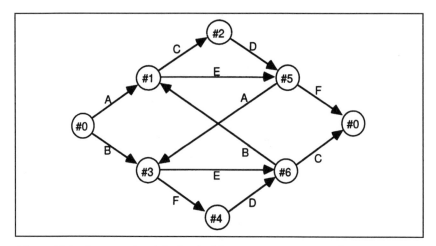

Figure 10.1. An example of the kind of finite-state grammar used to generate stimulus material in the Probabilistic Rule-Based sequence-learning paradigm.

NOTE: From Jiménez, Méndez, & Cleeremans, 1996. Note that the first and last nodes are one and the same.

based on contexts of Length 1. Analyses of the correlation between distributions of RTs and the corresponding distributions of conditional probabilities of appearance of different sequence elements in different selected contexts also showed that participants acquired detailed, graded, and statistical knowledge about the stimulus material.

How could the learning processes underlying the acquisition of such statistical knowledge be instantiated in the form of a set of computational mechanisms? We believe that this process is well captured by the SRN model. This model, first proposed by Elman (1990) and subsequently adapted by Cleeremans and McClelland (1991) to simulate sequence learning effects in SRT tasks, is shown in Figure 10.2. The network is trained using the back-propagation algorithm to predict the next element of a sequence based on the current element and on a representation of the temporal context that the network has elaborated itself. To model human performance, the network is presented on each trial with element t of the sequence, and is required to predict element $t + 1$. Its response is then compared to the actual successor of element t as prescribed by the sequence, and the error information is backpropagated to modify the connection weights. To enable the network to use the temporal context, its architecture includes recurrent connections from the hidden units.

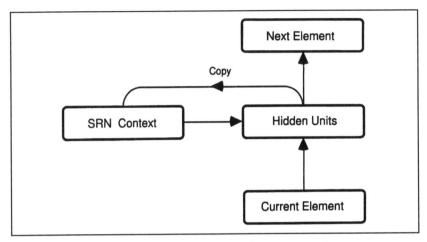

Figure 10.2. The Simple Recurrent Network (Elman, 1990; Cleeremans, 1993b).

The main assumption about how this process relates to human performance in choice reaction time tasks is that the prediction task that the network is asked to perform represents preparation in human participants. Thus, one expects the strong prediction responses that the network produces when the next element of the sequence is indeed predictable based on the temporal context to be associated with fast RTs to the same element in the corresponding human data. Likewise, random elements, which by definition are not predictable, tend to elicit weak prediction responses from the network and slow RTs from human participants. These correspondences between human and simulated data have been largely supported in previous research (see Cleeremans, 1993b).

How does the network come to be able to improve its prediction responses with training? A complete analysis of the learning process is out of the scope of this chapter, but we present a brief description in the following paragraph (see Cleeremans, 1993b; Servan-Schreiber, Cleeremans, & McClelland, 1991; for a full analysis).

When training starts, the network can only be sensitive to the information provided by the current element of the sequence, because its internal representations (which also act as context for the next trial) are completely unstructured and merely reflect the initially random connectivity between the network's units. The network will quickly become sensitive to the overall frequency of the various sequence elements, however, and will tend to activate more strongly the output units that represent these frequent elements. For instance, if trained on a four-element repeating sequence such as ABAC ABAC . . . , the network will first become sensitive to the fact that A is overall more frequent than either B or C, and its prediction responses will reflect this sensitivity in that the output unit associated with A will tend to be more activated than the others, regardless of which elements have previously occurred. At this point, the network's internal representations will contain information about the association between each sequence element and the entire set of its successors. This is what enables the network to become gradually more sensitive to the sequential constraints present in the stimulus material. Indeed, when copied over the context units on the next time step, this information can now be used by the network to base its predictions not only on the current element, but also on the context in which this element occurs. Soon, therefore, the network will come to predict that either B or C are equally likely to occur, but only in the context of an A, and that A itself is the only possible successor to either B or C. At this point, the network is thus sensitive to first-order sequential constraints.

Later in training, the network will further refine its prediction responses and will start to differentiate the two occurrences of A by incorporating information about the predecessor of each A token in their representation. For instance, A in the context of B will now elicit a different internal representation than A in the context of C. This differentiation will in turn enable the network to correctly predict that B is the only possible successor to the first A token, which is always preceded by C, and that C is the only possible successor to the second A token, which always occurs in the context of B. At this point, the network is thus sensitive to second-order sequential constraints, because its predictions are now based on the contingencies between subsequences of two elements and their possible successors. Throughout training, the network's responses thus reflect almost exactly the conditional probabilities of occurrence of each stimulus, given an increasingly large temporal context set by previous sequences of elements. This smooth integration of information about increasingly large temporal contexts matches participants' performance extremely well, regardless of whether the sequence contains only statistical information, as with probabilistic sequences, or whether it follows either a fixed sequence or a complex set of rules (for an extensive analysis and a number of relevant simulations, see Cleeremans, 1993b).

336

● Learning Statistical Knowledge With
Rule-Based and Deterministic Sequences

As described above, the SRN model appears to be able to account for a wide variety of data obtained with the Probabilistic Rule-Based paradigm (see Cleeremans, 1993b; Jiménez et al., 1996), as well as with both the Simple Repeating Sequence (e.g., Cohen et al., 1990; Curran & Keele, 1993) and Deterministic Rule-Based paradigms (Lewicki et al., 1988; Perruchet et al., 1990). In all three cases, the SRN model assumes that participants acquire specifically statistical knowledge about the distributional features of the ensemble of sequential regularities to which they are exposed. When people are presented with either short repeating sequences or with material that follows simple deterministic rules, however, they are also likely to develop a radically different kind of knowledge about the stimulus material: In some cases, they may end up memorizing the sequence altogether; in others, they may learn and use simple rules that enable them to better anticipate where the next stimulus will appear. The question we would like to focus on in this section is whether there are any grounds to assume that at least some of the knowledge that people acquire in such deterministic situations should also be thought of as essentially statistical in nature. To do so, we conducted a reanalysis of an interesting conceptual replication (Ferrer-Gil, 1994) of the classic experiment of Lewicki et al. (1988) and derived specific predictions based on four contrasting theoretical accounts of sequence learning: Rule-based accounts, accounts based on memory for instances, accounts based on sensitivity to frequency information, and accounts based on statistical learning.

STATISTICAL VERSUS RULE-BASED ACCOUNTS
OF RULED-SEQUENCE LEARNING

As described at the beginning of the section "An Overview of Sequence Learning," the sequence learning situation developed by Lewicki et al. (1988) is characterized by the fact that the sequence of successive stimuli was generated based on an arbitrary set of deterministic transition rules, rather than on the repetition of a specific sequence or on the output of a probabilistic finite-state grammar. Because the rules are deterministic, however, only a fixed set of sequences can be generated from them. Another way to think about Lewicki et al.'s material, therefore, is to consider that it consists of this fixed ensemble of sequences, each of which is presented several times during any training session. A third plausible account of learning in this situation was proposed by Perruchet et al. (1990), and involves sensitivity to the frequency of target movements. Finally, a fourth way with which to describe Lewicki's stimulus material is to focus on the statistical properties (specifically, the conditional probability of appearance of each element in different contexts) of the ensemble of sequences presented during training. Unlike other situations, Lewicki et al.'s (1988) task is therefore perfectly suited to serve as a test for the four theoretical accounts mentioned above, in that each theory at least affords some plausibility as a candidate framework with which to think about the data. In the following, we first describe Lewicki's paradigm in detail. Next, we formulate contrasting predictions based on each of the four accounts.

In the original experiment by Lewicki et al. (1988), participants were exposed to 4,080 trials of an SRT task during which they had to press on the key corresponding to the current location of a target character (an X) which could, on any trial, appear at one of four possible locations on a computer screen. The screen was divided by vertical and horizontal axes into four quadrants corresponding to each of the four possible target locations. The entire experiment was divided into 17 segments, each consisting of 240 trials. Unknown to subjects, each segment was structured in 48 logical blocks of five exposures each. In each such block, the first two trials (A and B) had been generated randomly (excluding repetitions) and were thus completely unpredictable. The last three trials of each block (C, D, and E), in contrast, were fully predictable based on the "move pattern" that the stimulus had followed during the previous two trials. Thus, the location at which the stimulus appears in Trial C depended on how the stimulus moved between Trials A and B. Trials D and E were similarly dependent on the transition between Trials B and C, and C and D, respectively. For instance, for Trial C, the rules were as follows: If the previous movement (i.e., between Trials A and B) had been horizontal, then the next movement (i.e., between Trials B and C) had to be vertical; if the previous movement had been vertical, then the next movement was diagonal; and if the previous movement had been diagonal, then the next one had to be horizontal (see Figure 10.3, left panel). Different but similar rules applied for Trials D and E. By following these rules, 12 different series of five exposures can be generated, and each one was presented four times during each training segment. After 15 of these training segments, participants were exposed to two additional transfer segments. In these last two segments, the generation rules were switched among Trials C, D, and E, so

338

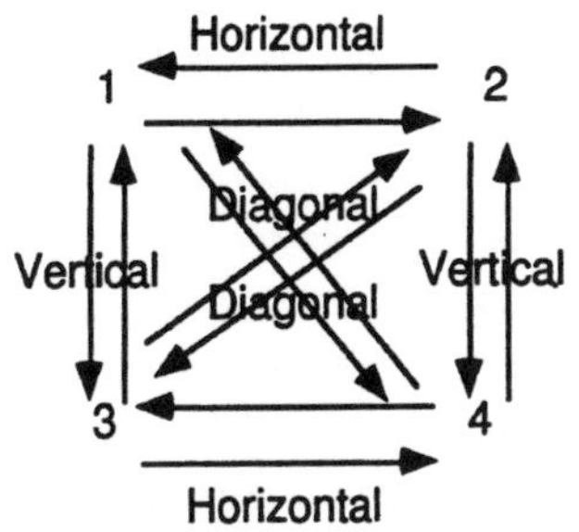

Lewicki et al's rules				Ferrer-Gil's rules			
A-B	B-C	C-D	D-E	A-B	B-C	C-D	D-E
Diagonal	Horizontal	Diagonal	Vertical	Diagonal	Vertical	Diagonal	Horizontal
Vertical	Diagonal	Vertical	Diagonal	Vertical	Horizontal	Vertical	Diagonal
Horizontal	Vertical	Diagonal	Vertical	Horizontal	Diagonal	Horizontal	Diagonal
Training Series				Training Series			
A	B	C	D	E	A	B	C	D	E

A	B	C	D	E	A	B	C	D	E
1	2	4	1	3	1	2	3	4	1
1	3	2	4	1	1	3	4	2	3
1	4	3	2	4	1	4	2	3	4
2	1	3	2	4	4	1	3	2	1
2	3	4	1	3	4	2	1	3	2
2	4	1	3	2	4	3	2	1	4
					Transfer Series				
3	1	4	2	3	2	1	4	3	2
3	2	1	4	2	2	3	1	4	3
3	4	2	3	1	2	4	3	1	4
4	1	2	3	1	3	1	2	4	1
4	2	3	1	4	3	2	4	1	2
4	3	1	2	4	3	4	1	2	3

Figure 10.3. Comparison between the rule system used by Lewicki et al. (1988) and by Ferrer-Gil (1994). Labels A-B, B-C, C-D and D-E stand for the transitions between adjacent trials in each series of five trials. Numbers from 1 to 4 designate the four possible locations.

that the rules that had previously determined the location of Trial C were now applied to Trial E, and so on. If participants had learned something about the rule system, then one would expect this knowledge to be useless during transfer.

The results showed that, with practice, mean efficiency[1] in response to unpredictable A/B trials fell below the efficiency expressed in response to predictable C/D/E trials. In other words, Lewicki et al. (1988) observed a progressively larger RT and accuracy advantage for the predictable trials. Crucially, the rule switch that took place during the last two segments resulted in the extinction of this difference, thereby suggesting that the effect observed over the first 15 segments was specifically related to the acquisition of knowledge about the regularities contained in the training material, but not in the transfer material.

To account for these effects, Lewicki et al. (1988) claimed that participants must either have incidentally learned the actual set of transition rules used to generate the material or, alternatively, that they must have memorized each of the 12 possible legal series. In post-task interviews, however, participants appeared to be fully unaware that the material contained regularities. For this reason, Lewicki et al. (1988) concluded that learning in this situation was unconscious.

Subsequent replications of these basic findings have attempted to clarify the nature of the acquired knowledge. For instance, Perruchet et al. (1990), based on a replication and a reappraisal of Lewicki et al.'s (1988) data, proposed the rather different theory that participants become consciously sensitive to the frequencies of specific movements of the target over training. By the same token, Ferrer-Gil (1994), based on new empirical evidence (described below) obtained within the same paradigm, claimed that memorization of specific sequences constitutes the better account.

In the rest of this section, we propose that these different theoretical accounts can be unified by assuming that learning in Lewicki et al.'s (1988) situation is statistical in nature and best instantiated by the mechanisms at play in the SRN model. We start by examining both Perruchet et al.'s (1990) and Ferrer-Gil's (1994) theories and data in detail, showing how each theory is in fact incapable of accounting for all the empirical findings associated with Lewicki's paradigm. Next, we describe new simulation work of Ferrer-Gil's (1994) data, which, together with previous simulations of both Lewicki et al.'s and Perruchet et al.'s (1990) empirical findings, clearly demonstrates that learning in this paradigm is best thought of as involving the gradual development of knowledge about which stimuli are likely to follow others in different contexts, that is, knowledge about the sequential constraints imposed by the generation rules on the stimulus material.

The Perruchet et al. Study. Perruchet et al. (1990) proposed that participants in Lewicki et al.'s (1988) situation may develop and use a set of simple and potentially conscious simple rules correlated with those used to generate the stimulus material. Specifically, Perruchet et al. (1990) suggested that participants encode the sequence in terms of event frequencies, where events are not single trials but target movements between two successive trials. Perruchet et al. assumed that participants represent the sequence essentially in terms of four types of movements (horizontal, diagonal, vertical, and salient three-trials "backward" moves, which reflect cases where the stimulus returns to the location it was in immediately after visiting another location, such as in 1-2-1). By conducting a detailed analysis of the frequencies with which these different types of movements are present in the different types of trials and experimental phases distinguished by Lewicki et al., Perruchet et al. showed that sensitivity to such information appears to be sufficient to understand most of the observed learning effects. Their analysis indicated that (a) backward moves never occur during C/D/E trials but are quite frequent (27%) during A/B trials, (b) horizontal moves are globally less frequent than either diagonal or vertical moves and occur less often during C/D/E trials (11%) than during A/B trials (34%), and (c) horizontal moves never occur for Trials D and E but can involve Trial C.

As Perruchet et al. (1990) noted, the first two factors are in fact sufficient to account for the observed results, in that participants may simply become sensitive to differences in the distribution of the movement types involved in the different trials. For instance, globally infrequent movements, such as horizontal or backward moves, tend to occur more often during the A/B trials than during the C/D/E trials. If one assumes that RT is sensitive to global frequency (which it is; see Hasher & Zacks, 1979), then it is perfectly reasonable to expect participants to produce slow RTs in response to trials involving infrequent target movements, and hence to observe slow RTs for A/B trials. This simple theory can also account for the extinction of the difference between A/B trials and C/D/E trials during transfer. Indeed, because of the specific way in which the rules are reorganized during transfer, globally infrequent movements now tend to also occur for D and E trials. Slower RTs to these trials are therefore expected, and observed.

Perruchet et al. (1990) also found further support for their theory through several fine-grained analyses of their replication data. Some aspects of these data indeed appear to be consistent with Perruchet et al.'s theory but not with earlier accounts. For instance, C trials should be as predictable as D or E trials by construction. Perruchet et al., however, observed slower average RTs to C trials than to D and E trials. Analyzing the stimulus material in terms of the frequency distribution of movement types offers a simple explanation for this result: Globally infrequent horizontal movements may indeed involve C trials, but never involve D or E trials in the training phase. RTs to trials of equal predictability in terms of constraints resulting from the rule system devised by Lewicki et al. (1988) can therefore be shown to be in fact strongly influenced by the frequency with which simple target movements involving such trials occur.

Perruchet et al. (1990) therefore concluded that sensitivity to such simple frequency information is sufficient to understand the data and that there is no need to assume that participants learn anything about the rule system used to generate the stimulus material, as hypothesized by Lewicki et al. (1988). By focusing on the details, this reinterpretation of a classical implicit learning study, whereby a seemingly complex implicit rule-induction process was reduced to sensitivity to simple frequency information, was thus instrumental in defining a new framework within which to interpret implicit learning phenomena (e.g., Perruchet & Gallego, in press; Shanks & St. John, 1994).

The Ferrer-Gil (1994) Experiment. A radically different explanation of the results obtained in this sequence learning paradigm has been proposed by Ferrer-Gil (1994). Ferrer-Gil started from Lewicki et al.'s (1988) claim that sequence learning could be accounted for either by a process of implicit rule induction or by a mechanism of implicit memory for the actual sequences generated based on the rules. To distinguish between these two alternative accounts, Ferrer-Gil proposed to follow the design adopted by Lewicki et al., but to train participants on only one half of the possible 12 sequences and to test them on the other half (see Figure 10.3, right panel). The interesting aspect of Ferrer-Gil's conceptual replication is that, in contrast to the original situation, the generation rules used during training and transfer are now identical. Because the actual sequences presented to participants differ, however, the transfer segments can now be thought of as a true generalization test.

The results of Ferrer-Gil's (1994) experiment are illustrated in Figure 10.4 (left panel) and are similar to those obtained by Lewicki et al. (1988): The difference between RTs to unpredictable A/B trials and to predictable C/D/E trials that is present during training disappears almost entirely during transfer.

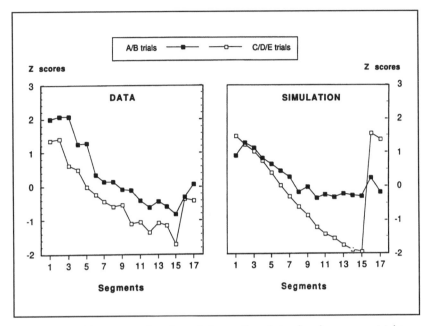

Figure 10.4. Human reaction times (left panel) and simulated responses (right panel) obtained over the 17 segments of Ferrer-Gil's (1994) situation, plotted separately for A/B and for C/D/E trials. Both human and simulated responses have been transformed into Z scores for comparison purposes.

Because the generation rules used during training and transfer are identical, these results exclude—even more strongly so than Perruchet et al.'s (1990) data—rule abstraction as a potential learning mechanism. According to Ferrer-Gil (1994), the most natural account of these results is simply that participants memorize the sequences presented over training: The random stimuli presented on Trials A and B of each block would act as recall cues, enabling participants to produce fast responses to the subsequent predictable C/D/E trials. Such knowledge would be useless during transfer, however, because all transfer sequences were new and instantiated never-seen combinations of Trials A and B.

This account, however, is at odds with the data collected by Perruchet et al. (1990). Indeed, if participants learned the entire set of sequences presented during training, as Ferrer-Gil (1994) assumes, then there would be no reason to expect that some predictable trials tend to systematically elicit slower responses than others, as Perruchet et al. have demonstrated.

TABLE 10.1 Relative Proportions of Horizontal, Diagonal, and Vertical Target Movements in Ferrer-Gil's (1994) Task, Represented Separately for the Training and Transfer Phases, and Broken Down by Trial Type						
	Training			Transfer		
	Trials A/B	Trials C/D/E	Total	Trials A/B	Trials C/D/E	Total
Diagonal	.500	.445	.466	.500	.445	.466
Horizontal	.250	.333	.300	.248	.333	.300
Vertical	.250	.222	.234	.252	.222	.234

Simple memorization of the stimulus material therefore appears to be insufficient to account for Perruchet et al.'s (1990) data and has to be rejected as a potential general mechanism with which to explain performance in Lewicki et al.'s (1988) situation. Let us now examine whether Perruchet et al.'s (1990) theory is successful in accounting for Ferrer-Gil's (1994) data.

To clarify this issue, we conducted a statistical analysis of the transition rules employed by Ferrer-Gil (1994). This analysis was similar to the one conducted by Perruchet et al. (1990) on Lewicki et al.'s (1988) stimulus material. We first generated 4,080 trials that followed Ferrer-Gil's stimulus-generation procedure exactly. Next, we computed the likelihood of all diagonal, horizontal, and vertical movements, both in general, and separately for A/B and C/D/E trials. Finally, we performed the same analysis on the transfer material. The results of both analyses are illustrated in Table 10.1.

The table makes several aspects of the frequency distribution of target movements clear. Focusing first on the training statistics represented in the left panel of Table 10.1, note that diagonal movements occur overall more frequently (in .466 of the cases) than either horizontal or vertical movements, both of which tend to occur about equally often (in .300 and .234 of the cases, respectively). Second, the distribution of target movements is sensibly similar for both A/B and C/D/E trials. It is therefore unlikely that differences in the distribution of target movements can account for the fact that C/D/E trials elicit faster responses than A/B trials in Ferrer-Gil's (1994) experiment. This hypothesis is further supported by the fact that both the most frequent and the least frequent movement types (diagonal movements and vertical movements, respectively) tend to occur more frequently during A/B trials than during C/D/E trials. Hence, it is rather unclear exactly what one should expect in terms of differences in response times for A/B and C/D/E trials based on an analysis of the distribution of target movements.

The hypothesis that participants' RTs reflect sensitivity to the frequency of target movements can perhaps be saved by considering that backward movements never occur during C/D/E trials, either in Lewicki et al.'s (1988) material or in Ferrer-Gil's (1994) material, whereas they are very frequent (35% of the cases) during the A/B trials of the training material used by Ferrer-Gil (1994).

Could such a single bias account solely for the effects observed by Ferrer-Gil (1994)? Exploring transfer performance in Ferrer-Gil's situation suggests otherwise. The transfer statistics are represented in the right panel of Table 10.1. The data show that the distribution of target movement types during the transfer phase of Ferrer-Gil's experiment is almost identical with the distribution observed for the training phase. Furthermore, backward movements also tend to occur at very similar rates during transfer, as they likewise occur exclusively during A/B trials (in 33% of the cases) and never during C/D/E trials.

There is thus nothing in the frequency distribution of the different target movement types during transfer that might account for the observed extinction of the difference between RTs to A/B versus C/D/E trials. To understand the data, it is therefore necessary to assume that participants are sensitive to some sequential information different from the frequency of target movements.

If the learning of simple target-movement frequency rules cannot account for the effects observed by Ferrer-Gil (1994), and if mere memorization similarly fails to account for some of the results obtained by Perruchet et al. (1990), what kind of theory may account for both sets of data? In the following, we show that the SRN model, which learns to exploit the emergent statistical properties of the stimulus material, is in fact capable of accounting for performance in all three empirical situations on which we focused.

The SRN Account. Cleeremans (1993b) has shown that the SRN can simulate the difference observed by Lewicki et al. (1988) between RTs to predictable (A/B) and unpredictable (C/D/E) trials and that it can likewise account for the more specific difference between C and D/E trials observed by Perruchet et al. (1990). As discussed above, the model relies neither on sensitivity to the relative frequencies of different target movements nor on rote memory for the material but instead develops representations of the conditional probabilities of appearance of sequence elements in (eventually optimal) contexts of previous elements.

To illustrate, consider for instance the finding that participants tend not to respond as fast to C trials as to D/E trials. This finding was taken by Perruchet et al. (1990) as solid evidence for the fact that participants, far from inducing the generation rules, are in fact sensitive to the regularity with which C trials can constitute the end points of globally infrequent movements of the stimulus, which is not the case for D/E trials. How does the SRN model account for these data? The model is sensitive to the conditional probability with which successive elements appear in the context defined by previous elements. Differences in RTs between C and D/E trials should therefore be the result of the fact that the most likely successors of all possible temporal contexts tend to appear more frequently during D/E trials than during C trials.

Thus, differences such as the one observed between responding to C or to D/E trials would simply arise from the fact that the most likely successors of all possible contexts often appear during the latter trials, whereas the less frequent ones tend to appear during C trials. Consider for instance the subsequence 2-3, using numbers from 1 to 4 to represent spatial locations, as shown in Figure 10.3. This subsequence is an instance of a diagonal movement and can span any pair of trials (i.e., A-B, B-C, C-D, D-E, E-A). Consider now the possible successors of this subsequence. There is only one instance where 2-3 acts as context for the elements that may appear in Trial C (i.e., the single case where Trial A is a 2 and Trial B is a 3), and its successor (i.e., the element that appears in Trial C) in that case is 4. There is one instance where 2-3 acts as context for Trial D, and its successor in that case is a 1. Finally, there are two instances where 2-3 acts as context for Trial E, and in both cases its successor is again a 1. Thus, in three cases out of four among the predictable trials, the subsequence 2-3 predicts a 1, and in all instances, this occurs during Trials D or E. Therefore, 4, which only occurs as a successor to 2-3 in Trial C, is less likely than 1 as a successor to 2-3, and hence it is not surprising that Trial C elicits a slower RT than Trials D or E. The same reasoning applies to other instances of diagonal movements. As shown by Cleeremans (1993b), this difference in predictability is in fact sufficient to produce the selective impairment observed by Perruchet et al. (1990) for the C trials, without assuming that participants are categorizing movements as diagonal, horizontal, or vertical ones.

Can the model also account for the results observed by Ferrer-Gil (1994)? To answer this question, we first consider how learning of the conditional probabilities of each successor in each context can account for these specific results, both during training and transfer phases. Next, we report on simulation work meant to determine whether the SRN model can learn Ferrer-Gil's material.

We first conducted an analysis that involved computing the conditional probability (CP) of occurrence of any element in the context of any given context of Length 1 and 2 for the entire training session. There are only four such contexts for Length 1 (each consisting of one of the four possible sequence elements), resulting in 12 CPs (given that immediate repetitions were forbidden, each of the four possible elements can only be followed by three successors). There were 36 such CPs for Length 2 (resulting from three possible successors to each of the 12 contexts of two elements that did not involve repetitions).

Next, we compared these global CPs with those obtained by conducting the same analysis, but limited to either A/B or to C/D/E trials. Finally, we also conducted these analyses separately for the transfer phases of Ferrer-Gil's (1994) experiment. The reasoning behind these analyses was as follows: If, as the SRN would predict, learning in this situation involves sensitivity to the global CPs with which the different sequence elements may appear in a variety of temporal contexts during training, then we should expect the CPs associated with C/D/E trials to be better correlated with the global CPs than the CPs associated with A/B trials are. In other words, predictable C/D/E trials should better reflect the sequential regularities present in the entire training set than unpredictable A/B trials. Furthermore, to explain the lack of transfer, one would also expect this difference to disappear during transfer, that is, the correlation between CPs for trials C/D/E and the global CPs should now be equally low as the correlation between CPs for Trials A/B and the global CPs.

The main results of these analyses are presented in Table 10.2. The data suggest, as predicted, that the correlation between training CPs and C/D/E CPs is indeed greater than the correlation between training CPs and A/B CPs, both for contexts of Length 1 (.817 versus .071) and for contexts of Length 2 (.851 versus .686). The former result is important because it suggests that enough information is already present in a single previous element to account for the difference in RTs observed between A/B and

TABLE 10.2 Correlations Between the Global Distribution of Conditional Probabilities of Appearance of the Different Sequence Elements in Contexts of Length 1 or 2 During Training in Ferrer-Gil's (1994) Experiment and the Distribution of Conditional Probabilities Observed Specifically for A/B and C/D/E Trials During Either Training or Transfer in the Same Experiment

	Training			Transfer		
	Trials A/B	Trials C/D/E	Total	Trials A/B	Trials C/D/E	Total
Length 1	.071	.817	1.00	−.186	−.626	−.335
Length 2	.686	.851	1.00	.352	.045	.184

C/D/E trials, despite the fact that the rule system used to generate the stimulus material erroneously conveys the impression that two previous elements are always necessary to predict the identity of the next element.

Turning now to the transfer data, one can see that the pattern of correlation between the global distribution of CPs during training and the A/B and C/D/E CPs computed for the transfer material also provides an account of the observed extinction of the difference between A/B and C/D/E trials during transfer. Indeed, and despite the fact that the transfer sequence was generated based on the same rule system as the training material, the global distribution of training CPs was no longer positively correlated with the CPs for C/D/E transfer trials (−.626 and .045 for contexts of Length 1 and 2 respectively) and tended to be even slightly better correlated with the distribution of CPs obtained for A/B transfer trials (−.186 and .352 for contexts of Length 1 and 2, respectively). These results therefore confirm that learning about the set of CPs of each successor after different contexts during the training phase constitutes a plausible account of both the training and the transfer effects observed by Ferrer-Gil (1994).

However, it remains to be determined whether the SRN model is capable of learning Ferrer-Gil's (1994) material and of reproducing his results. To find out, we trained an SRN in the conditions specified by Ferrer-Gil (i.e., for the same number of trials, and with the same material). The network (see Figure 10.2) used local representations on both the input and output pools (i.e., each unit corresponded to one of the four stimuli) and a pool of 15 hidden units. We used a learning rate of 0.15 and no momentum, as in the simulations reported in Cleeremans (1993b). The network used dual connection weights and running average activations on the output units to account for short-term priming effects, as described in Cleeremans (1993b). During training, the activation of each output unit was recorded on every trial and transformed into Luce (1963) ratios to normalize the responses. For the purpose of comparing the model's and participants' responses, we assumed (a) that the normalized running average activations of the output units represent response tendencies, and (b) that there is a linear reduction in RT proportional to the relative strength of the unit corresponding to the correct response. The network's responses were finally subtracted from 1.0, to make increases in response strength consistent with reductions in RT, which are both assumed to be associated with better ability to anticipate the next element of the sequence. To control for random variability, nine replications of this simulation (each initialized with a different set of random weights) were conducted and averaged together. Finally, to compare human and simulated responses, both sets of data were finally transformed into Z scores. The results are represented in Figure 10.4.

Visual inspection of Figure 10.4 (right panel) shows that the network is successful in reproducing the main pattern observed by Ferrer-Gil (1994), that is, (a) a growing difference between performance on A/B and C/D/E trials over training, and (b) a sudden extinction of this difference at the onset of the transfer phase. The global correlation between empirical and simulated data was .80. Despite this good degree of correspondence between human and simulated data, however, there are also some discrepancies between the human and the simulated data: First, differences in responding to A/B and C/D/E trials arise earlier in humans than they do in the model. Second, the model appears to be much more sensitive than human participants to the switch between training and transfer.

Which factors may account for these discrepancies? It is likely that human participants approach the task with several different explicit strategies that the SRN is incapable of modeling. For instance, if, as shown by Perruchet et al. (1990), human participants are indeed capable of discovering the rule that backward moves (e.g., 2-1-2) tend to be globally rare, they would tend to respond particularly slowly to the stimuli that constitute the end points of such movements. This sort of negative priming effect, where the response to a stimulus that appears again at a location it had already occupied shortly before is inhibited, is sufficient to understand both discrepancies between human and simulated responses. Indeed, backward moves, which are very salient, are relatively infrequent during training and appear exclusively during A/B in Ferrer-Gil's (1994) material. Human participants would thus tend to respond more slowly to A/B trials than would be predicted based exclusively on the CP of appearance of successive stimuli. Such a bias, if present, would result in the entire curve corresponding to A/B trials to be translated upward relative to the curve corresponding to C/D/E trials, and this upward shift would in turn result in (a) the observation of an increased difference between responses to A/B and C/D/E trials early in training, and (b) the observation of a smaller difference between A/B and C/D/E trials when switching to the transfer phase. To verify this hypothesis, we simply added a small constant bias to the model's responses to the A/B trials and verified that the resulting data exhibited both the early difference between A/B and C/D/E trials observed in human responses and an extinction of the difference between A/B and C/D/E trials during the transfer phase (rather than the inversion that the unbiased model's responses show).

To summarize, then, both the conceptual analyses and the simulations we reported in this chapter (see also Cleeremans, 1993b) strongly suggest that a process of statistical sequence learning similar to the one instantiated by the SRN can account for most of the effects reported by Lewicki et al. (1988), by Perruchet et al. (1990), and by Ferrer-Gil (1994). Some effects, however, probably require additional learning mechanisms (e.g., mechanisms based on explicit memory for salient aspects of the material) that are not at all captured by the model.

Having shown that statistical learning processes of the kind instantiated by the SRN appear to provide a unified and parsimonious account of sequence-learning effects in both the Probabilistic and Deterministic Rule-Based subparadigms, let us now turn our attention to the last kind of empirical situation through which sequence learning has typically been explored: The Simple Repeating Sequence subparadigm.

STATISTICAL VERSUS SERIAL ACCOUNTS
OF SERIAL-SEQUENCE LEARNING

Insofar as people presented with a sequence generated based on straightforward rules can induce some of these rules explicitly, it is only natural to expect people presented with a short, deterministic, and repeating sequence to be likewise able to memorize the sequence after a few exposures. The question is, therefore, not whether serial, and presumably conscious knowledge of a deterministic sequence can be acquired and used in a typical SRT task, but rather whether there is some evidence that allows us to conclude that performance also benefits from the statistical learning process described above for both probabilistic and rule-based sequential material.

Answering this question may prove difficult, however, because there may be a large overlap between the knowledge produced by memory for small fragments of a given deterministic sequence and the knowledge resulting from an encoding of the CP with which each element of the same sequence may appear in all possible contexts. This problem of separating the contributions of serial and of statistical knowledge may perhaps be circumvented provided one is willing to make an additional assumption: That serial knowledge is best characterized as explicit, conscious knowledge and that statistical knowledge is essentially implicit in nature. This assumption is motivated by different arguments spelled out in Cleeremans (in press). With this assumption in place, one may then hope to distinguish between both forms of sequence knowledge by contrasting conditions in which their acquisition and use are either facilitated or made more difficult. For instance, manipulating participants' orientation to learn or the availability of attentional resources should specifically influence the acquisition of serial knowledge and would therefore be expected to selectively interfere with the learning of deterministic sequences. Such factors, on the other hand, should not interfere with the processing of comparable probabilistic sequences if such material is essentially learned by means of mechanisms that induce the statistical properties of the material.

Thus, if two otherwise similar probabilistic and deterministic sequences can be shown to be equally learnable under conditions that strongly prevent explicit learning, one would tend to conclude that such a result lends support to the idea that both types of sequences are processed using the same mechanisms of statistical learning.

A study conducted by Curran and Keele (1993), which we already briefly described earlier, can be taken as providing a first step toward exploring these issues. In this study, Curran and Keele showed that participants exposed to a simple SRT task benefited greatly from instructions to memorize the sequence before the onset of the main SRT task compared with participants who had only received typical implicit learning instructions. Indeed, the results indicated that participants who were provided with serial information were systematically faster than "incidental" participants in responding to the SRT task when both groups performed under conditions of undivided attention. This difference disappeared completely,

351

however, when the same participants subsequently performed under conditions of divided attention.

Several different accounts of these data have been proposed. Curran and Keele (1993) interpreted these and other related findings as evidence for the existence of at least two forms of sequence learning, an attentional form and a nonattentional form. Only the nonattentional sequence-learning mechanism is impervious to the scarcity of attentional resources. Cleeremans (1993a) suggested that Curran and Keele's findings could be understood based on the joint action of a mechanism of automatic induction of the statistical structure of the sequence (i.e., the SRN), together with another mechanism that essentially fetches a literal representation of the series of elements (i.e., a buffer network). However, several alternative accounts of these results can also be conceived in terms, for instance, of the production of different pools of serial knowledge, which differ in their resilience to dividing attention. To decide between these alternatives, it could be interesting to compare the results obtained under these circumstances when participants are presented with similar probabilistic or deterministic sequences.

To address this question, we conducted an experiment in which we simultaneously manipulated several factors for otherwise similar deterministic and probabilistic sequences. For lack of space, we will only describe the relevant features of the design and results in this chapter.

In this experiment, participants were exposed to a six-choice RT task. We manipulated four different factors: Sequence Structure (unique versus ambiguous), Sequence Type (deterministic versus probabilistic), Attention (presence or absence of a secondary tone-counting task), and Orientation (intentional participants, who received instructions to memorize the sequence before the onset of the SRT task, versus incidental participants, who received typical implicit learning instructions).

Deterministic sequences could be either unique (i.e., each element t of the sequence is fully predictable based exclusively on element $t - 1$) or ambiguous (i.e., each element t can only be predicted based on the conjunction of elements $t - 2$ and $t - 1$). Six different unique sequences (each 6 elements long) and six different ambiguous (each 12 elements long) sequences were used. Probabilistic sequences were generated based on the deterministic sequences, in the following way: Whenever an element of the deterministic sequence was about to be presented, there was a 20% chance that another, randomly selected element would be presented instead (identity substitutions were forbidden).

Both Attention (i.e., availability of attentional resources), and Orientation (i.e., availability of explicit knowledge about the sequence) were manipulated in exactly the same way as Curran and Keele (1993): The secondary task consisted of monitoring a tone presented during the response-stimulus interval of the primary RT task. A high-pitched (2500 Hz) or low-pitched (1000 Hz) tone appeared after a randomly selected interval of 40, 60, or 80 ms after the response to the previous trial had been produced. The RSI was set to 120 ms. Participants in dual-task conditions were to count the number of high-pitched tones presented and to report this number at the end of each block. Availability of serial conscious information was manipulated by following Curran and Keele's (1993) intentional conditions, that is, by asking relevant participants to memorize the sequence before the onset of the task.

Crossing these four factors completely produced 16 experimental groups. Twelve participants, all undergraduates at the Université Libre de Bruxelles, were randomly assigned to each group. Each group was first exposed to a training phase consisting of 10 blocks of 120 trials each, performed under either single- or dual-task conditions. Next, each group performed 5 more blocks of 120 trials under dual-task conditions. Some participants therefore performed the entire experiment under dual-task conditions, whereas others first performed the task under single-task conditions and subsequently transferred to a dual-task situation.

This design allowed us to ascertain whether scarcity of attentional resources affects the expression of learning in a different way for groups that were trained under conditions that favor the acquisition of conscious, serial knowledge (i.e., deterministic, unique sequences, and instructions to memorize) and for groups trained under conditions that favor the acquisition of implicit, statistical knowledge (i.e., probabilistic structures, ambiguous sequences, and no specific instructions).

To assess learning, we adopted two slightly different measures for deterministic and probabilistic sequences. All groups exposed to deterministic material were exposed to the following series of 10 blocks during the training phase: Two random blocks (1-2), six structured blocks (3-8), one random block (9), and one structured block (10). The random material was matched with the structured material in terms of the frequencies of individual sequence elements. Learning was assessed by subtracting the average of the mean RTs produced in response to the structured blocks 8 and 10 from the mean RT obtained for the random block 9. The transfer phase consisted of 5 blocks, all of which involved structured material except for block 12. Learning during the transfer phase was assessed by subtracting the average of the mean RTs produced in response to the surrounding structured blocks (blocks 11 and 13) from the mean RT obtained for the random block 12.

The task design for groups performing with probabilistic material was simpler because control trials were interspersed within the sequences. All participants were merely first exposed to 2 blocks of random material followed by 13 blocks of structured material. The final 5 blocks (11 to 15) constituted the transfer phase and were performed under dual-task conditions. To make the measure of learning as comparable as possible to the measure used for deterministic material, learning during the training phase was assessed by subtracting the average of the mean RTs produced in response to the structured elements of blocks 8, 9, and 10 from the average of the mean RTs produced for random elements during the same blocks. Transfer performance was analyzed in the same way, using data from blocks 11, 12, and 13.

The results of this complex design are illustrated in Figure 10.5, which represents the RT differences (between structured and random material) obtained in both the training and the transfer phases for all 16 experimental groups. In the following, we first compare the transfer and training conditions, and we next focus on the effects of the grouping factors on performance during training.

To analyze the data, we first conducted an omnibus ANOVA with all four factors described above (Sequence Type, Sequence Structure, Attention, and Instructions) as between-subjects factors and with Experimental Phase (training versus transfer) as a repeated measure. Because the potential number of effects and interactions is rather large, we only report the most relevant results in the following paragraphs.

The interaction between Experimental Phase and Sequence Type was significant, $F(1, 176) = 11.63$; $MSE = 19868.7$; $p < .001$, suggesting that participants trained with deterministic sequences were more disrupted than those trained with probabilistic sequences when confronted with the transfer phase.

This interaction between Sequence Type and Experimental Phase was also clearly expressed through a significant triple interaction involving Sequence Type, Experimental Phase, and Attention, $F(1, 176) = 28.63$; $MSE = 48896.7$; $p < .0001$. Through this interaction, it is possible to distinguish between participants for whom transfer meant no change (i.e., participants who performed under dual-task conditions from the outset)

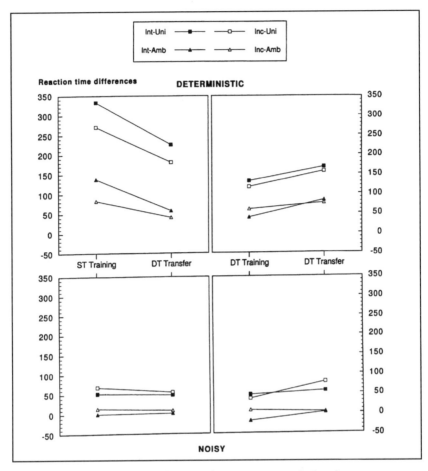

Figure 10.5. Reaction-time differences between grammatical and non-grammatical trials obtained with deterministic (top panels) or probabilistic (noisy) sequences (bottom panels), plotted separately for single-task (ST) training/dual-task transfer groups (left panels) and for dual-task (DT) training/dual-task transfer groups (right panels). The data are also represented separately for intentional (filled symbols) and incidental (open symbols) groups and for unique (squares) and ambiguous (triangles) sequences.

and participants for whom transfer involved switching from single-task conditions to dual-task conditions. The data suggest that transfer was specifically harmful for participants who had been trained with deterministic sequences under single-task conditions.

Focusing now on data from the training phase, some additional interesting results are worth reporting. As can be seen in Figure 10.5, there were significant main effects of Sequence Type, $F(1, 176) = 255.14$; $MSE = 699625.5$; $p < .0001$; of Sequence Structure, $F(1, 176) = 146.89$; $MSE = 402783.5$; $p < .0001$; and of Attention, $F(1, 176) = 79.49$; $MSE = 217980.6$; $p < .0001$. Instructions, however, failed to reach significance ($p > .30$). Thus, participants presented with deterministic material learned more than participants presented with probabilistic sequences (the difference between mean RTs in response to either structured or random trials was 147 ms for deterministic sequences and 26 ms for probabilistic sequences). Likewise, participants trained with unique sequences learned more than those presented with ambiguous sequences (132 versus 41 ms), and those who performed under single-task conditions learned more than those trained in the presence of the secondary task (120 versus 53 ms). The pattern of interactions also revealed significant effects involving Sequence Type, as follows: The difference between learning unique or ambiguous sequences was greater when the material was deterministic (213 versus 80 ms) as opposed to probabilistic (51 versus 1 ms), $F(1, 176) = 29.76$; $MSE = 81592.5$; $p < .0001$, and the difference between learning under single- or dual-task conditions was also greater when the material was deterministic (206 ms to 87 ms) rather than probabilistic (34 ms to 18 ms), $F(1, 176) = 47.01$; $MSE = 128892.2$; $p < .0001$.

Furthermore, an analysis of the interaction effects also indicated that the effects of asking participants to memorize the sequence before the outset of the task was beneficial for participants trained with deterministic sequences (161 versus 133 ms) but was ineffective, if not harmful when participants were trained with probabilistic material (20 versus 32 ms), $F(1, 176) = 6.77$; $p = .01$. Likewise, instructions to memorize tended to be beneficial for participants trained under single-task conditions (131 versus 109 ms) but had no effect for participants trained under dual-task conditions (50 versus 56 ms), $F(1, 176) = 3.31$; $MSE = 9084.2$; $p = .07$.

Two three-way interactions also reached significance and are worth reporting. First, the triple interaction between Attention, Sequence Structure (unique versus ambiguous) and Sequence Type (deterministic versus probabilistic) was significant, $F(1, 176) = 13.96$; $MSE = 38288.2$; $p < .001$. The effects of Attention were greater for unique than for ambiguous sequences, but only when the material was deterministic, $F(1, 88) = 19.33$; $MSE = 82720.0$; $p < .0001$. For probabilistic material, the effects of attention were similar regardless of whether the sequences involved unique or ambiguous transitions, $F(1, 88) = .98$; $MSE = 118.5$; $p > .75$.

Second, and most important, it appears that only participants learning deterministic sequences under single-task conditions actually benefited from the availability of explicit information about the sequence (233 ms versus 177 ms). All other combinations of structural noise and attentional conditions produced similar or less learning when participants had been instructed to memorize the sequence than when they had merely been given typical implicit instructions. These learning effects in deterministic, dual-task conditions were 86 ms for intentional participants and 89 ms for incidental participants. These same effects were 26 ms and 41 ms in probabilistic, single-task conditions, and 14 ms and 23 ms in probabilistic, dual-task conditions. The corresponding three-way interaction between Sequence Type, Attention, and Orientation was significant, $F(1, 176) = 4.96$; $MSE = 13590.1$; $p < .05$, and so was the interaction between Attention and Orientation in the deterministic condition: $F(1, 88) = 5.24$; $MSE = 22448.2$; $p < .05$. However, this same interaction failed to reach significance for groups trained with probabilistic material, $F(1, 88) = .19$; $MSE = 226.1$; $p > .65$.

To summarize, then, these results may be taken as indicating that conditions that favor explicit learning, such as learning unique sequences under single-task conditions and with full knowledge of the sequence, appear to be selectively beneficial to processing deterministic sequences, whereas conditions that hinder explicit learning tend to result in similar effects for both probabilistic and deterministic material. For instance, the finding that transfer from single- to dual-task conditions selectively influences the expression of learning of deterministic sequences strongly supports the claim that learning of probabilistic material is essentially a matter of implicit learning. Moreover, the fact that explicit information only helps participants trained with deterministic sequences also suggests that learning of such deterministic sequences can be selectively influenced by serial, conscious knowledge, whereas learning of probabilistic structures is not, and is therefore likely driven by different mechanisms. Finally, the observed three-way interaction between Orientation, Sequence Type, and Attention can also be taken to indicate that, under conditions of divided attention, both intentional and incidental learners tend to ignore or are incapable of using conscious information and instead base their responses on some other source of knowledge that is equally useful in processing either deterministic or probabilistic material.

We therefore believe that these results, when considered together with the material we described earlier concerning the mechanisms that might be responsible for the acquisition of statistical knowledge in both probabilistic and rule-based sequential settings, make it compelling that statistical learning as instantiated by the SRN is the core process that underlies learning in all the major sequence learning subparadigms.

SUMMARY AND FINAL REMARKS

Our main goal in this chapter was to show that implicit sequence learning can be understood in terms of the acquisition of representations of the statistical structure of the event sequences to which participants are exposed. Based on previous and on new results, we also showed that the Simple Recurrent Network (see Elman, 1990; Cleeremans, 1993b) appears to provide a good characterization of the processes through which such representations develop, both in situations involving probabilistic rule-based material (e.g., Cleeremans & McClelland, 1991; Jiménez et al., 1996) and in situations where the material is deterministic and consists of either simple repeating sequences or rule-based material. By analyzing in detail the classical study of Lewicki et al. (1988) and its conceptual replications by Perruchet et al. (1990) and by Ferrer-Gil (1994), we showed that the ensemble of results obtained with this specific empirical situation are in fact inconsistent with both instance-based and rule-based accounts. We showed that the SRN model, by contrast, provides a unifying account of these otherwise disparate empirical findings.

Finally, our empirical data suggest that although consciously held, explicit knowledge about the simple repeating sequences typically used in sequence-learning tasks may indeed play an important role in performance, it may still be the case that the kind of statistical learning process instantiated by the SRN also makes a large contribution. Indeed, our data suggest that the knowledge acquired by participants who performed under conditions that severely hinder explicit learning appears to be quite similar to the knowledge acquired by participants trained with otherwise similar, but probabilistic sequences.

Taken together, the different aspects of the research we described in this chapter suggest (a) that both explicit information (either in the form of rule-based knowledge or in the form of memory for instances or fragments) and implicit, essentially statistical information are produced simultaneously and can both influence performance in sequence-learning situations, and (b) that the latter knowledge is the default, core knowledge acquired when participants are exposed to a sequence-learning situation. This conclusion is grounded in results from both experimental and simulation studies and based on the analysis of paradigms that span the whole spectrum from deterministic to rule-based and probabilistic sequence-learning tasks. Nevertheless, there are some important caveats worth pointing out. We would like to discuss three such caveats in closing this chapter.

First, one might claim that interspersing random trials within deterministic sequences so radically changes the material that comparisons between otherwise similar deterministic and probabilistic sequences become meaningless. Support for such a dismissal of the procedure we described in this chapter may perhaps be found in the fact that although learning with both deterministic and probabilistic material tended to be equally insensitive to participants' orientation under conditions that maximally hinder explicit learning (i.e., dual-task conditions), deterministic sequences still tended to elicit more learning than probabilistic sequences (see Figure 10.5). Based on these data, one might be tempted to conclude that in addition to a source of statistical knowledge about the material, deterministic sequences also tended to benefit from additional sources of implicit knowledge (i.e., serial knowledge). We believe such a conclusion to be unwarranted, however, for the following reasons. A first factor is that learning was not assessed in exactly the same way for deterministic and for probabilistic sequences: The control (random) trials for deterministic sequences were indeed massed into a single block, whereas the corresponding control trials for probabilistic sequences were interspersed with the structured trials. We do not have a clear idea of how concentrating the random material can give rise to significant local drops in performance, but we surmise that this idea cannot be completely discarded, and that such an effect may in fact account for greater absolute effects to be obtained when contrasting blocks of deterministic material and blocks of random material. Another factor that may similarly contribute to the observation of better learning with deterministic material in our situation is that interspersing random material within the structured material makes the underlying sequence more difficult to learn because, by virtue of the resulting noise, the CPs of predictable and unpredictable successors become more and more similar. Indeed, if the noise interspersed within the structured material throughout the training blocks amounted to 20% in the conditions involving probabilistic material, it only amounted to 12.5% (1 out of 8 blocks) for conditions involving deterministic material. Further research is needed to make both conditions more comparable, but it is clear that, based on this difference, one should expect to observe larger learning effects with deterministic material even if only statistical learning were taking place.

Second, our analysis of learning in the Lewicki et al. (1988) paradigm leaves open the possibility that although the specific set of rules proposed by Perruchet et al. (1990) may not account for Ferrer-Gil's (1994) results, another set might. We see little reason to dismiss this possibility as a plausible account for all the data, but we would like to stress that the SRN model appears to provide the most parsimonious account of these data so far, and that the burden of proof therefore rests on defenders of the implicit learning as explicit rule-induction approach.

Finally, in closing, we would like to comment on several other theoretical approaches to sequence learning that are, like the SRN model, based on the acquisition of statistical knowledge. For instance, Stadler (1992, 1995) also proposed that implicit serial learning involves the development of sensitivity to the statistical structure of the material and described two alternative mechanisms capable of developing this sensitivity. The first mechanism, also described by Frensch and his colleagues (e.g., Frensch et al., 1994; Frensch & Miner, 1994), was inspired by Cowan's (1988) general model of information processing and essentially assumes that implicit learning involves the automatic association of the representations of all the events that are simultaneously active in short-term memory. This learning process is therefore limited, in that short-term memory capacity is itself severely limited and in that the traces it contains decay quickly with time.

A second mechanism discussed by Stadler (1995) and that bears important similarities to the first one, was originally proposed by Jennings and Keele (1990; Keele & Jennings, 1992) on the base of a connectionist model of serial learning previously developed by Jordan (1986). Although this model is endowed with a set of "plan" units that may be important in specifying its ability to explicitly learn hierarchical associations, its most relevant feature, in order to understand how it comes to implicitly encode the temporal context, is a temporal trace that would be represented over the input units, together with the activation corresponding to current element. Thus, temporal trace arises as the result of time-averaging the current activation of each input unit with its own previous state, according to a decay parameter that determines how long the trace of a particular past event is maintained available for blending with the next input.

Both this model and the framework proposed by Frensch and his colleagues have in common the fact that context sensitivity is fixed, in that it either depends on the temporal resolution of short-term memory or on the decay parameter that establishes how many previous elements can be considered as relevant to predict the next one. In contrast with these fixed-resolution models of sequence learning, the SRN's temporal window is flexible, in that the network progressively learns to base its responses on an increasingly large temporal context, up to the point that its responses finally come to reflect almost exactly the CPs of occurrence of each stimulus, given the largest informative context that the network can encode. This property of learning in the SRN actually results in specific predictions that have been shown to match participants' performance very well (e.g., Cleeremans & McClelland, 1991). In addition, it appears that only the SRN model can explain why the length of the context used to predict the next element can be different depending on the structure of the sequence. For instance, learning of sequential remote contingencies in the SRN can only take place if each element is useful in predicting the next one: The network tends to "forget" information about events that are not directly prediction-relevant (see Cleeremans, 1993b). Indeed, simulations of the SRN performance have shown that it learns to consider up to three previous elements of the sequence used by Cleeremans and McClelland (1991), but only up to two previous elements of that used by Jiménez et al. (1996). Accordingly, human participants in the experiments of Cleeremans and McClelland also learned third-order contingencies, but those presented with the structure of Jiménez et al. only appeared to be sensitive to the constraints set by the two previous trials. Other data (see Cleeremans, 1993b) have been shown to be inconsistent with the SRN's performance, however, and hence it is clear that further research is needed to help distinguish between the predictions of current statistical models of sequence learning.

As a whole, however, the SRN and similar models of sequence learning seem to capture most of the relevant features of the learning processes that take place when human participants are presented with a sequentially structured SRT task. We believe such models therefore provide a convincing unified perspective on the core processes involved in sequence learning, in that they make it clear how complex knowledge about the structure of the stimulus material can be produced through elementary learning mechanisms that involve neither tacit rule induction nor memory of instances.

NOTE

1. Efficiency is a combined measure of RT and accuracy (see Jiménez et al., 1996). Note that Lewicki et al. (1988) did not use such an efficiency measure, but relied instead on separate analysis of RT and accuracy.

REFERENCES

Altman, G. T. M., Dienes, Z., & Goode, A. (1995). Modality independence of implicitly learned grammatical knowledge. *Journal of Experimental Psychology: Learning, Memory, and Cognition, 21,* 899-912.

Cleeremans, A. (1993a). Attention and awareness in sequence learning. In *Proceedings of the XV Annual Conference of the Cognitive Science Society.* Hillsdale, NJ: Lawrence Erlbaum.

Cleeremans, A. (1993b). *Mechanisms of implicit learning: Connectionist models of sequence processing.* Cambridge: MIT Press.

Cleeremans, A. (in press). Principles for implicit learning. In D. Berry (Ed.), *What is implicit about implicit learning?* Oxford, UK: Oxford University Press.

Cleeremans, A., & McClelland, J. L. (1991). Learning the structure of event sequences. *Journal of Experimental Psychology: General, 120,* 235-253.

Cohen, A., Ivry, R. I., & Keele, S. W. (1990). Attention and structure in sequence learning. *Journal of Experimental Psychology: Learning, Memory, and Cognition, 16,* 17-30.

Cowan, N. (1988). Evolving conceptions of memory storage, selective attention, and their mutual constraints within the human information processing system. *Psychological Bulletin, 104,* 163-191.

Curran, T., & Keele, S. W. (1993). Attentional and nonattentional forms of sequence learning. *Journal of Experimental Psychology: Learning, Memory, and Cognition, 19,* 189-202.

Elman, J. L. (1990). Finding structure in time. *Cognitive Science, 14,* 179-211.

Ferrer-Gil, E. (1994). La unidad de aprendizaje en procesamiento no consciente: Un análisis experimental [The unit of learning in unconscious processing: An experimental analysis]. *Psicologemas, 7,* 195-217.

Frensch, P. A., Buchner, A., & Lin, J. (1994). Implicit learning of unique and ambiguous serial transitions in the presence and absence of a distractor task. *Journal of Experimental Psychology: Learning, Memory, and Cognition, 20,* 567-584.

Frensch, P. A., Lin, J., & Buchner, A. (in press). Learning versus behavioral expression of the learned: The effects of a secondary tone-counting task on implicit learning in the serial reaction time task. *Pychological Research.*

Frensch, P. A., & Miner, C. S. (1994). Individual differences in short-term memory capacity on an indirect measure of serial learning. *Memory & Cognition, 22,* 95-110.

Hasher, L., & Zacks, R. T. (1979). Automatic and effortful processes in memory. *Journal of Experimental Psychology: General, 108,* 356-388.

Jackson, G. M., & Jackson, S. R. (1995). Do measures of explicit learning actually measure what is being learnt in the serial reaction time task? *Psyche: An International Journal of Research on Consciousness, 2*(20).

Jennings, P., & Keele, S. W. (1990). A computational model of attentional requirements in sequence learning. In *Proceedings of the 12th Annual Conference of the Cognitive Science Society.* Hillsdale, NJ: Lawrence Erlbaum.

Jiménez, L., Méndez, C., & Cleeremans, A. (1996). Comparing direct and indirect measures of sequence learning. *Journal of Experimental Psychology: Learning, Memory, and Cognition, 22,* 948-969.

Jordan, M. I. (1986). Attractor dynamics and parallelism in a connectionist sequential machine. In *Proceedings of the 8th Annual Conference of the Cognitive Science Society.* Hillsdale, NJ: Lawrence Erlbaum.

Keele, S. W., & Jennings, P. J. (1992). Attention in the representation of sequence: Experiment and theory. *Human Movement Science, 11,* 125-138.

Lewicki, P., Hill, T., & Bizot, E. (1988). Acquisition of procedural knowledge about a pattern of stimuli that cannot be articulated. *Cognitive Psychology, 20,* 24-37.

Luce, R. D. (1963). Detection and recognition. In R. D. Luce, R. R. Bush, & E. Galanter (Eds.), *Handbook of mathematical psychology* (Vol. 1). New York: John Wiley.

Mayr, U. (1996). Spatial attention and implicit sequence learning: Evidence for independent learnng of spatial and nonspatial sequences. *Journal of Experimental Psychology: Learning, Memory, and Cognition, 22,* 350-364.

Nissen, M. J., & Bullemer, P. (1987). Attentional requirements of learning: Evidence from performance measures. *Cognitive Psychology, 19,* 1-32.

Perruchet, P., & Amorim, P. A. (1992). Conscious knowledge and changes in performance in sequence learning: Evidence against dissociation. *Journal of Experimental Psychology: Learning, Memory, and Cognition, 18,* 785-800.

Perruchet, P., & Gallego, J. (in press). An associative model of implicit learning. In D. Berry (Ed.), *What is implicit about implicit learning?* Oxford, UK: Oxford University Press.

Perruchet, P., Gallego, J., & Savy, I. (1990). A critical reappraisal of the evidence for unconscious abstraction of deterministic rules in complex experimental situations. *Cognitive Psychology, 22,* 493-516.

Reber, A. S. (1993). *Implicit learning and tacit knowledge.* New York: Oxford University Press.

Reed, J., & Johnson, P. (1994). Assessing implicit learning with indirect tests: Determining what is learnt about sequence structure. *Journal of Experimental Psychology: Learning, Memory, and Cognition, 20,* 585-594.

Reingold, E. M., & Merikle, P. M. (1988). Using direct and indirect measures to study perception without awareness. *Perception and Psychophysics, 44,* 563-575.

Servan-Schreiber, D., Cleeremans, A., & McClelland, J. L. (1991). Graded state machines: The representation of temporal contingencies in simple recurrent networks. *Machine Learning, 7,* 161-193.

Shanks, D. R., & St. John, M. F. (1994). Characteristics of dissociable learning systems. *Behavioral and Brain Sciences, 17,* 367-395.

Stadler, M. A. (1989). On learning complex procedural knowledge. *Journal of Experimental Psychology: Learning, Memory, and Cognition, 15,* 1061-1069.

Stadler, M. A. (1992). Statistical structure and implicit serial learning. *Journal of Experimental Psychology: Learning, Memory, and Cognition, 18,* 318-327.

Stadler, M. A. (1995). Role of attention in implicit learning. *Journal of Experimental Psychology: Learning, Memory, and Cognition, 21,* 819-827.

Willingham, D. B., Greeley, T., & Bardone, A. M. (1993). Dissociation in a serial response task using a recognition measure: Comment on Peruchet and Amorim (1992). *Journal of Experimental Psychology: Learning, Memory, and Cognition, 19,* 1424-1430.

Willingham, D. B., Nissen, M. J., & Bullemer, P. (1989). On the development of procedural knowledge. *Journal of Experimental Psychology: Learning, Memory, and Cognition, 15,* 1047-1060.

11

Implicit Sequence Learning From a Cognitive Neuroscience Perspective

What, How, and Where?

●────────────────────────────

Tim Curran

Implicit sequence learning has attracted a great deal of interest from researchers who seek to understand the neural mechanisms of learning, memory, and sequential behavior. Many studies of implicit sequence learning have adopted Nissen and Bullemer's (1987) serial reaction time (SRT) task. The present chapter will review much of this research, with an emphasis on how behavioral and neuropsychological research can be mutually beneficial for understanding two questions. First, *what* is the format or code of the learned sequence representations? That is, are subjects learning stimulus sequences, motor sequences, sensory-motor sequences, or more abstract formats that are neither sensory nor motor? Second, *how* are sequences learned? In other words, what are the

AUTHOR'S NOTE: Preparation of this chapter was partly supported by a W. P. Jones Presidential Faculty Development Award from Case Western Reserve University. I thank Steve Keele, Scott Rauch, Jon Reed, Paul Reber, and Mike Stadler for helpful comments. Address correspondence to Tim Curran, Department of Psychology, Case Western Reserve University, 10900 Euclid Avenue, Cleveland, OH 44106-7123. Email may be sent via Internet to tec3@po.cwru.edu.

rules or computations that underlie implicit sequence learning, and upon what sort of information does learning depend: event frequency learning, pairwise associative learning, recurrent associative learning, or hierarchic coding? I will begin by reviewing behavioral evidence that has examined these questions: what is learned and how is it learned? Next, I will review neuropsychological and neuroimaging results that are relevant to these questions and suggest *where* the processes underlying implicit sequence learning are implemented in the brain.

KEY QUESTIONS ABOUT THE COGNITIVE PROCESSES UNDERLYING IMPLICIT SEQUENCE LEARNING

Nissen and Bullemer (1987) introduced the SRT task to study sequence learning via performance improvement. On each trial, a visual stimulus is presented at one of three or four spatially distinct locations. The subject has an equal number of response keys and presses the corresponding key as quickly as possible on each trial. The visual signal disappears upon the subject's response; then another signal appears over a different position after a short interval. The visual signal follows a specific repeating sequence, but typically the subjects are not informed about the sequence. Nissen and Bullemer used four spatial positions and, designating the positions as 1 to 4 from left to right, their sequence was 4-2-3-1-3-2-4-4-3-2-1. The visual signal moves from position 4 to 2 to 3, and so on. The beginning and end of the sequence are not designated in any way, so the end of the sequence cycles directly back to the beginning. A typical block of trials contains 6 to 10 cycles of the repeating sequence.

Sequence learning is typically inferred from the reaction time (RT) difference between a block of trials that follows the repeating sequence and an adjacent control block that does not follow the sequence. The control block usually involves stimuli presented at random locations—actually, "pseudorandom" with the constraint that the same position is not immediately repeated (the repeating sequence typically does not have immediate repetitions). Faster RTs to sequence blocks compared to adjacent random blocks is the primary performance measure of SRT learning. SRT learning is often characterized as implicit when subjects' RTs improve with learning, but the subjects demonstrate little explicit knowledge on free recall tasks (Curran & Keele, 1993), recognition tasks (Willingham, Greenley, &

Bardona, 1993), or explicit prediction tasks (i.e., the generate task, Cohen, Ivry, & Keele, 1990; Nissen & Bullemer, 1987; Willingham, Nissen, & Bullemer, 1989). Of course, such claims for learning without awareness have not gone unchallenged (Perruchet & Amorim, 1992; Shanks & St. John, 1994). A complete discussion of the complicated issues surrounding the debate over awareness is beyond the scope of this chapter. However, I will address these issues when they have some bearing on the questions being considered in the chapter.

● **What Is the Format of SRT Learning?**

In the typical SRT paradigm, a one-to-one correspondence exists between stimuli and responses. Thus, the format of the learned representations conceivably could be based on stimulus properties, on response properties, on some form of stimulus-response learning, or on more abstract codes. One approach to studying the format of SRT learning is to test the extent to which sequence knowledge transfers from one mode of responding to another. Keele and colleagues (Keele, Jennings, Jones, Caulton, & Cohen, 1995; see also Cohen et al., 1990) had subjects respond with three fingers or one finger during a learning phase, then half of the subjects switched to the opposite response mode in a transfer phase. Subjects who switched response modes showed as much sequence knowledge in the transfer phase as did subjects who maintained the same response mode in both phases, so sequence knowledge appeared to be represented in a format that was not specific to particular effectors (for a similar result in a slightly different implicit learning paradigm, see Stadler, 1989). When Keele, Jennings, et al. (1995) tried a more dramatic change in response mode—from manual to verbal versus all verbal—the group who switched responses showed only about half as much sequence knowledge as the control group. Imperfect but above-chance transfer of sequence knowledge from manual to verbal responses suggests that the learned representation is neither completely response-based nor completely stimulus-based.

Willingham et al. (1989) reached a similar conclusion—in favor of a format that combines stimulus information with response information—from a different approach. Willingham et al. (Experiment 3) used stimuli that differed along two independent dimensions: four colors and four locations. Subjects learned to map each color onto one of four response keys. For one group of subjects, the stimulus locations followed a repeating sequence, but the colors/responses were random. Group 2 was given random stimulus locations but sequential colors/responses. Because the color/response sequence was learned, but the stimulus location sequence was not learned, Willingham et al. suggested that learning in the standard SRT tasks was unlikely to be purely visuospatial. Although Group 2 learned the sequence of color/responses, this knowledge did not transfer to a standard SRT condition in which responses were based on stimulus location, and the practiced response sequence was maintained. Thus, Group 2 must have acquired information that was not purely response-based. In general, these results suggest that stimulus characteristics as well as response characteristics are critical for learning. One possible format would be a form of stimulus-response learning in which the identity of a stimulus (n) becomes associated with the response to the next stimulus ($n + 1$). This kind of response priming might contribute to the performance improvements that arise from SRT learning.

More recently, Mayr (1996) has found evidence consistent with purely visuospatial learning in a paradigm that was similar to Willingham et al.'s (1989) Experiment 3. Mayr's subjects viewed stimuli that independently varied among four shapes and four locations, and key presses were made according to stimulus shape. Shapes/responses and locations were presented in co-occurring but independent sequences, and learning of each dimension was assessed by reverting to pseudorandom shapes/responses, locations, or both. Subjects were faster when the stimulus conformed to the location sequence than when locations were randomly determined. Subjects were also faster when stimuli conformed to the shape/response sequence than when these attributes were random. Thus, Mayr argued that visuospatial information can be learned independently of response information, and response/shape information can be learned independently of visuospatial information.

Recent research by Schmidtke and Heuer (in press) suggests that learned sequential information can be integrated across different stimulus/response modalities. Subjects practiced spatial/key-press sequences along with tone/foot-press sequences. When the two sequences were synchronized, subjects learned a multimodal combination of both sequences, so SRT learning is not necessarily tied to specific sensory or motor systems.

In summary, behavioral research has provided some useful information about the format of information that is implicitly learned within the SRT task. Although some research has failed to find purely stimulus-based learning (Keele, Jennings, et al., 1995; Willingham et al., 1989), Mayr's (1996) recent findings demonstrate that purely stimulus-based learning is possible.

Purely response-based learning has yet to be identified through behavioral methods. Arguments for stimulus-response based learning may, at first, suggest that SRT learning is a simple form of conditioning in which subjects learn an association between each stimulus location (n) and the next response ($n + 1$). However, research intended to characterize the SRT learning process has demanded more complicated models, so I will turn to a review of this research.

● How Are SRT Sequences Learned?

Research addressing the processes that underlie implicit SRT learning has often examined and/or manipulated the characteristics of learned sequences. First, Cohen et al. (1990) noted that each location in Nissen and Bullemer's (1987) sequence occurred in different pairwise orders within the overall sequence (e.g., 4-2-3-1-3-2-4-3-2-1 can be broken down into the following pairwise transitions: 1-3, 1-4; 2-3, 2-4, 2-1; 3-1, 3-2 [twice]; 4-2, 4-3). A mechanism that only learned pairwise associations between adjacent stimuli would not be very useful because pairwise associations are ambiguous within this sequence (i.e., the identity of stimulus/response n does not uniquely predict the identity of stimulus/response $n + 1$). Thus, the demonstration that subjects can learn sequences with such ambiguous pairwise transitions indicates that implicit sequence learning must be generally dependent upon a mechanism that takes more than just pairwise information into account.

Other investigators have noted characteristics of Nissen and Bullemer's (1987) sequence that might allow for learning mechanisms that use information that is even more rudimentary than pairwise associations (Jackson & Jackson, 1992; Reed & Johnson, 1994; Shanks & St. John, 1994). First, some positions occur more often than others within Nissen and Bullemer's sequence (e.g., 1 twice, 2 thrice, 3 thrice, 4 twice). When compared to a random condition in which each location occurs equally often, subjects might learn to respond faster by using probabilistic event frequency information. That is, by learning that 2 and 3 occur most frequently, priming these responses would speed RT in sequence blocks compared to random blocks. Second, an extension of this logic resurrects the possibility of pairwise learning—probabilistic pairwise learning (e.g., 3-2 is more likely than 3-1, which is more likely than 3-4; Jackson & Jackson, 1992). Demonstrations that subjects can learn such probability information in the absence of a truly repeating sequence (Stadler, 1992) make it important to account for these factors in studies of sequence learning.

The possibility that sequence learning depends exhaustively upon learning event probabilities or pairwise probabilities has been ruled out by demonstrations of implicit learning in which the frequency of individual elements and the frequency of pairwise transitions were equated between sequence and random conditions (Cohen et al., 1990; Reed & Johnson, 1994; Stadler, 1993). Following Reed and Johnson (1994), I will use the term *second-order conditional* (SOC) to refer to sequences in which each element can be predicted only from the identity of at least two previous elements, so pairwise and relative frequency information are insufficient for learning. It is also possible to analytically control for frequency learning and pairwise learning when sequence and control conditions are not properly equated. For example, Curran and Keele (1993) compared sequences like 1-3-2-3-1-4 with a pseudorandom control condition. Learning of individual event frequencies was ruled out by showing that RT to every element was faster than to random stimuli. If subjects only learned that 1 and 3 occurred more frequently than 2 and 4, RTs would have only been faster for positions 1 and 3. As a whole, appropriately designed experiments have suggested that implicit SRT learning can be based on higher-order information (i.e., more than pairwise information), but learning might be attributable to simpler information in experiments that have failed to take these considerations into account.

The exact nature of this higher-order information remains unclear. A number of hypotheses have emphasized related ideas such as grouping, chunking, and hierarchic representation (Cohen et al., 1990; Curran & Keele, 1993; Keele & Curran, 1995; Keele & Jennings, 1992; Servan-Schreiber & Anderson, 1990; Stadler, 1995). Two recurrent connectionist models have been successfully applied to SRT learning (Cleeremans, 1993a; Cleeremans, 1993b; Cleeremans & McClelland, 1991; Keele & Jennings, 1992; for review see Keele & Curran, 1995). Although details differ, both models show how learning can be accomplished by high-order associations between some combination of previous stimuli and the next stimulus and/or response. For example, in learning an SOC sequence like 1-2-1-4-2-3-4-1-3-2-4-3, these networks might learn that 1-2-1 is followed by 4, 2-1-4 is followed by 2, etc. More generally, the hidden-unit representation of each stimulus is shaded by the identity of all preceding stimuli with remote stimuli exerting a lesser influence than immediately prior stimuli (for an

370

excellent discussion of the representations developed by such recurrent networks, see Cleeremans, 1993b). Cleeremans and McClelland (1991) provided empirical evidence that the prediction of each element is influenced by the identity of at least three prior elements.

Questions regarding the nature of the mechanism(s) that underlie implicit sequence learning are further complicated by hypotheses of multiple learning mechanisms. Keele and his colleagues have advocated the idea that different mechanisms may be involved when subjects learn with distraction versus without distraction (Cohen et al., 1990; Curran & Keele, 1993; Keele & Curran, 1995; Keele, Davidson, & Hayes, 1995; Keele & Jennings, 1992). The effects of distraction on sequence learning were first explored by Nissen and Bullemer (1987), whose subjects failed to learn when required to perform a concurrent tone-counting task. Cohen et al. (1990) subsequently found that the effects of distraction interacted with sequence complexity such that a sequence with completely ambiguous first-order associations (e.g., 1-3-2-3-1-2) could not be learned under distraction, but a hybrid sequence (e.g., 1-4-3-1-3-2) with both unique and ambiguous pairwise transitions could be learned under distraction. Cohen et al. noted that hierarchic coding would be especially effective for learning the completely ambiguous sequence. That is, the sequence could be effectively represented by multiple chunks (e.g., 1-3-2 and 3-1-2) with higher-level control of the order in which these chunks are enabled. If learning of the ambiguous sequence was dependent on hierarchic coding, but learning of the hybrid sequence was not, and the hierarchic coding mechanism was disabled by distraction, this could explain the interaction between attention and sequence structure. Thus, Cohen et al. suggested (among other alternatives) that different mechanisms may be involved when learning with versus without distraction.

Despite initial evidence that ambiguous pairwise associations cannot be learned under distraction (Cohen et al., 1990; Nissen & Bullemer, 1987), subsequent studies have found that ambiguous elements of sequences can be learned under distraction (Curran & Keele, 1993; Frensch, Buchner, & Lin, 1994; Keele & Jennings, 1992) and that sequences composed of entirely ambiguous pairwise associations can also be learned under distraction after considerable amounts of training (Reed & Johnson, 1994). Heuer and Schmidtke (1996) have recently found that distraction can have similar effects on learning of unique versus ambiguous associations. Furthermore, Cleeremans and McClelland (1991) showed that Cohen et al.'s interaction between distraction and sequence structure could be simulated by a single serial recurrent network (SRN), when distraction was implemented by adding noise to the hidden-unit input. Thus, Cohen et al.'s results do not computationally demand separate learning mechanisms, and aspects of their results have been contradicted by recent research.

Curran and Keele (1993) subsequently tested some implications of the idea that separate learning mechanisms underlie learning with versus without distraction in a series of experiments that examined the ability of sequence knowledge to transfer to and from conditions of distraction. It was hypothesized that an attentional learning mechanism was only available when subjects were free from distraction, but a distinct nonattentional mechanism was always available. When subjects learned a hybrid sequence under distraction, only nonattentional learning should be operating. When subjects learned without distraction, both mechanisms should be operating. Thus, when one group learned without distraction and another learned with distraction, both groups should show equivalent sequence knowledge in a transfer phase with distraction (Curran & Keele, 1993, Experiment 2). Conversely, a group who learns with distraction should show no additional sequence knowledge when the distraction is removed, because only nonattentional learning was allowed to initially develop (Curran & Keele, 1993, Experiment 3). Cleeremans (1993a) noted that the original Cleeremans and McClelland (1991) model could not account for Curran and Keele's results. Therefore, a *Dual SRN* model included a short-term memory buffer that provided a source of sequence knowledge independent of the serial recurrent network.

Although Curran and Keele's (1993) results were consistent with the idea of separate learning mechanisms, others have expressed doubts about the necessity of separate mechanisms (e.g., Frensch et al., 1994; Heuer & Schmidtke, 1996; Stadler, 1995). For example, Stadler (1995) provided evidence that tone-counting distraction interferes with sequence learning by disrupting grouping processes. Stadler suggested sequences are learned as unique runs (or chunks) of stimuli, and the boundaries of these runs are influenced by extraneous cues (like distracting tones). By his theory, consistent grouping allows a relatively small number of chunks to be frequently encoded. Conversely, inconsistent grouping leads to encoding a large number of inconsistent chunks that are poorly learned due to fewer repetitions. Stadler suggested that transferring to and from conditions (in Curran & Keele, 1993) amounts to changing the organization of the sequence. By this explanation, Curran and Keele's finding that transfer from single to dual task gave equivalent sequence knowledge to learning with distraction throughout would have to be attributable to coincidence or lack of statistical power. However, Stadler's point is well taken—although consistent with distinct learning mechanisms, Curran and Keele's results could conceivably be handled by a single mechanism. It is difficult for purely behavioral research or formal modeling to resolve such issues.

In summary, behavioral research has investigated a number of important, yet unresolved issues, about the psychological mechanisms of sequence learning. First, aspects of sequential knowledge can be response-independent (Keele, Jennings, et al., 1995; Mayr, 1996). Purely stimulus-based learning has been demonstrated (Mayr, 1996), but purely response-based has not (Keele, Jennings, et al., 1995; Willingham et al., 1989). Insofar as we are able to differentiate between brain mechanisms involved in perception, motor control, sensory-motor integration, or more abstract forms of information processing, knowledge of the neural mechanisms of sequence learning can help resolve questions regarding the format of sequence representations. For an example of this logic from another domain, research showing that the visual cortex is critically involved with visual imagery has provided strong evidence for image-based rather than propositional codes underlying mental imagery (Kosslyn, 1994). Second, sequence learning is generally dependent upon a mechanism that is sensitive to more than pairwise association between temporally adjacent stimuli (Cleeremans & McClelland, 1991; Cohen et al., 1990; Reed & Johnson, 1994). This theoretical information can guide the search for neural mechanisms by appealing to other research that has addressed the associative learning capabilities of various brain areas. Furthermore, because our a priori understanding of these associative brain mechanisms remains incomplete, implicit sequence learning provides a useful paradigm for exploring the associative learning capabilities of various brain areas that have been implicated in learning and memory. Third, a primary effect of distraction appears to be the disruption of grouping processes (Schmidtke & Heuer, in press; Stadler, 1995), but it remains unresolved whether this disruption merely varies the effectiveness of a single learning mechanism (Cleeremans & McClelland, 1991; Stadler, 1995) or interferes with one learning mechanism but not another (Cohen et al., 1990; Curran & Keele, 1993; Keele & Curran, 1995; Keele, Davidson, et al., 1995; Keele & Jennings, 1992). The extent to which separable mechanisms underlie sequence learning can clearly be informed by an understanding of the underlying neural substrates.

WHERE ARE THE BRAIN MECHANISMS
OF SEQUENCE LEARNING?

I have previously provided a thorough review of research on the neural mechanisms of sequence learning (Curran, 1995; see also, Helmuth & Ivry, in press). Here I will summarize aspects of this review, describe newer research, and reexamine aspects that are particularly important to the questions outlined above. Research with neuropsychologically impaired patients is easily summarized. Patients with striatal dysfunction attributable to Huntington's disease or Parkinson's disease have typically shown impaired learning on the SRT task (Ferraro, Balota, & Connor, 1993; Jackson, Jackson, Harrison, Henderson, & Kennard, 1995; Knopman & Nissen, 1991; Pascual-Leone et al., 1993; Willingham & Koroshetz, 1993). In contrast, patients with anterograde amnesia have shown apparently normal learning (Nissen & Bullemer, 1987; Nissen, Willingham, & Hartman, 1989; Reber & Squire, 1994). The fact that implicit learning involves the striatum seems beyond dispute (also see neuroimaging results that are reviewed below), so I will not detail the relevant neuropsychological evidence here (for detailed review see Curran, 1995). However, later, I will provide a more detailed description of the existing research with amnesic patients and describe some new results from my own laboratory. First, I will review some recent neuroimaging research that is particularly relevant to questions regarding the format of learned sequential representations.

Neuroimaging Studies of SRT Learning

A number of recent studies have used modern neuroimaging techniques to explore the brain mechanisms of SRT learning—Transcranial Magnetic Stimulation (TMS; Pascual-Leon, Grafman, & Hallet, 1994), event-related brain potentials (ERP; Eimer, Goschke, Schlaghecken, & Stürmer, 1996), Positron Emission Tomography (PET; Grafton, Hazeltine, & Ivry, 1995; Hazeltine, Grafton, & Ivry, 1997; Rauch et al., 1995), and functional magnetic resonance imaging (Rauch et al., in press). I will review these neuroimaging studies and discuss their potential relevance to the theoretical questions outlined previously.

Pascual-Leone et al. (1994) used TMS to map the motor response fields of primary motor cortex before and after various stages of SRT learning. The motor cortex fields expanded in size and amplitude during the early learning blocks but declined back to baseline levels after more extensive practice. All five subjects were able to report the entire sequence at some point between blocks 6 and 9. Pascual-Leone et al. reported that motor-map expansion continued until the subject demonstrated full explicit knowledge. The motor map increases were interpreted as reflecting a motor cortex contribution to implicit learning, whereas the return to baseline was interpreted as a transfer to an explicit state that is presumably controlled by other brain mechanisms.

Stadler (1994) discussed a number of reasons that Pascual-Leone et al.'s (1994) results should be interpreted cautiously. First, subjects were asked if they noticed a repeating sequence after each block. This procedural departure from most SRT studies likely induced subjects to look for sequential regularities and to readily become aware of the sequence. Second, RTs became very fast before explicit knowledge had supposedly formed, and motor maps continued to grow when RTs were under 100 ms. RTs under 100 ms are typically interpreted as indicative of anticipatory responding based on explicit knowledge (Willingham et al., 1989), so this motor cortex expansion likely continued after subjects had actually acquired explicit knowledge. Third, Stadler noted that a purely motor basis for implicit learning is unlikely given behavioral reports that implicit learning transfers across motor effectors (as previously discussed). It is also inconsistent with Mayr's (1996) finding of purely stimulus-based learning. Stadler suggests that Pascual-Leone et al.'s results might be better interpreted as indicating a relationship between motor cortex expansion and explicit sequence learning, but the return to baseline reflected automatization or overlearning. Stadler's criticisms are sound, but recent PET findings of motor cortex activation related to implicit learning are not so easily dismissed.

Grafton et al. (1995; Hazeltine et al., 1997) have recently completed two PET studies of sequence learning that follow similar designs. Grafton et al. (1995) measured regional cerebral blood flow (rCBF) changes while subjects learned sequences with or without distraction (a tone-counting task). Grafton et al. used a six-element sequence with two unique and two ambiguous pairwise associations (called hybrid sequences by Cohen et al., 1990; e.g., 1-3-2-4-2-3 or 1-4-3-2-3-4) that subjects can learn when distracted (Cohen et al., 1990; Curran & Keele, 1993; Frensch et al., 1994). Subjects completed a 17-block phase (84 trials per block) with distraction, followed by another 17-block phase without distraction. Each phase included seven random blocks, followed by eight sequence blocks and then two random blocks; but different sequences were used in the two phases.

In each phase, PET activity was measured during the second, third, and final random blocks, and during the first, fourth, and seventh sequence blocks.

Behaviorally, subjects showed learning effects (RT differences between random and sequence) of about 50 ms when distracted and over 150 ms when not distracted (Grafton et al., 1995). Verbal reports suggested that subjects were predominantly unaware of the sequence when distracted, but 7 of 12 subjects reported awareness of the sequence after the nondistracted phase. Thus, Grafton et al. interpreted rCBF changes during Phase 1 as related to implicit learning under distraction and Phase 2 activity as related to explicit learning.

Evidence for learning-related brain activity was based on brain areas that showed monotonic increases or decreases in rCBF across the three sequence blocks that were scanned. A number of areas showed rCBF increases across the sequence blocks, but the areas associated with dual-task implicit learning did not overlap those associated with explicit learning. Grafton et al. (1995) found learning-related activity in left sensorimotor cortex, left supplementary motor areas, left parietal cortex, and bilateral areas within the putamen (a striatal nucleus of the basal ganglia). Grafton et al. noted that these areas are components of a motor circuit implicated in voluntary movement control (e.g., Alexander, Crutcher, & DeLong, 1990). Because subjects responded exclusively with their right hand, Grafton et al. emphasize that these areas of activation would be consistent with implicit learning being controlled by contralateral motor areas. During explicit learning, Grafton et al. found learning-related activity in right prefrontal, right basal ganglia (nucleus accumbens and/or putamen), and bilateral parieto-occipital areas. Right dorsolateral prefrontal cortex and parietal cortex have been implicated as subserving spatial working memory (Jonides et al., 1993; Wilson, Scalaidhe, & Goldman-Rakic, 1993) and other aspects of longer-term memory retrieval (Buckner & Tulving, 1995; Curran, Schacter, Norman, & Galluccio, 1997; Schacter, Curran, Galluccio, Milberg, & Bates, 1996).

Hazeltine et al. (1997) have completed an interesting extension of Grafton et al.'s (1995) study that is directly relevant to questions about the format of SRT learning. All aspects of the two experiments were identical except that the visual stimuli were different colors appearing in a central location (Hazeltine et al., 1997) rather than identical stimuli appearing at different spatial locations (Grafton et al., 1995). When subjects were distracted, learning-related activity increases were found in left primary motor cortex, left supplementary motor areas, left thalamus, and bilateral parietal areas. These findings are generally consistent with the contralateral motor areas identified by Grafton et al. when spatial sequences were learned.

Under single-task conditions, the results more dramatically differed between color sequences and spatial sequences. For color stimuli, right-lateralized learning-related activity was observed in the inferior frontal lobe, premotor areas, thalamus, temporal lobe, and occipital lobe. Bilateral activity was also observed in anterior portions of the cingulate gyrus. Taken together these results are consistent with a network including inferior prefrontal cortex and temporal cortex that is involved in explicit learning of color stimuli (Hazeltine et al., 1997), but a network involving superior dorsolateral prefrontal and parietal cortex for explicit learning of spatial stimuli (Grafton et al., 1995). Along with the results from conditions with distraction, these studies by Grafton's group indicate that implicit learning largely depends on contralateral motor areas that are stimulus-independent, whereas explicit learning recruits brain areas that are specifically suited to relevant stimulus attributes.

Rauch et al. (1995) used PET to study explicit and implicit sequence learning without distraction. Subjects practiced for three random blocks (144 trials per block), followed by three blocks with a 12-item SOC sequence (1-2-1-4-2-3-4-1-3-2-4-3), followed by another random block. After the random block, subjects were given two tests of explicit knowledge: a free-recall test and a recognition test. Next, explicit learning of the same sequence was examined by (a) informing subjects about the sequence, (b) giving subjects an opportunity to observe three slowly paced repetitions of the sequence, (c) giving subjects a training SRT block with the sequence and error feedback, and (d) giving two additional SRT blocks with the sequence (without error feedback and with instructions to respond as quickly as possible). Finally, the recognition and recall tests were repeated after this explicit learning phase. PET measurements were taken at six different blocks of the experiment: the second random block, the second and third sequence blocks (the implicit learning conditions), the last random block, and the last two explicit learning blocks.

Before describing the results, it is important to note some important methodological differences between our experiment (Rauch et al., 1995) and the studies by Grafton's group (Grafton et al., 1995; Hazeltine et al., 1997). First, Grafton et al. used a hybrid sequence with unequal event frequency and predictive pairwise associations (e.g., 1-3-2-4-2-3), but Rauch et al. used an SOC sequence (1-2-1-4-2-3-4-1-3-2-4-3). Second,

Grafton et al.'s subjects responded only with the right hand, but Rauch et al.'s subjects used the first two fingers of each hand. Third, Grafton et al. compared implicit learning of one sequence under distraction (which limited the development of explicit knowledge) and explicit learning of a difference sequence without distraction. Rauch et al. compared implicit and explicit sequence learning with no distraction tasks, a single sequence, and explicit training of all subjects. Fourth, Grafton's group assessed learning-related activity through monotonic increases or decreases across blocks with the sequence, whereas Rauch et al. used rCBF differences between random and sequence blocks. Finally, Rauch et al. were not able to completely image superior aspects of the brain that Grafton's group found to be related to implicit learning with distraction (sensorimotor cortex, supplementary motor areas, parietal cortex) or explicit learning (Grafton et al.: parieto-occipital cortex, premotor cortex, superior frontal cortex; Hazeltine et al.: premotor cortex, anterior cingulate).

Rauch et al. (1995) found significant learning of the SOC sequence, as indicated by the RT difference between the last implicit sequence block and the last random block. As would be expected, the learning effect was significantly greater in the explicit blocks. The recall and recognition tasks indicated that subjects did not have significant explicit knowledge after the implicit sequence blocks but did have significant sequence knowledge after the explicit blocks. Brain areas associated with implicit sequence learning were assessed by taking the difference between average PET activity in the two implicit sequence blocks and the average activity in the two random blocks. Similarly, for explicit learning, the random activity was subtracted from the average activity in the two explicit blocks.

Activity significantly related to implicit learning was observed in the right basal ganglia (ventral caudate nucleus and/or nucleus accumbens), right premotor, right thalamus, and bilateral visual (extrastriate) cortex. Using functional magnetic resonance imaging, we have recently replicated Rauch et al.'s (1995) findings that implicit SOC sequence learning is related to activity in the striatum, premotor cortex, and extrastriate cortex (Rauch et al., in press). A number of areas were active in the explicit condition: including left inferior frontal (Broadmann's area 45, near Broca's area), right thalamus, right middle temporal cortex, left fusiform cortex, bilateral cerebellum, and right brain stem. Like Grafton et al. (1995), Rauch et al. found little overlap between the areas involved in implicit versus explicit learning, with the exception of the right thalamus, which was active during both conditions in our experiment.

Although it is tempting to develop ad hoc explanations for differences between the findings of Grafton's group and those of Rauch et al. (1995, in press), direct comparisons are dangerous because the studies differ on a number of levels. Some of these differences are more theoretically interesting (e.g., sequence type, response hand, presence or absence of distraction, level of explicit knowledge) than others (different dependent measures: random versus sequences differences in Rauch et al.; monotonic increases or decreases across sequence blocks in Grafton et al., 1995). Systematic manipulation of these factors in future research could advance our understanding of sequence learning. For example, manipulation of distraction under otherwise identical conditions could test the idea that different mechanisms underlie learning with versus without distraction (e.g., Cohen et al., 1990; Curran & Keele, 1993; Keele & Curran, 1995; Keele, Davidson, et al., 1995; Keele & Jennings, 1992). Experiments by Grafton's group have met these conditions except that distraction was confounded with explicit knowledge. Because of these various methodological differences among the existing neuroimaging studies, I will focus on their commonalties.

● Neuroimaging Perspectives on the Format of SRT Representations

All of the aforementioned neuroimaging studies of sequence learning have emphasized brain areas involved with motor control: primary motor (or sensorimotor) cortex, premotor cortex, supplementary motor areas, and the basal ganglia. The finding that motor control areas are involved with learning spatial sequences (Grafton et al., 1995) as well as color sequences (Hazeltine et al., 1997) appears to provide strong evidence that the brain mechanisms of implicit sequence learning are primarily stimulus-independent and likely to be response-based. Such findings seem to contradict previously discussed behavioral studies that have suggested the format of sequence learning is not entirely response-based (as noted by Curran, 1995; Keele, Davidson, et al., 1995; Mayr, 1996; Stadler, 1994). When evaluating neuroimaging research, it must be kept in mind that these methods are essentially correlational. Thus, extant neuroimaging research provides little basis for distinguishing between brain areas that are involved with learning per se versus other brain areas that might be affected by learning but are not causally related to learning. With this caveat in mind, I will discuss a couple of ways in which the neuroimaging and behavioral research might be reconciled (for some other possibilities see Keele, Davidson, et al., 1995). The extent to which these behavioral and neuroimaging findings are truly contradictory depends upon some theoretical understanding of (a) the cognitive processes responsible for sequence learning, and (b) the properties of the motor areas that have been implicated by neuroimaging research.

Theories of sequence learning typically suggest that the learning system would be "trying to learn" during both random and sequence conditions (e.g., Cleeremans & McClelland, 1991; Stadler, 1995). In essence, the learning system extracts regularities among the stimuli/responses in both sequence and random conditions, but more regularities are present in the sequence conditions. With such theories in mind, it is useful to evaluate the potential of extant neuroimaging studies to provide information about such a learning system. Rauch et al. (1995) compared PET activity in random and sequence conditions, but the learning system may be similarly active in both conditions. Similarly, it is not clear if such a learning system would show monotonic increases or decreases with learning, as inferred by Grafton's group.

If activity in the system that is directly responsible for learning does not change across the conditions of these neuroimaging studies, what might the activity differences reflect? Activity could change in areas that use the learned information to improve performance rather than in areas responsible for learning per se. For example, an unidentified learning system may extract sequential regularities and feed this information to other brain areas that are responsible for advanced response preparation. Evidence for such advance response preparation has been provided by a study of SRT learning that measured ERPs (Eimer et al., 1996). An ERP component named the lateralized readiness potential (LRP) provides information about the timing of response preparation. The latency of the LRP was decreased as the amount of practice with a repeating sequence increased. Thus, response preparation became faster as subjects learned the sequence. Activation of motor cortical areas in PET studies may reflect this advance response preparation.

Each of the motor areas implicated by PET is involved with movement preparation as well as movement execution. Neurophysiological studies have shown that neurons in these areas fire before response execution when a monkey has some foreknowledge of an upcoming response and is merely waiting for a signal to respond: primary motor cortex (Georgopoulos, Kalaska, Caminiti, & Massey, 1984), premotor cortex (Mitz, Godschalk & Wise, 1991; Riehle & Requin, 1989), supplementary motor areas (Alexander & Crutcher, 1990b), and basal ganglia (e.g., putamen; Alexander & Crutcher, 1990b). Thus, PET activity in these areas should be increased in a condition with foreknowledge of the ensuing response that allows for preparatory responding (i.e., SRT conditions with a learned sequence) compared to a condition without such foreknowledge (i.e., random SRT conditions, or sequence conditions early in learning). By this view, some learning-related motor cortical activity may reflect a kind of priming in which motor areas receive a downstream influence from other brain areas.

If activation of motor areas represents response preparation rather than the activity of learning systems per se, this could account for behavioral evidence of response-independent learning. The learning system may represent sequences in a response-independent format and then feed the information to response systems that are required for the particular task. It should be noted that some level of response independence is still possible within the implicated motor areas. Contemporary understanding of these motor areas suggests that they operate at a somewhat abstract level. For example, Alexander and Crutcher (1990a; 1990b) have found that activity in a high proportion of neurons on the primary motor cortex, supplementary motor area, and putamen (of the basal ganglia) was related to movement direction but was independent of the actual muscles used to execute the movement. These particular studies compared identical movement directions that were accomplished by either flexing or extending the wrist (in monkeys). Relevant human evidence comes from a PET study of sequential visuospatial tracking that compared tracking movements made with the index finger, tongue, and toe (Grafton, Mazziotta, Woods, & Phelps, 1992). Although Grafton et al. (1992) found that activity in the primary motor cortex varied across effectors, activity in supplementary motor areas and parietal cortex did not. It seems conceivable that a similar level of muscle independence would exist between finger movements and arm movements (e.g., Keele, Jennings, et al., 1995, Experiments 1 & 2), but movement independence might not extend to radically different response systems such as between finger movements and verbal responses (e.g., Keele, Jennings, et al., 1995, Experiment 3). Thus, the involvement of these motor cortical areas may explain why learning transfers from finger movements to arm movements, more than from finger movements to verbal responses (Keele, Jennings, et al., 1995).

Despite the predominance of activity in areas classically related to motor control, learning-related activity in a number of nonmotor regions has been observed, such as visual (extrastriate, Rauch et al., 1995) and parietal cortex (Grafton et al., 1995; Hazeltine et al., 1997).[1] Grafton's group has also found learning-related decreases in the activity of various temporal lobe areas as well as the hippocampus. Memory-related decreases in visual cortex activity have been observed in stem-completion priming (Buckner et al., 1995; Squire et al., 1992), and decreases in temporal lobe activity have been observed in an auditory sentence-recognition task (Tulving, Kapur, et al., 1994). Such learning-related decreases in activity are entirely consistent with proceduralist views of memory, by which memory reflects a modification of information-processing systems (e.g., Kolers & Roediger, 1984). Thus, decreased PET activity may reflect a kind of priming whereby these information-processing systems in visual and temporal cortex do not need to work as hard to process repeated information (e.g., repeated sequences).

Keele, Davidson, et al. (1995) have considered the idea that activation of motor areas in PET studies reflects advanced response preparation (as discussed above), and they noted that this sort of response priming, if present under conditions of implicit learning, should also be present under conditions when sequence knowledge is explicitly available. Contrary evidence has been provided by the PET studies of SRT learning that have found virtually no overlap between activity related to implicit versus explicit learning (Grafton et al., 1995; Hazeltine et al., 1997; Rauch et al., 1995). Pascual-Leone et al. (1994) interpreted their results as showing that expansion of primary motor-cortex maps was limited to implicit learning, not explicit learning. However, as discussed previously, Stadler (1994) has offered reasonable arguments for the idea that motor cortex expansion was actually related to explicit learning in Pascual-Leone et al.'s experiment. Other explicit sequence-learning paradigms that have not used the SRT task have also found that the primary motor cortex changes with learning (Karni et al., 1995).

The particular question of how advanced response preparation could be observed for implicit but not explicit learning is pertinent to more general issues about the independence of implicit and explicit learning. Some cognitive research has advanced the idea that implicit and explicit learning operate independently (e.g., Curran & Keele, 1993). Thus, during explicit learning, the systems responsible for implicit learning should still be active. However, most of the previously reviewed neuroimaging results have found no overlap between the active areas in implicit and explicit conditions (compared with baseline conditions). As discussed by Hazeltine et al.

(1997), global blood flow remains stable across conditions because of standard normalization procedures, so activation increases in areas uniquely associated with explicit learning may obscure detection of significant activity in areas related to implicit learning.

In summary, neuroimaging experiments have identified a number of brain areas that are correlated with implicit SRT learning. Although areas related to movement control have been observed most consistently (primary motor cortex, premotor cortex, supplementary motor areas, basal ganglia), other, more perceptually oriented areas have also shown learning-related activity (extrastriate cortex, parietal cortex, temporal cortex, hippocampus). Behavioral evidence for response-independent learning could be reconciled with learning-related activation of motor brain areas if motor area activity reflects advanced response preparation. Motor response preparation may draw upon information from other brain mechanisms that are directly responsible for learning and that represent sequential information in a response-independent manner. In the next section, I speculate about the identity of this learning mechanism.

● Is SRT Learning "Normal" in Patients With Amnesia?

Neuroimaging results and studies of patients with Parkinson's disease or Huntington's disease converge on the conclusion that the basal ganglia are critically involved in implicit sequence learning. What about the relationship between the neuroimaging results and studies with amnesic patients? It is commonly understood that amnesic patients can learn SRT sequences normally (Nissen & Bullemer, 1987; Nissen et al., 1989; Reber & Squire, 1994), and neuroimaging studies have not emphasized learning-related brain areas that are related to amnesia. However, in what follows, I will argue that the sequence-learning capabilities of patients with amnesia remain an open question, so first I will point out a few relevant aspects of the neuroimaging results. First, Grafton et al. (1995) reported that right hippocampal activity decreased with learning. Although a learning-related decrease in hippocampal activity may at first seem paradoxical, it is entirely consistent with other evidence that hippocampal activity is related to the novelty of a stimulus (Stern et al., 1996; Tulving, Markowitsch, Kapur, Habib, & Houle, 1994), insofar as the novelty of a sequence decreases as it is learned. Another brain area that is specifically affected by Korsakoff's amnesia (the etiology of most amnesic patients who have been tested on the SRT task) is the thalamus, and learning-related increases in thalamic activity have been reported (Hazeltine et al., 1997; Rauch et al., 1995). Of course, the thalamus subserves a number of nonmemory functions and interacts extensively with the basal ganglia and other motor areas implicated in sequence learning, and PET does not have sufficient resolution to distinguish between different thalamic nuclei, so thalamic activity provides very weak evidence for a relationship to human amnesia. In general, however, aspects of the extant neuroimaging results are consistent with the idea that medial temporal (e.g., hippocampus) and diencephalic (e.g., thalamus) brain areas damaged in amnesic patients contribute to implicit sequence learning. Furthermore, as previously discussed, brain areas implicated by neuroimaging studies may reflect aspects of response preparation more than of learning per se, so systems directly responsible for learning might not have been identified in these studies.

The previous discussion of recent neuroimaging results exemplified how a knowledge of underlying brain mechanisms can provide information that is relevant to psychological questions about the format of sequential representations. In my discussion of sequence learning in patients with amnesia, the cross-fertilization between psychology and neuroscience flows in somewhat the opposite direction. In this case, our psychological understanding of SRT learning can be used to understand the nature of the learning deficit that is exhibited by amnesic patients—which may, in turn, advance our understanding of the general functions that are subserved by brain areas that are typically injured in cases of amnesia: the medial temporal lobe (e.g., hippocampus, parahippocampal gyrus) and the diencephalon.

Research on the neural mechanisms of sequence learning has primarily been approached from a perspective that is similar to Mishkin's influential distinction between memories and habits (Mishkin & Appenzeller, 1987; Mishkin, Malamut, & Bachevalier, 1984; Mishkin & Petri, 1984). A habit "is noncognitive: it is founded not on knowledge or even on memories (in the sense of independent mental entities) but on automatic connections between a stimulus and a response" (Mishkin & Appenzeller, 1987, p. 89). Mishkin and colleagues hypothesized that the striatum is the likely neural substrate of habit learning. In contrast, more cognitive forms of memory— which would more likely be accompanied by a greater awareness of what is learned—are critically dependent on medial temporal lobe structures (interacting with various cortical information-processing areas). The striatum has also been implicated as critical for skill learning (Gabrieli, 1994; Squire, 1992; Willingham, 1992), which may be similar to habit learning.

Neuropsychological research on SRT learning seems to fit nicely with the perspective that SRT learning is an example of habit or skill learning (Gabrieli, 1994; Squire, 1992; Willingham, 1992). SRT learning is typically considered to be spared in amnesic patients with medial temporal and/or diencephalic brain damage, but impaired in patients with striatal damage. However, the characterization of SRT learning in terms of habits or skills seems murky at a couple of levels. First, previously discussed behavioral evidence clearly shows that SRT learning involves more than first-order stimulus-response learning, so SRT learning does not neatly map onto Mishkin's ideas about habit learning. Second, although a clear definition of skill learning is difficult to find, it is not clear that SRT learning should be classified as skill learning (see also, Moscovitch, Vriezen, & Goshen-Gottstein, 1993). Most SRT researchers seem to have adopted a common-sense analogy between skill learning and SRT learning. For example, piano playing is easily classified as a skill, and like SRT learning, piano playing involves learning key-press sequences (e.g., Keele & Curran, 1995). However, the analogy becomes strained when two different aspects of piano playing are considered: learning a specific sequence of key presses (i.e., a song) versus learning more general aspects of piano playing (i.e., the mapping between keys and notes, proper cadence, etc.). As a child, I could play the main chorus of "Noel" on the piano but could play nothing else, so I would not meet most people's definition of a skilled piano player. As I learned to play only one specific song, most participants in an SRT experiment learn only a specific sequence. SRT participants may also learn general aspects of SRT performance, such as the stimulus-response mapping, but such nonspecific aspects of learning are typically removed by subtracting sequence performance from random performance.

Outside the domain of SRT research, more attention has been paid to the distinction between general versus specific aspects of skill learning. For example in a study of mirror reading, Cohen and Squire (1980) had subjects read word triads (e.g., BEDRAGGLE-CAPRICIOUS-GRANDIOSE) that were presented as mirror reflections. With practice, subjects specifically became faster at reading these same triads. However, subjects also became faster at reading new triads over the course of practice—reflecting general learning of a mirror-reading skill. Cohen and Squire found that amnesic patients learned the nonspecific skill as well as control subjects, but amnesic patients' improvement on specifically repeated words was less than control subjects' improvement. Whereas amnesic patients appear to learn the general skill of mirror reading normally, patients with Huntington's disease show normal item-specific learning, but impaired learning of the general mirror-reading skill (Martone, Butters, Payne, Becker, & Sax, 1984). Rotary pursuit provides another example of a skill-learning task that seems best characterized as nonspecific. Patients with Huntington's disease are impaired on rotary pursuit learning (Heindel, Butters, & Salmon, 1988; Heindel, Salmon, Shults, Walicke, & Butters, 1989), but amnesic patients perform relatively normally (Brooks & Baddeley, 1976; Cermak, Lewis, Butters, & Goodglass, 1973; Corkin, 1968).

In general, evidence for normal skill learning in amnesic patients and impaired skill learning in Huntington's patients seems to correspond best with general aspects of skill learning. Subjects may or may not learn such general skills in the SRT paradigm, but it is clear that they do learn information about specific sequences (for similar doubts about the classification of SRT learning as procedural, see Moscovitch et al., 1993). Of course, another reason that a person with amnesia would be expected to learn normally on the SRT task is that SRT learning can be implicit. Patients with anterograde amnesia appear to perform normally on most tests of implicit learning and implicit memory (Moscovitch et al., 1993; Schacter, Chiu, & Ochsner, 1993), so the suggestion that implicit sequence learning is normal in amnesic patients is accompanied by little surprise or debate (although the relevance of learning by amnesic patients to questions about awareness of the learned information is debatable, Reber & Squire, 1994; Shanks & St. John, 1994). However, SRT learning may be different from other implicit learning tasks in theoretically important respects. As Curran and Schacter (1997) recently discussed, amnesic patients often show deficits on implicit tasks that include an associative component (see also Bowers & Schacter, 1993; Cohen, Poldrack, & Eichenbaum, in press).

Many theories of the contribution of the hippocampus, medial temporal lobe, and related structures (areas often damaged in amnesic patients) to learning and memory emphasize aspects of higher-order associative learning (Cohen & Eichenbaum, 1993; Gluck & Myers, 1993; Mayes, Meudell, & Pickering, 1985; McClelland, McNaughton, & O'Reilly, 1995; Sutherland & Rudy, 1989; Wicklegren, 1979). Although the details of these theories differ considerably, they all generally hold that the brain areas damaged in amnesia are involved in a form of associative learning that is more complex than the kind of pairwise associative learning that underlies phenomena such as first-order conditioning. Such theories seem more promising than trying to cleanly delineate the learning ability of amnesic patients by classifying tasks as implicit or skill learning. Given the theoretical significance of understanding the associative learning ability of amnesic patients and the previously discussed evidence that SRT learning involves more than pairwise associative learning, the SRT learning ability of amnesic patients is of considerable interest.

Three published studies have investigated the sequence-learning ability of patients with anterograde amnesia (Nissen & Bullemer, 1987; Nissen et al., 1989; Reber & Squire, 1994). Nissen and Bullemer found a group by condition interaction, suggesting that the learning effect was greater for control subjects than for patients with amnesia attributable to Korsakoff's syndrome. In contrast, Nissen et al. (1989) found that the learning of Korsakoff's patients did not significantly differ from that of control subjects and also found that both groups showed similar retention of sequence knowledge after a 1-week delay. Interpretation of both of these studies is clouded by three factors. First, control subjects consistently showed more explicit knowledge of the sequence than did amnesic subjects (assessed by verbal reports). Thus, for example, the group difference in Nissen and Bullemer's original study might be attributable to control subjects' superior explicit knowledge because explicit knowledge typically increases SRT learning effects (e.g., Curran & Keele, 1993; Willingham et al., 1989; for contrary evidence see Reber & Squire, 1994). Second, Korsakoff's patients were consistently slower than control subjects, so the learning effects shown by these patients might be artifactually inflated (for an explanation of how RT differences can be inflated by overall slowness, see Chapman, Chapman, Curran, & Miller, 1994). Third, it is possible that amnesic subjects could have learned only lower-order aspects of Nissen and Bullemer's sequence (e.g., unequal probabilities of individual or pairwise elements). Thus, these studies do not unambiguously indicate whether or not SRT learning can be classified as "normal" in patients with Korsakoff's amnesia.

Reber and Squire (1994) subsequently performed two SRT experiments with amnesic patients that were primarily designed to include more stringent measures of explicit knowledge. In three separate sessions (Experiments 1a, 1b, and 2), amnesic patients showed SRT learning effects that were not significantly different from control subjects. Various measures of explicit memory showed that control subjects demonstrated explicit (or declarative, in Reber and Squire's parlance) knowledge of the repeating sequence, but that amnesic subjects did not. These results were interpreted as showing that sequential information can be learned in the absence of awareness of what is learned (i.e., implicitly), and that implicit and explicit learning are dependent on parallel brain systems. In addition to their careful assessment of explicit knowledge, Reber and Squire's experiments provide two other advances over previous research. First, amnesic subjects were not significantly slower than control subjects, so learning effects can be validly compared between groups. Second, Reber and Squire not only replicated amnesic learning of a 10-item sequence like those used in previous studies with amnesic patients (Nissen & Bullemer, 1987; Nissen et al., 1989; Reber & Squire, 1994) but also demonstrated that amnesic patients could learn a 12-item SOC sequence that cannot be entirely learned through first-order associations or through relative frequency of occurrence (2-3-4-2-1-4-1-3-1-2-4-3).

Reber and Squire's (1994) Experiment 2 clearly suggests that their amnesic patients were able to learn the SOC sequence, so the ability of these patients to learn higher-order associations might be considered to be normal. However, questions remain. Why did Nissen and Bullemer's (1987) amnesic patients show less learning than control subjects? Why did Reber and Squire's patients show learning effects that were smaller than those of control subjects (although not significantly different)? Given the importance of the question of higher-order associative learning in amnesia, I decided to reexamine the sequence-learning ability of amnesic patients (Curran, 1997).

Ten subjects with amnesia attributable to diverse etiologies were trained with an SOC sequence (1-2-1-4-2-3-4-1-3-2-4-3) in a modified SRT procedure (similar to Stadler, 1993). Rather than separate blocks of sequence and random trials, each block of 120 trials included a mixture of sequence and random cycles arranged as R-S-S-R-S-S-R-S-S-R (where R denotes 12 random trials and S denotes one cycle of the 12-element sequence). This design holds a number of advantages over between-block designs. First, mixing random and sequence cycles should obscure the presence of the sequence, so subjects are less likely to explicitly identify it. Second, a within-subjects measure of learning can be obtained in each block rather than only measuring learning near the end of training. The third advantage is directly related to the assessment of higher-order associative learning. Learning can be assessed while controlling for lower-order (pairwise and positional frequency) information by comparing the RT for each pairwise transition between the random and sequence conditions. That is, if subjects are faster responding to the pair (e.g., 1-2) in the sequence than to the same pair within a random cycle, the subject must have learned something other than the information within this pair to speed performance. Such an analysis of pairwise differences between random and sequence conditions is typically impossible in designs that only include a single random block because there is not enough data in the random condition.

The results of this experiment replicated Reber and Squire's (1994) finding that overall RT differences between random and sequence trials did not differ between amnesic patients and control subjects (Figure 11.1a). However, the analysis of pairwise differences suggested that amnesic subjects did not learn as much higher-order information as control subjects (Figure 11.1b). For example, Figure 11.1b shows that control subjects were 40 ms faster responding to the first occurrence of position C in the sequence (A-B-A-D-B-C . . .) than they were responding to the pair B-C in random conditions. Thus, subjects must have learned more than a pairwise relationship between B-C because pairwise information is equated between random and sequence conditions. Subjects must have learned at least second-order associations (e.g., D-B-C) to increase their speed in the sequence condition. Although the interaction between this measure of higher-order learning and group was not significant, an amnesic deficit was suggested by two other results. First, when groups were examined separately, control subjects but not amnesic patients showed a significant difference between sequence and random pairwise transitions. Second, individual *t* tests examined the difference between random and sequence for each sequence position separately. For control subjects these differences were significant for six positions, but only for three positions in amnesic patients. These effects are unlikely to be attributable to explicit knowledge because amnesic patients and control subjects did not differ on tests of explicit sequence recognition (and neither group differed from chance).[2]

Although these data are suggestive of an amnesic deficit in learning higher-order associations, the statistical support for this conclusion is not strong. However, any claim that amnesic patients show normal SRT learning also rests on shaky ground—failing to reject the null hypothesis with small sample sizes. As a whole, the sequence-learning ability of amnesic subjects remains an open question at least.

If one accepts the conclusion that amnesic patients show impairments in higher-order learning in the SRT task, it is important to clarify the implications of this result. First, this conclusion should not be taken as support for the claim that SRT learning is not truly implicit. As others have noted (e.g., Ostergaard & Jernigan, 1993), when control subjects outperform amnesic patients on nominally implicit tasks, it is sometimes claimed that performance was "contaminated" by explicit memory in the controls. Such an interpretation depends on the assumption that implicit learning or

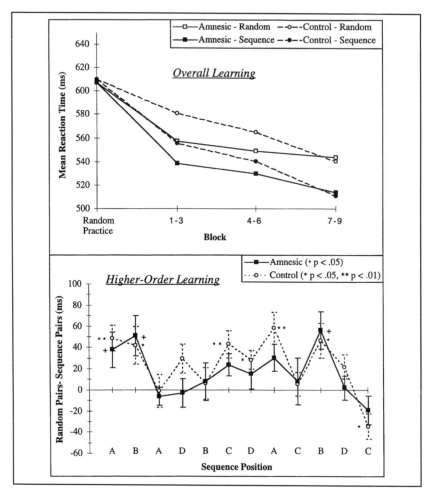

Figure 11.1. Top Panel (A): Overall learning is shown by plotting the mean of subjects' median reaction times in each condition. After a random practice block, there were nine blocks of intermixed random and sequence cycles; each set of three blocks are averaged together. Bottom Panel (B): Higher-order learning is shown by taking the mean reaction time difference between each sequence element and all random trials that followed the equivalent pairwise transition (e.g., the second points represent the reaction time difference between the second element of the sequence and all random trials in which B was preceded by A).

NOTE: Results in Figure 11.1b are collapsed across all nine training blocks. T tests were performed to determine which points were significantly different from zero (amnesic patients: $+p < .05$; control subjects: $*p < .05$. $**p < .01$).

memory is spared in amnesic patients, so group differences must be attributable to explicit learning or memory (which is impaired in amnesic patients). This reasoning can become circular when normal amnesic performance is taken as evidence that implicit learning or memory is spared, but impaired performance is taken as evidence for explicit contamination. Rather than using group differences as an indication of explicit knowledge, I used separate measures of explicit sequence recognition and found no evidence for significant explicit knowledge in either group.[3] Thus, learning was implicit, but amnesic patients learned less higher-order information than control subjects.

Although it is generally accepted that amnesic patients perform normally on implicit tasks (Moscovitch et al., 1993; Schacter et al., 1993), this may not be true in every case. Within the domain of implicit memory in priming tasks, there has been some recent controversy about the claim that priming is normal in amnesic patients (for the view that priming is typically normal in amnesic patients: Hamann, Squire, & Schacter, 1995; Squire, Hamann, & Schacter, 1996; against the view that priming is typically normal in amnesic patients: Ostergaard, 1994; Ostergaard & Jernigan, 1993, 1996). Sweeping generalities for either extreme position are probably unwarranted, but as previously noted, amnesic patients do exhibit impairments on nominally implicit tasks that include an associative component (Bowers & Schacter, 1993; Cohen et al., 1997; Curran & Schacter, 1997). A higher-order associative learning deficit in the SRT task would be consistent with this other evidence. Theoretically, this leads to the view that the medial temporal lobes and/or diencephalon may be necessary for explicit learning and memory, but these structures may also play a role in associative forms of implicit learning and memory. The associative nature of explicit learning and memory is well-known (e.g., Anderson & Bower, 1973). A perspective by which the functional contribution of the medial temporal lobe and/or diencephalon is related to higher-order associative learning, rather than awareness of the learned information per se, fits well with other theories (Cohen & Eichenbaum, 1993; Gluck & Myers, 1993; Mayes et al., 1985; McClelland et al., 1995; Sutherland & Rudy, 1989; Wicklegren, 1979). Higher-order associative representations may be necessary, but not sufficient, for the information to be consciously accessible. Because the majority of implicit learning and memory tasks are not associative, it makes sense that amnesics have typically shown normal performance on such tasks.

Returning more specifically to the SRT paradigm, it is notable that the level of theoretical development—although incomplete, as reviewed above—is rather advanced compared to many implicit tasks in which amnesic learning and memory have been addressed (for discussion of these theoretical gaps, see Hintzman, 1990; Ratcliff & McKoon, 1996). Behavioral research and formal modeling have shown that SRT learning depends on higher-order associative representations. My recent results with amnesic patients suggest a deficit that is specific to higher-order associative learning.

SUMMARY AND CONCLUSIONS

I have discussed the relationship between cognitive/behavioral and neuroscientific research on implicit sequence learning with the SRT task with two primary questions in mind: (a) What is the format of the learned sequential representations? and (b) How is SRT learning accomplished? First, behavioral research suggests that SRT learning may have stimulus-based as well as response-based components, and this has been upheld by a number of neuroimaging experiments implicating motor (primary motor cortex, premotor cortex, supplementary motor areas, and the basal ganglia) as well as nonmotor (extrastriate cortex, parietal cortex, temporal lobe) areas.

I have argued that activity in motor areas could reflect advanced response preparation rather than learning per se. Given converging neuropsychological and neuroimaging results, the basal ganglia seem especially critical for implicit sequence learning, but their functional role still remains elusive. At a general level, a number of researchers have suggested that the basal ganglia act as somewhat of an intermediary between brain areas that store sequential knowledge and others controlling behavior (for review see, Curran, 1995; Helmuth & Ivry, in press). According to Keele, Davidson, et al. (1995), for example, the basal ganglia coordinate selection among different sequence chunks stored in posterior perceptual areas (such as extrastriate, parietal, and temporal cortices) in a manner that allows the appropriate sequence chunk to be prepared and/or implemented by motor cortical areas.

Consideration of the second question—How are SRT sequences learned?—has led me to a somewhat unconventional view of where these sequence chunks are actually learned. Behavioral research and computational modeling have suggested that sequence learning must rely on higher-order associations (or chunks). My recent experiment with amnesic patients suggests that their ability to learn such higher-order chunks is impaired. Therefore, I have argued that medial temporal lobe areas may play a critical role in learning higher-order associations. By this view, medial temporal lobe regions are necessary for learning sequence chunks that are selected by the basal ganglia and used by motor cortical areas in order to prepare for an ensuing response.

NOTES

1. It should be noted that some theorists argue that parietal activity is directly related to movement control (e.g., Anderson, 1994; Goodale, 1993), so parietal activity is not necessarily response independent.

2. I also examine learning of a second sequence with more complicated structural characteristics (Curran, 1997b). For this sequence, both groups learned very little higher-order information, so no between-groups differences were observed.

3. Elsewhere, I have shown that the recognition measures used to test explicit knowledge in amnesic patients and their control subjects are sensitive to differences in explicit knowledge (Curran, 1997a).

REFERENCES

Alexander, G. E., & Crutcher, M. D. (1990a). Neuronal representations of the target (goal) of visually guided arm movements in three motor areas of the monkey. *Journal of Neurophysiology, 64,* 164-178.

Alexander, G. E., & Crutcher, M. D. (1990b). Preparation for movement: Neuronal representations of intended direction in three motor areas of the monkey. *Journal of Neurophysiology, 64,* 133-150.

Alexander, G. E., Crutcher, M. D., & DeLong, M. R. (1990). Basal ganglia thalamo-cortical circuits: Parallel substrates for motor control, oculomotor, "prefrontal" and "limbic" functions. *Progress in Brain Research, 85,* 119-146.

Anderson, J. A., & Bower, G. H. (1973). *Human associative memory.* Washington DC: V. H. Winston.

Anderson, R. A. (1994). Coordinate transformations and motor planning in posterior parietal cortex. In M. S. Gazzaniga (Ed.), *The cognitive neurosciences* (pp. 519-532). Cambridge: MIT Press.

Bowers, J., & Schacter, D. L. (1993). Priming of novel information in amnesic patients: Issues and data. In P. Graf & M. Masson (Eds.), *Implicit memory:*

New directions in cognition, development, and neuropsychology (pp. 303-326). Hillsdale, NJ: Lawrence Erlbaum.

Brooks, L., & Baddeley, A. D. (1976). What can amnesic patients learn? *Neuropsychologia, 14,* 111-122.

Buckner, R. L., Peterson, S. E., Ojeman, J. G., Miezin, F. M., Squire, L. R., & Raichle, M. E. (1995). Functional anatomical studies of explicit and implicit memory retrieval tasks. *The Journal of Neuroscience, 15,* 12-29.

Buckner, R. L., & Tulving, E. (1995). Neuroimaging studies of memory: Theory and recent PET results. In F. Boller & J. Grafman (Eds.), *Handbook of neuropsychology* (Vol. 10, pp. 439-466). Amsterdam: Elsevier.

Cermak, L. S., Lewis, R., Butters, N., & Goodglass, H. (1973). Role of verbal mediation in performance of motor tasks by Korsakoff's patients. *Perceptual and Motor Skills, 37,* 259-263.

Chapman, L. J., Chapman, J. P., Curran, T., & Miller, M. B. (1994). Do children and the elderly show heightened semantic priming? How to answer the question. *Developmental Review, 14,* 159-185.

Cleeremans, A. (1993a). *Attention and awareness in sequence learning.* Paper presented at the Proceedings of the 15th Annual Conference of the Cognitive Science Society, University of Boulder, Colorado.

Cleeremans, A. (1993b). *Mechanisms of implicit learning: Connectionist models of sequence processing.* Cambridge: MIT Press.

Cleeremans, A., & McClelland, J. L. (1991). Learning the structure of event sequences. *Journal of Experimental Psychology: General, 120,* 235-253.

Cohen, A., Ivry, R. I., & Keele, S. W. (1990). Attention and structure in sequence learning. *Journal of Experimental Psychology: Learning, Memory, and, Cognition, 16,* 17-30.

Cohen, N. J., & Eichenbaum, H. (1993). *Memory, amnesia, and the hippocampal system.* Cambridge: MIT Press.

Cohen, N. J., Poldrack, R. A., & Eichenbaum, H. (1997). Memory for items and memory for relations in the procedural/declarative memory framework. *Memory, 5,* 131-178.

Cohen, N. J., & Squire, L. R. (1980). Preserved learning and retention of pattern analyzing skill in amnesia: Dissociation of "knowing how" and "knowing that." *Science, 210,* 207-209.

Corkin, S. (1968). Acquisition of motor skill after bilateral medial temporal lobe excision. *Neuropsychologia, 6,* 255-265.

Curran, T. (1995). On the neural mechanisms of sequence learning. *Psyche* [On-line serial], 2(12). Available at URL:http://psyche.cs.monash.edu.au/volume2-1/psyche-95-2-12-sequence-1-curran.html.

Curran, T. (1997a). Effects of aging on implicit sequence learning: Accounting for sequence structure and explicit knowledge. *Psychological Research/Psychologische Forschung, 60,* 24-41.

Curran, T. (1997b). Higher-order associative learning in amnesia: Evidence from the serial reaction time task. *Journal of Cognitive Neuroscience, 9,* 522-533.

Curran, T., & Keele, S. W. (1993). Attentional and nonattentional forms of sequence learning. *Journal of Experimental Psychology: Learning, Memory, and Cognition, 19,* 189-202.

Curran, T., & Schacter, D. L. (1997). Implicit memory: What must theories of amnesia explain? *Memory, 5,* 37-47.

Curran, T., Schacter, D. L., Norman, K. A., & Galluccio, L. (1997). False recognition after a right frontal lobe infarction: Memory for general and specific information. *Neuropsychologia, 35,* 1035-1049.

Eimer, M., Goschke, T., Schlaghecken, F., & Stürmer, B. (1996). Explicit and implicit learning of event sequences: Evidence from event-related brain potentials. *Journal of Experimental Psychology: Learning, Memory, and Cognition, 22,* 970-987.

Ferraro, F. R., Balota, D. A., & Connor, L. T. (1993). Implicit memory and the formation of new associations in nondemented Parkinson's disease individuals and individuals with senile dementia of the Alzheimer type: A serial reaction time (SRT) investigation. *Brain and Cognition, 21,* 163-180.

Frensch, P. A., Buchner, A., & Lin, J. (1994). Implicit learning of unique and ambiguous serial transactions in the presence and absence of a distractor task. *Journal of Experimental Psychology: Learning, Memory, and Cognition, 20,* 567-584.

Gabrieli, J. (1994). Contributions of the basal ganglia to skill learning and working memory in humans. In J. Houk, J. L. Davis, & D. G. Beiser (Eds.), *Information processing in the basal ganglia* (pp. 277-294). Cambridge: MIT Press.

Georgopoulos, A. P., Kalaska, J. F., Caminiti, R., & Massey, J. T. (1984). The representation of movement direction in the motor cortex. In G. M. Edelman, W. M. Cowan, & W. E. Gall (Eds.), *Dynamic aspects of neocortical function* (pp. 501-524). New York: John Wiley.

Gluck, M. A., & Myers, C. E. (1993). Hippocampal mediation of stimulus representation: A computational theory. *Hippocampus, 3,* 491-516.

Goodale, M. A. (1993). Visual pathways supporting perception and action in the primate cerebral cortex. *Current Opinion in Neurobiology, 3,* 578-585.

Grafton, S. T., Hazeltine, E., & Ivry, R. (1995). Functional mapping of sequence learning in normal humans. *Journal of Cognitive Neuroscience, 7,* 497-510.

Grafton, S. T., Mazziotta, J. C., Woods, R. P., & Phelps, M. E. (1992). Human functional anatomy of visually guided finger movements. *Brain, 115,* 565-587.

Hamann, S. B., Squire, L. R., & Schacter, D. L. (1995). Perceptual thresholds and priming in amnesia. *Neuropsychology, 9,* 3-15.

Hazeltine, E., Grafton, S. T., & Ivry, R. (1997). Attention and stimulus characteristics determined the locus of motor sequence encoding: A PET study. *Brain, 120,* 123-140.

Heindel, W. C., Butters, N., & Salmon, D. P. (1988). Impaired learning of a motor skill in patients with Huntington's disease. *Behavioral Neuroscience, 102,* 141-147.

Heindel, W. C., Salmon, D. P., Shults, C. W., Walicke, P. A., & Butters, N. (1989). Neuropsychological evidence for multiple implicit memory systems: A comparison of Alzheimer's, Huntington's, and Parkinson's disease patients. *Journal of Neuroscience, 9,* 582-587.

Helmuth, L., & Ivry, R. B. (in press). Sequential movements. In M. Jahanshahi & R. Brown (Eds.), *The neuropsychology of movement disorders.* Amsterdam: Elsevier Science.

Heuer, H., & Schmidtke, V. (1996). Secondary-task effects on sequence learning. *Psychological Research/Psychologische Forschung, 59,* 119-133.

Hintzman, D. L. (1990). Human learning and memory: Connections and dissociations. *Annual Review of Psychology, 41,* 109-139.

Jackson, G., & Jackson, S. (1992). *Sequence structure and sequential learning: The evidence from ageing reconsidered* (Technical Report 92-9). Eugene: Institute of Cognitive and Decision Sciences, University of Oregon.

Jackson, G. M., Jackson, S. R., Harrison, J., Henderson, L., & Kennard, C. (1995). Serial reaction time learning and Parkinson's disease: Evidence for a procedural learning deficit. *Neuropsychologia, 33,* 577-593.

Jonides, J., Smith, E. E., Koeppe, R. A., Awh, E., Minoshima, S., & Mintun, M. A. (1993). Spatial working memory in humans as revealed by PET. *Nature, 363,* 623-625.

Karni, A., Meyer, G., Jezzard, P., Adams, M. M., Turner, R., & Ungerleider, L. G. (1995). Functional MRI evidence for adult motor cortex plasticity during motor skill learning. *Nature, 377,* 155-158.

Keele, S. W., & Curran, T. (1995). Modularity of sequence learning systems in humans. In E. Covey (Ed.), *Neural representation of temporal patterns* (pp. 197-225). New York: Plenum.

Keele, S. W., Davidson, M., & Hayes, A. (1995, December). *Sequential representation and the neural basis of motor skills.* Paper presented at the Third Biennial Motor Control and Human Skill Research Workshop, Perth, Australia.

Keele, S. W., & Jennings, P. J. (1992). Attention in the representation of sequence: Experiment and theory. *Human Movement Studies, 11,* 125-138.

Keele, S. W., Jennings, P., Jones, S., Caulton, D., & Cohen, A. (1995). On the modularity of sequence representation. *Journal of Motor Behavior, 27,* 17-30.

Knopman, D., & Nissen, M. J. (1991). Procedural learning is impaired in Huntington's disease: Evidence from the serial reaction time task. *Neuropsychologia, 29,* 245-254.

Kolers, P. A., & Roediger, H. L. (1984). Procedures of mind. *Journal of Verbal Learning and Verbal Behavior, 23,* 425-449.

Kosslyn, S. M. (1994). *Image and brain.* Cambridge: MIT Press.

Martone, M., Butters, N., Payne, M., Becker, J. T., & Sax, D. S. (1984). Dissociations between skill learning and verbal recognition in amnesia and dementia. *Archives of Neurology, 41,* 965-970.

Mayes, A. R., Meudell, P. R., & Pickering, A. (1985). Is organic amnesia caused by a selective deficit in remembering contextual information? *Cortex, 21,* 167-202.

Mayr, U. (1996). Spatial attention and implicit sequence learning: Evidence for independent learning of spatial and nonspatial sequences. *Journal of Experimental Psychology: Learning, Memory, and Cognition, 22,* 350-364.

McClelland, J. L., McNaughton, B. L., & O'Reilly, R. C. (1995). Why there are complimentary learning systems in the hippocampus and neocortex: Insights from the successes and failures of connectionist models of learning and memory. *Psychological Review, 102,* 419-457.

Mishkin, M., & Appenzeller, T. (1987). The anatomy of memory. *Scientific American, 256,* 80-89.

Mishkin, M., Malamut, B., & Bachevalier, J. (1984). Memories and habits: Two neural systems. In G. Lynch, J. McGaugh, & N. Weinberger (Eds.), *Neurobiology of learning and memory* (pp. 65-77). New York: Guilford.

Mishkin, M., & Petri, H. L. (1984). Memories and habits: Some implications for the analysis of learning and retention. In L. R. Squire & N. Butters (Eds.), *Neuropsychology of memory* (pp. 287-296). New York: Guilford.

Mitz, A. R., Godschalk, M., & Wise, S. P. (1991). Learning-dependent neuronal activity in the premotor cortex: Activity during the acquisition of conditional motor associations. *Journal of Neuroscience, 11,* 1855-1872.

Moscovitch, M., Vriezen, E., & Goshen-Gottstein, Y. (1993). Implicit tests of memory in patients with focal lesions or degenerative brain disorders. In H. Spinnler & F. Boller (Eds.), *Handbook of neuropsychology* (Vol. 8, pp. 133-173). Amsterdam: Elsevier.

Nissen, M. J., & Bullemer, P. (1987). Attentional requirements of learning: Evidence from performance measures. *Cognitive Psychology, 19,* 1-32.

Nissen, M. J., Willingham, D., & Hartman, M. (1989). Explicit and implicit remembering: When is learning preserved in amnesia? *Neuropsychologia, 27,* 341-352.

Ostergaard, A. L. (1994). Dissociations between word priming effects in normal subjects and patients with memory disorders: Multiple memory systems or retrieval. *Quarterly Journal of Experimental Psychology, 47A,* 331-364.

Ostergaard, A. L., & Jernigan, T. L. (1993). Are word priming and explicit memory mediated by different brain structures? In P. Graf & M. E. J. Masson (Eds.), *Implicit memory* (pp. 327-349). Hillsdale, NJ: Lawrence Erlbaum.

Ostergaard, A. L., & Jernigan, T. L. (1996). Priming and baseline perceptual identification performance in amnesia: A comment on Hamann, Squire, and Schacter. *Neuropsychology, 10,* 125-130.

Pascual-Leone, A., Grafman, J., Clark, K., Stewart, M., Massaquoi, S., Lou, J.-S., & Hallett, M. (1993). Procedural learning in Parkinson's disease and cerebellar degeneration. *Annals of Neurology, 34,* 594-602.

Pascual-Leon, A., Grafman, J., & Hallet, M. (1994). Modulation of cortical motor output maps during development of implicit and explicit knowledge. *Science, 263,* 1287-1289.

Perruchet, P., & Amorim, M. (1992). Conscious knowledge and changes in performance in sequence learning: Evidence against dissociation. *Journal of Experimental Psychology: Learning, Memory, and Cognition, 18,* 785-800.

Ratcliff, R., & McKoon, G. (1996). Bias effects in implicit memory. *Journal of Experimental Psychology: General, 125,* 403-421.

Rauch, S. L., Savage, C. R., Brown, H. D., Curran, T., Alpert, N. M., Kendrick, A., Fischman, A. J., & Kosslyn, S. M. (1995). A PET investigation of implicit and explicit sequence learning. *Human Brain Mapping, 3,* 271-286.

Rauch, S. L., Whalen, P. J., Savage, C. R., Curran, T., Kendrick, A., Brown, H. D., Bush, G., Breiter, H. C., & Rosen, B. R. (in press). Striatal recruitment during an implicit sequence learning task as measured by functional magnetic resonance imaging. *Human Brain Mapping.*

Reber, P. J., & Squire, L. R. (1994). Parallel brain systems for learning with and without awareness. *Learning & Memory, 1,* 217-229.

Reed, J., & Johnson, P. (1994). Assessing implicit learning with indirect tests: Determining what is learned about sequence structure. *Journal of Experimental Psychology: Learning, Memory, and Cognition, 20,* 585-594.

Riehle, A., & Requin, J. (1989). Monkey primary motor and premotor cortex: Single-cell activity related to prior information about direction and extent of an intended movement. *Journal of Neurophysiology, 61,* 534-549.

Schacter, D. L., Chiu, C. Y. P., & Ochsner, K. N. (1993). Implicit memory: A selective review. *Annual Review of Neuroscience, 16,* 159-182.

Schacter, D. L., Curran, T., Galluccio, L., Milberg, W., & Bates, J. (1996). False recognition and the right frontal lobe: A case study. *Neuropsychologia, 34,* 793-808.

Schmidtke, V., & Heuer, H. (in press). Task integration as a factor in secondary-task effects on sequence learning. *Psychological Research/Psychologische Forschung.*

Servan-Schreiber, E., & Anderson, J. R. (1990). Learning artificial grammars with competitive chunking. *Journal of Experimental Psychology: Learning, Memory, and Cognition, 16,* 592-608.

Shanks, D. R., & St. John, M. F. (1994). Characteristics of dissociable human learning systems. *Behavioral and Brain Sciences, 17,* 367-447.

Squire, L. R. (1992). Memory and the hippocampus: A synthesis of findings with rats, monkeys, and humans. *Psychological Review, 99,* 195-231.

Squire, L. R., Hamann, S. B., & Schacter, D. L. (1996). Intact baseline performance and priming in amnesia: Reply to Ostergaard and Jernigan. *Neuropsychology, 10,* 131-135.

Squire, L. R., Ojeman, J. G., Miezin, F. M., Peterson, S. E., Videen, T. O., & Raichle, M. E. (1992). Activation of the hippocampus in normal humans: A functional anatomical study of memory. *Proceedings of the National Academy of Science, 89,* 1837-1841.

Stadler, M. A. (1989). On the learning of complex procedural knowledge. *Journal of Experimental Psychology: Learning, Memory, and Cognition, 15,* 1061-1069.

Stadler, M. A. (1992). Statistical structure and implicit serial learning. *Journal of Experimental Psychology: Learning, Memory, and Cognition, 18,* 318-327.

Stadler, M. A. (1993). Implicit serial learning: Questions inspired by Hebb (1961). *Memory & Cognition, 21,* 819-827.

Stadler, M. A. (1994). Explicit and implicit learning and maps of cortical motor output. *Science, 265,* 1600.

Stadler, M. A. (1995). Role of attention in implicit learning. *Journal of Experimental Psychology: Learning, Memory, and Cognition, 21,* 674-685.

Stern, C. E., Corkin, S., Gonzalez, R. G., Guimaraes, A. R., Baker, J. R., Jennings, P. J., Carr, C. A., Sugiura, R. M., Vedantham, V., & Rosen, B. R. (1996). The hippocampal formation participates in novel picture encoding: Evidence from functional magnetic resonance imaging. *Proceedings of the National Academy of Sciences, 933,* 8660-8665.

Sutherland, R. J., & Rudy, J. W. (1989). Configural association theory: The role of the hippocampal formation in learning, memory, and amnesia. *Psychobiology, 17,* 129-144.

Tulving, E., Kapur, S., Markowitsch, H. J., Craik, F. I. M., Habib, R., & Houle, S. (1994). Neuroanatomical correlates of retrieval in episodic memory: Auditory sentence recognition. *Proceedings of the National Academy of Sciences, 91,* 2012-2015.

Tulving, E., Markowitsch, H. J., Kapur, S., Habib, R., & Houle, S. (1994). Novelty encoding networks in the human brain: Positron emission tomography data. *NeuroReport, 5,* 2525-2528.

Wicklegren, W. A. (1979). Chunking and consolidation: A theoretical synthesis of semantic networks, configuring in conditioning, S-R versus cognitive learning, normal forgetting, the amnesic syndrome, and the hippocampal arousal system. *Psychological Review, 86,* 44-60.

Willingham, D. B. (1992). Systems of motor skill. In L. R. Squire & N. Butters (Eds.), *Neuropsychology of memory* (pp. 166-178). New York: Guilford.

Willingham, D. B., Greenley, D. B., & Bardona, A. M. (1993). Dissociation in a serial response time task using a recognition measure: Comment on Perruchet and Amorim (1992). *Journal of Experimental Psychology: Learning, Memory, and Cognition, 19,* 1424-1430.

Willingham, D. B., & Koroshetz, W. J. (1993). Evidence for dissociable motor skills in Huntington's disease patients. *Psychobiology, 21,* 173-182.

Willingham, D. B., Nissen, M. J., & Bullemer, P. (1989). On the development of procedural knowledge. *Journal of Experimental Psychology: Learning, Memory, and Cognition, 15,* 1047-1060.

Wilson, F. A. W., Scalaidhe, S. P. O., & Goldman-Rakic, P. S. (1993). Dissociation of object and spatial processing domains in primate prefrontal cortex. *Science, 260,* 1955-1958.

12

Implicit Learning of Perceptual and Motor Sequences

Evidence for Independent Learning Systems

●───

Thomas Goschke

In a chapter published in 1951 on the "The Problem of Serial Order in Behavior," Karl Lashley highlighted the fundamental importance of sequential organization for an understanding of intelligent behavior. It is indeed easy to see that the acquisition of knowledge about sequences of events or actions is of essential importance for most higher organisms. Behaviors ranging from catching a prey to sophisticated human

AUTHOR'S NOTE: Part of the author's research summarized in this chapter was supported by a grant from the German Science Foundation (Go-720/1-1). The chapter was written during a stay at the Institute of Cognition and Decision Sciences at the University of Oregon at Eugene, which was supported by a grant from the German Academic Exchange Council (DAAD). I thank especially Steve Keele for his hospitality and numerous stimulating conversations, as well as for thoughtful comments on a previous version of this chapter. He made my visit not only intellectually rewarding, but also a very pleasant experience. I also thank Ulrich Mayr, Annette Bolte, Birgit Stürmer, Axel Buchner, Julius Kuhl, and Michael Posner for helpful comments on various topics discussed in the chapter, and Frauke Bastians, Kristina Gräper, and Bianca Pösse for their competent assistance in running some of the experiments summarized in this chapter. Some parts of this chapter are shortened and revised versions of parts of Goschke (in press-b). Correspondence may be addressed to Thomas Goschke, Fachbereich Psychologie, Universität Osnabrück, Seminarstr. 20, 49069 Osnabrück, Germany. Email may be sent to goschke@luce.psycho.uni-osnabrueck.de.

401

skills, such as typewriting, piano playing, or speaking are based on the ability to assemble elements into novel sequences of responses (finger movements on the piano keyboard or the phonemes forming a word) or to process on-line sequences of events (for instance, speech sounds).

According to an influential view, the acquisition of motor, perceptual, and cognitive skills can be conceived of as a process whereby declarative rules, initially communicated in a verbal form, are transformed into procedural knowledge in the course of extended practice (e.g., Anderson, 1983, 1987). However, contrary to this view, probably everyone has had the experience that mastery of a skill does not always depend on the prior acquisition of explicit, verbally expressed rules. For instance, someone knowing next to nothing about the structural relations inherent in the system of Western tonal music may nevertheless produce great guitar solos. On the other hand, having acquired an impressive amount of knowledge about the dynamics of moving bodies is not necessarily of much help when you find yourself on the tennis court. Apparently, many sequential skills are learned without ever encoding verbal rules and even without acquiring conscious knowledge about the underlying rules and regularities.

Such everyday observations find their tragic counterpart in cases of neurological patients who suffer from impairments of explicit conscious memory as a consequence of brain damage. These studies have revealed that the acquisition of cognitive and motor skills is sometimes more or less spared in amnesic patients, despite their severe impairment of declarative memory for facts and prior episodes (e.g., Cohen & Squire, 1980; Markowitsch, 1992; Moscovitch, Winocur, & McLachlan, 1986; Soliveri, Brown, Jahanshahi, & Marsden, 1992; Squire, 1994; Squire, Knowlton, & Musen, 1993).

During the last two decades, there has been an explosion of studies suggesting that not only the acquisition of perceptual motor skills, but also the learning of rulelike sequential structures can proceed independently of declarative memory and conscious knowledge (e.g., Lewicki, Hill, & Bizot, 1988). This type of learning has been termed implicit (Reber, 1967, 1993) and is conceived of as a process whereby knowledge is acquired incidentally, without attempts to discover rules or to use explicit hypothesis-testing strategies, and without an encoding of verbal rules. In addition, implicit learning is assumed to produce knowledge that is unconscious and difficult if not impossible to verbalize. As we will see, both defining characteristics have become the focus of considerable controversy.

In this chapter, I will discuss studies in which variants of the serial reaction time (SRT) task have been used to study implicit sequence learning. In the original version of this task, introduced by Nissen and Bullemer (1987), on each trial, an asterisk appears at one of four positions horizontally arranged on a computer screen. Participants have to respond to the position of the stimulus by pressing the response key directly below the stimulus. When the sequence of positions followed a fixed pattern (e.g., when the same sequence of 10 positions was constantly repeated), reaction times decreased with practice faster than in a condition in which participants responded to a random sequence. In addition, when the repeating sequence was unexpectedly switched to a random sequence after prolonged training, response times increased markedly. This shows that participants acquired specific procedural knowledge about the sequence structure (e.g., Cohen, Ivry, & Keele, 1990; Curran & Keele, 1993; Stadler, 1993; Willingham, Nissen, & Bullemer, 1989; for reviews, see Berry & Dienes, 1993; Buchner, 1993; Hoffmann, 1993; Seger, 1994). Performance increments in the SRT task have been observed for participants who were not able to verbalize the sequence after training or who performed poorly on direct tests of explicit knowledge (e.g., reproduction or recognition tests). It should be noted that this type of learning does not consist simply of acquiring pairwise associations. Reliable learning has also been observed with sequences in which each element followed each other element equally often, indicating that subjects learned more complex structures and took into account the sequential context in which individual elements appeared (Reber & Squire, 1994; Reed & Johnson, 1994). Moreover, sequence learning is not restricted to deterministic repeating patterns but has also been demonstrated with more complex probabilistic sequences that were generated by a finite-state grammar (Cleeremans, 1993; Cleeremans & McClelland, 1991; Jiménez, Méndez, & Cleeremans, 1996).

In this chapter, I will focus on three questions:

1. Is the knowledge acquired in SRT tasks actually unconscious?
2. What kind of knowledge is acquired in SRT tasks?
3. What brain systems underlie implicit sequence learning?

In the first part, I will discuss methodological problems in measuring explicit and implicit knowledge and review evidence on whether sequence learning is or is not implicit, including some of our own recent research, in which we applied the process-dissociation method (Jacoby, 1991) to separate explicit and implicit knowledge. In the second part of the chapter, I will defend the hypothesis that learning in SRT tasks is not restricted to the acquisition of sequences of motor responses, but that various types of stimulus sequences can be implicitly learned, even when there is no structured sequence of overt responses. In the third section, I will discuss neuropsychological, brain imaging, and electrophysiological evidence suggesting that different domain-specific brain systems are involved in sequence learning. This hypothesis derives from the general view that almost any part of the brain is plastic in the sense that it can be modified by experience and that different types of information are represented in a distributed network of neural systems specialized for the initial processing of the information. In the final section, I will briefly discuss whether, in addition to domain-specific sequence-representation systems, there is also a domain-unspecific sequence-acquisition device storing sequences in an abstract format. I will conclude with some speculative remarks on the functional properties of implicit and explicit learning.

HOW IMPLICIT IS SEQUENCE LEARNING?

Given that we do not have direct access to subjective phenomenal states of other people, we have to infer the presence (or absence) of conscious knowledge from observable behavior, verbal reports, or neurophysiological measures. The conclusion that a piece of knowledge is implicit rests on dissociations between performance in some task and some indicator of conscious knowledge (Shanks & St. John, 1994). For instance, when subjects in a sequence-learning experiment respond faster to a structured sequence of stimuli as compared to a random sequence, but they cannot verbalize or recall the sequence, this is considered evidence that subjects must have implicit knowledge of the sequence. Likewise, when a subject is able to verbalize, recall, or recognize fragments of the sequence, but this fragmentary knowledge is not sufficient to fully account for the performance increments in the indirect test, it is concluded that at least part of the knowledge is implicit. This type of dissociation can be called quantitative, because knowledge that is expressed in performance exceeds the conscious knowledge revealed by verbal reports or direct tests (Erderlyi, 1986).

● Criteria for Conscious Knowledge

The interpretation of quantitative dissociations has been the focus of considerable controversy (e.g., Goschke, in press-b; Reingold & Merikle, 1990; Shanks & St. John, 1994). Here I will focus on the distinction between subjective and objective criteria, which was originally introduced in research on subliminal perception (Cheesman & Merikle, 1984; Holender, 1986; Merikle, 1982; Reingold & Merikle, 1990). With respect to sequence learning, knowledge can be said to be unconscious according to a subjective criterion, when a subject shows performance increments in the SRT task but denies being aware of a structure and appears unable to recall the sequence. By contrast, an objective criterion requires that a subject performs at chance level in a forced-choice discrimination task, as when, for instance, he or she is unable to discriminate old and new sequences in a recognition test.

According to a subjective criterion, in most sequence-learning studies at least some subjects qualify as implicit learners. Reliable performance increments in the SRT task have been reported for subgroups of subjects who were not able to verbalize the sequence structure after training or who claimed that they had not even noticed that there was a structure (e.g., Cohen et al., 1990; Curran & Keele, 1993; Goschke, 1996b; Lewicki et al., 1988; Nissen & Bullemer, 1987; Pascual-Leone, Wassermann, Grafman, & Hallett, 1996; Reed & Johnson, 1994; Stadler, 1993; Willingham et al., 1989). Even when subjects were able to verbalize fragments of the sequence (e.g., chunks of two or three elements), detailed analyses suggested that this knowledge was not sufficient to account for the amount of learning shown in the SRT task (Cleeremans & McClelland, 1991).

The use of subjective criteria has been seriously questioned by Shanks and St. John (1994; see also Shanks & Johnstone, Chapter 16, this volume) in an influential article in which they argue that verbal reports are not sufficiently sensitive to reveal all explicit knowledge a subject has. For instance, a subject may be aware of small segments of two or three consecutive elements from the training sequence, but he or she refrains from reporting this fragmentary knowledge, because it is associated with low subjective confidence and the subject sets a strict response criterion. By contrast, in the SRT task, in which subjects have to respond as fast as possible, such fragmentary knowledge may suffice to produce reliable response-time increments (Cleeremans & McClelland, 1991; Perruchet, 1994). Shanks and St. John (1994) therefore recommend using objective criteria and consider discriminative behavior in forced-choice tests as a more sensitive measure of conscious knowledge. According to the authors, only if subjects perform at chance level in such tests is one justified in concluding that performance increments in implicit learning tasks are based on unconscious knowledge. Two commonly used forced-choice tests are prediction and recognition tests. In the prediction task, subjects are presented with the same stimuli as in the SRT task and are asked to predict at which location the next stimulus will appear. In recognition tests, subjects are presented short test sequences and are asked to decide whether these sequences were part of the previously presented sequence or not.

Studies in which prediction and recognition tests were used have produced less clear evidence for implicit learning than studies relying on verbal reports. Although, in some cases, performance on forced-choice tests was at chance level or did not differ from control subjects who had not been exposed to a structured sequence (Cohen et al., 1990; Reed & Johnson, 1994; Stadler, 1989), in most studies, average performance across subjects was above chance level, indicating that subjects possessed substantial conscious knowledge (Howard, Mutter, & Howard, 1992; Nissen & Bullemer, 1987; Perruchet & Amorim, 1992; Shanks, Green, & Kolodny, 1994; Shanks & Johnstone, Chapter 16, this volume; Willingham et al., 1989). However, this does not exclude the possibility that some participants performed at chance level in the direct tests but nevertheless did show reliable sequence learning. In fact, reliable sequence learning has repeatedly been reported for subgroups of subjects performing at chance level in forced-choice tests (Cohen et al., 1990; Frensch, Buchner, & Lin, 1994; Frensch & Miner, 1994; Stadler, 1989; Willingham et al., 1989; but see Hartman, Knopman, & Nissen, 1989).

Strong evidence against a dissociation between explicit and implicit knowledge has been reported by Perruchet and Amorim (1992). They noted various methodological shortcomings of previous studies, in particular, that often subjects had not been instructed that the sequence in the prediction tasks was the same as in the previous SRT task. In their own experiments, subjects received either a recognition task or a reproduction task in which they had to reproduce the previous training sequence, using the same keys as in the SRT task. After only 10 repetitions of a 10-trial sequence, subjects not only performed well above chance in both tests, but reaction-time benefits in the SRT task were highly correlated with performance in the direct tests. The authors concluded that performance increments in the SRT task are mediated by conscious knowledge about small fragments of the sequence. However, Willingham, Greeley, and Bardone (1993) could not replicate the correlation between reaction times in the SRT task and recognition performance (see Perruchet & Gallego, 1993, for critical discussion). Further evidence for genuine implicit learning stems from Jiménez et al. (1996), who used a more complex probabilistic sequence that was generated by a finite-state grammar. They performed a partial correlational analysis, which showed that response times in the serial reaction test were reliably correlated with the objective probabilities with which sequence events occurred in a given context of other elements, even when explicit knowledge (measured by a prediction task) was statistically controlled. This indicates that part of the sequential knowledge was only expressed through performance in the SRT task.

● The Sensitivity-Contamination Dilemma

At this point, it is advisable to step back for a moment from the complexities of the empirical findings and to consider a more fundamental theoretical problem underlying the distinction between subjective and objective criteria of consciousness. The use of forced-choice tests was motivated by the goal to use maximally sensitive measures of explicit knowledge. However, this strategy presupposes that forced-choice tasks are process-pure measures of explicit knowledge. For instance, Shanks and St. John (1994) state that "if subjects are instructed to try to predict events and are able to do so with above-chance accuracy, this is evidence of conscious knowledge, because their predictions *must* [italics added] be based on conscious expectancies" (p. 384). The problem is that we do not know whether and under what conditions this statement is true. Not only may performance measures be contaminated by explicit knowledge (Schacter, Bowers, & Booker, 1989), but allegedly direct tests may well be contaminated by implicit knowledge (Cohen & Curran, 1993; Goschke, in press-b; Jacoby, 1991; Reber, 1989; Reingold & Merikle, 1988). Recognition judgments may be based on conscious recollections or on feelings of familiarity that need not be accompanied by episodic memories (Jacoby, 1991; Mandler, 1980). Likewise, subjects who are simply guessing in a prediction task may nevertheless perform better than chance due to subtle response biases induced by implicit knowledge.

We are thus faced with a dilemma: whereas verbal reports probably underestimate the amount of conscious knowledge because of insufficient sensitivity, forced-choice tests may overestimate explicit knowledge due to a contamination by implicit knowledge. In some sense, we are back where we started, because to interpret the results from an objective forced-choice test, we apparently have to rely on subjective criteria. Whether performance in a forced-choice test does or does not indicate explicit knowledge depends after all on whether subjects do or do not base their responses on conscious knowledge. Probably most people would consider it odd to interpret above-chance performance in a recognition test as an expression of conscious knowledge when the subjects had the subjective impression of guessing. However, to determine whether subjects based their responses on conscious knowledge, we either can rely on their verbal report or confidence ratings or we can instruct the subjects accordingly and hope that they follow our instructions. Viewed this way, responses in a forced-choice test are essentially nonverbal speech acts expressing beliefs such as "I have seen this sequence before" or "I remember that Event A was followed by Event B." In conclusion, although Shanks and St. John (1994) are surely correct in assuming that forced-choice judgements are more sensitive measures of conscious knowledge than verbal reports, the problem remains how to decide a priori whether some discriminative behavior does or does not indicate conscious knowledge.

● Process Dissociation and Qualitative Dissociations

One attempt to escape the sensitivity contamination dilemma is the process-dissociation method, which was originally proposed for the study of implicit memory by Jacoby (1991; Jacoby, Toth, & Yonelinas, 1993). Rather than to look for dissociations between different tasks, this method is an attempt to derive separate estimates of conscious and unconscious knowledge within one task. This is done by setting intentional (explicit) and automatic (implicit) influences in opposition to each other by having subjects perform the same task under different instructions. We have recently applied this method to sequence learning (Goschke & Stürmer, 1997). Subjects performed the SRT task with an ambiguous repeating 12-element sequence either under a single-task condition or under a dual-task condition. In the latter condition, subjects' attention was distracted by a concurrent task, in which they had to count target letters that were presented simultaneously with the sequence events. After 40 repetitions of the sequence, subjects performed a sequence production task in which they were asked to generate a 100-trial sequence using the same keys as in the SRT task. To separate the influences of implicit and explicit knowledge on sequence reproduction, we compared performance in so-called inclusion and exclusion conditions. In our inclusion condition, subjects were instructed to try to remember and reproduce as accurately as possible the previous training sequence. Only when they were not able to recollect the old sequence were they allowed to press any key that would "feel" correct. By contrast, in the exclusion condition, subjects were instructed to produce a random sequence and not to reproduce the training sequence. In both conditions, we computed how often subjects produced chunks of Lengths 2 to 12 that were also contained in the training sequence. Following Jacoby (1991), we assumed that subjects with full explicit knowledge about the training sequence should produce only old chunks contained in the training sequence in the inclusion condition, whereas they should produce no old chunks in the exclusion condition. In this case, sequence production would be under complete intentional control. At the other extreme, subjects possessing no explicit knowledge at all should have no intentional control over performance and should thus produce an equal number of chunks from the training sequence in the exclusion and inclusion conditions. To the degree that subjects possess implicit knowledge, they should produce more old chunks in the exclusion condition than subjects who had been trained on a random sequence. This difference would reflect unconscious influences of the previous exposure to the structured sequence. By the same logic, the more explicit knowledge subjects have, the better should they be able to avoid producing old chunks in the exclusion condition. Expressed in a slightly more formal manner (cf. Jacoby et al., 1993), the probability of reproducing a chunk from the training sequence in the inclusion condition equals the sum of the probability of consciously remembering a chunk (E) and the probability of producing a chunk as a result of implicit knowledge (I) without consciously remembering it $I(1 - E)$: Inclusion $= E + I(1 - E)$. In the exclusion condition, a chunk from the old sequence will only be produced when it is not consciously recognized as old but is produced automatically: Exclusion $= I(1 - E)$. The probability of consciously recalling a chunk from the old sequence can thus be determined as $E =$ Inclusion $-$ Exclusion.[1]

In a series of experiments in which we used this method, we obtained a number of noteworthy findings (Goschke & Stürmer, 1997). First, we found reliable learning in the SRT task (that is, a reliable increase in response times when the structured sequence was switched to a different sequence at the end of the training phase), even in those subjects whose process-dissociation estimate of conscious knowledge was not larger than 0 (that is, whose number of correctly reproduced chunks in the inclusion condition did not exceed the number in the exclusion condition). Second, process-dissociation estimates of explicit and implicit knowledge were differentially influenced by the presence or absence of a secondary task. Subjects whose attention had been distracted during the SRT task showed reliably lower estimates of explicit knowledge than subjects in a single-task condition. By contrast, the secondary task had no reliable effect on sequence production in the exclusion condition. This finding fits with other studies showing that an attentional distraction impairs the acquisition of explicit knowledge more than implicit learning (Cohen et al., 1990; see also Curran & Keele, 1993) and constitutes a qualitative (in contrast to a mere quantitative) dissociation between explicit and implicit knowledge. This constitutes relatively strong evidence that the two forms of knowledge were mediated by different systems and/or processes (although this conclusion may not be unambiguous; see Dunn & Kirsner, 1988).

As one should expect, the process-dissociation method is not without problems (e.g., Graf & Komatsu, 1994). In particular, the procedure rests on theoretical assumptions about the way conscious and unconscious processes interact. Jacoby's (1991) proposal is based on the assumption that unconscious and conscious effects are independent of each other. This assumption has recently been questioned by Joordens and Merikle (1993), who proposed a redundancy model according to which situations in which performance is influenced by conscious processes are a subset of situations in which there are unconscious influences. At the other extreme, Gardiner and Java (1993) have proposed an exclusivity model according to which conscious and unconscious processes exclude each other. Although the different models arrive at the same estimate for conscious influences (that is, inclusion performance minus exclusion performance), they imply rather different estimates of unconscious influences. A further problem concerns the effects of guessing and response biases in the exclusion and inclusion conditions (Buchner, Erdfelder, & Vaterrodt-Plünnecke, 1995; see also Yonelinas & Jacoby, 1996). Here I cannot discuss these problems in more detail. Suffice it to say that I do not think that a decision about which of the different measurement models is to be preferred can be made on an a priori basis. Lacking empirically founded models of the interaction of conscious and unconscious processes, I consider it a fruitful strategy to systematically obtain process-dissociation estimates derived from different assumptions under different experimental conditions. The nomological network emerging from such studies, together with constraints from other fields (e.g., neuropsychological and brain imaging studies), should help both to validate our measurement models and to develop better founded theories of conscious and unconscious processes. In this respect, the problems of the process-dissociation methods are not unusual but reflect the general dilemma discussed by philosophers of science: We always have to decide when to trust our measurement models and adapt our theories to the empirical phenomena and when to question and revise the assumptions underlying our measurement models.

● Conclusions

There is convincing evidence that subjects often show reliable performance increments in SRT tasks even if they are not able to verbally report the structure of the sequence. This appears to be especially the case when attention is distracted or when knowledge is probed early in training. In most studies, however, lack of verbalizable knowledge was not complete, and subjects were able to report at least fragments of the training sequence. Moreover, after prolonged training, positive correlations between task performance and verbal knowledge have frequently been observed. Lacking systematic findings on the time course of the development of explicit and implicit knowledge, it must at present be considered an unresolved issue, whether such positive correlations indicate that performance increments in sequence learning tasks are based on the development of explicit knowledge, whether the development of explicit sequence knowledge is based on the development of implicit knowledge, or whether implicit and explicit learning are based on two independent learning systems operating in parallel (but see below on neuropsychological evidence concerning this issue).

The use of forced-choice tests for explicit knowledge has produced a more equivocal pattern of findings. In several studies, subjects performed above chance when their sequence knowledge was tested in recognition or predictions tasks, and in some cases, fragmentary sequence knowledge revealed by recognition or recall tests was highly correlated with performance in the SRT task (similar conclusions have been drawn for other types of implicit learning such as artificial grammar learning; see Berry & Dienes, 1993; Goschke, in press-a; Shanks & St. John, 1994 for reviews). However, it is unclear to what degree forced-choice measures are contaminated by implicit knowledge. Initial attempts to separate implicit and explicit influences with the process-dissociation method (Goschke & Stürmer, 1997) have yielded promising findings in favor of truly implicit learning. Moreover, these findings showed a qualitative dissociation between explicit and implicit knowledge within the same task. In contrast to quantitative dissociations, this result can less easily be explained in terms of differences in the sensitivity of different tasks.

WHAT IS LEARNED IN SERIAL REACTION-TIME TASKS?

Whereas research on implicit sequence learning has primarily focused on dissociations between explicit and implicit knowledge, far less attention has been paid to the question of whether sequence learning itself is a unitary phenomenon, or whether different processes and/or systems underlie the acquisition of different types of sequential structures. Three theoretical positions can be contrasted.

1. According to a motor view, implicit sequence learning reflects a form of perceptual motor skill acquisition, which is closely tied to experience-dependent modifications in motor-related output systems.
2. According to a unitary and abstractionist view, all forms of implicit sequence learning are mediated by some general unspecific learning system specialized for the unconscious registration and representation of sequential regularities.
3. According to a modular or multiple systems view, different forms of implicit sequence learning involve multiple functionally and structurally separable systems, which are specialized for the processing and retention of different kinds of sequential information.[2]

These theoretical positions can be discussed on a functional and a neurological level. Before I turn to neuropsychological studies on the brain structures involved in sequence learning, I will first focus on the functional level and ask what knowledge is and can be acquired in serial reactions tasks.

● **The Role of Motor Responses in Sequence Learning**

One obvious view holds that performance in SRT tasks reflects the acquisition of a sequence of motor responses or the formation of new motor programs and can thus be regarded as a form of motor skill acquisition. If this view is correct, motor responses should play an important role in sequence learning. Empirical support for this view has been obtained by

Nattkemper and Prinz (1993; cf. Nattkemper, 1993), who had their participants respond to regular stimulus sequences containing eight different stimulus alternatives, which were mapped to only four responses. That is, pairs of stimuli were mapped to the same response. Occasionally, a deviant stimulus, which violated the sequential structure, was inserted in the regular sequence. Deviants produced increased response times only if they required an unexpected response, but not when the deviant consisted of an unexpected stimulus that had to be responded to with the same finger as the regular stimulus would have been. The authors concluded that a sequence of responses rather than a sequence of stimuli was learned. One problem with this study is, however, that the type of sequence (responses versus stimuli) was confounded with the number of alternatives (four versus eight), thus making the information contained more complex in the stimulus sequence than in the response sequence.

Hoffmann and Sebald (1996) varied the relational structure (e.g., the number of runs like 1-2-3) in a sequence of stimuli and a sequence of responses independent from each other. They found that only the structure of the response sequence, but not the structure of the stimulus sequence, facilitated performance. However, as the authors noted, the relational structure in the response sequence (e.g., runs of adjacent key presses like 3-2-1) was much more salient than the structure in the stimulus sequence (e.g., runs of adjacent letters like E-D-C), and it thus remains an open issue whether more salient stimulus structures would reliably influence learning.

Willingham et al. (1989, Experiment 3) had their participants respond to the color of stimuli, which could appear at one of four locations. In a perceptual group, the sequence of colors was random whereas the sequence of locations followed a repeating pattern. In a response group, the sequence of colors followed a repeating pattern whereas the locations were determined at random. Reliable sequence learning was obtained only in the response group but not in the perceptual group. The interpretation of this result is rendered somewhat difficult, however, because instructing participants to respond to the colors presumably had the effect of distracting attention from the stimulus locations. As it is well-established that attentional distraction can impair learning of more complex sequences (Cohen et al. 1990; Curran & Keele, 1993; Nissen & Bullemer, 1987), this factor may explain the lack of learning in the perceptual group.

Zießler (1994) investigated the role of motor responses in sequence learning in an interesting novel task. Participants had to respond to targets that were embedded in a matrix of distractors. On each trial, the identity and location of the target predicted the location of the target in the next trial. Participants were much better at learning these sequential contingencies when each target was mapped to a specific motor response as compared to a condition in which different targets required the same motor response. Although these results suggest that motor responses play an important role in sequential learning, the author himself noted that it remains an open question whether sequence learning is restricted to situations in which sequential rules are linked to overt motor responses, or whether internal processes such as selective encoding or processing of a stimulus might play a similar facilitative role in learning.

In summary, irrespective of the methodological concerns I mentioned, it is fair to say that these studies provide convergent evidence that motor responses can play an important role in sequence learning. This does not imply, however, that specific sequences of low-level motor responses are in fact learned in SRT tasks, nor does it show that only response sequences can be learned. Regarding the first point, the question is whether sequential knowledge consists of a representation of effector-specific movements or whether more abstract representations are acquired. This question has been addressed in some detail by Keele and his coworkers, who performed transfer experiments in which subjects had to switch from one effector to another after they had performed the SRT task (Cohen et al., 1990; Keele, Jennings, Jones, Caulton, & Cohen, 1995). For instance, Cohen et al. (1990) had their participants first respond to a sequence consisting of stimuli that could appear at three different locations by pressing response keys with three different fingers. In a subsequent transfer phase, participants responded with one finger only. Despite this effector change, there was almost perfect transfer of the knowledge acquired during training. Analogous findings were reported by Stadler (1989) using a speeded visual search task (cf. Lewicki et al., 1988). More recently, Keele et al. (1995) have investigated transfer from manual key presses to vocal responses and still found substantial although much smaller transfer effects. Keele et al. (1995; cf. Keele & Curran, in press; Keele, Davidson, & Hayes, 1996) concluded that at least part of the knowledge acquired in SRT tasks is coded in a format that is more abstract than a sequence of specific movements and that can be used to control different effector systems. One candidate for such an abstract code is a representation of the spatial locations of the response keys that have to be pushed. In other words, what is learned is not so much a sequence of specific movements, but rather a sequence of intended effects of actions (for instance, a sequence of locations of to-be-pressed keys, irrespective of whether the intended effect is achieved by using three fingers, one finger, one's left foot, or even a vocal response that triggers a key-pressing device; cf. Goschke, 1992; Hoffmann, 1993; Prinz, 1990). If responses are mentally represented in terms of "the anticipation of the movement's sensible effects, resident or remote" (James, 1890, Vol. 2, p. 521), motor sequences differ from stimulus sequences primarily with respect to their representational contents. Moreover, rather than ask whether response or stimulus sequences are learned, or whether motor responses are a precondition for sequence learning, a more interesting question might be what kind of internal processing a sequence of stimuli must undergo in order to be learned.

● Independent Learning of Stimulus and Response Sequences

If these considerations are correct, it would be misleading to conceive of sequence learning exclusively as process in which new motor skills are acquired. Rather one should expect that very different kinds of sequences can be learned implicitly, even if they are not accompanied by a regular sequence of overt motor responses. From a functional view, it indeed appears hardly adaptive if organisms are able to learn sequential dependencies between events only if these events afford a regular sequence of motor responses. Rather, it appears prima facie to be important for adaptive systems to acquire knowledge about event sequences independently from specific motor responses. Everyday observation shows that humans are apt at learning sequential structures, even if no regular sequence of motor responses is required, as, for instance, in the case of musical apprehension. On the other hand, it would be equally dysfunctional if new sequences of motor responses could only be acquired when there was a perfectly correlated sequence of stimuli. Rather, one characteristic of skilled behavior is that each component response need not be triggered by a perceptual stimulus but that a sequence of responses can run off as a whole (cf. Lashley, 1951). If these considerations are correct, one should expect that knowledge about a sequence of stimuli can be acquired, even if it is not accompanied by a regular sequence of overt responses. Moreover, if learning of different kinds of sequences involves experience-dependent modifications in different domain-specific subsystems, it should be possible to learn two different kinds of sequences in parallel and without interference.

Some support for the view that both perceptual and response sequences can be learned stems from a study by Fendrich, Healy, and Bourne (1991,

Experiment 2), who used a task in which participants entered digit sequences with a computer keypad. When the keypad was switched after the acquisition phase, both old sequences of digits associated with new response sequences and new sequences of digits associated with old response sequences produced better performance as compared to completely new sequences. However, although consistent with the position I wish to defend, this study leaves open the possibility that stimulus sequences can only be learned when accompanied by a correlated response sequence during training. It would be more compelling if one could show that perceptual sequences are learned independently from motor responses. A study frequently cited as showing exactly this was performed by Howard, Mutter, and Howard (1992). They found that participants who first only observed a stimulus sequence and then later had to respond to the stimuli with key presses showed as much learning as participants who had to respond throughout the task. However, participants in the observation condition showed considerable explicit knowledge in a subsequent prediction task, and it thus remains an open question whether mere observation would also produce implicit learning.

To obtain more convincing evidence for response-independent sequence learning, I have recently developed a novel serial search task (Goschke, 1996b; see also Frensch & Miner, 1995, who independently developed a similar task). This task is an attempt to overcome the problem that, in the classical SRT task, various types of sequential information are confounded. For instance, in addition to a regular sequence of motor responses, there is also a sequence of locations of to-be-pushed response keys, a sequence of stimulus locations, a sequence of eye movements, and perhaps even a sequence of subvocalizations when subjects silently label different locations. Learning any of these sequential structures could influence overall performance. In contrast, the serial search task allows one to investigate learning of different sequences independent of each other under otherwise identical conditions. The basic idea of this task was to change the stimulus-response mapping from trial to trial. In each trial, four letters were presented at four locations horizontally arranged on the computer monitor. The four locations were mapped to four response keys. After a delay of 500 ms, one out of the four letters was presented auditorily, and the participant had to press the response key corresponding to the location of this letter on the visual display. For example, when the display CDBA was followed by the letter D, participants had to press the second key. The locations of the four letters in the visual display (that is, the stimulus-

416

response mapping) were changed from trial to trial, such that two conditions resulted. In the response/location sequence condition, the sequence of responses (and locations) followed a repeating 10-trial sequence, whereas the sequence of stimuli was quasi-random. In the stimulus sequence condition, the sequence of the auditorily presented letters followed a repeating pattern, whereas the sequence of responses (and locations) was quasi-random. Participants in the stimulus sequence condition can learn to anticipate the next stimulus (for instance, they may learn that ACB is followed by D), but it is not possible to predict the next response before the mapping display appears because there is no regular response sequence. Only after the mapping display has appeared can participants locate the anticipated stimulus and prepare the corresponding response. This condition thus allows one to test whether participants acquired knowledge about a sequence of stimuli in the absence of a regular response sequence.

The results showed that participants did in fact acquire knowledge about both kinds of sequences. Both in the stimulus and the response sequence condition, mean RT reliably decreased over the training blocks and increased reliably when a random sequence was unexpectedly presented after 90 repetitions of the sequence. There was no reliable difference in the magnitude of the learning effects for the two types of sequences. These results clearly show that procedural knowledge about stimulus and response sequences can be acquired independently of each other. To investigate whether the observed performance increments were due to explicit knowledge, participants were classified as explicit or implicit learners according to their performance in a sequence reproduction test. As described previously, this test was administered both under inclusion and exclusion instructions. Participants were classified as implicit learners when their probability of correctly reproducing chunks from the training sequence under inclusion instructions did not exceed the corresponding probability under exclusion instructions. Unsurprisingly, participants with at least some explicit knowledge of the sequence showed larger reaction time differences, especially when they were able to correctly reproduce longer chunks. However, when all participants showing at least minimal explicit knowledge were excluded from the analyses, the response time difference between structured and random blocks was still reliable both for the stimulus and the response sequence.

Similar results have been obtained by Frensch and Miner (1995), who used a somewhat similar sequential matching task. They also obtained reliable learning of sequences of visually presented letters as well as graphic symbols, even if the sequence of motor responses was random and even when subjects with explicit knowledge were excluded from the analyses.

A skeptic might insist, however, that even participants showing no explicit knowledge in the reproduction test may have been aware of fragments of the sequence while performing the serial search task, and such fragmentary conscious knowledge may have allowed subjects to anticipate events or responses. This "online" knowledge may simply have been forgotten at the time when subjects performed the sequence reproduction test (cf. Shanks & St. John, 1994). If this reasoning is correct, performance increments in the serial search task should reflect controlled search processes that are based on conscious expectations about what will happen next. By contrast, if knowledge was implicit, performance increments should rather reflect an automatic, involuntary orienting of attention to an (unconsciously) anticipated location (cf. Shiffrin & Schneider, 1977).

To separate the effects of conscious anticipations and automatic orienting, I varied the stimulus onset asynchrony (SOA) between the mapping display and the imperative stimulus (Goschke, 1996b). This SOA was set either to 200 ms or to 1000 ms. If performance increments in the stimulus-sequence condition are based on a voluntary search process, performance effects should become more pronounced when participants are given more time (1000 ms) to carry out the search. Conversely, shortening the time interval between mapping display and imperative stimulus to 200 ms should prevent a controlled search before the presentation of the imperative stimulus. Thus, in the short SOA condition, performance increments should reflect an automatic capture of attention by the anticipated stimulus. The results showed that the response time difference between random and structured blocks at the end of the training phase was reliably larger for the long as compared to the short SOA. This difference can be attributed to the fact that participants in the long SOA condition were able to locate the anticipated stimulus in the mapping display prior to the presentation of the imperative stimulus in the long SOA on the basis of a controlled search. By contrast, in the short SOA condition, there was no time for a controlled search process, and the residual performance increments were presumably due to an automatic capture of attention by the anticipated stimulus in the mapping display. This interpretation is further supported by the fact that the response time difference in the long SOA condition was reliably larger for explicit than for implicit learners. By contrast, in the short SOA condition, there was no reliable difference between explicit and implicit learners, which is consistent with the assumption that consciously controlled search processes were effectively suppressed. Most important, participants in the short SOA condition nevertheless showed a small but reliable learning effect. Thus, even in the absence of conscious expectations, implicit knowledge about the sequential dependencies was sufficient to induce an automatic anticipatory orienting of attention to the location of the next stimulus. Some participants did indeed spontaneously report after the experiment that they sometimes felt that their attention was automatically captured by a specific letter in the mapping display. In conclusion, conscious expectations and automatic attentional orienting appear to be separable subprocesses in sequence learning.

● **Parallel Learning of Two Different Sequences**

The experiments described so far show that a sequence of stimuli can be learned, even if it is not associated with a regular sequence of overt motor responses. Note that this does not imply that learning of a stimulus sequence involved no responses whatsoever. One might suspect that participants in the sequence-learning condition subvocally pronounced the auditorily presented letters and that a sequence of covert responses was learned. However, this does not call into question the conclusion: The important issue is not whether a sequence of stimuli is accompanied by a sequence of overt motor responses, but rather (a) how much and what kind of internal processing a sequence of stimuli must receive to be implicitly learned and (b) whether learning of different types of sequences is mediated by a single mechanism, which can be allocated to either the one or the other type of regularity, or whether there are multiple domain-specific systems working in parallel and mediating the acquisition of different sequences.

To answer the second question, it is not sufficient to demonstrate that different types of sequences can be learned in separate conditions. Rather, it would constitute much stronger evidence for the functional independence of different sequence-learning systems if one could show that two different sequences (for instance, sequences of letters and responses or of locations and objects) can be learned in parallel, even if both sequences are completely uncorrelated and events in one sequence cannot be predicted by events from the other sequence.

This question has been addressed by Mayr (1996) in a series of ingenious experiments. He presented geometric figures that could occur at different locations on the computer monitor. Both the sequence of objects and the sequence of locations followed a regular pattern, and both sequences were completely uncorrelated. Although subjects had to respond to the identity of the objects, they nevertheless showed reliable learning of the sequence of locations. When the sequence of locations was switched to a random sequence, there was a reliable increase in response times. This indicates that subjects had acquired knowledge about the sequence of locations, allowing them to respond faster to objects at expected locations while delaying responses to objects at unexpected locations. Most important, there were no indications that simultaneous learning of two sequences produced interference or attenuated the magnitude of the learning effect, which is consistent with the assumption of two independent learning systems.

Whereas in Mayr's (1996) study, the sequence of locations was response-irrelevant and the sequence of objects was associated with a sequence of key presses, I have recently investigated parallel learning in a situation in which the stimuli were response-irrelevant and the locations of the stimuli were associated with responses. I used the same serial search task as described earlier (Goschke, 1996a). The only difference was that the mapping display was changed from trial to trial, such that both the sequence of locations and the sequence of letters followed a repeating pattern. However, both sequences were completely uncorrelated. To measure the development of sequential knowledge, about 10% of the regular events were replaced by deviant events at unpredictable points. There were two types of deviant events: Stimulus deviants violated the sequence of stimuli but appeared at the expected location in the mapping display and thus required a response in accordance with the response sequence. Location/response deviants were in accordance with the stimulus sequence but appeared at an unexpected location and violated the sequence of responses.

The results showed that subjects did in fact learn both sequences. Across training blocks response times for all types of events decreased in both the stimulus- and the response-sequence conditions. However, this decrease was markedly smaller for deviants, and in the final block, both response and stimulus deviants showed reliably larger response times than regular events. It is important to note that this effect was not an artifact due to averaging across participants. One might suspect that each individual participant learned either the one or the other sequence, in which case averaging across all participants would create the faulty impression that the two sequences were learned simultaneously. If this was the case, one should expect a negative correlation between the two learning effects across subjects. Contrary to this prediction, the deviance effects (that is, the response time difference for deviant and regular events) for the stimulus and the location/response sequences were not reliably correlated (on a descriptive level, the correlation was even positive). This clearly shows that participants who acquired knowledge about one sequence also learned the other sequence.

Frensch and Miner (1995), who used a sequential matching task similar to the serial search task, came to similar conclusions. They presented a mixed 10-trial sequence in which two types of stimuli (letters and meaningless graphic symbols) were presented in alternation. After 105 repetitions of the sequence, different groups of subjects were transferred to one of two test blocks. In the letter-change group, the sequence of letters was random, but the sequence of graphic symbols was the same as in the training phase. In the graphics change group, the sequence of graphic symbols was random, but the letter sequence stayed regular. The results showed that in the letter-change group, only response times to letters increased reliably as compared to the training phase, whereas in the graphics-change group, only response times to graphic symbols increased reliably. The authors concluded that phonological and visual sequences were learned independent of each other. Moreover, the fact that response times for letters did not increase in the graphics-change group, and response times for graphic symbols did not increase in the letter-change group, suggests that no learning occurred across the two domains (that is, no associations between letters and graphics had been formed).

In conclusion, uncorrelated sequences of objects and locations, of letters and locations/responses, or of letters and visual forms can be learned in parallel and independent of each other. This finding is at least consistent with the assumption that learning of different sequences is mediated by independent learning systems.

NEUROPSYCHOLOGICAL AND NEUROIMAGING STUDIES OF SEQUENCE LEARNING

The evidence summarized so far suggests (a) that implicit and explicit sequence learning are qualitatively dissociable and (b) that different types of uncorrelated sequences can be learned simultaneously. Although these findings are consistent with the idea that there are separate systems for explicit and implicit learning as well as multiple domain-specific systems underlying different forms of implicit learning, it is difficult to establish this claim on the basis of behavioral evidence alone (cf. Anderson, 1978; Barsalou, 1990; Palmer, 1978). Dissociations between explicit and implicit memory can often be explained by different processes within a single system (e.g. Roediger, 1990). Likewise, simultaneous learning of two sequences may in principle be mediated by a unitary system with the capacity for learning two sequences in parallel. Therefore, data from neuropsychology and neurophysiology provide important additional constraints for deciding between competing theories (cf. Markowitsch, 1992; Schacter & Tulving, 1994; Squire et al., 1993). As neuropsychological and neuroimaging studies of sequence learning have been thoroughly reviewed by Curran (1995, Chapter 11, this volume), I will restrict my discussion to a few findings directly relevant for the present arguments.

● Sequence Learning in Amnesic Patients

The assumption that there are separate systems for implicit and explicit learning receives support from the study of brain-damaged patients suffering from amnesia. There is now relatively convincing evidence that damage to a number of localizable brain structures (in particular, the hippocampus and related areas such as the entorhinal, perirhinal, and parahippocampal cortices and the diencephalon) produce severe impairments of conscious memory for new episodes or facts (Kolb & Whishaw, 1990; Markowitsch, 1992; Schacter & Tulving, 1994; Squire, 1992). Despite their impaired declarative memory, amnesic patients often show more or less intact skill learning (Cohen & Squire, 1980; Kolb & Whishaw, 1990; Milner, Corkin, & Teuber, 1968; Moscovitch, Winocur, & McLachlan, 1986; Soliveri et al., 1992; Squire et al., 1993). Moreover, reliable learning in the SRT task has been demonstrated in amnesic patients suffering from Korsakoff's disease (Nissen & Bullemer, 1987; Nissen, Willingham, & Hartman, 1989) or Alzheimer's disease (Ferraro, Balota, & Connor, 1993; Knopman, 1991; Knopman & Nissen, 1987). Whereas control subjects often noted the repeating pattern, there was usually no evidence for conscious knowledge in the amnesic patients. It should be noted, however, that some of these studies have been criticized for methodological shortcomings (see Curran,

1995, Chapter 11, this volume, for discussion). For instance, in many studies, response times for a repeating sequence were compared with response times in a random block without matching the two blocks with respect to the frequencies of simple pairwise transitions. Many of these methodological issues were adequately addressed in a recent study by Reber and Squire (1994), who nevertheless demonstrated intact sequence learning in amnesic patients with diencephalic lesions and a smaller group of patients with hippocampal lesions.[3] In conclusion, the available evidence suggests that implicit sequence learning is independent of brain areas necessary for explicit declarative memory.

● **Brain Systems Underlying Sequence Learning**

Given that implicit learning is independent from explicit memory systems, what brain structures might be involved in it? More specifically, is there evidence that different forms of implicit learning are mediated by separable domain-specific systems? On first sight, the available evidence appears to stand in contrast to this hypothesis and to support the motor-skill view of sequence learning.

Effects of Striatal Dysfunction. The idea that sequence learning consists of the acquisition of a motor skill receives support from studies of patients suffering from Parkinson's or Huntington's disease, who show pathological degenerative changes in brain structures mediating motor behavior (e.g., the basal ganglia). These patients are impaired in procedural learning tasks (Butters, Heindel, & Salmon, 1990; Heindel, Butters, & Salmon, 1988). Moreover, patients with Huntington's disease (Knopman & Nissen, 1991; Willingham & Koroshetz, 1993) and Parkinson's disease (Ferraro et al., 1993; Jackson, Jackson, Harrison, Henderson, & Kennard, 1995) sometimes show impairments in the SRT task. It should be noted, however, that in the study of Knopman and Nissen (1991), only 5 of 13 patients actually showed an impairment of sequence learning, whereas the group as a whole showed normal response time savings in a retest after a delay of 20 to 60 minutes.

Functional Brain Imaging. Fascinating insights into the neuroanatomy of sequence learning stem from recent experiments in which functional brain-imaging technologies were used to study sequence learning in normal subjects (cf. Curran, 1995, Chapter 11, this volume, for a review). Grafton, Hazeltine, and Ivry (1995) measured regional cerebral blood flow with positron emission tomography (PET) while subjects performed the SRT task with the right hand. When subjects performed the task together with a distracting secondary task and acquired little explicit knowledge of the sequence, learning-related increases of cerebral blood flow across different training blocks were observed in a network of brain structures involved in motor control (including contralateral motor cortex, supplementary motor area, putamen), as well as in contralateral parietal areas. Interestingly, when subjects performed the SRT task without a secondary task and most of them became aware of the sequence, a very different network of brain areas was activated (including the right dorsolateral prefrontal cortex, right premotor cortex, and parieto-occipital cortex).

Further evidence that different brain structures are involved in explicit and implicit sequence learning was reported by Rauch et al. (1995). All subjects performed under single-task conditions, and learning-related changes in brain activity were assessed by computing differences between regional cerebral blood flow in blocks with random and repeating sequences. When PET scans were obtained early in training, when participants showed no reliable explicit knowledge of the sequence, learning-related increases in activation were observed in right-sided cortico-striatal areas (including ventral premotor cortex, ventral striatum, and thalamus), as well as in bilateral visual association cortex. Subsequently, additional PET scans were obtained after subjects had been fully informed about the repeating sequence and showed reliable explicit knowledge. Learning-related increases in activation now occurred in a left-frontal area roughly equivalent to Broca's area, bilateral temporo-parietal cortex, and bilateral primary visual cortex.[4]

Although these initial studies permit only preliminary conclusions, a number of points are noteworthy. First, sequence learning activates not a single area but a whole network of brain structures, which is consistent with the idea that different component processes are involved. Second, explicit and implicit modes of learning appear to be mediated by very different networks of brain structures. Third, when subjects had no explicit knowledge or performed under attentional distraction, learning-related increases in activation were obtained in a cortico-striatal network of brain regions related to motor control (although partly different areas were activated in different studies). Taken together with the observation that striatal dysfunctions are sometimes associated with impairments in the SRT task, this suggests that implicit sequence learning involves modifications in brain areas underlying the control of motor performance (cf. Curran, Chapter 11, this volume; see also Grafton et al., 1992; Pascual-Leone, Grafman, & Hallett, 1994).

However, this does not imply that implicit sequence learning is restricted to the learning of response sequences, nor does it show that sequences of low-level motor commands are acquired. As Curran (Chapter 11, this volume) notes, recent neurophysiological evidence suggests that so-called motor areas represent movements at a relatively abstract level, which is independent from the parameters controlling the activity of specific muscles. If this were correct, the learning-related activation of motor areas would be compatible with the effector-independence of sequence learning (Keele et al., 1995, 1996) and the evidence for motor-independent sequence learning (Frensch & Miner, 1995; Goschke, 1996b; Mayr, 1996).

Moreover, as I noted earlier, in the original SRT task, the sequence of stimuli or locations is completely confounded with the sequence of motor responses. Thus, the finding that implicit sequence learning is related to increased activation in brain areas involved in the planning and execution of motor responses may simply be due to the fact that subjects did learn a sequence of responses. Although this is an important finding in itself, it does of course not exclude the possibility that the learning of other kinds of (perceptual) sequences involves other brain areas. This possibility receives some support from the PET findings concerning explicit learning. Explicit learning of a sequence of locations produced increases of cerebral blood flow (among other structures) in the right dorsolateral prefrontal and parieto-occipital cortex (Grafton et al., 1995).

In a recent replication study, Hazeltine, Grafton, and Ivry (1996) found that explicit learning of sequences of colors produced learning-dependent activation in the right inferior frontal lobe, as well as in the premotor cortex, thalamus, inferior temporal lobe, occipital lobes, and bilateral anterior cingulate. Note that in both studies, activation of the prefrontal cortex was observed. However, the focus of activation was more ventral with the color as compared to the location sequence. This fits with the suggestion that different prefrontal areas are involved in different working memory functions, depending on the type of information to be held active (Goldman-Rakic, 1988; Smith & Jonides, 1995; Wilson, Scalaidhe, & Goldman-Rakic, 1993). Another difference between the two studies was that the location sequence produced activation foci in parietal areas, whereas the color sequence activated regions in the temporal lobe. It is tempting to relate this finding to the distinction between a what-system in the inferior temporal lobe, underlying the recognition of objects, and a posterior-parietal system, underlying the representation of spatial information and action-related information (Goodale, 1993; Ungerleider & Mishkin, 1982). Finally, in Rauch et al.'s (1995) study, explicit sequence learning was associated (among other areas) with activation in Broca's area. This makes sense if one takes into account the authors' remark that the response keys were labeled with letters and that subjects probably used these labels to maintain parts of the sequence in phonological working memory. That rehearsal of phonological information activates Broca's area has been shown in recent PET studies (Paulesu, Frith, & Frackowiak, 1993; cf. Frackowiak, 1994).

Although at present these findings must be considered preliminary, they suggest that different brain areas may be involved in the learning and/or representation of different kinds of sequential information. However, as these findings were obtained for subjects with explicit knowledge, it remains to be investigated whether implicit learning of different sequences is also mediated by domain-specific subsystems. It will thus be important to combine brain-imaging techniques with experimental paradigms that allow one to unconfound implicit learning of different types of sequences (e.g., Frensch & Miner, 1995; Goschke, 1996a, 1996b; Mayr, 1996).

● **Event-Related Brain Potentials and Sequence Learning**

Although brain-imaging studies have yielded important information concerning the anatomical structures involved in sequence learning, methods like PET are to date limited with respect to their temporal resolution. It is thus useful to complement these methods with electrophysiological measures, in particular, event-related brain potentials[5] (ERPs), that allow one to investigate the neural correlates of sequence learning on a more fine-grained time scale (albeit at the cost of less precise localization of the underlying sources of electrical activity; cf. Nunez, 1981). Eimer, Goschke, Schlaghecken, and Stürmer (1996) recorded ERPs while subjects performed a variant of the SRT task, where in each trial one of four letters (A, B, C, D) was presented at fixation, each of which was mapped to one out of four response keys. At unpredictable points in a repeating ambiguous 10-letter sequence, deviant letters were inserted, which were not allowed to occur at that specific position in the sequence. In two experiments, we found that reaction times for deviant stimuli were significantly slower than for standard stimuli and that this difference increased in the course of training. ERP waveforms that were averaged over deviant items showed an enhanced negativity in the range of 200 milliseconds post-stimulus as compared to ERPs elicited by regular items. This negativity tended to be larger in the second part of the experiment. This negativity effect was also larger for subjects showing at least some explicit knowledge in their verbal reports and a recognition test, suggesting that it is a reflection of explicit knowledge about the sequence. It may be noteworthy that negativities in the ERP (albeit with different latencies) have been obtained for deviations in other sequential structures, such as melodies (Besson & Macar, 1987; Paller, McCarthy, & Wood, 1992) and for syntactic-category violations in sentences (Friederici, Hahne, & Mecklinger, 1996). Although these effects all reflect in some sense the detection of deviations from a sequential structure, it is at present an open, although interesting question what the commonalities and differences in the underlying processes may be.

A second result of our study was evidence for anticipatory processes in sequence learning. An analysis of the Lateralized Readiness Potential (LRP), which can be considered an index of the selective activation of either a left- or right-hand response (Coles, 1989), showed that after extended training, correct responses were activated with shorter latencies than early in training. When deviant items, which had to be responded to with an unexpected hand, were occasionally inserted in the sequence, participants showed an initial activation of the incorrect, but to be expected response. This shows that the anticipatory preparation of responses plays an important role in sequence learning. However, although these data demonstrate the importance of motor preparation for performance increments, it must be stressed that they do not allow one to decide whether this preparation was actually due to motor learning or whether participants learned the sequence of stimuli and used this knowledge in an anticipatory way to prepare the next motor response. Results from the serial search task described earlier (Goschke, 1996b) support the latter alternative, because facilitative effects of an anticipation of the next stimulus were observed even though there was no regular sequence of motor responses. Irrespective of this question, our ERP findings fit with the assumption that sequence learning involves the formation of anticipations on the basis of a temporary context memory for previous events (Goschke, 1992, 1994; cf. Hoffmann, 1993). In terms of this model, the LRP effect may reflect the anticipation of what comes next, whereas the deviation-related negativity may reflect the registration of a deviation from the anticipated event and the updating of context memory.

One particularly attractive feature of ERPs is that they can measure sequence learning even if subjects do not have to respond overtly but merely observe an event sequence. This allows one to obtain nonreactive evidence that pure event sequences can be learned, even if subjects do not have to respond with overt motor actions (this does not, of course, exclude the possibility that our subjects did respond "covertly"). In an initial experiment (Goschke, 1996a), we presented participants in each trial one out of four letters (A, B, C, D) at one out of four different locations. Participants were instructed to fixate a point at the center of the screen but to pay attention to the letters appearing around the fixation cross. No overt responses were required. Both the letters and the locations appeared in a repeating sequence, but the two sequences were completely uncorrelated. At unpredictable points, two kinds of deviant events were inserted into the sequence. Letter deviations were letters that violated the letter sequence but appeared at the correct location (according to the location sequence). Location deviations were correct letters (that is, letters in accordance with the letter sequence) that appeared at a wrong, unexpected location that violated the sequence of locations. For instance, when the next regular event is a B at location 3, a letter deviant might be the letter D at location 3, whereas a location deviant might be the letter B at location 1.

The results showed that ERP waveforms for deviant events again exhibited an enhanced negativity in a similar time range as in our previous experiments. This was true for both the letter and the locations deviants. The deviation-related negativities for letter and location deviants were not significantly correlated, which indicates that the two sequences were learned simultaneously. This replicates the finding of parallel learning of two sequences in a condition, in which even eye movements were excluded as a possible source of response-based learning. Moreover, there were some indications that the deviation-related negativity for the location deviants had a shorter latency and a more central-parietal maximum as compared to the letter deviants, which showed a left-frontal maximum. However, before any inferences regarding different underlying neural generators of the two types of deviant effects can be drawn, these very preliminary results must be replicated. Irrespective of the issue of localization, our initial studies clearly show that sequences of locations and letters can be learned implicitly, even when no overt responses are required. From a more general perspective, the measurement of ERPs in combination with traditional chronometric methods is a particularly promising strategy to obtain nonreactive online measures of the development of sequential knowledge, measures that do not depend on the subject's overt responding and that allow for fine-grained analyses of the component processes involved in sequence learning.

CONCLUSIONS AND SPECULATIONS

Is There a Domain-Unspecific Sequence-Acquisition Device?

I have reviewed behavioral and neurophysiological evidence to support a modular view of implicit sequence learning. However, evidence for multiple domain-specific sequence-learning and representation systems by no means excludes the possibility that there is also a general purpose *sequence-acquisition device*. Such a domain-unspecific system might store abstract representations of sequential structures derived from, but independent of, their surface instantiations. If such a domain-independent system exists, one should expect that sequential knowledge acquired in one domain should transfer to other domains. By contrast, if implicit learning produces only domain-specific sequence representations, one might expect that this knowledge is relatively encapsulated and shows only limited transfer across domains.

Most studies of cross-domain transfer have focused on transfer across different effectors. As was noted earlier, such transfer has consistently been found, which indicates that relatively abstract sequence representations are acquired in SRT tasks, which can be interfaced with different output modules (Cohen et al., 1990; Keele & Curran, in press; Keele et al., 1995, 1996; Stadler, 1989). However, although these findings show that part of the sequential knowledge was more abstract than a specific sequence of motor movements, they do not necessarily prove the existence of an abstract sequence-learning system representing all kinds of sequences detached from their perceptual surface structure. According to an alternative account that is consistent with a modular view, transfer occurs to the degree that two different effector systems have highly overlearned connections to a common, but nevertheless domain-specific representation at some level. For instance, when a subject learns a sequence of locations of to-be-pressed keys, this representation can control movements of different fingers, the whole arm, or the feet, because all the different effector systems presumably have preexisting, highly automatized connections to representations of intended locations. By contrast, less transfer is to be expected when an effector system is not so easily accessed by the particular sequence representation that was acquired in the training phase. For instance, the finding that transfer from a sequence of manual key presses to an isomorphic sequence of vocal responses was less than perfect (Keele et al., 1995) fits with this account, if one assumes that the connection from a representation of spatial locations to verbal labels is less automatized than from spatial locations to different movement systems. No transfer at all should occur when the representation acquired during training has no preexisting links to the effector system used in the transfer phase. For instance, in preliminary pilot work, we found no transfer from a learning phase in which subjects had to name a sequence of letters to an isomorphic sequence of key presses in response to spatial locations, even if subjects were fully informed about the mapping between letters and locations. This is to be expected when subjects initially learn a nonspatial representation of letters, which has no overlearned links to spatial locations or manual responses. In conclusion, this view accounts for transfer effects by assuming that only domain-specific sequences are acquired (e.g., depending on the stimuli and the task, these may be sequences of key presses, spatial locations, verbal labels, visual objects) and that the amount of transfer depends on whether different effector systems can be accessed from a shared sequence representation.

Further indirect evidence against the idea that implicit sequence learning is subserved by a domain-unspecific system producing abstract knowledge stems from other fields of implicit learning research. In general, this research suggests that implicit knowledge about structured stimuli shows only very limited transfer to stimuli instantiating the same deep structure but differing in their perceptual surface features. Most of these studies concern the learning of artificial grammars, in which subjects study a list of meaningless letter strings that are generated by a finite-state grammar and are later able to classify new strings as grammatical or ungrammatical better than chance, even though they are limited in their verbal knowledge about the underlying rules (Reber, 1993). In some studies, it has been shown that subjects were still able to classify new stimuli better than chance, when the stimuli were constructed from a new set of letters or when there was a switch from letter strings to tone sequences generated by the same grammar (Altmann, Dienes, & Goode, 1995; see Goschke, in press-b; Reber, 1993; Redington & Chater, 1996, for reviews). However, these effects were usually very small, and it has been shown convincingly in recent computer simulations that the effects can be explained by assuming that subjects applied simple conscious rules and analogies to map stimuli across domains (Redington & Chater, 1996). Finally, research on implicit memory has also shown that repetition priming effects in indirect memory tests such as word-fragment completion are strongly attenuated when perceptual features such as type font or presentation modality are changed between study and test (Jacoby & Hayman, 1987; Kirsner, Milech, & Standen, 1983; Schacter, 1994). In conclusion, studies on transfer of implicit knowledge across changes of perceptual surface features of stimuli have yielded no convincing evidence for abstract, domain-unspecific implicit knowledge.

Toward a Neurocognitive Theory of Sequence Learning

I have tried to integrate various lines of research to defend the hypotheses that implicit sequence learning does exist and that it is not restricted to the acquisition of new motor skills but that different kinds of domain-specific sequential information can be learned. In this final section, I would like to draw some more general, admittedly speculative conclusions.

1. The available evidence is consistent with the idea that implicit sequence learning is relatively independent from the medial-temporal memory systems required for explicit, episodic memory. However, as I noted before, at present it is an unresolved issue whether the hippocampal system may be specifically involved in learning of higher-order, context-dependent sequential contingencies (see Curran, Chapter 11, this volume).

2. There is at least suggestive evidence supporting the idea that implicit sequence learning depends on experience-dependent modifications in different domain-specific brain structures, in particular, those structures that are also involved in the initial processing of the to-be-learned information (e.g., sequences of locations, objects, linguistic symbols, or motor responses). This hypothesis is consistent with findings from various other fields of cognitive neuroscience.

(a) Given the important role of attention in learning more complex types of sequences (Cohen et al., 1990; Curran & Keele, 1993; Stadler, 1995), the present view is consistent with recent distinctions between functionally separable attentional systems mediating spatial orienting, vigilance, and target detection (Posner & Peterson, 1990), or between sensory arousal versus motor activation (Pribram & McGuiness, 1975; Tucker & Williamson, 1984). It appears a promising hypothesis that learning of different types of sequences (e.g., locations versus responses) involves different attentional systems (e.g., for spatial orienting versus motor preparation).

(b) Likewise, the concept of working memory has been conceived in terms of separate subsystems for the maintenance of auditory-verbal and visual-spatial information (Baddeley, 1986; cf. Frensch & Miner, 1995). Recent PET studies have shown that rehearsal of phonological information activated Broca's area (Paulesu et al., 1993); short-term retention of spatial locations produced increased activation in prefrontal, parietal, occipital, and premotor regions of the right hemisphere; whereas short-retention of visual objects activated infero-temporal, parietal, and prefrontal regions of the left hemisphere (Smith & Jonides, 1995). Although the role of working memory in sequence learning remains controversial, it appears again an idea worth pursuing that domain-specific working memory systems are involved in the learning of different types of sequences (e.g., Frensch & Miner, 1995).

(c) Similar suggestions have been made with respect to long-term memory. Regarding visual processing, there has long been a distinction between what- and where-systems responsible for the recognition of object properties and the processing of spatial (and perhaps also action-related) information, respectively (Goodale, 1993; Ungerleider & Mishkin, 1982; Wilson et al., 1993). From a more general perspective, it has been suggested that various attributes of an experience (e.g., color, form, location) are represented in different neocortical areas involved in the initial perceptual processing of the information and that retrieval of information consists of a reinstantiation of distributed activation patterns in these cortical areas (Damasio, 1989; Goschke, in press-a; McClelland, Naughton, & O'Reilly, 1995; Squire, 1992). Electrophysiological evidence for this assumption was reported by Roesler, Heil, and Hennighausen (1995), who found that retrieval from long-term memory was correlated with slow negative brain-potential shifts lasting several seconds. The maximum of these negative shifts differed depending on the type of to-be-retrieved information: Retrieval of spatial information was associated with a maximum over parietal electrodes, retrieval of verbal information produced a maximum over left-frontal locations, and retrieval of colors produced maximal negative shifts over the right occipital cortex. Assuming that slow negative shifts indicate increased activity in the underlying cortical areas (cf. Birbaumer & Schmidt, 1990), these findings are consistent with the idea of a distributed network of areas representing domain-specific information.

Taken together, these two conclusions suggest a tentative theoretical model of the functions and mechanisms of implicit and explicit learning. According to this framework, implicit learning is based on gradual, incremental, and relatively slow changes in domain-specific representation systems. These changes are a by-product of processing sensory information or performing some task. A general class of computational models for this type of learning are connectionist networks in which information is represented in the pattern of connection weights, and novel information is acquired by gradual experience-dependent changes of connection weights (Cleeremans, 1993; Elman, 1991; Goschke & Koppelberg, 1991; McClelland et al., 1995; Rumelhart, McClelland, & The PDP Research Group, 1986). The adaptive function of such a learning mechanism based on relatively slow, incremental changes across many individual processing episodes can be seen in the extraction of invariances and repeating patterns from a large number of specific exemplars. With respect to implicit sequence learning, this mechanism presumably underlies the ability to form anticipations about what comes or what has to be done next in situations with invariant, regular, or repeating patterns of stimulation (cf., Goschke, in press-b; Sherry & Schacter, 1987).

In contrast, explicit memory systems reflect the opposite requirement, to retain single episodes in a spatio-temporal context and to store significant events even after a single exposure (Goschke, in press-b; Sherry & Schacter, 1987). Although the hippocampal system appears to play a crucial role in this type of learning, it is most probably not the anatomic locus at which declarative long-term memory traces are stored. This is shown by the observation that amnesic patients as well as animals with hippocampal lesions often (although not always) exhibit a temporal gradient of forgetting, that is, the longer before the lesion an event was experienced, the better it is remembered (cf. Squire, 1992). The hippocampus and related structures appear to play a time-dependent role in the consolidation of new episodic traces into long-term memory. The assumption of an extended consolidation process is supported by the observation that various factors such as electrical shocks or stimulation, inhibition of protein synthesis, blocking of certain neurotransmitters, and administration of hormones or peptides can impair or facilitate long-term memory in a time-dependent manner (McGaugh, 1989).

Based on neurological data and computational characteristics of connectionist learning procedures, McClelland et al. (1995; see also Squire,

1992) have recently proposed the specific hypothesis that the hippocampal system underlies the rapid acquisition of new memories, which are initially represented in a condensed format in the hippocampal system. These condensed representations support the reinstatement of distributed activation patterns representing the event in neocortical areas. Thus, initially, the hippocampal system is necessary to "bind" together different aspects of a newly encoded event into an integrated representation. During the consolidation process, repeated reinstatements of a new memory trace gradually lead to changes in the neocortical connectivity, which underlie the formation of permanent memory traces. Once established, these permanent traces can be retrieved in a content-addressable manner without intervention of the hippocampal system.

Although speculative in many respects, one attractive feature of the McClelland et al. (1995) model is that it provides a computational account for the different properties of explicit and implicit learning, one that is consistent with the above characterization of their complementary functions. The idea is that there are two contradictory constraints that a memory system must satisfy: on the one hand, it should be able to extract invariances and covariations across a large number of exemplars or episodes, thereby effectively ignoring variation and individual exemplars. On the other hand, it should be able to rapidly store significant new events even after a single encounter. To the degree that it is impossible to fulfill both requirements within a single system (Sherry & Schacter, 1987), multiple memory systems may have evolved.

Although the study of implicit sequence learning has revealed unexpected complexities, and although many theoretical ideas still have a speculative flavor, I think that this research is also particularly successful in exemplifying the advantages of a coevolutionary program, in which findings from experimental psychology, cognitive neuroscience, and computational modeling serve as mutual constraints for an understanding of the underlying systems and processes.

NOTES

1. Assuming that conscious and unconscious influences on performance are independent, one can also derive an estimate for the probability of automatically producing a chunk from the old sequence in the absence of a conscious recollection, $I = Exclusion/(1 - E)$ (see Jacoby et al., 1993, for details).

2. Note that modular and abstractionist views are not necessarily mutually incompatible. Different forms of sequence learning may involve experience-dependent modifications in different domain-specific subsystems, but there may in addition exist a general, domain-unspecific mechanism underlying the formation of more abstract sequential codes, which can be interfaced to different domain-specific systems (Greenfield, 1991; Keele et al., 1995).

3. It should be noted that, on a descriptive level, Reber and Squire's patients showed considerably smaller learning effects than control subjects (cf. Shanks & Johnstone, Chapter 16, this volume, for a critical discussion). Curran (Chapter 11, this volume) reports suggestive evidence that amnesic patients may be specifically impaired in learning more complex sequences containing only higher-order transitions. This would fit with evidence from the animal literature suggesting that the hippocampus is important for relational or configural learning and for the acquisition of higher-order contingencies (e.g., Rudy & Sutherland, 1994).

4. In contrast to Grafton et al.'s (1995) single-task condition, Rauch et al. (1995) found no activation of dorsolateral prefrontal cortex in their explicit learning condition. This may have been due to the fact that Rauch et al. were not able to measure completely activity in superior brain regions. That the dorsolateral prefrontal cortex may in fact play a role in explicit sequence learning is supported by another PET study, in which this region was activated when a sequence of key presses had to be learned explicitly (Nixon, Frackowiak, & Passingham, 1994). Interestingly, when sequences were very highly practiced, activation in the supplementary motor cortex increased, whereas there was less activation in dorsolateral prefrontal cortex.

5. ERPs are obtained by recording the electroencephalogram (EEG) from electrodes located on the scalp and averaging across a large number of trials, time-locked to the presentation of a stimulus or the execution of a response, in order to eliminate random fluctuations in the EEG. ERPs triggered by a specific task-stimulus combination typically consist of a relatively regular sequence of positive and negative voltage deflections or components, and it is assumed that these components reflect specific patterns of neural activity mediating perceptual, cognitive, or motor processes (cf. Hillyard & Kutas, 1983).

REFERENCES

Altmann, G. T. M., Dienes, Z., & Goode, A. (1995). Modality independence of implicitly learned grammatical knowledge. *Journal of Experimental Psychology: Learning, Memory, and Cognition, 21,* 899-912.

Anderson, J. R. (1978). Arguments concerning representations from mental imagery. *Psychological Review, 85,* 249-277.

Anderson, J. R. (1983). *The architecture of cognition.* Cambridge, MA: Harvard University Press.

Anderson, J. R. (1987). Skill acquisition: Compilation of weak-method problem solutions. *Psychological Review, 94,* 192-210.

Baddeley, A. D. (1986). *Working memory.* Oxford, UK: Clarendon.

Barsalou, L. W. (1990). On the indistinguishability of exemplar memory and abstraction in category representation. In T. K. Srull & R. S. Wyer (Eds.), *Advances in social cognition: Vol. 3. Content and process specificity in the effects of prior experiences.* Hillsdale, NJ: Lawrence Erlbaum.

Berry, D. C., & Dienes, Z. (1993). *Implicit learning: Theoretical and empirical issues.* Hillsdale, NJ: Lawrence Erlbaum.

Besson, M., & Macar, F. (1987). An event-related potential analysis of incongruity in music and other nonlinguistic contexts. *Psychophysiology, 24,* 14-25.

Birbaumer, N., & Schmidt, R. F. (1990). *Biologische Psychologie.* Berlin: Springer.

Buchner, A. (1993). *Implizites Lernen.* Weinheim: Psychologie Verlags Union.

Buchner, A., Erdfelder, E., & Vaterrodt-Plünnecke, B. (1995). Toward unbiased measurement of conscious and unconscious memory processes within the process dissociation framework. *Journal of Experimental Psychology: General, 124,* 137-160.

Butters, N., Heindel, W. C., & Salmon, D. P. (1990). Dissociation of implicit memory in dementia: Neurological implications. *Bulletin of the Psychonomic Society, 28,* 359-366.

Cheesman, J., & Merikle, P. M. (1984). Priming with and without awareness. *Perception and Psychophysics, 36,* 387-395.

Cleeremans, A. (1993). *Mechanisms of implicit learning.* Cambridge: MIT Press.

Cleeremans, A., & McClelland, J. L. (1991). Learning the structure of event sequences. *Journal of Experimental Psychology: General, 120,* 235-253.

Cohen, A., & Curran, T. (1993). On tasks, knowledge, correlations, and dissociations: Comment on Perruchet and Amorim (1992). *Journal of Experimental Psychology: Learning, Memory, and Cognition, 19,* 1431-1437.

Cohen, A., Ivry, R. I., & Keele, S. W. (1990). Attention and structure in sequence learning. *Journal of Experimental Psychology: Learning, Memory, and Cognition, 16,* 17-30.

Cohen, N. J., & Squire, L. R. (1980). Presevered learning and retention of pattern-analyzing skill in amnesia: Dissociation of "knowing how" and "knowing that." *Science, 210,* 207-209.

Coles, M. G. (1989). Modern mind-brain reading: Psychophysiology, physiology, and cognition. *Psychophysiology, 26,* 251-269.

Curran, T. (1995). On the neural mechanisms of sequence learning. *Psyche* [On-line serial], 2(12). Available at URL:http://psyche.cs.monash.edu.au/volume2-1/psyche-95-2-12-sequence-1-curran.html.

Curran, T., & Keele, S. W. (1993). Attentional and nonattentional forms of sequence learning. *Journal of Experimental Psychology: Learning, Memory, and Cognition, 19,* 189-202.

Damasio, A. R. (1989). Time-locked multiregional retroactivation: A systems-level proposal for the neural substrates of recall and recognition. *Cognition, 33,* 25-62.

Dunn, J. C., & Kirsner, K. (1988). Discovering functionally independent mental processes: The principle of reversed association. *Psychological Review, 95,* 91-101.

Eimer, M., Goschke, T., Schlaghecken, F., & Stürmer, B. (1996). Explicit and implicit learning of event sequences: Evidence from event-related brain potentials. *Journal of Experimental Psychology: Learning, Memory, and Cognition, 22,* 970-987.

Elman, J. L. (1991). Distributed representation, simple recurrent networks, and grammatical structure. *Machine Learning, 7,* 195-225.

Erderlyi, M. H. (1986). Experimental indeterminacies in the dissociation paradigm of subliminal perception: Comment on Holender (1986). *Behavioral and Brain Sciences, 9,* 30-31.

Fendrich, D. W., Healy, A. F., & Bourne, L. E. (1991). Long-term repetition effects for motoric and perceptual procedures. *Journal of Experimental Psychology: Learning, Memory, and Cognition, 17,* 137-151.

Ferraro, F. R., Balota, D. A., & Connor, L. T. (1993). Implicit memory and the formation of new associations in nondemented Parkinson's disease individuals and individuals with senile dementia of the Alzheimer type: A serial reaction time (SRT) investigation. *Brain and Cognition, 21,* 163-180.

Frackowiak, R. S. J. (1994). Functional mapping of verbal memory and language. *Trends in Neuroscience, 17,* 109-115.

Frensch, P. A., Buchner, A., & Lin, J. (1994). Implicit learning of unique and ambiguous serial transitions in the presence and absence of a distractor task. *Journal of Experimental Psychology: Learning, Memory, and Cognition, 20,* 567-584.

Frensch, P., & Miner, C. S. (1994). Individual differences in short-term memory capacity on an indirect measure of serial learning. *Memory & Cognition, 22,* 95-110.

Frensch, P., & Miner, C. S. (1995). Zur Rolle des Arbeitsgedächtnisses beim impliziten Sequenzlernen [The role of working memory in implicit sequence learning]. *Zeitschrift für Experimentelle Psychologie, 42,* 545-575.

Friederici, A. D., Hahne, A., & Mecklinger, A. (1996). Temporal structure of syntactic parsing: Early and late event-related brain potential effect. *Journal of Experimental Psychology: Learning, Memory, and Cognition, 22,* 1219-1248.

Gardiner, J. M., & Java, R. I. (1993). Recognizing and remembering. In A. Collins, M. A. Conway, S. E. Gathercole, & P. E. Morris (Eds.), *Theories of memory* (pp. 163-188). Hillsdale, NJ: Lawrence Erlbaum.

Goldman-Rakic, P. S. (1988). Cortical localization of working memory. In J. L. McGaugh, N. M. Weinberger, & G. Lynch (Eds.), *Brain organization and memory: Cells, systems, and circuits* (pp. 285-300). New York: Oxford University Press.

Goodale, M. A. (1993). Visual pathways supporting perception and action in the primate cerebral cortex. *Current Opinions in Neurobiology, 3,* 578-585.

Goschke, T. (1992). The role of attention in implicit learning of event sequences [Abstract]. *International Journal of Psychology, 27,* 110.

Goschke, T. (1994). *Mechanisms of implicit sequence learning: Evidence from dual-task studies and event-related brain potentials.* Poster presented at the 1994 European Summer Institute for Cognitive Neuroscience, Nijmegen, The Netherlands.

Goschke, T. (1996a). *Implicit learning of stimulus and response sequences: Evidence for independent learning systems.* Paper presented at the Max-Planck Institute for Cognitive Neuroscience, Leipzig, Germany.

Goschke, T. (1996b). *Learning stimulus and response sequences: Independence of perception and action in implicit learning.* Manuscript submitted for publication.

Goschke, T. (in press-a). Gedächtnis und Lernen: Mentale Prozesse und Hirnstrukturen. In G. Roth & W. Prinz (Eds.), *Kopf-Arbeit: Gehirnfunktionen und kognitive Leistungen.* Heidelberg: Spektrum Akademischer Verlag.

Goschke, T. (in press-b). Implicit learning and unconscious knowledge: Mental representation, computational mechanisms, and brain structures. In K. Lamberts & D. Shanks (Eds.), *Knowledge, concept, and categories.* London: University College London Press.

Goschke, T., & Koppelberg, D. (1991). The concept of representation and the representation of concepts in connectionist models. In W. Ramsey, D. E. Rumelhart, & S. Stich (Eds.), *Philosophy and connectionist theory* (pp. 129-162). Hillsdale, NJ: Lawrence Erlbaum.

Goschke, T., & Stürmer, B. (1997). *Explicit and implicit knowledge in sequence learning: A process dissociation approach.* Manuscript in preparation.

Graf, P., & Komatsu, S. (1994). Process dissociation procedure: Handle with caution! *European Journal of Cognitive Psychology, 6,* 113-129.

Grafton, S. T., Hazeltine, E., & Ivry, R. (1995). Functional mapping of sequence learning in normal humans. *Journal of Cognitive Neuroscience, 7,* 497-510.

Grafton, S. T., Mazziotta, J. C., Presty, S., Friston, K. J., Frackowiak, R. S. J. & Phelps, M. E. (1992). Functional anatomy of human procedural learning determined with regional cerebral blood flow and PET. *Journal of Neuroscience, 12,* 2542-2548.

Greenfield, P. (1991). Language, tools, and brain: The ontogeny and phylogeny of hierarchically organized sequential behavior. *Behavioral and Brain Sciences, 14,* 531-595.

Hartman, M., Knopman, D. S., & Nissen, M. J. (1989). Implicit learning of new verbal associations. *Journal of Experimental Psychology: Learning, Memory, and Cognition, 15,* 1070-1082.

Hazeltine, E., Grafton, S. T., & Ivry, R. (1996). *Neural loci of motor learning depend on stimulus characteristics.* Unpublished manuscript.

Heindel, W. C., Butters, N., & Salmon, D. P. (1988). Impaired learning of a motor skill in patients with Huntington's disease. *Behavioral Neuroscience, 102,* 141-147.

Hillyard, S. A., & Kutas, M. (1983). Electrophysiology of cognitive processing. *Annual Review of Psychology, 34,* 33-61.

Hoffmann, J. (1993). *Erkenntnis und Vorhersage.* Göttingen: Hogrefe.

Hoffman, J., & Sebald, A. (1996). Reiz- und Reaktionsmuster in seriellen Wahlreaktionen. *Zeitschrift für experimentelle Psychologie, 43,* 40-68.

Holender, D. (1986). Semantic activation without conscious identification in dichotic listening, parafoveal vision, and visual masking: A survey and reappraisal. *Behavioral and Brain Sciences, 9,* 1-23.

Howard, J. H., Mutter, S. A., & Howard, D. V. (1992). Serial pattern learning by event observation. *Journal of Experimental Psychology: Learning, Memory, and Cognition, 18,* 1029-1039.

Jackson, G. M., Jackson, S. R., Harrison, J., Henderson, L., & Kennard, C. (1995). Serial reaction time learning and Parkinson's disease: Evidence for a procedural learning deficit. *Neuropsychologia, 33,* 597-593.

Jacoby, L. (1991). A process dissociation framework: Separating automatic from intentional use of memory. *Journal of Memory and Language, 30,* 513-541.

Jacoby, L. L., & Hayman, C. A. G. (1987). Specific visual transfer in word identification. *Journal of Experimental Psychology: Learning, Memory, and Cognition, 13,* 456-463.

Jacoby, L. L., Toth, J. P. & Yonelinas, A. P. (1993). Separating conscious and unconscious influences of memory: Measuring recollection. *Journal of Experimental Psychology: General, 122,* 139-154.

James, W. (1890). *Principles of psychology.* New York: Holt.

Jiménez, L., Méndez, C., & Cleeremans, A. (1996). Comparing direct and indirect measures of sequence learning. *Journal of Experimental Psychology: Learning, Memory, and Cognition, 22,* 948-969.

Joordens, S., & Merikle, P. M. (1993). Independence or redundancy? Two models of conscious and unconscious influences. *Journal of Experimental Psychology: General, 122,* 462-467.

Keele, S., & Curran, T. (in press). On the modularity of sequence learning systems in humans. In E. Covey, R. F. Port, & H. L. Hawkins (Eds.), *Neural representation of temporal patterns.* New York: Plenum.

Keele, S., Davidson, M., & Hayes, A. (1996). *Sequential representation and the neural basis of motor skills* (Technical Report No. 96-12). Eugene: Institute of Cognitive and Decision Sciences, University of Oregon.

Keele, S., Jennings, P., Jones, S., Caulton, D., & Cohen, A. (1995). On the modularity of sequence representation. *Journal of Motor Behavior, 27,* 17-30.

Kirsner, K., Milech, D., & Standen, P. (1983). Common and modality-specific processes in the mental lexicon. *Memory & Cognition, 11,* 621-630.

Knopman, D. (1991). Long-term retention of implicitly acquired learning in patients with Alzheimer's disease. *Journal of Clinical and Experimental Neuropsychology, 13,* 880-894.

Knopman, D., & Nissen, M. J. (1987). Implicit learning in patients with probable Alzheimer's disease. *Neurology, 37,* 784-788.

Knopman, D., & Nissen, M. J. (1991). Procedural learning is impaired in Huntington's disease: Evidence from the serial reaction time task. *Neuropsychologia, 29,* 245-254.

Kolb, B., & Whishaw, I. Q. (1990). *Fundamentals of human neuropsychology.* New York: Freeman.

Lashley, K. S. (1951). The problem of serial order in behavior. In L. A. Jeffress (Ed.), *Cerebral mechanisms in behavior.* New York: John Wiley.

Lewicki, P., Hill, T., & Bizot, E. (1988). Acquisition of procedural knowledge about a pattern of stimuli that cannot be articulated. *Cognitive Psychology, 20,* 24-37.

Mandler, G. (1980). Recognizing: The judgment of previous occurrence. *Psychological Review, 87,* 252-271.

Markowitsch, H. J. (1992). *Neuropsychologie des Gedächtnisses.* Göttingen: Hogrefe.

Mayr, U. (1996). Spatial attention and implicit sequence learning: Evidence for independent learning of spatial and nonspatial sequences. *Journal of Experimental Psychology: Learning, Memory, and Cognition, 22,* 350-364.

McClelland, J. L., Naughton, B. L., & O'Reilly, R. C. (1995). Why there are complementary learning systems in the hippocampus and neocortex: Insights from the successes and failures of connectionist models of learning and memory. *Psychological Review, 102,* 419-457.

McGaugh, J. L. (1989). Involvement of hormonal and neuromodulatory systems in the regulation of memory storage. *Annual Review of Neurosciences, 12,* 255-287.

Merikle, P. (1982). Unconscious perception revisited. *Perception and Psychophysics, 31,* 289-301.

Milner, B., Corkin, S. & Teuber, H.-L. (1968). Further analysis of the hippocampal amnesic snydrome: 14-year follow-up of H.M. *Neuropsychologia, 6,* 215-234.

Moscovitch, M., Winocur, G., & McLachlan, D. (1986). Memory as assessed by recognition and reading time in normal and memory-impaired people with Alzheimer's disease and other neurological disorders. *Journal of Experimental Psychology: General, 115,* 331-347.

Nattkemper, D. (1993). *Processing structured event sequences.* Paper presented at the sixth conference of the European Society for Cognitive Psychology, Elsinore.

Nattkemper, D., & Prinz, W. (1993). *Processing structured event sequences.* Paper presented at the sixth conference of the European Society for Cognitive Psychology, Elsinore.

Nissen, M. J., & Bullemer, P. (1987). Attentional requirements of learning: Evidence from performance measures. *Cognitive Psychology, 19,* 1-32.

Nissen, M. J., Willingham, D., & Hartman, M. (1989). Explicit and implicit remembering: When is learning preserved in amnesia? *Neuropsychologia, 27,* 341-352.

Nunez, P. (1981). *Electrical fields of the brain.* New York: Oxford University Press.

Paller, K. A., McCarthy, G., & Wood, C. C. (1992). Event-related potentials elicited by deviant endings of melodies. *Psychophysiology, 29,* 202-206.

Palmer, S. E. (1978). Fundamental aspects of mental representation. In E. Rosch & B. B. Lloyd (Eds.), *Cognition and categorization* (pp. 259-303). Hillsdale, NJ: Lawrence Erlbaum.

Pascual-Leone, A., Grafman, J., & Hallett, M. (1994). Modulation of cortical output motor maps during development of implicit and explicit knowledge. *Science, 263,* 1287-1289.

Pascual-Leone, A., Wassermann, E. M., Grafman, J., & Hallett, M. (1996). The role of the dorsolateral prefrontal cortex in implicit procedural learning. *Experimental Brain Research, 107,* 479-485.

Paulesu, E., Frith, C. D., & Frackowiak, R. S. J. (1993). The neural correlates of the verbal component of working memory. *Nature, 362,* 342-345.

Perruchet, P. (1994). Learning from complex rule-governed environments: On the proper functions of nonconscious and conscious processes. In C. Umiltà & M. Moscovitch (Eds.), *Attention and performance XV: Conscious and nonconscious information processing* (pp. 811-835). Cambridge: MIT Press.

Perruchet, P., & Amorim, M. A. (1992). Conscious knowledge and changes in performance in sequence learning: Evidence against dissocation. *Journal of Experimental Psychology: Learning, Memory, and Cognition, 18,* 785-800.

Perruchet, P., & Gallego, J. (1993). Association between conscious knowledge and performance in normal subjects: Reply to Cohen and Curran (1993) and

Willingham, Greeley, and Bardone (1993). *Journal of Experimental Psychology: Learning, Memory, and Cognition, 19,* 1438-1444.

Posner, M. I., & Peterson, S. E. (1990). The attention system of the human brain. *Annual Review of Neuroscience, 13,* 25-42.

Pribram, K. H., & McGuiness, D. (1975). Arousal, activation, and effort in the control of attention. *Psychological Review, 82,* 116-149.

Prinz, W. (1990). A common coding approach to perception and action. In O. Neumann & W. Prinz (Eds.), *Relations between perception and action: Current approaches* (pp. 167-201). Berlin: Springer.

Rauch, S. L., Savage, C. R., Brown, H. D., Curran, T., Alpert, N. M., Kendrick, A., Fischman, A. J., & Kosslyn, S. M. (1995). A PET investigation of implicit and explicit sequence learning. *Human Brain Mapping, 3,* 271-286.

Reber, A. S. (1967). Implicit learning of artificial grammars. *Journal of Verbal Learning and Verbal Behavior, 5,* 855-863.

Reber, A. S. (1989). More thoughts on the unconscious: Reply to Brody and to Lewicki and Hill. *Journal of Experimental Psychology: General, 118,* 242-244.

Reber, A. S. (1993). *Implicit learning and tacit knowledge: An essay on the cognitive unconscious.* New York: Oxford University Press.

Reber, P. J., & Squire, L. R. (1994). Parallel brain systems for learning with and without awareness. *Learning & Memory, 1,* 217-229.

Redington, M., & Chater, N. (1996). Transfer in artificial grammar learning: Reevaluation. *Journal of Experimental Psychology: General, 125,* 123-138.

Reed, J., & Johnson, P. (1994). Assessing implicit learning with indirect tests: Determining what is learned about sequences structure. *Journal of Experimental Psychology: Learning, Memory, and Cognition, 20,* 585-594.

Reingold, E. M., & Merikle, P. M. (1988). Using direct and indirect measures to study perception without awareness. *Perception & Psychophysics, 44,* 563-575.

Reingold, E. M., & Merikle, P. M. (1990). On the interrelatedness of theory and measurement in the study of unconscious processes. *Mind and Language, 5,* 9-28.

Roediger, H. L. (1990). Implicit memory: Retention without remembering. *American Psychologist, 45,* 1043-1056.

Roesler, F., Heil, M., & Henninghausen, E. (1995). Distinct cortical activation patterns during long-term memory retrieval of verbal, spatial, and color information. *Journal of Cognitive Neuroscience, 7,* 51-65.

Rudy, J. W., & Sutherland, R. J. (1994). The memory-coherence problem, configural associations, and the hippocampal system. In D. L. Schacter & E. Tulving (Eds.), *Memory systems 1994* (pp. 119-146). Cambridge: MIT Press.

Rumelhart, D. E., McClelland, J. L., & The PDP Research Group. (1986). *Parallel distributed processing: Explorations in the microstructure of cognition* (Vol. 1). Cambridge: MIT Press.

Schacter, D. L. (1994). Priming and multiple memory systems: Perceptual mechanisms of implicit memory. In D. L. Schacter & E. Tulving (Eds.), *Memory systems 1994* (pp. 233-268). Cambridge: MIT Press.

Schacter, D. L., Bowers, J., & Booker, J. (1989). Intention, awareness, and implicit memory: The retrieval intentionality criterion. In S. Lewandowski, J. C. Dunn, & K. Kirsner (Eds.), *Implicit memory: Theoretical issues* (pp. 47-66). Hillsdale, NJ: Lawrence Erlbaum.

Schacter, D. L., & Tulving, E. (Eds.). (1994). *Memory systems 1994.* Cambridge: MIT Press.

Seger, C. A. (1994). Implicit learning. *Psychological Bulletin, 115,* 163-196.

Shanks, D. R., Green, R. E. A., & Kolodny, J. (1994). A critical examination of the evidence for unconscious (implicit) learning. In C. Umiltà & M. Moscovitch (Eds.), *Attention and performance XV: Conscious and nonconscious information processing* (pp. 837-860). Cambridge: MIT Press.

Shanks, D. R., & St. John, M. F. (1994). Characteristics of dissociable human learning systems. *Behavioral and Brain Sciences, 17,* 367-395.

Sherry, D. F., & Schacter, D. L. (1987). The evolution of multiple memory systems. *Psychological Review, 94,* 439-454.

Shiffrin, R. M., & Schneider, W. (1977). Controlled and automatic human information processing: II. Perceptual learning, automatic attending, and a general theory. *Psychological Review, 84,* 127-190.

Smith, E. E., & Jonides, J. (1995). Working memory in humans: Neuropsychological evidence. In M. Gazzaniga (Ed.), *The cognitive neurosciences* (pp. 1009-1020). Cambridge: MIT Press.

Soliveri, P., Brown, R. G., Jahanshahi, M., & Marsden, C. D. (1992). Procedural memory and neurological disease. *European Journal of Cognitive Psychology, 4,* 161-193.

Squire, L. R. (1992). Memory and the hippocampus: A synthesis from findings with rats, monkeys, and humans. *Psychological Review, 99,* 195-231.

Squire, L. R. (1994). Declarative and nondeclarative memory: Multiple brain systems supporting learning and memory. In D. L. Schacter & E. Tulving (Eds.), *Memory systems 1994* (pp. 203-232). Cambridge: MIT Press.

Squire, L. R., Knowlton, B., & Musen, G. (1993). The structure and organization of memory. *Annual Review of Psychology, 44,* 453-495.

Stadler, M. A. (1989). On learning complex procedural knowledge. *Journal of Experimental Psychology Learning, Memory, and Cognition, 15,* 1061-1069.

Stadler, M. A. (1993). Implicit serial learning: Questions inspired by Hebb (1961). *Memory & Cognition, 21,* 819-827.

Stadler, M. A. (1995). Role of attention in implicit learning. *Journal of Experimental Psychology: Learning, Memory, and Cognition, 21,* 674-685.

Tucker, D., & Williamson, P. A. (1984). Asymmetric neural control systems in human self-regulation. *Psychological Review, 91,* 185-215.

Ungerleider, L. G., & Mishkin, M. (1982). Two cortical visual systems. In D. J. Ingle, R. J. W. Mansfield, & M. S. Goodale (Eds.), *The analysis of visual behavior* (pp. 549-586). Cambridge: MIT Press.

Willingham, D. B., Greeley, T., & Bardone, A. M. (1993). Dissociation in a serial response time task using a recognition measure: Comment on Perruchet and Amorim (1992). *Journal of Experimental Psychology: Learning, Memory, and Cognition, 19,* 1424-1430.

Willingham, D. B., & Koroshetz, W. J. (1993). Evidence for dissociable motor skills in Huntington's disease patients. *Psychobiology, 21,* 173-182.

Willingham, D. B., Nissen, M. J., & Bullemer, P. (1989). On the development of procedural knowledge. *Journal of Experimental Psychology: Learning, Memory, and Cognition, 15,* 1047-1060.

Wilson, F. A. W., Scalaidhe, S. P. O. & Goldman-Rakic, P. S. (1993). Dissociation of object and spatial processing domains in the primate prefrontal cortex. *Science, 260,* 1955-1957.

Yonelinas, A. P., & Jacoby, L. L. (1996). Reponse bias and the process-dissociation procedure. *Journal of Experimental Psychology: General, 125,* 422-434.

Zießler, M. (1994). The impact of motor responses on serial-pattern learning. *Psychological Research, 57,* 30-41.

13

Aging and the Development of Learning

●——————————————————————————————————

William J. Hoyer
Amy E. Lincourt

Although it is well-established that there are age-related declines on measures of explicit learning, there is some evidence to suggest that learning in older adults is unimpaired on implicit measures of learning. One aim of this chapter is to review the available research on the effects of aging on implicit and explicit learning. A second aim is to try to describe the main sources of age effects on learning performance and to propose an account for how age-related differences can be found for some measures of learning and not for others. Our focus is on aspects of age-related differences in measures of learning that can be attributed to the specific characteristics of different learning tasks or task manipulations and to the information-processing abilities of the aging individual. With regard to processing abilities, we focus on research findings that suggest there are either task-general, age-related processing deficits (e.g., speed of processing), or task-specific age-sensitive mechanisms that correspond to different forms or conditions of learning. Although many different types of tasks have been used to study learning, and a variety of

AUTHORS' NOTE: Preparation of this chapter was supported by research grant AG11451 to William J. Hoyer and by training grant AG00185 to Syracuse University. Address correspondence to William J. Hoyer, Department of Psychology, Syracuse University, Syracuse, NY 13244-2340.

explanations have been advanced to account for the observed effects of aging on learning, our review suggests that age-related decline in general processing speed and in the efficiency of associative learning and instance learning can account for much of the data on age-related changes across tasks designed to tap explicit and implicit learning.

WHAT IS IMPLICIT LEARNING?

Frensch (Chapter 2, this volume) has pointed out that the term *implicit learning* has been used to refer to a variety of phenomena and that there are numerous definitions of implicit learning in the literature. To provide some needed clarification of the term, Frensch argued that the various meanings of the concept of implicit learning differ in whether *implicit* refers only to learning processes or to learning and retrieval processes and whether implicit refers either to the processing of information without awareness or to the nonintentional processing of information. Following Frensch's suggestions for giving better definition to the concept, we use the term *implicit learning* to refer to the nonintentional acquisition of knowledge about structural relations between objects or events.

Clarification of the meaning of implicit learning is especially important for understanding the interactions between developmental processes and learning processes because, as noted by Perruchet and Vinter (Chapter 15, this volume), the concepts of learning and development both refer to the acquisition of new skills or knowledge by a person as a consequence of his or her interaction with a structured environment. Learning and development can be distinguished mainly along three dimensions. First, in terms of the inclusiveness or scope of the behavior and the antecedents of time-related change, the term learning is more narrow in scope than the term development and refers exclusively to practice-related or experience-based influences on behavior. In contrast, the term *development* is unconstrained in terms of specification of the sources or antecedents associated with time-related change. It is generally accepted that developmental change is both multidetermined (e.g., by neurobiological as well as by proximal and distal experiential influences) and multidirectional (i.e., there are gains as well as losses across the life span). Second, development and learning differ in terms of the relative length of the interval or span of real time (e.g., minutes, years) in which time-related processes operate and in which the products or consequences of time-related processes endure. Third, learning is relatively constrained to practice-based improvements in the speed, accuracy, or efficiency of performing specific skills whereas development in regard to learning represents an expansive range or repertoire of capabilities and strategies for assimilation and accommodation in understanding and interacting with structured environments (e.g., see Baltes, 1987; Hoyer & Rybash, 1994, 1996; Karmiloff-Smith, 1992; Lerner, 1991).

Considering these issues, it is easy to see the implications of learning processes for the understanding of life-span development and aging. And furthermore, it is easy to see the significance of trying to describe and understand the consequences of age-related neurocognitive mechanisms and of other developmental processes on different types of learning performance. However, although differences between the implicit and explicit acquisition of knowledge of the regularities embodied in structured environments have received considerable attention in recent years, relatively little attention has been given to the interrelationships between learning and development. In this chapter, based on a review of the available literature, we propose a framework for organizing what is known about the effects of aging on learning processes and for guiding further exploration.

One point to begin our discussion is to call attention to the frequent observation that older individuals perform well in some kinds of learning situations and poorly in other kinds of learning situations. Furthermore, there are large individual differences in the observed patterns of intra-individual differences (e.g., Hoyer, 1985; Krampe & Ericsson, 1996). Can the study of implicit learning, and the bases of the distinction between implicit and explicit learning help us to describe the loci of age declines and the sources of maintained performance across the adult years? Is it the case that there is an implicit learning mechanism akin to a "structural sponge" that is unaffected by aging? If implicit learning processes are relatively unaffected by aging and neurological insult, in contrast to age-sensitive explicit processes, is it because implicit and explicit processes are disassociated in terms of neural substrates? Alternatively, is there a basic or general age-sensitive mechanism that accounts for performance differences between implicit and explicit measures because of differences in task demands? As discussed below, a careful examination of the research evidence reveals that there really is not much support for the position that implicit learning is spared or preserved in old age, or that implicit learning is distinct from explicit learning in terms of neural substrates or mechanisms. We begin with a brief review of what information is learned in implicit learning.

WHAT IS LEARNED IN IMPLICIT LEARNING
AND EXPLICIT LEARNING TASKS?

Current research and theory on implicit learning owes much to the pioneering work of Arthur Reber and his colleagues (e.g., Reber, 1969, 1989, 1993; Reber & Allen, 1978; Reber, Allen, Regan, 1985; Reber, Walkenfeld, & Hernstadt, 1991). Recently, Reber (1993) suggested that evolutionary considerations provide justification for the distinction between implicit and explicit cognitive processes. Reber argued that unconscious, implicit, covert cognitive functions must have predated the emergence of the conscious, explicit functions of mind. Because implicit learning is a phylogenetically older and more primitive system than explicit learning, implicit processes will be more *robust* than explicit processes in response to the neurological insults of age, dysfunction, and disease. Furthermore, Reber predicted that implicit processes will show little if any correlation with measurements of intellectual ability, whereas explicit measures of learning and memory are likely to be associated with general ability measures (see Feldman, Kerr, & Streissguth, 1995; Reber et al., 1991).

In contrast to explicit learning measures, which are designed to reflect deliberate or intentional aspects of learning, implicit learning measures presumably tap the nondeliberate acquisition of knowledge about the structure of a complex stimulus environment (e.g., Berry, 1994; Dienes, Broadbent, & Berry, 1991; Reber, 1989; Seger, 1994; Shanks, Green, & Kolodny, 1994). Two kinds of tasks, artificial grammar learning and serial reaction time (SRT) are frequently used to study implicit learning and the possible differences between implicit learning and explicit learning. The procedures and findings of a typical grammar-learning study by Knowlton, Ramus, and Squire (1992) are presented below, for illustration, and then we discuss what information can be learned in the grammar-learning paradigm. Later in this section, we examine the procedures of a typical SRT study by Howard and Howard (1992) and then examine what information can be learned in an SRT task.

Example 1: Artificial Grammar Learning. Knowlton et al. (1992) investigated whether the ability to classify on the basis of rules can be learned independently of memory for the specific instances that embody the rules. Amnesic patients and healthy controls studied letter strings generated by an artificial grammar, as illustrated in Figure 13.1a. After the study phase,

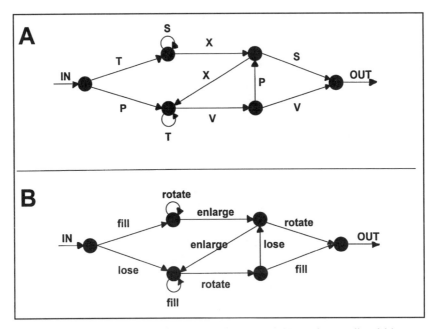

Figure 13.1 (Panels 1a and 1b). Grammar A was used by Reber, Walkenfeld, and Hernstadt (1991) to generate grammar-following strings of letter sequences. Strings were generated by traversing the diagram from the IN arrow to the OUT arrow, adding a letter to the sequence at each transition point. For example, the letter string, TSXXVV, is consistent with Grammar A. Grammar B was used by D'Eredita and Hoyer (in press) to generate grammar-following strings of figural sequences. Rule-following strings were formed by traversing the diagram from the IN arrow to the OUT arrow. Featural changes to the arrow stimulus were introduced at each point in the sequence (see Figure 13.2).

subjects were shown new letter strings and were instructed to classify them as grammatical or nongrammatical. Amnesic patients performed as well as normal subjects in classification learning. However, amnesic patients performed more poorly than control subjects on an explicit recognition test of the exemplars that had been presented. Amnesic patients also performed more poorly than control subjects when they were explicitly instructed to base their classifications on comparisons with the original exemplars. The results were interpreted to suggest that implicit classification learning can develop normally despite impaired explicit memory for particular exemplars. Knowlton et al. (1992) went on to suggest that classification learning depends on interactions between the neocortex and the neostriatum and that exemplar memory depends on interactions between neocortex and the limbic system.

One of the key issues bearing on the usefulness of the distinction between explicit and implicit learning has to do with what information is learned in grammar learning and SRT studies. In the example presented above, Knowlton et al. (1992) suggested that the learner acquires an understanding of the rules of the sequence or grammar without any awareness or intention of doing so. It was suggested that the learning of the abstract rules governing the task took place without explicit learning of the classifications and was not based on the surface features of the stimuli. Analogously, it seems that children learn to understand and speak their native language without deliberate or conscious effort to master the deep structure that governs language usage.

In contrast to an abstractionist interpretation of grammar learning, some researchers have argued that subjects learn probabilities of covariation of simple two-letter or three-letter sequences that happen to conform to the structure in grammar-learning tasks. That is, the subject learns fragments or instances, and the learning does not necessarily involve acquisition of the rules and structure of a grammar (e.g., Dulany, Carlson, & Dewey, 1984; Perruchet, 1994; Perruchet & Pacteau, 1990; Redington & Chater, 1996). In several careful analyses of what information is learned in implicit learning tasks, it has been shown that the acquisition of fragments and other relatively simple covariations inherent in the task can account for the observed performance in artificial grammar-learning tasks. For example, Perruchet (e.g., Perruchet, 1994; Perruchet & Amorim, 1992; Perruchet & Pacteau, 1990) showed that subjects learn fragments of the presented letter strings (i.e., bigrams or trigrams) and that fragment learning provides a satisfactory account of the findings of implicit learning. Perruchet and Pacteau (1990, Experiment 1) showed that knowledge of permissible letter pairs (i.e., bigrams adhering to the synthetic grammar) within letter strings could account for above-chance performance on grammaticality judgments. Grammaticality judgments of letter strings were compared for subjects trained with complete letter strings and for subjects presented with letter pairs composing the strings. If subjects were learning the artificial grammar, rather than just memorizing the bigrams composing the letter strings, then subjects presented with only the letter pairs would be unable to extract and learn the complex rules. However, subjects studying pairs of letters performed as well as subjects who studied the complete letter strings.

The results of Experiment 2 of the Perruchet and Pacteau (1990) study provided further support for the position that grammaticality judgments are based on the memorization of bigrams composing the strings, and not on the implicit learning of abstract rules. The type of grammatical violations presented in the test phase was manipulated in this experiment. It was predicted that subjects would judge a letter string as nongrammatical if the bigrams composing the string were incorrect (i.e., nonpermissable pairs), but would *not* judge a letter string as ungrammatical if the bigrams were simply presented in the wrong location within the string (i.e., nonpermissable order). As predicted, subjects made better judgments when ungrammatical strings were based on the presence of a nonpermissable pair rather than on a permissible pair presented in the wrong location.

It should be mentioned that the kinds of conclusions that can be drawn from the data from many of the studies of implicit learning using artificial grammars are limited because the designs of the studies are often flawed or lack the proper controls. Artificial grammar-learning studies generally do not have the necessary control conditions to determine if or to what extent subject performance is due to learning in the test phase. First, there is usually no control to determine if or to what extent grammatical and nongrammatical strings are distinguishable from each other without the benefit of training (e.g., Redington & Chater, 1996). Second, a comparison group of subjects given nongrammatical strings in the learning phase is usually absent. In most implicit learning experiments, subjects are first given a set of grammar-following strings to learn and are then asked to judge grammar-following strings as well as nongrammatical strings in a subsequent testing phase. Third, the extent to which grammaticality judgments are based on learning particular parts of strings versus learning relations across strings is usually not assessed.

Artificial Grammar-Learning Studies With Older Adults. Two recent studies examined possible adult age differences in implicit learning using versions of Reber's artificial grammar task (D'Eredita & Hoyer, in press; Meulemans, Van der Linden, & Denis, 1996). Meulemans, Van der Linden, and Denis (1996) reported that the ability to abstract rules from exemplars generated by a finite grammar was not affected by age. The mean age of the older subjects in this study was 64 years (range 60-69 years).

D'Eredita and Hoyer (in press) examined adult age differences in the implicit learning and explicit learning of abstract rules and of item-to-item covariations in figural sequences. Three age groups participated: young adults (17-23 years); middle-aged adults (35-45 years); and older adults (55-65 years). As shown in Figure 13.1b, D'Eredita and Hoyer substituted a sequence of changes in the features, size, and orientation of an object for the sequences of letters that are typically used in artificial grammar-learning studies (e.g., as shown in Figure 13.1a). To permit fair age comparisons, the learning requirements were made easier by limiting the number of operations to four. Reber used five letters (S, T, U, V, and X) in his grammar. By comparing the two panels (Figure 13.1a and Figure 13.1b), it can be seen that the structure of the rules was the same and that the use of four operations made the task easier. However, the grammar was sufficiently complex so as to minimize any explicit detection of the rules. In Phase 1 of the experiment, half the subjects in each age group learned sequences of three to eight items in which the item-to-item changes conformed to an artificial grammar. The other half of the subjects in each age group learned sequences in which the item-to-item changes were nongrammatical. All subjects were given sufficient practice so as to learn all strings to the same criterion.

In Phase 2, the implicit/explicit test phase, subjects made forced-choice judgments about the sequences they learned in Phase 1, under either explicit or implicit instructions. Subjects who were given explicit instructions were told that some of the strings would be the same as the ones they saw in the learning phase. Unlike previous studies, however, subjects were not told that there was a grammar that applied across the strings. The explicit instructions were intended to direct the subjects to make item selection decisions based on their explicit memory of the previously learned strings. The implicit instructions were intended to tap the subjects' implicit memory for the previously presented strings by asking them to complete the strings without reference to previous string learning or rule learning. Subjects were shown the same strings in the testing phase as were presented in the learning phase, but with two shapes removed, as shown in the lower panel of Figure 13.2b. Subjects were asked to complete each string by selecting one of two choices. Thus, instead of making judgments about the rule-based nature of each string, subjects were completing each string, either to make it the same as a previously seen string in the explicit instructions condition or to make a "better fit" in the implicit instructions condition. Analyses revealed evidence for the acquisition of item-to-item covariations, but there was no evidence of implicit learning of the abstract rules of the artificial grammar. An age-related deficit was found for explicit relearning of grammar-following sequences.

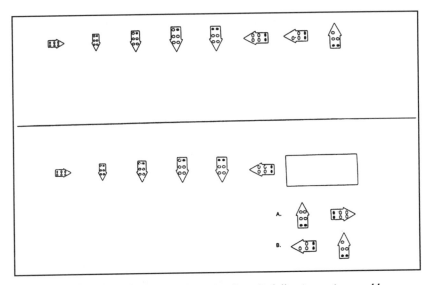

Figure 13.2 (Panels 2a and 2b). Example of a rule-following string used by D'Eredita and Hoyer (in press), Panel A shows the string as it was presented in the learning phase, and Panel B shows the string as it was presented in the testing phase with two items removed. Subjects made forced-choice responses (either choice A or B) to complete the strings using either explicit instructions or implicit instructions.

The difference in correctly judging grammar-following and nongrammatical strings was evident only for subjects who were explicitly told that they would be making judgments about the strings they learned in Phase 1. It is important to note that the instructions used in this study differed from those used in most previous studies (e.g., Dienes et al., 1991; Reber & Allen, 1978), in that no mention was made of the existence of a rule. Subjects in the D'Eredita and Hoyer (in press) study had the impression that their learning and memory for particular strings of items were being assessed, and they were given no clues that there were regularities across strings. For subjects in the explicit instructions condition, the correlation between performance and the derived covariations for the grammar-following and ungrammatical strings was significant for subjects receiving the grammar-following strings ($r = .50$) but was not significant for subjects receiving the nongrammatical strings ($r = .14$). For subjects in the implicit instructions condition, the correlation between performance and the derived covariations for the grammar-following and ungrammatical strings was significant for subjects receiving the grammar-following strings ($r =$ .36), but not for subjects receiving the nongrammatical strings ($r = -.05$). Thus, subjects use learned covariations when they are instructed to do so, or when there is a "cue" that instigates their applicability.

Because of the inefficiency of the grammar-learning paradigm in terms of the need and costs of proper controls, as well as other difficulties associated with interpreting performance in grammar-learning tasks, many researchers opt to use the SRT paradigm developed by Nissen and Bullemer (1987). Consider the study by Howard and Howard (1992) described below, for illustration.

Example 2: Serial Reaction Time. Howard and Howard (1992) examined changes in response times that occurred over a series of blocks containing a repeated pattern for the locations of asterisks on a computer screen. Response times improved with repetitions of the sequence for both younger and older adults. This increase in the speed of responding was due primarily to subjects' learning the pattern rather than to a general practice-based improvement in visual-motor speed, because it was found that response times nearly returned to their original level on blocks of trials in which the locations of the asterisks occurred in a random pattern. The increase in response times when the pattern was removed is considered to be an implicit measure of pattern learning, because the measure reflects the extent to which response times were influenced by the presence of the repeating pattern apparently without the subjects being consciously aware of learning any pattern. The lack of age differences on implicit measures of SRT contrasts with the data obtained from a comparable situation in which subjects attempted to generate or predict in advance the locations of asterisks; these explicit measures revealed reliable age-related deficits.

Because of its relative simplicity, tractability, and the improved precision of the dependent measure (i.e., response time), most researchers agree that the SRT task provides a somewhat better paradigm than the artificial grammar-learning task and other tasks (e.g., Lewicki, Czyzewska, & Hoffman, 1987) for investigating implicit learning (Reed & Johnson, 1994). Another advantage of the SRT procedure is that it affords a more direct assessment of what information is learned in implicit learning. The core claim of fragment-based accounts, that implicit learning is based on acquiring associations or chunks of letters, has been tested in SRT studies (e.g., Perruchet & Amorim, 1992; Shanks & St. John, 1994), and it has been found that fragment-based learning can account for the observed effects.

SRT Studies With Older Adults. In addition to the Howard and Howard (1992) study, these investigators have reported two other studies using the Nissen and Bullemer (1987) SRT paradigm with younger and older adults (i.e., Howard & Howard, 1989, in press). In the 1989 study, Howard and Howard asked younger and older subjects to respond to asterisks presented in four different locations on a computer screen whose positions followed a repeating pattern. Subjects were instructed to press the button that corresponded to one of four possible item locations. After a series of repetitions of the pattern, a random series of items was presented to the subjects. An increase in response times associated with the switch from the repeating sequence to the random sequence was used as a measure of implicit learning. Overall, older adults produced longer response times, but both young adults and older adults were equally disrupted by the switch from the patterned blocks to the random blocks. As an explicit measure of sequence learning, subjects were asked to predict the location of the next item to be presented based on previous learning. The explicit learning measure revealed an age-related deficit.

Howard & Howard (in press) examined pattern learning in younger and older adults under conditions designed to be more difficult for serial pattern learning. In this study, the sequences of the asterisks alternated between a repeating pattern and a random pattern. Subjects representing three age groups, including a group of six old-old adults ranging in age between 76 years and 80 years, were able to learn this relatively difficult and nonobvious sequence of covariations of locations. In contrast to earlier findings by Howard and Howard (1989, 1992), in which younger and older adults showed equal amounts of pattern learning on an implicit measure, there were age differences in the magnitude of pattern learning and in the sensitivity to patterns. The data suggested that only the younger adults showed sensitivity to the higher-order dependencies in the sequence.

Cherry and Stadler (1995) examined the implicit serial learning of relatively nonobvious sequences in a sample of young adults and two samples of older adults. The two groups of older adults differed in educational attainment, occupational status, and verbal ability. The ability differences between the two samples of older adults were associated with differences in degree of implicit learning. That is, the amount of disruption produced by changing from a repeated sequence to a random sequence in the Nissen and Bullemer task was not different for the samples of younger adults and high-ability older adults, but the sample of low-ability older adults showed less evidence of implicit learning compared with the samples of younger adults and high-ability older adults. Furthermore, the samples of younger adults and the high-ability older adults were more accurate on an explicit learning measure than the sample of low-ability older adults.

In addition to the difficulty of discerning a structure in the sequence, it has been reported that attentional demands associated with dual-task conditions and the complexity of the response required also affect the degree of implicit learning obtained by older adults. Frensch and Miner (1994) reported age differences in implicit learning under dual-task conditions, but not under single-task conditions. In the Frensch and Miner study (Experiment 1), implicit learning was found at short response-stimulus intervals (500 ms), but not at long response-stimulus intervals (1500 ms); explicit learning was found at both response-stimulus intervals, although it was less at the longer response-stimulus intervals. This finding suggests that implicit sequence learning depends on the co-activation of stimuli for associations to develop in short-term memory. Harrington and Haaland (1992) reported adult age differences in implicit learning for highly educated participants under single-task conditions when the task required complex hand movements to make the responses instead of simple button presses. Thus, age deficits do emerge in implicit learning tasks when the task is relatively difficult or when the older subjects are of relatively low ability.

Related to these findings, it is consistently reported that there are age-related differences in discerning higher-order dependencies in studies of the effects of adult age on explicit detection of relatively complicated event covariations (e.g., Kay, 1951; Mutter & Pliske, 1996). In an early study of the effects of age on explicit sequence learning, Kay (1951) showed that age differences in the accurate performance of a learning task depended on unlearning, then rebuilding a correct schema for performing a sequence task. Kay presented subjects with a row of five buttons and five lights. There was a correct sequence for pressing the buttons (2, 4, 3, 1, 5), and the task was to explicitly learn the sequence by trial and error. Feedback was signaled by a change in one of the five lights whenever a correct button was pressed. This task was very difficult for older adults, and the effects of age on reaching the criterion of two correct sequences increased from the 20s through the 30s, 40s, 50s, and 60s. In terms of current descriptive frameworks, Kay's findings are compatible with an account that emphasizes age-related declines in working memory because the correct response at each position had to be found before proceeding to the next, and the products of learning had to be held in memory. The results suggested that schema correction was required and that learning depended not just on a process of gradually eliminating errors.

Relative sparing of implicit learning, compared with deficits in explicit learning of a series, has been reported in studies comparing healthy and impaired older adults (e.g., Ferraro, Balota, & Connor, 1993; Knopman & Nissen, 1987; Mutter, Howard, & Howard, 1994; Mutter, Howard, Howard, & Wiggs, 1990). Dissociations between implicit and explicit measures of learning have been found in studies with clinically impaired samples of Korsakoff's patients (Nissen & Bullemer, 1987), Huntington's disease patients (Knopman & Nissen, 1991), and Alzheimer's disease patients (Ferraro et al., 1993; Knopman & Nissen, 1987). Also, Nissen, Knopman, and Schacter (1987) observed a similar dissociation in college students when they were administered the drug, scopolamine, so as to examine sequence learning under conditions of suppressed awareness and to simulate the effects of aging on learning systems. A connection between the distinctive characteristics of learning systems and the effects of aging and insult on particular brain structures and functions is an active topic of research in cognitive neuropsychology and neuroscience (e.g., Knowlton, Ramus, & Squire, 1992; Pascual-Leone, Grafman, & Hallatt, 1994; Rybash, 1996). There is some evidence to suggest that the neural substrates that support implicit learning and memory processes may be relatively unaffected by aging and by the kinds of disorders and dysfunctions that compromise explicit learning (e.g., see Curran, 1995; Rybash, 1996; Squire, Knowlton, & Musen, 1993). The available neural evidence suggests that implicit learning and explicit learning depend on nonidentical neural mechanisms (e.g., Baldwin & Kutas, 1997; Gabrieli, 1994; Seger, 1994; Squire et al., 1993). Implicit memory seems to depend on the integrity of the striatum, cerebellum, amygdala, and neocortex, whereas explicit learning seems to be associated with the integrity of limbic and diencephalic brain structures.

TOWARD A FRAMEWORK FOR DESCRIBING THE EFFECTS OF AGING ON LEARNING

Pronounced age differences have been reported for many types of learning, and smaller or no age differences have been reported for some types of learned tasks (e.g., Kausler, 1994; Salthouse, 1994). In this section, we briefly and selectively review the research on aging and implicit and explicit learning with an eye toward formulating a framework that can incorporate the major findings.

For some kinds of learning tasks, especially ones for which the subject has little or no prior knowledge, age differences in the initial level of performance are large, there are age differences in the rate of learning across training, and the age difference in performance remains after training or learning. For example, in an early study by Thorndike, Bregman, Tilton, and Woodyard (1928), right-handed young adults between the ages of 20 and 25 years and right-handed older adults between the ages of 35 and 57 years were given 15 hours of practice writing left-handed. Large age differences were found in the rate at which writing speed improved with practice. Recent studies of the effects of age on training of word processing skills have also revealed that the rate of learning is slower for older than for younger adults (e.g., Czaja & Sharit, 1993). Also, Salthouse, Hambrick, Lukas, and Dell (1996) have reported that adult age differences were initially large and were maintained across 25 sessions (3 days) in a complex or synthetic work task that involved managing several concurrent tasks (see also Kramer, Larish, & Strayer, 1995).

For other kinds of tasks, age differences in the initial level of performance are large, but there are equivalent rates of learning across training, and performance reaches an equivalent level for younger and older adults by the end of training. In the execution of well-learned, real-world skilled tasks, for example, it has been reported that older adults perform without noticeable deficits (e.g., Charness, 1981; Clancy & Hoyer, 1994; Krampe & Ericsson, 1996; Salthouse, 1984).

Perhaps the best-established accounts of the effects of aging on learning are the ones that give emphasis to age-related general slowing in the processing of information and to the consequences of age-related deficits in speed of processing for tasks that depend on working memory and the construction of new associations, as in digit-symbol substitution performance; of new instances, as in alphabet arithmetic tasks; or of new units or chunks of information, as in visual search and numerousity tasks.

The general slowing hypothesis is prominent because it offers a parsimonious account of a vast array of data on young-old differences. Meta-analyses reveal that a substantial amount of the age-related variance in cognitive function across a wide variety of tasks and situations can be described by a simple linear slowing factor (Cerella, 1990, 1991; Cerella & Hale, 1994; Myerson & Hale, 1993). That is, age-performance functions can be described by a simple overhead or ratio of 1.4 to 2.0 without any reference to differential aging of particular mechanisms or processes. Despite the success of the general slowing hypothesis in accounting for age variance, general slowing serves mainly as a default or a heuristic hypothesis, awaiting contrary evidence that is analytic of particular speed-sensitive mechanisms.

Such an account has recently been advanced by Salthouse (1996). This theory seems particularly useful for describing age-related declines in learning functions because reductions in the speed of processing are described in terms of their consequences for time-limited mechanisms and the simultaneity mechanism. Specifically, the concept of simultaneity rests on the notion that the products of early processing are lost by the time later processing is completed. Thus, information is no longer available, and this loss of information has consequences for learning new associations. Empirical work by Salthouse (1994) and Salthouse and Coon (1994) offers direct support for this theory.

Fisk, Hertzog, Rogers, and their colleagues have reported that older adults and younger adults do not show equivalent gains and that there is an age-related deficit in the development of an *automatic attention response* to consistently mapped items in visual search. However, a learning mechanism, referred to as *memory set unitization,* operates equally effectively for both younger and older adults in memory search (e.g., Fisk, Cooper, Hertzog, Anderson-Garlach, & Lee, 1995; Fisk & Rogers, 1991; Hertzog, Cooper, & Fisk, 1996; Rogers, 1992). One of the main points that can be derived from this work is that there are different age trends depending on the processing requirements for building new associations or units.

Differences in the efficiency of developing instance-based retrieval might also account for the effects of age on performance in learning tasks. Consistent with Salthouse's (1996) suggestion that the products of early processing are less available for later processing with age, it follows that more repetitions of a particular item would be required for it to be retrieved in an instance-based fashion. A recent study by Jenkins and Hoyer (1997) showed that age differences in how long it takes to develop automaticity were associated with differences in the efficiency of instance learning.

Lincourt and Hoyer (1996) also demonstrated that age differences in the efficiency of an instance-learning mechanism can account for differences in skill acquisition using an alphabet substitution task. Subjects were required to verify equations such as, H[4]M. The digit in brackets indicated the number of letters skipped in the alphabet. Strings were correct when the letter sequence followed the alphabet (e.g., H[4]M) and were incorrect when the letter to the right of the digit occupied the position in the alphabet that followed the correct one (e.g., H[4]N). The training data from one representative younger (18 years) and one older (66 years) subject are presented in Figure 13.3. Each histogram shows the distribution of 120 response times. In each of the session plots, the points represent responses to 20 presentations of six correct alphabet substitution facts. The data shown are for strings that contained no additional irrelevant computations; three of the strings had an addend of 3 (e.g., H[3]L), and three of the strings had an addend of 4 (e.g., H[4]M).

The means for the distributions of response times for the first session were 5,140 ms and 12,323 ms, for the young adult and older adult, respectively. The older adult performed more slowly early in training, and she continued to perform more slowly throughout training, compared with the young subject. Response times for Session 4 were 1,836 ms and 11,466 ms, for the two subjects. Initially, response times were more variable and skewed, especially for the older subject. The standard deviations for Session 1 were 2,686 ms and 4,718 ms for the young adult and the older adult. The older adult was also less efficient at reducing response time variability, suggesting that there is age-related slowing of the process responsible for reducing the proportion of algorithmic responses. The standard deviations for the distributions in Session 4 were 756 ms and 4,746 ms, for the young and older adult. For the age-group data reported in Lincourt and Hoyer (1996), examination of the differences in the mean response times and in the shapes of the learning curves and the distributions suggested that older adults were slower to develop instance-based responses. Thus, both Jenkins and Hoyer (1997) and Lincourt and Hoyer (1996) showed that the efficiency of the instance-learning mechanism is diminished with age.

We suggest that the findings reported above can be summarized in a way that provides a rough framework for describing the effects of aging on learning. Specifically, the available data lead us to the position that the effects of aging on learning can be described in terms of three principles.

First, learning at a fine-grained level in a wide range of tasks can be described in terms of a shift from algorithmic to instance-based responding, consistent with work by Logan (1988) and others. Furthermore, there are age-related differences in the efficiency of the qualitative shift from algorithmic to instance-based responding; this statement is supported by recent findings from the studies by Jenkins and Hoyer (1997) and Lincourt and Hoyer (1996), and others.

Second, the cognitive performance of healthy adults across a wide age range improves or can be maintained at an effective level to the extent that

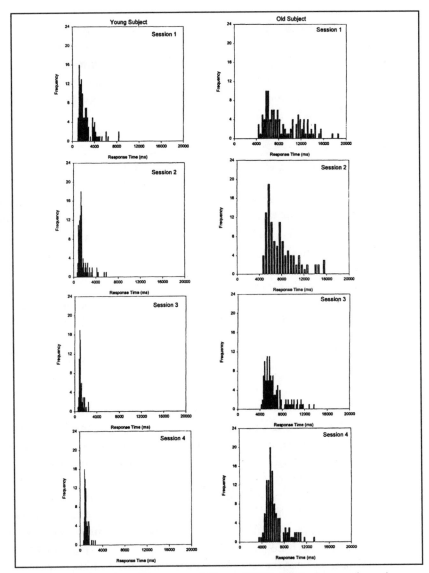

Figure 13.3. Data from Lincourt and Hoyer (1996). The columns of panels show session-by-session changes in the distributions of response times for a representative young subject (age 18 years) and a representative older subject (age 66 years). It can be seen that there are individual differences in mean response times and in the efficiency of the shift from slow responding based on algorithmic computation of the problem to fast responding based on retrieval of the instances. Mean response times for individuals by sessions do not adequately reflect the qualitative shift from algorithmic to instance-based responding, as shown in the distributions of response times.

461

domain-specific strategies or heuristics can be deployed to support effective performance. That is, if the individual knows how to approach a particular kind of problem or has already learned or knows how to perform a particular task, age limitations in the speed of processing or in learning new associations are likely to have negligible influences on performance. Findings of Charness (1981) and Krampe and Ericsson (1996) provide evidence supporting the compensatory role of strategic knowledge in understanding the maintained expertise of older adults in skilled domains.

Third, the research findings from many kinds of speeded cognitive tasks suggest that the efficiency of processing information that cannot be automatized in an instance-based fashion is unlikely to benefit from practice or learning (e.g., see Fisk et al., 1995). That is, the speed of performance of individuals is relatively immutable despite practice, in tasks that do not involve use of prior knowledge (e.g., Salthouse, 1996).

Applications and Implications of the Proposed Framework. Researchers have not paid much attention to how data from different age groups can be useful for evaluating and refining general experimental work in the area of learning. Can research on aging and learning advance the general understanding of learning? Specifically, we suggest that the proposed framework makes two kinds of general contributions.

Using Underwood's (1975) term, one kind of contribution has to do with using individual differences as a *crucible* for evaluation and extension of empirical work and theory building in the experimental psychology of learning. Subject characteristics, such as age-related differences in chunking and associative learning, serve as *manipulations* for investigating the kinds of processing required for task performance.

The proposed framework gives emphasis to research findings demonstrating that the development of automaticity is associated with a repetitions-based shift from deliberate processing to the direct instance-based retrieval. Although Logan and Klapp (1991) reported that the number of repetitions, and not the amount of material or the number of instances to be learned, affects the development of instance-based retrieval, their conclusion was based entirely on data from college students (presumably young adults). The results of Jenkins and Hoyer (1997), Lincourt, Hoyer, and Cerella (1997), and Lincourt and Hoyer (1996) clearly support Logan's position that the development of automaticity can be described as a shift from algorithmic responding to instance-based retrieval, but they add that the shift occurs more readily in some tasks than in others and that there are age-related differences in the efficiency of the shift mechanism. Our proposed framework suggests that the learning of new associations, regardless of the subject's intentions or strategies and other aspects of processing presumed to be related to the implicit-explicit distinction, is affected by age-related declines in the efficiency of the instance-learning mechanism.

Another example of an area where an individual differences approach contributes to the understanding of the general processes of learning has to do with possible clarification of the role of attention in implicit and explicit learning. Because it is well-established that the processes of selecting essential information, distinguishing relevant information from redundant task information, and limiting processing to relevant information are negatively affected by aging (e.g., see Kotary & Hoyer, 1995; Madden & Plude, 1993; Plude & Hoyer, 1986), developmental studies could help to clarify the role of attentional mechanisms in implicit and explicit learning. Individual differences data can serve to illuminate the possible effects of mediating factors on learning that are otherwise overlooked.

Second, the individual differences approach is helpful for teasing apart the sources of dissociations among learning systems within-individuals and across individuals, and it calls attention to the distinction between learning and the products of learning. That is, the on-line processes that produced the skilled performance of an individual may not be evident in measures of trained or maintained performance. William James (1890) was probably one of the first to clearly call attention to the differences between learning skills and performing skills:

> When we are learning to walk, to ride, to swim, skate, fence, write, play, or sing, we interrupt ourselves at every step by unnecessary movements and false notes. When we are proficient, on the contrary, the results not only follow with the very minimum of muscular action requisite to bring them forth, they also follow from a single instantaneous "cue." The marksman sees the bird, and before he knows it, he has aimed and shot. A gleam in his adversary's eye, a momentary pressure from his rapier, and the fencer finds he has instantly made the right parry and return. A glance at the musical hieroglyphics, and the pianist's fingers have rippled through a cataract of notes. (p. 86)

Sometimes the distinction between learning and the performing of learned skills is especially evident when observing the performance of older adults in skilled tasks, as the following quote from Talland (1965) suggests:

I am still puzzled by the contrast of the athlete, who at thirty, is too old for the championship and the maestro, who at eighty, can treat us to a memorable performance on the concert stage. Are our aged masters freaks of nature, paragons of self-discipline, or do they demonstrate the inadequacy of our present notions about the effects of age on human capacities? (p. 558)

Ericsson and Kintsch (1995) suggested that maintenance of chunks, units, associations, and instance-based representations may underlie the maintenance of expert performance in skilled tasks and that access to expert knowledge may be triggered by a cue. Thus, the availability of formed chunks, units, and instances may enable the older individual to bypass or circumvent speed of processing limitations. Our proposed framework suggests that learning as well as the outcomes of learning (i.e., the development of skilled performance) depends on instance-based retrieval supported by an associative memory system, such that quick access to learned knowledge is triggered by cues, and that such cuing or priming occurs without limitations associated with the execution of age-sensitive, resource-demanding processes.

Such an account does not apply to examples of expertise that involve extraordinary skill in abstracting and using complex rules; however, the manifestation of extraordinary skills of this type probably depends heavily on the status of the individual's repertoire of fluid mental abilities. Certainly, a comprehensive account of effective performance in real-world tasks depends on the status of the person's knowledge as it applies to the task at hand and access to that knowledge, and on the functioning of the person's fluid abilities as they apply to computational or processing demands of the task (e.g., Baltes, 1987; Hoyer, 1985, 1986; Krampe & Ericsson, 1996; Salthouse, 1984). These findings help us to understand how older adults perform competently in skilled situations despite age-related deficits in the speed and efficiency of acquisition processes.

SUMMARY AND CONCLUSIONS

The primary aim of this chapter was to describe and explain age differences in implicit and explicit learning in terms of what is known about the effects of aging on the processes of learning. We presented evidence to suggest that age-related differences in implicit learning and explicit learning are probably best understood in terms of age-related differences in the efficiency of processing speed and particular mechanisms (e.g., chunking or unitization, associative learning, instance-based learning). These age-sensitive mechanisms provide a satisfactory account for observed age differences in the course of implicit learning and explicit learning, and for the lack of age differences on simple or well-learned implicit or explicit tasks. The efficiency of basic learning mechanisms can affect performance on implicit and explicit learning tasks and may also underlie performance on a range of cognitive tasks, from detecting simple covariations (e.g., Mutter & Pliske, 1996) to solving complex problems (e.g., Kramer et al., 1995; Salthouse et al., 1996).

Further research will be needed to determine the extent to which intraindividual and interindividual differences in learning within and across tasks can be accounted for by general learning mechanisms, rather than by multiple learning processes.

REFERENCES

Baldwin, K. B., & Kutas, M. (1997). An ERP analysis of implicit structured sequence learning. *Psychophysiology, 34,* 74-86.

Baltes, P. B. (1987). Theoretical propositions of life-span developmental psychology: On the dynamics between growth and decline. *Developmental Psychology, 23,* 611-626.

Berry, D. C. (1994). Implicit learning: Twenty-five years on. A Tutorial. In C. Umiltà & M. Moscovitch (Eds.), *Attention and performance XV: Conscious and nonconscious information processing* (pp. 755-782). London: MIT Press.

Cerella, J. (1990). Aging and information-processing rate. In J. E. Birren & K. W. Schaie (Eds.), *Handbook of the psychology of aging* (3rd ed., pp. 201-221). New York: Academic Press.

Cerella, J. (1991). Age deficits may be global, not local: Comment on Fisk and Rogers (1991). *Journal of Experimental Psychology: General, 120,* 215-223.

Cerella, J., & Hale, S. (1994). The rise and fall of information-processing rates over the life span. *Acta Psychologica, 86,* 109-197.

Charness, N. (1981). Aging and skilled problem solving. *Journal of Experimental Psychology: General, 110,* 21-38.

Cherry, K. E., & Stadler, M. A. (1995). Implicit learning of a nonverbal sequence in younger and older adults. *Psychology and Aging, 10,* 379-394.

Clancy, S. M., & Hoyer, W. J. (1994). Age and skill in visual search. *Developmental Psychology, 30,* 545-552.

Curran, T. (1995). On the neural mechanisms of sequence learning. *Psyche* [On-line serial], 2(12). Available at URL:http://psyche.cs.monash.edu.au/volume2-1/psyche-95-2-12- seque nce-1-curran.html.

Czaja, S. J., & Sharit, J. (1993). Age differences in performance of computer-based work. *Psychology and Aging, 8,* 59-67.

D'Eredita, M. A., & Hoyer, W. J. (in press). Implicit and explicit learning of figural relations: Adult age differences. *Memory & Cognition.*

Dienes, Z., Broadbent, D., & Berry, D. (1991). Implicit and explicit bases in artificial grammar learning. *Journal of Experimental Psychology: Learning, Memory, and Cognition, 17,* 875-887.

Dulany, D. E., Carlson, A., & Dewey, G. I. (1984). A case of syntactical learning and judgment: How conscious and how abstract. *Journal of Experimental Psychology: General, 113,* 541-555.

Ericsson, K. A., & Kintsch, W. (1995). Long-term working memory. *Psychological Review, 102,* 211-245.

Feldman, J., Kerr, B., & Streissguth, A. P. (1995). Correlational analyses of procedural and declarative learning performance. *Intelligence, 20,* 87-114.

Ferraro, F. R., Balota, D. A., & Connor, L. T. (1993). Implicit memory and the formation of new associations in non-demented Parkinson's disease individuals and individuals with dementia of the Alzheimer's type: A serial reaction time (SRT) investigation. *Brain and Cognition, 21,* 163-180.

Fisk, A. D., Cooper, B. P., Hertzog, C., Anderson-Garlach, M., & Lee, M. D. (1995). Understanding performance and learning in consistent memory search: An age-related perspective. *Psychology and Aging, 10,* 255-268.

Fisk, A. D., & Rogers, W. (1991). Toward an understanding of age-related memory and visual search effects. *Journal of Experimental Psychology: General, 120,* 131-149.

Frensch, P. A., & Miner, C. S. (1994). Effects of presentation rate and individual differences in short-term memory capacity on an indirect measure of serial learning. *Memory & Cognition, 22,* 95-110.

Gabrieli, J. (1994). Contributions of the basal ganglia to skill learning and working memory in humans. In J. Houk, J. L. Davis, & D. G. Beiser (Eds.), *Information processing in the basal ganglia* (pp. 277-294). Cambridge: MIT Press.

Harrington, D. L., & Haaland, K. Y. (1992). Skill learning in the elderly: Diminished implicit and explicit memory for a motor sequence. *Psychology and Aging, 7,* 425-434.

Hertzog, C., Cooper, B. P., & Fisk, A. D. (1996). Age and individual differences in the development of skilled memory search. *Psychology and Aging, 11,* 497-520.

Howard, D. V., & Howard, J. H., Jr. (1989). Age differences in learning serial patterns: Direct versus indirect measures. *Psychology and Aging, 4,* 357-364.

Howard, D. V., & Howard, J. H., Jr. (1992). Adult age differences in the rate of learning serial patterns: Evidence from direct and indirect tests. *Psychology and Aging, 7,* 232-241.

Howard, J. H., Jr., & Howard, D. V. (in press). Age differences in implicit learning of higher-order dependencies in serial patterns. *Psychology and Aging.*

Hoyer, W. J. (1985). Aging and the development of expert cognition. In T. M. Schlecter & M. P. Toglia (Eds.), *New directions in cognitive science* (pp. 69-87). Norwood, NJ: Ablex.

Hoyer, W. J. (1986). On the growth of knowledge and the decentralization of *g* in adult intellectual development. In C. Schooler & K. W. Schaie (Eds.), *Cognitive functioning and social structures over the life course* (pp. 120-141). New York: Ablex.

Hoyer, W. J., & Rybash, J. M. (1994). Characterizing adult cognitive development. *Journal of Adult Development, 1,* 7-12.

Hoyer, W. J., & Rybash, J. M. (1996). Life-span theory. In J. E. Birren (Ed.), *Encyclopedia of gerontology* (pp. 65-71). San Diego: Academic Press.

James, W. (1890). *Principles of psychology.* New York: Dover.

Jenkins, L., & Hoyer, W. J. (1997). *Acquisition of memory-based automaticity: Adult age differences.* Unpublished manuscript, Syracuse University.

Karmiloff-Smith, A. (1992). *Beyond modularity: A developmental perspective on cognitive science.* Cambridge: MIT Press.

Kausler, D. H. (1994). *Learning and memory in normal aging.* San Diego: Academic Press.

Kay, H. (1951). Learning of a serial task by different age groups. *Quarterly Journal of Experimental Psychology, 3,* 166-183.

Knopman, D., & Nissen, M. J. (1987). Implicit learning in patients with probable Alzheimer's disease. *Neurology, 37,* 784-788.

Knopman, D., & Nissen, M. J. (1991). Procedural learning is impaired in Huntington's disease: Evidence from the serial reaction time task. *Neuropsychologia, 29,* 245-254.

Knowlton, B. J., Ramus, S. J., & Squire, L. R. (1992). Intact artificial grammar learning in amnesia. *Psychological Science, 3,* 172-179.

Kotary, L., & Hoyer, W. J. (1995). Age and the ability to inhibit distractor information in visual selective attention. *Experimental Aging Research, 21,* 159-171.

Kramer, A. F., Larish, J. F., & Strayer, D. L. (1995). Training for attentional control in dual task settings: A comparison of young and old adults. *Journal of Experimental Psychology: Applied, 1,* 50-76.

Krampe, R., & Ericsson, K. A. (1996). Maintaining excellence: Deliberate practice and elite performance in young and older pianists. *Journal of Experimental Psychology: General, 125,* 331-359.

Lerner, R. M. (1991). Changing organism-context relations as the basic process of development: A developmental contextual perspective. *Developmental Psychology, 27,* 27-32.

Lewicki, P., Czyzewska, M., & Hoffman, H. (1987). Unconscious acquisition of complex procedural knowledge. *Journal of Experimental Psychology: Learning, Memory, and Cognition, 13,* 523-530.

Lincourt, A., & Hoyer, W. J. (1996, November). *Aging and attention in memory-based automaticity.* Paper presented at the Psychonomic Society meetings, Chicago.

Lincourt, A., Hoyer, W. J., & Cerella, J. (1997). *Attention and learning mechanisms in the development of instance-based learning: Adult age differences.* Unpublished manuscript, Syracuse University.

Logan, G. D. (1988). Toward an instance theory of automatization. *Psychological Review, 95,* 492-528.

Logan, G. D., & Klapp, S. T. (1991). Automatizing alphabet arithmetic I: Is extended practice necessary to product automaticity? *Journal of Experimental Psychology: Learning, Memory, and Cognition, 17,* 179-195.

Madden, D. J., & Plude, D. J. (1993). Selective preservation of selective attention. In J. Cerella, J. Rybash, W. Hoyer, & M. Commons (Eds.), *Adult information processing: Limits on loss* (pp. 273-300). San Diego, CA: Academic Press.

Meulemans, T., Van der Linden, M., & Denis, C. (1996, July). *Implicit artificial grammar learning and aging.* Poster presented at the Second International Conference on Memory, Padova.

Mutter, S. A., Howard, J. H., & Howard, D. V. (1994). Serial pattern learning after head injury. *Journal of Clinical and Experimental Neuropsychology, 16,* 271-288.

Mutter, S. A., Howard, D. V., Howard, J. H., & Wiggs, C. L. (1990). Performance on direct and indirect tests of memory after mild closed-head injury. *Cognitive Neuropsychology, 7,* 329-346.

Mutter, S. A., & Pliske, R. M. (1996). Judging event covariation: Effects of age and memory demand. *Journal of Gerontology: Psychological Sciences, 51B,* P70-P80.

Myerson, J., & Hale, S. (1993). General slowing and age invariance in cognitive processing: The other side of the coin. In J. Cerella, J. M. Rybash, W. J. Hoyer, & M. L. Commons (Eds.), *Adult information processing: Limits on loss* (pp. 115-141). San Diego, CA: Academic Press.

Nissen, M. J., & Bullemer, P. (1987). Attentional requirements of learning: Evidence from performance measures. *Cognitive Psychology, 19,* 1-32.

Nissen, M. J., Knopman, D. S., & Schacter, D. L. (1987). Neurochemical dissociation of memory systems. *Neurology, 37,* 789.

Pascual-Leone, A., Grafman, J., & Hallatt, M. (1994). Modulation of cortical motor output maps during development of implicit and explicit knowledge. *Science, 263,* 1287-1289.

Perruchet, P. (1994). Learning from complex rule-governed environments: On the proper functions of nonconscious and conscious processes. In C. Umiltà & M. Moscovitch (Eds.), *Attention and performance XV* (pp. 811-836). Cambridge: MIT Press.

Perruchet, P., & Amorim, M. A. (1992). Conscious knowledge and changes in performance in sequence learning: Evidence against dissociation. *Journal of Experimental Psychology: Human Perception and Performance, 18*, 785-800.

Perruchet, P., & Pacteau, C. (1990). Synthetic grammar learning: Implicit rule abstraction or explicit fragmentary knowledge? *Journal of Experimental Psychology: General, 119*, 264-275.

Plude, D. J., & Hoyer, W. J. (1986). Aging and the selectivity of visual information processing. *Psychology and Aging, 1*, 1-9.

Reber, A. S. (1969). Transfer of syntactic structures in synthetic languages. *Journal of Experimental Psychology, 81*, 115-119.

Reber, A. S. (1989). Implicit learning and tacit knowledge. *Journal of Experimental Psychology: General, 118*, 219-235.

Reber, A. R. (1992). The cognitive unconscious: An evolutionary perspective. *Consciousness and Cognition, 1*, 93-133.

Reber, A. S. (1993). *Implicit learning and tacit knowledge.* New York: Oxford University Press.

Reber, A. S., & Allen, R. (1978). Analogic and abstraction strategies in synthetic grammar learning: A functionalist interpretation. *Cognition, 6*, 189-221.

Reber, A. S., Allen, R., & Regan, S. (1985). Syntactical learning and judgement, still unconscious and still abstract: Comment on Dulany, Carlson, and Dewey. *Journal of Experimental Psychology: General, 114*, 17-24.

Redington, M., & Chater, N. (1996). Transfer in artificial grammar learning: A reevaluation. *Journal of Experimental Psychology: General, 125*, 123-138.

Reed, J., & Johnson, P. (1994). Assessing implicit learning with indirect tests: Determining what is learned about sequence structure. *Journal of Experimental Psychology: Learning, Memory, and Cognition, 20*, 585-594.

Rogers, W. A. (1992). Age differences in visual search: Target and distractor learning. *Psychology and Aging, 7*, 526-535.

Rybash, J. M. (1996). Implicit memory and aging: A cognitive neuropsychological perspective. *Developmental Neuropsychology, 12*, 127-179.

Salthouse, T. A. (1984). Effects of age and skill in typing. *Journal of Experimental Psychology: General, 113*, 345-371.

Salthouse, T. A. (1994). Aging associations: Influence of speed on adult age differences in associative learning. *Journal of Experimental Psychology: Learning, Memory, and Cognition, 20*, 1486-1503.

Salthouse, T. A. (1996). The processing speed theory of adult age differences in cognition. *Psychological Review, 103*, 403-428.

Salthouse, T. A., & Coon, V. E. (1994). Interpretation of differential deficits: The case of aging and mental arithmetic. *Journal of Experimental Psychology: Learning, Memory, and Cognition, 20,* 1172-1182.

Salthouse, T. A., Hambrick, D. Z., Lukas, K. E., & Dell, T. C. (1996). Determinants of adult age differences on synthetic work performance. *Journal of Experimental Psychology: Applied, 2,* 305-329.

Seger, C. A. (1994). Implicit learning. *Psychological Bulletin, 115,* 163-196.

Shanks, D. R., Green, R. E. A., & Kolodny, J. A. (1994). A critical examination of the evidence for unconscious (implicit) learning. In C. Umiltà & M. Moscovitch (Eds.), *Attention and performance XV* (pp. 837-860). Cambridge: MIT Press.

Shanks, D. R., & St. John, M. F. (1994). Characteristics of dissociable human learning systems. *Behavioral and Brain Sciences, 17,* 367-447.

Squire, L. R., Knowlton, B., & Musen, G. (1993). The structure and organization of memory. *Annual Review of Psychology, 44,* 453-495.

Talland, G. A. (1965). Initiation of response, and reaction time in aging, and with brain damage. In A. T. Welford & J. E. Birren (Eds.), *Behavior, aging, and the nervous system* (pp. 526-561). Springfield, IL: Charles C Thomas.

Thorndike, E. L., Bregman, E. O., Tilton, J. W., & Woodyard, E. (1928). *Adult learning.* New York: Macmillan.

Underwood, B. J. (1975). Individual differences as a crucible in theory construction. *American Psychologist, 30,* 128-134.

14

The Role of Attention in Implicit Sequence Learning

Exploring the Limits of the Cognitive Unconscious

●───

Andrew T. Hsiao
Arthur S. Reber

All of the studies we will discuss here use one or another variation on a standard serial reaction time (SRT) procedure first developed by Nissen and Bullemer (1987). In this procedure, subjects are instructed to press as rapidly as possible one of four keys (or on occasion, more) in response to a simple visual stimulus target (such as a dot or an asterisk) as it appears at one of four (or more) locations arranged horizontally across the computer screen. The target sequence is either a sequence that repeats over and over (e.g., DBCACBDCBA is the one Nissen & Bullemer used) or one that is nonrepeating but follows a set of rules (see, e.g., Cleeremans & McClelland, 1991). Sequence learning is assessed either by comparing reaction times (RTs) to the target sequence with those obtained on a nonstructured or random sequence, or by introducing a random block of trials late in training and observing the extent to which RTs increase. The role of attention is explored typically by introducing a secondary task,

AUTHORS' NOTE: We would like to thank Mike Stadler, Asher Cohen, Tim Curran, Peter Frensch, Steve Keele, Dan Willingham, Matt Erdelyi, and Andy Delamater for their helpful feedback, discussions, clarifications, and/or comments on issues covered in this chapter. Correspondence should be addressed to Andrew Hsiao at Department of Psychology, Brooklyn College of CUNY, Brooklyn, NY 11210 or Email ahsiao@email.gc.cuny.edu.

most commonly a tone-counting task in which following each target stimulus, either a high- or low-pitched tone sounds, and subjects are required to keep a running count of one of them.

Using this procedure, Nissen and Bullemer (1987) first raised the question of whether implicit sequence learning demanded attentional resources. Their study and its intriguing conclusion—that sequence learning was inhibited by a secondary task—spawned a small but lively cottage industry within cognitive psychology. Nissen and Bullemer's research was based on the assumption of a limited central capacity in human information processing. In a series of experiments, they found that when performing the SRT task alone, subjects who responded to the repeating pattern displayed reliably faster RTs than those who responded to a random sequence. However, when a secondary tone-counting task was introduced, RTs for the two conditions did not differ significantly, prompting Nissen and Bullemer to conclude that sufficient attention is a critical condition for implicit sequence learning. In a subsequent experiment, Korsakoff amnesics, in the absence of the distractor, also succeeded in learning the sequence but were apparently unaware of what was learned, suggesting that conscious memory is not necessary for such learning.[1]

These tantalizing conclusions attracted a good deal of attention for at least two reasons. First, they made clear that a satisfactory account of attention will have to extend beyond topics concerned primarily with the apprehension of external stimulation, such as visual attention, focused or selective attention, and divided attention (Keele, 1973; Treisman, 1969; Treisman & Gelade, 1980) and take into account the role of attention in implicit, unconscious cognitive processes. Second, they cast new light on the finding that automatic processes, such as logging the frequency of events in stimulus displays, required few if any attentional resources (Hasher & Zacks, 1984). In this chapter, we review the now-extensive literature on the role of attention in implicit sequence learning and examine the different theories developed to account for the findings.

SEQUENCE CHARACTERISTICS AND THEIR DEMANDS ON ATTENTION

An early development in the research on the role of attention in implicit sequence learning was the not surprising finding that various characteristics such as the length and statistical structure of the sequence play important roles.

● Sequence Length

One sequence characteristic is its sheer length. Although different researchers have used sequence lengths varying from five elements (Cohen, Ivry, & Keele, 1990) to the length of an entire block of 96 trials (Reed & Johnson, 1994), Howard and her colleagues (Howard & Howard, 1989; Howard, Mutter, & Howard, 1992) were the first to examine the effect of sequence length on learning. They trained their subjects with either a 10-element (DBCACBDCBA) sequence or a 16-element (BCACDCDBADADA-CAD) sequence. The results revealed a more pronounced learning effect associated with the shorter sequence. Howard and Howard hypothesized that the longer sequence required more attentional capacity to encode because it had to be analyzed into more chunks to resolve inherent ambiguity. Similar findings were obtained by Pascual-Leone and his colleagues (1993), although they argued that longer sequences, simply by virtue of having more elements, place a greater demand on working memory. However, because other statistical properties were left uncontrolled (most notably, the basic frequency of occurrence of each component and the number of unique transitions, both of which are confounded with the effect of sequence length), both conclusions should be viewed with caution.

More recently, Stadler and Neely (in press), realizing that it is difficult to control for all the relevant characteristics of a sequence at the same time, attempted to unpack the length-versus-structure question by using different combinations of sequence length and levels of structural redundancy. In a series of three experiments, they found the latter to be the better predictor of implicit sequence learning. Specifically, a longer sequence with higher structure can be better learned than a shorter one with low structure, where *structure* can be taken to represent a metric akin to the classic Shannon and Weaver (1949) notion of information. Gauged by this information yardstick, highly structured sequences are ones whose subsequent events are highly predictable given the immediately preceding event(s). We will have more to say about this notion of structure later.

● Uniqueness and Ambiguity in Event Transitions

Cohen et al. (1990) investigated implicit sequence learning with three types of sequences having different inner structures, which they referred to as *ambiguous, unique,* and *hybrid,* respectively. An ambiguous sequence is one in which the occurrence of one event provides no information about the succeeding event (e.g., ACDBCABD). In contrast, if a sequence contains events each of which is determined reliably by the event immediately preceding it, it is called a unique sequence (e.g., ADCBADCB). A hybrid sequence, as the term suggests, is simply one that is made up of a mixture of unique and ambiguous transitions. Cohen et al. found that sequence learning under secondary task distraction is impaired only when the sequence is of the ambiguous type—which happened to be the sequence type used by Nissen and Bullemer (1987).

Cohen et al. (1990) theorized that unique sequences, which can be encoded as simple pair-wise associations, can be learned automatically, whereas ambiguous sequences, which require hierarchical encoding, require attention. This two-mechanism theory was buttressed by Curran and Keele (1993), who demonstrated that the nonattentional form of learning was operational in the presence or absence of the tone-counting task, whereas the attentional form appeared to operate only when freed from distraction. However, more recent work has complicated matters. Frensch, Buchner, and Lin (1994) reported that subjects were able to learn ambiguous transitions within the context of a hybrid sequence, even in a dual-task situation. Hsiao (1995) observed sequence learning in a dual-task setting for an ambiguous sequence, including a nonrepeating sequence generated by an artificial grammar, along the lines of the one used by Cleeremans and McClelland (1991). Other replications also yielded results that differed from the original findings (Keele, personal communication, 1995; Keele & Jennings, 1992).

It is not entirely clear why the picture changed as research on sequence learning progressed. One possibility is that measures of learning have attained greater sensitivity due to improved control—for example, by using pseudo-random transfer sequences that matched with the practice sequences in simple event frequencies. Another may be that subtle differences in instructions given to participants prior to practice on the sequence are playing a role (Hsiao, 1997). Yet another are the different data inclusion/exclusion criteria adopted by different researchers. For example, subjects with systematically long RTs are usually discarded—although the criterion for dropping them is not always the same. In addition, only the data from subjects whose accuracy on the tone-counting task exceeded a certain arbitrary percentage are used—although, again, not everyone uses the same cut-point. In spite of these procedural and methodological complications, we still feel that the evidence is sufficiently strong to conclude that, other factors notwithstanding, even sequences made up entirely of nonunique transitions can be learned under conditions of limited attention, although they are surely learned more slowly than unique sequences.

● **Overall Statistical Properties**

Stadler (1992), arguing that learning likely extends beyond the detection of simple event-to-event covariation, emphasized the importance of overall statistical structure. He varied the structural properties of learning sequences by creating three sequences, labeled as having *low, medium,* or *high* statistical structure. Specifically, he joined a six-element root string (e.g., BDBCAB) with one of three suffix strings (e.g., *ADAC, CDBC,* or *DBCD*) to build three sequences, BDBCAB*ADAC*, BDBCAB*CDBC*, BDBCAB*DBCD*, which correspond to the low, medium, and high structures, respectively. The addition of the suffix in the low-structure case only created new pair-wise associations; in the medium-structure case, it produced three instances of existing pair-wise associations (two BCs and a DB) and an instance of trio-repetition (DBC) that already existed. In the high-structure case, four instances of pair- and two instances of trio-repetitions were created (BD, two DBs, BC; BDB, DBC).

It was posited that, with the increase of structural constraints, certain event sequences become more predictable by virtue of the fact that these events have a greater probability of occurrence after certain other events. Indeed, the results showed differences in sequence learning commensurate with the three different levels of manipulation. The effect on learning is similar to what was found in Cohen et al. (1990), in that a sequence that contains highly probable event transitions is learned more easily. If the three sequences are analyzed in Cohen et al.'s terms, it can be seen that the low-structure sequence is composed of 10 transition types, none of which is unique; the medium-structure sequence is made up of 7 transition types with two unique transitions; the high-structure sequence contains 6 transitions types with two unique transitions, one of which repeated three times.

However, Stadler (1992) only used the single-task paradigm. It remains to be seen how subjects would perform with such sequences when attention is diverted. Nevertheless, the primary conclusion seems secure. The fewer the constraints, the more attentional resources will be required to learn that sequence.

● Higher-Order Contingencies

Cohen et al. (1990) had argued that ambiguous sequences are difficult to learn because higher-order contingencies must be encoded in order to resolve the ambiguity. Given time and sufficient attention, people can, and usually do, learn higher-order contingencies of events, which enables them to act effectively. Cleeremans and McClelland (1991) reported that subjects were able to benefit from sequential dependencies up to the fourth order, and Millward and Reber (1972), using the probability learning procedure, found sensitivities to events occurring seven trials back. The question now is whether this kind of sensitivity can be attained when attention is diverted.

Reed and Johnson (1994) were the first to address this issue using the SRT task. Unlike the standard procedure, in which the stimulus locations are determined by an n-element sequence recycled k times in a block, their procedure used a long sequence that was created by concatenating eight different 12-event sequences that shared the same set of second-order conditionals (SOC). In such a sequence, each event becomes predictable, given two other events preceding it. After extensive training (17 blocks), half the subjects were transferred to a different repeating sequence that had the same SOCs, whereas the other half received a pseudo-random sequence. This sequence had transitions selected randomly but similar simple event frequencies as the sequence used in training. Reed and Johnson found that the sequence-transfer subjects showed significant advantage over the pseudo-random-transfer subjects, implying that second-order dependencies could be learned even when attentional resources were diverted.

However, it may still be too early to consider the issue resolved. Recently, Heuer and Schmidtke (1996) conducted a study in which different groups of subjects performed an SRT task, either with or without a distractor. For some subjects, the behavior of the stimulus could be predicted accurately from the preceding event (i.e., with unique transitions); for others, the stimulus becomes deterministic only when two or three events before it were fixed (with higher-order contingencies). Sequence learning was assessed both in a single-task and/or a dual-task setting. The results run counter to Reed and Johnson's (1994) findings; only first-order dependencies seemed to have been learned when the SRT task was practiced under distraction. Learning of the second-order contextual information was impaired, even when both practice and test were done without distraction.

To sum up, recent research on implicit sequence learning seems to show that the SRT task is sensitive to manipulations on the type-of-sequence variable. Of particular interest for our discussion in this section is that the sequence-type variable interacts with the availability of attention. Nissen and Bullemer's (1987) initial conclusion regarding attentional requirements with respect to sequence learning under dual-task conditions has proven to be premature. Cohen et al. (1990) showed that Nissen and Bullemer failed to find learning because they had restricted training to the ambiguous type of sequence. As the studies reviewed in this section demonstrate, however, even Cohen et al.'s discovery appears to be less than conclusive. Later research yielded evidence that even the ambiguous type of sequence can be learned under attentional distraction, although sequences containing unique transitions were generally learned better. In their original report, Cohen et al. suggested that more complex sequential structure was best encoded using hierarchical representation, whereas simpler structures can be learned via paired association. But there seems to be no compelling reason to believe that the hierarchical encoding mechanism is inhibited when attention is diverted.

One difficulty in understanding the role of attention in sequence learning stems from a lack of a clear definition of attention itself. If we assume attention to be a central processor with a limited capacity and encoding information of various complexity requires more or less attention, we may attribute impairment in, or failure of, sequence learning to this central bottleneck when competing tasks are performed simultaneously. But it is conceivable that sequence learning that calls for more complex processing may still be possible in a dual-task setting because the secondary task may not deplete the attentional resources completely, or it may not demand attention at all times. Thus, the sequence-encoding mechanism can take advantage of the residual processing capacity in a phenomenon that can be called attention-sharing and/or attention-switching (Curran & Keele, 1993; Pashler & Carrier, 1996; Stadler, 1995). It follows from this theory that sequence learning will be achieved in a graded rather than all-or-none fashion. However, if different tasks are handled by parallel and independent mechanisms, or processing modules (Curran & Keele, 1993), and the function of attention is to monitor or coordinate certain processes, then it may be possible to observe dissociation between success or failure of task performance and overall system load. Progress made in cognitive neuroscience in recent years is shedding light on these issues, but the jury is still out on the exact role of attention in sequence learning.

THE ROLE OF THE SECONDARY
TASK IN SEQUENCE LEARNING

Since Nissen and Bullemer's (1987) original study, there is no doubt that performing the tone-counting task is disruptive because it invariably slows down subjects' responses to the primary SRT task. But the phenomenon that interests us here is that it also interferes with subjects' ability to learn, as reflected in various performance measures. In what follows, we will often refer to a *learning effect,* which unless otherwise stated, refers to a significant increase in RT on a block of trials in which the underlying structure of the sequence has been altered in some manner.

The Secondary Task Handicaps the
Hierarchical Encoding Mechanism

Cohen et al. (1990) observed that subjects were able to learn an ambiguous sequence when the SRT task was performed alone but were unable to do so under dual-task conditions. They hypothesized, as we discussed in the preceding section, that sequences with unique transitions can be learned by a mechanism that operates on associative principles whereas sequences with ambiguous transitions require one capable of hierarchical encoding. Because Cohen et al. assumed that performing the tone-counting task reduced attention available to the encoding of the structured sequence information, they maintained that the hierarchical mechanism requires attention to operate.

Curran and Keele (1993) further explored this dual-mechanism theory in a series of experiments. They referred to the two types of learning involving hierarchical encoding and associational encoding as the *attentional* and *nonattentional* forms, respectively. In one experiment, they had subjects practice the SRT task without distraction. Learning was first measured in a single-task setting and then in a dual-task setting. They found roughly twice as much learning in a single-task setting as in a dual-task setting. In a second study, they had subjects learn under dual-task conditions and measured learning first with the distractor present and then under single-task conditions. Surprisingly, the single-task advantage observed in the former experiment disappeared in the latter; the amount of learning was the same whether measured in a single- or a dual-task setting. Curran and Keele interpreted this result as meaning that both the attentional and the nonattentional forms of learning occur when sufficient attention is available in the learning phase, but only the nonattentional form operates when resources are diverted by a distraction task. Specifically, the tone-counting task reduces attentional resources necessary for parsing and encoding sections of an ambiguous sequence.

● **The Secondary Task Suppresses Expression of Learning**

There may be alternative explanations for Curran and Keele's (1993) results. One possibility is that the distraction task operates to impair expression of what has been learned. For instance, in their first experiment, where subjects practiced the SRT task in a single-task condition, learning was more pronounced in the single- than in the dual-task condition. In a separate experiment, one group practiced with the distractor and another without. Here, both groups exhibited similar levels of sequence learning. It is entirely possible that sequence knowledge acquired in a single-task condition failed to gain expression when the distractor task was added.

This notion has been embraced by Frensch, Lin, and Buchner (in press). In one experiment, they manipulated the amount of practice subjects received under single- and dual-task conditions and observed the effect of practice in the presence or absence of a distraction. All subjects received the same amount of practice on the primary SRT task. However, some subjects received more practice in a single-task situation whereas others received more practice in a dual-task situation. Hence, three groups were run, indexed by the number of blocks subjects practiced the SRT task in a single (ST) and dual task (DT) condition (i.e., 6DT/1ST, 4DT/3ST, and 2DT/5ST, respectively) before learning was assessed. The 6DT/1ST group, for instance, designates the group that first performed 6 blocks of the SRT task with a distractor, followed by 1 block without the distractor. Learning was evaluated in a single-task situation for all three groups in this experiment. It was found that, regardless of which practice schedule was used, the amount of learning was virtually identical.

In another experiment with a slightly different procedure, all subjects began by performing the SRT task in a single-task condition and then were shifted to a dual task at different times in the training phase (i.e., the three groups were: 6ST/1DT, 4ST/3DT, & 2ST/5DT). Here response rate was proportional to the amount of practice subjects received under the dual task condition, with the 2ST/5DT group showing the fastest overall RTs in the learning phase and the 6ST/1DT group showing the slowest. However, when the transfer effect was examined, all groups achieved similar levels of learning, despite overall RT differences. The results from these two experiments suggest that distraction during practice had little impact on sequence learning.

Frensch et al. (in press) noted that this latter observation is not totally inconsistent with Curran and Keele's (1993) formulation, as it can be argued that the learning essentially reflects the operation of the nonattentional mechanism. However, the dual-mechanism theory predicts differential amounts of learning associated with different practice schedules in the first experiment. Because learning was measured in a single-task setting where neither mechanism was inhibited and subjects of one group received more training in the single-task setting whereas those of another group received more training in the dual-task setting, subjects who received more single-task training are expected, according to the dual-mechanism theory, to exhibit more learning than subjects who received less such training. The dual-mechanism theory cannot accommodate this observation. The only door that is left open is to show that attentional learning can be complete within a single block of practice when the SRT task is performed without distraction.

Frensch et al. (in press) ran a second pair of experiments that ruled out this possibility. Groups that received only one block of practice before learning was assessed (1DT and 1ST) were compared with groups that received 5 blocks of practice (5DT and 5ST). The two experiments differed only in that the primary stimulus followed an ambiguous sequence in one and it followed a unique sequence in the other. Similar performance was observed, regardless of the type of sequence used. Of special interest was the finding that different amounts of practice yielded differential effects of learning. Specifically, subjects who received 5 blocks of practice learned better than those who received only 1 block of practice, whether learning was measured with or without the secondary task. Frensch et al. were therefore led to believe that implicit sequence learning may be mediated by a single learning mechanism that is not affected by the availability of attention, although such learning may not be expressed under conditions of severe distraction that interferes with retrieval.

● **The Secondary Task Disrupts Grouping in Sequence Learning**

In addition, the view that a secondary task disrupts implicit sequence learning because it reduces the amount of attention that is left to process the structural information underlying the stimulus events faces another challenge by Stadler (1995). Instead of arguing that the secondary task competes with the primary SRT task for a limited attentional capacity, Stadler argued that the secondary task impairs sequence learning because it disrupts organization of successive events during encoding. Stadler (1993) had previously demonstrated the importance of grouping in sequence learning by placing a longer (2000 ms) than usual (400 ms) response-stimulus interval (RSI), either at the end of each repeating sequence or between two trials of each sequence—determined randomly. The disruptive effect of the randomly occurring long RSI reduced learning significantly. Although this study used the single-task procedure, the suggestion is that the introduction of the dual task might operate in much the same way—that is, by interfering with the subjects' attempts to organize the ongoing sequence.

To test this prediction, Stadler (1995) had one group of subjects perform the SRT task with the secondary tone-counting task; a second group was required to retain a memory load of a set of letters while performing the SRT task; and a third group performed the SRT task as a single task but with inconsistent grouping cues. In addition, two other groups, who served as controls, received either the letter sets or the tones but were told to ignore them. Subjects who worked with the secondary tone-counting task closely resembled those with the inconsistent cues and both showed less learning than those with the separate memory load. Stadler's argument is that although memory load engages one's attention, it does not disrupt sequence grouping. In contrast, the randomly occurring long pauses place little extra demand on attentional expenditure, but they do impede consistent grouping. The functional similarity in subjects' performance in the tone-counting condition and the long-pause condition invites the inference that similar processes were disrupted during learning. Incidentally, it also suggests that the secondary tone-counting task may not be an effective means to manipulate the availability of attention because its detrimental effect on sequence learning may be attributable to its disruption in representational organization rather than a reduced attentional capacity.

The role of grouping in the SRT task had been examined earlier by Keele and Jennings (1992) in a study designed to test a connectionist model of the task based on the recurrent feedback algorithm developed by Jordan (1990). Both human subjects and a Jordan network produced similar data when trained with unique, hybrid, and ambiguous sequences. Of special interest was the finding that when an ambiguous sequence was suffixed with an additional unique element (e.g., 1323124), both the human subjects, who performed the task under distraction, and the neural network displayed sequence learning as if the sequence were of the unique type. Keele and Jennings argued that the salient suffix served as a grouping cue that facilitated the encoding of the sequence. The idea is further supported when a parsing mechanism was introduced in the computer model, which was implemented by resetting the state units to zero at the end of each repetition of the sequence. Consistent grouping induced by parsing soon led the neural network to produce near-perfect prediction.

As an aside here, it is worth noting that studies using the artificial grammar learning task provide additional support for the importance of organization in implicit learning. Servan-Schreiber and Anderson (1990) presented subjects with strings of letters that either were consistent with the rules of the artificial grammar or violated them in a subtle way. When the presentations followed the natural chunks of the grammar (i.e., groups of letters with high degree of covariation were presented together), subjects performed well, reliably distinguishing well-formed from ill-formed strings. When the chunks were assembled arbitrarily, performance was dramatically reduced. Interestingly, subjects who worked with unchunked displays performed like those who worked with the naturally chunked strings, suggesting that subjects use these kinds of organizational tendencies on their own.

Grouping, chunking, and hierarchical encoding are related ideas. They are hypothetical processes by which complex information is believed to be encoded and corresponding mental representations formed. Stadler (1995) may be right when he points out that both the secondary task and the irregular pauses disrupt grouping in the representation of stimulus events. However, demonstrating a common consequence of different disruptive procedures does not necessarily imply that the same mechanisms are actually involved in producing the disruption. The random pauses disrupt grouping because they encourage the subjects to encode the event sequence in many inconsistent ways, prompted by the pauses as grouping cues. The distraction task, however, disrupts encoding in a somewhat indirect way. To speculate, encoding a sequence with nonunique transitions involves extracting subsegmental covariations, identifying markers for these segments, and then integrating local rules pertaining to successive segments of the event sequence to form higher-order conditionals. In computational terms, carrying out these processes requires considerable amount of time and memory space in both encoding and retrieval. When the processing capacity is reduced by the secondary task, it is small wonder sequence learning, or the expression thereof, becomes more difficult. It should be noted, however, that the disruption in encoding due to inconsistent grouping cues cannot necessarily be blamed for all the difficulties of sequence learning in the dual-task paradigm. To support this cautionary note, let us just point out that although Stadler's (1995) tones control subjects were given the same inconsistent grouping cues, they nonetheless exhibited markedly better learning than subjects who had to tackle the tones in a way that taxes considerably more attention. The implicit learning machinery has evolved an ability to withstand noise in the environment. As another example, subjects in Jiménez and Cleeremans's (1994) experiment became sensitive to the sequence structure, even when the event sequence, which followed an artificial grammar, were interspersed with 15% random elements.

● The Secondary Task Reduces Short-Term Memory Capacity in Sequence Learning

Whereas Stadler (1995) contends that a secondary task impairs implicit sequence learning by disrupting consistent grouping, Frensch and his colleagues (Frensch et al., 1994; Frensch & Miner, 1994) have attributed the detrimental effect of the secondary task to a reduction in the capacity of short-term memory. This memory-based theory presumes two assumptions, namely, (a) the working memory has a limited capacity, which varies among individuals; and (b) contents in this memory decay rapidly (e.g., 500 ms or so). It was then pointed out that the disruptive effect of the secondary task could derive from simply lowering the probability that pieces of information about the target sequence are active in memory at any one time, thereby compromising the detection of covariation among elements.

To test this notion, Frensch and Miner (1994, Experiment 2) ran subjects with RSIs of either 500 or 1500 ms. Half of each group performed the SRT task alone, and half performed it with the tone-counting task. In the single-task conditions, all subjects learned, suggesting that a delay by itself may not necessarily prevent sequence learning because maintenance rehearsal can be used to bridge it. When the secondary task was performed together with the primary task, both groups showed less learning, but the 500 ms RSI subjects were significantly better than the 1500 ms. In addition, subjects' digit span, a measure of short-term memory capacity, correlates with sequence learning only in the RSI = 500 condition. Frensch and Miner argue that these results fit their short-term memory model.

The argument goes like this. In the typical SRT study, performing a secondary task tends to slow down RTs by some 200 to 300 ms, resulting in an RT, on average, of about 500 to 600 ms. When the RT on each trial is added to an RSI of 500 ms, the interval is approaching the duration limits of short-term memory. The probability of subjects detecting the covariations between elements of the sequence begins to diminish. In addition, the heavy demand of the secondary task means there will be little chance for maintenance rehearsal. This explains why sequence learning is usually poorer in a dual-task setting. With an RSI of 1500 ms, the likelihood of successive elements of the sequence remaining active in short-term memory drops dramatically, thus severely compromising subjects' ability to detect the associative links between adjacent events. Frensch and Miner (1994) believe that a model with a single associative learning mechanism is sufficient to account for observed data in sequence learning.

This theoretical framework makes moot the issue of the role of attention in sequence learning. However, the observation that short-term capacity correlates with sequence learning only when RSI is short (500 ms) and in the presence of a distractor suggests an interaction between timing and a capacity limit of some sort. What is interesting about this work is that the success or failure of sequence learning was not determined by the availability or shortage of time, because a longer RSI impaired rather than facilitated learning. Instead, it suggests that some critical processes related to learning may be compromised when two competing tasks are performed in the same time frame.

● **The Secondary Task Adds Complexity to the Learning Task**

Virtually all the work covered heretofore has focused on performance of the key-pressing SRT task. It is referred to as the primary task, whereas the tone-counting task was used as a distractor. As such, the primary task sequences have been programmed to follow certain orders, depending on the researchers' intent, whereas the secondary task has been largely left to vary at the mercy of random forces, except for a few weak constraints (e.g., a probabilistically defined proportion for the high- or low-pitched tone to occur). However, recently, Schmidtke and Heuer (in press) introduced a patterned secondary task.

In their experiments a patterned tone sequence was incorporated in some conditions. They also changed the nature of the secondary task.

Rather than having subjects keep a running count of the secondary stimuli, they were instructed to depress a foot pedal in response to a high-pitched tone (what they termed the "go/no go" task). The primary visual stimulus always followed a repeating sequence of Length 6. In one experiment, the performance of this group was compared with that of a control group that responded to a sequence of high- and low-pitched tones determined randomly, a group that received a six-element tone pattern, and one that received a five-element tone pattern. There was also a single-task control group, which performed the SRT task alone.

As would be expected, the single-task group demonstrated the best overall performance. Taking into consideration the likelihood that the overall RTs would be affected by response conflict when subjects had to respond both to the primary visual stimulus and the secondary auditory stimulus on the same trial when the high-pitched tone was presented, an analysis was performed on RTs from the "no go" trials only. The results showed that subjects exhibited the greatest amount of learning when both the primary and secondary tasks followed a six-element sequence and poorer learning when the primary stimulus sequence had six elements but the secondary stimulus sequence had five elements. The least amount of learning was found in the group for which the tones were random.

These observations were taken as support for Schmidtke and Heuer's (in press) notion of task integration. That is, subjects' behavior was affected by both the characteristics of the primary stimulus sequence and by the constraints of the secondary stimulus. When the secondary tone is random, subjects have to deal with a sequence of events in which every other event is stochastically determined. When the tone sequence coincides with the visual stimulus sequence in length, the task essentially becomes one of learning a 12-element visual-auditory pattern, which, although difficult, can be accomplished. The five-element tone sequence breaches this coherency, creating uncertainty in the larger context and compromising learning.

In another experiment, Schmidtke and Heuer (in press) showed that subjects' RTs to both the primary visual task and the secondary tone task were similarly affected by changes in sequence structure in the secondary task, further indicating that task integration takes place in such a situation. Nevertheless, the very fact that sequence learning was substantially superior when the tone followed a five-element sequence than when it was random suggests that learning of the visual stimulus sequence and that of the auditory stimulus sequence may have proceeded independently. The possibility of the existence of separate systems that are capable of implicitly acquiring information about complex dimensions was explored by other researchers (e.g., Mayr, 1996).

Although we find Schmidtke and Heuer's (in press) work provocative, we do note that their go/no go task is a major adaptation to the standard procedure. In one way, this modification is useful, because in the standard procedure, it has never been clear whether the tone-counting task directly disrupts encoding of the primary sequence or whether it merely affects short-term memory. However, it is unfortunate that it was introduced nonsystematically because it changes the procedure in ways that the findings of Frensch and his colleagues on the role of short-term memory would certainly suggest are important. Until more careful studies are carried out comparing these two variations, their findings need to be viewed as tentative.

● Section Summary

This section reviewed studies that proposed a number of possible roles the secondary task may play in sequence learning. Cohen et al. (1990) and Curran and Keele (1993) argued that the secondary task renders a specific learning mechanism inoperable. Stadler (1995) showed that the secondary task disrupts organization of the sequence during encoding. Frensch and colleagues first suggested that the secondary task makes learning difficult by occupying a capacity-limited working memory, which lowers the activation level of sequence elements in memory. Later, they (Frensch et al., in press) presented evidence that the secondary task suppresses the expression of learning rather than disrupting learning itself. Schmidtke and Heuer (in press) contended that the secondary task simply adds complexity to the original event sequence by inserting an auditory event between every two visual/spatial elements.

We think it's important to understand that each of these points of view can be correct to some extent without (much) conflict. The SRT task is clearly a more complex task than any of us initially appreciated. There are many ways in which performance on it could be compromised and, hence, many different processes that could be disrupted by the introduction of an attention-demanding secondary task. The secondary task impairs sequence learning, or it appears to do so, not because it distracts attention in a simple-minded way, but because it alters the context in which learning is supposed to take place or in which it is to be expressed. Finally, here we want to present some preliminary findings from our lab that suggest an even further complication caused by the delicate (and typically uncontrolled) timing relationships between the primary and secondary stimuli.

SEQUENCE LEARNING IS SENSITIVE
TO AVAILABLE ATTENTION

In a recent study, subjects in our lab demonstrated they were able to learn a 12-element ambiguous sequence in a dual-task situation. However, when they were required to practice on the secondary target-counting task prior to performing the SRT task coupled with the secondary task, the learning effect practically disappeared. These results first had us puzzled; why should additional practice lower performance? Here is what we think was happening; it is actually straightforward. Keeping a running count of the secondary stimuli requires a considerable amount of attention. However, pressing a key in response to an appropriate visual stimulus soon becomes nearly automatic. We view sequence learning as occurring in the background of the residual attention after the cost of the tone-counting task and the key-pressing task. If there is still sufficient attention available to the encoding of the sequence, learning will be successful; otherwise, failure will result. In the first case, performing the secondary task itself did not seem to have depleted attention enough to preclude sequence learning. But having subjects practice the secondary task before dual-task performance changed the way attention was allocated. Emphasizing that the secondary task was demanding and needed additional practice, subjects likely allocated more resources to that task, leaving attention relatively unavailable to sequence learning (Hsiao, 1997).

Our formulation presupposes a kind of bottleneck theory of attention, as proposed by Pashler and his coworkers (Fagot & Pashler, 1992; Pashler, 1994). In a typical dual-task performance situation, subjects start processing the secondary task (S_s) shortly before, or even after, the onset of the next primary stimulus (S_p). Pashler's work suggests that subjects are able to process S_p perceptually while attention is temporarily engaged by the response selection of the secondary task. But while they are deciding what should be done as a response to S_s, selection of a response to S_p cannot be processed; this has to await until the former is completed.

Now, let's apply this to the typical trial in the sequence learning situation. We haven't made much of this variable before, but it has long been a convention that the secondary stimulus (i.e., the tone) is presented on a variable schedule either 40, 80, or 120 ms after the subjects' response to the primary stimulus. This technique of using what we might call the *RSSOA* (for response-secondary stimulus onset asynchrony) was introduced to keep subjects from synchronizing the onset of the secondary stimulus with the onset of the next primary stimulus (Cohen, 1995, personal communication). The primary task timing, that between the button-pressing response and the next target (which is usually denoted as the RSI), is usually kept constant with 200 ms being a common RSI. If our arguments about the allocation of attentional resources are correct, then a short RSSOA (say, 40 ms) might have a lesser detrimental effect on sequence learning due to a smaller processing overlap than a longer one (say, 120 ms). The point is that this long RSSOA places the next target within the processing shadow of the distractor. If we are right about this, there are a lot of intriguing data buried in the literature because no one has varied RSSOA systematically.

The one published study that looked into the temporal perspective as an independent variable is reported by Frensch et al. (1994). In one experiment, they used a primary-secondary stimulus interval (SSI) of 0, 350, or 700 ms. They reported that subjects were able to learn the sequence with the SSI of 0 ms. The 350 ms SSI produced some but far less learning. The 700 ms SSI led to two different performance patterns, resulting from two different response strategies that subjects adopted. Some subjects pressed the key first, prior to the tone onset; others withheld their response to the primary task until after the tone sounded. The former strategy yielded the best learning and the fastest overall RTs, whereas the latter proved to be the least effective on both accounts.

Frensch et al. (1994) estimated that when the two tasks, that is, key pressing and tone counting, were performed in isolation, they took approximately 450 ms and 300 ms, respectively. It appears that when the two stimuli are presented simultaneously, subjects are able to attend to both perceptually and execute appropriate responses in succession. At onset 350, the tone is presented when subjects are just in the process of choosing a response, but the intrusion of the tone forces that task to be postponed until the tone is identified—the net effect being an impairment of sequence learning as well as an RT slowdown. At onset 700 ms, subjects who choose to respond to S_p first before they tackle the tone-counting task are performing the two tasks alternately. Conversely, subjects who withhold the response until they hear the tone are putting themselves in a situation where the response to S_p must be selected and/or executed after updating the tone count, which, as we suggested, should impair performance.

The success of attention sharing seems to be determined by task demands, as well as the timing of relevant events. When task demands are held constant, manipulating the temporal schedule of the two tasks will illuminate the locus of attentional demand of sequence learning. To put these ideas to the test, we (Hsiao & Reber, 1996) manipulated the onset of the secondary tone as a between-subjects factor with RSSOAs of 50, 100, and 150 ms. A standard RSI of 200 ms was used. We also introduced an Estimator control group, which performed the same tasks but was only required to estimate the tone count at the end of each block. Before the data were analyzed, experimental subjects were divided into two post hoc groups on the basis of their tone-count accuracy, Good Counters and Poor Counters.

The best learning was found, perhaps not surprisingly, in the Estimators and the Poor Counters. Presumably, Good Counters allocated more attention to the tone-counting task, leaving less attention available for the learning mechanism to process sequence information. There were also no effects of RSSOA in these groups. Among the Good Counters, however, there was an effect of RSSOA resulting from the 150 ms subjects showing impaired learning. Attempting to get an accurate tone count caused the central executive to allocate sufficient attention for the task, and a late tone onset caused it to overlap most with the next primary task. We take this finding to support the general argument that the availability of attention is an important determinant of sequence learning. We also take it as suggesting that a variety of what we like to call *microcognitive* factors are likely playing themselves out in these experiments—largely unnoticed.

CONCLUDING REMARKS AND SUGGESTIONS FOR FUTURE RESEARCH

We have attempted to present a general overview of the research on the role of attention in implicit sequence learning. In the decade since the initial study by Nissen and Bullemer (1987) first suggested that sequence learning requires attention, research has pointed to at least a few generalizations. Specifically,

1. Certain properties of the sequence, such as low predictability of component events (e.g., Cohen et al.'s ambiguous transitions and Stadler's low statistical

structures), make sequences more difficult (although not impossible) to learn under attentional load.

2. Learning and expression of what has been learned must be distinguished. Failure of subjects to display evidence of learning under secondary task constraints does not necessarily mean that they may not display knowledge of the sequence under other, less demanding conditions (Frensch et al., in press).

3. There is likely no single impact of the secondary task on learning. Rather, it appears that any of a variety of processes involved in the task are disrupted to some extent by an attention-demanding secondary task. Stadler (1995) has presented evidence implicating the disruption of organization of the sequence. Frensch and his colleagues (Frensch et al., 1994) find that short memory processes are interfered with. Hsiao and Reber (1996) showed that timing factors are important, and so is the actual allocation of attentional resources (Hsiao, 1997). We have little doubt that all of these (and probably other factors) are important. In short, the secondary task does not only add a source of attentional demand, it also changes the larger learning context (Schmidtke & Heuer, in press).

While working on this chapter, we have, from time to time, been seized by the possibility that the SRT task is psychologically empty and that the last several years of research on it have been little more than a modern version of that old theological puzzle of trying to ascertain how many angels can dance on the head of a pin. Although experimental paradigms like the SRT task can do this kind of thing to you, we actually believe otherwise. In fact, we suspect that the investigation of sequence learning under distraction has important implications for our understanding of cognitive processes and the architecture of the mind in general. For example, the very fact that the addition of a secondary task, even after extensive practice, makes subjects' responses to the primary task slower by about 200 to 300 ms suggests that there exists a bottleneck somewhere in the processing mechanism. Conceivably, a lot of processes are being carried out in distributed and parallel fashion, given the enormous amount of information being handled by the cognitive system. However, at least some of the processes in the performance of the SRT task and the secondary tone-counting task appear to be executed sequentially. The additivity of response latency suggests that at least some stages of the two tasks are carried out using a common mechanism that has a limited processing capacity and has a ceiling on the number of computations that can be carried out within a given time frame.

The realistic picture may be that the attentional mechanism is capable of switching among several jobs pending processing. Performance of each task can be broken down into a number of stages such as perception, response selection, and response production, as outlined by Pashler (1993). When the stimuli of two tasks are presented in such close succession that processing one stage of one task overlaps with the onset of another task, the system is forced to switch attention between two separate tasks, and sometimes while one process is being carried out, another one must be suspended. Depending on the complexity of each of the tasks and their temporal scheduling, capacity sharing may lead to compromised sequence learning in addition to disrupted performance of either or both tasks.

In addition, although we only touched on these issues, we suspect that the SRT task can be used to investigate a variety of other, microcognitive processes such as inhibition of return (if a segment of a sequence has an ABA structure, do we see reliably slower RTs on the second A?), priming (if a segment of a sequence contains repeats, as in ABBC, does the second B have a shorter RT—or a longer one, if inhibition of return operates here as well), completion (if an event "completes" a series, such as CADB, will this final B produce shorter RTs?), and modality effects (what happens if the secondary task and the primary task use the same modality?) (Goschke, 1992; Hsiao, 1995). These questions (and others, but we don't want to give away the entire store here) are ones that can be easily broached within the SRT framework. We look forward to the next decade.

NOTE

1. Although it lies outside the net we have cast for this chapter, the fact that patients with various lesions that compromise explicit functions perform at normal levels on implicit tasks is a topic of considerable importance in the emerging general picture of implicit learning (see Reber, Allen, & Reber, in press).

REFERENCES

Cleeremans, A., & McClelland, J. L. (1991). Learning the structure of event sequences. *Journal of Experimental Psychology: General, 120*(3), 235-253.

Cohen, A., Ivry, R. I., & Keele, S. W. (1990). Attention and structure in sequence learning. *Journal of Experimental Psychology: Learning, Memory, and Cognition, 16*(1),17-30.

Curran, T., & Keele, S. W. (1993). Attention and nonattentional forms sequence learning. *Journal of Experimental Psychology: Learning, Memory, and Cognition, 19,* 189-202.

Fagot, C., & Pashler, H. (1992). Making two responses to a single object: Implications for the central attentional bottleneck. *Journal of Experimental Psychology: Human Perception and Performance, 18,* 1058-1079.

Frensch, P. A., Buchner, A., & Lin, J. (1994). Implicit learning of unique and ambiguous transitions in the presence and absence of a distractor task. *Journal of Experimental Psychology: Learning, Memory, and Cognition, 20,* 567-584.

Frensch, P. A., Lin, J., & Buchner, A. (in press). Learning versus behavioral expression of the learned: The effects of a secondary tone-counting task on implicit learning in the Serial Reaction Task. *Psychological Research.*

Frensch, P. A., & Miner, C. S. (1994). Effects of presentation rate and individual differences in short-term memory capacity on an indirect measure of serial learning. *Memory & Cognition, 22(1),* 95-110.

Goschke, T. (1992). *The role of attention in implicit learning of structured event sequences.* Paper presented at the Annual Conference for Experimental Psychologists, Osnabrück, Germany.

Hasher, L., & Zacks, R. T. (1984). Automatic processing of fundamental information. *American Psychologist, 39,* 1372-1388.

Heuer, H., & Schmidtke, V. (1996). Secondary-task effects on sequence learning. *Psychological Research, 59,* 176-186.

Howard, D. V., & Howard, J. H., Jr. (1989). Age differences in learning serial patterns: Direct and indirect measures. *Psychology and Aging, 4,* 357-364.

Howard, J. H., Jr., Mutter, S. A., & Howard, D. V. (1992). Serial pattern learning by event observation. *Journal of Experimental Psychology: Learning, Memory, and Cognition, 18,* 1029-1039.

Hsiao, A. T. (1995). *Modality effect in sequence learning under attentional manipulation.* Paper presented at the 66th Annual Meeting of the Eastern Psychological Association, Boston.

Hsiao, A. T. (1997). *Implicit sequence learning depends on available residual attention.* Paper presented at the 68th Annual Meeting of the Eastern Psychological Association, Washington, DC.

Hsiao, A. T., & Reber, R. S. (1996). *Short (50-ms) distractor-target asynchronies disrupt SRT learning.* Paper presented at the 37th Psychonomic Society Annual Meeting, Chicago.

Jiménez, L., & Cleeremans, A. (1994). Direct and indirect measures of implicit learning. In *Proceedings of the 16th Annual Conference of the Cognitive Science Society* (pp. 445-550). Hillsdale, NJ: Lawrence Erlbaum.

Jordan, M. I. (1990). Learning to articulate: Sequential networks and distal constraints. In M. Jeannerod (Ed.), *Attention and performance* (Vol. 13). Hillsdale, NJ: Lawrence Erlbaum.

Keele, S. W. (1973). *Attention and human performance.* Pacific Palisades, CA: Goodyear.

Keele, S. W., & Jennings, P. J. (1992). Attention in the representation of sequence: Experiment and theory. *Human Movement Studies, 11,* 125-138.

Mayr, U. (1996). Spatial attention and implicit sequence learning: Evidence for independent learning of spatial and nonspatial sequences. *Journal of Experimental Psychology: Learning, Memory, and Cognition, 22*(2), 350-364.

Millward, R. B., & Reber, A. S. (1972). Probability learning: Contingent-event sequences with lags. *American Journal of Psychology, 85,* 81-98.

Nissen, M. J., & Bullemer, P. (1987). Attentional requirements of learning: Evidence from performance systems. *Cognitive Psychology, 19,* 1-32.

Pascual-Leone, A., Grafman, J., Clark, K., Stewart, M., Massaquoi, S., Lou, J.-S., & Hallett, M. (1993). Procedural learning in Parkinson's disease and cerebellar degeneration. *Annals of Neurology, 34,* 594-602.

Pashler, H. (1993). Doing two things at the same time. *American Scientist, 81,* 48-55.

Pashler, H. (1994). Graded capacity-sharing in dual-task interference? *Journal of Experimental Psychology: Human Perception and Performance, 20,* 330-342.

Pashler, H., & Carrier, M. (1996). Structures, processes, and the flow of information. In E. Bjork & R. A. Bjork (Eds.), *Handbook of perception and cognition: Memory* (2nd ed.). San Diego, CA: Academic Press.

Reber, A. S., Allen, R., & Reber, P. J. (in press). Implicit and explicit learning. In R. Sternberg (Ed.), *The concept of cognition.* Cambridge: MIT Press.

Reed, J., & Johnson, P. (1994). Assessing implicit learning with indirect tests: Determining what is learned about sequence structure. *Journal of Experimental Psychology: Learning, Memory, and Cognition, 20,* 585-594.

Servan-Schreiber, E., & Anderson, J. R. (1990). Learning artificial grammars with competitive chunking. *Journal of Experimental Psychology: Learning, Memory, and Cognition, 16*(4), 592-608.

Schmidtke, V., & Heuer, H. (in press). Task integration as a factor in secondary-task effect on sequence learning. *Psychological Research.*

Shannon, C. E., & Weaver, W. (1949). *The mathematical theory of communication.* Urbana: University of Illinois Press.

Stadler, M. A. (1992). Statistical structure and implicit serial learning. *Journal of Experimental Psychology: Learning, Memory, and Cognition, 18,* 318-327.

Stadler, M. A. (1993). Implicit serial learning: Questions inspired by Hebb (1961). *Memory & Cognition, 21,* 819-827.

Stadler, M. A. (1995). Role of attention in implicit learning. *Journal of Experimental Psychology: Learning, Memory, and Cognition, 21,* 674-685.

Stadler, M. A., & Neely, C. B. (in press). Effects of sequence length and structure on implicit serial learning. *Psychological Research.*

Treisman, A. M. (1969). Strategies and models of selective attention. *Psychological Review, 76,* 282-299.

Treisman, A. M., & Gelade, G. (1980). A feature-integration theory of attention. *Cognitive Psychology, 12,* 97-136.

15

Learning and Development

*The Implicit Knowledge Assumption
Reconsidered*

●————————————————————————————————————

Pierre Perruchet
Annie Vinter

INTRODUCTION

● **Learning and Development**

Many studies have addressed the question of whether the characteristics of learning differ between adults and children, or between children
of different ages. The focus of these studies, from the developmentalist's
standpoint, is one of investigating the evolution of a target behavior. Accordingly, learning as a target behavior has the same status as sensory-motor
or perceptual phenomena in other domains of developmental psychology.
From the learning researcher's standpoint, in contrast, the focus of age-
comparative studies is one of demonstrating dissociations between different
learning processes. Children, as the selected population, have the same
status as elderly people or neurological patients in other domains of the
psychology of learning. In virtually no case has the fact that learning and

AUTHORS' NOTE: Preparation of this chapter was supported by the University of Bourgogne
and the Centre National de la Recherche Scientifique (ESA CNRS 5022). We would like to
thank Peter A. Frensch, Pierre Mounoud, and one anonymous reviewer for their helpful
comments and constructive suggestions on an earlier version of this chapter.

495

development share an interest in the same fundamental issue, namely the acquisition of new skills or new knowledge by a person as a consequence of his or her interaction with a structured environment, led to the search for a common theoretical framework. Exceptions were the well-known early Watson and Skinner attempts to encompass child development within the models of conditioning, but these attempts have failed to generate a long-standing research program. By and large, learning and development have evolved as two independent fields of inquiry.

This independence has multiple determinants. For years, the main focus of interest for learning-oriented researchers has been elementary conditioning phenomena. At first glance, the situation of a subject faced with the repeated presentation of paired events, such as a tone and an electric shock, bears little resemblance to the real-world in which a child grows up. Likewise, theories elaborated in this context seem ill-suited for developmental issues. Of course, some authors have been concerned with more complex forms of learning, for instance, in research on concept formation. However, the nature of the problems, the mode of presentation of the data, the instructional demands for analytic and explicit modes of resolution, all appear to differ from the common situation of a child learning in his or her natural environment.

We believe that the recent upsurge of research on implicit learning provides a unique opportunity for a theoretical integration of the issues raised in the learning and developmental areas. The term *implicit learning* designates an adaptive mode in which subjects' behavior is sensitive to the structural features of an experienced situation, without the adaptation being due to an intentional exploitation of subjects' explicit knowledge about these features. Although there is little consensus within the literature, these two components, (a) the behavioral sensitivity to the structure of a situation, and (b) the lack of intentional, strategic causes for this sensitivity, have been included in virtually all definitions of implicit learning (e.g., Cleeremans, 1993; Reber, 1993). Many contributors to the area have added additional criteria. For instance, several researchers emphasize the point that explicit knowledge about the training situation is lacking or at least limited. Including this property in the implicit learning concept is obviously possible, insofar as terminological issues are arbitrary, but, as a matter of fact, doing so may well make the very existence of the phenomenon controversial (e.g., Shanks & St. John, 1994). The exclusive reliance on a lack of intentional exploitation of explicit knowledge, on the other hand, makes the existence of the phenomenon "real" at the phenomenological, introspective level, and it is confirmed by a large number of experimental investigations. This choice of definition has the additional advantage of unifying the meanings of implicit across the germane areas of implicit learning and implicit memory.

Examining the characteristics of the experimental situations usually involved in this field of research helps to understand why implicit learning is, a priori, relevant for development. First, implicit learning is generally observed while subjects are not asked to search for the rules structuring the situation they are tackling. Instead, subjects are generally instructed to engage in rote memory or any other activity ensuring attentional processing of the training display but diverting them from taking an analytical approach. Second, only well-structured patterns are displayed. For instance, in the category learning subarea, only positive instances of the to-be-learned category are shown to subjects. This condition contrasts with traditional concept-formation settings, in which subjects are shown both exemplars and nonexemplars of the concept (along with appropriate information). Note that this characteristic is a prerequisite for incidental conditions of learning because showing negative exemplars may well cause a shift within the learner toward adopting a problem-solving attitudinal set. The third characteristic of implicit learning situations is their relative complexity. On the whole, the implicit learning conditions are closer to most real-life situations encountered by children than were the conditions used in earlier, more traditional settings of learning.

However, we do not claim that the mapping between learning in an implicit learning situation and during development is perfect. The most salient differences between laboratory situations of implicit learning and the situations encountered in natural learning settings throughout childhood pertain to their duration and level of complexity. It may indeed appear absurd to draw a parallel between what happens during the few minutes of a typical implicit learning session and the full course of human development from infancy to adulthood. Likewise, the complexity of the typical implicit learning situation, although higher than in traditional laboratory studies, shows little resemblance to the complexity of natural languages or physical laws, for instance. This problem must not be ignored. In addition, parents, and mostly teachers, tend to design learning situations for children that do not necessarily display the characteristics of implicit learning situations. Our claim is, therefore, not that a laboratory learning session mimics the whole of development; our working hypothesis is only that an implicit learning session taps, at least partially, the same general acquisition processes that shape developmental sequelae.

This working hypothesis is tacitly adopted in most introductory texts on implicit learning. Many contributors to the implicit learning area endorse the view that implicit learning is responsible for at least some aspects of first-language (e.g., Chandler, 1993) and second-language learning (e.g., Carr & Curran, 1994), category elaboration, reading and writing acquisition, adaptation to physical constraints of the world (e.g., Krist, Fieberg, & Wilkening, 1993), and acquisition of social skills (e.g., Reber, 1993). Noteworthy, most of this learning takes place during childhood and constitutes the essentials of what a newborn must acquire to become an adult. However, the literature on the relation between implicit learning and development is sparse, to say the least. The few articles we are aware of (Maybery, Taylor, & O'Brien-Malone, 1995; Roter, 1995) have investigated whether the characteristics of implicit learning differ between children and adults, in line with the traditional approach described above. The integrative view we propose in this chapter goes further because theories of learning and development are considered jointly.

● Overview of the Chapter

Most of the many theoretical approaches to implicit learning share a basic postulate, namely, that behavioral sensitivity to the structural aspects of the environment, unmediated by an intentional exploitation of explicit knowledge, testifies to the formation and the use of an implicit knowledge base. However, the validity of this notion has been questioned in view of empirical data and theoretical arguments. A landmark feature of the perspective adopted here, which will be exposed below (see also Perruchet & Gallego, 1997; Perruchet, Vinter, & Gallego, 1997; Vinter & Perruchet, 1994), is that it leaves no room for the notion of implicit knowledge.

However, most of the dominant developmental theories adhere to the notion of implicit knowledge or implicit representation. At first glance, this situation deeply undermines the validity of our account, which has been derived from the most common laboratory situations of implicit learning, the sequence-learning and artificial grammar-learning tasks. Indeed, the apparent discrepancy between our account and dominant developmental theories suggests that our view may be unable to account for learning in complex natural settings. This inability, if confirmed, would seriously undermine our approach, even within its limited original context. However, in the implicit learning literature, the rejection of the notion of implicit knowledge stems from the reappraisal of earlier data and arguments that had been initially put forth in support of the notion. It is therefore conceivable that the same kind of reappraisal may be applied to the data and arguments currently put forth in the developmental literature to support the notion of implicit knowledge. In this chapter, we explore this possibility. In the next two sections, we present our theoretical framework of implicit learning. We then turn to a discussion of some dominant developmental theories that start from postulates opposite to ours. We will examine how some of the data on which these theories are based can be reanalyzed along the same principles that have led to a reinterpretation of the data in the implicit learning area. To anticipate, we will conclude that our account of implicit learning challenges the current focus on implicit knowledge in developmental theories more than the reverse.

As a last introductory remark, some words are necessary about what is meant by implicit knowledge in the implicit learning field, given that the rebuttal of this notion is at the core of the present chapter. This is difficult because the expression is generally used without further specifications. According to Berry and Dienes's (1993) synthesis, which appears to be one of the most systematic reflections on the topic, the main characteristic of implicit knowledge is its relative unavailability to consciousness. The authors write, "The inaccessibility of the knowledge seems to have been the starting point of most researchers' understanding of the claim for implicit knowledge" (p. 145). Berry and Dienes propose additional, secondary characteristics, such as a stronger robustness of implicit than explicit knowledge. The important point for our concern is that Berry and Dienes do not mention any differences pertaining to the contents of implicit and explicit knowledge. Although there are deep controversies about the actual content of implicit knowledge, with some authors positing that subjects abstract the rules underlying learning situations and store these rules in an abstract representational format (e.g., Reber, 1993), and other authors arguing that subjects memorize and store specific episodes of the learning situations (e.g., Neal & Hesketh, 1997), these properties are not construed as specific to a particular form of knowledge, implicit or explicit. Thus, a good approximation to the notion of implicit knowledge appears to be that it designates the same kind of knowledge that can be accessed introspectively (with possible variations on the dimension of abstractness), but that it is deprived, to some extent, of introspective availability. It is worth adding that the exact meaning of this last characteristic is itself controversial, with some authors arguing that unconsciousness is demonstrated only by chance level results in forced-choice tests (e.g., Shanks & St. John, 1994), and other authors contending that knowledge may be termed implicit when it is difficult to access with free-report procedures (e.g., Dienes & Berry, 1997). This issue will not be further elaborated in the present chapter. To provide more generality to our proposal, the term implicit will be used here with reference to its looser meaning.

A CASE STUDY: THE LEWICKI, HILL, AND BIZOT EXPERIMENT

Before we present our own theoretical account of implicit learning, let us begin with an example to illustrate how experimental data that, at first glance, support the notion of implicit knowledge, can be understood and interpreted in different terms. The paradigm under examination was initially designed by Lewicki, Hill, and Bizot (1988). In this paradigm, subjects are submitted to a four-choice reaction time (RT) task, with the targets appearing in one of four quadrants on a computer screen. Subjects are asked to track the targets on the numeric keypad of the computer as fast as possible. To subjects, the sequence appears as a long and continuous series of randomly located targets. However, in reality, the sequence is structured according to subtle, nonsalient rules. Specifically, the sequence is partitioned into a succession of logical blocks of five trials. In each block, the first two locations of the target are randomly selected, and the last three locations are determined by rules of the form: If the target describes a movement m while it moves from location $n - 2$ to location $n - 1$, then it describes a movement m' from location $n - 1$ to location n. As a function of whether n is the third, fourth, or fifth trial of the logical block, if m is horizontal (resp. vertical and diagonal), then m' is vertical or diagonal. Note that discovering these second-order dependency rules imperatively requires the segmentation of the entire sequence into a succession of five-trial subsequences. That is, any trial within the long sequence must be identified as the first, second, . . . , fifth trial within the logical five-trial block to which it belongs.

The results of Lewicki et al. (1988) were straightforward. Subjects were unable to verbalize the nature of the manipulation, and especially they had no explicit knowledge about the partitioning into logical blocks of five trials, which is a prerequisite for catching the rules. This finding is unsurprising, given the complexity of the situation (we suggest the skeptical reader conceive of a general purpose algorithm that could detect the presence of logical blocks in Lewicki et al.'s sequences). However, performance on the last trials of each block, the locations of which were predictable on the basis of the rules, improved at a faster rate and was better overall than performance on the first random trials.

Lewicki et al. (1988) accounted for these results by arguing that the structuring rules were discovered by a powerful, all-purpose unconscious algorithm abstractor. The rules thus became the constituents of subjects' implicit knowledge. Perruchet, Gallego, and Savy (1990), however, formed the basis for a radically different interpretation by demonstrating that subjects may have learned the task without ever performing the segmentation of the sequence into logical blocks. Rather, subjects may have been sensitive to the relative frequency of small units, comprising two or three successive locations. Some of the possible sequences of two or three locations were more frequent than others because the rules determining the last three trials within each five-trial block prohibited some transitions to occur. In particular, examination of the rules showed that they never generated back and forth movements (i.e., m' is never the inverse movement of m). As a consequence, back and forth transitions were less frequent in the entire sequence than the other possible transitions. The crucial point is that these less frequent events, which presumably elicit longer RTs, were exclusively located in the random trials. This stems not from an unfortunate bias in randomization but from a logical principle: The composition rules determined both the relative frequency of some events in the whole sequence and the selective occurrence of these events in specific trials. The validity of the Perruchet et al. interpretation was tested by deriving predictions for performance on specific features of the sequence, both from an abstractionist view and from our alternative view. Empirical data, confirmed by a connectionist modeling approach (Cleeremans, 1993), supported our reanalysis.

According to Lewicki et al. (1988), subjects acquire an implicit representation of the segmentation of the sequence into logical blocks. It could be argued that our reappraisal of the original data leads to a content modification of the implicit knowledge base, from abstract rules to representations of event frequencies. But let us go even further in our reconceptualization. There is in fact no need to postulate the formation of an implicit knowledge base that contains frequency representations. The subsequences of events considered by Perruchet et al. (1990), such as diagonal and back and forth movements of the targets, are presumably the events on which the subjects focus attention. These events are fully conscious to subjects, in the sense that they shape subjects' phenomenal experience with the task. What changes with training is the phenomenal experience itself. Some salient sequences of events are experienced as more familiar than other sequences. This change in the conscious, online perception of the task exerts direct influences on RTs. It may also exert influences on other tasks, notably so-called explicit knowledge tests. For instance, in the last phase of the Perruchet et al. (1990) experiment, participants were asked to predict the location of the next occurrence of the target. Their predictions turned out to be sensitive to the relative frequency of the salient events displayed during training.

It is important to emphasize the radical difference between the Lewicki et al. (1988) interpretation, which is taken here to instantiate the conventional account of implicit learning, and the interpretation introduced by the Perruchet et al. (1990) reappraisal of the data. In the former view, exposure to the material leads to the formation of implicit knowledge about its structuring features. Changes in performance are due to the unconscious exploitation of this implicit knowledge base, with all of the presumed processing being unavailable to subjects' consciousness. In the latter interpretation, there is no place for the notions of implicit knowledge or implicit representation. Exposure to the material shapes the way the material is consciously perceived and processed. The modification of the phenomenal experience triggers both the improvement in motor performance and the results in so-called explicit tests. Note that in this formulation, the debate on how to best assess consciousness becomes meaningless. The question of the extent to which knowledge acquired in an implicit learning episode is explicit no longer makes sense because conscious experience is construed as the end product of implicit learning.

A SUBJECTIVE UNIT-FORMATION
ACCOUNT OF IMPLICIT LEARNING

General Outline of the View

Our general view of implicit learning underlying the reinterpretation of the Lewicki et al. (1988) data will be outlined next (for a more extensive presentation, see Perruchet & Gallego, 1997). This view may be condensed into a few key points, listed below.

1. With their first exposure to the material displayed in any implicit learning situation, subjects begin to parse the material into small and disjunctive (i.e., nonoverlapping) units. These units are composed of the primitive features that are processed conjointly in the attentional focus, and as such, determine the conscious, phenomenal apprehension that subjects have of the material. The size of these units is determined by capacity limitations inherent to attentional processing, and their composition is induced by both subjects' background knowledge and surface-salient features of the material, such as those evidenced by Gestalt theorists. For instance, in the situation described above, the displacement of the target may be perceived as a succession of horizontal, vertical, and diagonal movements, back and forth displacements, or longer units, such as complete clockwise turnovers of the target around its different possible locations. These units will be referred to as sensory-based units hereafter.

2. While training progresses, the sensory-based units are selected and modified such that they provide a conscious coding of the material that is increasingly relevant to the structure of the task. This crucial phenomenon is a mandatory, automatic consequence of the attentional processing of the input data. The reason is that attention triggers the action of unconscious associative mechanisms, which have remarkable power to provide an optimal parsing of the material, as will be detailed later.

3. Concurrently, the sensory-based units become increasingly independent of the sensory input and form conscious internal representations. Sensory-based and internal units are not qualitatively different, and hence they may be seen as the end points of a continuous dimension. Hereafter, the term *subjective units* will be used to designate both sensory-based units and internal representations, the difference being their degree of dependence on sensory input. Subjective units are the constituents of phenomenal consciousness.

4. Subjective units form the new primitives of subsequent attention processing and can hence enter into the building of higher-level units. The possibility of hierarchical processing provides great explanatory power for learning in very complex settings.

5. The formation of subjective units that become increasingly congruent with the structure of the material is directly responsible for the improvement in performance observed in so-called implicit learning tasks. Thus, performance improvement is indicative of a change in the conscious perception and representation of the environment, due to the action of unconscious associative processes.

503

6. The mechanisms outlined above do not account for every form of behavioral adaptation. We are dealing here with implicit learning processes solely. Therefore, it is worth stressing that some forms of adaptive behavior are completely beyond the scope of this chapter because they necessarily require intentionally guided processes such as logical inference, hypothesis testing, or any form of abstract reasoning. For instance, genuine knowledge of the abstract rules governing Lewicki et al.'s (1988) situation cannot be achieved with the involvement of implicit learning processes alone, whatever the amount of training. This does not mean that human subjects are unable to find these rules. It means that these rules can only be discovered by means of an effortful inferential procedure. Note that implicit learning processes, by providing a coding of the material that tends to make its deep structure directly available to consciousness, provide a suitable preparation for a later analytical, problem-solving approach (see Vinter & Perruchet, in press, for a comment on this point).

To summarize, implicit learning forms the basis of conscious experience, that is, it shapes both subjects' perception and internal representation of the world. Because subjects have conscious perception and representations before starting any implicit learning episode, *implicit learning may be thought of as allowing to pass from earlier conscious perceptions and representations to later, generally better structured, conscious perceptions and representations through the action of intrinsically unconscious mechanisms.* Because our contention stands in straight opposition to the dominant stance of the literature (but see Dulany, 1997, for an exception), a bit of introspection may be needed to intuitively capture the likelihood that our proposal is correct. Let us consider any natural situation of implicit learning, whether this situation concerns the acquisition of language, reading and writing abilities, or sensitivity to musical structure. It is hardly defensible that our subjective experience of the part of the environment with which we interact, as well as our representation of it, remains unmodified while training progresses. Our claim is simply that the changes in the way we consciously perceive, represent, and interact with this environment are at the core of implicit learning.

In this account, the concept of implicit knowledge has no place. In any implicit learning setting, performance improves because subjects carry out a conscious coding of the material that is increasingly congruent with the structure of the material. What provides the illusion that there is some hidden knowledge is the increasing efficiency of the conscious coding.

This change is attributed to the action of intrinsically unconscious associative processes. Next, we discuss in more detail the way in which unconscious associative processes can provide an optimal parsing of the training material.

● The Formation of Optimal Subjective Units

The formation of subjective units is linked to the question of how information is parsed during processing. Such a question is particularly relevant for an understanding of early cognitive competence in childhood and has indeed received much attention from researchers who try to understand the abilities shown by neonates. Because we will argue that these early abilities rely on the same parsing mechanisms that are involved in implicit learning, a somewhat detailed discussion of this issue is worthwhile.

In the present section, we illustrate and analyze the parsing mechanisms using the artificial grammar-learning situation, which has been investigated far more extensively than the Lewicki et al. (1988) situation described above (note that Stadler, 1995, has proposed a theoretical account of implicit learning in serial reaction time [SRT] tasks that bears some resemblance to the following analysis). As is now well-known (see Reber, 1993, for a general discussion of the artificial grammar-learning paradigm), subjects in an artificial grammar-learning situation are familiarized, during the study phase, with a set of grammatical strings. There is considerable evidence that subjects partition this material during its coding. For example, when subjects are asked to write down the study items of an artificial grammar experiment, they frequently produce strings consisting of groups of letters (Servan-Schreiber & Anderson, 1990). Likewise, when subjects are asked to give verbal instructions to yoked partners during the study phase about what they should be looking for, they often refer to subunits, such as bigrams or trigrams (Mathews et al., 1989).

Our account of this ubiquitous form of coding is grounded on a general model of associative learning in which attention devoted to the stimulus is viewed as the major explanatory principle for the formation of subjective units. More precisely, the claim is that a new unit is formed as an automatic and mandatory consequence of the concurrent attentional processing of a few events (Frensch & Miner, 1994). Such a position has been expressed primarily in the conditioning field (e.g., Mackintosh, 1975), but also in other contexts. For instance, Ceraso (1985) has emphasized the role of initial perceptual processes in the formation of psychological units, and

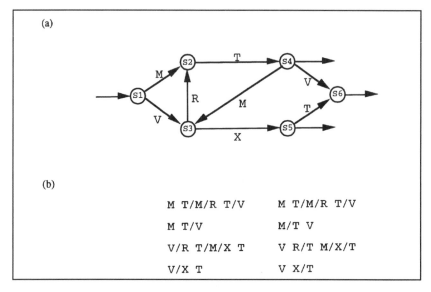

(a)

(b)

M T/M/R T/V	M T/M/R T/V
M T/V	M/T V
V/R T/M/X T	V R/T M/X/T
V/X T	V X/T

Figure 15.1. Panel (b) shows two modes of segmentation of four-letter strings generated by the finite-state grammar represented in panel (a). In the leftmost segmentation, only 5 different units are needed because they match with the main paths of the grammar. In the rightmost segmentation, which is random, 10 different units are necessary.

Logan and Etherton (1994) have highlighted the role of attention in constructing instances. In this kind of framework, subjective units stem from the concurrent processing of the primitives of the situation that may be simultaneously apprehended during the initial coding. If one considers that letters are the primitive features in artificial grammar-learning tasks for literate subjects, then the size of the units can be directly traced to the limited capacity of perceptual attentional processes.

Attentional limitations explain why continuous information is partitioned, but the fact we have to account for is that the resulting parts, which are initially induced by surface-salient features or determined by subject's background knowledge, increasingly match the structurally relevant units while training progresses. Let us consider the finite-state grammar shown in Figure 15.1a and two possible modes of segmentation of a few strings generated by this grammar in Figure 15.1b. In the first mode, the components match the main paths of the grammar, whereas they are at random in the second mode. Although the total number of units does not differ for the two modes of parsing (and hence the mean lengths of the units are identical), it may be seen that the strings can be described as composed of 5 or 10 different units, respectively. Clearly, describing the material with a smaller number of different units is much more economical. It is easier to learn few units, some of which are repeated, than a larger number of different units that are each presented once.

There exists empirical evidence suggesting that subjects effectively realize an increasingly efficient segmentation. In an unpublished experiment from our laboratory, subjects were asked to read each string generated by a finite state grammar and, immediately after reading, to mark with a slash bar the natural places of segmentation. Subjects repeated this task after a phase of familiarization with the material, which consisted either of learning items by rote, performing a short-term matching task, or searching for rules. Subjects formed the same number of total units before and after the training phase, thus indicating that they did not tend to form increasingly larger units. However, the number of different units reliably decreased, whatever the task during training. Our conclusion is that exposure to structured material modifies the natural coding of the material toward an increasingly more efficient segmentation (see also Servan-Schreiber & Anderson, 1990).

At first glance, selecting units that match the deep structure of a grammar implies sophisticated inductive tools. However, selection can be accounted for in a simplistic way within an associative framework. If one realizes all the possible partitions of a sequence into a succession of units of a given range of size, then the parsing matching the structure of the grammar most efficiently is the parsing in which the number of different units is minimized. A logical correlate of the minimal number criterion is that the final units are the most frequently occurring ones (for any fixed range of size). The detection by subjects of the most frequent units needs no special device but derives from the application of two fundamental principles.

First, in keeping with the ubiquitous beneficial effect of repetition on associative learning, the most frequent associations are privileged. Second, the formation of stable and optimal units may be strengthened by another process, referred to as overshadowing in the conditioning literature. This process prevents the formation of competitive, and infrequent, associative links. One of the major developments in the study of conditioning over the last few decades has been the discovery that associations between contiguous events tend to be selective and exclusive. For instance, if two events

A and B are paired with C, but for some reason (e.g., saliency, position, relative number of pairing), A is a better predictor than B, then the association between B and C is impaired (e.g., Kamin, 1969). Assume that for a string of five events (A, B, C, D, E), the segmentation matching a grammar is AB/CDE. This means that over the entire series of training, items AB and CDE occur more frequently than, say, ABC and DE. Association principles account for the formation of AB and CDE associations, but also for the neglect of less frequent associations because the associations of B with A and of C with D and E prevent the formation of a BC association. This overshadowing effect can be interpreted as an attentional effect, with the most frequent associations capturing all or most of the available attention (e.g., Mackintosh, 1975).

To summarize, the process of forming subjective units appears to be both extraordinarily powerful, insofar as the resulting units are consistent with the structure of the material, and accountable for by elementary and ubiquitous associative processes. Indeed, the only postulate needed is that units emerge as a mandatory consequence of the joint attention to a few primitive stimulus features.

THE CHALLENGE OF DEVELOPMENTAL THEORIES

Preliminary Considerations

Existing theories of development are strikingly heterogeneous, ranging from more nativist approaches to constructivist ones. Although some incursions in other models will be necessary to give more generality to our argument, we have chosen to focus mainly on a theory proposed recently by Karmiloff-Smith (1992), because this theory is grounded in the distinction between an implicit and an explicit knowledge format and thus deals with the relation between the two types of knowledge. To anticipate, we will argue that, as did Reber and Lewicki in their accounts of implicit learning phenomena, Karmiloff-Smith relates early acquired behavioral mastery to the progressive formation of implicit knowledge, which may later become explicit. Of additional interest in the Karmiloff-Smith theory is that not only is it devoted to accounting for specific age-related changes, but that this theory, in contrast to stage models such as Piaget's, also focuses on general acquisition processes in microdomains throughout development, which makes the comparison of learning processes in children and adults easier. Finally, we thought that taking Karmiloff-Smith's model as a privileged target is justified by the widespread interest and approval it has generated within the developmental area, as is evidenced by a recent *Behavioral and Brain Sciences* publication of the model (see Karmiloff-Smith, 1994, and the subsequent peer comments). The large appeal of the model is probably due to the fact that Karmiloff-Smith combined influences from the two main sources of theoretical inspiration in developmental psychology: the constructivist view of Piaget, on the one hand, and the modularist view of Fodor, on the other hand.

● The Notion of Implicit Knowledge in Developmental Theories

A brief presentation of Karmiloff-Smith's (1992) model is in order. Adopting a Piagetian constructivist view of development, Karmiloff-Smith argues that a unique (common) schema of development applies recursively to each domain of knowledge. For her, the cognitive architecture is modular, and domains or modules develop independent of each other. Inspired largely by Fodor's nativist view, Karmiloff-Smith also contends that development starts from an already existing basis of knowledge, that is, from innate predispositions or constraints. Consider the case of language acquisition, for example. According to Karmiloff-Smith, at least three kinds of premises are crucial for language acquisition to become a manageable learning problem for the infant: The continuous speech stream must be segmented into meaningful linguistic units, the visual array must be parsed into discrete objects and events, and the mapping between linguistic units and objects/events must be realized. In agreement with a large body of literature, Karmiloff-Smith argues that prestructured knowledge exists from birth with respect to these premises. Innately specified predispositions of the processing system simplify the learning task, guiding and constraining adequately where to focus attention and how to process information. Similar arguments are made for other domains of knowledge, such as the spatial, physical, and numerical domains. If we recall the Lewicki et al. (1988) learning situation, and try to make sense of this situation using Karmiloff-Smith's model, we would suppose that innate predispositions of the processing system would allow subjects to directly segment the incoming information into relevant blocks of five trials, hence making possible the progressive discovery of the second-order dependency rules that regulate the within-block events.

The first developmental phase described by Karmiloff-Smith (1992) is the result of a more or less prolonged period of continuous exposure to, and interaction with, the environment, adequately encoded due to the basic processing predispositions existing at birth. During this period, data-driven processes, such as associative processes, regulation through feedback, trial and error processes, and imitative processes directly shape the child's behavior. A phase of behavioral competence or mastery is thus attained by the child with respect to different skills pertaining to each domain of knowledge. Karmiloff-Smith shows that children aged 3 to 4 years old are perfectly able to manage the use of plurifunctional words in French, like *un* (which means both *a* and *one*), for instance, or to balance parallelepipedic objects on a narrow support even in difficult cases, such as when the center of gravity does not correspond to the geometric center.

Both because the child's cognitive system is adequately tuned to processing the relevant information and because the environment is coherently structured, the knowledge embedded in the efficient procedures making behavioral mastery possible will reflect the basic structural properties of the environment (e.g., objects, events), of the body, and of the actions. Karmiloff-Smith (1992) considers, for instance, that the knowledge appropriate for a metalinguistic understanding of the plurifunctionality of some French words is already embedded in the verbal procedures used by 3- to 4-year-old children. Similarly, she claims that the abstract notion of a gravity center is already embedded in the success of young children in object balancing. However, this knowledge is fundamentally nonaccessible. It is encapsulated in the procedure, in the sense that it is inherent to its functioning. Therefore, this first phase of development is called *implicit level*. The sensorimotor system of knowledge postulated by Mandler (1988, 1992) bears strong resemblance to this implicit level. The sensorimotor system includes procedural knowledge that does not require, according to Mandler, any accessible conscious information (i.e., reaching behavior, locomotion), and perceptual recognition that again does not need conscious access to information, as, for instance, perceptual recognition demonstrated in the habituation-dehabituation paradigm. This system embeds knowledge represented in an implicit format. Again, note how the Karmiloff-Smith model could account for the changes observed in adult behavior in the Lewicki et al. (1988) situation. During their exposure to the learning situation, subjects become increasingly sensitive to its structure, as revealed by RT measures, although they remain unable to report any rules. We could say that subjects are in a phase of behavioral mastery, in which the performance is grounded in representations that are instantiated in an implicit format.

However, despite the fact that a good degree of behavioral mastery is attained, development does not stop here (although it could, as observed for some sensorimotor skills, such as tying shoes, for instance). At a certain moment in time, an endogenous process that Karmiloff-Smith (1992) terms a *representational redescription* (RR), will be elicited. The reasons for the necessity of such a process can be found in the limitations of the previous phase. Efficient procedural skills have been formed during this first phase, which are completely independent, even if they finally embed similar or related knowledge. Furthermore, these procedural skills, and in consequence, the manifestation of the implicit knowledge, are completely under stimulus control, that is, they are completely context-dependent. The knowledge they embed cannot be accessed as a data source by other parts of the cognitive system. A RR process is thus necessary for extracting knowledge from the procedures, making it accessible, and for representing knowledge in a coherent and economical way. The RR process is internally guided and transforms implicit knowledge into explicit knowledge. Knowledge becomes accessible although it is still not conscious for Karmiloff-Smith. Consciously accessible knowledge will emerge in a further step, leading to verbally reportable knowledge in a final step, again through application of the RR process.

For our concerns in this chapter, we may pass over the details of the Karmiloff-Smith (1992) model and concentrate upon the gist of the model: Implicitly stored knowledge underlying early behavioral mastery is subsequently redescribed to become explicit knowledge, possibly verbally stateable at the end of the developmental process. Mandler (1992) seems to agree with this idea in the second version of her model, linking the appearance of image schemas (explicit knowledge) to a redescription of the previous perceptual schemas (implicit knowledge). Consequently, the idea that explicit systems of knowledge emerge in development as a result of a redescription process of implicit systems can be considered to have some generality.

A special case should however be made for one current developmental model (Mounoud, 1993; Mounoud & Vinter, 1981) that offers a quite divergent view on these issues. Basically, Mounoud assumes that the dynamic of development is due to the dialectic relations that exist continuously during development between two systems of knowledge: one that results from previous development, called a *practical system,* consisting of constituted, sedimented knowledge, and a second one, called a *conceptual system,* which consists of new in-built knowledge. The distinction between a practical and a conceptual system of knowledge does not rely on a difference in type of knowledge but designates qualitatively distinct states of development of the same knowledge system. We can illustrate this point with respect to the sensory-motor system of knowledge: It constitutes the conceptual system of knowledge under construction between birth and 2 to 3 years of age, and then the practical system of knowledge above 3 to 4 years of age. The transition between the two phases is gradual and skill-dependent. Reaching for an object, for instance, will achieve a practical form of behavior before locomotion. As Mounoud qualifies practical knowledge as immediate, non-accessible, and nonconscious, and conceptual knowledge as mediated, accessible, and conscious, it is attractive to consider the possibility that knowledge is implicit in the first system and explicit in the second. Although such a conclusion may indeed be acceptable for the conceptual system (consisting of explicit knowledge), it is far more contentious for the practical system, because practical knowledge is always the result of an earlier conceptually developed system and thus, of an earlier explicit form of knowledge. For researchers in the implicit learning domain, implicit knowledge is clearly to be differentiated from the kind of knowledge alluded to by Mounoud with the term practical, the meaning of which may be closer to *automatic.* In this perspective, we suggest that for Mounoud, knowledge is always explicit but becomes embedded in automatized behavior and, more-over, evolves from a conceptual to a practical form, and not the reverse. Finally, Mounoud's model contrasts also with Karmiloff-Smith's (1992) or Mandler's (1992) views of development with respect to the link between the two coexisting systems of knowledge: The conceptual system is not built through a redescription process.

Another notable exception to the idea that early behavioral competencies reflect implicit knowledge is provided by dynamic theories of development (e.g., Thelen & Smith, 1994). These theories strongly argue against any symbolic or computational view of cognition, claiming that our mind does not contain any representation or internal symbol. Perception, action, and cognition are considered as three undissociable facets of the activity deployed by any living organism in its environment. This activity is context-bound and continuously determined by both the environment's and the body's properties. Activity is defined by complex nets of relations established between a moving body in a specific environment, and cognition is necessarily embodied, distributed, and activity-driven. In this perspective, development relies on self-organizing processes of active living systems, and not on any redescription or abstraction process, basically because there is nothing to redescribe! Indeed, in the dynamic approaches, the notion of explicit knowledge is rejected like the notion of implicit knowledge, insofar as this knowledge is thought of as grounded in internal symbols. Symbolic thought is the result of the creation of external symbols for these authors. More precisely, activity can be described as symbolic thought when it operates on external symbols created by previous active exchanges with the environment. In summary, the very notion of internal symbolic activity, either implicit or explicit, is dismissed. We postpone a comparison of this approach to ours to the final section of this chapter.

● The Challenge

Our initial line of reasoning was that, due to the fact that implicit learning mechanisms seem, a priori, highly relevant to developmental phenomena, theories of development should provide some support to our challenging view of implicit learning, and notably, should support our rejection of the widespread notion of implicit knowledge. However, it turns out that the notion of implicit knowledge, notwithstanding some exceptions, finds a large echo in modern cognitive views of development. Note that the problem cannot be solved by arguing that the same term conveys different meanings in the two research contexts. On the contrary, the mainstream of the literature on implicit learning and of the literature on development confers the same general properties to implicit knowledge, namely, that it underlies initial behavioral adaptation and that it is closely related, in terms of its content, to knowledge that is available through introspection (this last point is made clear in the developmental literature by the assumption of a redescription of one form of knowledge into the other). Overall, this situation seemingly undermines the plausibility of our view. However, another possibility has to be explored, namely, that both the early behavioral mastery in children, and the subsequent emergence of explicit knowledge about the world, can themselves be reinterpreted along the same lines as the laboratory data on implicit learning in adults.

Our proposal is that the concept of implicit knowledge in the developmental literature, central to both nativist and constructivist approaches, stems from the same fundamental bias that has plagued implicit learning research for years, namely a misrepresentation of the source of the behavioral change. Briefly, our claim is that the construct of implicit knowledge, consisting of unconscious representations, becomes useless when one considers that improved performance of subjects, adults or children, is not grounded in an internalization of the structural properties of the environment.

In the next sections, we tackle the question of early behavioral competencies because most developmentalists appear to agree on the fact that these competencies rely on implicitly instantiated knowledge. As discussed above for Karmiloff-Smith's (1992) model, two types of early behavioral competence can be distinguished. The first type is linked to the functioning of the basic predispositions of the processing system. This type of behavioral competence exists at birth or soon after birth and embeds innate implicit knowledge. The second type is the result of learning through data-driven processes, as described by Karmiloff-Smith (1992) and Mandler (1988), and embeds acquired implicit knowledge. The first of the two next sections is devoted to a discussion of infants' predisposition of the processing system, and the second section is concerned with acquired behavioral competencies, particularly those revealed by habituation paradigms.

THE EARLY ABILITY TO
PARSE THE WORLD

Clearly, infants' behavior is testimony of an ability to segment continuous sensory input into discrete objects. Likewise, the ability to segment a continuous speech stream into meaningful linguistic units appears unquestionable. Most developmental psychologists or psycholinguists postulate that children's ability to parse sensory input into physically or linguistically relevant units is possible because there exist innate constraints and domain-specific knowledge (Bower, 1979; Karmiloff-Smith, 1992), assumptions (Markman, 1990), presuppositions or intuitive theories (Spelke, Breinlinger, Macomber, & Jacobson, 1992) about the structure of the world.

Our concern is to assess whether the hypothesis of innate implicit knowledge is needed to account for infants' behavioral competence. Our skepticism stems from the fact that the phenomenon of parsing is observed in laboratory situations of implicit learning where the arbitrariness of the material makes unrealistic the postulate of innate theoretical presuppositions about its structure. In this context, as argued above, the segmentation of material into structurally relevant units may be explained within a very parsimonious framework involving only elementary associative processes.

Our objective is to assess whether this framework is able to account for developmental phenomena as well.

The application of associative learning theory to child development is a priori justified because the postulated mechanisms have been shown to be ubiquitous along the ontogenetic and phylogenetic scales. Of course, some adaptations are warranted. For instance, the primitives of the system will no longer be letters, but, for instance, spatially oriented features. However, there are some deeper problems. For example, in artificial grammar learning, the number of possible units is limited because subjects' attention is oriented, via instructions, toward the primitive letters. In real life, infants may capture unrelated componential aspects of the environment, such as a sound frequency, with the orientation of a segment of a visual display in a single attentional focus. Under these conditions, the formation of relevant units looks like a serendipitous task indeed.

Our proposal is that the apparent problem raised by the unmanageable number of possible units in infants' environment is solved by considering more carefully the idea that units are formed by the concurrent attentional processing of a few primitives. The point is that infants' attention is captured by an array of stimuli sharing specific properties. One of these properties, for instance, is novelty (e.g., Kagan, 1971). If, at a given moment, several primitives are new for the infants, it is highly probable that they are processed conjointly in the attentional focus, hence forming a new unit. If several primitives are new for a subject, then they have a high chance to become components of the same meaningful unit. This same line of reasoning may be followed with respect to movement. It is well-established that infants' attention is drawn by a moving display (e.g., Bronson, 1982; Haith, 1978; Vinter, 1986). If several elementary features move concurrently, they have a high chance to be attentionally processed by infants and to belong to the same real object (of course, many objects do not move; however, it may be argued that the relative movement due to eye displacement in a 3-D visual field generalizes the phenomenon).

The same logic may be applied to the segmentation of the world into objects, the segmentation of the linguistic input into words, and the object/word mapping. To illustrate the latter issue, let us consider an example inspired from a question raised by Karmiloff-Smith (1992, p. 40). When an adult points toward a cat and says "look, a cat," how can the child pair the word *cat* with the whole animal, rather than, say, with the cat's whiskers, the color of the cat's fur, or the background context? The conventional response to this question consists in hypothesizing that children have assumptions about the mapping between words and their referents. For instance, Markman (1990) identifies three assumptions: the whole-object assumption, the taxonomic assumption, and the assumption of mutual exclusivity. Our account is far more simple and general. What is susceptible to becoming associated is what captures infants' attention, what is new and/or moving, for instance. Considering first the auditory input, *cat* is presumably newer than *look,* because look has been associated with many contexts before, so it is highly probable that cat, rather than look, enters into the momentary attentional focus. On the other hand, it is also highly probable that infants' attention is focused on the animal, which moves as a whole, rather than on any of its parts or other elements of the context, which are presumably both more familiar and motionless.

Of course, the process of mapping as described above may fail sometimes. The infant may be quite familiar with cats and surprised by the color russet of the fur of this specific cat. We predict that, in the latter case, infants would mismap the world cat with the color russet. It is worth noting that in real world settings this situation may be infrequent because adults tend to spell out what is presumably the most novel to infants and, more generally, what they infer to be infants' present object of attention. On the other hand, errors of mapping do occur during language development. What is needed therefore is not a theory predicting a perfect mapping from the outset but a theory able to predict the final achievement. Associative theory is precisely adapted to distinguish signals from noise. In general, the correct mapping will be the final outcome because infants will hear cat for animals that are not russet and will hear *russet* for animals that are not cats.

To summarize, data and theories from the implicit learning literature suggest a new account of infants' basic competencies. Recall that conventional accounts rely on the notion of domain-specific implicit assumptions or theories about the world. In our opinion, children's ability to code the world into meaningful units requires assumptions or presuppositions no more than the ability of infants to rest on the ground instead of floating in the air requires an assumption about gravity. In the latter case, subjects' behavior is constrained by physical mechanisms, whereas in the former case, subjects' behavior is constrained by physiological and associative mechanisms. Postulating assumptions about the world is irrelevant in both cases. The subjective units are the perceptual, phenomenal results of associative processes operating at the physiological level. The only innate properties of the system we assume is that attentional processes are driven by a few stimulus features, such as novelty or movement. Given the adaptive role of these properties, it is highly probable that they have been selected for by evolution.

EARLY INFERENCES ABOUT THE WORLD

In our view, there is indeed a redescription of knowledge, albeit in a sense very different from the one argued for in Karmiloff-Smith's (1992) model. Instead of children redescribing their early implicit knowledge into explicit knowledge, it is scientists who redescribe children's late explicit knowledge into (imagined) early implicit knowledge. In this section, our objective is to illustrate this general claim by discussing various examples of early behavioral mastery reported by Karmiloff-Smith, which illustrate, according to the author, the implicit phase postulated in her model. As a first target, we selected studies showing that infants possess knowledge about the properties of the physical world, dealing successively with object substance and object permanence. Then, we will focus on another type of knowledge displayed by older infants, which is related to the distinction between animates and inanimates. Finally, we will discuss a last example of implicit knowledge analyzed by Karmiloff-Smith, pertaining to the principle of gravity. For each of these examples, we begin describing a foundational experiment and the conventional interpretation of its results. Then, we show that a simpler alternative explanation is available in each case, which makes the postulate of implicit knowledge superfluous. The reader should be aware that this part of the chapter is clearly speculative, insofar as we propose alternative explanations without providing direct empirical support for them. However, some concrete suggestions for empirical testing will be offered.

Object Substance

A series of experiments by Spelke and her collaborators (1992) aimed at showing that 4-month-old infants have an implicit theory about the fact that an object cannot pass through another one. Infants were first habituated to the view of a ball falling on a supporting surface, as shown in Figure 15.2a. Then, the infants were shown either an event congruent with the laws of physics, in which the ball also falls on a supporting surface but in a different location, or an event not congruent with the laws of physics, in which the ball falls on the same surface as in the habituation trial, but after

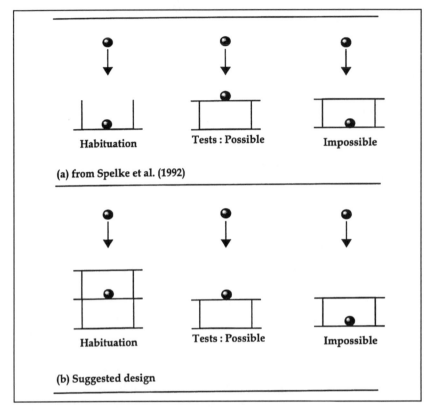

Figure 15.2. (a) Design of the Spelke et al. (1992) experiments, aimed at showing that 4-month-old infants have an implicit theory about the fact that an object cannot pass through another one. (b) Suggested design, intended to validate our alternative interpretation (see text for explanations).

falling through another potential supporting surface (to make this actually possible during the experiment, the final phase of the fall was masked, and the masking screen was subsequently lowered). Although the final location of the ball was different, and hence capable of capturing interest in the possible event, infants looked longer at the impossible events in which the final position of the ball was the same as in the habituation trials. Spelke et al. concluded that the behavior of 4-month-old infants demonstrated their knowledge that one solid object cannot pass through another one.

Now imagine the behavior of infants during the test trials when the masking screen is lowered. Presumably, infants are looking for a ball. In the possible-event condition, the ball is effectively the first object that appears. In the impossible-event condition, infants discover a new object (a blue surface; the previous floor was red). In Spelke et al.'s (1992) view, infants looked longer at the impossible event because they realized that the ball could not have crossed through the surface. In our view, the new surface draws attention because it is not the event expected on the basis of the habituation trials. This alternative interpretation is amenable to empirical tests. Figure 15.2b represents a case in which the two test events are the same as in Spelke et al., but infants are now habituated to an impossible event. The crucial difference is that infants are habituated to first discover a blue surface while the masking screen is lowered. Presumably, Spelke et al. would predict that infants look longer at the impossible test event, insofar as it violates a physical law (note that it is also more dissimilar to the habituation event if one considers the absolute spatial location, which is the similarity criterion used by Spelke et al.). In contrast, our prediction is that infants would look longer at the possible event because the first encountered object is no longer an empty surface (despite the fact that the final location of the ball is the same as in the habituation trials).

Our proposal is that infants form a perceptual representation of the habituation event in which the lowering of the masking screen reveals either the ball or a blue surface. Then, they react to the test display as a function of its similarity with the habituation display. If the habituation event is possible, as in Spelke et al.'s (1992) experiments, infants look longer at the impossible test event. If the habituation event is impossible, infants should look longer at the possible test event. There is no theory about the world here guiding infants' behavior, only a presumably short-lived effect due to familiarity with a specific display. Note that the hypothesis that inspection duration of the test event is due to its degree of similarity with the habituation event rather than to whether this event violates some physical law or not, finds support in the fact that, as is apparent in the figures of Spelke et al.'s article, the difference in looking time virtually disappears after the very first test trial. The very same criticism can be applied to all experimental studies provided in Spelke et al. that investigate infants' knowledge of a variety of physical laws.

● Object Permanence

As a second example, let us consider another well-known series of experiments (Baillargeon, Spelke, & Wasserman, 1985). In these experiments,

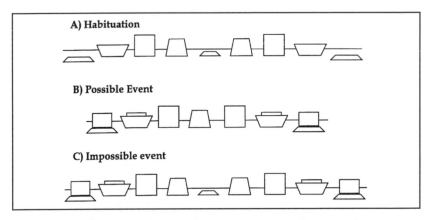

Figure 15.3. Schematic representation of what infants really saw in the Baillargeon et al. (1985) experiments, aimed at showing that 4- and 5-month-old infants have an implicit theory about some properties of physical objects, notably about their permanence (from Baillargeon et al., 1985; see text for explanation).

infants are habituated to the view of a screen moving back and forth through a 180-degree arc as shown in Figure 15.3a. Then, a solid box is placed behind the screen, preventing the complete rotation of the screen. Four and 5-month-old children are exposed to a series of possible or impossible events. For the possible events (Figure 15.3b), the screen was rotated until it reached the box (i.e., about 120 degrees), then it moved back to its initial position. The whole cycle lasted about 8 seconds. For the impossible events (Figure 15.3c), the screen completed a full 180-degree arc, covering the normal location of the box, which was no longer presented. Then, the screen moved back to its initial position, making the box visible again. The whole cycle lasted about 12 seconds. The reasoning of Baillargeon et al. (1985) was the following:

> If infants understood that (1) the box continued to exist, in its same location, after it was occluded by the screen, and (2) the screen could not move through the space occupied by the box, then they should perceive the impossible event to be novel, surprising, or both. (pp. 195-196)

In line with this prediction, infants looked longer at the impossible events than at the possible events. The authors concluded that infants as young as

5 months of age endow objects with some permanence and also realize that solid objects do not move through the space occupied by other solid objects.

Our point is that infants' performance may be explained when neither the first nor the second of Baillargeon et al.'s (1985) conditions are met. As evidenced by a comparison of Figures 15.3b and 15.3c, it suffices that infants looked longer at the more variable display than at the less variable one. When the possible event was cycled, infants saw a screen that occluded a motionless box repeatedly. When the impossible event was cycled, infants saw a screen that left visible the box only half of the time. It is highly probable that infants looked longer at the impossible event because the box appeared and disappeared while it was hidden by the screen, whatever the physical possibility of the scenario. An experimental setup testing our alternative hypothesis is easy to conceive, but it may be more economical to realize that this alternative hypothesis is supported every time a mother plays peek-a-boo with her baby.

● **The Animate/Inanimate Distinction**

According to Karmiloff-Smith (1992), 12-month-old infants have implicit knowledge of the distinction between animates and inanimates. This claim is grounded in the results of a series of experiments by Mandler and Bauer (1988), in which, for instance, infants were simply placed in front of toys comprising animals and vehicles. Infants did not touch the toys randomly but instead manipulated, for example, a series of vehicles, then a series of animals. Of course, the infants were unable to verbalize anything about what they were doing. Another series of observations, with 3- and 4-year-old children by Gelman (1990), shows that when children become able to state verbal criteria, they separate animate from inanimate as a function of whether the movement of the target object is endogenously driven or requires an external agent. The problem is one of assessing whether the distinctive touching pattern of young infants is grounded in the same knowledge that is revealed when older children are questioned, the only difference being the format, implicit or explicit, of the representation. According to Karmiloff-Smith, the answer is positive because the source of movement is the only feature that could account for the early behavioral pattern, given that Mandler and Bauer (1988) took great care to control some aspects of perceptual similarity between the two categories of objects.

We argue that Karmiloff-Smith's notion of early implicit knowledge is a theorist's redescription of the later explicit knowledge, instead of its genuine precursor. There is no evidence that the touching patterns of infants are grounded in their knowledge that inanimate objects, in contrast to living beings, require an external agent for moving. Moreover, there is no evidence that children have acquired any knowledge about a general distinction between the two categories. The only justified inference from the empirical data is that infants, on average, perceive two specific animals or two specific vehicles as more similar to each other than an animal and a vehicle. This may be accounted for in multiple ways. For instance, one may suppose that infants first focus on the toys that have eyes. This entails that they pick up a series of animals in which eyes are clearly visible. Then, they may become interested in the presence of wheels on some toys, and hence manipulate for some time a series of vehicles that have wheels, and so on. This explanation does not require that the successive features on which infants focus are really definitional features of the categories, that is, are both present in all the exemplars of a category and absent in all the exemplars of the other. The only postulates required are that infants are interested in some aspects of the toys, that these aspects change over time, and that there are more aspects in common within a (experimenter-defined) category than between categories.

● The Principle of Gravity

As a final illustration, we selected a series of experimental studies carried out by Karmiloff-Smith (1992) that provide, according to her, "a nice illustration of children's passage from behavioral mastery to verbally stateable theories" (p. 84). In these studies, children had to balance a series of parallelepipedic blocks on a narrow support. Some blocks were structurally homogeneous such that they balanced at their geometric center. Some other blocks, although apparently identical to the former ones, were filled with lead at one end, and thus their gravity center no longer matched their geometric center. Briefly, 4- and 5-year-olds moved every block along the support until it balanced by using the proprioceptive feedback about the direction of fall. They were in no way perturbed by the blocks with lead. Six and 7-year-olds placed every block at its geometric center. Doing so, they failed to balance asymmetrical blocks, which they pushed aside after a few unsuccessful trials. Eight to 9-year-olds succeeded in balancing each block, regardless of whether they were symmetrical or asymmetrical.

In Karmiloff-Smith's interpretation, implicit knowledge underlying the early behavioral adaptation is redescribed into two successive theories, the first focusing on the geometric center, which accounts for both successes and failures of 6- to 7-year-olds, and the second focusing on the gravity center, which accounts for the good performance of older children. By contrast, in our view, there is no continuity in the sources of the behavior, despite the fact that younger children behave as the older ones (at least on the very crude criterion that they balanced the blocks). We contend that initial mastery is the product of a trial-and-error procedure, which supports the existence of some pieces of (presumably explicit) knowledge, but which does not require an implicit theory of gravity. This claim finds support in the following pseudo-experiment. Suppose that the experimental arrangement is modified in such a way that the location for balancing the blocks is no longer their gravity center. (For example, the experiment is run in an orbital station, and the gravitational forces are replaced by magnetic forces, or some other fiddle). We would predict, as probably everyone would agree, that young children would be as successful as they are in natural contexts precisely because they solve the problem by a trial-and-error procedure. If children's performance were grounded in implicit knowledge of gravity, it should be impaired relative to an unfiddled situation. We fail to see how performance could be mediated by the implicit knowledge of a law without being affected when this law no longer applies.

Note that we do not question that children are able to form explicit theories. Rather, our claim is that these theories are built from a variety of sources, including earlier pieces of explicit knowledge, instead of being a redescription of the implicit knowledge presumably embedded in early procedural mastery. This theory building may be partially grounded in memory of past episodes. For instance, children may infer a general principle from the stored conscious representations of a number of previous trials in which the blocks turned out to balance when they were supported in their geometric center. Trial-and-error procedures may reveal some information about the structure of the world, but there is no sense in claiming that the success of a trial-and-error strategy is due to tacit knowledge about the structure of a task. A trial-and-error procedure provides information that can be used in a subsequent inferential process, but in the same way as the information provided through external sources. There is no privileged, intrasubject transfer of knowledge from an implicit to an explicit recipient.

To summarize, we have challenged the widespread idea that implicit knowledge underlies early behavioral adaptation by showing that the notion of implicit knowledge is not needed to account for several findings that have been construed as support for this notion. In each case, children's behavior can be accounted for by an acquired sensitivity to different aspects of the experimental situations, making them sensitive to factors such as the degree of novelty or the variety of displayed events. Of course, we do not deprive children of any competence. We assume that infants perceive eyes of animals, wheels of vehicles, a ball falling on a floor, a box, a screen, and so on, instead of their being the receptors of an unstructured beam of sensory excitations. Recall that we accounted for these primitive competencies in associative terms in the previous sections.

FINAL CONSIDERATIONS

Toward an Integrative View of Development and Adult Implicit Learning

In developmental psychology, the implicit knowledge assumption stems from the observation of a quite remarkable adaptation of the child to structured situations. The reasoning is that early behavioral adaptation necessarily requires processing of the structural properties of the situations and results from an internalization of these properties. This leads to the formation of knowledge, the content of which corresponds to a representation of the internalized properties of the situations, and the nature of which is implicit because it cannot be elicited independent of the context or the routine in which it is embedded. This view finds a large echo in mainstream theories of implicit learning in adults. However, in this chapter, we have proposed a different explanation in which the notion of implicit knowledge has no place.

The developmental literature we scrutinized shows that experimental data put forth in support of the notion of implicit knowledge can be conveniently reinterpreted within the same framework that led to reinterpretation of the data from adult implicit learning experiments. Of course, this demonstration can only have a provisional status. Our argument is undermined by the fact that we focused on a limited sample of the experimental literature. Although our analysis included some of the foundational experiments in current cognitive developmental psychology, many other studies were not considered. A larger synthesis is currently in progress in our laboratory (Vinter & Perruchet, 1997). Perhaps more important, our

524

alternative interpretation is mostly speculative, given that we provided no direct experimental support. Clearly, further empirical studies are needed before firm conclusions may be drawn. We suggested several experimental situations that may ultimately provide one possible basis for empirical testing.

Pending further evidence, it is worth providing the lineaments of a view that is potentially relevant for both development and adult implicit learning and that excludes the notion of implicit knowledge. The starting point for this view is that some features of a situation that the subject is exposed to capture attentional processes. The features capturing attention may be fairly different for newborn and older humans. Presumably, some properties such as movement and novelty trigger infants' attention as a consequence of hard-wired, innate mechanisms. In children and adults, attention is increasingly dependent on subjects' background knowledge, which itself is dependent on previous learning. However, the consequences of attentional processing are always the same. They consist in the parsing of incoming information into units. Because these units are composed of the primitive features that are processed conjointly in the attentional focus, they determine the conscious, phenomenal apprehension that subjects have of the material.

When the incoming information is structured or repeated, which is often the case when it comes from the natural environment, the composition of the subjective units is progressively modified in order to provide a conscious coding of the material, which becomes increasingly relevant to the structure of the task. This crucial phenomenon is a mandatory, automatic consequence of attentional processing. The reason is that attention triggers the action of unconscious associative mechanisms that have remarkable power to provide an optimal parsing of the material. The behavioral changes observed in infants, children, and adults are the results of this progressive formation of subjective units that map the structurally relevant components of the world. In this view, implicit acquisition phenomena, whatever the age at which they occur, may be conceived of as progressive changes in the conscious perceptions and representations of the world toward a better mapping with the world's deep structure through the action of intrinsically unconscious associative mechanisms.

In this conception, there is no longer any place for the notion of implicit knowledge. There are only unconscious processes shaping conscious experience. We alluded above to some models of development in which, in contrast to the dominant view, the notion of implicit knowledge is also dismissed. This is especially the case for dynamic theories (e.g., Thelen & Smith, 1994). These theories strongly argue against any symbolic or computational view of cognition, claiming that our mind does not contain any representation or internal symbol. Activity is described as symbolic thought when it operates on external symbols created by previous active exchanges with the environment. Thus, the existence of internal, implicit knowledge is negated, but the existence of explicit knowledge is rejected as well. Noteworthy, our account departs radically from the dynamic conceptions in the sense that we fully acknowledge the relevance of the notion of explicit knowledge. This notion is embodied in that of sensory-based or internal subjective units, which are at the core of our account. More generally, explicit knowledge is revealed through the existence of higher-level forms of thought, proceeding through conscious operations upon internal representations, although, as discussed below, this issue needs to be elaborated further.

● **Higher-Level Reasoning and Conscious Thought**

Any theory of development and learning must ultimately integrate an account of higher forms of thoughts, including the formation of abstract knowledge about the properties of the world whose existence is constitutive of adults' representations. The current literature on implicit learning is virtually mute on this point. Most of this literature is devoted to the demonstration of dissociations between implicit and explicit forms of knowledge. The emergence of any form of explicit knowledge, whether specific or abstract, is only considered a potential bias. By contrast, the literature on child development on which we have focused in this chapter provides an integrative view. Karmiloff-Smith's (1992) theory postulates that explicit knowledge about the properties of the environment is a progressive redescription of the implicit knowledge embedded in the performance. Likewise, Mandler (1992) suggests that conceptual propositional knowledge arises from a redescription of conceptual image-schemas, which themselves are the results of a redescription of perceptual schemas. The attractive aspect of such frameworks is that they introduce a link between the early behavioral adaptation to a task and the later formation of explicit knowledge about the properties of this task through the notion of implicit knowledge. Our reappraisal consists of showing that early behavioral adaptation is not grounded in implicit knowledge. However, insofar as this reappraisal may be considered successful, we are now faced with a question that may be put forth crudely in the following terms: If explicit knowledge about the structural properties of the world does not come from its earlier, implicit counterpart, where then does it come from?

We suggest that there is no continuity between the early behavioral adaptations and the subsequent knowledge of the properties of the world. In the remainder of this chapter, we illustrate this proposal with an analogy, which may also shed further light on both our criticism of the notion of implicit knowledge and the gist of our alternative account. The analogy concerns the ability to localize sound in space. As is well-known, humans are able to state the direction in space of a sound-emitting object due to the processing of binaural cues. The binaural listener makes use of the physical differences in stimulation that arise between the two ears because of their separation in space. For instance, a sound source can be located, under some circumstances, on the basis of differences in the time of arrival of stimulation to the two ears of as little as .0001 seconds (e.g., Handel, 1989). The responsible mechanism is the precedence effect, which results in the neural activity produced by the first tone partially inhibiting the response to the later one. This mechanism is efficient because it exploits a specific property of the sound waves, namely their speed of propagation. However, everybody would probably agree, we presume, that it makes no sense to endow laypeople with some implicit knowledge of the speed of propagation of sound, nor with any other properties of sound waves that the auditory system exploits. The neural mechanisms embed no hidden form of knowledge that could be made explicit with further effort or time. The speed of propagation of sound waves was assessed by scientific investigations, proceeding through an analytical, rational approach. These investigations were not made simpler or different because the scientists localized sound themselves: They could have been performed by deaf scientists as well.

Let us imagine now that, instead of being due to innate mechanisms, the neural substrate of which is at least partially known, the ability to detect the localization of a sound is learned during infancy. This scenario is not completely fanciful. The fact that, although present at birth, the mechanisms of sound localization are subsequently adjusted to accommodate the increasing distance between the two ears, due presumably to concurrent visual information, supports the view that this kind of ability is not out of reach of learning mechanisms. Another indication is provided by the remarkable use of auditory information in spatial localization by blind individuals who have had an early visual experience in orientation prior to losing their sight

(Veraart & Wanet-Defalque, 1987). But the likelihood of our assumption is not essential to our argument: our point is only to assess the consequence of this assumption upon the interpretation of the phenomena. Although we have no privileged insight into Karmiloff-Smith's mind, we suggest that it would be in the spirit of her model to assert that improved sound localization testifies to the acquisition of some implicit knowledge about the properties of the sound waves. In keeping with the same logic, the subsequent explicit knowledge that some people acquire about the properties of sound waves could be construed as the product of a redescription process of this earlier implicit knowledge.

Our proposal is that the same conception may apply, whether the ability at hand is the end product of a hard-wired innate mechanism or results from implicit learning episodes. The product of the mechanisms implemented in the auditory system is nothing other than the conscious experience of sound localization. We suggest that the neural modifications following an implicit learning episode affect our conscious experience of the world in the same way as the hard-wired mechanisms located in the auditory system shape our conscious representation of the sound space. These mechanisms embed no hidden knowledge. Insofar as the notion of knowledge makes sense here, it is only from the observer's (or scientist's) point of view. One can pass all of one's lifetime trying to redescribe the actual reasons that make one perceive the direction of a sound and yet never obtain knowledge about the speed of sound waves or even about the very existence of sound waves. Likewise, any attempts to redescribe, for instance, gravity laws from the mechanisms triggering the adaptation of the human body to these laws, is doomed to fail. Abstract knowledge is in no way a redescription of knowledge internally stored; it is a genuine construction. Explicit knowledge about the properties of the world is due to the engagement of inferential problem-solving processes, operating on a database comprising the conscious componential representation of the situation, such as is provided by unconscious associative processes.

● Summary

The dominant theories of implicit learning and the dominant theories of development share a common postulate, namely, that early behavioral adaptations are grounded in subjects' implicit knowledge bases. The goal of this chapter was to show that our previous reinterpretation of the data put forth in support of the concept of implicit knowledge in the implicit learning research area can be successfully applied to the developmental domain as well. We argue for a new integrative account of implicit learning and development in which implicit acquisition phenomena, whatever the age at which they occur, may be conceived of as progressive changes in the conscious perceptions and representations of the world toward a better mapping with the world's deep structure through the action of intrinsically unconscious associative mechanisms.

REFERENCES

Baillargeon, R., Spelke, E. S., & Wasserman, S. (1985). Object permanence in five-month-old infants. *Cognition, 20,* 191-208.

Berry, D. C., & Dienes, Z. (1993). *Implicit learning: Theoretical and empirical issues.* Hillsdale, NJ: Lawrence Erlbaum.

Bower, T. G. R. (1979). *Human development.* San Francisco: Freeman.

Bronson, G. W. (1982). *The scanning patterns of human infants: Implications for visual learning.* Norwood, NJ: Ablex.

Carr, T. H., & Curran, T. (1994). Cognitive factors in learning about structured sequences. *Studies in Second Language Acquisition, 16,* 205-230.

Ceraso, J. (1985). Unit formation in perception and memory. In G. Bower (Ed.), *The psychology of learning and motivation* (pp. 179-210). New York: Academic Press.

Chandler, S. (1993). Are rules and modules really necessary for explaining language? *Journal of Psycholinguistic Research, 22,* 593-606.

Cleeremans, A. (1993). *Mechanisms of implicit learning: A connectionist model of sequence processing.* Cambridge: MIT Press/Bradford Books.

Dienes, Z., & Berry, D. (1997). Implicit learning: Below the subjective threshold. *Psychonomic Bulletin and Review, 4,* 3-23.

Dulany, D. E. (1997). Consciousness in the explicit (deliberative) and implicit (evocative). In J. D. Cohen & J. W. Schooler (Eds.), *Scientific approaches to the question of consciousness* (pp. 179-212). Mahway, NJ: Lawrence Erlbaum.

Frensch, P. A., & Miner, C. S. (1994). Effects of presentation rate and of individual differences in short-term memory capacity on an indirect measure of serial learning. *Memory & Cognition, 22,* 95-110.

Gelman, R. (1990). First principles organize attention to and learning about relevant data: Number and animate-inanimate distinction as examples. *Cognitive Science, 14,* 79-106.

Haith, J. (1978). Visual competence in early infancy. In R. Held, H. Leibowitz, & H. L. Teuber (Eds.), *Handbook of sensory physiology: Vol. 3. Perception* (pp. 311-356). Berlin: Springer.

Handel, S. (1989). *Listening: An introduction to the perception of auditory events.* Cambridge: MIT Press.

Kagan, J. (1971). *Change and continuity in infancy.* New York: John Wiley.

Kamin, L. J. (1969). Predictability, surprise, attention, and conditioning. In R. Campbell & R. Church (Eds.), *Punishment and aversive behavior* (pp. 279-296). New York: Appleton-Century-Crofts.

Karmiloff-Smith, A. (1992). *Beyond modularity: A developmental perspective on cognitive science.* Cambridge: MIT Press/Bradford Books.

Karmiloff-Smith, A. (1994). Precis of beyond modularity. *Behavioral and Brain Sciences, 17,* 693-745.

Krist, H., Fieberg, E. L., & Wilkening, F. (1993). Intuitive physics in action and judgment: The development of knowledge about projectile motion. *Journal of Experimental Psychology: Learning, Memory, and Cognition, 19,* 952-966.

Lewicki, P., Hill, T., & Bizot, E. (1988). Acquisition of procedural knowledge about a pattern of stimuli that cannot be articulated. *Cognitive Psychology, 20,* 24-37.

Logan, G. G., & Etherton, J. L. (1994). What is learned during automatization? The role of attention in constructing an instance. *Journal of Experimental Psychology: Learning, Memory, and Cognition, 20,* 1022-1050.

Mackintosh, N. J. (1975). A theory of attention: Variations in the associability of stimuli with reinforcement. *Psychological Review, 82,* 276-298.

Mandler, J. M. (1988). How to build a baby: On the development of an accessible representational system. *Cognitive Development, 3,* 113-136.

Mandler, J. M. (1992). How to build a baby: II. Conceptual primitives. *Psychological Review, 99,* 587-604.

Mandler, J. M., & Bauer, P. J. (1988). The cradle of categorization: Is the basic level basic? *Cognitive Development, 3,* 237-264.

Markman, E. M. (1990). Constraints children place on word meanings. *Cognitive Science, 14,* 57-77.

Mathews, R. C., Buss, R. R., Stanley, W. B., Blanchard-Fields, F., Cho, J.-R., & Druhan, B. (1989). Role of implicit and explicit processes in learning from examples: A synergistic effect. *Journal of Experimental Psychology: Learning, Memory, and Cognition, 15,* 1083-1100.

Maybery, M., Taylor, M., & O'Brien-Malone, A. (1995). Implicit learning: Sensitive to age but not to IQ. *Australian Journal of Psychology, 47,* 8-17.

Mounoud, P. (1993). The emergence of new skills: Dialectic relations between knowledge systems. In G. J. P. Savelsbergh (Ed.), *The development of coordination in infancy.* Amsterdam: North-Holland.

Mounoud, P., & Vinter, A. (1981). Representation and sensorimotor development. In G. Butterworth (Ed.), *Infancy and epistemology.* Brighton: Harvester.

Neal, A., & Hesketh, B. (1997). Episodic knowledge and implicit learning. *Psychonomic Bulletin and Review, 4,* 24-37.

Perruchet, P., & Gallego, J. (1997). A subjective unit formation account of implicit learning. In D. Berry (Ed.), *How implicit is implicit learning?* (pp. 124-161). Oxford, UK: Oxford University Press.

Perruchet, P., Gallego, J., & Savy, I. (1990). A critical reappraisal of the evidence for unconscious abstraction of deterministic rules in complex experimental situations. *Cognitive Psychology, 22,* 493-516.

Perruchet, P., Vinter, A., & Gallego, J. (1997). Implicit learning shapes new conscious percepts and representations. *Psychonomic Bulletin and Review, 4,* 43-48.

Reber, A. S. (1993). *Implicit learning and tacit knowledge.* Oxford, UK: Oxford University Press.

Roter, A. (1995). *Implicit learning from a developmental perspective: Can children learn implicitly as well as adults?* Manuscript submitted for publication.

Servan-Schreiber, D., & Anderson, J. R. (1990). Learning artificial grammars with competitive chunking. *Journal of Experimental Psychology: Learning, Memory, and Cognition, 16,* 592-608.

Shanks, D. R., & St. John, M. F. (1994). Characteristics of dissociable human learning systems. *Behavioral and Brain Sciences, 17,* 367-447.

Spelke, E. S., Breinlinger, K., Macomber, J., & Jacobson, K. (1992). Origins of knowledge. *Psychological Review, 99,* 605-632.

Stadler, M. A. (1995). Role of attention in implicit learning. *Journal of Experimental Psychology: Learning, Memory, and Cognition, 21,* 674-685.

Thelen, E., & Smith, L. B. (1994). *A dynamic systems approach to the development of cognition and action.* Cambridge: MIT Press.

Veraart, C., & Wanet-Defalque, M.-C. (1987). Representation of locomotor space by the blind. *Perception and Psychophysics, 42,* 132-139.

Vinter, A. (1986). The role of movement in eliciting early imitations. *Child Development, 57,* 66-71.

Vinter, A., & Perruchet, P. (1994). Is there an implicit level of representation? *Behavioral and Brain Sciences, 17,* 730-731.

Vinter, A., & Perruchet, P. (1997). *De l'adaptation comportementale à la formation de la connaissance.* Paris: PUF.

Vinter, A., & Perruchet, P. (in press). Relational problems are not fully solved by a temporal sequence of statistical learning episodes. *Behavioral and Brain Sciences.*

16

Implicit Knowledge in Sequential Learning Tasks

●──

David R. Shanks
Theresa Johnstone

T he possibility that knowledge can exist in an implicit form—
whereby it is capable of affecting ongoing behavior without
being accessible to consciousness—has been the subject of much debate and
controversy in the last few years. In so-called *implicit learning* experiments,
subjects acquire knowledge about some complex domain and are then tested
for the degree to which this knowledge is consciously accessible. To the
extent that the knowledge can be deployed in some ongoing task without
being consciously available, it is said to be implicit.

A variety of experimental tasks have been used for studying the acquisition and use of implicit knowledge (see Berry & Dienes, 1993; and Shanks
& St. John, 1994, for reviews). The experimental task that is the focus of
the present article—and that in our view is particularly well-suited to

AUTHORS' NOTE: The research described here was supported in part by a project grant
from the United Kingdom Biotechnology and Biological Sciences Research Council to the
first author. The support of the Medical Research Council and the Economic and Social
Research Council is also gratefully acknowledged. The work is part of the program of the
ESRC Centre for Economic Learning and Social Evolution. We thank Zoltán Dienes, Peter
Frensch, Luis Jiménez, Peder Johnson, Paul Reber, and Larry Squire for their helpful comments
on an earlier draft. Correspondence concerning this chapter should be addressed to David R.
Shanks, Department of Psychology, University College London, Gower St., London WC1E
6BT, England. Email may be sent to david.shanks@psychol.ucl.ac.uk.

studying implicit knowledge—uses a serial reaction time (SRT) procedure first employed by Nissen and Bullemer (1987). In the typical procedure, a stimulus appears on a computer screen in one of four locations (1-4) on each trial, and the subject presses as fast as possible a button corresponding to that location. The subject is simply given standard-choice reaction-time (RT) instructions, but the twist in the experiment is that the stimulus follows a predictable repeating sequence of about 10 to 12 trials in length. After many cycles of the repeating pattern, subjects can be shown to have learned something about the sequential nature of the stimuli. This is established by unexpectedly transferring subjects either to a random, nonrepeating sequence or to an entirely different sequence. If subjects have indeed learned about the training sequence, they should on various (possibly all) trials have an expectation of where the stimulus will next appear and will therefore be able to anticipate that location. In the transfer stage, these expectations will be contradicted, and subjects will instead have to check themselves to avoid making incorrect responses. RTs will thus be increased. Critically, prior research appears to have shown that subjects can learn something about the trial sequence but be unable to access their knowledge consciously. Acquired sequence knowledge seems to be implicit in the same way that a typist's knowledge can be implicit (Annett, 1991).

The goal of the present chapter is to evaluate the evidence for implicit learning that has emerged from studies using the SRT task. We will both review the key results from previous research (e.g., Cleeremans & McClelland, 1991; Cohen, Ivry, & Keele, 1990; Frensch, Buchner, & Lin, 1994; Hartman, Knopman, & Nissen, 1989; Jiménez, Méndez, & Cleeremans, 1996; Nissen & Bullemer, 1987; Perruchet & Amorim, 1992; Reber & Squire, 1994; Reed & Johnson, 1994; Willingham, Greeley, & Bardone, 1993; Willingham, Nissen, & Bullemer, 1989) and also present some new data from our own laboratory.

Although fewer studies have used the SRT procedure than certain other procedures (e.g., artificial grammar learning; see Shanks & St. John, 1994), we believe that it is by far the best-suited of the available procedures for revealing implicit knowledge. The problem with most procedures is that they leave the experimenter to some extent in the dark about exactly what it is that is being learned and influencing the level of task performance. To decide whether task knowledge is implicit, we must be able to say exactly what the nature of the subject's acquired information is. Once we know the character of the information, we can then ask whether it is consciously accessible to the subject or not. But if we do not know for sure what form of knowledge subjects (implicitly) acquire in a certain task, then we have no idea what we should be looking for in the test of awareness (unless, of course, subjects deny being conscious of *any* task-relevant information, an unlikely outcome).

As an example of this difficulty, consider the famous demonstration by Greenspoon (1955) that subjects can be induced to say more and more plural words simply by being reinforced with an "umhmm" from the experimenter for each plural word, despite apparently being unaware of this reinforcement contingency. Subjects were simply asked to produce all the words they could think of. At face value, Greenspoon's result provides clear evidence of implicit rule learning, but the weakness is that subjects may have been responding on the basis of some other rule than one that links reinforcement to the production of a plural noun. That this weakness is significant was proved by Dulany (1961), who demonstrated that subjects were likely to remain within a given semantic category when they received reinforcement. If the subject said *diamonds* and received an "umhmm," the likelihood was that he or she would then produce something like *rubies* and *emeralds* as subsequent items. By staying within the category, there was a higher probability of continuing to emit plural words than would have been the case if a different category was chosen. But crucially, Dulany's subjects were all able to report adopting a conscious rule (e.g., to produce the names of precious stones), which was correlated with the plural-noun rule in the sense that using it tended to increase the frequency of reinforcement. In a nutshell, Greenspoon was misled into concluding that his subjects were responding on the basis of an unconscious rule because he did not know the true basis of his subjects' behavior.

In this context, the main attraction of SRT tasks is that the problem of knowing what information underlies task performance is a negligible worry because it must, at the very least, be *sequential* in some sense. Suppose a part of a training sequence is 1-2-3, and we wish to know whether subjects learn this pattern of target movements. All we have to do is test subjects on a transfer sequence identical to the training sequence, except that 1-2-3 is replaced by, say, 1-2-4, and if RTs to the 4 are slower than those to the 3, we have clear evidence (assuming certain methodological considerations are met) that subjects had indeed learned this part of the sequence. Nothing other than sequence knowledge would be capable of explaining a systematic RT difference like this. And if subjects are unaware of any sequential structure, then their knowledge can unequivocally be classed as implicit.

In sum, we feel that SRT tasks are ideally suited to revealing the existence of implicit knowledge. Accordingly, in the studies reported here, we use the SRT task to investigate a number of issues surrounding implicit knowledge. Our overall aim is to take a very critical look at the evidence for implicit knowledge in sequence-learning tasks and to see exactly what conclusions are justified concerning the nature of implicit knowledge.

MEASURES OF AWARENESS

It will come as no surprise to anyone to learn that a major topic of controversy in the study of implicit knowledge concerns the question of how one decides whether some knowledge is or is not conscious. In this section, we briefly consider the various ways in which awareness can be measured and some of the key theoretical issues surrounding them. Three possibilities have been extensively discussed (e.g., Dienes, Altmann, Kwan, & Goode, 1995; Reingold & Merikle, 1990) and these are explored in detail in the experiments presented in this chapter.

Verbal Reports

For many advocates of implicit learning, the dividing line between implicit and explicit knowledge is marked by whether or not the knowledge can be verbally reported. If some knowledge that is manifestly capable of influencing ongoing behavior is unavailable for free report by the subject, then it is implicit. We can simply ask the subject, via a series of probing questions, what he or she knows about the domain in question and consider the knowledge implicit if it is not reportable. This definition of *implicit* has much to commend it. On the positive side, the notion that subjects sometimes "know more than they can tell" (Nisbett & Wilson, 1977) accords well with what many laypeople would consider *unconscious* to mean. Moreover, there are clear implications for applied psychology from the fact that knowledge might not always be reportable. For instance, it might be futile to try to elicit an expert's knowledge verbally for the purposes of instruction or for the creation of an expert system if much of the relevant knowledge cannot be articulated.

On the downside, there are a number of potential problems with drawing the boundary between implicit and explicit knowledge at the verbal report threshold. We will discuss these problems in detail later, but for present purposes, it is simply worth noting the danger that a subject may fail to give an accurate verbal report of some knowledge not because it is unconscious but because it is weak or held with low confidence. In Reingold and Merikle's (1990) terminology, a test of verbal report may simply not be exhaustive. Teasing weak or low-confidence knowledge out of a subject may be a difficult thing to do.

● Objective Tests

A number of researchers (e.g., Jiménez et al., 1996; Reed & Johnson, 1994; Willingham et al., 1989) have suggested that instead of verbal reports, performance on so-called "objective" tests is the appropriate behavioral marker of consciousness. An objective test is like a test of implicit knowledge except that the instructions given to subjects should particularly encourage them to access conscious knowledge. The use of such tests to index conscious knowledge can be traced back to a parallel debate about the evaluation of awareness in studies of subliminal perception, where authors such as Eriksen (1960) and Holender (1986) advocated use of objective forced-choice discrimination tests.

As an illustration of the utility of objective tests in implicit learning, consider some data from an important SRT experiment by Willingham et al. (1989). Willingham et al.'s subjects performed a four-choice RT task. The actual sequence of signals was 4-2-3-1-3-2-4-3-2-1 . . ., which repeated many times with no break between cycles. Subjects' RTs improved across a total of 400 training trials. To see whether this knowledge was explicit, Willingham et al. then instructed their subjects to try to predict on each trial where the stimulus would appear next, with no requirement for rapid responses. Subjects simply chose response keys on each trial until they picked the one that corresponded to the target's next location, at which point they would then try to predict the next stimulus, and so on. If subjects explicitly knew the sequence, then they should have been able to predict the sequence of target locations in this test. However, Willingham et al. discovered that some subjects who showed clear speedup in the RT phase at the same time showed no evidence of being able to predict the target sequence; hence, their sequence knowledge was unconscious as assessed by the prediction task.

The particular results obtained by Willingham et al. (1989) have been the subject of some criticism (see Perruchet & Amorim, 1992; Shanks, Green, & Kolodny, 1994) on the basis of design and methodological problems, and so their results probably cannot be taken as strong evidence of implicit knowledge. Nevertheless, objective tests have the capability of providing very compelling evidence for unconscious knowledge. If subjects are unable to use their implicit knowledge on such forced-choice tests, it would be hard to argue, for example, that this is because the knowledge is held with low confidence. Objective tests are not without their own difficulties, however, particularly with respect to what one can infer when such a test does reveal significant levels of knowledge. We shall use two types of objective tests in the experiments reported here to examine the status of sequential knowledge in the RT task.

● Subjective Tests

The third and final way of evaluating awareness is to use a subjective assessment. Here, we assume that knowledge is unconscious if the subject claims to be unaware of it (Cheesman & Merikle, 1984) or claims to be guessing in some task requiring the application of that knowledge. To the best of our knowledge, the subjective confidence assessment has not been previously used in SRT tasks, but an example of its application to artificial grammar learning has been provided in a recent study by Dienes et al. (1995). After being exposed to strings generated from an artificial grammar, subjects made grammaticality judgments for novel legal and illegal strings, as in a standard grammar learning experiment. Subjects also stated how confident they were in their grammaticality decisions. The clear result was that subjects performed above chance in making grammaticality decisions even when they thought they were guessing. They lacked *meta-knowledge* about their own performance.

The use of a subjective criterion of unconsciousness is very appealing. Apart from anything else, most people would probably agree that when knowledge guides behavior in the absence of awareness that this is happening, then that knowledge is truly unconscious. However, there are again reasons to view with some caution this means of indexing awareness. As Reingold and Merikle (1990) have pointed out, a difficulty with the subjective confidence criterion is that it is left up to the subject to define what he or she means by "guessing," and of course, subjects may differ in their interpretation of this term. We discuss this problem in more detail later. First, we begin our empirical analysis of data from SRT experiments by describing the results of an important study by Reed and Johnson (1994). We follow this by describing the results of three new studies of our own in which verbal reports as well as objective and subjective tests are used to gauge implicit knowledge.

THE REED AND JOHNSON STUDY

Reed and Johnson (1994, Experiment 2) presented evidence that subjects can implicitly learn a sequence in a dual-task SRT experiment in which they performed a target-location and tone-counting task simultaneously. The tone-counting task was used to reduce the possibility that subjects would explicitly learn about the sequence of dot movements in the RT task. Reed and Johnson's evidence was based on the results of two tests. The first (indirect) test provided evidence of implicit knowledge by comparing RTs between a training phase and a transfer phase. In the training phase, subjects in the Indirect group were presented with dot movements based on a 12-location repeating sequence called SOC1, in which the dot moved between four boxes (1, 2, 3, and 4) on the computer screen, in the order 1-2-1-3-4-2-3-1-4-3-2-4. Subjects were asked to press one of four buttons on a keyboard, each of which corresponded to one of the four location boxes on the screen. The transfer phase again presented dots in a sequence (SOC2), but this time the order was 1-2-3-4-1-3-2-1-4-2-4-3. The finding that RTs increased significantly between the final block of the training phase and the transfer phase was the basis for concluding that subjects had implicitly learned something about the first sequence. To understand why this is the case, it is necessary to understand the composition of the sequences.

Both sequences were balanced for simple location and transition frequency. Each location (i.e., 1, 2, 3, 4) occurs three times in the 12 trial sequences and each possible transition (i.e., 1-2, 1-3, 1-4, 2-1, 2-3, 2-4, 3-1, 3-2, 3-4, 4-1, 4-2, 4-3) also occurs once in each sequence of 12 locations. But at the level of three (or more) consecutive locations, the two sequences differ. Reed and Johnson (1994) gave sequences of three locations the name *second order conditionals* (SOCs), which refers to the fact that the next location in the sequence of dot movements can be predicted from knowing the last two locations. For example in the training sequence SOC1, 1-2 is always followed by 1, whereas in the transfer sequence SOC2, 1-2 is always followed by 3.

The basis of Reed and Johnson's findings of implicit knowledge is that subjects had (unconsciously) developed an expectation that, for example, if they had seen a dot at location 1, followed by a dot at location 2, then the next dot would then be displayed in location 1, and that this expectation allowed subjects to respond rapidly. When the sequence was changed in the transfer block, subjects would now have to check themselves because 1-2 was no longer followed by the expected stimulus. Thus, a slowing of RT was anticipated. The increase in subjects' RTs in the transfer block was therefore attributed to them having unconsciously learned to predict specific locations at SOC sequence level or above in the training phase.

Reed and Johnson (1994, Experiment 2) used a second direct test to enable them to rule out the possibility that subjects had *explicitly* learned the sequence in the training phase. In this case, two further groups of subjects (Cued Generation Test and Cued Generation Control) were trained on sequence SOC1 and a nonrepeating sequence, respectively. The nonrepeating sequence was constructed to match the two repeating SOC sequences in terms of simple location and transition frequency information but contained no large-scale repeating structure. Subjects in both groups were told that in the training phase, the dot had followed a repeating pattern and that to assess their knowledge of this pattern, a cued-prediction test, similar to Willingham et al.'s (1989) prediction test, would be given. In this test, subjects were asked to respond to two locations of the sequence and then to generate the 10 dot movements they thought had followed these two cues in their training session, by pressing the appropriate keys. Each pair of locations that was presented corresponded to 1 of the 12 possible transitions, and performance was measured by counting how often the *first* key press created a correct continuation of the SOC1 sequence. No feedback was given to subjects about the accuracy of their generation responses. Of course, the expectation was that subjects in the Cued Generation control group would perform at about chance in this test, but the critical question was whether subjects in the Cued Generation test group would perform better than them or not.

Crucially, Reed and Johnson (1994) found no significant difference between the generation performance of the group whose members were trained and tested on the SOC1 sequence (Cued Generation test) and the control group, whose members trained on the nonrepeating sequence and were tested against the SOC1 sequence (Cued Generation control). The control group's performance was expected to be at chance levels, but the results from the sequence group are striking. Despite the fact that subjects in this group must have known something about the sequence (as indexed by the fact that subjects in the Indirect group, trained identically, showed a negative transfer effect when switched to sequence SOC2), they could predict target locations no better than subjects trained on a nonrepeating sequence. The result of this objective test of awareness was offered by Reed and Johnson as evidence that subjects had no explicit knowledge of the sequence.

AN ATTEMPT TO REPLICATE
THE REED AND JOHNSON STUDY

There is no doubt that the sequences and methodology developed by Reed and Johnson (1994) represent an important contribution to the implicit learning field and that their results provide, at face value, some of the best available evidence for true implicit knowledge. However, we believe that the specific design they used was flawed, and the objective of our Experiment 1 was therefore to demonstrate that their results do not stand up under closer scrutiny. The basic problem stems from the choice of different sequences for the transfer trials underlying the indirect test of implicit knowledge and for training the Cued Generation control group in preparation for the explicit generation test. This choice, we argue, inadvertently created conditions where the implicit test was more likely than the explicit test to show a significant difference.

The problem is that the SOC1 and SOC2 sequences used for the indirect test did not share any SOC triplets, whereas the SOC1 and nonrepeating sequences used for the Cued Generation test and control groups shared a high proportion of triplets. During the training phase, subjects in the Indirect group would have experienced 12 specific SOC-location triplets and would have learned that in each case, the third location of each SOC occurred with probability 1.0. For example, the two locations 4-1 were always followed by location 2 in the SOC1 sequence, but when the Indirect group switched to the transfer trials based on the SOC2 sequence, locations 4-1 were followed by location 3. This would cause maximum disruption to subjects' RT performance because a high expectation of location 2 had been created by the SOC1 sequence training trials.

However, subjects in the Cued Generation control group, trained on a nonrepeating sequence, would have seen many more than 12 SOC triplets in training and the probability of the third location of any particular SOC sequence would vary and in all cases be less than 1.0. The Cued Generation control group would therefore be more likely to generate an SOC triplet from the SOC1 sequence that they had never seen than if they had trained

TABLE 16.1	Sequences Used for Each Subject Group in Reed and Johnson's (1994) Experiment 2 and in the Present Experiment 1			
	Reed & Johnson (1994)		*Our Experiment 1*	
Group	*Training*	*Test*	*Training*	*Test*
Indirect	SOC1	SOC2	SOC1	SOC2
CG/CP Test	SOC1	SOC1	SOC1	SOC1
CG/CP Control	NRPT	SOC1	SOC2	SOC1

NOTE: Reed and Johnson (1994) used a cued generation (CG) test, whereas our Experiment 1 used a cued prediction (CP) test. SOC = second-order conditional. NRPT = nonrepeating sequence.

on the SOC2 sequence that underlay the indirect test. An example of this is that the Cued Generation control group may have seen locations 4-1 followed by 2 on three trials out of the eight specific SOCs beginning with locations 4-1 in each block. In addition, they may have seen 4-1 followed by 3 on a further three trials and 4-1 followed by 4 on another two trials. The Cued Generation control group would therefore have learned that there was some non-zero probability of any of locations 2, 3, or 4 following 4-1. The effect of this would be that subjects in this group, who trained on the nonrepeating sequence, would have been more likely to generate 4-1-2 from the SOC1 sequence than if they had trained on a nonoverlapping sequence such as SOC2. This would have the effect of reducing the difference in the number of correctly generated locations between the Cued Generation test group (trained on the SOC1 sequence) and the Cued Generation control group. Table 16.1 summarizes the sequences used by Reed and Johnson (1994, Experiment 2) and in our first experiment, where we attempted to avoid this problem.

We used the SOC1 training sequence to train both an Indirect group and a Cued Prediction test group. The original Reed and Johnson (1994, Experiment 2) transfer sequence, 1-2-3-4-1-3-2-1-4-2-4-3 (SOC2) was used in both the Indirect group's transfer trials and also to train a control group. This meant that both the implicit and explicit tests of sequence knowledge were based on sequences that had no overlap in terms of SOC sequence information. Reed and Johnson gave each subject 24 trials of a cued generation (CG) task. In our version of the experiment, we used a cued prediction (CP) test. Subjects were given only one location and were then required to predict the following 95 trials. Feedback was given on each trial, as the dot did not move until the subject selected the correct next location in the training sequence.

We had two hypotheses. The first was that the choice of a nonoverlapping pair of sequences should result in a greater difference between the CP test group's and CP control group's sequence prediction accuracy than was observed in Reed and Johnson's (1994) study. Second, we predicted that using the CP task would provide subjects with a greater opportunity to demonstrate explicit knowledge than the cued generation task used by Reed and Johnson, and as a result, we would find significant evidence of explicit knowledge.

A total of 93 psychology undergraduates at University College London carried out the experiment as part of a course requirement. Subjects were randomly assigned to three groups: Indirect group, CP Test group or CP Control group. After eliminating 11 subjects who made more than 10% tone-counting errors (see below), there were 29 subjects in the Indirect group, 27 subjects in the CP Test group, and 26 subjects in the CP Control group.

We followed Reed and Johnson's (1994) procedure as far as possible. Subjects were told that they were taking part in a simple computer-based choice RT experiment designed to see how fast people can become at responding to the location of a stimulus when they have to perform a concurrent tone-counting task. All subjects performed the two tasks for 16 blocks of 96 trials in the training phase. The Indirect test group then carried out the same two tasks for one further block of 96 trials based on a transfer sequence. The CP Test and CP Control groups carried out a CP task.

Four boxes were presented at the bottom of the computer screen, drawn with white lines against a blue background. The boxes were 3.5 cm wide and 2 cm deep. A dot (2 mm in diameter) appeared in the center of one of these boxes for each target location trial. Subjects were instructed to indicate the location of the target as quickly as possible by using the V, B, N, and M keys located across the bottom of the keyboard, to indicate locations 1 to 4, respectively. They responded to locations 1 and 2 with the middle and index fingers of their left hands, respectively, and to locations 3 and 4 with the index and middle fingers of their right hands, respectively.

Each block of target-location trials began with a random target location, and thereafter targets appeared according to the sequence programmed for that particular condition and block type. A target-location trial ended when a subject pressed the correct key, at which time the target was erased. The next trial began 200 ms later. Response latencies were measured from the onset of the targets to the completion of correct responses.

For each block of SRT trials, all subjects also performed a tone-counting task. A 100-ms, computer-generated tone was emitted 100 ms after each correct target-location response. Each tone was either low (1000 Hz) or high (2000 Hz), and subjects were instructed to count the number of high tones emitted during each block of trials. For each block of 96 trials, subjects heard from 31 (32%) to 64 (67%) high tones. At the end of each block, subjects were asked to provide their count, and if they made less than 5% errors, they were informed that their tone counting was accurate and asked to continue their good performance. If subjects made 5% or more errors, they were told their error percentage and encouraged to try harder to attend to their tone-counting accuracy.

Subjects in each of the CP groups trained for 16 blocks of trials and then carried out a CP task. Immediately after completing the 16th training block, they were informed that the dots had appeared in a regular repeating sequence and that in the final stage of the experiment, we wanted to see how much (if anything) they had learned about the sequence. Subjects were told that there would no longer be any tones for them to count, nor would their RTs be measured. Instead, when a dot appeared in one of the four boxes, they must press the key corresponding to where they thought it would appear *next*. The dot would not move until they pressed the correct key and once this had been achieved, they must again decide where it would appear on the following trial. This process was repeated for 95 trials. For both the CP Test and CP Control groups, the dot moved according to the SOC1 sequence. This meant that the CP Test group had trained on this sequence whereas the CP Control group had not. The CP Control subjects had trained on the SOC2 sequence.

Using the same criterion as Cohen et al. (1990) and Reed and Johnson (1994), subjects were eliminated from our analysis if their average tone-counting accuracy was in error by more than 10%. On this basis, a total of 11 subjects were excluded from the analysis.

Results. Figure 16.1 presents average RTs for each of the three groups in the training stage. RTs decreased across blocks by roughly equivalent amounts in all groups. The average RT in the Indirect group increased from Block 16 to Block 17 by 46 ms, and this effect was statistically significant.

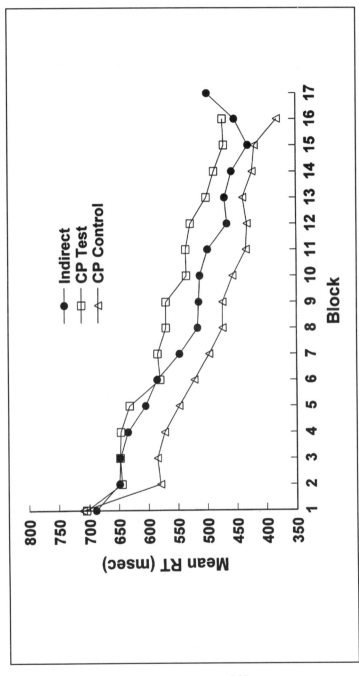

Figure 16.1. Mean reaction times (RTs) in ms across 16 blocks of training trials (all groups) and one block of transfer trials (Indirect group only) in Experiment 1. Groups Indirect and Cued Prediction (CP) Test were trained for 16 blocks on Sequence SOC1, whereas Group CP Control was trained on Sequence SOC2. RTs increased significantly on Block 17 in the Indirect group when the SOC2 sequence was introduced, indicating that some knowledge of the SOC1 sequence had been acquired during Blocks 1 to 16.

As the results showed a robust negative transfer effect on Block 17, we went on to investigate the individual transfer effects associated with each of the 12 SOC sequences. Mean RTs for the third location of each target SOC in Block 16 based on the SOC1 sequence were compared with the mean RT for the third location of transfer sequence SOCs based on the SOC2 sequence. For example, subjects were trained to expect the sequence 1-2 to be followed by 1 in the training phase but would encounter 1-2 followed by 3 in the transfer sequence, so we compared RTs to these two responses. Figure 16.2 shows the negative transfer effects at each of the 12 serial locations in the training sequence. The average RT in each of the 12 serial locations in Block 16 was subtracted from the average RT for the corresponding SOC sequence in Block 17. A positive result indicated a slowing of RTs in Block 17.

T tests were used to determine which specific locations of the sequence showed significant slowing of RT in the transfer trials and hence significant learning of the sequence. Those parts of the sequence that show a significant negative transfer effect at the level of $p < 0.05$ (one-tailed) are marked with an asterisk in Figure 16.2. The results suggest that subjects acquired knowledge at least as complex as SOCs but that this knowledge was not evenly distributed across all parts of the sequence. Reed and Johnson (1994, Experiment 2) reported that all SOCs showed a significant negative transfer effect, whereas our results show significant transfer effects for only 7 of the 12 locations.

Figure 16.3 shows how many accurate responses were made by each of the CP groups in each successive block of 12 CP trials. Correct predictions increased in number across trials because subjects were provided with an additional opportunity to learn the sequence, in the form of corrective feedback. The key result, however, is that the average number of correct predictions was 51.7 for the CP Test group and 42.8 for the CP Control group, a statistically significant difference. Plainly, in contrast to Reed and Johnson's (1994) findings, subjects in the CP Test group had considerably more knowledge of the sequence than those in the CP Control group.

To summarize the results of Experiment 1, we found significant evidence of sequence knowledge, as indexed by a reliable negative transfer effect in the Indirect group, but we also found that this sequence knowledge was at least partially explicit, because subjects in the CP Test group were quite good at predicting the sequence of target locations. We argue that these results challenge Reed and Johnson's (1994, Experiment 2) conclusions on two counts. First, we did not replicate their evidence of equivalent

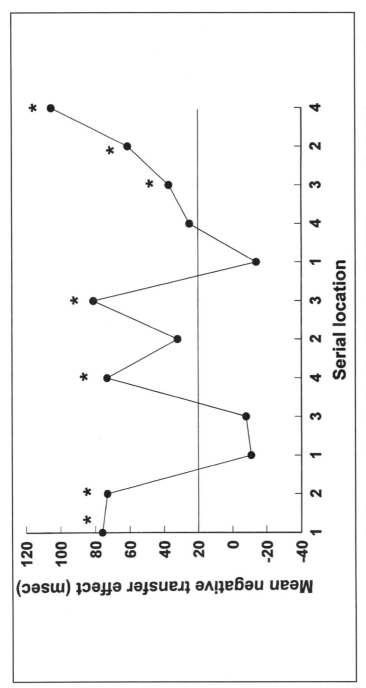

Figure 16.2. Negative transfer effects in ms for each of the 12 serial locations of the SOC1 sequence for the Indirect group in Experiment 1. Each point corresponds to the reaction time (RT) for a given part of the SOC1 sequence at the end of the training phase minus the RT for the corresponding part of the SOC2 transfer sequence. Thus, the rightmost data point is the difference between RTs to Location 4 in the SOC1 context 3-2-4 and RTs to the corresponding location (1) in the SOC2 sequence 3-2-1. The ordinate has been inverted so that positive values mean that RTs slowed down in the transfer phase.

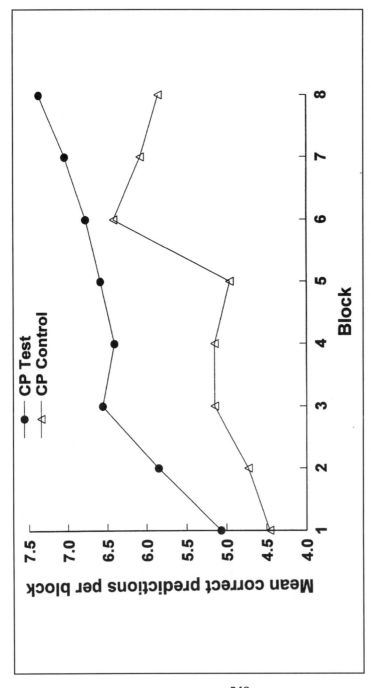

Figure 16.3. Mean number of correct cued predictions (CPs) in blocks of 12 trials for the CP Test and CP Control groups in Experiment 1. The CP Test group was trained on the SOC1 sequence whereas the CP Control group was trained on Sequence SOC2. Feedback in the CP test was based on the SOC1 sequence. Performance improved across trials in both groups as feedback allowed subjects to increase their knowledge of the SOC1 sequence, but the key result is that subjects in the CP Test groups made significantly more correct predictions than those in the CP Control group.

levels of performance in the explicit test and control groups. Instead, in our experiment there was a significant difference between the CP results for the CP Test and CP Control groups. Second, we argue that Reed and Johnson's use of a nonoverlapping sequence as the basis of their indirect test and an overlapping sequence as the basis of the direct test was a serious design flaw that makes their results impossible to interpret.

RELATIONS BETWEEN VERBAL, OBJECTIVE, AND SUBJECTIVE TESTS

The significant difference between the CP results of the CP Test and CP Control groups in Experiment 1 allowed us to refute Reed and Johnson's (1994, Experiment 2) claim that they had demonstrated true implicit sequence learning. We were also able to show that in the Indirect group, subjects had overall learned some parts of the 12-location serial sequence better than others. However, we wanted to examine conscious learning of sequences both at different levels (objective, subjective, and verbal knowledge) and at a much more detailed level for the objective measure of explicit knowledge. Our goals for Experiment 2 were therefore to collect verbal, subjective, and objective data, to use a *free generation* (FG) task, which has been claimed (Perruchet & Amorim, 1992) to be a more sensitive test of explicit knowledge than cued prediction, and to look in more detail at which parts of the 12-location sequence are learned best and whether the patterns of knowledge of specific subsequences are related in the direct and indirect tests. Of course, despite the fact that sequence knowledge seemed to be available both for the direct and indirect tests in Experiment 1, it remains a possibility that these two types of test produce dissociated results when a finer-grained analysis is used. For instance, the parts of the sequence that show significant negative transfer effects (Figure 16.2) may not be the same as the parts of the sequence for which subjects can make correct cued predictions.

In Experiment 2, we repeated the dual-task experiment, using the same sequences (SOC1 and SOC2) as in Experiment 1, but we replaced the CP task with a FG task (Perruchet & Amorim, 1992). In this test of explicit knowledge, subjects are asked simply to tap out a continuous sequence of key presses, trying to generate as many chunks or fragments of the training sequence as they can. When a key is pressed, the dot moves to the location corresponding to that key. In addition, we asked subjects about their knowledge of the repeating sequence before the FG task and about their confidence in the sequences they had generated after the FG task.

The important benefits of Perruchet and Amorim's (1992) FG task are that it does not disrupt a subject's performance by giving feedback; and because it does not demand adherence to the full 12-trial repeating sequence; it is sensitive enough to elicit partial knowledge of the full 12-location sequence. Moreover, Perruchet and Amorim (1992) found significant correlations between differences in RT improvement over the serial locations of their sequence and the corresponding freely generated knowledge. This gave us the opportunity to try to replicate Perruchet and Amorim's (1992) findings using different and longer sequences. We set out to compare the RT transfer effect in the Indirect group at each location in the sequence with the probability that the FG test group would produce a correct SOC sequence from SOC1.

The subjects were 49 students at University College, who were paid for taking part in the experiment. After eliminating seven subjects who made more than 10% tone-counting errors, we allocated 12 subjects to the Indirect group, 15 to the FG Test group, and 15 to the FG Control group.

The simple choice RT task and the SOC sequences used (SOC1 and SOC2) for the training phase and the implicit transfer test were exactly the same as in Experiment 1. However, (a) we questioned subjects about their conscious knowledge of the sequence, (b) we used an FG rather than a CP test of explicit knowledge, and (c) we asked subjects how confident they were about the accuracy of the sequences they had generated.

Subjects in each of the FG Test and FG Control groups trained for 16 blocks of trials on sequences SOC1 and SOC2, respectively, and were then asked to verbally describe their knowledge. As in Experiment 1, they were first informed that the dots had appeared in a regular repeating sequence and that in the final stage of the experiment, we wanted to see how much (if anything) they had learned about the sequence. Two questions were then asked:

1. While carrying out the choice reaction task, were you aware that the dot was moving in a repeating sequence?

and if the answer was yes,

2. Can you tell me any parts of the sequence that you were aware of?

The subjects then carried out the FG test.

Subjects were told that they would have to do a slightly different task in the final block of trials. There would no longer be any tones for them to count, nor would their RTs be measured. Instead, we wanted them to press the keys 96 times, attempting to freely generate sequences that they saw in the RT phase. They were told that each time they pressed a key, a dot would appear in the appropriate box and that this dot would remain on the screen until they pressed a further key. They were told not to worry if their memory of the sequence was poor, just to try to generate any sequences of key presses that seemed familiar. An important difference between the CP task used in Experiment 1 and the FG task is that in free generation, the dot moved whenever the subject pressed one of the four specified keys. A subject did not have to press the key that corresponded to the next correct location in the repeating sequence, as in cued prediction, in order for the dot to move.

Immediately after the FG test, subjects were asked a third question:

3. When you were generating the sequence did you feel that it was familiar or that you were guessing?

Results. Figure 16.4 presents mean RTs for each of the three groups in the training phase. As in Experiment 1, RTs decreased across blocks by roughly equivalent amounts in all groups. The negative transfer effect of changing the underlying sequence for the Indirect group on Block 17 was an average increase in RT of 49 ms and this was again reliable. These results are very similar to those obtained in Experiment 1, where there was a difference of 46 ms between RTs in Blocks 16 and 17.

Table 16.2 shows the main results of the experiment. The table lists the 12 individual SOC triplets from the SOC1 sequence. This is followed by three columns, based on the indirect test, showing the mean RT for the final location of each of the 12 SOCs in Block 16 (at the end of the training phase), the corresponding mean RT in Block 17 when subjects' performance was disrupted by using the SOC2 sequence, and the difference between Blocks 16 and 17, which is an indication of the negative transfer effect specific to that part of the sequence. Thus, if we take the part of the sequence where the target moved between locations 1-2-x, the second column in the table shows that in the final training-block subjects took on average 587 ms to press the button corresponding to the next location (actually Location 1) after 1-2. The next column shows that on Block 17, where sequence SOC2 was used, they took an average of 550 ms to press the button corre-

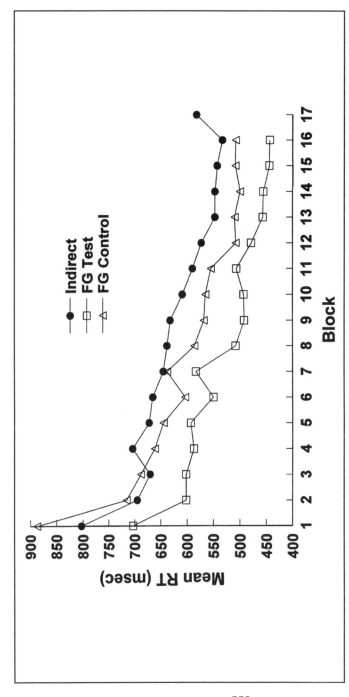

Figure 16.4. Mean reaction times (RTs) in ms across 16 blocks of training trials (all groups) and one block of transfer trials (Indirect group only) in Experiment 2. Groups Indirect and free-generation (FG) Test were trained for 16 blocks on Sequence SOC1, whereas Group FG Control was trained on Sequence SOC2. RTs increased significantly on Block 17 in the Indirect group when the SOC2 sequence was introduced, indicating that some knowledge of the SOC1 sequence had been acquired during Blocks 1 to 16.

TABLE 16.2 Mean Reaction Time (RT) and Free Generation (FG)
Performance Measures by Second-Order Conditionals (SOC)
for the Indirect and FG Test Groups in Experiment 2

SOC	Indirect Group, RT Block 16	Indirect Group, RT Block 17	Indirect Group, RT Blocks 17–16	FG Test Group, No. SOC Correct (a)	FG Test Group, No. SOC Incorrect (b)	FG Test Group, Correct SOC Generation Probability (a/(a+b))
12x	587	550	-37	42	92	0.31
21x	585	561	-24	39	54	0.42
13x	495	590	+95*	43	54	0.44*
34x	468	594	+126*	39	81	0.33
42x	540	592	+52	61	29	0.68*
23x	532	523	-9	53	75	0.41
31x	526	559	+33	49	41	0.54*
14x	492	559	+67*	47	46	0.51*
43x	508	610	+102*	68	50	0.58*
32x	566	594	+28	81	44	0.65*
24x	518	616	+98	73	52	0.58*
41x	567	588	+21	82	59	0.58*
Mean	532	578	+46*	45	45	0.50*

*$p < 0.05$, one-tailed.

sponding to the next location (actually Location 3) after 1-2. The difference
between these (–37 ms) given in the next column is an index of the transfer
effect. Looking down this column, it can be seen that the pattern of transfer
effects is roughly the same as that obtained in Experiment 1 (Figure 16.2).
In particular, the three locations where there is least evidence of sequence
knowledge (1-2-x, 2-1-x, 2-3-x) are the same in the two experiments.

The following three columns analyze the results of the FG Test group,
again by specific SOC sequence. The FG Test group created a sequence of

96 key presses based on what they had learned about the SOC1 sequence. We analyzed these strings of 96 key presses by dividing them into 94 consecutive triplets of responses and then looked to see how many of these triplets were consistent with the training sequence. First, the number of correct SOCs are shown, followed by the number of incorrect SOCs and then the calculated probability of the FG Test group subjects making the correct response. A triplet of responses is regarded as correct if it is one that appeared in the SOC1 training sequence. Thus, if the subject tapped out the sequence 1-2-1, it is scored as correct, whereas 1-2-3 and 1-2-4 are scored as incorrect. The chance likelihood of generating correct triplets is, of course, 0.33.[1] The critical hypothesis is that, having pressed keys 1-2, subjects will be more likely to press key 1 than either keys 3 or 4. Correct FG performance by SOC was examined using chi-square tests based on the number of correct and incorrect sequences. For example, 61 correct 4-2-3 sequences from the training sequence and 29 incorrect 4-2-x (i.e., 4-2-1 and 4-2-4) sequences that were not from the training sequence were generated. The eight asterisks in the FG Test group Correct SOC Generation Probability column indicate results that are significantly different from chance performance, $p < 0.05$, one-tailed.

Overall, a comparison of the mean number of SOCs correctly generated by the FG Test subjects ($M = 45.13$) against chance performance (31.33) yielded a significant difference. As a check, subjects in the FG Control group, who were trained on sequence SOC2, generated a mean of 36.07 SOC1 triplets, also reliably below the level of the FG Test subjects. Thus, at a global level, we have replicated the results of Experiment 1 insofar as subjects plainly have abundant explicit sequence knowledge. At the level of individual triplets, it can be seen from the transfer effects in the Indirect group that there is only evidence of this group learning SOC sequences ending on the four locations marked with asterisks. However, the probabilities of the FG Test group generating a correct SOC sequence show explicit knowledge of eight locations of the 12-trial repeating sequence. Thus, the results overall do not support the hypothesis that knowledge is generally more available on the indirect test than on the FG test. But despite this, note that there is some evidence of genuine implicit sequence knowledge, in that the triplet 3-4-2 yielded a significant negative transfer effect but not a reliable FG effect. That is, on the indirect test, subjects slowed down when the transfer sequence (3-4-1) was introduced, but they showed

554

no tendency to press 2 after 3-4 in the explicit test. We regard this as only minimal evidence for implicit learning, however, because we have not replicated the effect in further studies using more sensitive within-subjects designs.[2] Instead, these additional studies confirm the general picture of the present experiment that free generation is if anything more sensitive to sequence knowledge than the magnitude of the negative transfer effect.

We went on to explore more globally whether the subjects in the Indirect group showed greatest transfer scores for the same areas of the sequence that subjects in the FG Test group were most likely to generate. The relationship between these two measures of implicit and explicit learning were compared with a Pearson product-moment correlation, which yielded a nonsignificant value of $r = 0.20$. We therefore failed to replicate the findings of Perruchet and Amorim (1992) that implicit knowledge measured by slowing down of responses correlates with explicit FG knowledge. However, because Perruchet and Amorim (1992; see also Feldman, Kerr, & Streissguth, 1995) used a within-subjects design and correlated each subject's RT speedup over the training trials with his or her own FG performance, the likelihood is that our procedure was insufficiently sensitive to detect a correlation. Again, in other studies we have conducted using within-subjects designs, we have found the correlations between transfer effects and FG probabilities to be significant.

Interestingly, Jiménez et al. (1996; see Cleeremans & Jiménez, Chapter 10, this volume) concluded in a recent study that performance on direct and indirect tests can be dissociated. Their task used probabilistic rather than deterministic sequences, such that the probability of a signal occurring at a certain location in a given context could vary between 0 and 1. When performance on a direct test of knowledge was controlled for in a partial correlation analysis, there remained a significant correlation between the probability of the signal occurring in a given context and the RT to that signal. Jiménez et al. concluded from this finding that subjects can possess sequence knowledge that they are unable to deploy on a direct test. The results of Jiménez et al.'s study and our own Experiment 2 seem to be in conflict, because their global finding suggests that there should be specific parts of a sequence for which subjects have indirect but not direct knowledge, yet we have been unable to identify clear examples of such sequence fragments in our own studies. Plainly, further work is needed to reconcile these contrasting results.

EVALUATION OF OBJECTIVE CRITERIA

The two objective tests we have used in the present experiments (cued prediction and free generation) have yielded very interesting data. At the global level, these tests appear to show that subjects' sequence knowledge is to quite a considerable degree explicit. In Experiment 2, there was a hint at a more fine-grained level that some sequence knowledge may be truly implicit, but further experiments of ours have failed to turn this into a robust demonstration. Conservatively, then, we must conclude that there is no evidence of true implicit knowledge in these SRT tasks.

This assumes, of course, that objective tests such as cued prediction and free generation are acceptable ways of indexing conscious knowledge. However, a major (and understandable) criticism of these objective tests is that instead of being pure measures of conscious knowledge, they may be contaminated by unconscious knowledge (i.e., these tests are not *exclusive* in detecting conscious knowledge; Reingold & Merikle, 1990), in which case conclusions based on them may be flawed. How might such "contamination" arise? One possibility—particularly plausible in a four-choice RT task—is that during the generation test, finger movements are guided by unconsciously applied perceptual-motor programs. After making a certain sequence of key presses, a finger simply gets programmed unconsciously to press the next button in the sequence. Such perceptual-motor programs would be created during the extensive practice afforded by the training stage. Essentially, the fingers get dragged automatically toward the next location, not because of the subject's conscious knowledge of the sequence but because of the automatization of a simple finger-movement skill.

If performance on an objective test tends not to dissociate from that on an indirect test (as is the case in our studies), this can be used by opponents of unconscious knowledge to argue that implicit knowledge is invariably conscious, but the same result can equally plausibly be interpreted by friends of implicit knowledge to argue that the objective test was not exclusive. Thus, it may not be the case that sequence knowledge in RT tasks is invariably conscious: It may instead be the case that it is unconscious but that the objective tests used to evaluate conscious knowledge are contaminated by unconscious knowledge. Of course, this problem would be avoided if the tests yielded different results, but in our view, no such results exist. We do not believe that the literature contains any compelling examples of knowledge being available on an indirect test but unavailable on an objective test. A number of claimed examples of such dissociations (e.g., Cohen et al., 1990; Hartman et al., 1989; Howard & Howard, 1989; Knopman, 1991; Nissen & Bullemer, 1987; Willingham et al., 1989) can be discounted because of methodological problems already rehearsed elsewhere (Perruchet & Amorim, 1992; Reed & Johnson, 1994; Shanks et al., 1994; Shanks & St. John, 1994). We chose to attempt to replicate the Reed and Johnson (1994) study precisely because it stood out as providing an apparent exception.

What the debate boils down to is this: If knowledge appears not to be detected by an objective test, then that is good evidence of implicit knowledge. However, if the objective test is successful in detecting the relevant knowledge, then that may imply that the knowledge is explicit, but it may equally imply that the test is not exclusive. Of course, it would be nice to have some independent evidence that a test such as free generation is contaminated by unconscious knowledge, but even without such evidence it is clear that other types of tests will need to be explored to evaluate the true status of implicit knowledge.

VERBAL REPORTS

Having established that the objective FG test fails to indicate that sequence learning in these RT experiments is implicit, we went on to look at two other criteria for explicit knowledge: verbal reports and subjective confidence levels. Recall that in Experiment 2, we questioned subjects about their sequence knowledge prior to the FG test. What do their answers reveal? We analyzed the answers subjects in the FG Test and FG Control groups gave to two specific questions. We did not question subjects in the Indirect group because they carried out a transfer block immediately after their 16 blocks of training, with no break point at which to ask them any questions.

The first question was: While carrying out the choice reaction time task, were you aware that the dot was moving in a repeating sequence? Out of the 30 subjects in the FG Test and FG Control groups, 16 said yes, and 14 said no. But in answer to the second question (Can you tell me any parts of the sequence that you were aware of?), only 7 of the 16 who answered yes to the first question could verbally generate correct fragments from the sequence. We therefore concluded that if the test of conscious knowledge of the sequence was based on verbalizable knowledge, 23 of our 30 subjects did not have explicit knowledge. The seven aware subjects were able to generate small fragments, such as 1-4-3-2, 4-3-2-4, 4-3-2, and 4-1-2 (FG Test subjects), and 4-1-3, 1-2-3-4, 1-2-3-4-1, and 1-2-3-4 (FG Control subjects).

Because this experiment used a between-subjects design, we cannot determine whether subjects unable verbally to report the sequence did nonetheless manifest significant sequence knowledge. Our evidence for sequence knowledge requires transfer to a different sequence, and, of course, this did not happen for subjects in the FG Test and FG Control groups. However, the negative transfer effect in the Indirect group was sufficiently robust (8 of 10 subjects responded more slowly in Block 17 than in Block 16) that we have little hesitation in concluding that our 23 verbally unaware subjects would have shown evidence of sequence knowledge if they had been transferred to a different sequence rather than doing the FG test. Thus, our data provide tentative evidence that sequence knowledge can be truly implicit by a verbal report criterion.

In fact, a number of prior studies have attempted to show the same effect. In one of the best examples, Willingham et al. (1993) used an SRT task similar to that of Reed and Johnson (1994), except that subjects responded under single-task conditions. For some subjects, a random sequence of signals was presented whereas for others a repeating 16-trial sequence was present. Subjects who saw the repeating pattern showed a greater degree of RT speedup across blocks than those exposed to a random sequence, demonstrating that they were learning the location constraints imposed by the sequence. At the end of the training phase, subjects were extensively tested for their explicit knowledge, using both verbal report and recognition tests. Some sequence subjects were unable to verbally describe the sequence they had been trained on and hence were classified as unaware. The key result was that these unaware subjects still showed faster speedup in the training stage than subjects in the random group. Thus, an inability verbally to report the sequence is not necessarily an impediment to having implicit knowledge of that sequence.

On the face of it, verbal report provides a plausible dividing line between implicit and explicit knowledge, consistent with the intuition that when some knowledge is conscious, we can usually describe it. But the problem is that it is not always the case that we can describe our knowledge, even when it is fully conscious. For example, we may simply lack the vocabulary to describe our experience, or more important, the demand characteristics of the task may make us reluctant to report weak or low-confidence knowledge. As Reingold and Merikle (1990) have pointed out, an adequate test of consciousness must be exhaustive: It must be possible to show that our test of awareness is powerful enough to reveal all of the subject's conscious knowledge. The reason for demanding this is that if the test is not exhaustive, then a dissociation between indirect and direct tests may come about simply because the indirect test recruits more conscious knowledge than the direct test. Yet, it is very hard to see how verbal reports could ever be shown to be exhaustive. There will always be the possibility that subjects choose not to report some low-confidence but potentially verbalizable knowledge because they have set their report criterion too high.

This problem of unwillingness to report near-threshold information has plagued other areas in which unconscious mental processes have been studied. For instance, one interpretation of blindsight is in terms of response criterion. Blindsight refers to the striking observation that patients whose visual cortex has been damaged and who are experientially blind across some portion of the visual field may nonetheless perform above chance on certain objective forced-choice tests of visual knowledge (see Cowey & Stoerig, 1995; Weiskrantz, 1986). For instance, blindsight patients may be able to judge in a forced-choice test whether a stimulus consists of horizontal or vertical stripes while denying any visual experience of the stimulus. But a straightforward, albeit controversial, explanation of such findings in terms of signal detection theory, proposed by Campion, Latto, and Smith (1983), is simply that subjects have a different response criterion when making forced-choice responses than they do when reporting their visual experience. On this theory, there is no need to posit unconscious visual knowledge in blindsight. Knowledge about the visual properties of the stimulus may be conscious (but close to threshold); however, because of differences in response criteria, this knowledge may be detected on the forced-choice but not on the verbal report test.

SUBJECTIVE CONFIDENCE

In Experiment 2, we asked a third question of our FG subjects to assess their subjective confidence in their performance. The question was: When you were generating the sequence, did you feel that it was familiar or that you were guessing? The key result from subjects in the FG Test group was that three subjects felt that to some extent, some of the sequences they had generated were familiar and that they had actually generated fragments of the training sequence. The result of excluding these three aware subjects was that the performance of the remaining 12 unaware subjects ($M = 42.92$) remained significantly above chance (31.33) in terms of the number of SOC1 triplets they generated. Our conclusion from this analysis is therefore that if subjective confidence were the criterion by which we determined conscious knowledge, we again would have demonstrated implicit knowledge of the sequence. Subjects who believed they were guessing had actually performed at above-chance levels on the FG test.

One problem with this sort of analysis is that it is left up to the subject to define consciousness and guessing. The problem has been persuasively stated by Reingold and Merikle (1990):

> Many investigators . . . feel uncomfortable measuring conscious awareness solely in terms of subjective reports. A major reason for caution is that it is difficult to know what criteria individuals use to decide they are guessing. . . . Statements expressing no subjective confidence may simply reflect biases introduced by either the experimental instructions (i.e., demand characteristics, in psychological jargon) or an individual's preconceived ideas concerning the value of particular types of perceptual experiences for making decisions. . . . Thus, statements indicating an absence of subjective confidence may only reflect an individual's own theories of how perceptual experience guides behavior rather than a true absence of conscious perceptual experience. . . . The fundamental problem with the subjective confidence approach is that it transfers the responsibility for operationally defining awareness from the investigator to the observer. (p. 17)

To put this objection another way, the subject may be conscious of the knowledge that is guiding his or her behavior, but this conscious experience may be extremely fragmentary and elusive. Subjects may simply require a fairly high degree of confidence that their responses are nonrandom before they are willing to report this to the experimenter. We therefore conducted one further experiment to look more closely at subjective confidence.

In this third and final experiment, we repeated the dual-task paradigm, using the SOC1 sequence for a Sequence group and a nonrepeating sequence for a Nonrepeating group. The nonrepeating sequence matched the SOC sequence in terms of location and transition frequencies but contained no repeating structure. All subjects were exposed to 16 blocks of training under dual-task conditions and then freely generated 96 dot locations, which were compared to the SOC1 sequence. Immediately after the FG task was completed, all subjects were asked to give a subjective confidence rating indicating how successful they thought they had been at generating parts of the sequence they saw in the RT phase of the experiment on a scale from 0 to 100. Because this test does not mention the word *guessing* but merely asks for a numerical judgment about perceived success at free generation, it is not susceptible to the sort of problem articulated by Reingold and Merikle (1990).

Using this design created a between-subjects measure of subjective confidence in the Sequence and Nonrepeating groups. The Sequence group was expected to perform at above-chance levels on the FG task, whereas the Nonrepeating group was expected to perform at chance levels. The measure of interest is the difference in subjective confidence ratings between the two groups. Will the Sequence group show greater confidence in their FG performance than the Nonrepeating group? Or is their sequence knowledge characterized by chance levels of subjective confidence?

Thirty-three subjects performed the experiment. After eliminating three subjects who made more than 10% tone-counting errors, there was a total of 30 subjects, with 15 in each of two groups. The simple choice RT task, the SOC1 sequence task, and the FG task were exactly the same as for Experiment 2. The only difference was that subjects in Experiment 3 were asked to give a subjective confidence rating. Each subject was given a standard form with the following instructions:

> Please indicate on the line below how successful you think you have been at generating parts of the sequence you saw in the reaction time part of this experiment. The line represents a scale from 0 to 100, where 0 indicates that you felt unable to generate any part of the sequence and 100 indicates that you feel all your responses conformed to the sequence you saw.

This was followed by a line 5.75 inches long, which was created from 100 dashes. A 0 was placed at one end of the line, with the description: *unable to generate any parts of the sequence,* and at the opposite end, a 100 was placed with the description *all responses conformed to the sequence in the RT task.*

Results. Figure 16.5 presents mean RTs for each of 16 training blocks and for each of two groups of subjects and shows roughly equivalent RT

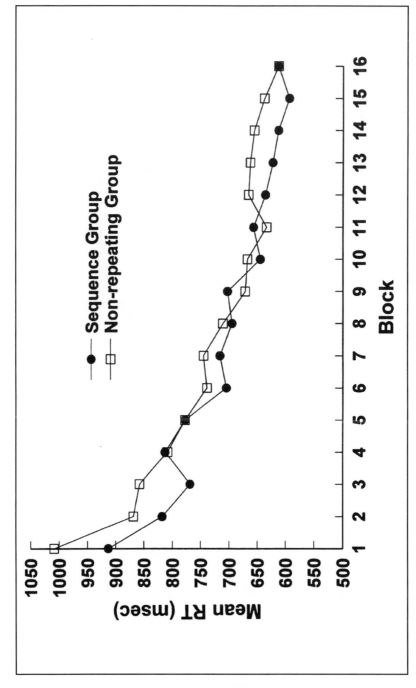

Figure 16.5. Mean reaction times (RTs) in ms across 16 blocks of training trials in Experiment 3. Group Sequence was trained for 16 blocks on Sequence SOC1 whereas Group Nonrepeating was trained on a matched nonrepeating sequence.

TABLE 16.3 Mean Free-Generation (FG) and Subjective Confidence Rating
Scores for the Sequence and Nonrepeating Groups in Experiment 3

Group	Mean Number of Correct SOCs Generated	Mean Subjective Confidence Rating
Sequence	40.60	42.13
Sequence/Unaware	44.43	23.14
Nonrepeating	33.27	21.80

decreases in the two groups. It might be expected that the Sequence group
would have speeded up across blocks more than the Nonrepeating group,
but the results do not support this. Because subjects in the Sequence group
do have sequence knowledge (see below), it seems that RT speedup across
blocks is not a particularly sensitive index of learning.

Table 16.3 shows the results of the FG and subjective confidence ratings
for the Sequence and Nonrepeating groups. Each group created a sequence
of 96 key presses based on what they had learned about the SOC1 and
nonrepeating sequences, respectively. We analyzed these strings of 96 key
presses for all subjects by counting the frequency of correct three-location
SOC sequences from the SOC1 sequence. Chance performance is again
31.33 correct SOC sequences. The Sequence group produced a mean of
40.60 correct sequences, whereas the Nonrepeating group produced a mean
of 33.27, and there was a significant difference between the FG performance
of these two groups. Confirming the results of Experiment 2, subjects
trained on a repeating sequence are able to generate fragments of that
sequence.

All subjects gave a subjective confidence rating indicating how successful they thought they had been at generating parts of the sequence they saw
in the RT task. The mean Sequence group rating was 42.13, whereas the
mean Nonrepeating group rating was 21.80, and this difference was significant. Thus, this more detailed examination of subjective confidence
reveals that, when pressed, subjects do admit to being aware that they were
somewhat successful in generating the training sequence. Their confidence
ratings are greater than those seen in a group trained on a nonrepeating
sequence.

However, another analysis that can be performed on these data is to
select a subgroup of Sequence subjects who give low confidence ratings and

to see whether their FG scores are above or equal to those of subjects in the Nonrepeating group. Seven subjects in the Sequence group gave reasonably low confidence ratings ($M = 23.14$), approximately matching the mean in the Nonrepeating group (21.80). How did these subjects do in terms of free generation? Table 16.3 shows that despite giving low subjective ratings, these subjects nevertheless freely generated far more SOC1 triplets than subjects in the Nonrepeating group, and this difference was statistically significant. Thus, there are subjects in the Sequence group who have knowledge of the repeating structure of the RT stimuli but who lack meta-knowledge: They do not appear to know that they know this structure.

To summarize the results of Experiment 3, we found a significant difference between the two groups of subjects with both the objective measure of FG performance and the subjective confidence ratings of how successful subjects thought they had been at generating parts of the sequence they had seen in the training phase. However, some subjects whose subjective confidence was as low as that seen in the Nonrepeating group nevertheless did have sequence knowledge. These results suggest that with an experimental design that forces subjects to give a fine-grained, quantitative assessment of their subjective confidence, confidence can be dissociated from the content of prior learning.

These findings corroborate nicely the results of the study by Dienes et al. (1995) mentioned earlier. Recall that after being exposed to strings generated from an artificial grammar, Dienes et al.'s subjects made grammaticality judgments for novel legal and illegal strings and also stated how confident they felt they were in their grammaticality decisions. The outcome was that subjects performed above chance in making grammaticality decisions even when they thought they were guessing, thus demonstrating a dissociation between grammatical knowledge and subjective awareness.

PERFORMANCE OF AMNESIC PATIENTS ON THE SRT TASK

Experimental analyses of SRT performance in normal subjects have not proved that sequence knowledge can be below an objective threshold. But perhaps more clear-cut evidence can be found in the performance of memory-impaired subjects. A number of investigators have looked to the performance of amnesic patients for clues concerning the status of implicitly acquired knowledge (e.g., Cleeremans, 1993; Nissen & Bullemer, 1987;

Nissen, Willingham, & Hartman, 1989; Reber & Squire, 1994). Here we will briefly review the principal findings from these studies.

In the first application of the four-choice SRT task, Nissen and Bullemer (1987; see also Nissen et al., 1989) showed that Korsakoff's amnesic patients were able to learn a 10-trial repeating sequence. After four blocks of training with a repeating sequence, RTs increased significantly when the signals appeared at random. None of the patients reported noticing the repeating sequence. In a further study, Nissen, Knopman, and Schacter (1987) induced amnesia-like effects in normal subjects via the administration of scopolamine and found that this had no detectable effect on an indirect assessment of sequence knowledge (but see Knopman, 1991, for evidence that scopolamine can affect sequence learning). Subjects injected with scopolamine were impaired, however, in their CP performance. Unfortunately, in neither of the above studies were the repeating and random sequences matched for location frequencies, in which case the negative transfer effects observed on the random trials cannot be unambiguously interpreted as evidence of *sequence* knowledge (see Reed & Johnson, 1994; Shanks et al., 1994).

Probably the most extensive analysis of amnesic performance on the SRT task was undertaken by Reber and Squire (1994), and their results demand careful scrutiny. These studies were actually quite complex, but we will describe the aspects most relevant to our present concerns. In their first experiment, Reber and Squire presented amnesic ($n = 9$) and control subjects with 400 RT trials in which the signal appeared according to a repeating 10-trial sequence. At the end of the training phase, subjects were questioned about their knowledge of the sequence and then given a prediction test similar to that used in Experiment 1 above. Some weeks later, subjects were trained on a different sequence, again questioned about their knowledge of the sequence, and finally given an FG test similar to that used in Experiment 2 above. Thus, the interesting data come from an analysis of how much subjects know about the sequence as assessed (a) indirectly, (b) via verbal report, (c) via a prediction test, and (d) via an FG test.

Turning first to the results of the verbal report test, the amnesic patients were significantly less aware than the control subjects of the repeating sequence and less able to report specific parts of the sequence. Hence, via a verbal report assessment, amnesics were impaired in their ability to become consciously aware of a repeating sequence. The results of the objective tests, however, were more ambiguous. The amnesics were significantly worse than the controls at predicting sequence continuations, but they were statistically no worse at freely generating sequence fragments. Thus, our conclusions concerning the performance of amnesics relative to controls on objective tests of awareness must remain tentative: There is some evidence of a difference, but not on all objective tests. In fact, given evidence that free generation is a less biased test of sequence knowledge than cued prediction (Perruchet & Amorim, 1992), it could be argued that more weight should be given to the negative results of the FG test.

Be that as it may, it is still the case that Reber and Squire's (1994) amnesic patients were poorer than their control subjects at verbally reporting the sequence structure. If the two groups were indistinguishable in the extent to which an indirect test illustrated sequence knowledge, then this pattern of results would provide strong evidence of a dissociation between awareness and knowledge. The data would suggest that comparable degrees of knowledge (as assessed indirectly) could be accompanied by varying degrees of awareness, indicating that awareness and knowledge do not necessarily go hand in hand. So what is the evidence that Reber and Squire's amnesics and controls were indeed matched in terms of their underlying (implicit) sequence knowledge? The key data come from a final set of RT trials administered after the generation test. Here, subjects were given 100 trials with the same repeating sequence they had originally been trained on, followed by 100 trials with a random sequence. One problem with this comparison, as Reber and Squire acknowledge, is that the repeating and random sequences were again not matched for location frequencies, in which case any negative transfer effect observed does not provide unambiguous evidence concerning sequence knowledge. But even putting this problem aside, the results are unconvincing. Although Reber and Squire found that the negative transfer effect caused by switching to the random sequence was not significantly greater in the control as compared to the amnesic patients, close examination of the block means suggests that the effect was quite considerably larger for the control (86 ms) than for the amnesic (49 ms) subjects. Thus, it is far from clear that the amnesics' implicit learning of the sequence was comparable to that of the controls.

The results of Reber and Squire's (1994) second experiment are no more clear-cut. This time, subjects were trained on a 12-trial SOC sequence, and as before the amnesics ($n = 8$) were significantly less able verbally to describe this sequence than were the controls. After the verbal report test, a negative transfer score was determined by giving subjects a further block of repeating trials followed by a block of random trials as in the first experiment. Because the SOC and random sequences were roughly matched in terms of location and transition frequencies, this test provides a much better index of true sequence knowledge. However, again the amnesics showed a smaller negative transfer effect (27 ms) than the controls (39 ms). As with Reber and Squire's first experiment, the small number of subjects means that it is difficult to rule out the possibility that low statistical power could have obscured a real group difference.

Analyses of the performance of amnesics and controls on the SRT task are in principle capable of yielding very strong evidence concerning the true unconscious nature of implicit knowledge. If amnesics are *selectively* worse at verbally reporting a sequence or at performing an objective test of sequence knowledge, given the level of sequence knowledge they demonstrate in an indirect test, then that would provide compelling evidence that knowledge of a structured sequence can be unconscious. However, to date, the results obtained from amnesic subjects performing SRT tasks—like those obtained from normals—can be satisfactorily explained by the null hypothesis that the level of knowledge they manifest on direct tests is entirely consistent with the level of knowledge they manifest on indirect tests.

CONCLUSIONS

Let us begin by briefly summarizing our main conclusions. In the absence of a single, agreed behavioral index of consciousness, researchers have considered various different possibilities, which may be overlapping or which may be entirely independent. We have reviewed previous research and presented new findings concerning the conclusions one reaches about the implicit nature of sequence learning when verbal report, objective, and subjective criteria are adopted. First, there is little doubt that subjects may possess sequence knowledge that they are unable to verbally report when questioned, but this fact is hard to interpret—it may simply reflect unwillingness on the part of the subject to report weak or low-confidence knowledge. Turning to subjects' performance on objective forced-choice tests of sequence knowledge, a review of the literature indicated that Reed and Johnson's (1994) results seemed to provide impressive evidence of a dissociation between knowledge and awareness. However, in each of the three experiments we have reported in this chapter, subjects were able to deploy their sequence knowledge in objective tests (cued prediction and free generation), and we argued that Reed and Johnson's experimental design contained a flaw that biased them toward failing to obtain evidence of above-chance CP performance. Finally, in Experiment 2, we obtained some suggestive evidence that subjects may lack subjective confidence in or meta-knowledge about their own performance. This was confirmed in Experiment 3, where it emerged that a subgroup of subjects trained on a repeating sequence who had no greater confidence in their FG performance than subjects trained on a nonrepeating sequence nevertheless outperformed them on that test.

Given previous claims, our conclusions concerning objective tests may seem unduly negative, so we will end by offering what we hope is a more positive view of implicit knowledge. We have argued elsewhere (St. John & Shanks, 1997; Shanks, Johnstone, & Staggs, 1997; Shanks & St. John, 1994) that the interesting distinction between implicit and explicit knowledge lies not so much in their respective accessibilities to consciousness but rather in their information-processing properties. Briefly, we see implicit knowledge as being largely based on the accumulation of instances in a superpositional memory system, such as a connectionist network, with the instances representing aspects of the distributional statistics of the surface elements of the domain in question. In contrast, explicit knowledge can be much more abstract and rule-based and can transcend the specific items on which learning is based. With respect to the SRT task, this means that implicit knowledge consists of associative chains between representations of the stimuli and their accompanying responses (see Cleeremans, 1993, for a specific connectionist model of this type of knowledge). Such knowledge is surface-based in that it reflects very specific perceptual and motor attributes of the RT task and is unlikely to transfer well across changes in the format of the task (see Willingham et al., 1989). Explicit knowledge, on the other hand, might consist of abstract knowledge of the sequence of stimuli and might be coded in a form that allows transfer to a completely different stimulus or response modality. On this conception, implicit and explicit knowledge do not differ in any fundamental way with respect to their conscious accessibility. Instead, it is their representational contents that differ.

We believe that although the conscious-unconscious debate has proven problematic, there is clear evidence for a distinction between surface-based and abstract knowledge (e.g., Chater & Hahn, 1996; Nosofsky, Palmeri, & McKinley, 1994; Perruchet, 1994; Regehr & Brooks, 1993; Shanks, 1995; Shanks et al., 1997). Unfortunately, most of the evidence has come from concept- and artificial grammar-learning studies rather than from experiments on RTs in sequence learning studies (but see Perruchet, 1994, for an exception). But this should encourage researchers to look more closely at the possibility that implicit and explicit forms of sequence learning, differing in their information-processing characteristics rather than in their availability to consciousness, may exist.

NOTES

1. This assumes that subjects know that the target never appears in the same location on consecutive trials. In fact, there were a small number of location repetitions in the subjects' FG responses, but these have been excluded from the data analysis.

2. One reason why the significant transfer effect for the 3-4-x part of the sequence may have been an artifact in the present experiment is that our procedure, like Reed and Johnson's (1994), does not control for the latencies of different finger movements. That is, subjects may simply be faster at pressing Button 2 in the SOC1 training sequence 3-4-2 than Button 1 in the SOC2 transfer sequence 3-4-1. The transcription-typing literature (e.g., Salthouse, 1986) has identified numerous reasons why different finger movements in sequences of key presses may differ in latency. In later studies, we have been careful to control for these latencies, and as a result, the transfer effects obtained have probably been more unbiased.

REFERENCES

Annett, J. (1991). Skill acquisition. In J. E. Morrison (Ed.), *Training for performance: Principles of applied human learning* (pp. 13-51). Chichester: Wiley.

Berry, D. C., & Dienes, Z. (1993). *Implicit learning: Theoretical and empirical issues*. Hove: Lawrence Erlbaum.

Campion, J., Latto, R., & Smith, Y. M. (1983). Is blindsight an effect of scattered light, spared cortex, and near-threshold vision? *Behavioral and Brain Sciences, 6*, 423-486.

Chater, N., & Hahn, N. (1996). *Similarity and rules: Distinct? Exhaustive? Empirically distinguishable?* Manuscript submitted for publication.

Cheesman, J., & Merikle, P. M. (1984). Priming with and without awareness. *Perception and Psychophysics, 36*, 387-395.

Cleeremans, A. (1993). *Mechanisms of implicit learning*. Cambridge: MIT Press.

Cleeremans, A., & McClelland, J. L. (1991). Learning the structure of event sequences. *Journal of Experimental Psychology: General, 120*, 235-253.

Cohen, A., Ivry, R. I., & Keele, S. W. (1990). Attention and structure in sequence learning. *Journal of Experimental Psychology: Learning, Memory, and Cognition, 16,* 17-30.

Cowey, A., & Stoerig, P. (1995). Blindsight in monkeys. *Nature, 373,* 247-249.

Dienes, Z., Altmann, G. T. M., Kwan, L., & Goode, A. (1995). Unconscious knowledge of artificial grammars is applied strategically. *Journal of Experimental Psychology: Learning, Memory, and Cognition, 21,* 1322-1338.

Dulany, D. E. (1961). Hypotheses and habits in verbal "operant conditioning." *Journal of Abnormal and Social Psychology, 63,* 251-263.

Eriksen, C. W. (1960). Discrimination and learning without awareness: A methodological survey and evaluation. *Psychological Review, 67,* 279-300.

Feldman, J., Kerr, B., & Streissguth, A. P. (1995). Correlational analyses of procedural and declarative learning performance. *Intelligence, 20,* 87-114.

Frensch, P. A., Buchner, A., & Lin, J. (1994). Implicit learning of unique and ambiguous serial transitions in the presence and absence of a distractor task. *Journal of Experimental Psychology: Learning, Memory, and Cognition, 20,* 567-584.

Greenspoon, J. (1955). The reinforcing effect of two spoken sounds on the frequency of two responses. *American Journal of Psychology, 68,* 409-416.

Hartman, M., Knopman, D. S., & Nissen, M. J. (1989). Implicit learning of new verbal associations. *Journal of Experimental Psychology: Learning, Memory, and Cognition, 15,* 1070-1082.

Holender, D. (1986). Semantic activation without conscious identification in dichotic listening, parafoveal vision, and visual masking: A survey and appraisal. *Behavioral and Brain Sciences, 9,* 1-66.

Howard, D. V., & Howard, J. H. (1989). Age differences in learning serial patterns: Direct versus indirect measures. *Psychology and Aging, 4,* 357-364.

Jiménez, L., Méndez, C., & Cleeremans, A. (1996). Comparing direct and indirect measures of sequence learning. *Journal of Experimental Psychology: Learning, Memory, and Cognition, 22,* 948-969.

Knopman, D. (1991). Unaware learning versus preserved learning in pharmacologic amnesia: Similarities and differences. *Journal of Experimental Psychology: Learning, Memory, and Cognition, 17,* 1017-1029.

Nisbett, R. E., & Wilson, T. D. (1977). Telling more than we can know: Verbal reports on mental processes. *Psychological Review, 84,* 231-259.

Nissen, M. J., & Bullemer, P. (1987). Attentional requirements of learning: Evidence from performance measures. *Cognitive Psychology, 19,* 1-32.

Nissen, M. J., Knopman, D. S., & Schacter, D. L. (1987). Neurochemical dissociation of memory systems. *Neurology, 37,* 789-794.

Nissen, M. J., Willingham, D., & Hartman, M. (1989). Explicit and implicit remembering: When is learning preserved in amnesia? *Neuropsychologia, 27,* 341-352.

Nosofsky, R. M., Palmeri, T. J., & McKinley, S. C. (1994). Rule-plus-exception model of classification learning. *Psychological Review, 101,* 53-79.

Perruchet, P. (1994). Learning from complex rule-governed environments: On the proper functions of nonconscious and conscious processes. In C. Umiltà & M. Moscovitch (Eds.), *Attention and performance XV. Conscious and nonconscious information processing* (pp. 811-835). Cambridge: MIT Press.

Perruchet, P., & Amorim, M.-A. (1992). Conscious knowledge and changes in performance in sequence learning: Evidence against dissociation. *Journal of Experimental Psychology: Learning, Memory, and Cognition, 18,* 785-800.

Reber, P. J., & Squire, L. R. (1994). Parallel brain systems for learning with and without awareness. *Learning and Memory, 1,* 217-229.

Reed, J., & Johnson, P. (1994). Assessing implicit learning with indirect tests: Determining what is learned about sequence structure. *Journal of Experimental Psychology: Learning, Memory, and Cognition, 20,* 585-594.

Regehr, G., & Brooks, L. R. (1993). Perceptual manifestations of an analytic structure: The priority of holistic individuation. *Journal of Experimental Psychology: General, 122,* 92-114.

Reingold, E. M., & Merikle, P. M. (1990). On the interrelatedness of theory and measurement in the study of unconscious processes. *Mind and Language, 5,* 9-28.

St. John, M. F., & Shanks, D. R. (1997). Implicit learning from an information processing standpoint. In D. Berry (Ed.), *How implicit is implicit learning?* Oxford, UK: Oxford University Press.

Salthouse, T. A. (1986). Perceptual, cognitive, and motoric aspects of transcription typing. *Psychological Bulletin, 99,* 303-319.

Shanks, D. R. (1995). *The psychology of associative learning.* Cambridge, UK: Cambridge University Press.

Shanks, D. R., Green, R. E. A., & Kolodny, J. A. (1994). A critical examination of the evidence for unconscious (implicit) learning. In C. Umiltà & M. Moscovitch (Eds.), *Attention and performance XV: Conscious and nonconscious information processing* (pp. 837-860). Cambridge: MIT Press.

Shanks, D. R., Johnstone, T., & Staggs, L. (1997). Abstraction processes in artificial grammar learning. *Quarterly Journal of Experimental Psychology, 50A,* 216-252.

Shanks, D. R., & St. John, M. F. (1994). Characteristics of dissociable human learning systems. *Behavioral and Brain Sciences, 17,* 367-447.

Weiskrantz, L. (1986). *Blindsight: A case study and implications.* Oxford, UK: Oxford University Press.

Willingham, D. B., Greeley, T., & Bardone, A. M. (1993). Dissociation in a serial response time task using a recognition measure: Comment on Perruchet and Amorim (1992). *Journal of Experimental Psychology: Learning, Memory, and Cognition, 19,* 1424-1430.

Willingham, D. B., Nissen, M. J., & Bullemer, P. (1989). On the development of procedural knowledge. *Journal of Experimental Psychology: Learning, Memory, and Cognition, 15,* 1047-1060.

17

Implicit Learning and Motor Skill Learning in Older Subjects

An Extension of the Processing Speed Theory

Daniel B. Willingham

Learning continues throughout the life span. A question of some interest, therefore, is the extent to which aging affects one's ability to learn. There has been considerable research on learning and memory in older subjects, but most of this research has focused on a small set of tasks, namely, recognition and recall, usually using verbal materials. For these tasks, a consistent pattern of age-related performance has emerged. Older subjects are more impaired in tasks that require a greater contribution from memory-search strategies; thus, older subjects usually show good recognition memory but impaired cued recall and still more impaired free recall (Craik, 1977, 1994).

The effect of aging on motor skill learning is less clear, but there is reason to think that age-related effects might be qualitatively different for motor skill learning tasks. Recognition and recall rely on *declarative* memory (Cohen & Squire, 1980). Declarative memory is memory for facts and events, and its normal operation depends on the integrity of structures in the medial temporal lobe and diencephalon (Squire, 1992b). The processes that search declarative memory and appear to be difficult for older subjects

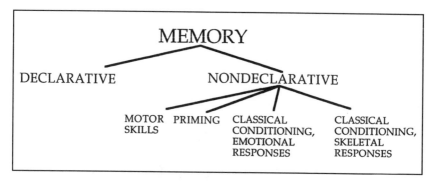

Figure 17.1. Taxonomy of memory systems.

are subserved by prefrontal cortical areas, as revealed by recent neuroimaging studies (Mulder et al., 1995), and it is known that there is frontal lobe degeneration associated with normal aging (Raz et al., in press).

Declarative memory may be contrasted with *nondeclarative memory* (Squire, 1992a). Nondeclarative memory is proposed to have a number of subsystems, including those supporting repetition priming, classical conditioning of skeletal responses, emotional conditioning, and motor skill learning, as shown in the memory taxonomy depicted in Figure 17.1 (for a brief review of memory systems, see Willingham, 1997).[1] Implicit learning is also thought to be supported by the nondeclarative systems. These various subsystems are neurally independent of one another and are independent of declarative memory.

Motor skills are considered to be nondeclarative due to the pattern of data from patients with anterograde amnesia. These amnesic patients have a profound deficit in declarative memory due to damage to the medial temporal lobe structures, such as the hippocampus, or to the diencephalon and therefore are grossly impaired in standard recognition or recall tasks. Nevertheless, amnesic patients learn novel motor skills at the same rate that neurologically intact subjects do (Corkin, 1968; Eslinger & Damasio, 1986; Nissen, Willingham, & Hartman, 1989). Thus, an amnesic patient who has practiced a motor skill task will deny having performed the task before, claim never to have seen the apparatus, and then perform the task quite skillfully.

A second reason that motor skills are considered nondeclarative is their relationship to awareness. Motor skills can be learned outside of awareness, meaning the participant is not necessarily aware that he or she is learning.

For example, Pew (1974) had subjects track a target on a video monitor using a joystick. Unbeknownst to the participants, the middle section of each trial used the same pattern of target movements. With practice, participants' performance improved on this repeating segment relative to the other parts of the trial that used random target movement. It is also relevant that on other motor skills in which the participant might be aware that performance is improving, the participant does not have conscious access to the knowledge used to improve performance. One might know that one can ride a bicycle, but one cannot consciously access the knowledge on which that skill depends. Thus motor skills have the two important characteristics of nondeclarative knowledge: They do not depend on the medial temporal lobe or dienchephalon, and the representations that support learning are not available to awareness.

Thus, although age-related deficits have been demonstrated on some of the tasks that tap declarative memory, age-related effects on motor skill learning tasks may be quite different, because these tasks tap a memory system that is neurally independent of declarative memory.

Which brain structures support motor skill learning, given that the medial temporal lobe and diencephalon do not? Candidate structures are the basal ganglia, supplementary motor area, and primary motor cortex (Salmon & Butters, 1995). Although all motor skills could be classified as nondeclarative, that does not mean that all motor skills have the same characteristics, and as will be seen, older subjects are impaired in learning some motor skills but learn others at the same rate as young subjects.

This chapter considers the effect of aging on motor skill learning. As described below, motor skill learning is neither uniformly impaired nor uniformly spared in older subjects. This pattern of data is considered, along with several potential accounts that have been offered. None of the extant theories, including the implicit/explicit learning distinction, appear to explain the pattern of data. A new account of aging and motor skill learning is offered, based on Salthouse's (1996) processing speed theory of aging.

MOTOR SKILL LEARNING IN OLDER SUBJECTS

It is important to be clear about the distinction between motor performance and motor skill learning. Motor performance refers to subjects' ability to execute a motor task with accuracy. Accuracy may be taken to mean temporal or spatial accuracy, or both. Motor skill learning refers to a subject's ability to improve accuracy with practice.

There is little doubt that motor performance is compromised in older subjects. Older subjects are impaired in most or all features of motor performance, showing longer movement times (Stelmach & Nahom, 1992), impoverished perception in perceptual motor tasks (Verillo & Verrillo, 1985), poor tracking of a target on a computer with a joystick (Jagacinski, Liao, & Fayyad, 1995), greater difficulty in using a spatially incompatible stimulus-response mapping, and so forth (for a review, see Welford, 1984). The picture is not so clear for motor skill learning, however, as older subjects appear to improve performance at the same rate as younger subjects on some tasks but not others.

A number of researchers have examined motor skill learning with the pursuit rotor task, in which the participant must keep the tip of a hand-held stylus in contact with a small target that moves in a circle. The dependent measure is the number of seconds the subject can keep the tip of the stylus in contact with the target during a 25-second trial. Older subjects are impaired in learning this task. They improve their time-on-target, but more slowly than younger subjects do (Gutman, 1965; Ruch, 1934; Wright & Payne, 1985).

Two of these studies also tested subjects' ability on the pursuit rotor task when they could view the apparatus and their hand only in a mirror. Again, researchers reported that older subjects learned more slowly (Ruch, 1934; Wright & Payne, 1985). In a related paradigm, Snoddy (1926) asked subjects to trace a star-shaped pattern in a mirror. This task is different because the target does not move, and the task is therefore paced by the subject. The dependent measures are speed to complete one circuit around the star and the number of errors. Snoddy reported that older subjects were impaired, although he did not publish the actual data or results of the statistics.

On the other hand, older subjects consistently show normal learning (relative to younger subjects) on the serial response time (SRT) task. This is a four-choice response time (RT) task in which the stimuli appear in a repeating 12-unit sequence. Younger subjects typically show progressively faster RTs with continued training on the task when the stimuli appear in the repeating sequence. If a block of randomly appearing stimuli are introduced, RTs abruptly increase. This increase shows that some of the knowledge is specific to the sequence, and subjects' improvement is not simply due to learning more general aspects of the task, for example, the stimu-lus-response mapping.

Subjects are not told that the stimuli appear in a sequence, and nothing demarcates a sequence's beginning or end, and so many subjects believe that the stimuli appear randomly; indeed, they report being unaware that the stimuli were sequenced, even though their RTs make it clear that they have some knowledge of the sequence (Willingham, Nissen, & Bullemer, 1989). Thus, this learning can be largely implicit, although whether the learning is motoric, perceptual, or something else is still under debate (see Howard, Mutter, & Howard, 1992; Mayr, 1996; Willingham et al., 1989). Older subjects show normal implicit learning of the sequence in the SRT task (Howard & Howard, 1989, 1992).

Cherry and Stadler (1995) have argued that broad generalizations about implicit learning in older subjects may be ill-advised because there are sizable individual differences. They tested two groups of older sub-jects—what they called lower-ability and higher-ability older subjects—as well as younger subjects on the SRT task. Lower-ability older subjects had lower educational attainment, occupational status, and verbal ability (as measured by the Wechsler Adult Intelligence Scale, 1981) than their higher-ability counterparts. Higher-ability older subjects showed implicit learning on the SRT task comparable to the younger subjects, but the lower-ability subjects showed less implicit learning. As Cherry and Stadler point out, the interpretation of this study is complicated by the lack of a younger control group of lower-ability subjects; it may be that age is less important to the poor performance of the lower-ability older subjects than the fact that they were low ability.

THEORETICAL ACCOUNTS OF AGE-RELATED MOTOR SKILL LEARNING EFFECTS

The Implicit/Explicit Distinction

A candidate explanation for the pattern of spared and impaired mo-tor skill learning in aging is the implicit/explicit task distinction (Graf & Schacter, 1985). Explicit tasks are those in which the subject is directly queried about the to-be-remembered material, and remembering is accom-panied by a feeling of conscious awareness on the part of the subject. In implicit tasks, subjects are not directly queried; rather, they are simply asked to perform a task, and learning is inferred from task performance, which is biased or changed by previous experience. The performance of implicit tasks is not necessarily associated with subjective awareness of remembering on the part of the subject.

In general, it is thought that explicit tasks tap declarative memory, whereas implicit tasks tap nondeclarative memory. It is generally true that patients with anterograde amnesia (who have a deficit in declarative memory) only learn implicit tasks normally, but it should be noted that the distinctions are different; implicit/explicit is a distinction of types of tasks, whereas declarative/nondeclarative refers to hypothetical memory systems. Thus, it is not necessarily the case that there is perfect concordance between the two distinctions.

There is good reason to hypothesize that the pattern of age-related performance might be different in implicit tasks compared to explicit tasks and that this distinction might account for the motor skill-learning data. As described earlier, older subjects have difficulty with recall and cued recall (explicit tasks), and the difficulty in explicit learning appears to be closely tied to memory-search strategies. Memory-search strategies become important when only minimal cues to the to-be-remembered material are available, as in free recall (What happened yesterday?). Search strategies are less important when the environment offers richer cues to the to-be-remembered material, as in a recognition task, where the cue is the actual thing to be remembered (Did you see this picture yesterday?). If the cues provided in the environment offer sufficient support, older subjects are less impaired. In fact, Craik (1994) has argued that environmental support is the key factor in the explicit memory performance of older subjects.

A cardinal feature of most or all implicit learning tasks is that the environment constrains the response the subject may make (Nissen, Willingham, & Hartman, 1989). By definition, implicit learning is measured indirectly by how a subject's response is biased or facilitated by experience; the task must provide sufficient information to generate a response even if the subject has absolutely no experience to guide performance. Thus, the feature of explicit tasks that appears to give older subjects the most trouble—generating a response given few cues—is absent from implicit tasks.

A number of studies have shown normal learning or marginal, statistically unreliable impairment in implicit memory tasks in the elderly; these tasks are not restricted to motor skill tasks but include repetition priming (e.g., Light, Singh & Capps, 1986), classical conditioning (e.g.,

Woodruff-Pak, 1988), and others. In contrast to these marginal effects, older subjects are consistently impaired on explicit memory tasks, leading some researchers to suggest that implicit memory is impaired in the elderly, but less so than explicit memory (for reviews, see Graf, 1990; Howard, 1991; Light, 1988).

Does the implicit/explicit distinction capture the age-related deficit on some motor skill tasks? It is true that the motor skill task on which old people are consistently successful—the SRT task—is implicit. This seems still more plausible in light of another aspect of the older subjects' performance on the SRT task. Although subjects are not told about the repeating sequence, some typically notice the sequence and learn it explicitly; among younger subjects, as many as half might report being aware that the stimuli were sequenced (although they might not be able to recall all of it; Willingham, Nissen, & Bullemer, 1989). But fewer older subjects become aware that the stimuli are sequenced, and if they are later asked to explicitly learn the sequence, they are slower to do so than younger subjects (Howard & Howard, 1989).

What of the motor skills on which older subjects are impaired? The mirror tracing and pursuit rotor skills are definitely nondeclarative; patients with global amnesia with damage to the medial temporal lobe or diencephalon are able to learn these tasks as quickly as normal subjects (Eslinger & Damasio, 1986; Gabrieli, Corkin, Mickel, & Growdon, 1993). Still, these tasks are not *necessarily* implicit. Although subjects are not directly told that they should try to use prior experience to improve performance, it may be obvious to the subject that mirror-tracing is a learning task. After all, they are asked to repetitively trace the same figure in a mirror as quickly and accurately as possible. It is further possible that subjects' learning is accompanied by some feeling of awareness; this question has not been closely examined. Thus, one might argue that there is at least some explicit contribution to these tasks, and that is the source of the age-related deficit.

Harrington and Haaland (1992) sought to test directly whether all motor skills that are implicit would be intact in older subjects. They administered a task that was similar to the SRT task but used a more complex stimulus-response mapping. Subjects responded to stimuli not with key presses but with hand postures. As in the SRT task, some of the stimuli followed a repeating sequence, and the researchers found that younger subjects showed steadily decreasing RTs when the stimuli were sequenced and then slower RTs when the stimuli appeared randomly. The task was implicit because no specific reference to prior experience was made in the task instructions, and subjects were not necessarily aware that learning had occurred, nor that stimuli were sequenced. Older subjects showed this RT pattern less dramatically; when the authors transformed RTs to a log scale, the age-related difference in learning was reliable. When they did not do the transformation, the difference was marginal. Harrington and Haaland argued that the analysis using the transformation was more decisive and concluded that a task being implicit was not sufficient to guarantee that it would be learned. They specifically pointed to the more complex mapping as the possible reason that older subjects failed to learn the skill; the more complex mapping places greater demands on subjects for integrating multiple sources of information and for specifying more dimensions of each movement.

In sum, the implicit/explicit distinction does not seem to account for age-related deficits in motor skill. Some of the tasks on which older subjects are impaired (pursuit rotor, mirror tracing) may have an explicit component, but they fail to learn at least one implicit task (hand posturing).

● Striatal Damage

Another possibility is that striatal damage accounts for the age-related motor skill learning deficit. Patients with striatal abnormalities due to Huntington's disease or Parkinson's disease show impaired motor skill learning (Harrington, Haaland, Yeo, & Marder, 1990; Heindel, Salmon, Shults, Walicke, & Butters, 1989; Willingham & Koroshetz, 1993). Reduction in striatal dopamine function is a concomitant of aging (e.g., Martin, Palmer, Patlak, & Caine, 1989; Van Gorp & Mahler, 1990), although it is not as severe as that found in Parkinson's disease.

Older subjects' general impairment in motor skill learning is consistent with striatal dysfunction, but their normal learning of the SRT task (Howard & Howard, 1989, 1992) is not. Huntington's and Parkinson's disease patients have been shown to be impaired on this task in a number of studies (Jackson, Jackson, Harrison, Henderson, & Kennard, 1995; Knopman & Nissen, 1991; Willingham & Koroshetz, 1993). As noted earlier, Cherry and Stadler (1995) report that lower-ability older subjects (as measured by occupational status and educational achievement) seem not to learn the SRT task normally, and it is possible that these individual differences are correlated with individual differences in striatal dysfunction. Such data are not available, as yet, and it would be premature to propose a brain-behavior relationship in Cherry and Stadler's data.

Willingham and Winter (1995) sought to test the proposal that older subjects' difficulties in motor skill learning are due to depleted dopamine levels in the striatum. They administered four motor skill learning tasks to older, middle-aged, and younger subjects. Two of these tasks are known to be impaired in striatal patients. One was the SRT task (Jackson et al., 1995; Knopman & Nissen, 1991; Willingham & Koroshetz, 1993), and the second was called the key-maze task. This was a stepping-stone maze task administered on a computer, in which the path through the maze was continuously visible. Participants were asked to navigate the maze by using a keyboard equipped with four keys, enabling them to move up, down, left, or right through the maze. The same pattern was used for 20 trials, and subjects were then transferred to a different maze for 5 trials. Huntington's disease patients were impaired in learning this task (Willingham & Koroshetz, 1993).

Willingham and Winter (1995) administered two other tasks that striatal patients learn normally. One was an incompatible response time task, in which subjects performed a four-choice response time task but were required to push the response key one position to the right of where the stimulus appeared. The stimulus positions were random, so there was not a sequence to be learned; all subjects could learn was the new, incompatible mapping. The other task was called the mouse-maze task, a different version of the stepping-stone maze. This version was identical to the other version, except that subjects responded by using the mouse. None of the subjects had used a mouse before, and so the primary thing that participants might learn in this task was how to manipulate the cursor using the mouse. Patients with Huntington's disease learned both the incompatible SRT and mouse maze tasks normally (Willingham & Koroshetz, 1993), which I have elsewhere argued is due to a neural separation of two types of skill learning (Willingham, 1992; Willingham et al., 1996): learning novel sequences of movements (which depends on the striatum) and learning new stimulus-response mappings (which depends on the posterior parietal and premotor cortices). The prediction, then, is that if the motor skill-learning deficit in older subjects is due to dopamine depletion to the striatum, older subjects should show the same pattern of spared and impaired learning that striatal patients do. Instead, older subjects showed learning equivalent to middle-aged and younger subjects on all four tasks. Thus, older subjects learn normally some tasks on which striatal patients show impairment, indicating that striatal dysfunction is not the cause of a motor skill deficit in normal aging.

It is possible that older subjects are in fact impaired in learning all motor skills but that some tasks (e.g., pursuit rotor) are more sensitive measures of striatal dysfunction than other tasks (e.g., SRT). Older subjects only appear impaired on the sensitive tasks, whereas striatal patients, whose damage is more severe, are impaired even on the less sensitive tasks. This explanation is difficult to refute because it is post hoc. The sensitivity of a task to striatal dysfunction can only be assessed by subject performance. For this reason, although the explanation cannot be ruled out, it is not very helpful.

● **Motor Slowness**

It is well-established that older subjects respond more slowly than younger subjects on a variety of simple motor tasks (Welford, 1984), and indeed on the motor skill-learning tasks described, older subjects consistently respond more slowly than younger subjects. The apparently complex pattern of spared and impaired motor skill learning in older subjects may be an artifact of the consistent use of response time or movement time as the dependent measure in all of these tasks. When older subjects are reported to learn a task normally, it is always in terms of the absolute decrease in response time. One might ask whether this is the appropriate measure of performance change. If an older subject's initial response takes 2000 ms and with practice decreases to 1900 ms, can one say that this subject has shown learning equivalent to a younger subject, whose initial response takes 400 ms and after practice 300 ms? Is it not in some sense easier to improve 100 ms if one starts very slowly (2000 ms) than if one's response is initially rapid (400 ms)? Put another way, perhaps one should consider not the absolute improvement in RT, but the percentage improvement, in which case in the previous example older subjects improvement (5%) would be inferior to the younger subject's improvement (25%).

As pointed out by Harrington and Haaland (1992), this is a thorny, persistent, and pervasive problem throughout the literature on aging (and indeed, the literature on neurological patient populations as well). Older subjects will always respond more slowly than younger subjects, so the problem will always be present, and given current methods, the problem is not soluble in an absolute sense. Two considerations are worth mentioning, one theoretical, the other practical.

First, it should be pointed out that this issue is really one of scaling. In saying that it is easier to improve from 2000 to 1900 ms than to improve from 400 to 300 ms, one is saying that the response time scale does not have equal intervals, psychologically; the 400 to 300 interval is larger, or harder to traverse, than the 2000 to 1900 interval. The next question must be this: if a linear scale is not an appropriate representation of the intervals, then what is? If the linear scale is abandoned, what is an appropriate replacement? To my knowledge, there is not at this time a principled basis on which to select another scale for this purpose.

Also, one must closely consider the reason to suppose that the intervals are not equal across the scale. Why should it not be equally difficult for older subjects to improve RTs 100 ms? It makes sense that it would be easier to improve one's response time at longer RTs, but what are these RTs longer than? One must consider whether the older subjects' RTs are long not relative to younger subjects, but relative to the asymptotic performance the older subjects could achieve. Suppose that asymptotic performance for younger subjects is 200 ms, and for older subjects, it is 1800 ms. In that case, improvement for each group of (respectively) 400 to 300 ms, and 2000 to 1900 ms, appears equivalent. In discussions of the scaling problem of RTs, researchers frequently neglect the fact that asymptotic performance of the two groups is almost certainly different.

A second point to consider regarding motor slowness and motor skill is practical. As with the striatal dysfunction account of the age-related motor skill-learning deficit, motor slowness as an account cannot make any predictions about learning. Why do older subjects learn the SRT and the maze tasks but fail on pursuit tracking and mirror tracking? This explanation can only predict that older subjects are always impaired but that sometimes the baseline difference in performance will be sufficient that scaling effects will cause older subjects' performance to appear normal, whereas other times the baseline difference will not be sufficient. This post-hoc account is not really satisfactory.

PROCESSING SPEED AS AN ACCOUNT OF AGE-RELATED EFFECTS IN MOTOR SKILL LEARNING

Processing Speed

Following other proposals (Birren, 1974; Cerella, 1985; Myerson, Hale, Wagstaff, Poon, & Smith, 1990), Salthouse (1996) has proposed a simple, far-reaching account of age-related deficits in cognition. He suggests that most or all of the deficits in a variety of memory, problem-solving, reasoning, and spatial tasks can be traced to a deficit in what he calls *processing speed*. The theory assumes that the speed with which many cognitive processes can be executed is reduced in normal aging. There are two mechanisms by which this slowing causes cognitive deficits: a *limited time* mechanism, which assumes that, if there is a constraint on how long the subject has to complete a task, the slow processing means some processing will not be completed in the allotted time; and a *simultaneity* mechanism, which assumes that slow processing reduces the amount of information that is simultaneously available for higher-level processes to use. This occurs because the products of earlier processing may be lost by the time later processing is complete (assuming that as time passes, information becomes less available). The simultaneity mechanism is akin to working memory capacity (Baddeley, 1986), but it is a more specific term because it specifies that the bottleneck to capacity is the slowness of later processing, causing the loss of the products of earlier processing (as opposed to, for example, a rapid decay rate being the bottleneck).

Two primary sources of evidence have been offered in support of Salthouse's (1996) proposal that differences in processing speed underlie many of the age-related differences in cognition. There are large age differences in the scores of processing speed tests. Salthouse argues that processing speed can be assessed by measuring quite elemental cognitive operations, for example, by timing subjects' ability to compare two letters or two digits. The age-related differences in scores on processing speed tests are similar to differences in more complex cognitive skills, for example, solving arithmetic problems or geometry analogies or performing a working memory task. If one uses the processing speed scores as a covariate in an analysis of the more complex cognitive abilities, the age-related effects disappear (see Salthouse, 1996, for a review). Second, path analyses indicate, as the theory predicts, a relationship between age and processing speed and between processing speed and high-level cognitive processes, but no direct relation between age and high-level cognition (Salthouse, 1991, 1994).

● Processing Speed Applied to Motor Skill Learning

The slowing of processing speed may account for the motor skill-learning deficit observed in older subjects on some tasks, and it also predicts when motor skill learning should be intact. First, the operation of the limited time mechanism indicates that tasks that are experimenter-paced may be impaired in older subjects, whereas those that are subject-paced may not be. As Salthouse (1996) notes, the limited time mechanism will come into play when the subject cannot set the speed of processing; external time constraints force a response, and the response must therefore be made before processing may be complete.

Second, the operation of the simultaneity mechanism indicates that motor skill-learning tasks that demand that multiple processes be active simultaneously in working memory will more likely be impaired in older subjects, because if multiple processes are needed, the slow processing makes it more likely that critical information will be degraded or unavailable when it is needed.

It is difficult to develop an independent measure of the extent to which a task demands that multiple processes be active stimultaneously, but it should be possible to compare specific tasks on this dimension. For example, it appears evident that an RT task that requires a spatially incompatible stimulus-response transformation will be more demanding that an identical task using a spatially compatible mapping.

The processing speed theory applied to motor skill learning makes a final prediction. The theory predicts that older subjects will be less likely to spontaneously become aware of an effective strategy that could be applied to a motor skill-learning task. In some motor skill tasks the subject might adopt a nonobvious strategy that will greatly improve performance. For example, in the SRT task, the subject is not told that the stimuli are sequenced, but the subject might spontaneously notice that they are and explicitly memorize the sequence. Doing so greatly decreases RTs (Willingham et al., 1989). It is reasonable to assume that developing and testing hypotheses about new ways to respond in a motor task is demanding of working memory. Older subjects will be less likely to spontaneously develop a new strategy in a motor skill because of the simultaneity mechanism; their slower processing speed makes it more difficult to simultaneously perform the task and maintain in working memory processes that might generate new strategies.

● Processing Speed Predictions as an Account of Extant Data

Table 17.1 summarizes results from motor skill-learning tasks on which older subjects have been tested. As described in this section, older subjects

TABLE 17.1 Summary of Motor Skill-Learning Tasks Comparing Older and Younger Subjects

Task	Elderly Impaired	Experimenter Paced	Mapping to Be Learned	Sequence to Be Learned	Investigator
Pursuit rotor	√	√		√	Wright & Payne, 1985
Mirror tracking	√	√	√		Wright & Payne, 1985
Hand posture	√		√	√	Harrington & Haaland, 1992
Mirror tracing	√		√		Snoddy, 1926
Mouse maze			√		Willingham & Winter, 1995
Key maze				√	Willingham & Winter, 1995
Serial response time				√	Howard & Howard, 1989
Incompatible serial response time			√		Willingham & Winter, 1995

generally learn normally, unless the motor skill is experimenter-paced or unless the task requires learning two things at once, which arguably calls for maintaining multiple processes simultaneously.

Because of the limited time mechanism, older subjects should be impaired on tasks that are experimenter-paced. In the pursuit rotor (Gutman, 1965; Ruch, 1934; Wright & Payne, 1985) and the mirror tracking tasks (Ruch, 1934; Wright & Payne, 1985), the speed of the target that the subject is to track is set by the experimenter. Older subjects are impaired on these tasks.

The theory predicts that older subjects will also have difficulty learning tasks that demand the simultaneous maintenance of multiple cognitive processes. Although it is difficult to find a metric by which to compare disparate tasks on this dimension, it may be noted that for some tasks there are two things to be learned, whereas for others, only one thing needs to be learned.

As noted in Table 17.1, for some motor skill-learning tasks, the stimuli appear in a repeating sequence, and the chief way the subject may improve performance is through learning the sequence; for example, in both the SRT and the key-maze tasks, the required series of responses is repeated again and again. Subjects' performance degrades when new sets of stimuli are presented, indicating that the performance improvement is due, in large measure, to learning the repeating sequence. In other tasks, the chief thing the subject may learn is a new mapping between stimuli and responses. In these tasks, there is not a sequence to be learned (i.e., the stimuli are random) or the stimuli may be sequenced, but subjects fail to learn the sequence; this can be adduced by perfect transfer to novel stimuli. In tasks like the mouse-maze, mirror tracing, and the incompatible SRT task, subjects improve performance by learning a novel mapping between stimuli and responses.

As shown in Table 17.1, older subjects learn motor skills normally when they demand that subjects learn either a sequence or a new stimulus-response mapping (and when the task is not experimenter-paced). Just one task has been administered that required learning both a sequence and a new stimulus response mapping. That was Harrington and Haaland's (1992) hand-posturing task, in which subjects responded to lights as cues with different hand postures and the lights sometimes appeared in a repeating sequence. The argument made here is that the failure of older subjects to learn this task is due to processing speed limitations, through the simultaneity mechanism. Harrington and Haaland did consider the processing speed hypothesis. They had administered a measure of processing speed to their subjects (the Digit Symbol subtest of the Wechsler Adult Intelligence Scale, 1981) and found that it did not correlate with learning on the hand-posture task. Still, the correlation may have been reduced due to the restricted range of scores.

The mirror tracing data reported by Snoddy (1926) are not well accounted for by the theory. The mirror tracing task is subject-paced, and it should require learning only a new stimulus-response mapping. Although the same figure is presented on each trial, subjects typically do not learn the particular sequence of movements necessary to traverse the star—they learn a more general transformation for movement, and the skill they acquire transfers well to tracing novel shapes (e.g., Gabrieli et al., 1993; see also Bedford, 1993). Why, then were Snoddy's older subjects impaired in mirror tracing? This study is often cited as an example of an age-related deficit in motor skill learning, and yet the details of the study are lacking.

The aging effect was not central to Snoddy's purpose, and he therefore merely mentions the effect in one paragraph of the monograph, providing no statistical analysis or data, but he does mention that there were large individual differences in learning. One might also question whether, in 1926, the subject population was as carefully screened for Alzheimer's and other dementing diseases, as would be done today. The age-related deficit in learning mirror tracing should be replicated before one assigns too much significance to the result.

The theory also predicts that older subjects will be less likely to spontaneously notice a strategy that could lead to improved performance. As noted earlier, older subjects notice that the stimuli are sequenced less often than younger subjects do, in tasks such as the SRT task. One other study addresses this question, using a different paradigm (McNay & Willingham, 1995). Older and younger subjects were asked to trace a line appearing on a computer screen, using a graphics tablet and a stylus. An occluding screen prevented subjects from seeing their hand, the tablet, or the stylus. Subjects first performed some *practice* trials, tracing the line by using the stylus and graphics tablet. Then they performed *training* trials, during which the relationship of the stylus movement and cursor movement was altered, so that the cursor moved at a 90-degree angle from the stylus movement (e.g., if the subject moved the stylus straight away from the body, the cursor moved to the right). The movement of the cursor on the screen left a visible trail. Blocks of training trials were alternated with shorter blocks of test trials, during which the subjects were told that the odd relationship between the stylus and cursor movement was no longer present. Subjects were told that they should respond as they had during the practice trials, except that their movements would no longer be echoed on the screen; they would have to judge where the cursor was, based on their movements.

Learning on training trials occurs through two sources. First, there is unconscious recalibration of vision and proprioception. The training trials introduce a discordance between the proprioceptive feeling of where the hand is moving and the visual feedback on the screen of where the hand is moving. With practice, proprioception becomes recalibrated so that it is in agreement with the visual feedback. A second source of learning is through conscious strategy. The subjects may deduce that the transformation is a rotation and adopt a strategy to guide their hand movements (e.g., rotating the presented line; cf. Redding & Wallace, 1996) so that they essentially move their hands in a way that *feels* wrong. Performance on the training trials could be influenced by both sources of learning. Performance on the test trials, however, is influenced only by recalibration. On test trials, subjects consistently trace at a slight counterclockwise angle to the line presented. This happens because they have no visual feedback to guide their movements; the cursor is not visible. Movements can only be guided by proprioception, which has been recalibrated by the training trials. Although subjects might adopt a conscious strategy to aid performance on the training trials, this strategy cannot be applied to the test trials. Subjects are told that the transformation is no longer present on the test trials, so any strategy they adopted for the training trials is rendered irrelevant.

Thus, the processing speed theory predicts that older subjects will be impaired in learning (i.e., reducing error) during the training trials because younger subjects will often adopt a conscious strategy to guide their movements, whereas older subjects will do so less often because they are less able to deduce the nature of the transformation relating cursor movement to hand movement. Performance on the test trials, however, should be equivalent in the two groups, because recalibration occurs outside of awareness and without the need for any strategy on the part of the subject. McNay and Willingham (1995) reported finding just this pattern of results when comparing groups of older (mean age = 64.2 years) and younger subjects (mean age = 19.9 years).

CONCLUSION

Although there is a paucity of data regarding the effect of age on novel motor skill learning, those studies that have been done show that older subjects are impaired in learning some skills but learn others at the same rate that younger subjects do.

The extension of Salthouse's processing speed theory (e.g., Salthouse, 1996) to motor skill learning offers several important advantages compared to other accounts of age-related effects in motor skill learning. First, the theory appears to account successfully for extant data, unlike the implicit/explicit distinction. Second, the theory is specific about the mechanism of the deficit when it occurs and therefore makes testable predictions, which appears to be a problem for the motor slowness account and for the striatal dysfunction account. Third, and perhaps most important, the account offered here is rooted in a broad-based theory that has been quite successful in accounting for aging data in a number of domains. This gives the account offered here more credibility and may also serve as a starting point for thinking about the relationships of motor skill learning and other types of cognitive abilities, such as problem solving and explicit memory.

Considering processing speed as an account of age-related differences in motor skill learning may also serve as a bridge between behavioral and neural studies of motor skill learning. There has been increased interest in motor skill learning in neuropsychology in the last 10 years, but this work has not been closely related to the more behavioral work in aging. If age-related deficits in motor skill learning are due to a slowing of processing speed, that might lead to work that would seek to uncover the brain mechanism of the processing speed slowdown and a consideration of how that relates to the brain bases of other types of motor skill-learning deficits (e.g.,striatal or cerebellar dysfunctions).

Finally, it should be noted that preferring processing speed to the implicit/explicit distinction as an account of age-related effects in motor skill learning does not bear on the usefulness of the implicit/explicit distinction in other domains or with other subject groups. To date, it appears that age-related differences determined by processing speed cut across many tasks, including implicit and explicit tasks. This pattern of data is an important reminder of the logic of dissociations. It is perfectly possible for various distinctions to be important in accounting for data in different subject groups; it need not be the case that one distinction or the other will apply to all subject groups. It is also a reminder that each new dissociation need not call for a new subdivision among memory systems that have already been proposed. New distinctions may be orthogonal to those already proposed, as the processing speed distinction is orthogonal to the implicit/explicit memory distinction.

NOTE

1. Squire's (1992a) distinction between declarative and nondeclarative memory is one among many characterizations of the differences among memory systems. For a number of different perspectives, see Schacter and Tulving, 1994.

REFERENCES

Baddeley, A. (1986). *Working memory.* Oxford, UK: Clarendon Press.

Bedford, F. (1993). Perceptual learning. *The Psychology of Learning and Motivation, 30,* 1-60.

Birren, J. E. (1974). Translations in gerontology: From lab to life: Psychophysiology and speed of response. *American Psychologist, 29,* 808-815.

Cerella, J. (1985). Information processing rates in the elderly. *Psychological Bulletin, 98,* 67-83.

Cherry, K. E., & Stadler, M. A. (1995). Implicit learning of a nonverbal sequence in younger and older adults. *Psychology and Aging, 10,* 3793-3794.

Cohen, N. J., & Squire, L. R. (1980). Preserved learning and pattern-analyzing skill in amnesia: Dissociation of knowing how and knowing that. *Science, 210,* 207-210.

Corkin, S. (1968). Acquisition of motor skill after bilateral medial temporal lobe excision. *Neuropsychologia, 6,* 255-265.

Craik, F. I. M. (1977). Age differences in human memory. In B. J. Schaie & K. Schaie (Eds.), *Handbook of the psychology of aging.* New York: Van Nostrand Rheinhold.

Craik, F. I. M. (1994). Memory changes in normal aging. *Current Directions in Psychological Science, 3,* 155-158.

Craik, F. I. M., & Jennings, J. M. (1992). Human memory. In F. Craik & T. Salthouse (Eds.), *The handbook of aging and cognition.* Hillsdale, NJ: Lawrence Erlbaum.

Eslinger, P. J., & Damasio, A. R. (1986). Preserved motor learning in Alzheimer's disease: Implications for anatomy and behavior. *Journal of Neuroscience, 6,* 3006-3009.

Gabrieli, J. D. E., Corkin, S., Mickel, S. F., & Growdon, J. H. (1993). Intact acquisition and long-term retention of mirror-tracing skill and Alzheimer's disease and in global amnesia. *Behavioral Neuroscience, 107,* 899-910.

Graf, P. (1990). Life-span changes in implicit and explicit memory. *Bulletin of the Psychonomic Society, 28,* 353-358.

Graf, P., & Schacter, D. L. (1985). Implicit and explicit memory for new associations in normal and amnesic subjects. *Journal of Experimental Psychology: Learning, Memory, and Cognition, 11,* 501-518.

Gutman, G. M. (1965). The effects of age and extroversion on pursuit rotor reminiscence. *Journal of Gerontology, 20,* 346-350.

Harrington, D. L., & Haaland, K. Y. (1992). Skill learning in the elderly: Diminished implicit and explicit memory for a motor sequence. *Psychology and Aging, 7,* 425-434.

Harrington, D. L., Haaland, K. Y., Yeo, R. A., & Marder, E. (1990). Procedural memory in Parkinson's disease: Impaired motor but not visuoperceptual learning. *Journal of Clinical and Experimental Neuropsychology, 12,* 323-339.

Heindel, W. C., Salmon, D. P., Shults, C. W., Walicke, P. A., & Butters, N. (1989). Neuropsychological evidence for multiple implicit memory systems: A comparison of Alzheimer's, Huntington's, and Parkinson's disease patients. *Journal of Neuroscience, 9,* 582-587.

Howard, D. V. (1991). Implicit memory: An expanding picture of cognitive aging. In K. W. Schaie (Ed.), *Annual review of gerontology and geriatrics* (Vol 11., pp. 1-22). New York: Springer.

Howard, D. V., & Howard, J. H. (1989). Age differences in learning serial patterns: Direct versus indirect measures. *Psychology and Aging, 4,* 357-364.

Howard, D. V., & Howard, J. H. (1992). Adult age differences in the rate of learning serial patterns: Evidence from direct and indirect tests. *Psychology and Aging, 7,* 232-241.

Howard, J. H., Mutter, S. A., & Howard, D. V. (1992). Serial pattern learning by event observation. *Journal of Experimental Psychology: Learning, Memory, and Cognition, 18,* 1029-1039.

Jackson, G. M., Jackson, S. R., Harrison, J., Henderson, L., & Kennard, C. (1995). Serial reaction time learning and Parkinson's disease: Evidence for a procedural learning deficit. *Neuropsychologia, 33,* 577-593.

Jagacinski, R. J., Liao, M.-J., & Fayyad, E. A. (1995). Generalized slowing in sinusoidal tracking by older adults. *Psychology and Aging, 10,* 8-19.

Knopman, D., & Nissen, M. J. (1991). Procedural learning is impaired in Huntington's disease: Evidence from the serial reaction time task. *Neuropsychologia, 29,* 245-254.

Light, L. L. (1988). Preserved implicit memory in old age. In M. M. Gruneberg, P. E. Morris, & R. N. Sykes (Eds.), *Practical aspects of memory: Current research and issues* (Vol. 2, pp. 90-95). New York: John Wiley.

Light, L. L., Singh, A., & Capps, J. L. (1986). Dissociation of memory and awareness in young and older adults. *Journal of Clinical and Experimental Neuropsychology, 8,* 62-74.

Martin, W. R. W., Palmer, M. R., Patlak, C. S., & Caine, D. B. (1989). Nigrostriatal function in humans studied with positron emission tomography. *Annals of Neurology, 26,* 535-542.

Mayr, U. (1996). Spatial attention and implicit sequence learning: Evidence for independent learning of spatial and nonspatial sequences. *Journal of Experimental Psychology: Learning, Memory, and Cognition, 22,* 350-364.

McNay, E. C., & Willingham, D. B. (1995). Aging-related deficit in implicit perceptuomotor learning. *Society for Neuroscience Abstracts, 21,* 1709.

Mulder, G., Wijers, A. A., Lange, J. J., Buijink, B. M., Mulder, L. J. M., Willemsen, A. T. M., & Paans, A. M. J. (1995). The role of neuroimaging in the discovery of processing stages. *Acta Psychologica, 90,* 63-79.

Myerson, J., Hale, S., Wagstaff, D., Poon, L. W., & Smith, G. A. (1990). The information loss model: A mathematical theory of age-related cognitive slowing. *Psychological Review, 97,* 475-487.

Nissen, M. J., Willingham, D. B., & Hartman, M. (1989). Explicit and implicit remembering: When is learning preserved in amnesia? *Neuropsychologia, 27,* 341-352.

Pew, R. W. (1974). Levels of analysis in motor control. *Brain Research, 71,* 393-400.

Raz, N., Gunning, F. M., Head, D., Dupuis, J. H., McQuain, J., Briggs, S. D., Loken, W. J., Thornton, A. E., & Acker, J. D. (in press). Selective aging of the human cerebral cortex observed in vivo: Differential vulnerability of the prefrontal gray matter. *Cerebral Cortex.*

Redding, G. M., & Wallace, B. (1996). Adaptive spatial alignment and strategic perceptual-motor control. *Journal of Experimental Psychology: Human Perception and Performance, 22,* 379-394.

Ruch, F. L. (1934). The differential effects of age upon human learning. *Journal of General Psychology, 11,* 261-286.

Salmon, D. P., & Butters, N. (1995). Neurobiology of skill and habit learning. *Current Opinion in Neurobiology, 5,* 184-190.

Salthouse, T. A. (1991). Mediation of adult age difference in cognition by reductions in working memory and speed of processing. *Psychological Science, 2,* 179-183.

Salthouse, T. A. (1994). The nature of the influence of speed on adult age differences in cognition. *Developmental Psychology, 30,* 240-259.

Salthouse, T. A. (1996). The processing-speed theory of adult age differences in cognition. *Psychological Review, 103,* 403-428.

Schacter, D. L., & Tulving, E. (1994). *Memory systems 1994.* Cambridge: MIT Press.

Snoddy, G. S. (1926). Learning and stability. *Journal of Applied Psychology, 10,* 1-36.

Squire, L. R. (1992a). Declarative and nondeclarative memory: Multiple brain systems supporting learning and memory. *Journal of Cognitive Neuroscience, 4,* 232-243.

Squire, L. R. (1992b). Memory and the hippocampus: A synthesis from findings with rats, monkeys, and humans. *Psychological Review, 99,* 195-231.

Stelmach, G. E., & Nahom, A. (1992). Cognitive-motor abilities of the elderly driver. *Human Factors, 34,* 53-65.

Van Gorp, W. G., & Mahler, M. (1990). Subcortical features of normal aging. In J. L. Cummings (Ed.), *Subcortical dementia* (pp. 231-250). New York: Oxford University Press.

Verillo, R. T., & Verrillo, V. (1985). Sensory and perceptual performance. In N. Charness (Ed.), *Aging and human performance* (pp. 1-46). New York: John Wiley.

Wechsler, D. (1981). *Wechsler Adult Intelligence Scale-Revised.* San Antonio, TX: Psychological Corporation.

Welford, A. T. (1984). Psychomotor performance. *Annual Review of Gerontology and Geriatrics, 4*, 237-273.

Willingham, D. B. (1992). Systems of motor skill. In L. R. Squire & N. Butters (Eds.), *Neuropsychology of memory* (2nd ed., pp. 166-178). New York: Guilford.

Willingham, D. B. (1997). Systems of memory in the human brain. *Neuron, 18*, 5-8.

Willingham, D. B., Koroshetz, W. J., & Peterson, E. (1993). Evidence for neurally dissociable motor skill systems in Huntington's disease patients. *Psychobiology, 21*, 173-182.

Willingham, D. B., & Koroshetz, W. J. (1996). Motor skill learning has diverse neural bases: Spared and impaired skill acquisition in Huntington's disease. *Neuropsychology, 10*, 315-321.

Willingham, D. B., Nissen, M. J., & Bullemer, P. (1989). On the development of procedural knowledge. *Journal of Experimental Psychology: Learning, Memory, and Cognition, 15*, 1047-1060.

Willingham, D. B., & Winter, E. (1995). Comparison of motor skill learning in elderly and young human subjects. *Society for Neuroscience Abstracts, 21*, 1440.

Woodruff-Pak, D. S. (1988). Aging and classical conditioning: Parallel studies in rabbits and humans. *Neurobiology of Aging, 9*, 511-522.

Wright, B. M., & Payne, R. B. (1985). Effects of aging on sex differences in psychomotor reminiscence and tracking proficiency. *Journal of Gerontology, 40*, 179-184.

Author Index

Editor's Note: Page references followed by f or t indicate figures or tables, respectively.
References followed by "n" indicate endnotes.

Subject Index

Editor's Note: Page references followed by *f* or *t* indicate figures or tables, respectively. References followed by n indicate endnotes.

About the Contributors

Dianne Berry is a reader in psychology at the University of Reading (UK), where she has been working since 1990. Prior to this, she was a research fellow at Oxford University. Her academic qualifications include a first degree in psychology and a doctorate in experimental psychology, the latter of which she gained at Oxford. She has been researching in the area of implicit learning for the past 15 years. She has many publications on this topic, including a co-authored book with Zoltan Dienes, called *Implicit Learning: Theoretical and Empirical Issues,* which was published in 1993. She has also recently edited a book called *How Implicit Is Implicit Learning?*

Axel Buchner is Assistant Professor of Psychology at the University of Trier, Germany. He received his Ph.D. in psychology at the University of Bonn, Germany, in 1992. His research interests are in cognitive psychology, especially human attention, learning, memory, and problem solving.

Axel Cleeremans received degrees in psychology from the Université Libre de Bruxelles and from Carnegie Mellon University, where he completed his Ph.D. with Jay McClelland in 1991. He is a research associate with the National Fund for Scientific Research (Belgium) and is affiliated with the Université Libre de Bruxelles, where he heads the Cognitive Science Research Seminar and teaches in the Department of Philosophy. He also serves as an associate editor for the *Quarterly Journal of Experimental Psychology* and the *European Journal of Psychology*. His research focuses on implicit learning and on the formulation of computationally explicit theories. He authored *Mechanisms of Implicit Learning*, the first book entirely dedicated to implicit learning.

Barbara P. Cochran recently completed her Ph.D. in cognitive psychology at Louisiana State University. She combines an interest in language acquisition with an interest in implicit learning. Her dissertation focused on the acquisition of American Sign Language by hearing adults. She has also recently completed a series of studies on the nature and acquisition of generative systems, inspired by George Miller's *Project Grammarama*.

Josephine Cock is a research fellow in the Department of Psychology at the University of Reading, where she took her doctorate in experimental psychology. Her other academic qualifications include a first degree in psychology and a master's degree in counseling psychology. Prior to joining the Reading department, she carried out voluntary work in the tropics for many years.

Tim Curran is Assistant Professor of Psychology at Case Western Reserve University. He received a B.S. in psychology from the University of Wisconsin (1989), received a Ph.D. in experimental psychology from the University of Oregon (1993), and completed a postdoctoral fellowship in cognitive neuroscience at Harvard University (1993 to 1995). He serves as a consulting editor for the *Journal of Experimental Psychology: Learning, Memory, and Cognition* and the *Journal of Experimental Psychology: General*. His primary research interests are related to human learning and memory.

Peter A. Frensch studied electrical engineering, psychology, and philosophy at the Universities of Darmstadt and Trier, Germany, and at Yale University, where he received his M.S., M.phil., and Ph.D. He worked as an assistant and associate professor in the Department of Psychology at the University of Missouri-Columbia, from 1989 until 1994. In 1994, he moved to the Max-Planck-Institute for Human Development and Education, Berlin, Germany, where he is a senior research scientist. In addition, he is professor of psychology at Humboldt University in Berlin. He is co-editor of the journal *Psychological Research*. His research interests include learning, memory, and problem solving.

Thomas Goschke holds a postdoctoral position in the Department of Psychology at the University of Osnabrück, Germany. He studied psychology and philosophy at the Ruhr-University of Bochum and received his Ph.D. from the University of Osnabrück in 1992. He also worked at the University of Oregon at Eugene and taught at the Technical University of Braunschweig. Current research interests include: (1) experimental and electrophysiological studies of implicit sequence learning; (2) cognitive control, task-set switching, executive functions, and volitional action; (3) connectionist models of implicit learning and theoretical work on mental representation.

Joachim Hoffmann is Professor of Psychology at the University of Würzburg, Germany. He received his Ph.D. from the Humboldt University, Berlin, in 1972 and has worked and taught at the Humboldt University; at the Academy of Science, Berlin; at the Max Planck Institute für Psychological Research, Munich; and at the University of Munich. His research interests are behavioral control and perception, knowledge representation, and learning. He published the monographies *Das aktive Gedächtnis* [The active memory], *Die Welt der Begriffe* [The world of concepts], and *Vorhersage und Erkenntnis* [Anticipation and Cognition].

William J. Hoyer is Professor of Psychology and Director of the Graduate Training Program in Experimental Psychology at Syracuse University. He received a B.S. in psychology and mathematics from Rutgers University in 1967 and a Ph.D. in experimental psychology from West Virginia University in 1972. The focus of his research interests is the study of cognitive aging, especially the effects of aging on learning and skilled cognitive performance.

Andrew T. Hsiao is a doctoral student in the experimental psychology subprogram of the City University of New York. He is interested in the processes and mechanisms of learning and memory and the phenomenology of consciousness. His current work focuses on the role of attention in implicit learning. He takes an approach that attempts to understand unconscious cognitive functions from a microscopic temporal/spatial point of view.

Luis Jiménez received his Ph.D. in 1993 from the University of Santiago (Spain), where he teaches the Human Learning course. During the last four years, he has authored several articles on sequence learning, and has made extended stays in Brussels, where he collaborated with Axel Cleeremans on a number of projects focused on the analysis of methodological and conceptual issues in implicit learning and on connectionist modeling. His main research interests are now focussed on the role of attention in implicit sequence learning, and on the conceptual issues underlying the definition of implicit learning.

Peder J. Johnson received his Ph.D. in cognitive psychology from the University of Colorado in 1965. After an additional year at Colorado as an NSF Research Fellow, he joined the faculty of the University of New Mexico in 1966, where he is currently a professor of psychology. Over the years, his research has focused upon factors influencing abstractions in children and adults, allocation of additional resources, assessment of automatic processing, and the effects of involuntary processing of context on speeded classification. His current research interests are divided between implicit learning and knowledge assessment.

Theresa Johnstone is currently undertaking doctoral research at University College London. She received her BSc in Psychology from the University of Surrey in 1996. Prior to studying for her first degree, she was a systems development manager responsible for derivative product risk-management systems with Chase Manhattan Bank in New York. Her specific research interest is the relative effectiveness of instance memorization versus hypothesis testing as learning strategies.

Iring Koch is research assistant at the University of Würzburg, Germany. He received his diploma in psychology from the Universitity of Frankfurt am Main, in 1994. His present research topic is sequential learning, especially the question as to which factors contribute to the formation of sequential structure.

Amy E. Lincourt received a B.A. in psychology from the University of North Carolina–Charlotte, an M.S. in experimental psychology from Villanova University, and a Ph.D. in 1997 in experimental psychology from Syracuse University. The focus of her research is in the general area of cognitive aging, with special emphasis on the effects of visual selective attention on learning rates across the adult lifespan.

Louis Manza is Assistant Professor of Psychology at Lebanon Valley College in Annville, Pennsylvania. He graduated from the State University of New York at Binghamton in 1988 with a B.A. in psychology, followed by a Ph.D. in cognitive psychology from the City University of New York in 1992. He previously taught in the psychology departments of Brooklyn College (1989-1992) and Gettysburg College (1992-1995). His research specialty is implicit learning, with specific interests in implicit emotional preference formation and how this process manifests itself under different clinical, developmental, and laboratory-based conditions. He teaches a variety of courses, such as general psychology, history of psychology, learning and memory, cognitive science, and social psychology.

Robert C. Mathews is Professor of Psychology at Louisiana State University and he directs LSU's Office of Human and Machine Cognition. His work on implicit learning began in the late 1980s with studies examining transfer and verbalization of implicitly acquired knowledge of artificial grammars. Since then, he has published several studies concerned with acquisition of implicit knowledge in a variety of domains. He also explored classifier systems as an architecture for modeling implicit learning and for exchanging information between humans and machines. More recently, he has become interested in techniques to enhance expertise by integrating experiential and reflective knowledge.

Pierre Perruchet is currently a research director at the National Center of Scientific Research (CNRS), a position he has held since 1990. He has been attached to the CNRS research unit on learning and development (LEAD) of the University of Burgundy since 1994. He received his Ph.D. at the University Rene Descartes in Paris in 1976, with a thesis on human classical conditioning. He began his career as a lecturer at the University of Lille (France), then was a research scientist at the University Rene Descartes. His main current interests are in the domain of learning and memory, especially the issues surrounding the implicit/explicit distinction.

Arthur S. Reber is Professor of Psychology at Brooklyn College and The Graduate Center of The City University of New York. His abiding interest is in implicit learning, the problem of how information about a complexly structured environment is acquired largely independent of awareness of both the process and products of acquisition. In recent years, his theoretical work has taken two paths. One has been to tuck the work on the cognitive unconscious within an evolutionary biological framework. The other has been to explore the manner in which current psychological thinking about implicit processes dovetails with recent developments in the philosophy of mind. Recent experimental work has focused on such problems as the role of implicit processes in the formation of preferences, the problem of individual differences in implicit and explicit cognition, and the role of attention in implicit learning.

Jonathan M. Reed received his Ph.D. in cognitive psychology from the University of New Mexico in 1995. He is currently a postdoctoral research fellow in the Psychiatry Department of the University of California, San Diego, investigating aspects of human amnesiac syndromes.

Henry L. Roediger III is Professor and Chair of the Department of Psychology at Washington University in St. Louis. After receiving his Ph.D. at Yale University in 1973, he was on the faculty at Purdue University from 1973-1988 and Rice University from 1988-1996. His research has centered on human learning and memory. A consulting editor to several journals, Roediger was editor of the *Journal of Experimental Psychology: Learning, Memory, and Cognition* and is founding editor of *Psychonomic Bulletin & Review*. He is also coauthor of three textbooks. Roediger is a Fellow of several professional societies, was Chair of the Psychonomic Society (1989-1990) and President of the Midwestern Psychological Association (1992-1993), was elected to the Society of Experimental Psychologists in 1994, and held a Guggenheim Fellowship (1994-1995).

Carol A. Seger is a visiting scholar in the Psychology Department at Stanford University. She is supported by an NRSA postdoctoral fellowship from the National Institute of Mental Health. She received an A.B. in psychology-cognitive science from Harvard and Radcliffe Colleges in 1987 and a Ph.D. in cognitive psychology from the University of California, Los Angeles, in 1994. Her research interests include learning and memory, high-level visual perception, and implicit cognition. She uses behavioral and cognitive neuroscience methods in her research.

David R. Shanks is a Reader in Experimental Psychology at University College London, where he has been since 1993. He previously held an appointment at the Medical Research Council's Applied Psychology Unit, Cambridge, England, and was a research fellow at the Cognitive Science

Department, University of California, San Diego. He received his M.A. and Ph.D. from the University of Cambridge, England. He is currently director of the Experimental Division of the ESRC Centre for Economic Learning and Social Evolution at University College London. His research interests are in cognitive psychology and neuropsychology, especially human learning, memory, and decision making.

Michael A. Stadler is Assistant Professor of Psychology at the University of Missouri in Columbia, where he has been on the faculty since 1992, after 3 years on the faculty at Louisiana State University. He received his B.S. in psychology from Wright State University in 1985 and his Ph.D. in cognitive psychology from Purdue University in 1989. He serves as a consulting editor for the *Journal of Experimental Psychology: Learning, Memory, and Cognition.* His research focuses on human learning and memory.

Annie Vinter is Professor of Developmental Psychology at the University of Burgundy (Dijon, France), and she is attached to the research unit on learning and development of the National Center of Scientific Research. She was trained in psychology in Geneva (Switzerland), where she obtained her Ph.D. in 1983. Her research interests are in cognitive and developmental psychology, especially motor development and learning.

Daniel B. Willingham is Assistant Professor of Psychology and a member of the Neuroscience Graduate Program at the University of Virginia where he has been on the faculty since 1992, after 2 years on the faculty at Williams College. He received his B.A. in psychology and English from Duke University in 1983 and his Ph.D in cognitive psychology from Harvard University in 1990. His research centers on the cognitive and neural basis of motor skill acquisition.

Werner Wippich is Professor of Psychology at the University of Trier, Germany, a position he has held since 1981. He received his Ph.D. in psychology in 1969 at the University of Göttingen, Germany, where he worked until 1980. His research interests are in cognitive psychology, social cognition, and developmental psychology, especially in the memory domain.

Diane Zizak is a native New Yorker who is a Ph.D. candidate in the experimental psychology program at the City University of New York. She received a B.A. from Hunter College in psychology and Chinese and earned an M.A. in experimental psychology from Brooklyn College. In addition to her research on the role of implicit learning in the determination of preferences, she is currently employed by the New York City Board of Education, where she is working as a reading teacher/coordinator in an alternative junior high school.